UNEASY STAGES

Books by JOHN SIMON

ACID TEST
PRIVATE SCREENINGS
FILM 67/68 *(coeditor with Richard Schickel)*
FOURTEEN FOR NOW *(editor)*
MOVIES INTO FILM
INGMAR BERGMAN DIRECTS
SINGULARITIES
UNEASY STAGES

UNEASY STAGES

BY John Simon

A Chronicle of the New York Theater, 1963~1973

RANDOM HOUSE   New York

All rights reserved under International and Pan-American
Copyright Conventions. Published in the United States by
Random House, Inc., New York, and simultaneously in
Canada by Random House of Canada Limited, Toronto.

Library of Congress Cataloging in Publication Data

Simon, John Ivan.
    Uneasy stages: a chronicle of the New York theater,
    1963-1973
    1. Theater—New York (City)—Reviews.   I. Title.
PN2277.N5S53   1976   792.9'09747'1   75-10262
ISBN 0-394-49805-4
ISBN 0-394-73117-4 pbk.

These reviews originally appeared in slightly different form
in *New York* magazine, *Commonweal* and *The Hudson
Review.*

*Manufactured in the United States of America
Designed by Anita Karl*

24689753

FIRST EDITION

To my ever-present teachers:
>   Harry Levin
>   Renato Poggioli
>   Jean Seznec
>   Karl Viëtor

And you, a would-be player too,
Will give those angry ghosts their due
Who threw their voices far as doom
Greatly in a little room.

Suite for Recorders
LOUIS MACNEICE

CONTENTS

x

INTRODUCTION:
ON BEING AN ELITIST CRITIC

V ERY WELL, I confess: the reviews that follow were written by an "elitist" critic, an epithet that has been hurled at me only a trifle less frequently than "acerbic." That "acerbic," by the way, has popped up everywhere, attached to my name as if the two of them were Siamese twins—in national magazines, provincial newspapers, talk-show and lecture introductions. I wonder sometimes whether my having grown up in Belgrade, the capital of Serbia as well as Yugo-slavia, made me first into "a Serb" and then, by homonymy, acerb or acerbic. In any case, *acerbic* is not worth discussing, beyond pointing out how unfastidious most journalism is; otherwise it could surely come up with an occasional synonym. Why can't I sometimes be the barbed, biting, acidulous, peppery, sharp, tart or sardonic John Simon? (For that last, I suppose, I would have had to be born in Sardinia.)

The *elitist*, however, is worth consideration. Criticism is, by defi-nition, one of the most elitist activities extant. It is highly presump-tuous to sit in judgment—to be paid for sitting in judgment—over other people's work and talent; to pronounce, in a democratic society, on what is superior and what inferior, and know, even while doing it, that masses of people will not comprehend such discrimination, feel threatened by it, and resent it bitterly. The only kind of critic who is not considered an elitist at all is one who likes most things; the trouble with such a critic is that he is not a critic at all. To be choosy, to be stern, is to be elitist; yet what is discrimination and tough-minded-ness except strong conviction based on intense comparative evalua-tion, which might just as easily be called practical, shrewd and energetic. In his own domain, a critic is simply a rugged individualist; what makes him an elitist would, in almost any other field, make him a good American.

If I were to ask the mirror on my wall who is the greatest elitist of them all, it would, if it is an honest mirror, have to answer "Time," or else "Oblivion," which is time's pen name when meting out unfavorable criticism. No critic is harsher, more exclusive—more elitist—than time. Where are thousands upon thousands of yesterday's celebrities today? Where will the even more thousands of today's celebrities be tomorrow? Winnowed out by time and buried in a potter's field by oblivion. And some of these denizens of unmarked graves were once critics' darlings. The ideal critic, therefore, would be the one who could prefigure the judgment of time and anticipate the voice of posterity. But obviously none of us can quite do that, time-bound creatures that we are, to a greater or lesser extent. Pauline Kael once chided me for being so Olympianly concerned with speaking to and for the future rather than for and to my contemporaries, as she feels a critic should. I disagree. A critic who glories in being of his day may lose his usefulness in time to come—except for a limited interest to scholars. But the critic who tries to accord with the judgment of the future must ipso facto speak to people with a sense of perspective in his own time. And to whom else is it really worth talking?

Well, yes, one tries to teach the untutored. There is good in that; but if they become tutored merely by adopting the critic's opinions and insights rather than by finding in his views a confirmation and refinement of their own, they will be sedulous apes at best. The ideal reader is one who is already about as discriminating as the critic—in other words, just as much of an elitist. Still, the critic does teach, so perhaps it would be most accurate to say that he teaches potential, budding elitists to become consummate and mature ones. Only let us make sure that we know what we mean by elitism. I have in mind an aristocracy of the spirit, which has nothing to do with birth or social standing or wealth or academic background (though this last may in some cases help—and in others hinder). It has to do with something else: with whether, for whatever reason, one prefers high art to the other kinds, and whether one has the power of discrimination to tell them apart, for it is very easy to have the preference without the discrimination.

And, really, how is one not to appear an elitist among today's critics? Said Karl Kraus: "An intellectual elevator service ought to be instituted to spare one the unheard-of exhaustion stemming from the descent to the level of today's writing. When I regain consciousness, I am always quite out of breath." Substitute the word "criticism" for "writing," and you have pretty much the current state of affairs. But, one might ask, do the prevailing standards of newspaper and magazine criticism matter all that much? And if they do, can they afford to be as aristocratically fussy as I would have them be? That I believe them to matter goes without saying; otherwise I would not bother to write criticism for such publications. Whether they can afford to have such high standards is another question, and here the answer must be more circumspect.

The theater today, as the reviews that follow will make abundantly clear, is in fairly desperate shape. Even paranoiacs have enemies, Delmore Schwartz quipped, and even a fabulous invalid, as Broadway has come to be known, may eventually have to die. Broadway is not the American theater, of course, still less the theater, *tout court*. But it is the nucleus of theater in America, around which the rest rightly or wrongly revolves, either in emulation or in revulsion—and, in both cases, in envy. It is incontestable that if Broadway were to disappear, the shape of American theater would undergo a radical change, probably for the better, but just possibly for the worse. After all, a strong nucleus is of paramount importance for any institution, even if for genuine imagination and innovation one may have to look nearer the periphery.

So, contrary to what some of the Great White Way's stalwarts claim, I am far from being the sworn enemy of Broadway—using the term to include such related phenomena as, say, the Lincoln and Kennedy Centers. The amount of attention I devote to it is in itself an index of my concern, however strict my assessments or gloomy my expectations may be. But whereas I am not eager to see it go, or exultant in its putative proximate demise, I cannot help feeling that it may have outlived its usefulness as the cornerstone, cement or lodestar of our theater.

This is not the occasion for raising the thorny question of what the theater of the future might be like, even assuming that I had the answer. But it seems to me not at all unlikely that under the never-before-experienced triple onslaught of film, television and rock concerts (undoubtedly the most cherished medium of today's youth), theater may have to restructure itself—in contradistinction to those more popular mediums—into an elitist art form. It may have to give up competing with film in the grandioseness of its *mise en scène*, with television in its undemanding frivolity, with rock music and lyrics in their simple-minded accessibility. In other words, theater may have to become a minority art, rather like chamber music. The latter, though not a crowd pleaser and gold mine, nevertheless need not go begging for a small but supportive audience of enthusiasts. We tend to remember only one of Procrustes' nasty habits: that of lopping off those parts of his guests that protruded beyond his bed. Yet he had another, no less unsavory custom: that of stretching travelers shorter than his bed until they exactly matched its length. We must not try to rack an uninterested public into filling up the obsolete gigantism of our theatrical edifices.

Of course, as things stand, theater is so much more expensive than chamber music concerts that it requires much more extensive box-office returns. However, enormous as it is, this problem may in time be resolved. There will have to be less costly production values, greater governmental and private subsidies and, above all, some way of putting the various theatrical unions in their places, from which they cannot make their present murderous—and ultimately suicidal—demands. The task ahead—involving, as it surely does, also the establishment of a National Theater—is tremendous but not impossible. I can say not impossible because no major art form that has been with us for centuries, indeed millennia, has ever died out, with the single exception of the epic.

Yet on closer inspection even the epic has not become extinct, merely transformed into the novel. Which may be precisely the sort of transmutation the theater may have to endure, *transmutatis transmutandis*. If the critic, by being not so much severe as simply scrupulously honest (which, in juxtaposition with current critical practice, may come to the same thing), should accelerate this rebirth into a more selective, aristocratic, minority-oriented—in short, elitist—theater, so much the better. In an interview with a Rochester paper, Clive Barnes, the drama critic of *The New York Times,* was holding forth on what he considers the general overestimation of the critic's power and importance. Asked by the interviewer whether he thought that "the acerbic John Simon . . . subscribed to that philosophy," Barnes replied, among other things, that "John Simon subscribes to John Simon," and went on to describe his own position as "I say what I think. I think sometimes I hold back on grounds of compassion." Whether or not the grounds are compassion, and whether or not there is a great deal to hold back there, Barnes, like other reviewers, certainly holds back.

Not so I. It seems to me that a critic needs a great many other tools far more than he does compassion, and that the person dealing in compassion has a choice of numerous charitable vocations—of which criticism does not happen to be one. *Amicus Plato, sed magis amica veritas:* I cannot serve the cause of friendliness when I am trying to serve the cause of theater by being as passionate, subjective and truthful as I can be.

And even if this makes me into an elitist, I do subscribe only to myself. Whom else can a critic subscribe to?

UNEASY STAGES

SPRING, 1963

BEYOND THE FRINGE
   by Alan Bennett, Peter Cook,
     Jonathan Miller and Dudley Moore

THE BEAUTY PART
   by S. J. Perelman

THE PINTER PLAYS: THE DUMB WAITER
and THE COLLECTION
   by Harold Pinter

THE MILK TRAIN DOESN'T STOP HERE ANYMORE
   by Tennessee Williams

THERE OUGHT TO BE a wistful little fairy tale somewhere—in Perrault or preferably Andersen—about an unhappy drama critic who must review bad play after bad play until he is kept alive only by a transcendent yearning for the one good play that someday, somehow he will live to see and write about. Then, after an indescribably long wait, that play does come along, but the wretched fellow is so overwhelmed that his mind and fingers go numb and he cannot even roll a ball-point across the page. It is somewhat in this situation that the British nonmusical revue *Beyond the Fringe* leaves one. It is thoroughly witty, adultly satirical, civilized down to its sharp-nailed fingertips: an evening in the theater when the excitement of stage history is in the air. But there is little or nothing one can say about it.

Not, perhaps, for lack of the appropriate vocabulary, but for the no less valid reason that further jokes must not be given away. Already there is the cast recording, the various newspaper accounts, and enthusiastic quoting and misquoting at cocktail parties. But even if the four sumptuous pranksters on stage were better yet than they are—which, without selling their souls to the devil, they could scarcely be—unless a G-string's worth of surprise is decently left them, they cannot maintain their efficacy undiminished.

So it is "Down, wanton, down!" to the urge to quote profusely, and let there be merely a few words about each of the four author-performers. Together, they constitute a large amiably misanthropic mosaic, depicting every absurd stridency of our world with hilariously condign distortion. There is Dudley Moore, a fallen cherub who carries his particular hell with him in the shape of a piano; but, deprived of that instrument of torture and self-torture, he can play gratingly atonal jokes direct on your funny bone. There is Alan Bennett, so jolly decent, so frightfully shy, such an awfully good sort, that—out of sheer reserve—he seems to be backing into his devastating impersonations, which humbly bowing in turn, knife each of our pretensions in the back. There is Peter Cook, looking like every cultured or pseudo-cultured Briton there ever was, from Lucky Jim to Commander Whitehead, a veritable Cook's tour of all forms of charlatanism and cant. And there is Jonathan Miller, who looks like a Wystan Auden condemned to be the jester of a Borgia Pope, flits about like a hopped-up springbok, and makes faces piteous enough to melt the snowcap off an Alp.

Nothing, I am happy to say, is sacred to these four: everything from Harold Macmillan to Shakespeare, from religion to the atom bomb, from the shiniest alpha to the crummiest omega gets it from them both coming and going. Sublimely mad hatters, they whip up instant dunce's caps for everybody, and as we take off our hats to them, full of laughter and admiration—wham! the dunce's cap is already on our own heads.

WHAT A CRAVEN and witless affair, by comparison, is S. J. Perelman's *The Beauty Part*. With eagle eye, Mr. Perelman spots every cultural and social pretension that has been around long enough to become the cliché-monger's butt, or is so grossly exaggerated as to be attackable with impunity: harebrained Hollywood hulks, illiterate film producers, phony art buyers, artists who sell out, best-seller writers, publishers of cheap magazines, reactionary, senile tycoons, flighty faggots, artsy cocottes and Bennett Cerf. When Perelman was writing for the Marx Brothers, he had to be merely preposterously zany; when he was writing for *The New Yorker,* he needed to be only elaborately whimsical. Suddenly, confronted with a Voltairian theme— the painful initiation of a wide-eyed Yalie into the fraternity and so- rority of swindlers and hypocrites—he is obliged to be satirical and can't make it.

There are further reasons for this failure. At times, Perelman seems to be peering through both halves of his bifocals, and images get superimposed and blurred. The Fleur Cowles-like publisher of a fancy magazine, surrounded by her flimsy battery of yea-saying no-men, cannot do double duty as the ruthless editor of a sexy-horror-story magazine ("A naked girl tied to a bedpost with a chimpanzee bran- dishing a whip? No more punch than a seed catalogue!")—obviously two entirely different breeds. Also, why ridicule things so monstrously laughable in themselves that any parody, even a far cleverer one than Perelman's, must turn into piddling anticlimax? The courtroom scene where justice is being jazzed up for the benefit of television cannot begin to compare with actual TV shows like *Divorce Court.*

Furthermore, Perelman's lines are simply not funny enough. "Our son, which he is home from Yale for midyear," or "I thought there was a colored gentleman in the woodpile," or "Suppose Simone Signorette [sic] didn't shack up with that guy in *Room at the Top,* where would this great industry be today?" or "He was on the Dean's List, morning, noon and night," or "It's Christmas Eve and the land- lord shut off the gas and he's starving.—The landlord?" and oodles more of the same just don't do the trick. When everything else fails him, Perelman promptly pulls out a bit of Yiddish and sticks it into the mouth of whoever is stage center ("You'll be the chief *shames* of the whole goddam production," or "A public disturbance at the inter- section of La Paloma and Alte Yenta Boulevards," or "Author of *The Joy of Cooking* and *Love and Knishes,*" and so on)—and everything else fails him altogether too often. Add to this such abject lapses of taste as having Bert Lahr do a scene in drag even though there are several overripe character actresses in the cast who could have done it at least as well, and you have an idea of the spirit that informs this mature entertainment.

Matters are not helped by Noel Willman's uningenious direction, William Pitkin's uninteresting sets, Don Walker's unsavory incidental music, and performances that are, all but one of them, undistinguished. That one is not Bert Lahr's, which is routine, but Larry Hagman's appealing Candide *après la lettre*. Every once in a while Perelman gets off a viable joke, as when a sculptress is working in Castille soap on a Procter and Gamble fellowship, but for most of the time *The Beauty Part* is a jejune and, for the audience, degrading affair.

But Off-Broadway boasts at least one half of a rewarding evening in *The Pinter Plays*. *The Dumb Waiter,* to be sure, is in Pinter's worst eclectic manner. Two inept hired killers are waiting for orders in the basement of an abandoned restaurant, and receiving crazy requests for food through a dumb waiter, which they frantically try to meet with the measly contents of their lunch basket. The final order reveals that the awaited victim is one of them, whom the other must kill. Throughout the play one is acutely conscious of Pinter waiting for Beckett to write him some better lines. But the second play, *The Collection,* written for television and so presumably obliged to be a little more communicative, does evoke splendidly the queasy ambience of two unwholesome households, one homosexual, one heterosexual. The kept boy and the wife who wears the pants may have committed adultery, which leads to blackmail, threats, minor violence and a barely breathable atmosphere of domestic nastiness. The question at the center remains unanswered in a somewhat Pirandellian fashion, but around the grain of mystery the play secretes its substance like an ominously glittering black pearl. It is cogently directed by Alan Schneider; and Henderson Forsythe, James Patterson, Patricia Roe, James Ray and a lovely little white kitten act it most persuasively. No one, to my knowledge, has captured more compellingly than Pinter has done here, the mingled playfulness and malice so typical of homosexual "marriages."

One may well shudder at the horrid neologism "anymore" in the title of Tennessee Williams' latest play, *The Milk Train Doesn't Stop Here Anymore*, but the play itself promptly supplies many far better causes for shudders. One would have to go back as far as *The Purification* to find a comparably abortive play in the Williams corpus. The characters are either wooden or preposterous, the plot could not involve one less, and the dialogue surpasses anything in Williams for long stretches of barren waste littered only with the skeletons of jokes gone astray. Take the pretentiousness of *Camino Real*, the dishonesty of *Cat on a Hot Tin Roof* or *Sweet Bird of Youth*, and the dullness of *Period of Adjustment*, roll them into one, and you have an inkling of *Milk Train*.

The rich Mrs. Flora Goforth is dying simultaneously in three villas on an Italian hilltop. Night and day, she is dictating her inane memoirs through ubiquitous walkie-talkies to her harassed secretary. To her comes a starving young poet in *Lederhosen*, Christopher Flanders, bringing a three-day-old hunger, a slender volume of his verse, translations of Hindu lore, a mobile he has constructed, and great good looks despite the advanced age (for a gigolo) of thirty-four. The secretary warms up to him, but the selfish and ludicrous Mrs. Goforth, who is absurdly deluding herself about her impending death, will not feed him unless he sleeps with her. Another despicable hag from a neighboring island informs her that Chris is known as The Angel of Death, because the elderly ladies he had attached himself to all died shortly thereafter. But this neighbor may be lying, for she wants Chris for herself, and he has a downright charismatic account of what he was able to do for those ladies while they lasted. There ensues a contest in which Mrs. Goforth tries to starve Chris into making love to her, but fails; he, however, manages to implant the seeds of salvation in her before he leaves.

That indefatigable mystagogue, *Time* magazine, with a little help from *The Pilot* (more overtly devoted to scholasticism), has already explicated for us the profound allegory of the play. Chris is a combination Christ and St. Christopher, Mrs. Goforth errant mankind about to kick off unsaved, the neighbor is the Devil tempting Christ on the mountain top, the four days without food a tithe of Christ's forty-day fast, Chris is thirty-four to denote that the action takes place after the crucifixion, and so on. How they could miss out on the mobile as the *primum mobile* with its planets and fixed stars, I cannot imagine, for Flora is left at play's end contemplating a slightly Calderized version of the army of unalterable law. No doubt much of this elucidation is, alas, relevant, but however heavenly *Milk Train* may be on the anagogical level, on the literal, it is of the earth, muddy.

Consider first the language. For wit, we get "Men clutched at my legs trying to dismount me so they could mount me," or "Do you trust anyone, Mrs. Goforth?—Certainly not. Not anyone human. I trust dogs, all except poodles. I've never trusted a poodle." For repartee: "You have nice teeth.—Thank you.—Don't thank me, thank the dentist.—I never go to the dentist.—Then thank the Good Lord for the calcium you sucked in with your mother's milk." Or "We could play double solitaire.—That's all we are playing now: solitaire without cards." This last, of course, verges on profundity, of which we also have examples like "Has it ever struck you that life is all memory, except for each passing moment?" And for poetry, we get "His lovely, lovely young head—it broke like the shell of a songbird," a certifiable synecdoche, to be sure, or "Dying under that angry old lion, the sun; under the faraway stars . . ."

But that is not all. The play gives us once again that pederastic image of the coveted bedfellow transubstantiated into an angel— sometimes, as in Cocteau's *Orphée,* an angel of life, but frequently, as in Albee's *The Sandbox,* an angel of death. Now, I find it difficult to accept a Christ whose loincloth is a pair of gibbous *Lederhosen,* a Savior whose sayings are apt to be "I'm all through with that loveless love bit—I can't make that scene any more." (Pardon me—"anymore.") Aberration should not be confused with salvation: the sacramental bread is not to be found in a basket. Or take the scene in which the bloated, repugnant old Mrs. Goforth, who has just spat blood, tosses out her nightgown from offstage and tries to lure Chris into her bed by alternately enumerating her hippopotamus charms and insulting or threatening. Is this parabolic? Is it supposed to be a proof of Chris's holiness? God knows, little as it means to resist a siren out of Hieronymus Bosch, it is the only concrete specimen of Christian morality we are treated to. Or is all this just a ghastly *frisson?* I seriously doubt that such total absence of aesthetic values could prove ethically valuable.

The play is not improved by Hermione Baddeley's anile crudeness or by Paul Roebling's uniform blandness and finishing-school vocalization. The sets of Jo Mielziner and the staging of Herbert Machiz are equally devoid of style and invention; but Mildred Dunnock, as the reptilian neighbor, and Ann Williams, as a harried, somewhat soured innocent, give irreproachable performances that are oases for the eye and ear. Mr. Williams' scatological eschatology notwithstanding, I don't believe you can get to heaven by milk train.

Summer, 1963

Mother Courage and Her Children
    by Bertolt Brecht

Six Characters in Search of an Author
    by Luigi Pirandello

Strange Interlude
    by Eugene O'Neill
    produced by The Actors Studio Theatre

Photo Finish
    by Peter Ustinov

Enter Laughing
    by Carl Reiner

Dear Me, the Sky Is Falling
    by Leonard Spigelgass
    based on a story by Gertrude Berg and James Yaffe

Tovarich
    book by David Shaw
    music by Lee Pockriss
    lyrics by Anne Croswell

It took *Mother Courage and Her Children* a quarter of a century to get to the New York stage, and it will take at least that long for the bad taste this production left in our mouths to be rinsed away.

The strange thing is that everyone concerned wanted to make the Broadway production as Brechtian as can be—except for little compromises which everyone also felt impelled to make. Thus *Mother Courage* manages to fall solidly between two stools and be neither good Brecht nor good Broadway theater.

Blame attaches to every aspect of this production. Eric Bentley, the translator, has devoted himself to Brecht to the point where he combs his hair à la Brecht, dresses Brechtianly, and behaves with Brecht-like waspishness. By all means let Brecht be God and Bentley his prophet—only what comes out in English? To begin with, Bentley is quite unable to catch the racy folksiness of the German, and his occasional use of slang merely emphasizes the middle-class colorlessness of his basic language. Next, he has cut (or been obliged to cut) about one sixth or seventh of the play, leaving hardly a longer speech undecimated. From such a key statement, for instance, as the Chaplain's in scene six about the harmlessness of war, the magnificently ironic basic utterance *"Der Krieg befriedigt nämlich alle Bedürfnis, auch die friedlichen darunter"* is missing, along with several juicy details. The big social-political speeches in scenes three and six are cut to the bone, and the mixture of cynicism, opportunism, bitter common sense and, on the other hand, hero worship and folly which the scenes contain becomes unperspicuous and uncompelling. Bentley presumes, however, to smuggle in little inventions of his own. In scene one, Courage, showing her papers, says, "Here's a Bible—picked it up somewhere to wrap my cucumbers in," which is taking us, humoristically, back to Methuselah; but there are even more banal interpolations, as when the Chaplain is made to remark "War is like love."

Worst, however, are Bentley's mistranslations. Often he misses jokes. Thus *"Und hat das Maul nicht aufgemacht, ausser wenn er gegessen hat. Und dann muss er,"* says the Chaplain to prove that Swiss Cheese was silent; but Bentley translates "Never once opened his mouth except to eat, which is necessary," where the "necessary" now refers to eating instead of to opening his mouth. It should have been something like "Never once opened his trap except to eat. And then he's got to." Again, explaining the Cook's nickname, Peter Piper, Yvette says *"Weil er die Pfeif nicht aus dem Maul genommen hat dabei,"* yet Bentley translates this highly sexual *dabei* with a non-committal "the whole time" which the audience managed beautifully to misunderstand. Still more serious are the downright mistranslations. Thus Courage's ironic comments in scene eight on her one man *"wo solid war"* become pointless because Bentley translates *solid* as "sound" instead of as "respectable." Or again, the Chaplain's warning not to treat peace as an *"altes, verrotztes Sacktuch"* (a filthy, old snotrag) loses all its meaningful brutality in Bentley's cozily familiar "snotty old hanky."

To have picked Jerome Robbins, an able choreographer and clever but chichi musical-comedy director, to stage *Mother Courage* was a curious whim. Robbins, with gingerly care, attempted to turn this into a near-Brechtian production. But all he achieved is self-consciousness in the performers, amateurish clichés in the stage movement, and a sense of emptiness rather than spiritual aridity. One had the funereal feeling of watching the show through its own semitransparent cerements. The few times Robbins dared invent something, it was foolish. Thus he had the Swedish commander in scene two pretend to offer the Chaplain some wine, only to splash it over the fellow's robes and hand, dyeing it blood-red—a piece of sensationalism quite out of key with the requisite cynicism. Even Kattrin's death scene is impaired: she is not allowed to show sufficient concern for her mother, the wagon and her own safety, but must drum away with almost unrelieved heroism. When she is shot, the few last drum beats—a real *coup de théâtre*—are jettisoned in favor of immediate collapse and death.

But it is the casting and acting of the play that must be reckoned the weakest link in this brittle chain. Only the Angel of Perversity, or Broadway, could have chosen Anne Bancroft to play Courage, the archetypal peasant turned small businesswoman. Miss Bancroft, who grew up in the Bronx and prepared fo this part by studying the peddlers of the Lower East Side, makes the canteen woman a smart-aleck, slightly snappish, city proletarian. That her Bronx-Brooklyn speech and mannerisms effectively preclude her being a seventeenth-century Bavarian peasant is bad enough, but that she is young, light-weight, and tries very hard not to play realistically (in accordance with "epic theater") and as a result gives only a promising high-school performance, is a more serious matter. Graver yet is that she is totally incapable of summoning up a kind of basic humanity, that she cannot weld cunning, pigheadedness, greed, obtuseness, primeval femininity, occasional grudging sentiment and ultimate preposterousness into the figure of a more-than-life-size pigmy, an eponymous worm, a creature hovering between pathos and absurdity, enduring in her fierce triviality. Worst of all, Miss Bancroft and Mr. Robbins contrive to make Courage indomitable. She ought to be merely dogged. Yet dismal as Miss Bancroft's fiasco is, it is not just one person's inadequacy. It is the failure of the whole American theater system and stage life to produce an actress of such thoroughgoing humanity and roundedness as Therese Giehse or Helene Weigel, the two great German interpreters of Mother Courage.

The other performances were no better: a typically American wise guy of a Cook, a sly young jokester of a Chaplain, an Yvette laden with the commonplaces of cabaret theater, and so on. Only Zohra Lampert's Kattrin was a respectable, indeed a solid, performance, though she unfortunately conceives of muteness as verging on feeble-mindedness.

Ming Cho Lee's settings missed the mark by retaining a slightly Oriental elegance in the midst of dilapidation and squalor. Thus the main piece of décor is a kind of orangey cyclorama forming four fifths of the horizon. On it are painted faint ghosts of horizontal clouds, and it is propped up by slender ascending ribs which are cleverly—too cleverly—not quite parallel. Between scenes, this entire large canvas was covered with slide projections showing the disasters of World War II, retreating armies or harried lines of refugees, and serving merely to clutter up the stage with giant tautologies.

The music also suffered. The Soldier's Song in scene six was left out, as was the Chaplain's in scene three; of the Solomon Song only one half (not including Solomon!) remained. The Lullaby in scene twelve was omitted at one performance I attended, and reinstated at another but without orchestral accompaniment, thus making that scene more heartrending, the very thing against which Brecht repeatedly warned. And there were quite a few times when the orchestrations sounded more like Richard Rodgers than Paul Dessau. Even when a song was all there, as the one about the pleasures of settledness which is supposed to come as a terrible taunt to the ragged, hungry, homeless Courage and Kattrin, who hear it as they pass a prosperous farmhouse, it was made to issue, instead, from a speaker system, as if a jukebox were providing a pause that refreshes.

The reviews of *Mother Courage* ranged from the hypocritically respectful to the enthusiastically asinine. The main audience reaction is vapid laughter, shocked tsk-tsking, and dutiful but unconvinced applause. Unless Anne Bancroft's Hollywood-sent Oscar keeps the play running, it stands a good chance of a short unhappy life. And, with heavy hearts, Brecht-lovers will have to speed it along to oblivion.

•   •   •

It is amazing what a good production and fine translation can do even for a play that is securely accepted as a masterpiece. For all the respect and admiration we might have had for *Six Characters in Search of an Author,* it takes a rare production such as the one now at the small, semicircular Martinique Theatre to make us relish the play with spontaneous joy. What William Ball, the director, and Paul Avila Mayer, the translator, have done is to rescue a classic from sinking ever deeper into its own classicism—without resorting, however, to that vulgar and obfuscating horseplay with which Tyrone Guthrie studded his revival at the Phoenix. Suddenly Pirandello stands before us as the peer of any great nineteenth- or twentieth-century playwright, the worthy heir of Shakespeare.

We realize now that *Six Characters* is not only a brilliant examination of the insoluble problem of illusion and reality, but also a humane study of compassion and indifference; a thorough analysis of the relation of the author to his work, of the created character to the public, to posterity, and to his playwright—which last, by extension, may also be the relationship of man to God; and finally a magnificent imaging of the theater: its magic, callousness, and disturbing dual citizenship in fact and dream, which may, after all, be the greater fact.

All this is brought out beautifully by William Ball's direction—by its boundless inventiveness and energy, its ceaselessly flowing pictorial suggestiveness. As the audience sits in the theater, things begin to happen quite imperceptibly. Technicians and actors seem to be preparing their work on a brightly lit stage; they murmur words semi-audibly and move about casually. This cannot be the play. When the Director enjoins us to watch a rehearsal quietly, we are persuaded that nothing more than just that is happening. Suddenly, the lights go out, as though a fuse had blown, there is protestation and cursing, then one light goes on again. There, dressed in black, undulating in eerie unison, in an uncanny, penumbral, as it were, underwater lighting, is an at first indeterminate number of presences compressed into a kind of living cube—rather like some deep-sea fish pressing hungrily against the glass of their aquarium.

I cannot dwell in detail on the extraordinarily imaginative manner in which Ball has staged the tantalizing interaction of these six very alive fictions with the far more inchoate but supposedly real Actors and Director—as real, that is, as you and I, however real that may be. Never is this production allowed to bog down; things are continually happening: on the stage, along the sidelines of it, in the audience, around and behind the spectators, sometimes just audibly in the corridors outside. And however much our attention may be engaged in several places at the same time, whatever is confusing is confusing the way the dramatist intended it, the way life is when it is lived by us, or, perhaps, when we are being lived by it.

Ball's great achievement is that he has found movements and actions to go with every bit of what in other productions of the play is merely exposition or philosophizing or recrimination, so that what might have looked like opera without music becomes an intellectually disturbing, emotionally tugging three-ring circus in which the funny, the frightening, and the unbearably sad are enacted simultaneously to our delight and awe. When, in the last scene, the Director leaves the stage, he brushes, deeply shaken, against the only remaining source of light: a bridge of spots that is left swaying anxiously to and fro on the empty stage—an objective correlative for all of our minds wrenched from their conventional assumptions.

Ball's direction and Mayer's translation, abetted by Jules Fisher's almost dialectically penetrating lighting, make this a major occasion in the theater, even though the acting is generally only adequate; with very interesting work contributed, however, by Michael O'Sullivan as the Director and Richard A. Dysart as the Father.

AND WHAT did another revival, this one by the celebrated—or is it legendary?—Actors Studio in its first public appearance since its formative days, bring to light? The play was Eugene O'Neill's *Strange Interlude,* revived by an all-star cast and directed by José Quintero, the entire production meant to testify to the contribution the Studio, Lee Strasberg and the "method" have made to the American theater. On the evidence of this production, it is nothing more or less than setting it back a good thirty years.

In his early plays, O'Neill wrote sympathetically and straightforwardly about the life in the merchant marine that he knew. In his last plays, when his intellectually shaping and linguistically lifegiving faculties had finally matured, he wrote two or three incisive, many-sided, fully fleshed plays whose humanity will not wither with years. But in between he turned out some of the worst plays ever concocted by a major talent, plays based on imperfectly digested European influences meant clearly *pour épater les bourgeois,* not the least impressionable bourgeois being O'Neill himself. To dig up one of the most turgid and turbid plays of this middle period, *Strange Interlude,* a nine-act, five-hour megatherium, even more edentate in its present fossilized form, to conceive of it with bloody literal-mindedness and direct it with pious stodginess, is in itself a disaster. To populate it with a nebula of Actors Studio luminaries—Geraldine Page, Ben Gazzara, Pat Hingle, Jane Fonda, Geoffrey Horne—and a few other "names" drawn into the Studio orbit—Franchot Tone, Betty Field, William Prince—has turned it into a carnival of egomaniacal circus horses each pulling in its own direction. Everybody is playing his trademark: Miss Page is back there summer-and-smoking it up, Gazzara is still wallowing on a hot tin roof, Hingle is still spreading around some leftover Inge and MacLeish. Granted that if they were playing what O'Neill wrote, things would scarcely be improved, this much is certain: *Strange Interlude* remains a dreadful cross between uncomprehended Freud and unfunny Coward; and the Actors Studio cannot even foster the minimum requirement for such a group: homogeneous ensemble acting.

NEXT THERE IS Peter Ustinov's *Photo Finish,* which, if one could see it through the wrong side of the telescope, might make an acceptable ten-minute bauble, but blown up into a three-act play it is only a large bladderful of blather. It bursts sooner or later, according to how much tolerance one has for exchanges like "He works for the Government of Southern Australia, refusing immigrants.—Well, if he refuses them, he probably accepts some of them.—Oh no, they've got another man for that." Even this may be a little racier than most of the wit, which is on the level of "He's the kind of person who'd take blondes dancing vertically at first, horizontally later" or "You used to grunt and groan in my arms like a small warthog."

What passes for the idea here is to confront a novelist of eighty with his earlier selves, aged sixty, forty and twenty, respectively, as well as with his long-dead father (which allows for further witticisms on the order of "You have no right to forbid me anything: you may be my father, but I am older than you are!") and to make the present and its past, and the past and its future intermingle like a garbled lesson in conjugations. "Writing," says the protagonist's octogenarian self, "is not difficult. It's thought, and protecting that thought against wit and ornament." Mr. Ustinov, who despite the wanness of his jokes is only forty-two, has not yet made this discovery of his future self. As of now he is still protecting his wit and ornament against thought, and at this, I must confess, he is quite successful. Which would be all right if the wit were worth protecting against anything at all, but facile ironies like "She's an old lady, and her beastliness has real sweep and majesty to it" might just as well be left to drown in the martinis that must have begotten them.

Ustinov's main concern is clearly not art but economics: how to make his single self go farthest. Time was when he could write, direct and act in a play whose principals were four colonels, only one of whom he could portray. Now, however, he has perfected his technique, and besides writing, directing and starring, gives us four principals who are all aspects of the same vaguely autobiographical self. It is to be hoped that ultimately he will achieve a form of mitosis enabling him to play all the parts himself. For the time being, though, Ustinov has to put up with such other actors as Dennis King and Paul Rogers who summarily outdo his own rather hammy performance.

BOTH *Enter Laughing* and *Dear Me, the Sky Is Falling* are comedies based on the ascendancy of one supposedly riotously funny character. In *Enter Laughing*, it is a nice little Jewish young man who decides to become an actor instead of working in a shop, and who triumphs finally over all odds, including his own complete lack of talent. In *Dear Me*, it is a sweet, middle-aged Jewish mother who decides she will not run everybody else's life (after having made a total mess of things thereby), goes to a psychiatrist, learns to lay off interfering—until the various members of her family end up asking her to manipulate them and proceeding to do on their own what the beloved autocrat used to coerce them into. And everything settles down again into pristine prosaicism. The only thing that recommends *Enter Laughing* is the very special comic talent of Alan Arkin, who possesses what I can describe only oxymoronically as a charming stolidity, a dogged grace, a volubly brooding, seductive schlemihlhood that makes his corner of *Enter Laughing* jocund and bright indeed. As for Gertrude Berg, who is coauthor and star of *Dear Me*, her self-satisfaction assumes such heroic proportions that it actually borders on adequacy. The real acting in the play—as much as a performance in an obviously contrived work can ever be real acting—is that of the always excellent William Daniels, and a noteworthy newcomer, Ron Leibman. But the true interest of this three-act contraption lies in the fact that—O temerity!—it dares pit two of America's most sacred cows, Mom and the Psychoanalyst, against each other. Needless to say, the bout ends in an honorable draw, satisfying to both parties, and permitting the audience to have a good laugh at its idols while cherishing the feeling that this laughter itself is a kind of incense.

One thing, at least, becomes more and more clear: how right Kenneth Tynan is in his contention that if you took the Jews away from the Broadway scene, there would be no comedy left. I know, I know, but I am not resigned. There must be other sources of merriment besides the eternal ambitious mothers who want their sons to be respectable professional men, their daughters married to doctors or lawyers, and all members of their family eating heartily. Jokes must be derivable from other subjects besides harried fathers, lovably bossed by their wives and dreaming of homes in Florida and holes-in-one, who feebly side up with their children and comically sink in the quicksands of "the Business." But most of all I am sick unto death of the ugliness of Jewish speech: of its clichés, its barbarisms, its whining inflections. And of the gratuitous collusion that engulfs the playhouses in which these shows are on view: the confidence on both sides of the footlights that because two such vacuous mirrors as the commercial theater and the commercial audience can repeat any paltry object caught between them unto infinity, the nugacity and dreariness of that object are somehow remitted, and the object itself ennobled to the point of deserving its pestilential permanence. It is entirely probable that if what I am showered with were to be plays about Welshmen, Yorkshiremen, Sicilians or Patagonians, my reactions would be no less vehement; but *this* is what I am drowning in, and while even one corner of my mouth remains above it, I shall intone my protest against *this*.

Tovarich is a large show—as large and frozen and barren as Siberia, to which its authors deserve to be banished. David Shaw's book manages to dilute Jacques Deval's original (which, I admit, is an achievement of sorts); Lee Pockriss' score resembles music only when it resembles somebody else's, and then it certainly resembles; Anne Croswell's lyrics are a trifle better, or more exactly better trifles; Herbert Ross's dances are in this gifted but erratic choreographer's erratic manner—though here and there a touch of the gifted Ross does rear its toes; Peter Glenville supplies his customary slick and soulless direction; and whereas Rolf Gerard's settings alternate between the routine and the resourceful, the usually excellent costumes by Motley are, in this show, steadily mediocre.

And the performances? Well, both Jean Pierre Aumont and Vivien

Leigh have an undeniable savoir-faire and some of that dubious appeal which, with a lump in my throat, I shall call glamour; and for the benefit of those impressed by such things, I can declare both stars extremely well preserved, and in fact rather too young for their parts. Miss Leigh, indeed, is still in full possession of that kittenishness with which she so magisterially mucked up Shakespeare's Cleopatra a dozen years ago, and which so ill befits the Grand Duchess Tatiana's personality and the diva's age. But when she does a charleston—a quite ordinary charleston, mind you—she brings the house down, as though the Pope were condescending to make a personal appearance at the Broadway Theater singing "Home on the Range." For the rest, such able performers as Louise Kirtland, Alexander Scourby and George S. Irving are wasted on spineless parts; and there are two juveniles, Byron Mitchell and Margery Gray, who perform their absolutely distasteful material as though they were convinced they could make it worse. And, by God, they are right.

WINTER, 1963-1964

THE REHEARSAL
  by Jean Anouilh

LUTHER
  by John Osborne

CHIPS WITH EVERYTHING
  by Arnold Wesker

SPOON RIVER
  by Edgar Lee Masters

CORRUPTION IN THE PALACE OF JUSTICE
  by Ugo Betti

THE PRIVATE EAR AND THE PUBLIC EYE
  by Peter Shaffer

PHÈDRE
  by Jean Baptiste Racine
  produced by the Compagnie Marie Bell

THE FIRST THREE successful plays of the Broadway season are all English imports, all of them with English casts.

First came *The Rehearsal*, by Jean Anouilh, as translated by

Pamela Hansford Johnson and Kitty Black, in its London production but with a different English cast. In French, this is one of Anouilh's best plays, and was originally staged at the Théâtre Marivaux— appropriately enough, since it concerns a group of decadent twentieth-century aristocrats rehearsing a play by Marivaux for the amusement of next week's dinner guests, while performing the ghastly drama which is their life and which just barely manages to amuse them. As played by Barrault and his company, this was memorable theater. How a brave, lovely, innocent girl is destroyed by the elegant and cruel artifice, the genteel and sophisticated viciousness of a jaded society, has been Anouilh's theme more than once. But here, against the background of the play within the play, which echoes, underlines, anticipates, winds itself in and out of the events of the play proper, Anouilh has created a cat-and-mouse tale the more horrible because, shockingly, the mouse is all alone in a world of cats who kill with predatoriness, with cattiness and even with kindness. And if the mouse escapes with her life, though irreparably mauled, and even if the blackest tomcat dies an expiatory death, this does nothing to miti-gate the horror of all those other cats going on as if nothing had hap-pened, with their lives of charming, gracious, utterly ruthless *mari-vaudage.*

Though lacking the precision of the original—notably in its gram-mar—the translation is serviceable enough. But what else is? Peter Coe's direction is unfailingly heavy-handed and banal: scene after scene is played *at* the audience, and speech upon speech is made aggressively overemphatic. One of the main points of *The Rehearsal* is lost: that these Carborundum-hearted aristocrats can hurt and destroy even while playing with velvet paws, and that the epigram is the shortest distance between style and the stiletto. Coe is not helped by his actors, either. That Keith Michell should be a much-employed classical leading man in England can have no natural causes; he makes the Count not into the one redeemable character he should be, spoiled but at least not rotten; rather, he turns him into a brat and a boor, who moreover is always quite literally leading with his chin. The nobleman drunk with his own rhetoric becomes a punch-drunk prize fighter; at best he mistakes oiliness for polish. True suavity is lacking also in the rest of the cast, and Alan Badel, a good realistic heavy, makes a ludicrous tragic villain. (One thinks with regret of what Jean Servais and, after him, Jacques Dacqmine were able to do with this part.) Only Coral Browne, as the Countess, brings off a well-rounded performance, though even this is not free from a slight odor of fishwifery. The very sets and costumes are merely adequate, which in a work full of precarious and exquisite balances is simply not good enough.

WITH JOHN OSBORNE's *Luther*, quite the opposite obtains. Here the production is highly proficient in almost every detail, but the play itself is hollow. Hollow and shallow, to be exact. What Osborne has tried to do is to write a genuine English Brechtian play, modeling himself largely on *Galileo* (which possibly is not one of Brecht's best works and certainly not one of the best models), but he has produced only a brazen simulacrum. It is hollow in the sense that Osborne's Martin Luther is not a complex, rousing, captivating, charismatic leader: underneath Albert Finney's stinging performance there is only a neurotic mishandled by his father, tortured by inadequate bowel movements, obsessed by images of defecation with which he torments himself and others. No doubt all this was so, and the porcine, constipated, scatological Luther assuredly did exist. But no less assuredly there must have been more to him.

Two factors contribute largely to the hollowness of the protagonist. One is that Osborne tried very carefully to stick to historical data and put together the preponderant part of Luther's speeches out of the reformer's actual preserved utterances. But here several difficulties arise: not enough intimate material by and about Luther is recorded, what there is does not necessarily provide suitable speeches and incidents for a play, and Osborne's selections from the available sources are not always the most judicious. How, for instance, in a Freudianly oriented play, can one omit Luther's public proclamation that his first and foremost reason for taking a wife was that it would please his father? Above all, dramatic and verbal invention is mandatory even in a historical play; Brecht, for that matter, had no compunction about making up all but a few basic facts of the Galileo story.

The other reason for this hollowness is Osborne's insistence on making something negative, doubting, unsure under the arrogance, the key to Luther's revolt. Even if that were all there was to it—and I cannot help feeling that this rebellion without cause, or nearly, is more characteristic of Osborne than of Luther—it does not make for strong drama or a convex, alive hero. The very father-son conflict in

Luther is not commandingly developed, yet that is the farthest Osborne sticks his nose into Lutherian nosography.*

As for the shallowness, it stems from Osborne's inability to make the people, places, and issues come to life. Since Brecht is the model, where is the portrait of an age (real or imaginary, it matters not) that we get in *Mother Courage;* where is the dramatic pot running over with hot, bubbling incidents, minor characters, curious inventions? What could be more schematic and stolidly conceived than Osborne's Knight who is supposed to convey Luther's betrayal of the peasants; what could be more perfunctory and unintegrated than the sudden emergence and disappearance of a Mrs. Luther?

But, of course, this is Osborne's weakness: he writes dazzlingly about single characters who fulminate in deprecation and imprecation, who can scorch and blast a whole human landscape with their tirades; but when it comes to interrelating characters, presenting complementary or conflicting views with equal vivacity and conviction, Osborne's powers flag. The one strong exception is the second act of *George Dillon,* but one does not know to what extent this achievement is owed to Osborne's collaborator on that play, Anthony Creighton.

Within these limits, though, *Luther* is still a vigorous, splashy, perfervid piece of theater, if only for secondary reasons: Tony Richardson's resourcefully and relentlessly forward-thrusting direction, Albert Finney's boldly sculptured Luther compensating with winning idiosyncrasy for the lack of individuality in the writing, efficient supporting performances among which John Moffatt's Cajetan is *primus inter pares*, Jocelyn Herbert's simple but suitable scenery, and John Addison's finely integrated music.

ANOTHER ENGLISH IMPORT, however, manages to combine a decent play with a superlative production; this is Arnold Wesker's *Chips with Everything*. Wesker's talent has progressed hearteningly from play to play—from *The Kitchen* to *Chicken Soup with Barley* to *I'm Speaking About Jerusalem* to this new work, all—with the possible exception of *Roots*—mark not a step but a jump ahead.

Chips with Everything has a minuscule plot: it tells of how an

---

* It is a sad comment on Osborne's play that even such a relatively clumsy book as Erik H. Erikson's *Young Man Luther* makes Luther more interesting, and that a mere short poem such as W. S. Merwin's "Luther" leaves a livelier image in the mind.

upper-class young man, Pip, becomes an enlisted man in the RAF and insists on throwing in his lot with lower- and middle-class youths whom he manages to turn quietly against their sneering superiors in rank and caste, until these break him. They break him not by savaging and punishing him, but by slowly and sinisterly convincing him, with persistent and pliant pseudo-solicitude, that his motive is personal pride, that his refusal to become an officer is only his arrogant urge to be a two-bit (or, I should say, penny-halfpenny) saint and leader of the benighted and undiscriminating. Needless to say, the play is an allegory of how British class consciousness perpetuates itself by blandly devious means in a world where Draconic measures are no longer practicable, but where mock-tolerant absorption proves as effective as bloody repressions did formerly.

If that were all, however, the play would not be more than deserving; what makes it impressive is that it goes beyond local allegory into universal symbolism. For, as Wesker himself has stated, *Chips with Everything* is about the way society neutralizes the hand grenade that is genius, not by wrenching out its firing-pin, but by melting down the whole contraption in the heat of paternalistic, pharisaical approval. This phenomenon is as American as it is English (I stress this because a frequent objection raised here is that the play is scarcely relevant to our purportedly classless society). As Gerald Weales has justly noted about the United States, "Any man who lifts his voice to criticize our society today is in danger of becoming a popular idol . . . permissiveness has become our weapon against criticism. Our society, largely through the activity of the mass media, has learned to absorb any criticism by celebrating the critic."

There is still more to *Chips*. For though the play is mainly naturalistic, as Wesker's earlier plays have been, there are moments when the language slowly becomes unreal: reduced to bare, essential phrases that do not answer any questions, but whose repetition with increasing intensity or a desperately dying fall ends up by suggesting the deserts that lie beyond the reiterated platitudes—deserts of barren isolation where the wind of words scarcely leaves even a tracery in the sand.* There are two such scenes between Pip, that Sancho-Panzized Don Quixote, and Charley, a quixotic, idolizing Sancho; as played by Gary Bond and Derek Fowlds, and directed by John Dexter, they are extremely hard to forget.

Dexter's staging, the entire cast in a spectacular display of ensem-

---

* It may be that Wesker is here undergoing the influence of two fascinating young British playwrights, Ann Jellicoe and Henry Livings.

ble acting, Jocelyn Herbert's spare, mobile, and amply suggestive décor, along with Wesker's neat device of using fanatical RAF drill as a connecting thread between scenes (besides allowing it to constitute some of the liveliest scenes themselves), infectious and wholly authentic army humor that is ready at the drop of a rifle to turn into pathos or drama, all these contribute to an evening of perhaps not great—because intellectually oversimplified—but total, and totally affecting, theater.

SPOON RIVER began as *Spoon River Anthology* but dropped the last third of its title because, as the producer announced, many intelligent and educated people were put off by the fact that they did not know the meaning of the word "anthology." Actually, a better edited title would have been *Anthology*, for a good many intelligent people must have been put off by the fact that they did know the meaning of the words "Spoon River."

To sweep the sepulchral dust off Edgar Lee Masters' "poetry" and put it on the stage where it belongs even less than on the shelf is an idea that could have occurred only to an American actor. The American actor is a species that knows nothing whatsoever about poetry, but knows what he likes: Sandburg, Stephen Vincent Benét, Edna St. Vincent Millay, and if someone calls his attention to him, Edgar Lee Masters. (No one has yet suggested Eugene Field, Bliss Carman or John G. Neihardt, but that too may come to pass.) And before you know it, you get—along with suitable interludes on the guitar—an Evening with Carl Sandburg, a Night with Edna St. Vincent Millay, or a Spoon River with or without Anthology.

In case any of you have been fortunate enough to forget what Masters' free verse reads like, here are a few representative reminders:

(DRAMATIC)

From the dust I lift a voice of protest:
My flowering side you never saw!
Ye living ones, ye are fools indeed
Who do not know the ways of the wind.

(LYRICAL)

She took my strength by minutes,
She took my life by hours,
She drained me like a fevered moon
That saps the spinning world.

(SOPHISTICATED)   *One night, in a room in the Rue de Rivoli,*
I was drinking wine with a black-eyed cocotte
And the tears swam into my eyes.

(IRONIC)   *Seeds in a dry pod, tick, tick, tick,*
Tick, tick, tick, like mites in a quarrel—
Faint iambics that the full breeze wakens—
But the pine trees make a symphony thereof. . . .
Tick, tick, tick, what little iambics,
While Homer and Whitman roared in the pines.

Imagine now four actors, with interludes from two folk singer-guitarists, with tricksy costume and bogus accent changes, reciting and acting out this American classic. Particularly when Joyce Van Patten is an abject vulgarian, and of the others only Charles Aidman has any real dignity (but on his shoulders rests the indignity of conceiving this adaptation). This First Melodrama Quartet labors desperately; but you cannot make an old, perfumed silk purse into anything as real even as a sow's ear.

The reviewers, naturally, ladled out the superlatives reserved for something cultural like *Spoon River*. But the public has a healthy resistance to fare like this, and, while Walter and Taubman roared in the aisles, refused to make a symphony thereof. Yet as I write this, advertising of the triune sort—buttering up the consumer, categorical imperatives, and cut-rate tickets—threatens to take *Spoon River* out of the soup. Well, if the audience wants to see deadly verse epitaphs deadeningly dragged onto the stage, that is no doubt the theatrical subdivision of the American way of death.

WE ARE CONTINUALLY being told by a fairly vocal minority that Ugo Betti is a major playwright; some assure us that the early Betti is the real thing; some blame the English versions for obscuring his merits. Of the three Betti plays I have seen prior to *Corruption in the Palace of Justice*, only *Goat Island*, with its final *coup de théâtre*, lingers in my memory, and I would be greatly interested to learn who these "most critics in Italy" are, who, according to a program note by the producers of *Corruption*, regard him "as a greater dramatic artist" than Pirandello. It may, of course, be that as a "dramatic artist" he was greater; as a playwright, he is considerably inferior.

Corruption begins promisingly, with an atmosphere of guilt and intrigue in a high court where corruption has thoroughly possessed one of the justices (but which?) and apparently tainted the others. Tentacular suspicion, the clamminess of culpability, and the viscous fear of being culpable are neatly evoked by the first act. But the Kafkaesque suggestiveness soon coagulates into cough syrup full of sticky philosophizing and bittersweet sentimentality. Anouilh and existentialism make their entrances—but an Anouilh without the verbal felicity, and the existentialism not of Sartre's drama but of Gabriel Marcel's. Nor is Betti content with propagating the thesis that evil triumphs only to find in its very triumph condign punishment; no, he must, with his customary Christering, show us supreme evil repentant at last, rather like Iago going off on a pilgrimage to Lourdes.

Betti's one unquestionable though theatrically dangerous virtue, his dogged moral earnestness, loses out at the hands of a motley cast and Richard Altman's mediocre staging. The acting styles include everything from Muni Seroff's Yiddish Art Theatre at its flamboyantly tawdry worst to Maria Tucci's Methodized amateurishness. In between, there are Leonardo Cimino's B-movie plug-ugliness and David Hooks's perfect nullity trying to make itself interesting with meaningless changes of vocal pace, and as unsavory a bunch of inexpensive character actors as ever struck poses as though to strike them dead.

In a very important sense, Peter Shaffer's double bill, *The Private Ear and The Public Eye*, is satisfying theater. Because it proves that without writing a work of lasting literary merit, one can still produce something intelligent, entertaining, and best of all apperceptible and appreciable on all levels of audience sophistication. It is the kind of theater that aims for neither heights nor depths, but sweeps cleanly across all members of an audience that for years now have been painfully drifting apart, and amiably reunites them. Breadth is Mr. Shaffer's dimension, and the young Englishman takes possession of it with modesty and good taste.

In *The Private Ear* a shy, innocent young man is being pushed into the seduction of a pseudo-shy, seeming-innocent young woman by his friend, a certifiably unshy non-innocent. The sexual theme, amusingly handled in itself, gains interest by mirroring the sociological. In this lower middle-class milieu the hero's atypical love of serious music and his hi-fi, the pandering friend's donjuanism, the girl's specious respectability, all become attempts, ludicrous or pathetic, to ascend socially. The funny sexual skirmish is part of the class war. It is all done with good humor, exemplary economy of means, and a sympathy that never strays into either sogginess or smart-aleckry. A potentially static situation is further enlivened by merrily meaningful stage business, and it is amazing how much relevant action can be got into the putting on of socks or application of underarm deodorant. The only lapse comes at the end, when the hero's cherished Puccini record has failed to seduce the girl for him; he brutally scratches it, and sits listening to the crippled music. The symbolic flourish might work in a short story; on stage, at the end of a nice, realistic little play, it rings a false note.

The Public Eye is a more ambitious affair, and though it has wonderful exuberance and ample comic invention, it does ultimately miss the mark. It cannot quite decide whether it wants to be Peter Sellers' type of farcical comedy verging on dropping pants, or something more metaphysical and "absurd" in the manner of Ionesco, which leads to contradictions and eventual wobbliness. I can willingly suspend my disbelief or believe in unwilling suspenders, but I cannot do both at once. Absurdist farce is as possible as farcical absurdity, but one or the other element must predominate and set the tone.

In both plays, acting and direction are delightfully aglimmer, though occasionally exaggerated. In the first piece, Geraldine McEwan does put on her commonness rather too thickly, and in the second, both Barry Foster and Moray Watson are seduced into a burlesque swishing it up by the talented but overeager director, Peter Wood. Nonetheless, all give generous evidence of comic mastery, and Brian Bedford's lovable music-lover is, succinctly, perfect.

IMPORTING FROM FRANCE, on the other hand, seems less profitable nowadays than importing from England. The Compagnie Marie Bell opened with a *Phèdre* that made mincemeat of everything, from Racine to common decency. Marie Bell, never a great actress but always a competent one, has not improved with decrepitude. Her diction is still fine, her technique accomplished but a craft rather than an art, and her mezza voce remains good. But when this apparition of a transvestite Halloween pumpkin—a grotesque plaster of Paris mask topped by a flaming, five-bell-alarm wig—attempts to emote, let us say to suffer, she immediately reminds us of a grinning bust of Voltaire. The voice, when elated, turns into a croak; when tearful, into a cackle. As for the movements of that heavily shrouded body, it goes the aged Bernhardt more than one better: the Divine Sarah had one wooden leg; the Demonic Marie may have one fleshy limb. The rest of the cast do their level best to reduce the long, straight, parallel lines of the alexandrine to wiggly hachure, and manage, it must be granted, to find each his individual way of being frightful. The shining exception is Danielle Volle as Aricie: lovely, dignified, her voice rich and well modulated, she is the ray of sunshine dancing on the morass.

THE HERO of Howard Teichmann's *A Rainy Day in Newark* is named Kodiak; everything else about the play is grizzly.

SPRING, 1964

THE RESISTIBLE RISE OF ARTURO UI
  by Bertolt Brecht

THE BALLAD OF THE SAD CAFÉ
  by Edward Albee
  from the novel by Carson McCullers

THE TROJAN WOMEN
  by Euripides
  produced by the Circle in the Square Theater

IN WHITE AMERICA
  by Martin B. Duberman

PLAY
  by Samuel Beckett

THE LOVER
  by Harold Pinter

SOME FAILURES deserve anatomizing. Not such things as Tennessee Williams' revised *Milk Train*, which actually managed to be worse than the unrevised version, no mean feat. But what of *Arturo Ui?* Brecht and Broadway simply were not made for each other. *Mother Courage* failed rapidly last season; this season, *Ui* lasted less than a week. It is a dated play, nowhere near so good as *Courage,* but again the fault is much more Broadway's than Brecht's: the same forces that whittled down the title from *The Resistible Rise of Arturo Ui* to just plain *Arturo Ui* are responsible for the play's irresistible fall.

Brecht wrote this work in 1941 in exile in Finland. The Nazis were at the height of their power: neutral countries might be impressed by the Nazi successes and still ignorant of the extent of Nazi bestiality. At such a time there was every reason to write a play that transposes Germany to the ganglands of Chicago, and turns Hitler and his cohorts into an Al Capone and his henchmen who control an absurd but sinister Cauliflower Trust and gradually exterminate or expropriate the supposedly honest world around them. As Brecht put it in his notes to the play, it is to be performed "in the grand style . . . but pure travesty must, of course, be avoided; even in the midst of the grotesque, the atmosphere of gruesomeness must not give way for a minute." In the recent, and very bad, film *The Condemned of Altona* we see one brief, brilliant sequence from *Arturo Ui* as performed by Brecht's Berliner Ensemble. It is grotesque and it is gruesome, and it works. The Broadway production, a house divided against Brecht as well as against itself, collapsed miserably.

Almost all the blame must rest with the adapter, George Tabori, and the director, Tony Richardson. What they turned out was olla podrida mixed with bouillabaisse and tutti-frutti. First of all, they plagiarized from Chaplin's *The Great Dictator,* and gave the whole show a circusy, burlesque tone that was ridiculous without being frightening. Here were Chaplin's sagging costumes, hypertrophic shoes, tomfoolery with pistols, cowerings under tables, but quite without Chaplin's genius. The next layer imposed on the play was Damon Runyonish Brooklynese farce. Brecht's Ui was born in the Bronx, but to Brecht this merely meant poverty and grubbiness. Tabori and Richardson superimpose a guys-and-dolls atmosphere of homey jocularity which proceeds to clash both with the Chaplinesque and the Brechtian. A further layer is manifest in some of the sets, costumes, and make-up. Here the designer Rouben Ter-Arutunian echoes what he did some years ago for the Brecht-Weill *Seven Deadly Sins:* a satire in the manner of George Grosz on Berlin in the porcine thirties; indeed, in the last scene, the Cauliflower boys emerge in full-fledged Nazi uniforms, further muddling the tone of the play.

But it is Tabori's adaptation that adds still another stratum, possibly the worst: unfunny pastiche. Brecht has written some of the play in blank verse, some in rhyming couplets with various mock-heroic allusions to Shakespeare and Goethe's *Faust*. Tabori, an unwitty would-be wit, seized upon this to write into the text not only some of the ghastliest doggerel this side of Christmas cards, but also every kind of parody of Shakespearean and other famous lines, distorted references to music-hall songs, bathroom humor galore, anachronisms, and what have you. This vintage vandalism yields in quick succession gems like "There's something rotten in the state of Illinois," "Friends, what's in a name?" "Friends, countrymen, Brooklynites, lend me your faiths!" and a whole gallery of wreckage from *The Tempest*, like "Blue cops carousing full of airs and graces," "Have you dropped your ideas about a City Loan?—Dropped five fathoms in the earth and deeper," "She hates the smell of cauliflower now.—A very ancient, fish-like smell it is," and so on and on. When Brecht alludes to the wooing scene in *Richard III*, Tabori, nothing loath, transcribes nearly the whole scene verbatim. But when Brecht alludes to *Faust*, poor Tabori misses the point completely. Further, he tries to get every sort of easy and inappropriate laugh out of references to or paraphrases from "Barbara Fritchie," *Sturm und Drang*, John Birch, "My Melancholy Baby," "Miss Otis Regrets," and even uses out-of-place slang like "fink" or stoops to lifting a gag out of *Chips with Everything*. Other jokes run as follows: "Where are the thugs of yesteryear?" "Is this the face that launched a thousand tricks?" and "Sheet has kicked the bucket, let's all kick him while he's down!"

Add to this the fact that every scene was introduced by garish, flickering lights from an arch of lightbulbs framing the proscenium, and that Jule Styne composed some background music that may well be the most cacophonously offensive imitation jazz ever concocted. What, then, was left? A resourceful and commanding performance by Christopher Plummer as Ui—the Canadian actor's mastery of Brooklynese was in itself prodigious—but what he so magisterially embodied was Tony Richardson's totally misguided notion of the part. Also, there was some rather good scenery. Nothing, however, was left of Brecht's intention which is most trenchantly summarized in another note to the play: "Crime itself often elicits admiration. I never heard the burghers of my native town refer with anything but devout reverence and enthusiasm to a mass murderer called Kneisel, so that I have remembered his name to this day. It was not even considered necessary to invent for him those proverbial kindnesses to little old ladies; his murders were good enough."

If I dwell at such length on a pathetic fiasco, it is because it is not only pathetic but also symptomatic. What happens on Broadway?

Brecht is finally understood to be in great demand. Very well: we begin by choosing one of his least apposite plays. Next, we pick as adapter a man whose own plays have all been deserved failures and who, not content with this, has begun a thriving business of palming off his third-rate irrelevancies on the texts of writers like Brecht and Max Frisch. Then we get a hokey, gimmicky director, a typical musical-comedy composer, a bunch of hammy actors like Lionel Stander and Michael Constantine, and the original has about as much chance of survival as a virgin in a novel by the Marquis de Sade.

But the most important single fact is that everybody involved wants to achieve commercial success by explaining the obvious. Take a typical example. In a scene of *Arturo Ui*, a gangster's moll, engaged to impersonate the disconsolate widow of a slain accomplice, intones a phony lament for herself and somebody's small child she is clutching to her bosom. "My little girl only six years old," she weeps; half a minute later it is "my little girl only five years old." The adapter wasn't satisfied with this. He had to bring in still another reference to "my poor little boy . . . er . . . girl, only five . . . er . . . six years old." Now, the joke is hardly esoteric in its original form, but to reduce it to the six . . . er . . . five-year-old level is not going to improve the play for even a halfway civilized audience. Yet this is the pattern of Broadway: to translate good plays not into English but into baby-talk and baby-thought, and ultimately dissatisfy everyone.

In my book *Acid Test* I enunciated a theorem: "There is a simple law governing the dramatization of novels: if it is worth doing, it can't be done; if it can be done, it isn't worth it." Edward Albee himself had serious doubts about whether fiction can be dramatized, and in order to find out he undertook the adaptation of Carson McCullers' novella *The Ballad of the Sad Café*. There is between Mrs. McCullers' and Albee's worlds a certain consanguinity: both have a view of sex that is aberrant and a view of mankind that is abhorrent. Each in his or her way writes a kind of American Gothic, and a publicity photograph showing the two of them together gave the uninitiated viewer some pause as to who is which. But even though a novella about a town that had only three good people in it might obviously appeal to Albee, the McCullers grotesquerie and the Albee nastiness are not really sisters under the scab. A statement from the novella, "It is better to take in your mortal enemy than face the terror of living alone," might have served as epigraph for *Who's Afraid of Virginia Woolf?*, but the McCullers and Albee modes are ultimately different.

Consider this exchange from *Virginia Woolf* in which the young instructor and middle-aged associate professor drunkenly discuss how the former might get ahead. Nick says he will ". . . take over a few courses from the older men, start some special groups for myself . . . plow a few pertinent wives . . ." "Now that's it!" George exclaims. "You can take over all the courses you want to, and get as much of the young élite together in the gymnasium as you like, but until you start plowing pertinent wives, you really aren't working. The way to a man's heart is through his wife's belly, and don't you forget it." This is very different stuff from Mrs. McCullers' tiny Southern mill town, where "Life could become one long dim scramble just to get the things needed to keep alive. And the confusing point is this: All useful things have a price, and are bought only with money, as that is the way the world is run. You know without having to reason about it the price of a bale of cotton, or a quart of molasses. But no value has been put on human life; it is given to us free and taken without being paid for." Note how the bleakness of this view is humanized, as it were, by the chattiness of "the confusing point is this," by the folksiness of "as that is the way the world is run"—especially by that colloquial "as." We might say that Mrs. McCullers tries to humanize the horrible, whereas Albee is bent on viewing the all too human in the most horrible light.

The Ballad of the Sad Café concerns Miss Amelia, a rich, solitary, sexually abnormal giantess, in whom meanness and the power to heal people are curiously entangled (in Albee's version, by the way, the healing is significantly slurred over). There is also Marvin Macy, a ne'er-do-well who completely reforms in order to marry her, is then physically rejected and financially bled dry by his wife, until he runs off to a life of crime and eventually the penitentiary. And there is Cousin Lymon, a shiftless dwarf with whom the giantess falls in doting love, and who becomes her tyrannical parasite. When the husband returns from jail to wreak vengeance on Miss Amelia, the dwarf whom he despises and insults falls abjectly in love with him. With Cousin Lymon's help, Marvin Macy beats up Miss Amelia and wrecks her prosperous café. The wreckers leave town together, and Miss Amelia lets her thriving business lapse and turns into a wretched recluse.

Now, in the novella these characters and their story are sick; but the sickness is redeemed by the author's amiableness and style, and also by the fact that, not having to see the characters, we are free to palliate them in our imagination. The stage, on the other hand, forces us to see and hear the full ugliness, and Albee's additions, few and poor though they are, operate further in the direction of enforced tangibility. Moreover, Albee's antipathies, e.g., women, superadded to those of Carson McCullers, e.g., men, leave no stone unturned for whatever might crawl out from under it.

Another difficulty lies in the fact that the novella contains very little dialogue. Albee resorts, first of all, to a narrator, but there is something blatantly untheatrical and disconcerting about this non-existent character shuffling around the place, sticking his nose into everything, sitting around like an eternal *terzo incomodo,* and talking a literary language that clashes violently with the lingo of all the others. And what a lingo! Where Mrs. McCullers had her folk talking perfectly acceptable English, Albee invents a kind of pseudo-hillbilly baby-talk full of "I were saying" and "he be going," double negatives and "ain't"s.

But the negatives at least are only double; everything else is multiple. To pad his play, Albee takes the most banal statements like "Good evening!" or "Where be she?" and repeats and repeats them— "Who is Marvin Macy?" actually manages to get asked eight times by Cousin Lymon, if I did not lose count—till much of the dialogue sounds like a Da Ponte libretto without the Mozart music, translated into dude-Ozarkian. There is, moreover, an occasional lapse into jarring city slang, as when Marvin Macy is said to be "up-ending girls from here to Cheehaw," whereas in the book he "degraded and shamed" them. In short, the play is a vast emptiness in which a lot of measly dialogue and a few miserable actions cheerlessly rattle around.

To increase the grayness, two of the three principals are inadequate. Lou Antonio as Marvin Macy callowly combines the sidewalks of New York with the dead ends of Method-acting, but Colleen Dewhurst's Miss Amelia is a more complicated failure. Miss Dewhurst is supposed to play a large, weird, uncharming woman. But there is about her, in part after part, such an absence of charm, grace, loveliness, femininity—call it what you will—that one eventually cannot divorce what may be the oafishness appropriate to a role from her very own ungainliness and uncouthness. As Miss Amelia, she does everything right, but she does it without being in the least winning. There is some basic attraction, fascination, or grace that a player must have, no matter how disgraceful or dilapidated the character to be portrayed. Miss Dewhurst, alas, repels. Michael Dunn, though, is just right as the dwarf, achieving the proper blend of distastefulness and pathos, mischief and magnetism, to re-create some of that iridescent atmosphere between drollery and evil that the book possesses and the play fundamentally lacks. Yet another adaptation of a piece of fiction has proved bad theater.

Off Broadway's most honored showcase, Circle in the Square, put on Euripides' *The Trojan Women* as staged by Michael Cacoyannis, the Greek film director, some of whose films have been extremely interesting and some thoroughly overrated. Euripides' play, though to my mind one of the finest of all Greek tragedies, presents, like Greek tragedy as a whole, an almost insuperable problem for the contemporary theater. We have seen, for instance, the attempts in Greece today to re-create these plays in the most austere, starkly archaic, grand manner; the result, for a twentieth-century theatergoer, was stupefying boredom. In our theater, the superhuman imperceptibly bleeds into the infrahuman. We have also seen drastic efforts at cutting and modernization, such as Cocteau's bird's-eye views of *Antigone* and *Oedipus Rex* (Brecht, too, tried his hand at the former), but simplification of great poetry must inevitably strike us as oversimplification. Neither method works.

Cacoyannis has aimed at something like an amalgam of the two modes: stylization, but modernistic stylization. Thus the main characters must move as in a controlled, intellectualized *Grand Guignol* verging on ballet, while the chorus disports itself in a modification of Swedish movements, sometimes even applying Swedish massage, but more often in a ritual reenactment of a football game. Now it is the team going into a huddle, now the crowd roaring in a frenzy of *unanimisme*, now the bands between halves spelling out the names of their colleges. Then again, it is the cheer leaders at work, and at times even a bit of tearing down the losers' goal post—always, of course, heightened in artfulness by tricky lighting. Up and down a set of stairs or slithering, intertwining, crawling across the flat of the stage, the nine women of the chorus assume every grouping that geometry—within the limits of its poor, old three dimensions—can be made to cough up. Since the play is performed in the three-quarters round, the possible permutations of constellations are abundant, and if this and balletified calisthenics did a tragedy make, we might have been deeply moved.

Instead the evening was studied, arch, and above all unmoving. That this shattering play in which injustice and suffering are orchestrated with uncanny skill from the melancholy to the unbearable, from subtle, individual pain to great concerted agonies, until at last we don't know which hurt is more staggering—indeed, the play can be conceived as a contest in which each character and the chorus compete in adducing profounder wretchedness: a striving, as it were, to excel in abjection—that this play should come out as a cold piece of theory seems inconceivable. But there it is: a study in stylized, gyrating shadowboxing with the abstraction of war, with the mere concepts of slavery, enforced concubinage and death—the sheer ghost of grief.

Among the performers, only the lovely Carrie Nye is up to her arduous assignment: she makes Cassandra into a trinity of fragile virgin, pathetic madwoman and inspired prophetess of vengeance. There is both delicacy and asperity in this rendition, and watching it we are filled with the requisite pity and awe. As Andromache, Joyce Ebert, too, has some authentic moments. The others are at best pallid, and at worst like Jane White's Helen, a bad joke, or like Mildred Dunnock's Hecuba, a desiccated schoolmistress suffering from delusions of persecution by pupils and fellow-teachers alike—and what's that to us that we should weep for her? Jean Prodromides, however, has composed a score that captures all that acting and direction fail to. It sounds like percussion and brutalized strings of a barbaric, faintly Oriental sort, vitalized by amplifying electronics: at once ancient and modern, it emerges superbly timeless.

One wishes that somebody would try producing a play like *The Trojan Women* (in a less pedestrian translation than Edith Hamilton's, by the way) in a manner as naturalistic as possible without tampering with the text. In that case, the principals and the chorus would be men and women behaving like human beings. Some of the grandeur would be sacrificed, but a modern audience would at long last be able to believe in what is happening. We have learned to take some necessary liberties with Shakespeare—who after all is not a naturalistic playwright either; with the Greek classics, too, it is time to respect nothing but the integrity of the text and proceed to rid ourselves of all conventions or approximations of conventions. Otherwise, we might just as well bring back the masks, megaphones, cothurnuses, and do the plays in Greek. Following the performance, the shrieks of delight from the assembled academicians would provide a suitable satyr play.

A MORE SATISFYING evening is provided by *In White America*, a documentary of the Negro's trek through the jungle of white American injustice (and occasional decency), from his arrival here to this very day which is, if not a day, at least a dawn. From letters, journals, journalistic accounts, trial records, and similar sources, Martin B. Duberman has assembled a piece of history that makes good theater because it is true, interesting and overwhelmingly important. And it is theater —even if not art—in the best sense: moving, funny, humane, genuine and, best of all, unflaggingly provocative, coming as it does from sources most of us would always have been unaware of, and the worse off for it. It is well staged and consummately acted by three Negro actors and, a little less expertly, three white ones. Perhaps the most touching thing was to see, at about the thirtieth performance, Claudette Nevins, a white actress, watch Gloria Foster, her Negro colleague, act out the part of a fifteen-year-old Negro girl trying to go to an integrated school in Little Rock and nearly getting lynched. Miss Foster was magnificent, but no less so was the fact that there were tears in Miss Nevins' eyes. It must have been at least the sixtieth time that she was, from the sidelines, witnessing this scene, but the tears were brand new and absolutely real. I am a fairly hardened soul, and I am fully willing to admit that this manifestation had, in a sense, nothing to do with drama. But there are moments when the theater transcends drama, and my everlasting thanks go out to them.

THE BECKETT-PINTER double bill at the Cherry Lane is another civilized, literate and, in the Beckett half, not inconsiderable bit of theater. It is hard to pinpoint what it is exactly that Beckett has been persisting after in his later fiction and drama. You might say that he has been steadily painting himself into a dramatic corner. He has been lopping off action and space around his characters, and even pumping out whatever surrounding air they might breathe. But out of that last corner Beckett's personages manage to fulfill some harrowing, furiously funny dramatic possibilities; and their author, after having painted the entire floor a vivid shiny black, leaves—conjurer that he is—through the walls. Or might it be more accurate to say that Beckett, just when he seems up a dramatic tree, is in fact going down it: down Yggdrasill, the tree of the world, to its very roots, and is there gnawing away at the ineffable beginning, burrowing after unfathomable meanings; that the crunch-crunch that reaches us is that of a magnificent mole digging into the darkest dark for daylight, for enlightenment. All of which is to say that, minor and mysterious as it may be, Beckett's *Play* is eminently worthy, and is impeccably directed by Alan Schneider and solidly performed in a mesmerizing, macerating monotone. Pinter's *The Lover* is a British television play that makes one yearn for the B.B.C. It is a kind of Noël Coward—Sacha Guitry ultra-sophisticated marital farce, but given such ominously yet funnily Freudian overtones as to shimmer with a comically wicked sheen. It is a slight play, but it produces tingles on both spine and intellect.

SUMMER, 1964

DYLAN
by Sidney Michaels

AFTER THE FALL
by Arthur Miller

HAMLET
by William Shakespeare
with Richard Burton directed by John Gielgud

BAREFOOT IN THE PARK
by Neil Simon

HELLO, DOLLY!
book by Michael Stewart
music and lyrics by Jerry Herman

NOT THE LEAST AWFUL of all possible awful plays is the kind that indulges the solid burghers in the illusion of an artistic and intellectual experience, while in fact it hasn't the vaguest notion of what art is, and makes a mockery of the intellect. Such a play is Sidney Michaels' *Dylan*, which fails not only as a play and production, but also as a gossip column.

I remember once congratulating Dylan Thomas on his performance as the Raven in Louis MacNeice's radio play *The Dark Tower*. "Whenever the B.B.C. needs any kind of bird," he replied, "they always come to me." Sidney Michaels has made Thomas into a combination promiscuous park pigeon, exhibitionist peacock and scrapping gutter sparrow. That this blithe bird was also a spirit, a poet, to be exact, you would never guess from the play. Oh, the word "poet" is flashed in your face often enough, and there are even two poems of Thomas' dragged in by their bristling hairs. Perhaps it is too much to ask of a commercial play to be literate and sensitive in its treatment of a poet's life, let alone to convey something of what it is like to be a poet. But must it shuttle between boozing and brawling, between lewd propositions and pinched posteriors, practically without respite? Just about the only glimpse of Thomas the poet is an ineptly contrived monologue in which he is made to analyze "Baa, baa, black sheep" in a mirthless parody of the New Criticism and turn it into the story of his life. Bah to that!

Since Mr. Michaels had not the talent—nor, very possibly, the intention—to give us a work of the imagination, he might at least have produced a piece of sharp journalism, a *chronique scandaleuse* with some psychosociological interest—which, I assume, was his intention. But even here he has failed. He has obviously not made a thorough study of the scattered source material, or he would have come up with far more outrageously funny anecdotes and more pungent epigrams than he has assembled. Thus the very first unpublished Thomas letter which Ralph Maud, that dedicated Thomist, stuck under my nose contained the following: "The women of the world, perpetually out of perspective, cry, Focus, Focus. Is it our fault that we misinterpret them?" There is a profusion of such gems wherever one looks, but Michaels was quite content to draw almost all his material from John Malcolm Brinnin's and Caitlin Thomas' well-known books, both of which tell more about their writers than about Dylan. Yet even out of these—especially with a little reading between the lines—something fairly provocative could have been constructed. But partly because of a shallow reading of the books, and partly because of an understandable fear of possible lawsuits, such insights were not extracted. The result is an unrevealing revelation, an unshocking shocker, a clean dirty joke.

Nor does Alec Guinness, in the title part, fully succeed. I gather that he is trying to play Dylan against the grain, the coarse grain in which he is depicted. I understand also that Guinness is not particularly in sympathy with Thomas the man. But beyond all that, the interpretation is inapposite: an ithyphallic incubus is somehow reduced to an impotently impish leprechaun. Guinness' Dylan Thomas is really an aging Walter de la Mare with a pinch of Rupert Brooke for spice. The other actors are as drab as their stereotyped parts, except for Kate Reid as Caitlin, who does manage to wrest a second dimension from her one-dimensional role. As an example, however, of how to write a play with absolutely no point of view whatever, *Dylan* can scarcely be surpassed.

A FAR MORE imposing dramatic gossip column, and a considerably more massive example of how to *épater les bourgeois,* is Arthur Miller's *After the Fall.* Miller's mind has always loomed bulky on the stage—not like a genuine largeness, but like the elephantiasis of a flea. Imagine, to be precise, an enormous photographic enlargement of a microbe: instead of being majestic, it is merely distorted, grotesque, and blurred in its detail. This is emblematically manifest in the very opening stage direction of *After the Fall:* "The action takes place in the mind, thought and memory of Quentin." Though *mind* would seem to cover the whole thing very nicely, one might, pedantically, wish to throw in *memory.* But what on earth is that pleonastic *thought* for? To satisfy Miller's need for magnifying grandiloquence: Damn the tautologies, full speed to the stars!

The most painful flaw of *After the Fall* is its megalomania combined with hypocrisy. A forthright, smiling self-love can be harmless and even likable. But here we have Miller telling us that he is relentlessly baring his, or his blatantly autobiographical hero's, chest—only to emerge as someone whose faults are as nothing compared to those of almost everybody else. True, Quentin is a bit cold to his women; true, when as a lawyer he undertakes to defend a man forsaken by all his other friends as he comes up for congressional investigation, Quentin is scared about his own future and momentarily relieved when the man commits suicide. But at least Quentin reasons patiently with these women and freely admits his small failings; whereas they, unself-critical, hurl castrating abuse or violently absurd demands at him—in fact, we see four wives in the play calling their husbands "moron" or "idiot," and at crucial points maltreating them accordingly. And at least Quentin does stand up for the victim of McCarthyism when no one else will. In short, a classic case of what Wilde called washing one's clean linen in public.

And the megalomania! What are we to make of a play whose chief purpose, or at any rate only lively element, is the laying of Marilyn Monroe's ghost, but which cannot do this without dragging in everything from McCarthy to Auschwitz, from the Communism of the thirties to the Garden of Eden and a symbolic self-crucifixion? Quentin-Miller's humdrum peccadilloes are played out under the gaze of a Nazi death camp; a characteristic stage image shows us Quentin towering over three prostrate, spurned or adoring, women; and in a particularly gross scene "Maggie" Monroe's naked mating-dance is superimposed on a congressional hearing. Similarly, in statements about his play, Miller is regularly invoking Goethe, Tolstoy, the Book of Genesis, or the attacks on Hannah Arendt's *Eichmann in Jerusalem* (which he equates with unfavorable notices of his play), or informing us that it reveals "a hidden process which underlies the destructiveness hanging over this age," as though *After the Fall* had made some giant psychic discovery that hitherto eluded all analysis. Actually the play's only discovery is a new form of contrition called *tua culpa*.

Perhaps the most preposterous statement of Miller's is this: "*After the Fall* is experimental in any terms. It involves what is not a new theatrical style so much as a new style of thinking about the world, the unification, the synthesis of individual psychology and social and moral considerations to make a moral biology on the stage. Instead of having a work concentrate on one element of man, I have tried to put him on in totality." This about a play that has for its sum total of newness a narrator who comments on or steps into remembered events —muddying their sequence and creating formlessness—and that has for its only solution to all the injustice, lovelessness, cruelty, loneliness, disaffection in this world an utterance made by the character representing Miller's new wife to the effect that "one must finally take one's life in one's arms" and "kiss it" even though it has the "dreadful face" of an idiot child. *O altitudo!* The playwright is requested kindly to refrain from making a moral biology on the stage—or on the rug, either.

What Miller woefully lacks here is the imagination to digest, transpose, transubstantiate the givens of his life, never mind about kissing it. It is this incapacity for any translation beyond the changing of a few names and professions—including the awkward one of turning the theater and writing of plays into the law and writing of briefs—that forces an audience to see the play, as it were, through a keyhole; that makes the viewer a voyeur, and the critical cogitator a gossip-monger in spite of himself. There would be nothing shocking about a sentence like "But how can you speak of love, she had been chewed and spat out by a long line of grinning men!" (except, perhaps, the triteness of the writing) if one's nose weren't being

rubbed in the fact that this is Arthur Miller talking about Marilyn
Monroe, his ex-wife. And so it goes, from intimate premarital dis-
closure to garish marital fracas and all the way to suicide, and we
are every man his own gossip columnist.

Space allows me to itemize only some of the other lapses. There
is the inconsistency in character when Maggie hurtles from a paragon of healthy sexuality to a pathetic, abject, neurotic bitch. There
is the incredibly poor taste of showing one's two previous wives as
failures, while one's new one (with whom one hasn't had time to
fall out as yet) is presented as a wartime heroine and peacetime
angel of goodness, wisdom and, above all, self-abnegation—the key
to a woman's success with Mr. Miller. There are ghastly flights of
pseudo-prose poetry (as in "How few the days are that hold the
mind together like a tapestry hung on four or five hooks"); there is
the autobiographical hero's grammar, so bad that it verges on illiteracy. There is the humorlessness, both in the few, feeble attempts
at wit and in the ability to write, in complete seriousness, a line like
"And in the morning, a dagger in that dear little daughter's heart!"
Add to this Elia Kazan's uninventive, musical comedy-style direction
on a grandiose open stage on which you would expect to see, at the
very least, *Prometheus Bound,* and performances which, with the
exception of Barbara Loden's penetrant Maggie, are undistinguished,
and you have a picture of what the mountain of Lincoln Center
Repertory Theatre has labored to give birth to. Instead of toiling
away at this overlong brief, Miller should have quietly settled out of
court.

To DO *Hamlet* in appropriate modern dress is, perhaps, permis-
sible. But, as in the current revival, to do it as a dress rehearsal with
actors wearing the most outlandish and jarringly irrelevant rehearsal
motley is so disturbing as to require constant effort to ignore the
frippery even fitfully. Indeed, during the first twenty minutes the
air of *faux naïf* is so overpowering that instead of bringing the highly
sophisticated words closer to us, it turns us into dazed victims of
dissociation of sensibility. Again, the set, which is not really a bare
stage, but a set pretending to be a bare stage, with a gimmick or two
built in, is a thoroughly disorienting phenomenon. There are more
ambiguities in this production than were dreamt of in Mr. Empson's worst nightmares.

When I first saw Richard Burton in *The Lady's Not for Burn-*

ing, I was struck by the promise this young actor held out. But the promise is beginning to outlive the youth, and it would be most unnerving if he were to become a promising middle-aged actor. Burton's present Hamlet is handsome, virile, less intellectual than intuitive but possessed of supreme intuition, dazzlingly mobile in mind and body, and whether boyish or brooding, making the stage reverberate with his moods. However, the passion of him is almost always spurious: the arms flailing too choreographically ("sawr the air," as he pronounces it), the eyes rolling in too fine and pale a frenzy, the voice trying to make up for everything with mere dynamics. There may be the rub: Burton's voice—as, to a certain extent, his expression—tends to become marooned in plangency, moored in near-surliness, which may form a striking contrast with the sudden flashes of merriment but makes lesser fits of passion disappear into their background and forces emotional climaxes to o'erleap themselves and fall flat. On the whole, the comic moments and those that require manly alacrity without intense feeling emerge full-fledged; others are apt to remain sketchy or grandly hollow. I was delighted by such bits as the "O, my prophetic soul!" projected almost laughingly with an amateur sleuth's pride at being proved right, and the reactions to the Ghost's subterranean "Swear!" full of conspiratorial satisfaction only at the very last yielding to sad awareness. On the other hand, "How all occasions . . ." was delivered throughout in a drooping, tenebrose monotone, and the fight with Laertes in Ophelia's grave was utterly wan, possibly because too much energy had been spent in the Closet Scene in an exhibition of Greco-Roman wrestling with Gertrude.

Of the rest of the cast, the less said the better. Hume Cronyn remembers something of the way Tyrone Guthrie directed Polonius last summer in Minneapolis, and these scraps of memory are pleasant ornaments on an otherwise routine performance. Alfred Drake does Claudius in three different styles, all of them wrong. There is drawing-room comedy, musical comedy and melodrama, and sometimes he switches in midsentence. "Alas, how should this bloody deed be answered?" is spoken in lavishly portentous fashion and presto, "Where is he gone?" with the prissy exasperation of a long-suffering television parent. Enough: the supporting performances were either terrible or unforgivable, and to distinguish between the two would be not only ungracious but also rather difficult.

John Gielgud has staged the Ghost interestingly as a waggling shadow on the wall (though it would have made more sense for those addressing it to face it rather than turn their backs on it), and he has taped a voice for that shadow that is perhaps a shade too richly creamy but at least suggests that speech in the hereafter is more mellifluent than in the here. That, however, is where Gielgud's good offices end; the rest of his staging is no better than his casting. When Claudius is upset by the play (I mean "The Mousetrap" just now, not *Hamlet*), he does not simply leave, but takes several steps toward Hamlet, who takes several steps toward him: there they stand, glowering and practically rubbing noses. When Hamlet considers killing the praying King, he comes close enough to the royal nape to scratch it with his sword, or even with his nose, and delivers his lines full blast into the regal occiput. When at the very end Claudius stands fully unmasked, he literally stands: stage center and mildly interested, and only gradually joining his unarmed retinue, none of whom comes to his defense, until Hamlet slaughters him in his own good time. And in general two men seldom talk to each other in this *Hamlet* without thoroughly pawing each other, or at the very least searching each other's faces for blackheads. Again, when Horatio hears "the cock that is the trumpet to the morn," the lights helpfully begin to come up. On "it faded on the crowing of the cock," the lights, to illustrate the fading, obligingly go down again. But on "the morn in russet mantle clad," cheerfully up go the lights again. Altogether a flickering affair, this *Hamlet;* and when Burton's candle goes out, we are left darkling.

BAREFOOT IN THE PARK is a farce about the difficulties of a young newly married couple whose problems stem about equally from the fact that their expectations from each other are too high not to produce letdowns, and that their small apartment, a sixth-floor walk-up, is too high not to produce exhaustion in those who make the climb. It is a variation on an old theme which we could call *omne post matrimonium animal triste,* and the situational comedy involving also a marriageable mother-in-law, an unorthodox neighbor and various tradesmen, is full of jokes wheezing not so much from having to ascend six flights of stairs as from plain old age. But Neil Simon has managed to squeeze hidden bits of laughter out of the old jokes, just as one can always get a little more toothpaste out of an empty tube and feel more elation in getting it than in the luxurious first squeeze from a brand new tube. Mike Nichols has directed the play with a knowing verve that understands how to whip up bizarre truths out of the least likely ingredients, and some of the performances—especially that of Robert Redford, a young man with seemingly inexhaustible histrionic resources and a sense of economy to do a Keynes proud—add a mirror polish to the proceedings.

THERE ARE ALSO two musical comedies to report on. *Hello, Dolly!* is an adaptation of Thornton Wilder's *The Matchmaker*, itself a revision of an adaptation of an adaptation! Though the book, lyrics, and tunes are undistinguished, the sets, costumes, and performances are for the most part immensely likable. But what makes the show remarkable is the staging and choreography of Gower Champion. The basic unit is a kind of stylized movement which with a little push can spill over into dance; or with a slight shove in the other direction can become a mere heightened strut that accommodates itself to the burlesque character of the non-dancing scenes. No effort is made to justify logically the cropping up of dancers, or to make the dances more elaborate than mere high jinks; but for these and similar reasons a continuous onrushing flux is maintained, with dances tapering off into sheer grotesque locomotion which, in turn, grows in dynamism until it swells into dance. The irresistible force of Gower Champion's staging should establish *Hello, Dolly!* as an immovable object at the St. James Theatre.

As for *What Makes Sammy Run?*—for longer than a week, that is —I really don't know.

AUTUMN, 1964

BLUES FOR MISTER CHARLIE
by James Baldwin

DUTCHMAN
by LeRoi Jones

KING LEAR
by William Shakespeare
produced by the Royal Shakespeare Company

THE KNACK
by Ann Jellicoe

HOME MOVIES
by Rosalyn Drexler

THE THREE SISTERS
by Anton Chekhov
produced by the Actors Studio Theatre

SINCE THE NEGRO "protest novel" has been around for some time, our theater, which nowadays follows fiction at a respectful distance, could have been expected at this point to erupt with the Negro "protest play." Accordingly we now have on Broadway James Baldwin's *Blues for Mister Charlie,* and off-Broadway, LeRoi Jones's *Dutchman.*

A "protest play," unfortunately, always has a hard time of it artistically, and even more so if, like Baldwin, the playwright doth protest too much. And not only too much but too much too soon. Right at the outset we are clobbered with a tirade that is an inflammatory inventory of all the injustices against the Negro, and justified as these grievances are, they strike a false note: you do not paint a picture that is to be a work of art with air brush and poster paint—unless, that is, you are a pop artist—and Baldwin would shudder at the thought of having written a pop-art play. But that is what it is: pop art and agit-prop.

Baldwin is undoubtedly one of our ablest essayists and literary journalists—terms I use with respect—but as a novelist he has always struck me as a failure, and a progressively worse one at that. Somewhere hedged in by fact and opinion lies the domain of fiction, which is neither brute reality nor the spinning out of speculation, however profound or piercing. In fiction—and in drama too—certain moods, experiences, states of being and insights achieve a solidity of texture through psychological exactness, tasteful selection of detail, architectural structuring, and (most important, though least definable) a poetic sensitivity to words. In these things, Baldwin is more or less deficient, and his assumption of the mantle of embattled prophethood and the consequent thickening of his voice have made matters worse.

Blues for Mister Charlie is the story of Richard, a Southern Negro minister's son who, disgusted with his father's weak-kneed acceptance of the killing of his wife by whites as a mere accident, goes North. In eight years there, he has been a successful jazz musician and conqueror of numerous white women; revolted by them, he takes to dope, loses his money, and finally submits to a voluntary but painful cure at Lexington State Hospital. The play proper concerns his return to his strife-torn home town, to which he brings an even more bristling vengefulness and hate. He clashes especially with a poor white shopkeeper, Lyle, the prototype of stolid backwardness and already the unprosecuted killer of a Negro whose wife he had made his mistress. Richard taunts Lyle and his dim, mousy wife, Jo, to the point where Lyle kills him. Parnell, the white newspaper editor, Lyle's friend, is also a friend to the Negroes; in his youth, a Negro girl gave him his one bit of true happiness. He is now instrumental in bringing Lyle to trial. The dead boy's father, Reverend Meridian Henry, his girl Juanita, his grandmother, and various Negro friends perform bravely or cunningly on Richard's behalf at the phony trial; but when even Parnell is sucked, impotent, into this white conspiracy, Lyle is acquitted, only to boast afterward of being Richard's murderer. But at least, in defending his son, Reverend Henry has achieved true manhood, and the very violence that was in Richard has taught Juanita to love better—which, I suppose, means (if it means anything) to fight better.

The fact that the play begins with the shooting of Richard, and thence proceeds alternately forward and backward by a sort of free-associational movement is, in itself, neither good nor bad. The conventional flashbacks in the courtroom scene are somewhat mechanistic; but this is not a serious flaw. Other things are. What is most serious is that the play pretends to be about racial injustice and the Negro's struggle for his human rights, while it is actually about something else. I am not saying that Baldwin is deliberately deceiving us, which would be bad enough, but that he is deceiving himself, which is, artistically speaking, worse.

It is, or ought to be, clear to anyone who reads Baldwin's fiction— and the author is, if anything, eager to reveal it—that what we have come to call normal sexuality is here found wanting. Plainly enough in *Giovanni's Room,* and still more so in *Another Country,* Baldwin has suggested the superiority of inversion over heterosexuality. Every man is, of course, entitled to his convictions and to the freedom of campaigning for them; but not when, disguised as in this drama, they masquerade as and distort other more important ones. Thus Richard becomes a heroin addict not because of a sense of inferiority brutally imposed on Negroes, but because of some mysterious superiority of his over white women: their disgusting insufficiency in bed drives him from the embraces of these antiheroines into the arms of heroin. Now there is no need for a Negro repelled by white women—dried-up, pale-arsed bitches, he calls them—to choose a remedy more drastic, and less logical, then simply switching to black women. If, instead, he picks dope, we might assume that mere women, or even men perhaps, cannot satisfy him: that there occurred some profound sexual fiasco.

In the first act alone there are some twenty references to the sexual inferiority of the whites and their consequent craving for Negroes, and concomitantly to the superiority of the Negroes, both sexual and —it follows like the night the day—human. Both the "bad" white, Lyle, and the "good" white, Parnell, can find fulfillment only with Negro women; Jo, the one important white woman in the play, is introduced as unyielding to her husband, objecting that he comes to her "grunting . . . in the wee small hours of the morning." Conversely

Juanita, the Negro heroine, pulsates with life and healthy sexuality, as do other Negro women mentioned in the play. But whenever a Negro girl is praised, like a certain Ruthie who, done in by whites, "is never again going to be the swinging little chick she used to be," the girl "swings." Now, where is "swinging," i.e., promiscuity, particularly common and esteemed? Richard says of white women, "I want to screw up their minds forever," and adds that he could hardly restrain himself from beating them to death (who, by the way, is corrupting whom?). Where is sexuality most apt to couple itself with sadism? One of the main themes of the play, stated climactically in Richard's dying words, is that the white man wants to cut off the Negro's genitals. Where, other than among women, is what the Freudians call penis envy most prominent?

It seems to me that *Blues for Mister Charlie* is a homosexual play, which would be fine if it came out and admitted it. But far from doing this, it actually sneers at homosexuality: according to Richard, all white women, however eagerly they make love to Negroes, have "got some piss-assed, faggoty white boy on a string" whom they will cravenly marry. Yet persecuted blacks and persecuting whites seem to become subliminally identified with victimized but sexually free, noble homosexuals and tormenting, sexually frustrated heterosexuals; it is typical for the sexual misfit to blame the society's sexual mores for all his troubles. Why else would the racial issue be reduced here to sexual terms, and sex be seen as the true, secret strength of the Negro, the ultimate cause of white discrimination against him, fear and hatred based on sexual envy?

Out of this comes the most monumental falsification of all: the myth of Negro supremacy. Agreed that the myth of white supremacy is as unscientific as it is deleterious, but is the opposite myth any more justifiable, any more salubrious? It is one thing to fight fire with fire, but another to believe in fire—in its necessity, justice, excellence. Baldwin seems not merely to resort to fire, but to preconize it. The simple old Negro woman says of the whites: "I don't hate them no more. They too pitiful." The Negroes, says Reverend Henry, have no right to be as bad as "anybody else" because they "know better." The white editor tells the Negro preacher and his flock, "You must have mercy on us. We have no other hope." And so it goes: white arrogance must bow down before black arrogance, rather than all arrogance come to an end.

The private and public worlds of James Baldwin appear to have become hopelessly entangled in each other. And this confusion tends to be couched in language such as this, from Juanita's speech on the witness stand, "He fell on—fell on me—like life and death. My God. His chest, his belly, the rising and the falling, the moans. How he clung, how he struggled—life and death! Life and death! Why did it all seem to me like tears? That he came to me, clung to me, plunged into me, sobbing, howling, bleeding, somewhere inside his chest, his belly, and it all came out, came pouring out, like tears!" And so on, for some two pages of tendentious bombast. And night after night an audience of understandably hate-ridden Negroes and less understandably self-hate-crazed whites frantically applauds this piece of incendiary bad writing whose ineptitude even that inspired actress Diana Sands, for all her passionate delivery, can scarcely mitigate.

Quite rightly, *Blues for Mister Charlie* was to have closed after a handful of performances. Promptly, however, some prominent but literarily, as well as literally, insensitive folk contributed sizable sums of money and took out large advertisements for the play, so that it now seems solidly ensconced: a triumph of bad taste and bad judgment. No one seems to have grasped the meaning heralded by the very title: blues for Mr. Charlie, i.e., a dirge for the white man, whom Negro slang calls Mr. Charlie—a *Götterdämmerung* for the whole piss-assed, faggoty, or not faggoty enough, white race.

In LeRoi Jones's *Dutchman,* an intellectual, artistic young Negro is picked up on the subway by a weird, taunting white temptress. He is to take her along to a party he is going to, in exchange for which she'll later take him home and to her bed. The girl provokes him with jeers at his attempts to become assimilated into white society and culture; hers is a vicious combination of inviting nymphomania and castrating rejections. He finally explodes in a philippic hurled as much at some other white passengers as at the girl herself; when she further provokes him into swinging at her, it is she who pulls out a switchblade knife, kills him, and, with the help of the other passengers, dumps the body onto an empty platform. As the play ends, she has spotted another well-dressed, bookish young Negro who has just boarded the subway car, and she prepares to repeat the entire bloody ritual.

That the play is preposterous on the literal level is obvious enough. Yet allegory or symbolism, to be effective, must first function properly on the literal level. But does *Dutchman* work even figuratively? Does the white society woo the Negro with a mixture of promises and rebuffs only to destroy him utterly when he shows his just resentment? Perhaps. But it looks to me as if resentment were finally beginning to pay off. Whites, moreover, have been treating Negroes with a simpler, though no less damnable, cruelty. They have been neither so Machiavellian nor so psychotic as *Dutchman* implies. Add to this Jones's often consciously arty language and the vacuity of his symbols: the girl plies her victims with apples, an assembly-line Eve; the title presumably refers to the Flying Dutchman, but whether this describes the girl, fatally traveling up and down the subway line, or the boy, needing to be redeemed by the true love of a white girl, is unclear and, in either case, unhelpful. *Dutchman* and *Blues for Mister Charlie* are merely propaganda, which can add some fuel to a sometimes necessary fire; they are not truth, which alone can free us from our eternal enemy, ignorance.

"THE ADVANTAGE of doing the King in the traditional Senecan style—the 'tyrant' role of Greek drama—is that we get the effect of something strong and imposing, almost monumental, with its own magnetism and power . . ." This plea against a "natural" King, voiced twenty-six years ago by Stark Young, was made on behalf of Claudius in *Hamlet;* how very much more urgently it must be made on behalf of the royal personage that dominates the early scenes of *King Lear.* But in the Royal Shakespeare Company's recent *King Lear,* the "royal" was confined to the name of the company. Peter Brook, the director, and Paul Scofield, the principal actor, have contrived a Lear who, if not exactly "natural," is stylized down rather than up.

Brook got the idea from the Polish critic Jan Kott, who perceives *Lear* as a play related to the "theater of the absurd" and particularly to Beckett's *Endgame. Quot* (or Kott) *homines, tot sententiae,* and I am certainly not wanting in respect for the misotheist fantasies of the mirthfully macabre Irishman. But if anyone tells me that the pinnacle of English poetic drama—perhaps the greatest tragedy of all time—was merely laboring toward *Endgame,* I must exclaim with Kent, "Is this the promis'd end?" and smite that slanted Polack on the thin ice of his Marxist ideology. Brook, in any case, has gone about his Beckettizing and Brechtification systematically and ruthlessly, with the perverse predilection for the ghastly or unsavory that has generally marked his work. Accordingly whatever is kindly must be excised. Cordelia must come on as arrogant in her modesty, Lear's knights must become teddy-boys smashing a seaside resort to bits, Albany an amorphous, lily-stomach'd weakling who vomits upon hearing ugly news, Gloucester a bigger fool even than intended. The lines in which his servants show Gloucester kindness are omitted in favor of cruelties directorially inserted; Edmund's conversion is cut; and so on, as if the readiness to cut were all. Conversely whatever is evil must be mitigated, made natural, and if possible attractive. Thus Regan and Goneril emerge almost more sinned against than sinning (there is some justification for this in the text, but not much); Edmund towers over Edgar almost to the very end; even Oswald is cruelly put upon by Lear, Kent and the knights, and his fight with Edgar is turned into an impressive, resourcefully choreographic affair. But the climactic duel between Edgar and Edmund is reduced to a little ritual Indian wrestling: the moment in the tragedy when right seems closest to winning out over wrong must not only be brief and inconclusive, as it already is—it must also be made uninteresting.

It is, of course, Lear himself who is obliged to suffer most from this leveling process. "That Titan spirit," as Granville-Barker called him, must be divested not only of the thunder in his outbursts, but also of much of the gentle rain of quiet pathos. Instead, the entire conception is enveloped in a chill mist of alienation. Typically, the great line "Let me wipe it first; it smells of mortality" managed to elicit laughs on both nights I attended. All that was needed was to avoid a pause at the semicolon. But no—the pause was stubbornly held. Or consider how "Then kill, kill, kill, kill, kill, kill!" was reduced in size. Lear picked up his boots and manipulated them like a troop of horses shod with felt: they sneaked up on an imaginary insect colony, and then on each dully muttered "kill," some invisible beetle was pettishly swatted. There were no verbal cataracts here, let alone emotional hurricanes—though Goneril, conversely, was allowed to roll out her speeches in the grand style.

But let us not rob Peter to pay Paul: Scofield deserves as much blame as Brook. That Scofield is an actor of unusual stature would be senseless to deny, but he is an actor suspicious of poetry and a sworn enemy of passion—rather large handicaps for playing Lear. By the time I heard Scofield do his first scene in an elaborately artificial old man's voice complete with rustic overtones, saw him look stolid and move as in weighted astronaut's boots, heard him equip his grayish utterances with little, ascending, crotchety curlicues at the end, my spirits began to sink. They went right on sinking as inner and outer storms began to rise, or rather fail to rise. True, there were affecting scenes with Alec McCowen's saucily sophisticated Fool;

there was, later, a moving encounter with Gloucester and Edgar; and all the moments when Lear must impose desperate control on his emotions and sanity had the proper thwarted momentum.

But emotional control is not, after all, what the part calls for—at least not till the final sections of the play. And in Scofield there was never an unloosing of the ache, despair, fury that alone could purge and chasten that proud man, that alone can bridge the gap between maniac and saint. And what of the poetry, the one element of the play that does not crack or spill, that reaches the most painfully precarious heights of magnificence while at the same time fulfilling the pious, well-nigh humble, task of being the one luminous thing that reconciles us to the universal darkness? This indispensable poetry was willfully cast out by Scofield and Brook, by readings that were clouded, arid, deliberately antipoetic. The later scenes with Cordelia thus proved dismal anticlimaxes.

Oddly enough, there was, besides tendentious cutting, some uncouth manhandling of the text. So Scofield would change the famous "Through tatter'd clothes small vices do appear;/ Robes and furr'd gowns hide all" to "great vices," for which he has the authority of the Folio, but not that of good sense. But neither Folio nor Quarto—nor even a duodecimo—explains his rewriting of the no less famous "let them anatomize Regan" as "atomize Regan," unless he was simply trying to fall in with the general atomizing process of the production. Again, John Laurie, as Gloucester, addressing the mad Lear, emended "O ruin'd piece of Nature! This great world/ Shall so wear out to naught" to "fall out to naught," which is nonsense.

As for Brook's costumes, they were, for the most part, rather nice in their burlapy or leathery timelessness; his sets were a cross between Isamu Noguchi and Teo Otto: vaguely non-objective objects appearing out of nowhere and disappearing into it, or carried onstage and off. Sometimes they suggested known places and things, though not necessarily the appropriate ones: a railroad crossing is not a palace interior. Sometimes they were unknowable: three corrugated copper squares which could be suspended along walls or in midair, singly, doubly or all together. In the storm scene, which was played in bright lights, with no heath, and with only the people straining and toiling against arbitrary gusts of wind which might strike one actor and not the other and come from opposite directions simultaneously, all three copper squares oscillated and buzzed like a cubist beehive. When just one square was lowered, I always expected it to bear a legend—say: "January 1636. Mother Courage loses her daughter and trudges on alone."

As for the supporting cast, it ranged from Irene Worth's heroic monolith of a Goneril, Ian Richardson's nonchalantly scintillating Edmund, and Alec McCowen's almost too intellectual Fool, through some adequate performances, all the way to Tom Fleming's obvious Kent, John Laurie's pathetically decrepit but otherwise boring Gloucester, Brian Murray's callow Edgar, and Clifford Rose's scurvy little Albany. The best moments of this production were stage images or stage business: Lear's knights conducting their tumultuous *dolce vita* at Goneril's court; the miserable, near-dead, half-naked Gloucester cowering stage center, while a beautifully orchestrated but invisible battle majestically rages and wistfully dies away offstage. But typically, this is all peripheral, not to say adventitious; nothing that is germane to the text and inherent in the poetry was allowed to have anything like the same forcefulness and life. To liberate *King Lear* from the awesome splendor of its teeming poetry is not to bring it closer to our time, but to deprive it of that which now, as ever, is the one thing that can humanize its horror.

THE ENGLISH theater has developed a brand of Absurdism of its own, more socially conscious, more concerned with quaint but real types, more prosaic than its French counterpart. In the plays of N. F. Simpson, Henry Livings, Ann Jellicoe and a few others, the Absurd has been domesticated: it has been swathed in flannels and tweeds, a pipe has been stuck in its mouth, and it has even developed a taste for tea. Certainly the amount of tea consumed in Ann Jellicoe's *The Knack* compares favorably with the quantity ingested in a play by James Bridie, J. B. Priestley or whoever the current West End favorite may be. But Miss Jellicoe strains her tea through some curiously barren, bizarrely monochromatic, almost basic-English dialogue, but an always slightly off-base basic.

She gives us three young men in a lodging house: one a sort of Soho satyr who measures out his life with petty seductions; the other a foolishly likable ninny, starved for women; the third an *homme moyen sensuel*, full of outrageous fancies but quite sensible underneath. The teddy-boy picks a little provincial guinea pig for the teddy bear to practice on under his sinister guidance. The nice chap tries to humanize the experiment. The guinea pig revolts. There are all kinds of crosscurrents, cross purposes, double crosses, and minor mayhem. Amiable decency seems, in the end, to assert itself.

Miss Jellicoe has said in an interview that "people should forget their intellect for a while and lead fuller and richer sensory and emotional lives," and *The Knack* certainly capitalizes on the most visceral aspects of conversation, so to speak, garnished by charmingly feminine flights of comic fancy. Her play is a kind of good-natured fat lady, naked but wearing a funny hat—a daintily comic cloche over a Gaston Lachaise body. Typically, the girl's dialogue for half a page or more consists of the word "Rape!" Simple but not ordinary: she is screaming about a rape that hasn't been committed, though she wishes it had; and calling for help which, however, she doesn't want to come. It is the victim raping the rapists, who are really rapists in spite of themselves. It is a topsy-turvy world, seen upside-down through an old-fashioned camera, but all the time we know that we will get from it a picture that is comfortingly right-side-up. I found *The Knack* amusing and endearing; Brian Bedford's performance as flawlessly tactful, gracefully understated a piece of comic work as I have ever seen; Roddy Maude-Roxby a bit too cabaretish but overwhelmingly droll; and the other two performers at least adequate. Mike Nichols' direction may insist on high gear even when the terrain is momentarily level, but it is full of beans and unencumbered by any of that intellectualizing that Miss Jellicoe so stoutly abhors.

AN AMERICAN woman playwright who is also a pop artist and an ex-wrestler (good qualifications for absurdist drama) has come up with a kind of woman's version of *Oh Dad, Poor Dad;* I refer to Rosalyn Drexler's off-Broadway musical *Home Movies*, which has all the slaphappily perverse, bluish, artfully anti-arty qualities which "home movies" nowadays suggest. There is no point in describing this farrago whose chief virtue is that it is indescribable: outrageous, incoherent, and, when not solidly boring, monstrously funny. The whole thing is really less a play than a hypertrophied play on words, and Al Carmines' music is sufficient to the evil thereof, as are the suitably grotesque staging and acting. *Home Movies* is a collage with *arrière-pensées,* and its innocuous wickedness is not without charm.

As WE BEGAN with an Actors Studio Theatre production, so let us end. (Another A.S.T. item, *Baby Want a Kiss*, is too sleazy to dwell on; suffice it to say that those who possess the key to this *pièce à clef* will find it even less appetizing than those who don't.) A.S.T. has finally come around to a good, indeed a great play, *The Three Sisters*—and what hath Strasberg wrought? For it is with intense curiosity that one awaited the appearance of Lee Strasberg as director before the general public for the first time since his withdrawal to become the guru of the Actors Studio, the Zen master and den mother of the Method.

The result is reverent and utterly stodgy. What is serious in Chekhov, emerges funereal; what is funny, comes out ludicrous; and what is sad, becomes dead. The play neither moves us nor moves along: in the gaping interstices of this production, a whole other one could be staged, faster and better. But the trouble is not so much lack of tempo as lack of humor, sensitivity, and imagination. Let us merely consider the cast.

As Masha, Kim Stanley is up to her tried and trying tricks: the long pause before speaking, the soft and slightly quavering delivery, the staring off into astral space, the lurking threat of hysterics. The actress is not only immense, she somehow suggests hollowness as well, and as she lounges about in scene after scene, one seems to be looking at a giant piece of *puri*, or whatever the round, inflated bread of India is called. No actress should allow herself to look so, and no director should permit her to appear so on his stage. Geraldine Page, as Olga, merely trundles out every one of her Tennessee Williams-heroine mannerisms, but without their former conviction. The most appalling moment comes when Olga declares that watching people being cruel makes her sick, and Miss Page promptly repairs to the washstand and starts retching. Shirley Knight's Irina is a hysterical wraith you expect to see take off for Moscow through the air. Luther Adler's Chebutykin is an itinerant bagel peddler, and Robert Loggia's Solyony is a silent-movie ham unable to decide whether he is Valentino or Barrymore, and sporting a voice which the silents, bless them, would have denied us.

James Olson's Tuzenbach is at least inoffensive, but excessively weak; Kevin McCarthy's Vershinin, a road-company Chocolate Soldier; Gerald Hiken's scholarly Andrei, straight Lower East Side; Albert Paulsen's Kulygin is a burlesque straight man obliged to go on for the ailing comic, and managing merely to snivel earnestly. Most frightening of all is Barbara Baxley's Natalya, something just escaped from Vincent Price's laboratory, its voice, behavior, and appearance far from ready to start impersonating a human being. Even Salem Ludwig, as Ferapon—a gentle, touching old man of the Firs variety—must turn into a bewhiskered feeble-minded weight-lifter.

After this, you will want to spare me—and yourselves—further descriptions of *The Three Sisters*, though you might want to know that

Randall Jarrell's otherwise colorless English version (based on what previous translation?) does rise to one ludicrous height when Chebutykin is made to pronounce himself "snug as a bug in a rug." Here lies the A.S.T.

R.I.P.

WINTER, 1964-1965

THE LAST ANALYSIS
by Saul Bellow

I F THERE IS one thing the American theater cannot afford to throw away, it is a play. And yet after twenty-eight painfully eked-out performances, Saul Bellow's *The Last Analysis* had to close, as though it were another confection, another soufflé that did not quite rise to the occasion. The truth is that the production was frightful, but no amount of superimposed opacity could obscure the underlying translucence and purity; what was here being rejected was rarer than a pearl in an oyster: a play in a Broadway playhouse.

I am not saying that Bellow's farcical fantasy about a once hugely successful comedian restaging his life as a closed-circuit TV show for an audience of psychiatrists at the Waldorf-Astoria, in order to shed light on the terrible disease Success, is a flawless dramatic creation. But there are things in it that we must hold dear. There is, first of all, the intense rhetoric that makes the word become flesh before our very ears and eyes: such throbbing flesh that it scarcely matters if the personages uttering it are somewhat less than people. Nor does it matter all that much (though it does matter) that this galaxy of galvanic words does not compose itself into a well-shaped entity; this, at least, is a case where the sum of the parts is greater than most other wholes.

The Last Analysis is a title whose significance is various. Bummidge, the comic, is carrying psychoanalysis to its most grandiose extreme. He has at one end not one but a whole battery of analysts; at the other, not just the fragments and figments which are the stuffing of the mind, but his real-life family and friends—most of them bitter foes—coerced into acting out his human, all too human, past, his fierce suffering from "humanitis." But the play attempts a last analysis in even simpler or, if you will, more complicated terms: understanding what makes life so barely livable, so little alive. Bummidge, the comedian gone unfunny not from staleness but from fresh, horrible awareness, becomes a symbol for the Jew, the American, the artist, the simple naked man—symbolizing them not by turns, but all at once. Or yes, by turns: by comic turns which manage to be only faintly weirder than comedians' routines—just as the psychiatric jargon is only slightly exacerbated—but render with woebegone humor all the sadness of the human comedy.

When a cynical exploiter comments, "The audience are tired of the old nonsense-type nonsense; they're ripe for serious-type nonsense," the linguistic garishness falls in with the grotesqueness of paradox and anticlimax to elicit a kind of thinking laughter, which is probably the best kind there is. It is not Bellow's only kind, however. There is also the purely rhetorical one, as when Bummidge inveighs against his parasitical son, "You're lying, you crumb, you ex-sperm! . . ." And there is a lyrical laughter: "Today's heart is a rotten cantaloupe"—for isn't a cantaloupe both too big and too small for the chest of this poetically personified Today, thus achieving something more concentratedly absurd than can be wrung from mere prose.

As Bummidge relives every horror from birth, against which he is kicking already in the womb, through copulation, which results in a shotgun wedding, to the death of individuality, which turns him into the chattel of a success-wielding society; as everyone from a dead father to a deceitful mistress falls into place under the roving eyes of television cameras rolling around Bummidge's ramshackle hangout; as mock-crucifixion jostles mock-birth, and mock-psychiatry mingles with mock-TV production numbers—the whole mess finally transcends itself into illumination. It appears that if you can carry self-dramatization (or self-comedization), exhibitionism, absurdity to their extremes, you come out at the other end universally admired, Olympianly laughing, and ready to love your fellow-freaks. "Watch from the fringes and you'll get benefits" says a lurking schemer; the arch-clown Bummidge watches from the center of his being and invites the world to watch with him. Zany self-revelation proves valid artistic creation and is acclaimed both by the social science of psychiatry and the exact science of show business. Bummidge goes off to found a school for despondent comics.

I wish there were not this final deterioration of the divine spirit of comedy into a mere mechanical device, so that the play ends with the emergence of a machine from a god. Instead of Bummidge's self-styled Platonic Academy, it could use a little Socratic *aporia*. But the work suffered less from this arbitrary ending than from chaotic direction and clumsy acting. We know that Bellow wrote originally a very much longer and in many respects quite different play. What changes were wrought, by whom and to what effect, we can only gloomily surmise. What is unmistakable is that Joseph Anthony's direction, with its vaudeville sight gags and George Abbottish bustle, descended like a pall on the play, and that Sam Levene's incomprehension of Bummidge contributed another shroud's-worth. Levene played his standard Jewish comic nonentity, and could not begin to make Bummidge larger than lowlife-size. Whatever testifies to the character's seeing through cultural clichés, became in Levene's delivery merely dialectal mouthing, rather as if Milton Berle were reading the lines of, say, Coriolanus. The rest of the cast did not distinguish themselves, and Alix Elias as a sexpot in spite of herself managed to be downright offensive, but here again the sleazy staging must bear part of the blame.

Yet when all this is said, there is still no excuse for reviewers and audiences not to have come to the rescue of *The Last Analysis*. It was, in the last analysis, far more provocative than anything else around.

SPRING, 1965

TINY ALICE
by Edward Albee

LUV
by Murray Schisgal

THE TOILET *and* THE SLAVE
by LeRoi Jones

THE OLD GLORY
by Robert Lowell

THE CHANGELING
by Thomas Middleton and William Rowley

INCIDENT AT VICHY
by Arthur Miller

TARTUFFE
by Molière
produced by the Repertory Theater of Lincoln Center

THE ORIGIN of Edward Albee's *Tiny Alice* seems to be the old homosexual joke about the identity of God, whose punch line is "Actually, she is black." Since, however, it is no longer safe socially, let alone financially, to be jocular about Negroes, the God of *Tiny Alice* is, outwardly at least, white. But she is a bitch.

It is impossible to outline a plot so complex, elusive, digressive, self-contradictory and, I admit it, imperfectly comprehensible even after two viewings. A summary would err by being too long, too short, or too clear. The play deals with the superhumanly wealthy Miss Alice, her weird castle in which scale models within scale models repeat themselves perhaps to infinity, and her two associates in intrigue, a sinister lawyer and a cynical butler. These three, for an astronomic sum to be paid to the Church, buy from a cardinal his secretary, the simple and pious Brother Julian. It is, to be sure, unclear whether they buy his body, his soul, or his faith; or what good any or all of these commodities are to them, or to the Alice whom they serve. Do they, by humiliations, seduction and murder, make a fool or a martyr or both out of him? We cannot tell—nor why they leave him, dying, to an invisible Alice who may or may not exist.

It has been contended that *Tiny Alice* is based on Manichaeanism, or on Genet's notions of evil being good, and good evil. Accordingly, Alice may be God, or the devil, or both in one; she may also be anything one wants her to be (the lawyer explains that we do not get what we want but want what we get); or she may not be at all. Julian may be Everyman, Christ (he dies crucified or, at any rate, spreadeagled, crying, "Alice—God, why hast thou forsaken me?"), Julian the Apostate (he spent six years in an asylum when he lost his faith; when he marries Miss Alice, Alice's tiny earthly representative, he forsakes his lay brotherhood), the Holy Ghost or Joseph (in the asylum, he may have had—unless he hallucinated it—intercourse with a patient who claimed to be the Virgin Mary; now he becomes Alice's consort); or he may be any martyr for his faith, with all that implies of heroism or folly or both.

Nor is it clear whether Julian finally triumphs or fails, though his end seems to be aloneness and annihilation. It is certainly unclear what the three agents spent "two billion" on: humiliating the Catholic Church; supplying almighty Alice, the female Eternal, with men; creating a martyr—yet they would prefer to keep Julian alive, though alone, in the castle; or ridiculing and discrediting martyrdom—yet there is no one there to profit from the lesson.

The agents may be the World (the worldly, flippant butler), the Flesh (Miss Alice) and the Devil (the vicious lawyer); or they may be devilish angels working for the good, bad or nonexistent deity. But then there are statements by and about them to the effect that they are human, too human—and yet they must go on till the world ends or they are "replaced," whatever that means. The time, place and duration of the action are left deliberately vague, with contradictory hints about each; the concentric castles, moreover, are supposed to suggest worlds within worlds, each repeating the other. Typically, Albee has already instructed us to enjoy ourselves without trying to understand, but that we can do just as well without seeing the play, if not better.

People have discovered allusions in *Tiny Alice* to such far-fetched but not impossible sources as Preston Sturges' *The Lady Eve* and Disney's *Snow White*. There are borrowings from Eliot, Graham Greene and Pinter in the dramaturgy. Alice, large or tiny, equated once with a mouse imprisoned in the model castle, suggests Carroll's Alice and dormouse. The name Alice may stand for "all is," in the sense that everything or anything can exist, or for its Greek word from which it is derived, *alethea*, truth, meaning that such is the supreme truth, God. One can multiply sources, allusions, interpretations, but demonstrably none of them fits all parts of the fable.

Tiny Alice fails as symbolism because of its inconsistency and incredibility on the literal level; without firm footing in literalness, there is no working metaphor—just as without viable dramatic characters, there are no compelling symbols. But the work fails also as pure fantasy, because it lacks even that homogeneity that lends dreams, hallucinations and fairy tales their own kind of logic. Why, when an inexplicable fire breaks out both in the castle's and in the model's chapel, should Alice be praying. "Let us not be consumed, oh God!" as well as "Let it all come down, let it all go"? Why God and not Alice? And why should God, or Alice, have sent the fire? And if we are not to be consumed, why should it all come down? Above all, if we were to follow Albee's jesuitic advice, and merely let the play envelop us and wash over us, how would we cope with the gritty nodules of realism and grating dialectical rugosities that refuse to dissolve in the bath water?

Even hostile critics, however, have joined Albee in admiring his play's language—he went so far as to insist on English actors as alone capable of doing justice to his linguistic demands. Actually, the language leaves much to be desired. Thus Albee uses "replica" for both enlargement and miniature, though it can mean only exact duplication. We are given "removed people" for remote or withdrawn, "quixotic" for perverse or capricious. There is something about being "answerable *to* your own temptations" and about memory being "the same as *it* having happened," and someone announces "Exit all!" We reach the neighborhood of gibberish with "wonders that may befall a man least where he is looking, least that he would have thought." There is also the persistent, supposedly witty or ominous, repetition of one character's phrases by another, until the stage fairly turns into an echo chamber. The subtlety of the word play is exemplified by the frequent and unctuous emphasis on "*lay* brother," or by the lawyer's reference to Julian as "a bird of pray, P-R-A-Y" and his boast of what further puns he could make on this, or by his description of the cardinal, "His Eminence is a most eminent man." Again, the lawyer asks Miss Alice about Julian, "When are you having him again?" and she retorts, "On business or privately?" Worst of all, though, are the sticky attempts at being poetic, in which, for instance, sex becomes "sweet, sweaty slopping," "a milky white gladiator's belly" and "the great, sweet, warm breath of a lion . . . his soft, hard tongue," and so on.

But the awkwardness is not limited to words alone. Some scenes— almost all of act three, in fact—are so attenuated as to float off before our very eyes into nothingness; others, like the conclusion of act two, are crammed so full as to fall resoundingly flat. In the latter, Miss Alice and Julian, back from an outing on horseback, discuss where on a male body hair is sexually desirable (in an earlier scene, we were enlightened about where it is not). Julian is fiddling with his crop, which arouses sado-masochistic yearnings in Miss Alice; he is tempted for a moment, but when he refuses to whip her, she laments, "No one does things naturally any more." Next he reenacts for her his youthful visions of martyrdom, in which being devoured by a lion in the Roman arena somehow merges with being raped by a gladiator, which, in turn, merges with being penetrated by the lion or, more precisely, by his tongue. Miss Alice then seduces Julian in the name of that Alice whose surrogate she is. When she throws open her black negligee to him, Julian goes down on his knees and lunges in. As Miss Alice enfolds him, moaning, "Alice, he will be yours . . . Ah . . . Aaaah . . . Aaaa-liiice," the curtain comes down on the one true mystery of the play: what does Sir John Gielgud do for twenty seconds with his head inside Irene Worth's deshabille? This is wasteful dramaturgy: Albee throws away on one brief scene fetishism, flagellomania, homosexuality, zoophilia, fellatio, cunnilingus, and (though this one is foisted off on the audience rather than on the characters) voyeurism. Out of all that, Tennessee Williams could have made half a dozen full-length plays.

There is, moreover, a homosexual strain running through *Tiny Alice,* but remaining just barely supraliminal and certainly unintegrated; it thus adds considerably to the general confusion. The butler and the lawyer address each other as darling and dearest, there is much hinting about the cardinal's and Julian's being "buddies," the sexuality of the play is largely oral, and there is throughout that suggestive waspishness that characterizes many homosexual relationships. This is particularly evident in the opening scene, in which the lawyer and the cardinal engage in a protracted contest of bitchiness laced with references to pederasty past and present, which may yet give rise to a neo-Greek dramatic device to be known as the fagon. Is all this relevant to the main theme or not? Or is it, perhaps, the main theme? Is the whole play a piece of camp metaphysics or metaphysical camping?

A line in *Tiny Alice* about "the same mysteries, the evasions, the perfect plot" describes not only the play but also the stratagems surrounding it and the utterances of Albee and his associates concerning it. The décor is magnificent, but for an evaluation of the staging and the acting, one would have to be a mite clearer about what it all means. Richard Gilman has declared *Tiny Alice* "the most significant play of the season." To me, it appears to be completely nonsignificant: neither its physical nor its metaphysical world is coherent enough to signify anything. If Gielgud seems at times too theatrical and Miss Worth too portentous, I suspect that the fault, dear Edward, lies not in our stars.

It may be that Albee is the victim of self-delusion and genuinely thinks that he has made a meaningful statement. It seems at least as likely that he is being a *fumiste*, giving vent to his scorn for the great washed. But neither private masturbation nor public provocation is in itself so dramatically adequate that it can dispense with significant form.

MEDIOCRITY AND LESS than mediocrity have been, as usual, living it up on Broadway, having found, as usual, staunch champions in the reviewers or in ad hoc committees of theatrical personalities taking out advertisements in behalf of the plays. Disappointingly, the tone of these paid advertisements proved to be on no higher a level than that of the daily reviews. Such items as *The Sign in Sidney Brustein's Window, Poor Richard, The Owl and the Pussycat* and *Slow Dance on the Killing Ground* have not lacked enthusiastic support, though at best they can claim a few good performances by such gifted young people as Gabriel Dell, Alan Bates, Alan Alda, Carolan Daniels and

Clarence Williams III. Probably the most rapturously acclaimed of all these plays is Murray Schisgal's *Luv*. Mr. Schisgal, according to Walter Kerr, domesticates the Theater of the Absurd on these shores by taking a more humanely American look at the lives of noisy desperation led by certain purportedly prototypical grotesques in New York City. And whoever likes his Beckett in bobbysox, his Ionesco on a bagel with lox, may relish this occasionally funny and largely insipid lampoon.

In *Luv* (which here preserves inexplicably a title appropriate to the version Schisgal had put on in London), a now highly successful businessman comes upon the genius of his high-school class trying to jump off a bridge. He has failed at everything and proudly wallows in his monumentally miserable childhood and supercolossal failures thereafter. But his friend competes with him for the possession of the most atrocious childhood, and convinces him that LUV is the solution to all problems; he is even eager to let him have his wife who will not give him the divorce he needs to marry another girl. The wife herself presently appears, boasting of a childhood (she hopes) even more horrendous, and a marital sex life—she produces a huge chart to illustrate it—that has long since reached absolute zero. The rest of the play comprises a game of marital chairs, various inept and presumably hilarious attempts at suicide and murder, and a resolution leaving everything exactly as it was before.

What this is, of course, is not devastating social satire, still less avant-garde theater; it is plain and simple burlesque or vaudeville. (The fact that the avant-garde may also draw on burlesque is irrelevant: you can lead a horse to water but you can't make him a water buffalo thereby.) Indeed, *Luv* might make a perfectly acceptable fifteen- or twenty-minute sketch in a jauntier night club or revue, but it is by no means a full-length play. The old burlesque device of repetition by way of a slow comic build-up serves a dual purpose here: it stretches out a mere playlet into the more marketable commodity of a play, and it allows the playwright's essentially commonplace mind to revel in its natural habitat. I am not saying that there aren't some genuinely snappy jokes, as when the husband complains to his ex-wife that his current wife has grown a mustache, and the ex-wife tries to be helpful with "You should have given her sympathy, not criticism," to which he retorts "I should have given her shaving cream." But a large part of the dialogue crawls like this: "I didn't want to marry Harry.— You didn't want to marry Harry?—I didn't want to marry Harry!" Or the gags will be funny in a passé and déclassé way that makes laughter stick in one's craw: "All I want is you, sweetheart, and the opportunity to be incredibly rich sometime."

One of the troubles is that Schisgal is not quite up to what he is trying to poke fun at. Thus the wife is presented as an overeducated genius, maladjusted because of her unwomanly female superiority. But how does her brilliance manifest itself? In nothing more than a photographic memory and a headful of frozen facts available at a moment's defrosting. Now, if the point were that this is what passes for intelligence in our society, Mr. Schisgal would at least have had a tired little idea; but no! he sets this up as a bona fide superiority and then proceeds to debunk it—and what sadder delusion than that of a man who thinks he is pulling out pedestals from under false idols, when in fact he is only pulling out the rug from under his own sorry conceits. Significantly this high-IQ wife says of her husband, "He lays in the corner . . ." Another and more serious trouble is that the playwright scatters his shots in all directions, in an attempt to puncture whatever he can hit, without committing himself to any point of view. And that, in anything but a piece of unpretentious zaniness, is immoral.

Anne Jackson and Eli Wallach do well enough by their parts, but Alan Arkin is spectacular as the perennial loser. However, even his charms eventually pall; partly because the material stops dead like a too short carpet, leaving Mr. Arkin barefoot on a cold stone floor; partly because a comic technique geared to cabaret skits is not quite sufficient for straight theater. Still, he and Mike Nichols, the raucously inventive director, emerge as the heroes of the evening. If they work at times too frenziedly, it is only out of an instinctive *horror vacui;* yet who but Nature herself could fill the vast vacuum at the heart of this play? Nature, however, is not allowed anywhere near it.

IF, ON THE OTHER HAND, you want nature *au naturel,* without the palliative presence of thought or art or narrative or just a shred of restraint—not to mention taste—there is *The Toilet,* the first of two one-acters making up a double bill by LeRoi Jones. This is a vignette about nine assorted Negro high-school boys beating up a tenth who has made the mistake of sending a love letter to one of them. What adds spice to this triviality is that a) the tenth boy, the victim, is white; b) the locale is the school toilet, allowing for the free flow of scatology and obscenity—something like a third of the dialogue could have been, until recently, identified as "unprintable"; c) the boy who received the love letter is the intellectual type, and though he is perfectly happy to help beat the sender to a pulp, he does sneak back later to wash and embrace the bloody and unconscious epistolarian's head.

Now, the truth about this bit of vulgarity is that it exploits the Negro-white hostility totally adventitiously and meretriciously, there being no good reason for the particular color scheme of the play; that it raises the equally sensationalistic issue of homosexuality (the white boy defiantly shouts out the content of his letter, an offer of fellatio) without shedding any genuine light on it; that it capitalizes on (forgive the archaism) smut, without even having the sense of using it sparingly for greater effect; that it purports to tell us something about the innermost of life while merely spelling out the inside of a latrine. But the cross section of a toilet, which Larry Rivers' set helps to evoke with full pop-art *verismo,* is not yet the nation in crosscut, which LeRoi Jones so arrogantly pretends, and fails, to represent.

It is typical that Taubman of the *Times,* in his not quite sacred simplicity, should be moved by this alleged parable of love forced by everyday brutality into manifesting itself pathetically on the sly; but I wonder just what higher values are embodied in one high-school boy's offer to take another one in his mouth—regardless of what racial barriers would thus be crossed over or under.

The other Jones play, *The Slave,* is even more offensive. Here the obscenities come less fast, though still pretty thick—"Oh, fuck you, fuck you . . . just fuck you, that's all. Just fuck you! I mean really, just fuck you," runs one of Jones's verbal orchestrations. Far worse is the sheer obtuse nastiness. It is true that this hate-filled piece is supposedly mitigated by a prologue whose swampy rhetoric seems to be saying that violence is no solution, and by a supposedly high-flown diction. Unfortunately, the pious sentiments and the brackish grandiloquence are both merely stuck onto the surface of the play, and not even with glue but with spittle.

This is a tale of the future in which a Negro leader whose black soldiers are about to take over America enters at gunpoint the home of his white ex-wife, and kills her present white professor husband after reviling him for his intellectualism and alleged repressed homosexuality. He continues to terrorize the woman, who is still desperately attracted to him physically (note that!), and after one of his bombs blows up the house and mortally wounds her, he reveals that he has just killed their two daughters who had been living with her. Wounded himself, he limps away, after a good day's work of hate and destruction.

Once again, we get here and there a sham gesture of compassion, but the only thing that is real under the bogus language ("sometimes the place and twist of what we are will push and sting, and what the crust of our stance has become will ring in our ears and shatter that piece of our eyes that is never closed") and pretentiously nonsensical ideas ("the worst thing that ever happened to the West was the psychological novel") is the naked, snarling hatred of the author for anything thoughtful, polite, unviolent or—merely—white. This is the sort of exacerbation of racial conflict that is particularly unjustified and cowardly coming from one who is indulged, lionized, and above all, produced by whites—whites blinded either by feelings of guilt or by plain stupidity. It is deplorable to see a predominantly white audience hysterically cheering this kick in their groins. Mr. Jones calls his play "a fable." If it is that, the only talking animal in it is the author.

IT WOULD BE pleasant to be able to report that over this desolation we can at least hoist with pride *The Old Glory*, Robert Lowell's three one-acters based on tales by Hawthorne and Melville. Here, once again, we face the almost insuperable problem of adaptation; but, like Lowell's verse translations, these are versions rather than transcriptions, and Lowell, however much of a theatrical tyro, is not the tired hack who usually undertakes to "dramatize the classics." Nevertheless, what comes out is scarcely more viable on the stage than the usual Henry James novel that shows up on Broadway every three or four years.

My Kinsman, Major Molineux was turned by Lowell and his director, Jonathan Miller, into a series of tableaux, in which everything down to the *grisaille* of costumes and make-up imitated eighteenth-century political cartoons. This immediately reduces Hawthorne's nightmare atmosphere to comic garishness. The fact that the hero's solitary wanderings through the nocturnal city become, by dramatic requirements, a shuffling about in one place with a kid brother for confidant, further reduces the effectiveness of the original concept. That Lowell has cast it all into absurdist dialogue and stage business, and that Miller has directed it accordingly, reduces the horror of reality (heightened reality, if you will) to a string of arch, enervating *frissons*. There is even some claptrap about the ferryman being Charon, and Boston the City of the Dead, which is worthy of little poets' theaters battening on poetic colloquies by women with three names and men with one bad one.

Benito Cereno, on the other hand, tries to shoot Melville full of foresight-like hindsight by turning it into a parable of the coming racial violence. The point that there is guilt on both sides emerges with some novelty but, in the light of the present situation, little validity. (I doubt that Lowell wishes to play John the Baptist to LeRoi Jones.) Melville's unity of tone and metaphysical speculation is here obtruded on by devices out of Genet's *The Blacks*, previous adaptations of *Billy Budd*, and Hollywood epics of the sea with their shoot-em-up finales. Indeed, Lowell's ending makes the revolted slaves out to be exemplary boobies falling into the most perspicuous trap. The play proceeds at a pace I can describe only as putting one *longueur* before the other, and when everything else fails one can always borrow a scream out of the *Heart of Darkness*. Intelligence is discernible among the pregnant pauses, but it is not yet a dramatic intelligence.

A few special performances of the third play, *Endicott and the Red Cross*, were also given, but these did not even benefit from Miller's cleverness. Instead, the production was restaged by Wynn Handman as an oratorio without music. The play has more stasis in it than was packed into the Pyramids, but not nearly so much shape. It does, however, contain the thought that may be the cornerstone of *The Old Glory*: "A statesman can either work with a murderous efficiency and leave a graveyard, or work in a hit-or-miss fashion and leave a cesspool."

For it is Lowell's conceit that "the old glory" of the founding of this republic was more gory than glorious, that no party had a monopoly on guilt; Church of England or Puritans, English or Colonials, white or black—it is only a question of whose foot the shoe is on: the kicks are always coming, with always a behind to receive them. But the point becomes more and more monotonous as Lowell keeps verbalizing instead of dramatizing. The American Place Theatre, however, did nicely by at least two of the plays, giving them a smooth and attractive, though not unblemished, production. Roscoe Lee Brown's Babu and Yehudi Wyner's incidental music were especially noteworthy.

Of the three new Lincoln Center offerings, one, *The Changeling*, managed to die quickly, the very thing repertory theater is supposed to protect against. Nothing, however—neither moly nor bathing in dragon's blood—could have prevented the early demise of Elia Kazan's misreading and misproduction of this fine play; everything in the production collaborated harmoniously on the creation of total catastrophe. The next item was Arthur Miller's *Incident at Vichy*, which marks a step up from *After the Fall*—but, then, what play would not?

Incident at Vichy concerns some Frenchmen rounded up by the Nazis and awaiting questioning; those who are neither Jews nor Communists will be let go, the others will never again be heard from. The play examines, rather synthetically, the various attitudes of victims and victimizers, and ends with a grand gesture in which an Austrian prince gives his papers to a Jewish psychiatrist and goes to die in his stead. The work is full of pseudoprofundities such as that everyone, even the Jew, has his Jew (i.e., scapegoat), and that what the Jew wants from the gentile is not his guilt but his responsibility. But underneath the catchy phrasing, these are the same doleful, senescent truisms we have had from all the social-commitment wholesalers. The final gesture, which is supposed to be laden with symbolic significance, emerges as a cross between a *beau geste* and an *acte gratuit;* it makes little sense, and proves or promises nothing.

Miller is sincere enough in his grappling with the problems, but just as the events presented never surpass the achievement of the anti-Nazi movies of the forties, the intellectual insight does not even approach the best thinking on the subject achieved in the fifties and sixties. Miller's externals manage to hold our interest, but his essence is merely a tract for former times. Above all, the playwright has no sense of other people in other places: his Jewish Frenchman is patently a Lower-East-Side Jew, his French merchant a Brooklyn shopkeeper, his Austrian aristocrat a pack of clichés, his gypsy nobody at all. And one gets the uncomfortable feeling that the Jewish doctor-hero is a heroic projection of Miller himself, and that the final message is that the world owes the platitudinous homilist a living. Harold Clurman's direction is entirely suitable; among the generally nondescript performances, Hal Holbrook's stands out for its excellence, and David J. Stewart's and David Wayne's for their awfulness.

Translation is the art of losing gracefully. The original is pointed to, accosted and engaged in an embrace that partakes equally of wrestling and love; but as the good translation goes down before the ultimately unconquerable original, it goes under so gallantly, so generously exalting its conqueror, that the defeat turns into a kind of victory. Such a translation is Richard Wilbur's *Tartuffe*, and *it* is the hero of the evening. Only very, very rarely does a solecism like "how aggravating!" or a cacophony like "They crucify their *foes* in heaven's cause" mar an English verse texture as poised, pointed and elegant as Molière could have wished for.

Unfortunately, William Ball, our most talented young director, has not truly succeeded either with his stylization of movement or with his handling of rhyme on stage, and his interpretation of the play is less than convincing. The movement consists largely of flouncing promenades by one or two characters, while others, usually whole groups, stand like a troupe of ballet dancers immobilized in midaction by a cosmic-ray gun. Then, from *tableau vivant* to *tableau vivant*, there is a bit of frantic scrambling to get to the next frozen position in time. It is nice, but it is both too much and not quite enough. And to make rhyme palatable to untutored ears, Ball drives his cast into racing through the lines in the assumption that this will make the rhyming unnoticeable. What actually happens is that the rushing sense slips through our cognition, and we are left with whole earfuls of sound and—precisely—rhyme. Moreover, Ball seems to have taken literally Wilbur's statement that *Tartuffe* is the *Lear* of comedy, and tried for all kinds of wistful and serious moments in the midst of the bustle, which unhappily clash with the nature and movement of the play—as does his interpretation of outrageous comic figures such as Orgon as mere pathetic simpletons. The earnestness of *Tartuffe* must register in the comedy, in the preposterousness; not from somewhere beside it, and beside its point.

Michael O'Sullivan's Tartuffe is highly implausible: not farce, but travesty of farce—a comic strip with a bad case of the fidgets. This once promising actor is rapidly sinking in a sea of fussiness, affectation and self-indulgence. There are equally painful and even less interesting performances from Joyce Ebert, Salome Jens, Patricia Roe and Hal Holbrook; Larry Gates and Claude Woolman are at least up to what the director wanted; but Sada Thompson's intelligent, assured and stylish work as Dorine sets the standard for what might have been. What is, is a clever and by no means contemptible production. But Ball is a brilliant director, and such cleverness is a miscarriage of brilliance no less saddening than any other form of miscarriage.

DEAD SOULS
a dramatization of the novel by Nicholai Gogol
produced by the Moscow Art Theatre

THREE SISTERS *and* THE CHERRY ORCHARD
by Anton Chekhov
produced by the Moscow Art Theatre

WAR AND PEACE
by Leo Tolstoy
produced by the APA-Phoenix Repertory Company

JUDITH
by Jean Giraudoux
produced by the APA-Phoenix Repertory Company

HARRY, NOON AND NIGHT
by Ronald Ribman

AND THINGS THAT GO BUMP IN THE NIGHT
by Terrence McNally

THE THING, nowadays, is Happenings. In a recent interview in *Art International*, Allan Kaprow, their putative pop, announced that he is working on international Happenings, to take place concurrently in various parts of the globe. Susan Sontag has hailed them as one of the most interesting forms of contemporary theater, and she may, heaven help us, be right. Now we have the first critical anthology of them, *Happenings*, written and edited by Michael Kirby.* This ludicrous nonbook should delight Kaprowphiliacs, but others too may learn from it: if, for example, a girl comes crawling at you across the floor and starts untying your shoelaces, you should know it is a Happening and kick her in the face. If, however, one does not belong to the privileged few who get to attend Happenings, there was something not unlike them available for mass consumption at the City Center. I am referring to the visit of the Moscow Art Theatre, with a repertoire consisting of a dramatization of *Dead Souls, Three Sisters, The Cherry Orchard* and a piece of agit-prop dramaturgy by one Pogodin, entitled *Kremlin Chimes*. The remarkable things were not going on onstage.

What went on up there was merely slightly pathetic and slightly risible. It will be recalled that even in the Moscow Art's heyday under Stanislavsky, Chekhov used to be quite upset about some of the things the great director did to his plays. But what the Moscow Art has been doing to both Chekhov and Stanislavsky over the decades is far worse. The Soviets love embalming. In Red Square, one can see Lenin embalmed. In the Soviet Writers' Home in Moscow, one can see the embalmed body of Samuil Marshak lying in state. And at the Moscow Art, one can see Chekhov embalmed, the actors lying in state-approved interpretations of the plays. For Chekhov is being done as nearly as possible as under Stanislavsky and Nemirovich-Danchenko, except for some added horseplay and some tendentious changes. Thus, Lopakhin, the boorish arriviste of *The Cherry Orchard*, becomes a basically correct and gentlemanly fellow, to show that the lower classes really deserved to take over. Or Chebutykin, at the end of *The Three Sisters*, is interpreted not as a cynical old parasite, but as someone who through compassionate understanding points to a better Russia to come. In various ways, things are made more acceptable politically, or simply more upbeat, which amounts to the same thing.

The changes, however, are far less distressing than the lack of change. The customary defense that admirers of the Moscow Art's incredibly old-fashioned productions will proffer is that, yes, these are museum pieces, presented reverently behind glass cases, but don't we enjoy old paintings and sculpture and furniture in our museums?

* *Happenings*, ed. by Michael Kirby. E. P. Dutton and Co., 1965.

So why not Chekhov's plays as they were done by a master director in a renowned theater, exactly as the author and his contemporaries beheld them? The answer, of course, is that paintings and furniture are objects and cannot, should not, be changed—though even they are not allowed to gather the dust of the ages, but are removed from time to time for cleaning or restoring or whatever is needed to show them off to best advantage. Now, where living people are concerned —and not only the actors, but also and above all the characters they portray are living people—there must be keeping up with the times, not embalming. Besides, it takes a lot of living to make a mausoleum a museum.

We got slow tempos, insufficient or uninteresting movement, ponderous delivery and chilling attitudinizing, uncharming actors, antiquated notions of stage design and uninventive costumes, caricatures drawn with a sledge hammer in Gogol, bovine attempts at farce in Chekhov—including some rather tasteless interpolations. There were exceptions, to be sure. Alexei Gribov, for example, proved himself an actor completely versatile and always commanding; one or two others were scarcely less accomplished. But others, like Pavel Massalsky, Mikhail Zimin, or most of the women . . . Can you imagine a Gaev who is an utter, gray nonentity even in his moments of flamboyant self-dramatization? No. But here you could see one. Can you conceive of a Masha carrying on like Nita Naldi when vamphood was in flower? No. But here she was.

Well, that is what happens with embalming. People who see Lenin's mummy tend to think that it is a phony—a wax figure. But the point about a mummy is that even if it is real, it is phony. A production of Shakespeare that tells us how it was when people feared the rebellious Essex or Catholic plots against the Queen, or reconstructs what it was like to perform at the Globe Theatre in broad daylight, or tries to re-create the English pronunciation of Shakespeare's time, is of no serious interest to us. The purpose of art is not to take us into a given time, but to take us out of time altogether, into a realm of truth where the temporal ceases to matter. And this can be done only by making the play as new as possible—as if every performance were the world première. And it is surely easier for a work of art to move ahead in time, for genius to keep up with the shifting ways of ordinary mortals, than for us with our earthly limitations to become our own ancestors. But this is something that the Moscow Art taxidermists fail to understand. And, alas, there will always be people for whom poetry is "thou" and "yond" and "e'er" and not what some daring young poet is writing today, people for whom the stuffed owl on their desk is more real a bird than the one glimpsed on the wing, in a flash.

But I had not thought that the death of taste had undone so many. What went on in the auditorium was more pathetic than *The Three Sisters*, more absurd than *The Cherry Orchard*, more grotesque than *Dead Souls*—even had they been done well. The audience consisted, first, of Russian emigrés, who understand Russian, to be sure, but not the theater—for whom this was a sentimental journey back to their childhood and the enchanted theater of their youth. Then there were all the semiliterate theater people, theater buffs, cultural snobs, rememberers of the Moscow Art's first visit to New York in '23 and descendants of these rememberers, former or current leftists to whom the Moscow Art for doctrinaire reasons represents the acme of dramatic achievement, and all that piously well-meaning bourgeoisie to whom it has been brought home that repertory is a blessing, but not as we might conceive it, only as those illustrious, tradition-drenched foreign companies can. And of course there were the campy homosexuals, to whom a play like *Kremlin Chimes*, performed in Russian, seemed a screamingly hilarious mating of the Bolshoi Ballet with *Dracula's Daughters*.

For those in the audience who wished to pay extra, the management provided transistorized closed-circuit radios, over which a quavering-voiced Russian-accented crone and a callow young Britisher supplied poor running translations croakingly or lethargically read; it was, as someone observed, like listening to one's childhood piano teacher and a BOAC purser indulging in an improbable party game. When people grew tired of this equivocal hearing aid and removed their earphones, these emitted a nasty little buzz—so that the auditorium was at all times invaded by a horde of angry crickets. Added to this was the noise of frantic explanations circulating among the audience, frenzied applause for the exit of every bit player, hectic laughter at any little stage joke both from those spectators who understood Russian and from those who felt obliged to emulate them; in sum, quite a concert. Moreover, for all their professed love of art, many people were subconsciously eager to miss as much as possible of these foreign-tongued goings on, so that for at least fifty minutes after curtain time late arrivers were still causing minor commotions on the way to their seats. After the first fifty minutes, there were others (admittedly not many) who, insufficiently primed about the glories of martyrdom in the cause of culture, began to leave, causing minor commotions on the way out. All this coming and going was, of course, a boon for those who had not been able to rent transistors (of which there was a limited supply), or whose transistors had given out (as quite a few did), for it provided them with a spectacle they could enjoy without a language barrier.

In the intermissions, I had some interesting experiences. A retired actress was raving to me about how wonderful it all was: true ensemble playing, real Chekhov as she had never seen it done before. When I ventured to ask whether she thought that Gaev, for example, was being played with distinction, she asked, "Gaev? Which one is Gaev?" A highly successful young producer-director informed me how great it was to hear Chekhov, at last, in Russian. I asked him whether he knew the language. "Of course not," he replied. Leaving *The Cherry Orchard* after the second act*—as was the director of perhaps the most important repertory company in the country—I noticed one of our most dazzling young directors lingering in the lobby. He told me he didn't care if the acting was nothing special, the mere pleasure of watching such masterpieces performed was enough. The bell had rung long ago; there was no one left in the foyer. With heavy feet, he shuffled back into the auditorium.

Seldom indeed have I seen such an orgy of mass enthusiasm so imposingly incommensurate with what was being offered. Thousands of people were applauding and cheering themselves hoarse to prove to the Russians that we love them and would they, please, spare us with their bombs! (God knows what the things that hit the City Center stage were supposed to be.) Others, perhaps, were expressing their political sympathies. Still others were proving that they knew true art when they saw it. Some, possibly, were reacting against the dearth of good repertory and ensemble acting in this country by exalting the first foreign aggregation that crossed their path. A good many, no doubt, had read the abjectly deferential notices in the papers. Altogether, you could tell by the noise that an artistic event of the first magnitude had been successfully detonated.

And how does repertory thrive on our own shores? The Association of Producing Artists has been doing bang-up business at the Phoenix, banging the hell out of Tolstoy and Giraudoux. (I could not

---

* The management saw fit to grant me reviewers' tickets for only two of the productions. On tickets that have to be paid for, I do not feel obligated to hope for last-minute miracles.

bring myself to go to their third offering, *Man and Superman:* the thought of Ellis Rabb and Nancy Marchand incarnating—if that is the word—the eternal male and the eternal female, respectively, is more than this flesh can bear.) Of *War and Peace,* not much need be said. I beg the reader to stifle his distaste while I repeat for the two hundred and ninety-eighth time (it's just as unpleasant for me) that great novels cannot be dramatized, only prostituted on the stage. When a narrator comes on and announces that the material from *War and Peace* has been "selected, arranged, and even invented in the hope of serving Tolstoy's purpose," we know that what is going to be served is not Tolstoy's purpose but smorgasbord. Good performances by Sydney Walker, Rosemary Harris, and Keene Curtis as Napoleon, were all but drowned out by the poor acting of everybody else and by a dreary script, which, among other things, obliged Natasha to walk away from Andrei's deathbed right into Pierre's arms without even a decent period of mourning—say, thirty seconds. Peter Wexler's devising of a miniature Battle of Borodino was fine; unfortunately, just about everything else was miniature, too.

Judith, though not one of Giraudoux's best plays, might still yield lyrical and stinging theater, for even here Giraudoux could turn the drama into something like a Provençal sestina laced with Parisian wit. Instead, we got a translation by John K. Savacool, which, though not gone bad, tasted rather like the remnants of a gourmet dinner by the time it reaches the servants' table. Thus Walter Kerr squarely blamed Giraudoux for having written "a paroxysm of passion and humanity"; but if the "critic's critic" had bothered to check the French, he would have found "*un accès de passion et d'humanité,*" or, simply, "a fit of passion and humanity." Yet the translation was less culpable than the various cuts. Some things (like a reference to a "fine Jewish nose") were omitted lest they give offense, others presumably just to speed things up. Only, this is precisely what the play cannot stand: its reversals come so thick and fast that cutting causes one *peripeteia* to stumble over the next; indeed, parts of the play seemed to be more Feydeau than Giraudoux.

This was the fault of Ellis Rabb's direction, as well. For one thing, Rabb did all he could to keep this comic tragedy as close to comedy as possible; for another, he did his best to strip it of contemporary relevance by hiding its saucy anachronisms as though they were painful catachreses. Lastly, he missed or ignored what the play really is: an argument with God, a demonstration of how the supernal—whether it exists, or is merely believed to exist—infiltrates and takes over the human will. And partly, too, because of the direction, partly because of her own limitations, Rosemary Harris failed to give us a Judith who goes from charming socialite *allumeuse,* through frightened virgin and profoundly aroused woman, all the way to a fanatic who allows God's angel—if it is God's angel—to persuade her to bask in a macabre sanctity she herself had most disclaimed. What we got was a rather good impersonation of Audrey Hepburn—in other words, the imitation of an imitation. As Holofernes, Paul Sparer gave his usual pompously overlubricated performance: he was dripping with leers and squeezing out greasy words complacently. As a hotly desirable courtesan, Nancy Marchand perfectly suggested a sleepwalking New England spinster, and others performed no less approximately. As a homosexual Assyrian officer, Keene Curtis alone managed to make a mark.

APA is the ideal repertory company for a middlebrow culture: any group that offers Ibsen, Chekhov, Shaw and other worthy staples; that very carefully never puts on anything more experimental than a farce by George M. Cohan; that has its summer base at a large Midwestern university and its winter season in New York; that clusters several American character actors around a genteelly British star; that has a young or at any rate youngish look onstage, will be forgiven anything, even the feeblest actors and flabbiest directors.

MORE DISPIRITING is Ronald Ribman's *Harry, Noon and Night,* scenes from a young Jewish American's life in postwar Munich. There are three essentially unconnected vignettes that have very little point individually, and none whatever taken as a whole. But they do allow for elaborate pawing of a whore's breasts (an organ for which the author rattles off a thesaurus' worth of vulgar synonyms, and goes on to top this with a Homeric catalogue of different types of animal dung), a mock copulation, a hunchback picking his nose and toes, and peddling his nails as sacred relics, the chopping up of a mackerel into countless tiny pieces (you can even smell it), a man going to the toilet while another watches through a chink, the toilet not flushing and assaulting the man with his own excreta, all kinds of jolly references to gas ovens and lampshades made of human skin, various sadomasochistic scenes between two men in and around a bed (the bedding does not change, but the men do), and several other goodies that I have happily managed to forget.

There were able performances by everyone except the lead, Joel Grey, who was, if possible, worse than his material. But what made this production interesting was that it was done at St. Clement's Church by The American Place Theatre, whose president is the Rev. Sidney Lanier, and with money from the Ford Foundation. It is comforting to know that there is a way—gratuitous scatology and brutal obscenity—of pleasing both God and Mammon.

THE PRIZE HORROR of the season, however, is Terrence McNally's *And Things That Go Bump in the Night.* This is a devilishly embarrassing situation for those of us who, along with Philip Roth, deplored the crypto-homosexual play in which the pederast appeared disguised as an aging actress, a rebellious Negro or Everyman. Well, now we have an honest-to-goodness homosexual play, and is it ever an abomination! Anything is better than the hero as mother-craving-and-hating, alternately poetic and bitchy, sadistic but oh-so-red-blooded-American, smart-aleck little creep. And the mother and little sister who are his sidekicks—the perfect mother and sister for a homosexual: females clever and imaginative enough to envy, selfish and ruthless enough to want to strangle!

Let us dismiss the ostensible plot, which makes no sense anyway: something about an unknown, seemingly atomic "It" that murderously rules the streets by night, though by day life continues unchanged, and about people locking themselves in bomb-proof cellars surrounded by high-voltage fences to be safe at night. Let us ignore also the paraphernalia of the play: fancy sound and light effects, tape-recorded dialogue, intercoms, PA systems, slide projections (of two men going to bed together) and whatnot. No need to detain ourselves with the borrowings, obvious and heavy, from *The Zoo Story, Who's Afraid of Virginia Woolf?* and *Tiny Alice,* though translated back into homosexual relationships. A little harder to disregard is the writing: "SIGFRID: The sadness of Shakespeare, the enduring sadness of Florence, and the necessarily greater sadness of someone alone in the park. CLARENCE: What do you mean? SIGFRID: And that's the sadness of Clarence . . . I'm not your friend—and that's the sadness of Sigfrid."

What matters is the basic situation of that supremely vicious mother-son-daughter triangle that would die of internecine blood-lust if it were not for an endless line of victims, male or (though these, typically, we are not shown) female, whom sonny-boy lures into the family's nocturnal lair; he has sadomasochistic sex with them, and

later, with the help of mother and sister and all-revealing slides and
tape-recordings, humiliates the victims beyond endurance—in the
case of the present victim, Clarence, to the point of suicide. All of
which makes for wonderful family fun. The idea is that these three
incubi and succubi are infinitely appealing despite their ghoulishness
or even because of it; that the so-called normal people in the play
are represented as paralyzed or insensate, living in the past or escaping into sleep, doomed to extinction of one kind or another; that even
among the inverts, the "nice" ones die because they can't take it; that
the monsters shall endure and inherit the earth.

However, even the obnoxiousness of this premise might be made
tolerable if the insights or at least the language were interesting.
But no, it is all campy trivialities couched in poeticizing baby talk
(with camp refrains like "Sssh, *caro*, sssh; double-sssh, *caro*, double-
sssh" repeated ad nauseam) intertwined with sadistic bitchery, as in
this exchange between the ex-operatic diva mother and her son:
"SIGFRID: Well, your bazooms have dropped! RUBY: Of course, there's
no one I especially want to keep them up for . . . But aside from my
fallen grapes, how do I look? SIGFRID: . . . I wish you'd slip on the
Valkyrie outfit with the cast-iron boobies—they always make you
look so feminine."

And that whole long scene in which endless fun is squeezed from
the fact that poor Clarence is forced to wear nothing but a dress:
they stole his clothes, and there he is, barefoot in a frock, the poor,
gangly, likable, naïve, idealistic, uneffeminate queer. And the hearty
double entendres on words like "queen" and "basket." And the
poetic outbursts, like twelve-year-old daughter Lakme's "Dead is
bad, Ruby! Why didn't you tell us how bad dead was?" And son
Sigfrid's fundamentalist *de profundis*, "I buggered him! I buggered
him good! And we can't have buggered saints!" It fair makes one
long for the Albertine strategy again. Come back, Albertine, all is
forgiven! For it would seem, on the evidence of this play and certain
others related to it, that the homosexual theater cannot as yet be
merely homosexual: it has to wallow in every kind of nastiness, exhibitionism, vulgarity, and destruction. It is not the homosexuality
that offends, but all that hysterical ugliness that seems to be its
Siamese twin.

Just for the record, the production, too, and especially Michael
Cacoyannis's untalented direction, failed miserably. Only Ed Wittstein's lugubrious set and Marco St. John's touching Clarence could
pass muster. And, as always, Jules Fisher's masterly lighting.

WINTER, 1965-1966

PHILADELPHIA, HERE I COME!
by Brian Friel

THE LION IN WINTER
by James Goldman

SWEET CHARITY
book by Neil Simon
music by Cy Coleman
lyrics by Dorothy Fields

DIE MITSCHULDIGEN
by Johann Wolfgang von Goethe
produced by the Bavarian State Theatre

WOYZECK by Georg Büchner
produced by the Bavarian State Theatre

DIE RATTEN
by Gerhart Hauptmann
produced by the Bavarian State Theatre

BROADWAY has come up with one viable play, unsurprisingly enough an import, but this time from Ireland: *Philadelphia, Here I Come!* by Brian Friel. It is particularly interesting as a rather successful attempt to get out of a cultural rut. Just as we have the Thirties Mentality to shake off (in which all artistic activity was subsumed by some form of radical politics, style was ideologically suspect and aesthetics atrophied), Ireland has to rid itself of the "Irish Play." Either in the form of naturalist comedy-drama, or in that of fantasy, the Irish theater has, with few exceptions, belabored the theme of blathering nonentities boozing and dreaming away impotently while someone in their midst accomplishes a deed of rare chivalric (and quixotic) magnificence; but this act of lightning nobility promptly sinks into the morass of liquor, loquacity and lethargy. O'Casey's later works are but a depressing record of doomed efforts to break the mold; the Johnstons and Carrolls, with less talent to start with, fared no better. Now Friel has almost done it.

Philadelphia chronicles the last comic-pathetic night of young Gareth O'Donnell in the oppressive village of Ballybeg before emigrating to a new life in the City of Brotherly Love; it also reveals a night of the soul that, for all its being traversed by flashes of death-defying, daredevil wit, may never lead to a dawn. In essence, the play is a duologue between the Public Gar and the Private Gar, played by another actor, in which this conscience (let me refer to it mathematically and punningly as Gar^1) upbraids, flatters, mocks and bullies Gar into action that is never forthcoming, or joins with Gar in sardonically deploring the world around him, or more precisely around his neck. What makes this unusual and stimulating is not the doubleness of Gar; such devices are not new but go back at least as far as Jean-Victor Pellerin's *Intimité,* and conceivably even to the two angels in *Doctor Faustus.* It is the interaction of the Gars, their whimsical and acerb relationship, that captures our attention and sympathy. Sometimes they become a vaudeville act doing song numbers or comic turns together; sometimes they participate in a tragicomic agon; sometimes Gar is shamefacedly silent while Gar^1 rattles off corrosive tirades and pasquinades that could turn the whole community upside down—which, in this case, would be right side up—if the words could ever get beyond the lips of the mind. Certain reviewers who were bothered by the discrepancy between the brilliant inner satirist and the taciturn outer noninterventionist missed the very point; that the humble, worn outer garment could uncover a rich lining inside if only convention and habit could be defied to the extent of daring to wear oneself inside out. The disparity between the Gars works beautifully for the author: the more preposterously grotesque it is, the funnier it becomes; but the more the implications of the preposterous rift dawn on us, the more frightening and tragic the experience. Friel's comedy is his tragedy, and that is one of the very best things a playwright can achieve.

But there is more. If the characters around the duple (and therefore unintentionally duplicitous) protagonist were just the traditional "Irish Play" figures—the faithful female retainer, the bleakly unreachable father, the local politicians, priests and teachers—the old Hibernian microcosm would once again be revolving around its creaky axis bent with helpless laughter and rusted with impotent tears—although it must be stressed that even these traditional figures are drawn with a winning deftness. Friel, however, brings in two other worlds as well: that of the drunken, uprooted, vulgarized Philadelphia aunt who is making Gar's transplanting possible, but who, with her retinue, suggests that the New World is not such a brave one; and that of Gar's rowdy pals, the disaffected youth of the Auld Sod who, in the perishableness of their revolt, indicate that this brave world is not such a new one. Thus Friel's scope fans out into a broader perspective; and his language, though not consistently fresh and poetic, often manages to bring Ballybeg remarkably close to Llareggub.

The weaknesses of the play come out in the occasional easy pathos, as in two scenes with the sweetheart whom Gar lacks the courage to marry and who becomes the languishing bride of another—though this part suffered also from the uninspired performance of Lanna Saunders. The aunt, though nicely projected by Mavis Villiers, verges on a stock character, a kind of Irish Shelley Winters. But most of the acting is expert, and that of Donald Donnelly as Gar[1]—arrogantly charming and drolly pertinacious, with a singlemindedness that succeeds, paradoxically, in being mercurial—is of the very first rank. Hilton Edwards' direction is graphic in its groupings and musical in its well-modulated rhythms. The production is worthy, and Brian Friel's sobering play is the thing our dreams are unmade on.

JAMES GOLDMAN's *The Lion in Winter* is an attempt to endow a psychologizing family soap opera with dignity by having the family be that of Henry II of England, and by dousing the semblances of plot and character with a heavy perfume of epigrams. As the King and his hissing kin wrangle over the succession to the throne—and how little the author cares about story and dramatis personae is evident from there being neither resolution of the one nor development of the other—we are sprayed with witticism after witticism until the auditorium is fairly awash on essence of Wilde Flower. But the trouble with the epigram is that unless it is very startling and cuts deep, it has no great literary value; and if, moreover, it has nothing to latch onto by way of substratum except more epigrams, it drowns in a surfeit of itself. In *The Importance of Being Earnest* the epigrams both heralded a shocking new cultural dispensation and illuminated recognizable human traits; furthermore, their phrasing had a perfection bordering on the algebraic. But when in *The Lion in Winter* we are told that "in a world where carpenters are resurrected, anything is possible," it is too late in the game to be shocked, and much too early to look for any depth in Mr. Goldman's thought.

All too often Goldman settles for easy anachronistic effects: "The year is 1183 and we are all Barbarians!" or facile anticlimaxes, as when after murderous family intriguing and clashes Eleanor of Aquitaine sighs, "All families have their little ups and downs," or exhausted jokes like "They threw the baby out and kept the afterbirth," which figured in the repertoire of generations of medical-school raconteurs. But Goldman waxes more desperate. He uses every ploy from the manuals on How to Dress Up Your Comedy. There is the tastefully simple basic black paradox: "When can I believe you, Henry? —Always, even when I lie." There is diamond solitaire hyperbole, which one dresses down with a neat little aside, preferably in tasty bad taste: "Henry's bed is his province; he can people it with sheep for all I care—as, I believe, on occasion he does." (Zoophilia is always good for a clean dirty laugh.) A fancy *haute couture* label never misses its effect on the sophisticates: "Ask Praxiteles why he doesn't work in butter." Particularly affecting is the reverse English, whereby what looks at first glance like a very expensive boutique design, turns out to be a sensible little thrift-shop verity: "Time hasn't done a thing but wrinkle you." And, for the groundlings, one must feature an occasional bit of strong (off) color: "Piss on your peace!"

But, of course, the year is 1183: rapiers have not been invented yet, and the wit is broadsword. Once in a while the broadsword will hit home: "There's no point in wondering if the air is good if there's nothing else to breathe"; and Noel Willman has staged what there is of the play with a certain easeful directness and a sculptural quality in the blocking that makes for at least a seeming solidity. He has got his actors reading their lines with bounce and precision, avoiding both slurring and overemphasis. Amazingly, he has unearthed several young men to play English and French princes and not sound like American or (if that is not synonymous) method actors; he accomplished this by choosing mostly actor-singers whose very sound-production lends them unparochial, indeed princely, stature. Robert Preston is able to rely on his manly charm and a kind of energy that laughs at itself to make the King both sturdy and delightfully fantastic. But Rosemary Harris once again demonstrates the difference between a highly competent, technically proficient actress and a truly fine or even great one: her Eleanor is always calculated for maximum effect, with nothing smacking of mere humanity allowed to peep through.

SWEET CHARITY purports to be based on Fellini's *Nights of Cabiria*, but might as well come from the Kabyles, the Kaffirs or the Khyber Pass. For the original's bittersweet seediness verging on the sentimental, Neil Simon's book substitutes sheer sentimental comedy verging on idiocy. Prostitutes become dance-hall hostesses, predators become bumblers, sex becomes a running gag, a bootless pilgrimage to the shrine of a miraculous Virgin becomes the apparition of a comic fairy-godmother in Central Park, and what was a nice enough film becomes an unholy mess. Add to this unimpressive songs, and repartee that tastes and stretches like used chewing gum, and you would expect to have nothing. But astonishingly the first act of the show is almost rescued, and at times even made to glow by Bob Fosse who (I quote the program credits) "conceived, staged and choreographed" it with razzle-dazzle inventiveness, though gradually losing out to the book, music and lyrics. In the second act, stiltedness and listlessness preponderate, but there were those two or three glittering dance and production numbers in the first. Gwen Verdon is appetizing and resourceful, but her bag of tricks is not bottomless; John McMartin has a cunning comic simmer that can flare up into triumphantly nasal trumpetings, but there is not much substance to apply his adroit, idiosyncratic style to. Helen Gallagher is her usual sassy self, but the lackluster mealy-mouthedness engulfs her, too. Something always undercuts *Sweet Charity:* if Robert Randolph's scenery is going great guns, Irene Sharaf's costumes will conk out; when a bedroom scene has comic potential, it is well-nigh exaggerated out of its life, and an inept actor (James Luisi) finishes it off.

THE BAVARIAN STATE THEATRE was short on traditional Bavarian cheer. Goethe's *Die Mitschuldigen* is a wispy comic vignette that was performed with a good deal less than the requisite scintillation—it was Mark Lothar's music that came off best. Georg Büchner's breathtaking masterpiece *Woyzeck* was given an unutterably arid production under Hans Lietzau's cloddish direction. Lietzau tried to make this an expressionist play by sticking to the same ghostly pace throughout. Starting the play with the woodcutting scene, which gives us a demented Woyzeck, is already a huge mistake; by beginning with the shaving scene, one conveys the social conditions that drive the man mad. But the errors of taste, judgment, and simple under- standing were legion. The grandmother's tale, for example, surely one of the most moving and terrifying moments in all dramatic litera- ture, was deprived of all terror and pathos by the staging and acting alike. The overwhelming line, "Man is an abyss, you get dizzy looking down," was no longer addressed by Woyzeck to Marie's eyes, but to his own image in the water—tragedy reduced to narcissism. The pathetically stolid Andres was played as a handsome, sensible young man; the animalistically sexual drum major became a marionette with Nazi overtones. The transcendent poetry was consistently lost, as was even the humble tenderness; little of the social and intellectual satire remained. Jürgen Rose's permanent set, a roofed-over inner court- yard, made scenes that were supposed to represent the countryside look laughable; and the time it took to roll out a box set for some of the interiors was almost longer than the duration of some of the in- tensely compressed scenes themselves. The cast, with the exception of Max Mairich's Captain, was mediocre at best, Heinrich Schweiger playing Woyzeck like a dazed gorilla and Elisabeth Orth not begin- ning to bring out Marie's complexities. Almost the only purpose served by this *Woyzeck* was to prove that Lincoln Center is not the only place where Büchner gets fractured.

The other presentation of the Bavarians, Hauptmann's *Die Rat- ten,* was so unwieldy and unconvincing a play that the rather better, though conventional, treatment it got under Helmut Henrichs was of no appreciable help. Here there was some forceful acting by Maria Wimmer, a tragedienne of stature, and Peter Fricke and Max Mairich contributed some especially handsome supporting work. (Peter Fricke had been quite remarkable in an excellent production of *The Awak- ening of Spring* a couple of seasons ago at the Residenztheater; why on earth could not that incisive and swift production, demonstrating how much good there is in Wedekind's play, be brought over instead of Hauptmann's clumsy posturing in the direction of Greek tragedy?) Rose's sets were acceptable this time, and the first half of the play, where comedy predominates, was passing fair. Later on, how- ever, the murk took over, at first melodramatically, thereafter risibly.

SPRING, 1966

THE PERSECUTION AND ASSASSINATION OF
JEAN-PAUL MARAT, AS PERFORMED BY THE
INMATES OF THE ASYLUM OF CHARENTON UNDER
THE DIRECTION OF THE MARQUIS DE SADE
   by Peter Weiss

INADMISSIBLE EVIDENCE
   by John Osborne

THE COUNTRY WIFE
   by William Wycherley
   produced by the Repertory Theater of Lincoln Center

THE WHITE DEVIL
   by John Webster
   produced by the Circle in the Square Theatre

A TRICKY FELLOW, Peter Weiss. He writes or speaks in such as yet insufficiently explored art forms as the open letter and the interview, and has refined them to a point of Brechtianly artful dodging. He revises his political position and artistic intentions from one public statement to the next, and he has raised charges of misquotation, bowdlerization, and unauthorized publication to the level of dazzling rhetorical figures. Into this world of shifting meanings and stances, Weiss's play *Marat/Sade* fits perfectly. (I use the dehydrated version of the title; quoted in full, it feels too much like an infringement of the copyright laws.) The play is a house of mirrors, a fun palace, a many-bottomed valise whose final bottom is infinity. It is highly sophisticated theater, but only a slender addition to the drama.

Günter Grass described *Marat/Sade* as a fine scenario for a ballet. More indulgently, one might call it a splendid stage metaphor. Historically, the play takes place in 1808, but the action of the play-within-the-play is laid in 1793, with flashbacks to still earlier times; however, the use of anachronism situates the play in our present—if not, indeed, in anybody's. Politically, the play is an extended and often interrupted agon between Sade the individualist and rational antirationalist, and Marat the fanatical populist and would-be reformer, so that the debate would seem to be between aristocratic and hedonistic self-realization and Marxism—except that this Marat is a brainchild of Sade's and, therefore, not real, and that Sade may be a madman, and therefore likewise unreal. Which brings us to the philosophical plane, where the question is who is mad and who is sane, or what is reality and what illusion? The dramatis personae are almost all lunatics, but they are, to the best of their abilities, performing a text, presumably sane. They tend, however, to revert to themselves—at times manifestly, at times perhaps covertly. When are they real? When they are performing an ostensibly coherent play by a possible madman, or when they burst into the very genuine symptoms of their madness? And how sane is the madhouse director who encourages this dubious psychodrama for therapeutic reasons, but who, whenever the play moves toward disquieting truths, resorts to crass censorship? Can truth become dangerous, unhealthy, insane? And how real and sane are we, the theater audience made to impersonate those thrill-hungry worldlings who flocked to Charenton, like so many voyeurs, to see the inmates disport themselves dramatically or, better yet, dementedly? We see ourselves attacked in the play, our weaknesses magnified (but not falsified) by the madmen, and we laugh and applaud. Madness this side of the footlights, or that side—or both?

Even anecdotally the play is an ambiguity: in the final chaos, it is impossible to assess who or what triumphs, if anything does. And formally, the play fluctuates between the doggerel of the medieval morality and the free verse of contemporary looseness. The raucous song interludes contribute yet another disturbing dimension. In every possible labyrinthine way, the implicated spectators are confounded and disoriented, until their *dépaysement* is complete. *Marat/Sade* begins at the confluence of Brechtian alienation, Pirandellian illusionism and Artaudian shock treatment, and follows them to where they conjointly debouch into the sea of the absurd.

Beyond this complex and absorbing conceit, the play offers little more than a handsome occasion for a spectacular production. Indeed, a brilliant Polish stage director, Konrad Swinarski, helped Weiss with the play, and no doubt contributed largely to its remarkable stageworthiness. The play, whose confrontations and clevernesses fail to crystallize into true insight, will survive as one of the dandiest theatrical pretexts, showering its largesse on the director. And Peter Brook has seized the opportunity and kneaded it into what I do not hesitate to call a perfect production.

The set consists of brick walls of a grayish beige, benches alongside the walls, various tiled pits (this is the bathhouse of the asylum) and slatted wooden screens to cover some of these pits. The screens are first seen in a circular arrangement on the raked floor, but subsequently undergo the wildest transformations to suggest a variety of objects or settings constantly reshaping an evidently putty world. In come the madmen, putty-colored themselves, a breathing compendium of aberrancies, a staring, stumbling, mumbling, gesticulating, tic-ridden or catatonic mass, now scurrying about like balls of mercury on a glass surface, now lapsing into drained, comatose blankness. On stage left is a podium on which sit the smug asylum director and his insipid ladies who mostly ogle and chirp at the audience. In the proscenium boxes are bands of lunatic musicians (this is one of many Brookian improvements; according to the original text, the band is nonhistrionic and is onstage) who, besides playing Richard Peaslee's animated tunes in hectic arrangements, provide a running commentary of addled reactions to the play. And there is one solid object on a centerstage dais: the tub in which Marat is confined by his skin disease (or the cage in which the paranoiac playing Marat is constrained): a large, dark metal boot, a symbol of might that crushes but also constricts.

I wish I could itemize some of the sardonic, tantalizing, unnerving stage images—as often out of Brook as out of Weiss—that ensue, a ceaselessly bubbling cauldron of laughing horrors and satanic whimsies. Thus Brook has conceived of having the mock-executed madmen jump into one of the bath pits, till only a heap of heads bobs above stage level; as the decapitations occur, a bucket of blood is casually emptied: red for plain folks, blue for aristocrats, black for a villain . . . and white for a savior like Marat. Imagine a welter of visual and aural devices among which the dialogue weaves in and out, modest enough to begin with and forced into increasing self-effacement.

It is true that Brook's production shows some departures from the excellent, though often rather ungrammatical, English version, whose prose sections are by Geoffrey Skelton and verse sequences by Adrian Mitchell.* The English text, moreover, takes not infrequent liberties with Weiss's original. But this hardly matters when the acting itself is enough to overwhelm one. It would be an insult to single out any actor as better or worse than the rest: the entire cast is a marvelous, macabre, tentacular monster with some forty heads and one hundred and sixty limbs, rehearsed to grim perfection by that master monster-trainer, Peter Brook. However much one may regret the rudimentariness of the ideas and their development, however little the words may climb above flat adequacy, the production is something like an ironic and thoroughly successful set of illustrations for Dante's *Inferno,* adding what such illustrations usually lack: the hellish laughter.

ANOTHER, SMALLER-SCALE, postlapsarian freak show is afforded us by John Osborne's *Inadmissible Evidence.* Here damnation has made its filthy lair in the first form of the divine, the word. Osborne is one of the foremost writers of monologues for the modern theater; though he can compose a passage for several voices, give him that single instrument, the angry or whining human voice, and he will wrest from it all kinds of double stops: comic plangencies, torrential trivialities, staccato fusillades of all-consuming spite, and whimpering cadenzas of self-pity and self-hate. The play relates the crack-up of Bill Maitland, a seedy East-London solicitor: the crazily spiraling tensions with his staff, clients and women—wife, mistresses, daughter—leading up to the ultimate breakdown.

As usual with Osborne, there are two deficiencies: lack of sufficient form and lack of wholly convincing motivation. It is as though neurosis were its own begetter, its own sustenance, and its own final cause; it is not to be questioned any more than arrested, its reasons and consequences the unshakable *données* of the protagonist's life. Can it be that this is as it should be: is the case history of Bill Maitland really the case of Maitland vs. Maitland, or of Maitland vs.

* Published here by Atheneum, 1966.

Everything? Is what is required not psychological analysis but litigation? What is surely not required is a red herring of a prologue, the sterile repetitiousness of the second act, and such total irrelevancy as the semi-ironic, semi-abject paean to the younger generation that Maitland delivers to his bored and resentful daughter, not half so bored and resentful as I was in the audience.

But the first act, and even a fraction of the second, can be marveled at and enjoyed as the fusion of a mighty cataclysm with a bagful of bitter jokes, combining in extraordinary defiance of all scientific and dramatic laws. Maitland is a mini-Machiavel of engrossing, though festering, vitality; he is as witty and funny as he is beastly, but his very beastliness is shot through with twitches of abortive humanity. This petty character manages to loom large; his defeat, or self-defeat, concerns us: there but for a stroke of luck sink we into the quicksands of the irrational.

Perfectly embodying Osborne's sourly scintillating humor, there sits, slouches and sidles, groans, grumbles and fulminates Nicol Williamson, an actor whose looks, sounds, and movements have a heroic asymmetry, who emits a truculent lopsidedness that mauls our eyes and ears. Take his face: is it cadaverous or fleshly? It squiggles in both directions. Take his voice: is it an outrage or a joke? Mere phonemes become laden with ambivalence. Never absent from the stage throughout the play, Williamson prestidigitates more than he acts: our stock responses to Maitland are kept dextrously in abeyance. Around him, there is a highly efficient cast, in which only Ted van Griethuysen and Madeleine Sherwood, the two un-British members, prove unequal to the needed flexibility. Jocelyn Herbert has designed a properly dreary set, and Anthony Page has directed with a nice sense of pacing and spacing. The virtues of this play and production should outlive the flaws, though one wishes that the penetrating Osborne who wrote the first act had not yielded his typewriter to the diffuse and prolix Osborne who wrote the second.

THE NEW Repertory Theater of Lincoln Center has followed up its mishandled production of *Danton's Death* with an almost equally mismanaged rendition of *The Country Wife*. Contrasted with Etherege, Wycherley reveals, according to Rudolf Stamm, *"einen gröberen Witz,"* but also the skill of constructing *"wirksamere Handlungen."* In this production, the action may not prove particularly effective, but the wit certainly is coarse. Yet for this coarseness to mean anything—a rake's passing himself off as impotent in order to cuckold husbands with their blessing, and a country lass's taking to adultery as a tot to making mudpies—the wit must play off its crudeness against the pseudo-refinement of the ambience. What cynicism and corruption are here; what crazed extremes, from Pinchwife, who is more turnkey than husband to his bride, to Sparkish, who keeps throwing his intended at his lustful crony's head. For these men and women the world revolves around a genital axis; one thinks of the apostrophe to the vagina in *Sodom*, "This is the ware house of the world's chief Trade,/ On this soft anvil all mankind was made." Only, in *The Country Wife* reproduction is not even mentioned, mass production, "Trade," is all—but always in the kid gloves of style, under the rose of elegance, with the firm conviction that wickedness is the supreme form of innocence.

Precious little of all this reaches the stage of the Vivian Beaumont. The Repertory Theater does indeed command a repertoire of accents from Bay Area to Brooklyn, but the polished British tones that alone can make the cadences of Restoration phraseology fall pleasurably on our ears are scarcely within its compass. The acting itself is undistinguished, though Priscilla Pointer's Lady Fidget is definitely on the right track, and for a glimmer or two Stacy Keach captures something of Horner. Robert Symonds' direction is erratic: to make Sparkish (whom Symonds himself plays) into a pathetic buffoon rather than a preposterous, possibly homosexual, fop, is novel but untenable. Sets and costumes are perfunctory, and whenever the production is in doubt, it hopefully rolls out the turntables. Alas, they might as well rely on a centrifuge, for all the homogeneity they achieve.

At that, *The Country Wife* never sank to the level of Circle in the Square's *The White Devil*, directed by Jack Landau. *The White Devil* is arguably as good as *The Duchess of Malfi*, which makes it very good indeed. After Landau and his cast get through with their severely cut modern-dress version, it might as well be called *The Poor Devil*. If there is such a thing as ensemble non-acting, this is it. By the time I caught the production, Eric Berry was no longer in it; but of all the actors I saw, only Frank Langella as Flamineo displayed understanding of what he was doing and a sense of style. Even so, the part could have used a little more masculinity, and Langella did not rise to its ultimate tragic heights. Of the others, it is more charitable to say nothing, though I cannot help wondering how such a major part as that of Lodovico could have gone, even in this production, to a performer without a shred of presence or a minimum of intelligibility.

Landau's staging is uninspired and crude to the point of allowing Frederic Warriner to camp up the part of Camillo, and letting Cornelia deliver one of the most beautiful English dirges, "Call for the robin-redbreast and the wren," in the manner of a rambling madwoman—for the sake of a bit of misplaced naturalism, farewell poetry! But not even to Webster's most explicit lines does Landau pay attention. Francisco is played with a Hathaway eye patch, though at one point he plainly refers to closing his (plural) eyes. Vittoria's hair is compared to a "blackbird's feather," yet Carrie Nye is stridently blonde. Even the costuming makes no sense: Francisco's Moorish disguise becomes a monk's hood and cape, and, of all things, dark glasses. To prevent the hood from slipping too far back, Robert Burr must nod continually like a worry-bird, and it is a mystery how Zanche can fall in love with him on first sight through all those integuments. Ah well, what are we to expect from a production in which "alms" is pronounced "olms"? May ablivion engolf it!

Winter, 1966-1967

A Delicate Balance
by Edward Albee

The Investigation
by Peter Weiss

The Killing of Sister George
by Frank Marcus

ALBEE IS progressing. *Who's Afraid of Virginia Woolf?* was about the emptiness that surrounds and threatens to swallow our relationships; *Tiny Alice* was about the void lurking behind our deepest beliefs; now, *A Delicate Balance* is about the nothingness, the bare nothingness of it all—it is a play about nothing. "Nothing will come of nothing" was not spoken of the theater: *there* nothing has been known to yield glittering and even golden returns. *Heartbreak House,* for example, is a play more or less about nothing, and so are most of Beckett's plays. But Shaw fills his nothingness with incisive speculation, so that the mind, though working in a near-vacuum, begets its own thrilling parabolas; Beckett raises nothingness to fierce tragicomic, almost epic, heights. But the nothingness—perhaps more accurately *nothinginess*—of Albee's play is petty, self-indulgent, stationary. Albee's nothing is as dull as anything.

Tobias and Agnes, a genteel middle-aged couple, are the pillars of suburbia. They drink, vegetate and speechify. With them lives Agnes' alcoholic younger sister, Claire, between whom and Tobias there may or may not be some hanky-panky. Claire and Agnes loathe each other, which allows Claire to pour out a steady stream of wise-cracks floating out over the stream of liquor flowing down. The daughter of the house, Julia, aged thirty-six, returns as her fourth marriage is breaking up; this phenomenon occurs every three years, and her parents keep her room ready to soothe the postmarital de-pression. This uneasy ménage could just barely be kept in a delicate balance if it weren't for the neighbors and best friends, Harry and Edna, who, sudden preys to a terrible but nameless fear, arrive un-announced and intending to stay, apparently forever. They are given Julia's room, which causes that ungay divorcée to have hysterics and almost shoot the intruders. After much soul-searching and several storms in a martini glass, leading up to a frenzied tirade of Tobias' full of instant self-contradiction, Harry and Edna go home, after all, leaving the family quartet to play, in precarious equilibrium, sour-sweet music on one another's heartstrings.

The first thing to strike one about all this is its rank improbability. Why are any of these people here? Why should Agnes tolerate Claire's sniping, and why would Claire want this ungenial hostess, even with free drinks and the rather square host thrown in as an ice cube? Why should Julia rush home to recuperate, when she and her parents do not seem particularly in tune, and she is wealthy and big enough to undertake a hotel? Why should the neighbors wish to move in? Edna was at her knitting, Harry at his recorded French course, when the mysterious terror seized them. But what makes them think that they can move in with their friends indefinitely or, rather, definitively? And why; when in that vacuous household, amid jangling cocktail glasses and nerves, there is plenty of room for the fear to move right in with them? Finally, the key problem makes no sense: should one put up one's neighbors, in the name of friendship, in perpetuity, or shouldn't one? No halfway sane people would arrive with such a request, and no halfway conceivable people would seriously entertain the notion of so entertaining them. Yet in Albee's play this is presented with a straight face, earnestly, though the idea belongs in absurdist farce, where, however, it would be handled with Ionescoan wit or Pinterish balefulness.

But presumably there is a deeper meaning: something, no doubt, like what is a marriage, a family, friendship, and how does one keep these relations going in the face of a world grown meaningless? Now, first of all, I am tired of this mythical "meaningless world" when the playwright fails to create or suggest any outer world (one isolated reference to income taxes might as well have been to Chinese calligraphy), and when he neglects to indicate what meaningfulness might have been before it got mislaid. This posturing play abounds in the cocktail-party profundities and family-reunion soundings that bloated up Eliot's drama, but at least Eliot was, however flatfootedly, after some sort of myth or metaphysic. Albee, too, must drop little hints: one can play with Claire's clairvoyance, with Julia as a latter-day Juliet, with Tobias and Agnes as Tobias and the Angel—but, as Elizabeth Hardwick notes, "a reading of the *Book of Tobit* did not produce any deepening allegory."

That may still leave Albee's language, which, according to a chorus of reviewers, is a marvel and a joy. Now, it is true that Albee is in love with language, which sets him above your average play-wright who does not even realize that language exists, but, for all that, Albee's love affair is sadly one-sided. The language of *Virginia Woolf*, for example, often lapses into subliteracy: "He is breathing a little heavy; behaving a little manic," "A son who I have raised," "I have never robbed a hothouse without there is a light from heaven," the curious notion that *ibid* means something like "in the same way," which frequently recurs in the stage directions, e.g., "NICK (*very quietly*) . . . GEORGE (*ibid*)" etc. In my review of *Tiny Alice*, I quoted a goodly number of similar lapses and, mind you, always in the speech of supposedly cultivated persons. So again here, as in "You're not as young as either of us were" or in Claire's dogged distinction that she is not "an alcoholic" but "*a* alcoholic," which is supposed to be amusingly portentous, but manages to be merely nonsense, linguistically and otherwise.

But there is a much more profound insensitivity to language at work here, and the more painful since Albee (as he did in *Tiny Alice*) has one of his characters apologize for his alleged articulate-ness. But Albee's "articulateness" is either self-conscious poeticism, "When the daylight comes, comes order with it," or long, syntactically overburdened sentences and paragraphs, or putative shockers like, "Your mummy got her pudenda scarred a couple of times before she met daddy," where "pudenda" is rather too recherché for Tobias, and "scarred" much too sadistic: it may be consistent with his char-acter to be sardonic, but not to be beastly. Or, again, consider, "And if we were touching, ah, what a splendid cocoon that was!" How inept to use the weak word "touching" for sexual contact (as it is here used) and to match this up with "cocoon," which does not sug-gest two beings becoming one, but, on the contrary, one ego narcis-sistically shutting itself off. Or take this exchange: "You are not young, and you do not live at home.—Where do I live?—In the dark sadness, yes?" Is this supposed to be irony or lyricism? In either case, I say, the dark sadness, no. And even Albee's usually dependable bitchy wit fails him all too often here, as in "AGNES: Why don't you go to Kentucky or Tennessee and visit the distilleries? CLAIRE: Why don't you die?"

What, one wonders, was the real motive behind *A Delicate Balance?* I, for one, still believe in Albee's perceptiveness and even in his talent (he did, after all, write *The Zoo Story* and *Virginia Woolf*); why would he hurtle into such utter pointlessness? It occurs to me that, at least since *Virginia Woolf*, Albee's plays and adaptations have been viewed by many as dealing overtly or covertly with homosexual matters; Albee may have resolved here to write a play reeking with heterosexuality. To be sure, the edges are fuzzy. The good friends Harry and Tobias spend a summer sleeping with the same girl, a practice about which psychoanalysis has a thing or two to tell. When an unprepossessing and gauche saleswoman tries to help Claire with a bathing suit and asks her what she could do for her, Claire replies with a nasty smirk fraught with double entendre, "Not very much, sweetheart," a piece of repartee appropriate only to an invert. And there is a whole sequence in which Agnes and Tobias figuratively (and sneeringly) reverse sexes and roles in their relationship with Julia. But all this is not at the heart of the play. At the heart of the play things are heterosexual and totally lifeless.

Under the circumstances, it is hard to evaluate the production. It would seem that Rosemary Murphy, as Claire, gives the best performance, but then she gets most of the good lines and few of the terrible ones; it would also seem that the others act passably, except for Marian Seldes whose Julia is unconvincing, and Carmen Mathews who makes Edna so smug and odious that no one, I should think, would let her cross his threshold. Alan Schneider's direction may be all that can be done for the play, and William Ritman's set has the proper look of an expensive, well-furnished cavern, to match the general hollowness. Liquors are by Renfield Importers, Ltd., and without them the play might be close to an act shorter.

PETER WEISS's *The Investigation* is, for quite other reasons, not a play either. It is an abridgment of the 1964–65 Frankfurt trials of former Auschwitz personnel, which Weiss has edited but, as he maintains, not added to. It is, in other words, a theater documentary that relates untold unspeakable horrors; shows that the men who perpetrated them still believe, most of them quite sincerely, that they were only doing their duty; and points out that those few who miraculously survived live in a world in which their former torturers and would-be executioners are, for the most part, better off than they. *The Investigation* implies that we are all only too capable of such bestialities if encouraged or ordered to commit them, and is presumably intended as a memento and a warning.

The play (I call it that merely for convenience) raises two liminal questions: is the stage the place for a documentary, and does this particular documentary serve a valid purpose? I am not against documentary theater, as long as no one goes around calling its author a full-fledged dramatist. About the appropriateness of the subject— well, the Austrian humorist, Helmut Qualtinger, playing on the German title of Pirandello's masterpiece (*Sechs Personen suchen einen Autor*), quipped, "Sechs Millionen Personen suchen keinen Autor," and there is some validity in the argument that no theatrical presentation can grapple with the enormity of this crime. The argument runs that making a "play" out of it either commercializes and cheapens the event, or (more plausibly) that so many horrors cancel one another out, and that the audience ends up hardened rather than moved. There is also the corollary argument that this kind of play reaches only those already converted, and that—as the play itself demonstrates—those prone to such brutality cannot be kept from it by any easy means.

It is undeniable that *The Investigation* is not a work of art. That brings to mind Hochhuth's remarks on the fifth act of his *Deputy*, which takes place at Auschwitz. After claiming that "documentary naturalism" is an inadequate "stylistic principle" for the purpose, Hochhuth nonetheless warns that "an approach such as was so effectively used in Paul Celan's masterly poem *Todesfuge*, in which the gassing of the Jews is entirely translated into metaphors . . . despite the tremendous force of suggestion emanating from . . . metaphors, still [screens] the infernal cynicism of what really took place. . . ." Since Hochhuth is right on both counts, his own last act fails, and so, on one level at least, does all of *The Investigation*.

I would like to think that the way to produce the impact that might make an impression on people is through art, though whether anything can soothe the savage breast more than fleetingly is highly debatable. Art, however, can cope only with a narrower range: it can show fear in a handful of dust, but not in ovenfuls of human ashes.

Even so, I am for anything that might in any way remind us of our *maxima culpa* of not being better than we are, for anything that does whatever it can to deanonymize the victims of persecution. Yet it must be admitted that films can do this documentary memorialization better than the stage. I am thinking of Alain Resnais' *Night and Fog,* and more recently of a Hungarian short, *St. Matthew Passion* by Tamás Czigány, which, to the accompaniment of Bach's music, had the camera shuttling between paintings of the crucifixion and actual shots from the death camps.

It would seem necessary, however, that any theatrical reenactment be staged and acted with utmost subtlety and restraint: even outbursts should be managed with a kind of impersonality transcending the histrionic. This has proved too much for the director, Ulu Grosbard, and most of the cast. Sitting in tiers of a stylized wooden beehive, and costumed in gray (witnesses for the prosecution), charcoal (witnesses for the accused) and black (defendants), surrounded by more wood, and indeed revealed by the drawing apart of two halves of a heavy wood and wire wall, the performers, like the scenery by Kert Lundell, look more or less right. But as one becomes more precisely aware of them, trouble begins. Fellows like Tom Pedi and Richard Castellano, for instance, look like Brooklyn truckdrivers, and, once they open their mouths, no amount of reverse English could turn them into Teutonic torturers or symbols of universal inhumanity. Others, like Gordon B. Clarke, Ferdi Hoffman and John Marley, though they look right, either overact or go off on histrionic tangents. Still others, like Ward Costello or Leslie Barrett, can make powerful stuff sound garbled or dull. Henry Oliver, for example, manages everything right, except making you forget that he is an actor. The judge and the two attorneys, besides being awkwardly placed in the orchestra pit with their backs to the audience, are all ineffectual. A particularly offensive performance is given by Vivian Nathan, as a composite of various Auschwitz inmates: she literally bristles with a variety of cheap little tricks meant to extort sympathy from the audience; and even genuine tears, on her, become cultured pearls.

A few people, on the other hand, emerge commendably. Peter Brandon makes a stolid, callous Nazi corporal almost pitiable; and Wendell K. Phillips, Sr., and Ivor Francis make two lesser defendants thoroughly credible. It is significant, though, that the butchers tend to come out more substantial, more real, than the victims. Still, on the other side of the fence, Alice Hirson looks and sounds right, with a lurking hysteria almost completely buried under layers of hard, petrified tissue. And as for Graham Jarvis, here was a witness in the truest sense of that word, all clarity, simplicity, penetration. His pauses were not for effect, one felt—only to find the most nearly adequate words for the inexpressible. The most horrible things were uttered most soberly. Always there was the suggestion of patience and humility before the facts, and though the lips sometimes came close to trembling, there was no quaver in the voice, no gratuitous tearfulness. Even while merely sitting and listening to others, Jarvis tilted his body, neck, and face into the exact angle of acute concern, and was the very image of troubled decency.

But as I look at the German text of *The Investigation,* I become troubled too. There is something faintly disturbing (and not in the right sense) about an author who can take this material, transcribe it as free verse, call it "an oratorio in eleven cantos," and even if he gives the royalties to charity, takes the credit for a "play."

THE NEW ENGLISH FARCE *The Killing of Sister George* concerns a beloved character on a popular BBC radio serial who is to be killed off in order to make the program more contemporary. This character, Sister George, is a hymn-singing, motorbike-riding, rough-and-ready nurse, and has become second nature to June Buckridge, the aging actress who portrays her. But June's first nature is still very much there, nice and unnatural: she is a tippling lesbian termagant. Her flat- and bed-mate is an infantile girl of thirty-four, nicknamed Childie, who can be rather exasperating and mercenary—a sort of inverted, postgraduate Lolita. Into this alternatingly jovial and sinister ménage (there are violent quarrels after which Childie has to do ritual, masochistic penance) comes Mrs. Mercy Croft, an oh so politely steely executive of the BBC, bringing tidings of Sister George's fate that drip with elocutionist's honey and leave an aftertaste of pure wormwood. The play depicts the deterioration of June's and Childie's relationship as Sister George's foothold on the serial becomes more and more precarious. (A drunken assault on a pair of nuns in a taxi just outside Broadcasting House doesn't help either.) Finally, Sister George is dispatched in a traffic accident which the BBC, in its infinite wisdom, has coincide with Road Safety Week. George is mourned by the BBC on the air along with, it would seem, the entire nation. Mrs. Croft steals Childie from June, who is offered the ultimate ignominy of playing a cow on a children's serial but, never fear, a contemporary, "a flawed, credible cow." As the curtain falls, June is drinking alone and practicing her mooing.

But the problem with Frank Marcus' play is that it cannot find its tone. There are elements of domestic comedy cheek by jowl with absurdist farce, just as there is pathos jostling satire. Sometimes one is not even sure about what is which: thus Childie's having to kneel and kiss the hem of June's dress, or eat June's cigar butt or drink June's bath water may be the semijocular enactment of a fantasy, or may have to be taken more seriously as tokens of the beatings Childie claims to receive at other times. There are moments when the play functions effectively on one plane or another, but eventually the tug of its conflicting aspirations confuses and cheapens the issues. And though the humor, consistently on target in the first act, is still well aimed much of the time thereafter, it broadens out excessively without being able to hoist itself fully into satire or to burrow deep enough into the absurd.

The two principal performances, however, are gloriously irreproachable. In Beryl Reid's George *cum* June all of the author's complex and sometimes contradictory intentions are frighteningly, funnily, frangibly reconciled; and Eileen Atkins' Childie is a paradigm of gawky pathos and seductively jolly bitchiness. They can be exceedingly amusing together, as when they practice a Laurel and Hardy routine for a drag party and make the fetching humor go sour and ominous at the drop of water into a hat. Indeed, they turn their whole being together into a comic routine that teeters breathlessly between tease and torment. Lally Bowers is, like her BBC accent, a trifle overstated, and Polly Rowles, as a Russian clairvoyante, can pass. Val May has directed shrewdly, and *The Killing of Sister George* emerges uneven but with with quite a swarm of tickles and stings.

AND NOW I want to tell you about what was, for me, the most thought-provoking event of the season so far. It happened at the opening night of three one-acters by Thornton Wilder (nothing thought-provoking about them!), the first production of the year. Here was an audience of double first-nighters: the first night of the first play; surely these were true sophisticates. Well, when the curtain went up on the third playlet, the nauseatingly *Happy Journey to Trenton and Camden*, it revealed a bare stage with a few folding chairs and the permanent brick wall at the back of the stage. This sight was greeted with enthusiastic applause.

Now, let us reflect on what this might mean. Was the audience made up of such profound seekers after truth that genuine bricks in a genuine wall were more welcome and precious to them than any scenery the talented Ed Wittstein might have devised? Or did the audience consist of such simpletons as mistake a piece of building construction for ingenious *trompe-l'oeil* scenery and then give vent to their passion for *verismo*? Or could our first-nighters, even the more advanced, off-Broadway kind, be utter imbeciles who think that every set must be applauded—even if the emperor isn't wearing any—because it proves one's appreciation of Art? Ponder this one, dear readers, for here might lie the answer to certain vexing, ecumenical puzzlers.

SUMMER, 1967

GALILEO
by Bertolt Brecht
produced by the Repertory Theater of Lincoln Center

YOU KNOW I CAN'T HEAR YOU
WHEN THE WATER'S RUNNING
by Robert Anderson

THE DEER PARK
by Norman Mailer

MACBIRD
by Barbara Garson

BRECHT'S *Galileo* is remarkable for several reasons. A comparatively compact play, it nevertheless covers vast ground; a relatively uncomplicated play, it says a great deal about politics, power, psychology, science, the workings of history; a seemingly historical play, it is intensely autobiographical, enlightening us about that curious, repellent and attention-riveting master that was its author. Brecht was a devious, rebarbative, inconsistent and infuriating creature, but through a maze of contradictions he managed to steer toward his own ultimate advantage in a world intellectually unreceptive, politically hostile and historically cataclysmic. Like his Galileo, Brecht was never without a Scylla to his left and a Charybdis to his right. Like his Galileo, he managed to save his skin and his work by means of all manner of unsavory maneuvers. Like his protagonist, he must have had his moments of self-hate, though never of self-doubt. Like him, he was neither hero nor villain but both in one—in other words, a genius.

Consider this Galileo. Repeatedly we are told that he approaches truth and science as a voluptuary: "Knowledge will be a passion, and research sensual pleasure!" he exclaims, and also, "My sense of beauty would be offended if Venus in my cosmology were without phases." Brecht himself proclaimed in the *Kleines Organon,* "Do not forget it: he thinks out of voluptuousness." But despite or because of his sensualism, this man is an intellectual and dedicated champion of truth, his dedication sometimes taking the expedient form of servility, "A man like me can attain a halfway decent position only by crawling on his belly. And you know I· despise people whose brains aren't capable of filling their stomachs." No one should expect this Galileo to die for the truth when he can, however duplicitously, live for it. Even though he declares, "Whoever doesn't know the truth is merely a fool. But whoever knows it and calls it a lie is a criminal!" he becomes just such a delinquent. But Brecht does not let us think of him so for long. When Andrea, the very disciple who turned most bitterly on his master for recanting, discovers that this act enabled Galileo to finish his invaluable *Discorsi,* he exults, "You hid the truth. From the enemy. Even in the field of ethics you were centuries ahead of us!"

At this point something amazing happens. The Galileo who just after the fateful moment topped Andrea's reproachful "Unhappy the country that does not have a hero!" with the brilliant "No, unhappy the country that needs a hero," is, in his old age, reviling his own strategy, praised though it now be by that very Andrea. "I consider it the sole aim of science," says the Galileo of scene fourteen, "to alleviate the arduousness of mankind's lot." Yet how dashingly the Galileo of scene eleven announced, "I have written a book about the mechanics of the universe, that is all. What is or isn't done with it is no concern of mine." What happened in between? Brecht became a more militant Communist and rejected Galileo's "bourgeois" compromise. Also, by the time the second version of the play was completed, the atom bomb had become a reality, and Brecht, not content with making Galileo step out of character, makes him glaringly step out of his period: "The gulf between you [scientists] and it [mankind] may someday become so great that your shout of joy about some new achievement may be answered by a universal cry of dismay." This is clearly a reference to the Bomb, and the parallel between the recanting Galileo and the militaristically exploited atomic scientist is implicit. But Brecht is being more than usually tendentious here: there is a huge difference between a scientist's denying the truth and giving up experimentation to satisfy a regressive and repressive Church, and a scientist's proceeding with his research even though he knows that it may lead to military devastation. If humanity is evil and stupid enough to destroy itself by discovering certain truths, it is not within the power of the individual scientist to prevent this, and there is some doubt about whether such a humanity is worth saving. Allowing the truth to knuckle under to dogma is something else again.

From the dramatic point of view, however, this reversal is not without interest: it can be taken as Galileo's self-hate at work. In any case, it is yet again reversed when Andrea, who has now been defending his old master, leaves for Holland with the *Discorsi* as precious contraband and says by way of a coded farewell, "Concerning your evaluation of the author we were discussing, I can't give you a reply. But I cannot imagine that your murderous analysis will be the last word on the matter." To which Galileo answers, "My sincerest thanks, Sir," and proceeds to consume a goose someone has sent him. I, in turn, cannot imagine that this last was not intended as a palinode's palinode: Galileo acquiescing in Andrea's view of the situation and, by immersing himself in gastronomic if not astronomic pleasure, reasserting his delight in sensual pursuits of which science was, for him, the foremost. So when Brecht, just before his death, told the actors he was directing in *Galileo* that the protagonist "must be shown as a social criminal, a total scoundrel," he knew what he was doing: while he, as author-director, was espousing the party line which called for heroes, his protagonist and play would be giving him—gloriously—the lie. Thus Galileo joins the company of such other Brechtian heroes as Mother Courage and Azdak, who cannot be taken at face value because the truth has more faces than one.

The production of *Galileo* at Lincoln Center is a cause for considerable jubilation: we can finally say of the Repertory Company, *"Eppur si muove!"* The second version of the play here used could have profited by judicious collating with the first and third, and by a little less wanton cutting, especially in the ballad singer scene. Yet the Laughton translation was, after all, supervised by Brecht, whose English was better than his machiavellianism would let on, and as further adapted here, this translation is quite a good one.

John Hirsch, whose direction was promising in *Yerma,* staged a clean and efficient production in which the rambunctious is generally controlled and the potentially static not permitted to sag, and which tends to adhere to the author's imaginative stage directions. But it is unfortunate that some of the play's intellectual values are allowed to get lost in the shuffle. Still, Hanns Eisler's catchy musical underpinnings are mostly there; and Robin Wagner's towering jungle gyms that frame the middle distance, and on which peripheral figures are sporadically perched, nicely suggest earthly if not celestial mechanics, and convey the drafts blowing from an open universe onto a no longer fixed earth. There is also much wonderfully bizarre period astronomical equipment, and James Heart Stearns's costumes are adequate, though those for some of the higher prelates deviate into high camp.

Most of the acting is at least functional, although the comedienne Estelle Parsons is miscast as the pathetic Virginia, and among several hams Charles Siebert, as her fiancé, and Edgar Daniels, as a ballooning cardinal, are the worst. Zestful contributions are made by Philip Bosco and Robert Symonds, but Shepperd Strudwick, though he looks just right as the Cardinal Inquisitor, continues his long career of colorlessness. That brings us to Anthony Quayle's Galileo: dependable, assured, meticulous in elocution, and ultimately unexciting. Quayle has a provocative all-purpose slouch and a serviceable pucker of the eyes and areas adjoining, but he never ventures far beyond this utility base, and his performances, instead of gallant conquests of uncharted seas, are mere *periploi.* Still, one is thankful that the originally scheduled Rod Steiger did not do the part: better make Galileo than the entire audience quail.

The skill with which Brecht has us participating in the not readily dramatizable excitement of scientific discovery is surpassed by his ability to create suspense where none can really exist. The scene in which the daughter and assistants of Galileo await with profound but conflicting emotions whether he will recant or die a martyr like Giordano Bruno—if he forswears his discoveries, there will be a great tolling of bells—is every bit as breathtaking and shattering as if we did not know the outcome. But it was shocking to hear an audience that, all along, had accompanied the play with little clucks of hindsighted self-righteousness (applauding hardest when reason seemed triumphant, though there is little doubt about whose side they would have been on at the time), burst into laughter at the sound of the bells. Still, what is one to expect from an audience having for su-

preme mentor Walter Kerr, whose two reviews of *Galileo* were masterpieces of cantankerous niggardliness: he actually complained that
Brecht did not dwell at length on the differences between old-style
and new-style chess, or let us peer through the various telescopes,
which would have made this, for Kerr, a much better play.

BUT KERR, like all other reviewers, was lavish with praise for a
piece of shoddy goods called *You Know I Can't Hear You When the
Water's Running* by Robert Anderson, whose career in the theater
began with the meretricious success of *Tea and Sympathy* and proceeded through a string of well-merited flops to this foursome of
tawdry one-acters. In the first, a puritanic young playwright insists
that the producer keep in his play a scene in which an actor walks
about naked, while the worldly producer argues against it, and a desperate actor proves only too willing to oblige. This purports to be a
stinging comment on the new realism in the performing arts, about
which, however, it says nothing; it is really, like most of the evening,
an excuse for a cento of clean dirty jokes. The second play has a middle-aged husband and wife bickering in the bedroom furniture section of a department store about whether they should switch to separate beds; a faggoty salesman and a floppy girl who limbers up the
husband's libido provide padding for the bedding humor ("The family that lies together dies together"). The third episode, about the
evils of sedulous sex education in a typical middle-class family tries to
be serious as well as funny and succeeds in being mawkish ("Suppose
they couldn't find a drugstore open—as we couldn't, if you will recall." "There's nothing wrong with it [masturbation], except that it's
awfully lonely"). The last play concerns a superannuated married
couple who reminisce about their sex lives and cannot get anything
straight, not even whom they are married to now. This is supposed to
be theater of the absurd, of which it is known that it originated in
vaudeville; but its achievement was to rise above its origins, to which
Anderson handily returns it.

Beneath all these smirking but anodyne, tasteful little tasteless-
nesses ("All I know is that if I had known earlier in our marriage the
peculiar little things you like . . ." [aposiopesis, naturally, the author's]) there is a solidly retrograde mentality at work, whose aim is to
titillate the audience while in the same breath assuring it that the
author is, at bottom, for all the middle-class virtues and art forms, and
finds sex more honored in the breeches than in the observable. The

trouble with some masturbation is that, so far from being lonely, it is communal, acclaimed and supremely lucrative.

A DIFFERENT, though scarcely more compelling, sexuality informs Norman Mailer's adaptation of his novel *The Deer Park*, which illustrates usefully the cleft in Mailer's writing. On one hand there is the by now duly recognized journalist of verve and talent; on the other, the still not properly assessed novelist of verve and very little talent. So desperately eager are we for substantial novelists in our post-Faulkner era, that we are fanatically loath to relinquish hope in a Mailer, a Baldwin, and many even less likely pretenders, compared to whose chances those of the Bourbons and Hapsburgs to regain their thrones are positively rosy. The one defense consistently advanced in Mailer's behalf as a creative writer is his energy, but no amount of it is going to extricate an author who has stuffed himself into *An American Dream*, which is not a novel but an orgone box.

In *The Deer Park*, there are shrewd bits of observation about the ubiquitous chicaneries, colossal viciousness and bottomless dishonesty of Hollywood, recorded from life by an alert reporter with radar eyes and sonar ears; there is also enough pseudo-tough, pseudo-poetic maundering about art, love, and sex to make the staunchest sophomore giddy. Examples of the former: a ghastly Louis B. Mayer figure who, among other things, bullies a homosexual actor and a nymphomaniac star into a publicity marriage with the most nauseating apple-pie-pieties ("You think you can buy good publicity? Good publicity is a gift of God!"), and his more forthrightly crass son-in-law who wants to produce "something with angels' voices in the background, only not full of shit!" These figures and some others are aptly drawn, and their almost innocent monstrosity is as funny as it is fearsome.

But then comes the other Mailer, with a dreary triangle involving a brilliant director who was ruined by blacklisting (even unbrilliant ones, in real life, were not); a marginal actress, his off-and-on mistress, whose life's work seems to be the search for the nonstop orgasm; and a vile pimp who lusts after both of them but succeeds only, occasionally, with the girl. Here, Mailer indulges in philosophizings such as these: "Love may be murder and murder an act of love. . . . As if Elena were not only my woman but my balm. . . . You don't want me and yet you want every bit of me. . . . You're the only woman who has made me cry more than once, so, yes, let's get married. . . . I worship you—it's better with you than it is with anyone. . . . We have to take it from each other: to dare the fury of the murderous —" In this last quotation I cannot read my own jotting: the final word may be "heart," "beast" or "cunt," but the statement is, I dare say, equally profound with any of the three endings. When you further consider that the play is in eighty-eight scenes and has a framework that assures us that the locale is Hell and these are the Damned, and that Mailer plainly wants us to take this literally, you get some idea of the pretentiousness and vapidity of the proceedings. But it must be stated that Rip Torn, Will Lee and Mickey Knox give juicy performances, and that Leo Garen's direction could be a great deal worse.

ABOUT *MacBird* so much has been written by now, and so much more will be by the time these pages are printed, that I find it hard to forestall a sense of *déjà lu*. Lacking the charming optimism of my friends Robert Brustein and Dwight Macdonald, I cannot perceive in *MacBird* the rebirth of political satire, an almost extinct bird in the American theatrical landscape; but neither, on the other hand, can I condone Walter Kerr's belittling of the play. *MacBird* is neither a macphoenix nor a macturkey: it is a piece of exuberant collegiate fun, based on a very clever idea and executed with much skill and not a little sloppiness. The anxious pleas that Mrs. Garson does not really mean that Johnson murdered Kennedy seem to me as super-erogatory as the hopes that this will prove the fountainhead of a new kind of theater seem premature. The blending of Shakespearean language with various forms of contemporary idiom produces some genuine merriment, but if we have laughed at MacBird's "This here is the winter of our discontent," we are no longer likely to do so at his "This here's a solemn moment." Though we may be amused by "sweet chuck" becoming LBJ-ified into "sweet woodchuck," when we get something like "Stars, hide thy fires! . . ." we are almost more offended than entertained.

Still, *MacBird* must, I suppose, be considered from the point of view of its political efficiency first, and here its greatest strength is also its ultimate weakness. It must be said for Barbara Garson that her virulence is directed at everyone; rather than being a mere anti-Johnsonian, she is almost equally antipathetic to all: LBJ, JFK, Bobby, Teddy, Stevenson, Morse, beatnik demonstrators, old-time leftists, militant Negroes—anyone who gets involved in politics. While this lifts the play above propaganda, it also projects it into a realm of nihilism where greater powers than the author possesses are re-

quired to avert a feeling of window-smashing for its own sake. There
may be something liberating about breaking windows from within to
let in fresh air, but *MacBird* as often shatters them schoolboyishly
from without, proclaiming things to be equally foul on both sides of
the pane. To carry this off, Mrs. Garson's satire lacks sufficient stature.
Discontent can afford to be sophomoric; despair must be Swiftian to
score.

Nevertheless, there is fun to be had from this production, in which
the leading parts of MacBird and Robert Ken O'Dunc are manfully
handled by Stacy Keach and William Devane, especially the latter,
who manages to look and sound awesomely like his prototype. And
indeed a germ of meaning does emerge, thanks in part to their able
playing: that in politics both low and high cunning are sinister,
whereas other more decent modes are not even operative. Unfortunately, the rest of the cast is at best undistinguished, and at worst
inept; but Roy Levine (with help from Gerald Freedman) has directed with brio, the scenery and music are helpful, and Jeanne
Button's costumes, of a style describable as moth-eaten Wagnerian,
just right. I particularly relished a stuffed, deciduous eagle MacBird
carried about as a scepter, and the Wayne of Morse's lance that
looked like the perfectly preserved backbone of a brontosaurus that
died of rickets.

Autumn, 1967

Rosencrantz & Guildenstern Are Dead
by Tom Stoppard

Tom Stoppard's *Rosencrantz & Guildenstern Are Dead*, the hit presumptive of the season, may well be hoist with its own Stoppard. For the idea of the play is a conception of genius, which requires genius to develop it, whereas, in the event, it gets only cleverness and charm. The play turns the action of *Hamlet* inside out like a glove, and makes the story of Rosencrantz and Guildenstern its subject, with Shakespeare's main characters wandering in at appropriate moments to speak snatches of the Bard's lines as a sort of background music.

R and G are seen as typical bystanders sucked into a great event, playing their bit parts in it almost unaware of what they are doing—which is, in fact, mostly waiting around—and ending up crushed by the wheels of mighty circumstances: that is, the action of *Hamlet*. Stoppard has his twin homunculi—no one, not even they, can remember which of them is which—mostly playing games: flipping coins, bantering with the strolling players on their way to Elsinore, and above all, wallowing in word games with each other. These range from silly party pastimes played with alarming earnestness, to grand speculations on the last causes bandied about as if they were least—or lost—causes. For R and G are just as obsessed with words as their great antagonist Hamlet; only, whereas he can turn them into sublime poetry, they make of them a kind of subliminal prose. They are so overcome by the sense of their marginal existence that their entire protracted dialogue is a long tuning up of instruments: squeaky, scratchy, now and then shot through with shreds of poignant melody.

Yet when these two peripheral woodwinds actually play—when they enter the stage of *Hamlet*—they contribute but a few small, semi-submerged sounds to the mighty symphony. Willingly R and G embrace their deaths, as relief from their insignificance.

The play, in which can be seen squeezing large chunks of Beckett, Pinter and Pirandello, like sliding bulges on a python as he digests rabbits swallowed whole, is concerned with free will versus predestination, and illusion versus reality, the two pairs of antinomies that have paid off best in the theater. The first pair is represented by the plot of *Hamlet*, which here stands for fatality—Hamlet, Ophelia, Polonius, R and G and the rest die in the ordained way at the time appointed by destiny or dramaturgy; and by the feeble attempts at selfhood embodied in R and G's twitchings and wisecracks, which stand for free will. Illusion and reality are brought on by the itinerant actors, a mute prophetic chorus foretelling the events to come in dumb show and commented on by the Player, the chorus leader, who is full of sardonic epigrams on the greater reality of staged death than real death, and on the precariousness and wispiness of the debased reality we live in. He and his tragedians enact R and G's fate before it happens—for life merely comes to imitate art—by way of an objective correlative that neatly ties in a bundle both pairs of antinomies. In this enactment, illusion is seen as illumination, of which reality is only the shadow, while the voluntary playacting invites the inevitable acting out of the tragedy in the greater *theatrum mundi*.

The shortcomings of the play are three inconsistencies and one consistency. First, language. To go from Shakespeare's blank verse to Stoppard's ultracontemporary idiom and back again is—to adapt Frost's famous trope—like playing tennis with two balls simultaneously: if you miss one, you score with the other; if you miss both, the mere fact that two balls were in motion at the same time is enough to dazzle the laity. Secondly, character. Shakespeare's R and G (as Robert Brustein has pointed out) are calculating opportunists; Stoppard's, though their actions are still those of their prototypes, poor fish innocently hooked by higher villainy. But this fails to convince: two such pikers, congenitally incapable of action, could scarcely do what they are made to do here; if they could, however, they could no longer pass for such innocents. Thirdly, roles. R and G are derived from Beckett's Estragon and Vladimir; but whereas Beckett's characters maintain their identities as the simple soul and the intellectual, Stoppard's get confused. Though R is basically the clown and G the cogitator, they tend to overlap and blur. Now, this contradiction, like the previous one, can be defended as the very paradox of existence; but where characters are used as counters in the first place, there had better be less self-contradicting. R is sometimes far too smart for the rest of him, and G has a way of dropping inordinately below his intellectual level. In life, this may be possible; in a highly stylized play, it looks like irresponsibility. In fact, it *is* irresponsibility.

But however one might defend these inconsistencies, the basic consistency is indefensible. For three acts R and G indulge in interminable word play, some of which is amusing and linguistically stimulating, but the total of which is cloying. Consider this sample page (printed vertically rather than continuously, it constitutes a page): "G: I think I have it. A man talking sense to himself is no madder than a man talking nonsense not to himself. R: Or just as mad. G: Or just as mad. R: And he does both. G: So there you are. R: Stark raving sane. (*Pause.*) PLAYER: Why? G: Ah. (*to* R) Why? Exactly. G: Exactly what? R: Exactly why. G: Exactly why *what?* R: What? G: *Why?* R: Why what, exactly? G: Why is he mad?! R: *I* don't know!" Stoppard can keep this sort of thing up indefinitely—or, at any rate, for three acts, and it proves a fatal consistency.

Derek Goldby has directed the production with intelligence and energy, and Desmond Heeley has designed it with the proper grandeur gone to seed. Brian Murray's R is superlative as an existential jack-in-the-box, and John Wood's G is duly academic and forensic, although somewhat too manneredly elocutionary. Paul Hecht's Player will do in a pinch, and the itinerant mimes are acceptably handled, but for the rest, the play is sicklied o'er by the pale cast. The Hamlet and Ophelia, though, are not just pale; they are offensively, unforgivably bad. These major characters are, after all, supposed to be the mighty opposites between whose fell incensed points our poor shrimps perish; if they are themselves only cardboard shadow-boxers, everything drifts away.

But, even at best, Mr. Stoppard's ingenious, witty, provocative charade seems to me less a play than a play on words. The author has reduced a stroke of genius to a tour de force.

WINTER, 1967-1968

THE LITTLE FOXES
by Lillian Hellman

IPHIGENIA IN AULIS
by Euripides
produced by the Circle in the Square Theatre

EVERYTHING IN THE GARDEN
by Giles Cooper
adapted by Edward Albee

PANTAGLEIZE
by Michel de Ghelderode
APA-Phoenix Repertory Theater

THE SHOW-OFF
by George Kelly
APA-Phoenix Repertory Theater

YOUR OWN THING
book by Donald Driver
music and lyrics by Hal Hester and Danny Apolinar

THE PRIME OF MISS JEAN BRODIE
by Jay Presson

LILLIAN HELLMAN enjoys the reputation of a major American playwright, and the current revival of *The Little Foxes* should make everyone wonder why. It is easy enough to find a place in the short and simple annals of the poor American stage, but is that any reason for an author who is so clearly a melodramatist rather than a dramatist to usurp a position of prominence? Certainly Miss Hellman knows how to construct a play, just as a tailor knows how to make a suit, but unless that tailor is also a designer, unless he creates a style, are we to call him a *couturier?* The fact is that *Watch on the Rhine* is a good piece of melodrama, and *The Children's Hour* a sometimes brashly effective broadside, but as plays they are inferior to *The Little Foxes* by almost as much as it is inferior to Chekhov, whom, in its best moments, it tries to resemble. But unfortunately its best moments—I mean its attempts at psychology, language, drama—are really its weakest. Only when villainy snarls or smiles as it stabs does the work come to life—and then only to the second-rate life of melodrama.

The acting in this Lincoln Center revival is, with one exception, a mixed bag, not in the sense that some of it is good and some bad, but in the sense that some of it is quite adequate and some awful. Richard A. Dysart, as Horace Giddens, the doomed cardiac case, who wants to do something good before he dies, plays with remarkable restraint, and makes us care for a part that is undistinguishedly written and has little depth and variety in it. Dysart's presence is commanding: a look followed by a monosyllable followed by a silence erect a mighty, almost literally visible arch across the stage. As Ben, the most scheming of the foxy Hubbards, George C. Scott erupts into his usual seemingly bluff bluster. It is the jovial belching of bullfrogs by a summertime pond, while underneath the Ice Age is on the march to swallow up the world. But I must confess that I am getting tired of this baked-Alaska performance, particularly since the outer warmth is too blatantly phony, and Scott of the Antarctic too visible beneath it. Moreover, Scott's diction is really too sloppy for a leading actor in anything but a theater for convalescent throat patients.

Margaret Leighton's pathetic Birdie is rather too young, too shrill, too deliberate to be truly pathetic, and her accent is just a little bit south of Vivien Leigh's Scarlett O'Hara and just as convincing. But at least she tries. Most of the others either don't try for the accent, which is defensible, or try when they can remember—and never before have I seen so many amnesiacs foregathered in one place. Worst at the accent business, as at everything else, is Anne Bancroft in the central role of Regina. Miss Bancroft is cursed with a commonplace, even vulgar voice, and her accent, which may indeed be Southern Bronx, is distressing. But all this is as nothing to her acting, which suggests —in basic quality, artistry and mere technique—a high-school girl with undue hopes of becoming the star of her college dramatic club. If my image is facile, I am sorry, but the shallowness and cynicism with which she approaches her part—staying always at a safe distance from it—do not merit any more invention on my part.

In lesser roles, there is no less unevenness. E. G. Marshall, a dependable and sometimes outstanding actor, makes the littler of the foxy brothers a gaping, gasping, blithering cliché. As Leo, the littlest fox, Austin Pendleton is suitably smarmy, but he goes the others one better by forgetting not only his accent but also his lines. Maria Tucci, as Alexandra, is (as always) a typically nasal ingenue, with a range extending from adenoids to tonsilitis. She is simply dripping with fake, lacrimose sincerity. As the Negro housekeeper, Beah Richards gives a glittering, finely honed performance, but here Mike Nichols, the director, makes his first error in updating the play. These turn-of-the-century Negro servants are not supposed to be undercover agents for SNCC, and turning them into that makes their ruthless exploiters seem less antipathetic.

Supremely clever as Mike Nichols is with bright, brittle comedy, here he is out of his element. He has tried again to rely on cleverness, keeping the volume ominously low through most of the outbursts (and thus making things weaker instead of subtler, for subtlety is not in this script), and he has borrowed a device from Orson Welles of having characters talk over one another's lines (which does not help either, because it occurs during moments of vehemence and nastiness in which the author is at her best and should be heard). At times Nichols introduces a good comic touch, as when Leo is pushed into Horace's empty wheelchair and scoots upstage in it, but the main thing in a play of this kind, solid ensemble playing, he has not been able to elicit.

Howard Bay's set is decent enough, and greatly enhanced by Patricia Zipprodt's tastefully inventive costumes. As a woman remarked to her escort during the second intermission, "Look, there's Mike Nichols! He is brilliant, just brilliant! Did he direct this play?" I had been asking myself the same question. And also "Why?"

EURIPIDES' *Iphigenia in Aulis* is a beautiful and intelligent play. Tragedies, like people, are often comely but brainless, or bright but unsightly; this play lacks nothing. It is the very model of a Greek tragedy in which there is no villain, only guiltless guilt. The gods (if it is they) make an impossible demand: to obtain a wind enabling the Greek army to sail to Troy, Agamemnon must sacrifice his daughter Iphigenia on the altar of Artemis. At first, he unwillingly consents in the public interest, then countermands his initial order. But the fatal mechanism has been set in motion, and no mortal can stop it.

Others, too, make mistakes. Menelaus, itching to recover Helen, at first sides with the gods against Iphigenia, thus helping the initial error—or the machinery of fate—along its way. He, too, repents and changes his mind; too late—he has already made his small but necessary contribution to the girl's doom. By now, the high priest having broadcast the will of the gods, the entire army clamors for the innocent blood: *vox dei* has become *vox populi* and there is no gainsaying it.

One champion comes to the aid of the princess: Achilles. It was on the pretext of betrothal to him that Iphigenia was lured to Aulis, where the fleet lies becalmed. His honor has been trifled with, and to avenge it, as well as in deference to the frantic Clytemnestra, he undertakes to rescue her daughter. When he meets the girl, smitten with her beauty and courage, he is ready for civil, rather than recriminatory and colonial, war.

But here the individual achieves true greatness by rising to the terrible demands of destiny. Iphigenia, a moment ago a child childishly rejoicing in her engagement, turns suddenly but believably into a woman, a human being, a heroine, engaged—*engagée*—in a far deeper sense. Transcending a mother's grief, a lover's needs, a father's harrowing impotence, she shoulders her fate with naked nobility, and becomes, as the chorus proclaims, the true victor of Troy. And more than that: she becomes the exemplar for every human being who, in his last hour, must accept the unacceptable. She becomes a model for us all.

Euripides' sublime work has this final quality to make it precious to us: it is extremely modern. For in it, implicitly and even explicitly, the challenge to God rings out: God is cruel, or he does not exist; either morally or literally, God is dead. And it is for such a universe that Euripides speaks his words of courage and consolation.

Michael Cacoyannis, a director whose work I have lately deplored, rouses himself here to considerable heights. This is a much more controlled and judicious production than his *Trojan Women* of some years ago, to say nothing of his other plays and movies since. Here stage movement has become more purposive, less frilly; people are even allowed to stand still at times and just be heard. Occasionally, the chorus will assume a grouping from a Greek frieze, but antiquity is not rubbed in any more than modernity is. To be sure, the chorus is an insuperable problem for today's directors: there is almost no way of making that institution look wholly different from Founder's Day at Bryn Mawr or Wellesley, or wherever the drama of hoop-racing flourishes. But Cacoyannis at least gets his chorus looking only distracted, not demented, and in Erin Martin he has an intense and nimble chorus leader. He may have allowed his cast to declaim a shade too much, but excess in the opposite direction would have been worse.

Irene Papas' Clytemnestra unfortunately speaks as if English were Greek—or, rather, not Greek—to her; she also moves less than gracefully. But she has a regal aspect and a dark intensity that make up for much. Mitchell Ryan, on the other hand, lacks royalty in speech as in bearing; but if one wants a weak Agamemnon, he certainly is that. Alan Mixon is astonishingly good as Menelaus; I've always had an impression of stiffness and monotony from him before. Christopher Walken, as Achilles, suggests the beach at Malibu more than the one at Aulis, but at least he is good-looking and well-spoken. The lesser roles are played without distinction, but Jenny Leigh's Iphigenia is magnificent. Starting as almost a child, she next turns into a somewhat dizzy debutante; then as tragedy overtakes her, she shoots up to meet it. Suddenly, but not so suddenly as to be unconvincing, this Iphigenia has become a heroine: superb at something that is neither superhuman strength nor unbearable pathos but simply humanity. Humanity in its uncompromised nakedness: so gentle, defenseless, and beautiful that its sacrifice would tear us apart if it were not an act of triumph. Miss Leigh brings off heroism without ceasing to be winsome; she is transcendent yet still one of us. If anyone questions the concept of catharsis, this performance will dispel his doubts.

Michael Annals has designed a set of steps that seems properly doubled up with grief, but his costumes have a bargain basement look; Annals can do very well on a big budget, but scrimping is not his forte. Marvin David Levy, a genuinely undistinguished composer, has provided music that is at least unassertive except for one moment of highly obtrusive obstreperousness. Jules Fisher's lighting is, as always, a paragon of inconspicuous inventiveness, and his last slow fadeout on the agonized face of Clytemnestra is the perfect spelling out of *finis* with lights. But the great light is shed by Euripides, of whom a later and lesser Greek poet, George Seferis, has aptly said,

"He saw man's veins / as a net the gods made to catch us in like wild beasts; / he tried to pierce it."

S_AY_ _WHAT_ _YOU_ will against Edward Albee's *The Zoo Story* and *Who's Afraid of Virginia Woolf?*—and, like me, you can surely say plenty—they remain two of the best plays written in America. It is, therefore, sad to see what has been happening to Albee since, and nothing—not even the instant coffining of *Malcolm*—was as disheartening as the current *Everything in the Garden,* regardless of whether it runs or vanishes into the thin air that it already so closely resembles.

Everything in the Garden is a 1962 play by the English dramatist Giles Cooper, which Albee was to change only minimally so as to transpose it to America, but which he proceeded to rewrite extensively—though not nearly so extensively as he has since claimed. That Cooper recently died is a misfortune not only for him but also for Albee, whose adaptation thus changes from simple rape to an act of necrophilia. And Albee makes matters worse by patronizing Cooper, whose play is considerably better than this parasitic paraphrase. In an article in the *Times* Albee owned that he was "terribly proud" of Cooper—presumably for having provided him with a rough draft for his master recension. At times, terrible pride could be better described as infernal cheek.

Cooper's play was a smooth and cool contribution to the absurdist theater. A struggling suburban middle-class couple, particularly concerned with keeping up their garden and appearances, become suddenly rich; it turns out that the wife has been lucratively selling herself in a London house of assignation. Her husband is about to throw her out when guests arrive, and it emerges that all the wives in the group work for the same outfit with their husbands' approval. So our husband acquiesces, and when an unmarried bibulous friend stumbles on the guilty secret, he ends up buried in the garden, which now, besides other expensive improvements, can boast human fertilizer.

The English play, no masterpiece by a long shot, nevertheless scores by keeping a surface of almost unruffled hypocrisy: a stiff upper lip while lower organs, including the heart, indulge in most un-British activities. With impeccable understatement, this society is shown consuming its pot of honey—or gold—on the grave of the last remaining decencies. But Albee cannot leave it at that: he has to hype up the comic parts into his well-known bitchy barb-tossing contests, and the grim ones into shrill, self-righteous hysteria. Thus where in Cooper's play the bachelor, Jack, says of the wife, Jenny, "Isn't she beautiful?" in Albee he comments, "I find Jenny so attractive—not that I am going to jump her." Or where Cooper uses the word "madam," Albee gives us a drooling "prostitootsie." And he blithely writes in scenes of sneaky nastiness among spouses, where the original has only anger, or nothing at all. Then, to lend his play a truly high tone, he inflates the character of Jack into a part-time narrator-*raisonneur*, who addresses the audience with choice inanities, often no more than the repetition of the line just spoken by himself or another character, only now in a faggoty drawl and with a sarcastic leer.

Albee particularly fanaticizes the anti-Semitic and anti-Negro attitudes of this country-club set, thereby turning the sociological clock back some dozen years and the dramatic one at least a score, all in the interest of up-to-dateness. For the trouble with Albee is that he desperately wants to be daring but lacks one required ingredient: courage. Thus he changes the character of the madam from a Jewish survivor of the concentration camps, hardened and cynical—a character that on Broadway, with its vast Jewish clientele, would have required audacity—into a slick, affluent Englishwoman, almost a Tiny Alice, and a perfectly uncontroversial target. Again, he wants to heighten the viciousness of Jack's death; in the original, this was caused by his being inadvertently hit too hard with a bottle. Now we have the whole group smothering him, Desdemona-like, with a pillow; nevertheless, the group then tries sheepishly to revive him. So Albee makes his characters into deliberate murderers while yet giving them a burst of posthumous goodwill that makes no sense whatever.

The play is ploddingly directed by Peter Glenville, and unhappily cast with men who suggest homosexuality and women who could never make a hundred dollars an hour as whores—only as actresses, the requirements of our stage being laxer than those of our stews. Still, Barry Nelson as the husband manages to squeeze some life out of his role (he must have practiced by squeezing blood out of stones), whereas Barbara Bel Geddes is only ridiculous as the wife. When the outrageously effete Jack of Robert Moore speaks of "jumping" the shapeless and dowdy Jenny of Miss Bel Geddes, Albee's play, for once, does reach the heights of the Absurd.

What possessed Albee to take a less than outstanding English play, remove its occasional funny lines and genuine restrained horror, and insert his own brashly unfunny nastiness and screechy moral indignation, only to end up with an outstandingly bad play? "I wonder whether you can read into other breasts than your own?" George

Meredith once wrote to Alice Meynell. Albee's case is the opposite: when it comes to reading his own breast, he proves totally illiterate. For what is going on here is projection. In his crudely vehement castigation of these characters' venality, whorishness, need to impress others at all costs, he is blindly lashing out against his own need for the limelight, for dazzling the Broadway theater at any cost except courage, even if it means misadapting Carson McCullers, James Purdy, Truman Capote or Giles Cooper. I realize that it is hard to come up constantly with new, original plays, but if Albee is allowed to adapt away unchecked, he will end up not only witless in himself, but the cause that witlessness is in a good many others.

Next to taking candy from a baby and not helping a blind old lady across the street, knocking a repertory company in America may well be the most heinous crime. Thus I have always noted with pleasure the alacrity with which our halt reviewers lead on the blind efforts of the APA-Phoenix Repertory Company with the most candied superlatives. It makes me, in my dissent, feel less of a curmudgeon—only a critic.

The current APA season has begun with *Pantagleize* and *The Show-Off*, and at first glance this seems both judicious and ecumenical. Michel de Ghelderode, the great Flemish playwright, was something like a merger of the paintings of James Ensor with a Gothic cathedral. His characters are gargoyles taught to speak with the tongues of fallen angels and revealing themselves hideously, heart-rendingly human. It is therefore unfortunate that APA picked one of the few plays in which Ghelderode forsook his wonderfully unnatural habitat, the medieval but timeless carnival, to write about a contemporary carnage: an abortive revolution in which an innocent is caught up, briefly carried aloft, and then ruthlessly discarded.

Pantagleize is half exalted poet, half paltry buffoon, the whole somehow adding up to a wistful, winsome nonentity. By one vast, resounding mistake, fate—of which it is impossible to tell whether it never makes mistakes, or never anything but mistakes—has Pantagleize pronounce accidentally a harmless phrase that proves the password and call-to-arms of the brewing insurrection. Chaplinesque, he stumbles through a series of highly successful misunderstandings and missteps, which, for a moment, set the state rocking. But most of the revolutionaries are as corrupt as the rulers, and, after some grotesque bloodletting, things revert to the shabby and cynical norm.

Pantagleize is executed; but for a day—poet, puppet, or mankind's conscience—he lived and uttered his shining impossibilities.

The text has been drastically cut by the APA, but it has been buoyantly and sweepingly staged by John Houseman and Ellis Rabb. On a well-nigh bare stage, movement, both balletic and burlesque, is allowed to zigzag all over like the encephalogram of a world gone mad—or, rather, refusing to go sane. But the acting lets down the staging. Ellis Rabb is a clever, mannered miniaturist, good at portraying cameo parts; in a lead, he is at best finical, at worst cute. His Pantagleize is not so much an inspired innocent as an impish invert brimming with curdled coyness. The rest of the cast is almost uniformly undistinguished (including the usually redeeming Sidney Walker, here miscast), with several performances worse than that— notably Nicholas Martin's poet, loathsome rather than ludicrous. A special demerit goes to Jack O'Brien's inept lyrics, including couplets like "She's got a blue tattoo / Right on her you know who," which degrade not only wit but even grammar. Still, for the chance of seeing Ghelderode on an American stage, I would recommend reading the play and then going to see the APA production out of the corner of your eye.

LESS CAN BE said for *The Show-Off*. When casting about for a comic playwright in the American twenties, the mind affectionately recalls George Kelly. And, I dare say, in a suffocating desert one cannot look a gift oasis in the palm. But from the vantage point of the present, or merely from that of any serious artistic standard, *The Show-Off* simply won't do. It concerns a swaggering social climber and small-time charlatan who captures the heart of a nice middle-class Philadelphia girl, infiltrates her family by marrying her over her mother's living and her father's dead body, and, after wreaking every kind of havoc, proves, first, pathetic deep down, and secondly, shrewdly practical deeper down yet. Thus he ends up instrumental in making the family's fortune.

The aim of the play, to demonstrate that there is a sense profounder than common sense, is all to the good, but the first two acts of the demonstration are, alas, all to the bad. Here are the perennial jokes of domestic comedy, and nothing, in the long run, proves as deciduous as these hardy perennials. In the third act, which probes deeper, and in which character unveils surprises beyond the permutations of the predictable, our interest is engaged. But we are given too little too late. There is a born dramatist in George Kelly, but he is almost all born and not nearly enough made.

Under Stephen Porter's direction, things move on with efficiency but without effervescence, let alone imagination. The acting, once again, is consistently unnoteworthy, with two rather unfortunate exceptions. As the crusty, sensible mother, Helen Hayes does everything under the sun—or, more precisely, under the spotlight—to make an audience drool, shriek with helpless and headless laughter, and eat her up alive. She's as American as cutie-pie, as adorable as a big fat baby that has just peed in your lap, and if canny, senescent whimsy could be bottled, there is enough here to make an entire convention of geriatricians pie-eyed drunk. As the protagonist, Clayton Corzatte gives another one of his shrill, charmless performances, like an emery board to the nerve edges. His Aubrey Piper emerges so repulsive that little mounds of dead plausibility pile up around him into mountainous barrows. His guffaw is the death rattle of a laughing hyena, his walk that of a Saint Bernard sashaying in on little cat's feet, and his entire personality flaps about in a just barely invisible pair of baggy pants.

Again, the American theater has a crying need for repertory groups. Between crying over the need and crying over the APA, the latter may be preferable. But only just.

Happy Elizabethans! They could suspend their disbelief when Rosalind in boy's clothes fooled Orlando, or Mariana in no clothes passed for Isabella in Angelo's bed. Today, when hair styles, clothes or bed partners no longer reveal anyone's sex, let alone identity, there is no more disbelief left to suspend. Thus what in *Twelfth Night* was fanciful, becomes in its current rock-musical adaptation, *Your Own Thing*, the soul of credibility.

The twins Sebastian and Viola lose each other in a real swinging shipwreck and are washed ashore on the seacoast of New York's bohemia. A rock-'n'-roll quartet, the Apocalypse, have lost their fourth member, Disease; Viola, in her very own boy's clothing, replaces him —except when Sebastian, unbeknown to all including himself, replaces *her*. They get tangled up in the moribund love affair of Orson, an agent, and Olivia, a discothèque-owner. Olivia has reached thirty, the age of untrustworthiness, and hankers after youth: she lures Viola but is bedded with what turns out to be, to her immense relief, Sebastian. Orson falls for Viola, sweats out what seems to be his ungainsayable homosexuality, only to be saved at the eleventh hour by the revelation of Disease's, i.e., Viola's bosom.

The Apocalypse comments on the mix-up with songs that have the salt of wit and, when set to Shakespeare's lyrics, even the salt of tears. The pepper is supplied by a running commentary from a chorus of slide projections ranging from Arthur Godfrey to God, and including along the way "Duke" Wayne, Bogey, the Bard of Avon with his Virgin Queen, Pope Paul VI between Buddha and Christ. With appropriate tones and apposite mentalities, they proffer maxims and minims of wit and wisdom that I would not take down for fear of missing the next, and equally uproarious, one.

Donald Driver's book and staging are as apt as they are frolicsome, the freshets of bubbling irreverence never eroding the bedrock of humanity beneath. When the dialogue occasionally reverts to Shakespeare, the effect is exhilarating and never gross as in Joseph Papp's current inane *Hamlet;* it proves an affectionate, lefthanded compliment to Shakespeare rather than a right to the jaw. The music and lyrics by Hal Hester and Danny Apolinar are not the best of their kind (I preferred the ones in *Hair*), but they help break down the stupid resistance of the American musical to genuine innovation: if *Man of La Mancha* could hear them, it would drop dead, not once but twice. The technical aspects of the show are handled with great charm, and the cast is as talented and fetching as any I have encountered.

The outstanding performance is Leland Palmer's Viola. Miss Palmer is a wispy dynamo of a girl with eyes like outraged hemispheres of a schizoidly split world. She is suffering from advanced tomboyishness and seems to have no control over her body beyond the knees, where strange jack-knifings occur with crazy *désinvolture*. She is rather like a mechanical doll just turned into a human one, and everything fills her with a tart mixture of stupefaction and exaltation. She is sexless yet irresistible, and it is small wonder that Tom Ligon's dapper Orson is sufficiently enamored of her to resign himself to homosexuality as the apparent price of fulfillment. When she finally reveals (in part) an adorable little bosom, not only is Orson relieved, but also every spectator's bosom swells with a sense of well-being.

THE PRIME OF MISS JEAN BRODIE is Jay Presson's, an American woman's, adaptation of a novella by the Britisher, Muriel Spark, and as the play takes place in Edinburgh, was first done in London, has been directed here by Michael Langham, a Canadianized Englishman, and stars a London-trained Australian woman, we may safely refer to it as British. It has a serious, even important, idea underlying it, but handles it on a fairly superficial level. The problem is whether Miss Brodie, a rousing eccentric of a teacher in a staid Scottish girls' school of the thirties, who takes possession of her pupils' minds and souls lock, stock and barrel, is, in fact, a benefactress or a menace. For she does teach her eleven- and twelve-year-olds extraordinary, thrilling things about Giotto and *La Traviata* and her lover who died "for them" in Flanders Field, which fire their imaginations; and she foretells brilliantly gaudy futures for them, which whet their ambition. But fecklessly and incurably romantic, she also propels them into premature love affairs as well as spiritual dalliance with Fascist dictators whom she sees as Robin Hoods, and actually drives one girl into the arms of Franco and death.

Miss Brodie—absurd, lovable, stimulating and pernicious—is indeed an absorbing character, and the interplay of her private and public lives, her compacts and conflicts with her wards, and the disentangling of her merits and guilt are well worth dramatic scrutiny. But the trouble with the play is, first, that it concentrates so hard on Jean Brodie that she alone achieves roundedness, while all other figures remain in a state of more or less well-painted cardboard two-dimensionality. Secondly, Miss Brodie herself is seen preponderantly as an eccentric, a very human caricature but a caricature all the same, so that her wellsprings remain ultimately unexplored. And the work keeps fluctuating betwen farcical comedy and (not wholly unfarcical) drama, which is bothersome, too: if your characters are solid, you can play around with the tone; to have both of them brittle and unsteady makes me feel in a glassware store whose very floors are made of glass.

Zoë Caldwell, though a greatly competent actress, makes Miss Brodie into a burlesque. Miss Caldwell may be aware of her militant homeliness that makes the overwhelming passion for her of a profligate artist and fellow-teacher seem less than credible; and perhaps she is overcompensating for this by turning herself into a "character" every mercilessly idiosyncratic inch of the way. I must plead earnestly for not casting insuperably plain women in the parts of bewitching ones—I have seen on past occasions Miss Caldwell, for all her consummate technique, ruin Ophelia and Millamant. Here it is not a question of ruining anything, only of undermining it. An additional difficulty is the Americanness of the various schoolgirls. There is a kind of precocious gentlemanliness or ladylikeness, an odd combination of maturity and innocence, about British children that the far less disciplined Americans (whatever the performers' actual ages may be) simply cannot render.

Michael Langham has directed the play routinely in Joe Mielziner's utilitarian scenery. *The Prime of Miss Jean Brodie* is far from being prime theater, but at least it does concern itself with ideas, which are sorely missing from today's American drama that subsists entirely on gags, situations and posturing.

SPRING, 1968

The Price
by Arthur Miller

[A Day in the Death of] Joe Egg
by Peter Nichols

Loot
by Joe Orton

Tiger at the Gates
by Jean Giraudoux

The Seven Descents of Myrtle
by Tennessee Williams

Cyrano de Bergerac
by Edmond Rostand
produced by the Repertory Theater of Lincoln Center

Hair
by Gerome Ragni and James Rado

I would like to be able to like the plays of Arthur Miller. The man is patently honest, dedicated, responsible, and, when talking about the drama (as distinct from talking about *his* drama, and from writing it), discerning. Which is not to say that *The Price* is undiscerning. But it is improbable, uncompelling, old-fashioned, humorless for all its jokes, and undramatic. It is a well-meaning, respectable, middlebrow anachronism and, I am afraid, a bore.

As often before, Miller's model is Ibsen, but with a fatal difference—leaving aside the question of whether one could meaningfully write even good Ibsen in 1968. *The Price* concerns two brothers, Victor and Walter, who have not seen each other for 16 years. When their father lost all his money in the Crash, Walter was working his way through medical school and sending home a measly five dollars a month. Victor gave up the study of science, became a policeman, and supported their father as best he could. Walter, later on, refused even a loan of five hundred dollars to Victor, which would have enabled him to finish college.

As the play begins, Victor, a police sergeant, comes to the attic crammed with family furniture which, Pop being dead and the building condemned, is to be sold to an antiques dealer. He has notified Walter about the impending sale and his intention to go halves with him, even though Walter is now an extremely prosperous surgeon. Esther, Victor's wife, is a practical creature, striving both for some hard-headed understanding with Walter and for a good price on the furniture. Solomon, the antiques dealer and appraiser, is ancient and wily, all bittersweet shrewdness—a kind of living, squawking compendium of Jewish humor.

Finally Walter arrives, and the past is resurrected: new facts (or are they fictions?) come to light, and the problem of what price one must or must not pay out of filial duty is passionately batted around. Charges and countercharges are made; the questions of whether duty is really self-indulgence, ruthlessness really common sense, and whether the old man was really worth it (it turns out he had four thousand dollars nicely tucked away somewhere) are inconclusively argued and agonized over. The brothers part again, and nothing seems to be changed, let alone resolved.

Now, it is perfectly true that in most of Ibsen's plays the past—as something that fills our closets with skeletons or casts its grim shadow over the present—figures prominently as it is gradually unraveled and revealed. Then, however, there is the present. There is what *does* happen to Rosmer and Rebecca, Solness and Hilda, and the rest. There is a dramatic situation in the present, or even a contemplation of the future (as with Nora or Dr. Stockmann) that is developed and that absorbs us. In *The Price* the entire play looks backward and argues about what really happened back then, or should have happened, and why. But in the present of the play there is next to nothing, and in its future nothing at all. This makes for a dramatic movement as of a man in a gale who tries to advance by backing into the wind, but is continually swept toward his starting point, and cannot even face the future that lies behind him.

For a realistic play, moreover, there is far too much here that is improbable—such as Walter's having the information about Pop's cache that Victor lacked, or Walter's attempt to give Victor the five hundred dollars after all, only the message was delivered to Pop who selfishly withheld it from Victor. Most incredible of all is the sixteen-year blackout of communication between brothers, to the point where Victor doesn't even hear of Walter's divorce and protracted nervous breakdown. And upon all this, the casual way in which the brothers resume their bickerings and *politesses* as if nothing had happened.

Then there is the awkwardness of even what lopsided construction there is. Thus, for example, Mr. Solomon is kept in the other room during much of the play, to be brought on whenever it is time for a little comic relief: periodically he pops out, like a joke-in-the-box, with lox-flavored yaks like "Water I don't need; a little blood I could use." The problem is that Miller cannot imbue his principal characters with any humor ("You were grinding your teeth again last night," says Esther, to which Victor's comic rejoinder is "Well, no wonder my ear hurts," which Esther, in turn, tops with "It sounded like a lot of rocks rolling down a mountain"); nor can he raise their dialogue to the heights of poetry—"We are dying, that's what's true!" is about as high as his language can lumber up that mountain. For Miller's language is an instrument that has an accurately defined middle range, but lacks both the bass of real wit and the treble of poetry.

Moreover, Miller continues here to be obsessed by his two interconnecting themes: the family and guilty consciences. Always there are brothers and sisters, parents and children, husbands and wives clashing over excessive demands on, or real or imagined neglect of, each other. I do not know whether this set of problems is exhausted, or whether it has merely exhausted Miller, but I seem to detect, along with the smell of midnight oil, the smell of stale sweat from running behind the times. Finally, can one really care about the lost potentials and troubled consciences of these insufficiently plastic, insufficiently moving characters? One does not even get the sense of any great waste—except of one's time at the theater.

In *After the Fall,* Miller disguised himself as Quentin, a lawyer.

But if we note all those exact figures in *The Price*—$5, $500, $4,000—we begin to wonder whether he is not, in the deepest sense, an accountant in playwright's disguise. And, to keep the account straight, we must note that the acting, particularly Kate Reid's, is good, and that Boris Aronson's setting is a monumental pile of antiquated bric-a-brac. I wish it were not such a perfect objective correlative for the dramaturgy.

A DAY IN THE DEATH OF JOE EGG (as it is called in England; here, where death does not sell, it became plain *Joe Egg*) is a two-act play with a strong first act, a shaky second, and a sorely missed third. You should see it: though Peter Nichols, the author, will someday do better, you could right now do a great deal worse.

Joe Egg concerns a young teacher, his wife, and their spastic vegetable of a daughter, the eponymous Joe Egg. The mother loves the child and hopes; the father, though also loving, finds solace in jokes. Brian and Sheila's marriage is undermined by this child, whom Sheila thinks of as punishment for her (rather mild) premarital promiscuity, and Bri as a chunk of the world's preposterousness and a potent rival for his wife's affection. The first act is a series of boldly etched, deftly linked vignettes in which the couple's past and present are shown, as it were, in superimposition. Bri converts the pitiful yet sometimes ludicrous highlights of Life with Joe into a spate of comic turns in which he satirically enacts anyone out of the past: doctors, nurses, Viennese specialists, vicars who believe in the laying on of hands, even imaginary radio commentators. Sheila usually plays the straight man—meaning herself—in order to humor Bri; Joe is impersonated by a cushion that gets cradled, pummeled and tossed.

Much of this is very funny, and none of it strikes me as a sick joke. The butt of these routines is never the child; rather it is the world and people around it whose inadequacies and crassness are ridiculed, with Joe merely the catalyst. Moreover, these vaudeville turns represent a last-ditch stand against the collapse of morale and marriage, which lends them a peculiar dignity, almost a nobility. But there is more: what is an age that has found its hopes unfounded, its faiths obsolete, to fall back on? It can either, like Sheila, hope against hope; or, like Bri, jest at scars. The joke becomes the ultimate defiance hurled at cosmic despair, an indictment of a universe ruled over, at best, by "a manic depressive rugby footballer" whose *nom de guerre* is God; it is an attack on the hypocrisies committed in his name, hypocrisies that ultimately upset our apple cart with its wormy yet sweet apples.

Coiled around these comic routines and occasionally popping up right in the middle of them is the couple's present: affection, frustration, and a steady flow of almost benign bickering. Bri is a mother's boy, extremely clever but unstable and spoiled. Sheila is full of womanly and motherly love, thwarted by not being able to have more babies besides these two, Joe and Bri, neither of whom will grow up. So she dabbles (untalentedly) in amateur dramatics, he tinkers (talentedly) with painting, and both play constantly, lovingly and maddeningly, on each other's nerves.

There is also a four-piece band halfway into the wings stage left, which actually plays a few bars before the characters of the play launch into soliloquies. This device is borrowed from a *A Taste of Honey*, where it didn't work either. The only other borrowing is less marked: something about the relationship of Brian and Sheila, down to the very game-playing, suggests Jimmy and Alison in *Look Back in Anger*. I cannot think of a specific source for the soliloquies, though I would like to be able to blame them on something external. Actually they are not bad, but there is something a bit too easy about the device.

The second act, like the marriage, falls apart. It is not so much that the affluent couple who come to visit are, though frequently funny, very close to caricature; or that Bri's mother, though a skillful blend of the idiosyncratic and the universal, remains somehow marginal; it is rather that the play now turns melodramatic, unconvincing, and, in its ending, factitious. I think the trouble here is that in the first part Mr. Nichols was drawing on his own experience (life in Bristol, a spastic child, teaching school and hating it) which he enriched with his imagination. In the second half, he was trying for a "plot," and had going for him neither lived experience nor true imaginative and emotional involvement in an "action" tacked onto what is essentially a static situation. Yet there are perfectly good ways of making stasis dramatic, as playwrights from Aeschylus to Beckett have discovered.

There are also lesser weaknesses in *Joe Egg*. Thus, I counted five instances of the joke of mistaken reference, when a character connects some remark with the wrong antecedent, e.g., "I should have her destroyed" with Joe, when what is actually meant is "The cat— if she has fleas." But lesser flaws disappear behind the delightful performances. Albert Finney is—he can't help it—a star, which is too much for the will-o'-the-wisp Bri; yet how charmingly he plays down his bravura, how intelligently he conveys the ambiguities of wit, the ambivalence of feelings that did not grow up. And his impersonation of an Oxbridge vicar, the last word in muscular Christianity ludicrously trying to be with it—indeed, just the way his pipe smokes 'him rather than vice versa—is a piece of unalloyed histrionic brilliance.

As Sheila, Zena Walker is absolutely right: sweet without cloying, sturdy without the least loss of femininity, absurdly hopeful without becoming absurd. Among the three able supporting players (Joe is not done very well, but the part hardly exists) I especially liked Joan Hickson as Bri's mother. She has flawless comic decorum, which means getting every possible laugh without pushing, and every bit of implied seriousness without stepping outside comedy. And Michael Blakemore has directed with unobtrusive efficiency.

In his "Observations on Egges," Sir Thomas Browne describes a curious hen's egg that some might think derived from "the coition . . . of a duck wh. sometimes will follow & at least attempt to tread henns." There is something as ill-mated about the two acts of Mr. Nichols' ovoid. Nevertheless, for the good parts of *Joe Egg* and for what Nichols will yet, I believe, give us, I am willing to forgive him much—even his collaboration on the screenplay of *Georgy Girl*.

FROM THE OXFORD gray of *Joe Egg* to the Hades black of Joe Orton's *Loot* is enough of a jump to have insured well-nigh instant failure for the latter, probably the most interesting and deserving play of the season. A true black comedy—as opposed to a mock one, like *Scuba Duba*—sees the world as a thoroughly hopeless place, redeemed only by one's being able to laugh at it and perhaps even write a black comedy about it. Joe Orton, the homosexual English playwright, was brutally murdered at the age of thirty-four by his roommate—to whom, it turned out, he had left all his money. The latter was unable to collect because (a) under British law, a murderer cannot inherit, and (b) he had committed suicide right after bludgeoning Orton. So the money went to Orton's father, whom the playwright ridiculed in his plays. A man who dies, and undoubtedly lived, a black comedy, should be able to write a good one; still, Orton's first play, *Entertaining Mr. Sloane*, had struck me as too conventionally commercial for the unconventional attitudes it was promulgating as well as ridiculing; nor did it seem to me as entertaining as its title. *Loot*, however, is something else again. Its tone and characters are properly absurd, yet they retain a great deal of authentic London lower-class wryness. The plot is totally preposterous. It involves a brand new Catholic widower about to marry the sweet Catholic nurse who actually killed his wife and who, after marrying him, will kill him, too—she has a record of such crimes. It also involves the man's son, who, with his equally bisexual chum working for the undertaker, has robbed a bank, and must hide the loot in his mother's coffin. And there is the idiot-savant policeman, doggedly sleuthing and bullying away, but ultimately most interested in getting the lion's share of the loot. The play takes the form of a crazy juggling act, with the money and the corpse continually switching hiding places, if not actually flying through the air. The characters are all Catholics, policemen, or criminals, or a combination of these, plus that flying, incessantly undressed or wrapped-up and otherwise manhandled cadaver. And, as you might expect, the jugglers of our lady's corpse end up thriving in direct proportion to their wickedness.

All this, of course, would be scant recommendation if Orton's writing were not, most of the time, breezily, bruisingly equal to his somberly uproarious vision. Take a gag described by Walter Kerr as "no joke at all": when the son says of his pal and himself, "We shared the same cradle," the nurse inquires, "Was that economy or malpractice?" At the lowest level, this illustrates the nurse's dirty-mindedness. But on second thought, the boys did apparently grow up to be sexually involved with each other—may not the child be father to the fag? And, further, is this not a highly suggestive bracketing of economy and malpractice—of economics and malfeasance—which become casual, almost synonymous, alternatives? But Kerr sees no joke at all there, and "no goal" in the play.

"THE TROJAN WAR WILL NOT TAKE PLACE," as *Tiger at the Gates* should be called, is a much maligned play. It should not be translated into English, least of all by Christopher Fry; it should not be performed by an American cast, least of all by the Repertory Theater of Lincoln Center; and it should not have to be reviewed by New York reviewers, least of all by Clive Barnes.

Jean Giraudoux wrote the most gossamer, translucent, opalescent prose ever written; and if prose cannot be all of those things simultaneously, why, then, his is all of them by turns. It is also precious, sparkling, ironic and imbued with profound pessimism. That, too, I imagine, is paradoxical; and so is Giraudoux. Seldom if ever has the language of clearest poetry and ravishing wit carried such a load of bitterness, misanthropy, despair. To translate him into English, though, you would need a Samuel Beckett rewritten by Robert Herrick; Giraudoux is like a battering ram carved by Cellini out of pure alabaster. Jean Cocteau wrote about Giraudoux, when he was drawing him on his deathbed, "You were telling me my drawings were a kind of writing. I find your writing a sort of drawing, or rather, something like those astonishing rosettes that form at the core of a folded and refolded piece of paper that one cuts out at the corners."

What does Mr. Fry do to Giraudoux? He gilds the lily: "You poet with dirty feet" becomes "You filthy-footed iambic pentameter." He loses the flavor: Ajax, *"le plus brutal et le plus mauvais coucheur des Grecs"* (which calls for something like "the meanest plug-ugly among the Greeks") becomes limply "the most impossible and unruly man among the Greeks." Something snappy like Cassandra's retort to Andromache about a war having been the last, *"C'était la dernière. La suivante l'attend"* (which should run roughly, "It is the last. Now comes the next"), is dragged out into "It is the last. The next is still ahead of him." These may not be the best examples of Fry's misadapting, but they are what I got down on my program. To think that there was a time not so long ago when Fry was considered a major poetic dramatist! I think of this when I look at some of today's luminaries; it gives me hope.

There has been much carping about Giraudoux's lack of realism —wars supposedly don't break out the way this Trojan War does, the leaders trying to avert it but the old men, the fanatics, the rabble precipitating it anyway. I wonder whether these same Newer Critics who find Giraudoux unreal and old hat would claim that Genet's *The Screens* is a true representation of what happened in Algeria, or whether they would complain that social exploitation is not accurately depicted in *Waiting for Godot?* The truth is that the opposition of our youth and of some of our more responsible civic and intellectual leaders to the Vietnam War is very much like the efforts of Hector and Ulysses to avert war; if Giraudoux translates reality into witty or poignant metaphors (like Ulysses' reason for wanting peace: "Andromache bats her eyelashes exactly the way Penelope does"), surely this cannot make the play less valid as a dramatic poem.

The cast, however, is barely dramatic, let alone poetic. There is, in fact, a kind of pathetic fallacy in the way some of these clods attempt to be lyrical and airy, like elephants tripping the light fantastic. Philip Bosco's Hector is not a bad performance for an American actor in the present parochial state of our theater; but as of now, he does not have it in him to carry the weight—especially the airy, feathery weight—of a whole play on his shoulders. One thinks of accounts of what Louis Jouvet did with the oration for the dead in the original production: he delivered it all in a heartrending monotone. (But of course Jouvet's monotone was full of subtle half- and quarter-tones.) Bosco declaims and barnstorms, and the thing falls flat.

But flat is good compared to some of the other performances: Robert Symonds' unbearably sniveling Demokos, Roger de Koven's peevish Priam, Jennifer West's vulgar Marilyn Monroe *cum* Jackie Kennedy Helen, Diana Sands's unrelievedly sneering Cassandra (as if the ironic epigram required a tone of heavy, contemptuous sarcasm), and so on, quite literally, ad nauseam. Only Tony van Bridge, as Ulysses, proved once again what a figure a professional cuts among amateurs: with such a Greek, what chance did the Trojans have?

Stanley Silverman contributed his usual totally meaningless musical score; David Hays's sets were aggressively cute, and Fred Voelpel's costumes, as always, militantly unsightly. In fact, there was a separate war going on between Hector's and Ulysses' costumes: the one's paratrooper's plus-fours against the other's feather-boa-like cloak, each trying to outhorrify the other.

The whole thing was strenuously misdirected by Anthony Quayle. The pace was uncertain, and the stage movement always either schematic or studiedly hectic, with chorus-like crowds along the sidelines sounding off ploddingly on cue. Even obvious details were muffed: if Helen is spoken of as adjusting her sandals offstage, she comes in barefoot. The stage directions explicitly call for a brilliant last image: as the Gates of War are opened again, they are to reveal Helen unconcernedly kissing Troilus. Quayle allows the gates to open first, and then has Helen slinking over to kiss the boy. This makes it all deliberate, calculated, instead of spontaneous and truly horrible—all for sex, and the world well lost.

The scenes involving the gods were, regrettably, cut. This left the mortals, as usual, holding the bag: whether they were dead, like Giraudoux, or technically alive, like the cast.

•   •   •

OTHER DRAMATISTS write plays; Tennessee Williams rewrites plays. He does this in two ways. There is hardly a recent full-length drama of his that wasn't first a short story, then a one-act play, then tried out in one long version in Florida and another at Spoleto, then came out in *Esquire* in revised form, then was further revised for Broadway, where it was sometimes, after failing, revived in a rewritten version which also failed. Sometimes there is a slight departure from this schema: there may, for instance, be a London or a San Francisco recension; or Broadway may settle for one disastrous production. There may or may not be a further revision for the movies.

All this would be merely laughable—no, let me revise that, pathetic; what is heartrending is the *other* rewriting Williams does: the appalling self-parroting and self-parody. *The Seven Descents of Myrtle* (called originally, like the story on which it is based, *Kingdom of Earth*) is almost completely plagiarized from other Williams works. If one had the stomach for it, one could play a game with one's theater companion: who can spot the source of this speech or scene first? In dismal sequence, almost all of Williams' works parade through this pastiche—always coarsened or reduced to the absurd.

The Seven Descents of Myrtle concerns Lot, a young Southern mother's boy, dying of TB, and his half-brother, Chicken, a roughneck to whom the ramshackle house by the river will go upon Lot's death. It is the time of periodic floods that drive the inmates to the roof, where Chicken (hence his name) quenches his thirst by biting the head off a chicken and drinking its blood. Lot is still clinging to the ghost of his dead, refined mother, and wants to keep Chicken, whom their crude father begat on a black, from inheriting. So he marries Myrtle, an amiable tramp, on a television program on which she has already won any number of household appliances. He brings her home, but, as his lung condition worsens, retires to the upstairs bedroom. He seems to be impotent and homosexual as well as tubercular, and now concentrates on sending the frustrated Myrtle down to the kitchen to get Chicken drunk and steal the deed to the property from him.

Now the descents of Myrtle begin. There are only four left in the play, which had forty-five minutes cut during tryouts; four plus a very important fifth one. As Myrtle peregrinates between Chicken and Lot, and keeps getting drunker herself, Lot becomes more hostile to her, and Chicken, though he too insults and humiliates her, more attracted. As the flood keeps rising, Lot's life sinks; he dons his beloved mother's clothes, stumbles down the stairs, and dies *en travesti*. Meanwhile, Myrtle and Chicken have sealed their compact with her final and supreme descent: she goes down on him. In exchange, he will take her up on the roof with him, and will, when the waters settle, settle down with her in the house that is now his.

The basic agon of the play is "the subduing of the woman" motif which we know best from such plays as *Summer and Smoke*, *A Streetcar Named Desire* and *Night of the Iguana*; it is here enacted comically between Chicken and Myrtle, in a way reminiscent of *The Rose Tattoo*. The subsidiary contest between Lot and Myrtle is the motif of "the unfulfilled woman," which can be found in every Williams story, novel or play. The particular variant here—"vital woman failing with exquisite young man"—we know from *Suddenly Last Summer*, from Blanche's monologue about her marriage in *Streetcar*, and in a less pure form, from *Cat on a Hot Tin Roof*.

But the self-plagiarism and self-parody are particularly blatant in the dialogue. In his earlier plays, Williams, who started out as a poet, often managed to be quietly, pervasively poetic. Now we get things like "The moon is out, like the bleary eye of a drunkard"; or, more philosophically, "What are you laughing at?—At life.—I think it's a bad dream.—A bad dream can be funny." For psychology we get, "There's two ways to treat a hysterical woman: one is to slap her face, the other is to lay her. Sometimes you've got to do both." Or a statement about there being more to love (or sex—I forget which, but I doubt that Williams ever distinguished between them) than "jumping up and down on each other's eggs"—which seems to me particularly inept in a supposedly heterosexual context.

Worst of all is the humor. Thus, a utensil elicits the following exchange: "MYRTLE: Oh, that's a man-size instrument. CHICKEN: Well, don't you like a man-size instrument?" Or this, apropos some French fries: "Still hot?—Who?—I meant the potatoes.—Oh, is that what you meant?" And sometimes this turns real tough (a throwback to Stanley and Blanche), as when Chicken disputes Myrtle's claims to living off the musical theater: "You kick up your right leg, and you kick up your left leg, and in-between your legs you make your living." With writing like that, what do you need symbolic overtones (the flood) or social undertones (Chicken's mixed blood) for? You kick up your symbols, you kick up your social significance, but it's in between that you make your living.

Jo Mielziner has parodied his own previous sets for Williams plays; José Quintero has again directed flaccidly and aimlessly; and the actors are left pretty much to their own devices. Brian Bedford, as Lot, barely takes any of it seriously; Harry Guardino, as Chicken, falls back on his good comic timing and his good looks; both come off relatively unscathed. But Estelle Parsons minces movements and words, and generally tries to be a giant, sexy panda, which, I am afraid, comes out nauseating. But why should the actors and director know what to do with the play when the author didn't? Thus, Chicken, who begins as an illiterate brute, ends up as a poet who rhapsodizes about owning one's house and land, one's "kingdom of earth." None of it makes sense. There are two ways to treat a hysterical play: one is to slap it down, the other to lay it to rest. In this case, you've got to do both.

The Repertory Theater of Lincoln Center is finishing its commercially most successful season with yet another artistic disaster, a *Cyrano de Bergerac* that is one of the hundred neediest cases in theatrical history. First, it lacks a protagonist: Richard Basehart, who was to have starred, acquired a mysterious case of chronic laryngitis and dropped out. Secondly, it lacks a stage: without a proscenium arch, none of its illusions truly comes off. Thirdly, it lacks a suitable director: Carl Weber, a graduate of Brecht's Berliner Ensemble has imposed all kinds of alienation effects on a play that cries out for our emotional involvement. Fourthly, it needs a better English version than James Forsyth's seems to be; I say "seems" because the way the actors have been instructed to alienate the verse into skittering prose that hides its rhymes like a guilty secret, one can't be sure. Fifthly, it needs far more dashing and evocative sets and costumes. Sixthly and desperately, it needs a cast that has charm, bravura, or at least proficiency. But with the exception of Dennis Cooney's Christian, a nice combination of loutishness and delicacy of soul, and the Roxane of Suzanne Grossmann, at least intermittently alive, the acting was at best nonexistent, at worst frighteningly in evidence. Even the usually able Philip Bosco reduced De Guiche to a night-club impersonation of John Gielgud.

What *Cyrano* decidedly does not need is Robert Symonds, who inherited the title part, which should have died intestate. Symonds has the voice and vocal mannerisms of a Midwestern mortician, his every quavering syllable dripping with a mixture of sanctimoniousness and embalming fluid. He almost gets away with the farcical passages, but when it comes to pathos, poetry, swashbuckling, or wit, he gives us a Cyrano whose panache has been plucked, and whose exiguity is plainer even than the nose on his face.

The text has been mercilessly cut, but what is left is subjected to the unkindest cut of all: misdirection. Thus, the Gascon Cadets are a bunch of sottish bumpkins, the expansive balcony scene is squeezed together into a tiny corner upstage left, the battle scenes are a veritable batrachomyomachy, and Cyrano's death has been staged with Roxane, Le Bret and Ragueneau standing center stage in a row, like three lamp posts, while the dying hero, left to his own devices, cavorts and collapses down front. Yet, as invariably happens, the play got most of the blame. If I may quote my program note for the Caedmon recording of *Cyrano* (with Ralph Richardson as a fine, though somewhat hoary, protagonist), "It is rather more theater than literature, but in that honorably second category, the play has not been surpassed . . . *Cyrano* can be said to finish ahead of many more ambitious efforts by a nose, a long nose." At Lincoln Center, it does not even show.

As PERFORMED last fall at the off-Broadway Public Theatre, *Hair* was an unpretentious, charming, swinging little musical. Not without flaws, it was nevertheless youthful, zestful, tuneful and brimful of life. In its new Broadway version, it is merely fulsome. What happened? It would seem that the new producer was hellbent on giving uptowners a sensational revelation of how it *really* is; as part of that endeavor, he hired Tom O'Horgan (of Café La Mama, *Futz* and *Tom Paine* fame) as director. Now, O'Horgan is a sort of off-off-Broadway Peter Brook: clever, chic and, at bottom, quite commercial. Given his first go at Broadway, he was, like the producer, out to *épater les bourgeois* for all he was worth (which, in my book, is not very much); but at the same time, care had to be exercised only to titillate the middle class, not to offend it. So, with shock and inoffensiveness as its contradictory aims, *Hair* was off on an internal collision course.

Typically, nudity, perversion, four-letter words were built up, whereas the story with its antiwar but also antibourgeois bias was either soft-pedaled or transmogrified into stingless farce, when not actually thrown out altogether. Thus, there appeared throughout the original *Hair* a burlesque middle-class couple, who were also the hero's parents, but mostly the epitome of smug squareness. These figures have been turned into a transvestite posing as a *bourgeoise* with a *castrato* sidekick; or, in the family scene, a father and mother each in triplicate, the main third of the mother again a man in drag. The wistfully comic and, granted, somewhat uninspired plot has yielded to something worse: pseudoimprovisatory extravaganza. Even such a fetchingly bittersweet number as a girl hippie's lament for a lover who just yipped in and out, surrounded by all those overproduction values, loses its fragile nostalgia. Where Gerald Freedman's original direction really scored, as in a dance number showing, in bizarre superimposition, the history of America and of Vietnam as the tragicomic slaughter of one race or religion by the next in an unending vicious circle, O'Horgan goes out of his way to make his staging gratuitously different, and succeeds in killing the point.

Some members of the original company remain very funny and endearing. Gerome Ragni, one of the authors of the late book and lyrics, is still outrageously droll; though James Rado, his co-author and new to the cast, is pallid. Two of the original girls, Sally Eaton and Shelley Plimpton, are irresistible: the one a nearsighted, concupiscent teddy bear; the other all ethereal poignancy. The new leading lady, Lynn Kellogg, though pretty, has the personality of a cornflake; her sprightly and full-voiced predecessor, Jill O'Hara, is now wasting her gifts on the vacuous musical *George M.*, which also preempted the zest of Susan Batson and Jonelle Allen. Galt MacDermot's music is still delicious, though the new numbers are not up to the old. So it is a *Hair* both overgrown and shorn; but for those who missed it downtown, still guardedly recommended.

SUMMER AND
AUTUMN, 1968

FUTZ
by Rochelle Owens

DIONYSUS IN '69
by Richard Schechner

A MOON FOR THE MISBEGOTTEN
by Eugene O'Neill

THE BOYS IN THE BAND
by Mart Crowley

LOVERS
by Brian Friel

THE MISANTHROPE
by Molière
produced by the APA-Phoenix Repertory Theater

IT WOULD, I think, be idle to dispute whether the theater began as word or gesture; the two, ultimately, flourished conjointly and redounded to the theater's glory. But today's theater has decided that the word is unimportant, a mere pretext for gesture; gradually and disastrously, the word is being squeezed into the background, if not elbowed out altogether. And the gesture is becoming ruder and ruder, to be reduced finally to a single symbolic—indeed, literal—obscenity.

Two current productions corroborate these melancholy speculations: Rochelle Owens' *Futz* and *Dionysus in '69*. *Futz* is a very short play—the author cannot sustain dialogue—and what words there are are mostly hollow, uncouth, obscene, or even meaningless grunts. The play concerns one Cyrus Futz, a farmer who prefers to have intercourse with his pig, Amanda. This drives the spurned village whore, Majorie Satz, wild with rage, and her family mad with vengefulness. The village idiot, Oscar Loop (like all Miss Owens' characters, he inclines toward self-contradiction, and can at times be her metaphysical mouthpiece) observes Cyrus and Amanda *in flagrante,* and commits a sex murder for which he is hanged. Whereupon the combined fury of the Satzes, the villagers, and the law lead to Futz's imprisonment and eventual murder.

Miss Owens wants us, I suppose, to see in this the calvary of the nonconforming individual, the greater bestiality of the supposedly normal majority, and society's cowardice in not daring to espouse an animality it secretly craves. But even assuming that we agree with the author's theses—one of which seems to me old hat, one questionable and one ludicrous—they are not couched in a dramatic event, a set of characters, a language that can move any part of us other than the stomach.

The construction of the play is awkward: tiny open-ended vignettes in which the characters burble pretentious nonsense or infantile naughtiness, while the narrator recites the action. The people are all demented, depraved or retarded, and not even Futz, who under pressure cravenly denies Amanda, commands our interest or sympathy. As for the language, it has three modes. (1) Pretentious and preposterous: "sticking his fingers out like stone worms," "how can well I go describing on?" "his kneebones high like the two hemispheres," "my choppers say yes to your head under their feet." (2) Synthetic hillbilly, a cross between Dogpatch and Volapük: "You make it wus tan it is mentionin' the pig . . . O o o o so indecent I am, and now the filty dreams 'ill come. O Gods help meee that we shoulda both laid with a sow." (3) Scatology, obscenity, baby-talk and grunts: "HAHA-Haaaah-shhhhhushy yeah yeah," "Yeeeiiiiiey Oyu Big man-bloke!" and much more, less suitable for quoting. Each of these elements is painful in itself; together, they are well-nigh unendurable.

The play, however, is only a skeleton, albeit an indecently jig-

gling one. To put flesh on it required the services of the chief purveyor of bare meat to off-Broadway (*Tom Paine*) and Broadway
(*Hair*), Tom O'Horgan. He has developed a directorial scenario
encasing the play that is almost totally independent from and even
at odds with the text, which it matches only in beastliness. The
actors, and more particularly a chorus encircling the action, crawl,
wallow, leap and roll over one another, sometimes piling up in a
human pyramid, more often simulating various types of human,
porcine or mixed intercourse. At the same time, they have been arbitrarily assigned lines of the narration, which they deliver, singly or
chorically, in speech, whispers, singsong or shouts, all perfectly
divorced from any inner logic. The stage sound and movement become an amorphous weltering and word-mongering, a veritable ho-
gomachy. The actors, moreover, accompany themselves on peculiar
instruments with O'Horgan's rather ordinary tunes.

Fluid staging is, of course, a good thing, but exactly what is
flowing here? Things are either pointless, as when Oscar Loop's
mother, visiting her doomed son in jail, sticks her foot in his shirt,
and he whirls her around by it like a windmill. Or there is a point,
but a crude and hardly relevant one, as when Mrs. Loop suddenly
bares her breasts and starts suckling Oscar, who then sticks his head
under her skirt as she says "A son and his mother are holy," while
the chorus makes obscene clucking sounds and symbolically ejacu-
lates in their direction. But Miss Owens herself is fully capable of
ending a scene with Oscar raising his toes to his nose "with a monkey's grace and whiff[ing them] deeply." On Miss Owens' Ossa,
do we need O'Horgan's Pelion?

The acting is disciplined enough, if neatly executed group copulation is a standard. Of performances as such there can be little
question here, though John Bakos as Futz and Peter Craig as the
Sheriff produce the right attitudes and tonalities. Seth Allen's Oscar
and Sally Kirkland's Narrator strike me as pure—or, rather, impure—
ham; and, as Majorie, Beth Porter is so pungently porcine as to
outswine Amanda. Amanda herself never appears, presumably because a proper pig wouldn't stoop to such an enterprise.

After it is all over, including some ten minutes of introductory
screening from Ed Emshwiller's film, *Relativity*, showing the slaught-
ering of hogs, I am left with little more than the realization that if
there is anything worse than a pig in a poke, it's a poke in a pig.
But no doubt this will prove another triumph for O'Horgan, the
hot new director who has shot up in our sky like an inverted meteor,

and who will now be lauded for the brilliance with which he converted the entire stage into one vast pigsty. I wonder, though, what he and Miss Owens thought they were doing: liberating in a grand, obscene gesture our dangerously repressed animal instincts? Or are they both just trying, with shrewd commercialism, to live high off the hog?

RICHARD SCHECHNER, professor of drama at N.Y.U. and editor of *The Drama Review,* has started something called The Performance Group. From his spoken pronunciamentos and printed manifestoes, one gathers that the group is dedicated, first, to exploring their own and one another's bodies via such exercises as aboriginal simulated childbirth rituals and the "group grope," which involves blindfoldedly groping and smelling out a partner with whom one pairs off for the evening. Secondly, they want to develop a theater of total involvement, derived from Artaud, Peter Brook, and two Poles, Jan Kott and Jerzy Grotowski.

The Performance Group has now let us in on their arcane doings with Schechner's version of *The Bacchae* of Euripides, *Dionysus in '69,* a title meant to function both in writing and orally. As those familiar with Kott's treatment of Shakespeare and other classics will guess, Euripides and Schechner's reverse bowdlerizing of him are Poles apart. What we get here, in a specially constructed "environment" at a converted garage, consists of one third Euripides and two thirds ritual birthings, group therapy for the actors, group gropes for both actors and such members of the audience as allow themselves to be lured into frugging with performers or being groped by them, and a great deal of hippie talk. Dionysus, for example, is described as "a god who eats food and women, smokes cigarettes, and with a social security number"; he promises people "freedom, real freedom, not bullshit American freedom"; in other words, gloriously terrible things "like burning down slums and listening to the screams." And William Finley, who enacts, or engropes, Dionysus, proclaims: "I come from the flowering slum to the East, but I live to the West on Christopher Street, Number 69+22," and "To quote Euripides, etcetera, let the truth be told: there is no God greater than Bill Finley!"

The environment consists of a central playing area surrounded by numerous and diverse crudely jointed wooden—what shall I call them: towers? erections?—on, under, and around which both actors and audience sit or disport themselves. The mixture of mumbled Euripides, bellowed Schechner, and actors' therapeutic improvisations ("Rozanne, why are you so afraid of being a woman?"); of actors' stripping down to diminutive jock straps affording tower-seated pederasts (and unfortunately the rest of us) perfect views of anuses; of actresses baring their unnoteworthy bosoms; this mixture, I say, crawls, leaps, wallows, tumbles and grumbles (elocution, of course, is anathema) all over this converted, or deconverted, garage.

I shall cite only two examples of the crude and pointless goings-on. One is Pentheus' delivering a speech while turning somersaults round and round the central stage. The other is Agave, enacted at this point by two girls simultaneously, killing and performing fellatio on a single Pentheus in duplicate, while the entire cast smear themselves with and roll about in simulated gore.

There seem to be at least two glaring fallacies at work in all this. The first is the assumption that nonentities like Schechner and his gropers can liberally insert their foolishness into a work of art and come up with a viable fusion—as if you could add apples and horsebuns. The second is that you involve people by jostling, tickling, ad- or un-dressing them. An audience is willing to suspend its disbelief *as an audience*, and for this there are any number of useful conventions like the picture-frame stage, special lighting and so on, and above all, that greater and deeper thing which is art. But why should a spectator be moved by groups of actors, sweaty and smelly, rolling over his legs and tumbling into his lap? This means being accosted not as audience but *as a private citizen*, and there is no reason why I as a private individual should suspend my disbelief, or lend my ears and nose to The Performance Group's bad diction and worse odors. (O, for the good old days when all you might have inhaled in this garage was a little carbon monoxide!) In other words, the methods here used work not for the play but against it, in the name of some nebulous communion with persons whom my senses and taste urge me to stay as far away from as possible.

There is a well-wrought and poignant revival of O'Neill's *A Moon for the Misbegotten*. This is not one of the master's best plays, but it runs a fairly close and highly estimable second. The theme, as in all of O'Neill's mature works, is people reaching for someone or something, only to find their yearnings unfulfilled, regardless of whether their objective eludes or submits to their grasp.

So here the would-be lovers dance a harrowing emotional minuet—barefoot, on broken glass—and can touch only in the mind, share only mutual abdication.

The beauty of O'Neill's full-blown dramaturgy is that it is so very much of a piece. The same tremulous frustrations, the same shyly hopeful yet dashed expectations, the same violence ending by turning inward on itself that inform the play as a whole are to be found in almost every scene, in nearly every bit of dialogue. That is what makes this rowdy and heartbreaking play finally so exhilarating and even restful: its consistency, its homogeneity. A look at it through either end of the opera glasses yields the same pattern of things, large or small. The drunken, guilt-haunted hero exclaims at one point, "There is no present or future—only the past happening over and over again—now." Similarly, O'Neill's tragic vision rears up before us over and over again, even in the midst of the often very funny humor.

What is best about this play is that it has the double rhythm of O'Neill's finest writing. The language proceeds in four-quarter time: A provokes, B takes umbrage, A apologizes, B forgives; this pattern is repeated over and over. Underneath, however, the emotions proceed in counterrhythm in three-quarter time: a reaching out from deep down, a grasping that crumbles in mid-clasp, a lapsing back into forlorn but proud aloneness. And this duple rhythm, which propels almost every scene, finally becomes the schema of the whole work, O'Neill's vision of life.

Already at the beginning of O'Neill's career, Hugo von Hofmannsthal cogently observed that these plays were "theater through and through, and from the roots up." Looking at *A Moon for the Misbegotten* in Theodore Mann's conservative but penetrating production, we feel how applicable to O'Neill are Mallarmé's marvelous words about Poe, *"Calme bloc ici-bas chu d'un désastre obscur"*; the play is a self-contained monolith dropped on earth from some great, distant cosmic disaster.

PEOPLE FREQUENTLY ASK me (as a reader did recently in a letter) what my critical yardstick is, or (as a girl just did at a symposium) what I want the theater to be. This reminds me of a radio commercial for a recording of Handel's masterpiece I keep hearing: "Send no money—simply write to *Messiah!*" People—perfectly good people—would love to send no money, do no extensive reading of a critic's work, just shoot a question, *the* question, at him, and get a nice, encapsulated, reusable, all-purpose Messianic answer.

Unfortunately for them as for the critic, no such answer exists. I don't know what the theater ought to be like, or I'd be writing plays. I don't have a yardstick, or I'd become a carpenter. But as I go or drag myself from play to play, I struggle toward a greater understanding of what makes theater theater; to which is later added the further struggle of conveying this in readable expository prose. I think of Rilke's semiautobiographical hero, Malte Laurids Brigge, who writes about poetry in his diary: "One should wait with it, and gather meaning and sweetness a whole life long, and a long one if possible, and then, at the very end, perhaps one could write ten lines that are good." Of course the drama critic cannot, any more than the poet, follow this sage advice; but it is hard work nevertheless to write good poetry or criticism, and the reader, too, should be prepared to put in some work.

As for prescribing a direction for the theater—why, it's hard enough to recognize what is or might be truly valuable, and to warn people about what strikes one as factitious and sterile. For example, I would not have believed until the day I saw it that a play about a clutch of homosexuals, ranging from closet to screaming queens, who celebrate an internecine birthday party would prove one of the very few good shows of the season. Not, of course, because I am against the subject matter; on the contrary, along with several others, I have been pleading all along for frankly homosexual drama instead of plays in drag, in which the homosexual appears disguised as an aging nymphomanias, a gigolo-consuming termagant, or a virgin dying of being misunderstood.

No, the reason Mart Crowley's *The Boys in the Band* ought not to be good is, first, that it is a basically realistic play, and that the realistic drama has temporarily run dry, producing crushing tautologies like *The Price*, or mere sniffings of subjects demanding the incisiveness of imagination, like *The Prime of Miss Jean Brodie*. Secondly, it is a cross-section play—the kind in which, say, a group of entertainers are trapped in a sandstorm in the basement of an Ethiopian charity bazaar, and one of them proves to be a tyrannical psychotic, one an angelic whore, one a saucer-eyed innocent, and you fill in the rest. This sort of thing always ends up being schematic, whether it is schematic in Kansas City or on a spaceship headed for Sirius. Thirdly, it is one of those mixtures of comedy and drama that requires extremely deft handling of not readily miscible ingredients, which frequently tripped up no less a man than Sean O'Casey.

But *The Boys in the Band* manages to overcome these handicaps. It is realistic, but in an area that stage realism had not yet explored, perhaps because our social climate has until now demanded that homosexuality be viewed as a shameful or pathetic lapse in the midst of a heterosexual world (*Cat on a Hot Tin Roof, Tea and Sympathy*), or as something so monstrous as to be almost heroic or hilarious (*And Things That Go Bump in the Night, Gorilla Queen*). But now along comes a view of it that is knowing rather than sensationalistic, sympathetic rather than apologetic or defiant, and, above all, unruffled. Straightforwardness toward this subject proves an original achievement.

Yes, it is a cross-section play, and to some extent it suffers from it. If eight or nine people's problems are to be examined in some psychological and dramaturgical detail, chances are that they will not be individuals so much as types; a good play usually cannot be fully honest about more than four people. (There are exceptions.) But here the semi-individuals, semi-types are all related and held together by their homosexuality, are all aspects of the same sociosexual problem, and together form a collective protagonist.

True, the tone changes frequently and quickly, but in the very nervousness lies the salvation. It is never any one thing long enough for the next thing to be a recognizable contradiction; moreover, the precarious yet embattled position of the homosexual, along with his theatrical tendency to exaggerate toward delirium or dejection, makes the mercurial moods, the chameleon characterizations psychologically relevant and dramatically justified.

The acting is, with a couple of exceptions, so good and homogeneous that when the French director Roger Planchon saw the show, he thought he was seeing a repertory group and asked what the women in the company were like. The point about this all-male cast, and about the director and author as well, is that there is missionary zeal in their work. The homosexual part of the audience is to feel purged and to some extent vindicated by this play and production, whereas heterosexual spectators are to be made more aware of homosexual life styles and, if possible, sympathetic to them. (Nastily obtuse reader letters to the *Times* indicated that there is still a lot of learning to be done.) It is enlightening to watch the homosexual spectators laugh ecstatically, while, alongside them, middle-aged married couples and very young girls absorbedly strain to keep up and comprehend. It may prove a lesson in majority and minority coexistence—though at *The Boys in the Band* (as, often, elsewhere) it is hard to tell which is which.

·　·　·

Last night I dreamt that, as we were sitting at a theater bar, I asked Kenneth Tynan what he thought of Brian Friel's *Philadelphia, Here I Come!* Tynan, looking more debonair than ever, suddenly stretched out among the full and empty glasses on the bar, and replied amiably, "It is the nicest kind of sentimental theater." That seems to me a bit hard on that remarkable play, but it might just fit Friel's current double bill, *Lovers.*

The first play, *Winners,* is a comic tragedy. A male and female narrator—in black, motionless, on highbacked chairs flanking the stage—tell the story of Mag Enright and Joe Brennan, both seventeen, three weeks before their impending wedding precipitated by her pregnancy. The story begins on a hilltop on a summer morning, with the kids studying for their finals, dreaming about the future, quarreling and making up. That afternoon they went boating on the lake and drowned. Reading impersonally from quaintly bound manuscripts, the fatidic antiphonal choruses unfurl what happened from the point of view of the bereaved families, the small Irish town, and history itself. Meanwhile, on the stage between them, Mag and Joe argue and frolic on their last day on earth. At first, the narration and the events on stage are synchronous; then the fatelike narration speeds ahead to disappearance, discovery of bodies, inquest, grim aftermath, and the world's final oblivion. But on stage, the young pair is still loving and cavorting about.

The contrapuntal discrepancy develops into thrilling dramatic tension—a splendid stage metaphor. It suggests the interweaving of joy and horror in every strand of life; it embodies the clash between how the lovers see themselves and how they must appear—and disappear—under the aspect of eternity. It conveys the double time we live in. For these lovers, there is only the passionate now, which becomes their eternity. For the rest, there is slow transience, nibbling at everything, even grief.

The idea must be as old as literature itself; frequent in Yeats's poetry, it has been heard most poignantly on the Irish stage in Synge's *Deirdre of the Sorrows.* About to kill herself over the body of her murdered lover, Deirdre exclaims, "I have put away sorrow like a shoe that is worn out and muddy . . . It is not a small thing to be rid of grey hairs, and the loosening of the teeth. It was the choice of lives we had in the clear woods, and in the grave, we're safe, surely." But here's the difference: Deirdre and Naisi chose to die for their love; Mag and Joe die in spite of it, seemingly by accident. Friel is aware of the comedown in this, and shrouds the deaths in mystery: it was a warm, windless day, and the boat was in perfect working order. We are left to feel obscurely that the lovers died by something bigger than chance.

Still, the stakes are somehow small: the very language of the lovers, though always fresh and perky, never transcends into poetry. Sometimes we are reminded of Giraudoux at his worst (Irma's soliloquy in *The Madwoman of Chaillot*) or of Thornton Wilder at his Wilderest. True, these kids must be ordinary, but they must also be more than that. For they are up against an extraordinary dramatic device, and, as it is, the device wins hands down. The language and characterization seldom if ever rise above the resources of so typical an Irish commercial playwright as the late Lennox Robinson, author of such Hibernian staples as *Is Life Worth Living? or: Drama at Inish*.

What further weakens the production at the Vivian Beaumont Theatre is that the star, Art Carney, has been allowed to enact both commentators. Instead of an immobile, androgynous Fate, a man and woman vaticinating on either side of the stage, we get Carney, slightly vulgar, invincibly commonplace in his street clothes, moseying around from stage left to right and back, squatting down to watch the action, and every now and again blowing a line. For the suprahuman we get the all too human, and the metaphysics are blurred.

But the lovers, in Hilton Edwards' otherwise intelligently modulated and handsomely spread out staging, are captivating. Eamon Morrissey is an expansive, bumptious, earnest and winning Joe; but whenever Fionnuala Flanagan as Mag takes over the stage (which she does with the greatest of ease), it is changed, changed utterly: a terrible beauty is born. A face, a body and a voice make themselves into the gleeful instruments of the universe; what Miss Flanagan does is not a way of laughing, crying, being silly or wise—it is the very paradigm of horseplay and horse sense, of absurdity and adorableness, of being alive.

The second play, *Losers*, is a tragic comedy and tells a typical Irish story of middle-aged lovers (later spouses) tyrannized and finally beaten down by the woman's mother. This widowed monster, a fake cardiac case and genuine religious fanatic, piously chains her household to her bedstead; she withstands the unmasking of her patron saint as a fraud, and succeeds in turning her spunky daughter into a bad wife but good nurse. The tale is told with a wry, often strikingly funny, but somewhat coarse and derivative wit.

Anna Manahan is first-rate as the bouncy but hagridden daughter, whose defiant spirit is eventually forced into permanent genuflection before her bedridden mother. Art Carney is amusing as the unsuccessfully rebellious and finally castrated husband, though his Irish-American tones contrast pitifully with the rich, resplendent Irishness of most of the others. But the second panel of Brian Friel's diptych is, unfortunately, altogether within the reach of Lennox Robinson, author of *Killycreggs in Twilight*.

The APA PRODUCTION of *The Misanthrope* is as bad as . . . as . . . it is hard to find an adequately monstrous simile. As bad—let me try —as its review by Clive Barnes, who had high praise for this production. In the theater, I am as good a masochist as anybody and have been known to sit through entire productions at Stratford, Connecticut, and in the lofts of Greenwich Village; but this *Misanthrope* sent me packing after the second act.

To begin with the speaking of verse—granted, no easy problem: I recall a story about a Viennese box office that answered inquiries about whether a play was in verse with the comforting reply, "Yes, but you can't notice it." Well, there are some members of this cast whose solution is to make Richard Wilbur's brilliant rhymed-verse translation sound like Paddy Chayefsky. There are others whose approach is to singsong along as if they were following the ball from syllable to syllable, and who thus translate Molière into a Hallmark Christmas card. Some of the cast have British accents, others jog along in plain, honest Amurrican. Some rattle away like a Singer sewing machine trying to make like an Alfa Romeo; others labor painfully as if each iambic pentameter were a giving of birth to quintuplets. The total effect is far worse than the sum of its parts.

The scenery by James Tilton and the costumes by Nancy Potts are a disaster. It must have seemed a hellishly clever idea to use nothing but black and beige in both, with here and there an inconspicuous dab of white. A certain type of book illustration was meant to come to life. But what looks good on paper does not necessarily make sense on stage: as you watch this veritable army of Black and Tans parade across the scene, the drabness of the acting and directing is given ghastly corroboration.

Stephen Porter's direction is the apogee of boredom. Again, it must have seemed a good idea not to move the actors around excessively, and to let Molière's wit and profundity cascade forth untrammeled. Porter, however, becomes fixated on stasis: his characters repeatedly immobilize themselves in the same positions and places, as if ships at sea had to chart their courses by them. Thus, Célimène spends enough time in a certain spot halfway left of center stage with her left profile to us for coins bearing her likeness to be designed and struck. The stage is strewn with enough anonymous corpses to become a potter's (or Porter's) field. But when a character does move, as when Eliante delivers her second-act speech about love (in a mincingly self-congratulatory manner), the movement is as schematic and predictable as if, instead of being directed, it had been drawn by a pair of compasses.

The acting is almost uniformly bad. The exception is the Oronte of Keene Curtis. Curtis manages to make the character first obsequious but not smarmy, then pretentious without undue bluster, and finally seething on a nice, low flame. Brian Bedford's Acaste is at least a poised performance, though it scarcely begins to suggest the blood-less, overrefined elegance that is called for. But the rest!

Richard Easton works hard on his Alceste, and if acting were like ditch-digging, one could commend him for a devotedly wielded pickax, and the unstinting sweat of his brow. Alceste, to be sure, is a character second only to Hamlet in complexity. He has been played for extremes of tragedy and comedy, and all stages between. As with verse speaking, I feel that a judicious middle way must be found. The character must not be played either for our sympathy or our hilarity: he is a cross between Timon and Benedick, a sort of Thersites out of Giraudoux. Easton plays him as a country bumpkin with some horse sense and lots of horse. At best, he approaches Jonsonian comedy of humors; at worst, he is profoundly humorless. In his fright wig, he looks like a broomstick with a collapsed broom on top, and his basic sound is a bellow collapsed into a groan.

The others are perfectly hopeless. Christine Pickles' Célimène is nothing more than a series of prestissimo crepitations, an unending stream of verbiage trailing behind her like a hysterically unwound roll of toilet paper. Her gestures are devoid of grace, and her face lacks refinement: this enchantress is a scullion affecting the ways of her mistress. At that, she may be better than the other two women, whose performances are deep-frozen postures. Sydney Walker has been known to be good; his Philinte, though, is an elderly, retired butcher, chopping couplets instead of cutlets. Joseph Bird's Clitandre is merely gross.

This raises the question of aesthetics. It is painful, when the acting is not good enough to make us forget it, to watch a company so patently lacking good looks and charm. Furthermore, the women all behave as if they were men in drag—exaggerated travesties of feminine behavior—while the men seem hardly able to wait till the next performance, when it will be their turn to play the female parts. Yet Mr. Barnes urges us not just to buy a ticket but to give the company a donation as well. If the money is to be used as an instant retirement fund, I shall be glad to contribute. There is undeniably a crying need for repertory in America, but I would rather cry over the need than over the APA.

Winter, 1968-1969

Box *and*
Quotations from Chairman Mao Tse-tung
  by Edward Albee

The Great White Hope
  by Howard Sackler

We Bombed in New Haven
  by Joseph Heller

The Living Theatre

The Tea Party *and* The Basement
  by Harold Pinter

King Lear
  by William Shakespeare
  produced by the Repertory Theater of Lincoln Center

Promises, Promises
  book by Neil Simon
  music by Burt Bacharach
  lyrics by Hal David

Jimmy Shine
  by Murray Schisgal

Hadrian VII
  by Peter Luke

THE HOUSE OF ATREUS
by Aeschylus
produced by the Minnesota Theatre Company

AKROPOLIS
by Stanislaw Wyspianski

CELEBRATION
book and lyrics by Tom Jones
music by Harvey Schmidt

IF ALBEE were not so arrogant, one would view his desperate stratagems with pity. When you have failed with every kind of play, including adaptations of novels and other people's plays, the last remaining maneuver is the nonplay. Finding himself in a box, Albee has contrived two interlocking nonplays, based, apparently, on a mathematical error: it is by multiplying, not by adding, minuses that you get a plus. *Box* and *Quotations from Chairman Mao Tse-tung*, when run together like two ink blots of different colors, raise the Rorschach test to new dramatic heights.

Box is a fifteen-to-twenty-minute taped monologue piped into a darkened theater with only the outlines of a large empty box gleaming in ultraviolet light on the black stage. As you gaze at this piece of hollow geometry for a *mauvais quart d'heure*, Ruth White's voice from the P.A. system flutteringly harangues you with platitudes and non sequiturs about life and art, including some impudent but prestigious references to Bach and to our arts slipping into mere crafts—as if this redundant message were necessary when we have *Box* before or, considering the placing of the loudspeaker, behind us. Albee's renowned command of language once again manifests itself in such hearty solecisms as "off of."

Lights go on as the box gradually fills up with a schematic setting: on the deck of an ocean liner, Chairman Mao stands erect, an old woman squats in a corner by her shabby suitcase, and a minister and a "Long Winded Lady" (as the program identifies her) lounge in deck chairs. There ensues what Albee no doubt thinks of as a fugue for speaking voices. The old woman recites a trashy piece of thirties doggerel, "Over the Hill to the Poorhouse," by one Will Carlton or Carleton, whoever he may be, about a poor, creaky critter whose ungrateful children consign her sunset years to the poorhouse. This is interrupted periodically by Chairman Mao (who strips off a rubber Mao mask to reveal beneath it—a Mao face; he is nothing but a walking set of Chinese boxes); he recites endlessly from his aphorisms. This is interrupted in turn by the Long Winded Lady, who relates her life with her husband, his death, her estrangement from her daughter, and her attempted suicide by leaping from just such an ocean liner. The clergyman responds to her with various more or less commensurate gestures, but never utters a syllable. This is, presumably, the Cagey element in the fugue. Mao paces about the stage and the entire auditorium; the old woman makes one slow symbolic trajectory toward an upstage perch; the LWL and the minister walk about a little. The three voices spell one another, and are joined, toward the end of the play, by the taped voice from *Box* interjecting some of its own previous pronouncements in what is supposed to be an ironically pregnant *stretto*.

But, alas, even though some members of the sparse audience laughed relentlessly at the satiric depths they perceived in the random juxtapositions of these unrelated voices, I felt doused with discrepancy. Rather than as a fugue, the exercise struck me as a piece of vocal *cadavre exquis*, without even the amusing *trouvailles* bequeathed by chance on that famous surrealist parlor game. One can perhaps extract some quasi-meanings (like teeth from a toothless mouth): the commonplaces of communism vs. the banalities of the bourgeoisie; the parallel miseries of the rich and the poor; the shibboleths of Mao's gospel vs. the silences of the man of God. But these are not so much legitimate explications as counsels of despair. In a fugue, in any case, there is development. Here, once the quartet is visually and vocally presented, there is nowhere to go. The grandam recites her WPA poetastery with ever campier emphases, and with increasingly dogged repetition of the wretched verses; Mao, sprouting successively from opposite proscenium boxes, spouts the same minimal maxims; the clergyman produces more and more D. W. Griffithish faces and gestures. The one thing that moves on freely is the LWL's narrative—but that is just what it is: a rambling, pettifogging, pseudoliterate monologue of strictly nondramatic verbiage.

We get the same ambitious, artificial, circumlocutory prose Albee keeps elaborating in his later, sterile works. It consists of false starts,

emendations, indirections, apologies, and general syntactic deviousness. One guesses that Albee imagines this to be some wonderful
cross between Beckett and Joyce; in fact, it is a barren, puerile mannerism. It suggests a kind of doddering pedantry that Albee might
attribute to a particular character—if it were not so often out of
character, and if a good many of his more recent favorite personages
did not speak exactly, or inexactly, like this. And always that pathetic
intellectual climbing of the (insufficiently) self-educated: "They
didn't know who Trollope was!—that is a life for you," complains the
LWL, and one winces for Albee. For behind such outcries we have
come to recognize the genteel author's feelings of superiority over,
and especially *against,* the unwashed that surround him, or that he
chooses to surround himself with. Significantly, this motif is equally
frequent in Tennessee Williams. And Trollope as status symbol! Next
thing it will be Rupert Brooke.

But suppose it were the character that is being ridiculed. So
much the worse for play and playwright; it would mean that they are
suffering from delusions of being Beckett, who alone can get away
with this sort of thing by virtue of much greater sensitivity to words
and to the essential foibles of human nature. There is even a conscious or unconscious allusion to Beckett in the LWL's repeated
references to falling and "all that falling," including, if my memory
isn't playing Albeesque tricks on me, falling *upward.* Typical of this
monologue is a line like "that was more seeing than landing—if you
like a pun," with that built-in escape clause yielding irritation rather
than mitigation. Or take this, from an evocation of the LWL's husband: "His scrotum was large, and not only for small men. His penis
also long and of a neat proportion...I cupped my hands around
his lovely scrotum..." Balls, if you like a pun. Though, obviously, it
is testicles that are large, "scrotum" is one of the few remaining words
that have not been heard on the stage, and Albee wants to get there
first with the absolute most. And, of course, it should be "for a small
man"—or could this be deliberate catachresis? And who but a poor
stylist would write "His penis also long and of a neat proportion,"
which is both fancy and vague. And who would describe a scrotum as
"lovely"? Surely not this woman. What need is there, above all, for
this entire, here abbreviated, speech? But Albee's pretensions are
large, and not only for a small man.

Shock value is always the last resort of the impotent. Indeed,
when the taped voice joins in, pseudosignificance runs amuck as darkness engulfs the scene. Alan Schneider has made resolute but arbi-

trary attempts at moving the characters around a little, but to no great effect, except perhaps to make the "fugue" sound stereophonic. Sudie Bond continues to play the one part she has played ever since *The Sandbox* and *The American Dream,* and there may be some perverse glory in having built a career on Albee's granny. The parts of Mao and the minister are equally nonexistent, but Nancy Kelly makes the LWL as amiable as possible. Ruth White's taped voice babbles on almost as magisterially as Ruth White in the flesh. As for Albee, where does he go from here? He could perhaps eliminate the third dimension from his box, or have us sit in a voiceless dark. We'll get to the grass roots of theater yet, even if it means burrowing underground like a mole.

This season's most interesting offering so far is *The Great White Hope.* Howard Sackler's play, transferred from Washington's Arena Stage, revised and partly recast, generates considerable excitement. Generating excitement is not nearly so good as generating art, but in these lean times may have to do. How nice if Sackler, who had the good sense to use Shakespeare and Brecht as his models, had come up with something worthy of them; unfortunately, the writing is only hard-working, competent but overambitious middlebrow stuff.

The play is the semifictionalized story of Jack Johnson, the first Negro heavyweight champion of the world. In the play, Jack Jefferson (could the name Johnson be too dirty a word for a white liberal to apply to his black hero?) wins the championship against mighty odds, and, to the despair of white America, seems unbeatable. Worse yet, he has a white girl friend; this, however, enables his enemies in and out of the FBI to frame him under the Mann Act. He beats a trumped-up three-year rap by escaping to Europe with Ellie, his girl, Goldie, his Jewish manager, and Tick, his Negro trainer. He defeats all contenders, but it becomes harder and harder for him to get fights or even to remain unmolested in any country for very long: in various ways America continues to hound him. He performs in shabby night-club acts and stoops to other indignities, but refuses lucrative offers to throw the championship in a rigged fight. When his mother dies back home and he can't even attend her funeral, Jack angrily leads his faithful band to Mexico, whence he hurls defiance across the border while, in dire financial straits, he keeps in training for a possible fight. His bitterness is so great that he ends by driving his devoted girl to her death. Broken by this as well as by the Mexican government's expulsion order (under U.S. coercion), Jefferson agrees to fight "the great white hope" who has finally been found and groomed against him; he agrees, furthermore, to lose in exchange for not only money but also the dropping of charges against him. The Negroes are still solidly behind him, but when he loses the big fight in Havana (apparently honestly), they too reject him.

Many things seem wrong to me with this sprawling three-act and nineteen-scene play. My first objection may seem irrelevant, but I consider it extremely unfortunate that boxing should be made into a heroic and noble thing. This so-called sport, which strikes me as the ugliest and most anachronistic of pastimes, can hardly be squared with our supposed discouragement of blood lust and our curbs on most (unfortunately not all) sports involving similar cruelty to animals. The leading Swedish newspaper, *Dagens Nyheter,* in its campaign against boxing, keeps unearthing numerous deaths in or just after the ring, which elsewhere go unreported. Jack Johnson may be a perfect symbol of the black hero-victim, there may have been no other avenues to fame for Negroes in the early 1900's, and Howard Sackler may certainly not have *intended* to glorify prize fighting, but all this and Pindar notwithstanding, I find the central positive value of the play a profoundly distasteful one, which diminishes the work ipso facto.

Scarcely more attractive is the ideological oversimplification. The play's moral universe is about as simplistic and false as LeRoi Jones's, with this difference: there is a *tertium quid* between all those lovable Negroes and appalling whites—Ellie and Goldie, who are good though white, apparently because they are Jewish. The world, I fear, just isn't that black-and-Jewish-and-white. At least this notion strikes me as equally open to doubt as the one that performing a musical-comedy version of *Uncle Tom's Cabin*—an eminently respectable pursuit in Siam, as Rodgers and Hammerstein have taught us—should, in a Budapest cabaret, be appreciably worse than beating or being beaten to a bloody pulp in the arena.

Next comes the problem of focus. By trying for a personal tragedy as well as a racial one, scope as well as intimacy; by including even a proleptic view of the future in the unlikely character of Scipio, a Black Panther *avant la lettre*; by further adding vignettes satirizing the faults of various nationalities; by trying to write in high and low style successively when not simultaneously, Sackler finds himself in the position of the man who wants to paint a giant fresco and illuminate an initial both at once. Shakespeare could do it, true; but he could do anything. Brecht could do it, sometimes. Sackler cannot do it, or at least not smoothly and compellingly.

There are also some disturbing evasions. We never see the crucial events, the prizefights, which remain offstage. But the same holds true for such diverse masterpieces as *Oedipus Rex* and *Penthesilea*, for example. There, however, we have the dramatic poetry of Sophocles and Kleist to compensate for the lack—even to surpass the actual events in the most brilliant representation. Sackler's last scene, with fight fans reporting the bout from the top of a ladder in barely comprehensible shouts, falls flat. More crippling, however, is the cop-out: did Jefferson throw the fight or lose it fair and square? Sackler seems to be too much in love with his hero to accept either alternative; he leaves the matter hanging, and when the now victorious challenger is carried onstage, his face is one bleeding gash, as if a bomb had carried off most of it, whereas Jack's still has a human shape to it. At this point, Sackler has definitely thrown *his* fight.

But the main weakness of the play is its attempt at poetry. No viewer, myself included, could begin to smell blank verse behind what is heard at the Alvin Theatre. Yet on consulting the printed text, there it suddenly is. This is the school of blank verse extending from T. S. Eliot to Rolf Hochhuth, noted for the unnoticeableness of its pentameters. Which raises the legitimate question: why bother at all? Is anything gained by the meter in this passage typical of most of the play:

> *Why, it juss like whut Presden Teddy say,*
> *Square Deal for Evvybody!—come on, les treat em right,*
> *git some chairs out here, they gonna stay, OK,*
> *no use they standing, some old-timie folks*
> *long with em here . . .*

But observe that even in the rarer, more poetic passages, as in this meditation by Cap'n Dan, a former champion and now Jack's nemesis, nothing much is achieved:

> *Now you'll say, Oh, that's only your title in sports—*
> *no, it's more. Admit it. And more than if one got to be*
> *world's best engineer, or smartest politician,*
> *or number one opera singer, or world's biggest genius*
> *at making things from peanuts. No calamity there.*
> *But Heavyweight Champion of the World, well*
> *it feels like the world's got a shadow across it,*
> *Everything's—no joke intended—kind of darker,*
> *and different, like it's shrinking . . .*

I cannot help feeling that it is *lèse-majesté* to haul dramatic blank verse out of its mausoleum for such street-corner turns. And it's no use saying that that is what such people sound like. Fine, but let them sound like that in prose, where they belong.

Nevertheless, the play has energy and variety. It knows when to hurtle and when to sashay forward, there is humor in it, and it does generate a growing sense of entrapment and doom. The Negro speech patterns are accurate and flavorous, and the protagonist, for one, does emerge a full and appealing human being. The other parts, even when they are no more than stereotypes, are at least swirlingly animated stereotypes. The device of addressing the audience is positively run into the groundlings, but some of the text's more awkward speeches are mercifully cut in the stage version. Sackler has at any rate sketched in a historical play conceived in the grand style; some credit is due for the very boldness of his concept.

The production is better than anything currently on view in New York. Edwin Sherin, the director, has coaxed every spark to be had out of rapid movement, lightning transitions, connecting music and disconnecting voices shrilling and sputtering. His one fault is to have driven his actors to shouting overmuch; given the initial problem some of them have with diction, a goodly proportion of lines never makes it comprehensibly across the footlights. This, regrettably, goes most for James Earl Jones. Otherwise, his Jack Jefferson is a magnificent creation, so much so that the play is unimaginable without Jones. Physically, he is just the shiny-pated, swift-footed, barrel-chested, debonair giant Johnson must have been; quick-witted, too, and jovial, charmingly embodying that real or imagined animality that white men fear for real or imaginary reasons. His emotional range is no less colossal: from bubbling badinage through ironic jabs to overwhelming grief at the death of his girl—human, animal, titanic—Jones encompasses everything with the precision and ease of a master. Particularly fine is his timing: the entire performance is paced with the sensitivity to tempo and inflection of a virtuoso *Lieder* singer. His breakdown over Ellie's body is as unbearably moving a piece of acting as I have ever seen.

Barely, if at all, behind him is Jane Alexander as Ellie. A *jolie laide* if ever there was one, she plays the part with an endearing firmness and modesty—almost a primness, if you can imagine primness as the vehicle for tenderness, warmth and passionate resolve. Whether she is quietly defending her relationship against various legal bloodhounds or feverishly clinging to it in the face of her lover's seemingly brutal rejection, she maintains (along with flawless diction) a sturdy grip on the human dignity of the part. It is Miss Alexander's triumph that without the slightest bid for our sympathy she has us loving her, suffering with her, mourning her. There is something virginal about her acting: every gesture and utterance comes as a first awakening, an emergence from deep, shy reserve into daylight, exaltation and pain.

Most of the supporting parts are at least capably handled. Even such often erratic actors as Lou Gilbert, George Mathews, and Jon Cypher give performances to be relished, and some of the briefest appearances manage to register. Equally to be commended are Robin Wagner's efficiently spare sets, David Toser's sensibly restrained costumes, John Gleason's graphic lighting, and Charles Gross's suggestively arranged musical underpinnings. Even the playwright deserves, after all, a lefthanded salute.

No SALUTE is due Joseph Heller's rather self-indulgent antiwar and anti-universal indifference play, *We Bombed in New Haven,* a belated foray into Pirandellism covering ideological and technical ground that is already flyspecked with footprints. Actually, the play has flunked out of every school it attended. At the Pirandello Academy it failed to master the basic precept that there can be no easy answers: here, when Sergeant Henderson unmistakably dies before our eyes and Captain Starkey sends his own son (however expressionistically depicted) to perish as the logical consequence of having sent all the other young men entrusted to him to their deaths, all the suggestive ambiguity evaporates and we are left with simple, tearful preachment. At the Absurdist Institute it did not learn the first lesson: to create figures that transcend reality (usually downward); here, at best, we have bitterly funny naturalistic types who fall on their fannies when the rug of reality is pulled out from under them. At the Brecht Cram School it never absorbed that racy deviousness that makes all characters tangily complex. At the Pinterian Mysteries, it was never initiated into the power of the unspoken. *We Bombed in New Haven* is a well-intentioned universal dropout. While Ron Leibman and Anthony Holland give incisive performances, Jason Robards is perfunctory. As for Diana Sands, as a comic Red Cross girl (a part that in this revised and cut version had shrunk to very little even before Miss Sands assumed it), how long will it take people to realize that, despite the wonderful fact of her negritude, she is an exceedingly limited, repetitious, uneuphonious and defiantly smug performer?

THE LIVING THEATRE strikes me as one vast act of revenge; as such, and only as such, it was moderately successful. Judith Malina and Julian Beck were imprisoned for non-payment of income taxes; they left the U.S. in indignation. Now they are back to incarcerate each viewer of any of their productions in hours of intermissionless hatred in the guise of justice, claustrophobia-producing closeness in the guise of communion, and semicontrolled hysteria in the guise of theater.

I have seen three of the LT's four productions, but I can recall those three only slightly more clearly than the fourth. Whether the basis for the LT's productions is Sophocles, Mary Shelley, Brecht, or actors' exercises, the result is one Hydra-headed monster behind whose slightly different heads lurks the same heart of bitterness, aggression and ferocity. What is the use of lurching into the aisles and mingling with the audience, of luring the audience up on the stage into mindless communal chanting and wallowing, when the only coherent words that issue from the performers are recriminations, imprecations and assaults on everyone and everything. It is all rather like the naked display of a body with one hideously hypertrophied organ: a vast fist shaken in the collective face of the audience.

The essence of the act is repetition. Some forty or fifty lines of dialogue (not counting ad hoc insult agons with equally incoherent hecklers) are reiterated over and over again, accompanied by assorted leaps, tumbles, fits, collapses, gyrations, crawling, strutting and running around. There is also a concert of inchoate noises from hums to shrieks, from moans to howls, including a few that are unclassifiable. The scene is a three-ring circus in which each ring strives to outshout and outbore the others. There is the center stage where the various rebarbative charades take place; the rest of the stage, along with the aisles and lobby, where performers and spectators commingle in an orgy of thoughtless and pointless bustle; and the seating area, from which people continually rise to hurl cheers, witless encouragement or dissent, or just decibels upon decibels of applause.

Let me illustrate. At one point various voices from the stage yell out: "Fuck the Jews! Fuck the Arabs! Fuck means peace!" A spectator sagely corrects: "Fuck means a piece of arse." But note the LT's typical aggression. Is this pacification? Is this a political program? Is this comic theater? Why should Jews or Arabs, or even hyenas in heat, submit to the embraces of the unwashed, unsightly, uncivilized untouchable members of the LT? And, significantly, the entire ensemble now howls in chorus: "Kill! Kill! Kill!" In the name of peace, of course. And there are four and a half hours of this, without intermission or even remission.

Not since the devils of Loudun has there been such an outburst of possession by demons in the name of religion—for the LT is a kind of religious pep pill for the disaffected and disoriented. Like those dark effusions of medievalism, this too is a form of ghastly therapy for performers and spectators in which they can release inferiority feelings that have festered into hatred in what seems like a new and triumphant form of theater.

During one phase of the evening, large numbers of spectators made a pilgrimage to the stage, formed an enormous circle with the performers, and proceeded to hum and sway, sway and hum. Several reviewers with reputations participated in this ritual. One young girl hobbled up on the stage on crutches. I am sorry to have to report that no miracle occurred; she had to hobble back to her seat. Rather like Lourdes, I imagine. But this is not theater, and if it were only labeled "mass therapy" two ends would be achieved: the exhibition would be an honest one, and people interested in theater would be spared the tedium of having to watch and review it.

If I must attempt a further description, let me do it in terms of four lacks. Wordlessness—merely sound, or sound disguised as utterance; humorlessness—no repartee from the performers when an occasional spectator does come up with a witty or pertinent comment; lovelessness—for nothing that is done here, even though some of it is adroit and well-rehearsed, has beauty in it, which is the only way to translate love onto the stage; and looklessness—there is almost no one on that stage (and this goes also for the spectators who join in) who looks even moderately worth contemplating. One reviewer gushed about how nice it was to see actors who don't look like actors. Why should they—when they aren't. The trouble is, most of them don't even look like people.

In sum, The Living Theatre treats us to a threefold fascism: the fascism of mercilessly inflicted vulgarity and boredom, the fascism of global intolerance, and the fascism of profound disrespect for human creativity and art.

·　　·　　·

"You seem a little subdued lately," says a wife to her husband. "No. Reading a life of Napoleon, that's all," he replies. It is a non sequitur. But it could mean something. A great man's life cramps a small man into nothingness. Or it might mean that to a frivolous woman concentration looks like dejection. Or it might show the husband's evasiveness scaling absurd heights. Or it could just be a putdown. Or . . .

This same husband is interviewing a sexy girl applying for the job of secretary to him. "I understand your last employer touched your body too much." "Not too much. One touch was enough." "Oh, you left after the first touch?" "No, not quite." The girl is a fake: at the first jolt, she tumbles off her high moral horse. No, that's not it; we pretend to hate something, yet we temporize, compromise, live with it. No, no: the whole thing is absurd—what business have employer and job applicant to discuss such an intimate, ticklish subject—and in such matter-of-fact terms? But no, isn't it rather that . . .

These are the ambiguities, ambivalences, verbal ambidextrousnesses that we have come to expect from Harold Pinter—some of us with delight, some of us with awe, and some of us (myself included) with a skepticism tapering into indifference. The above quotations are from *The Tea Party*, which, along with another one-acter, *The Basement*, has insinuated itself onto the stage of the Eastside Playhouse. Originally, both plays were written for television, but like a previous and better Pinter TV play, *The Lover*, they have infiltrated the stage. Either the theater is so impoverished that it must reach into such godforsaken corners as television for its sustenance, or Pinter is so great a playwright that even his marginalia must be mounted. A pretty pass, either way.

In *The Tea Party*, a leading bidet manufacturer and self-made man marries a young and pretty second wife the day he hires a seductive new secretary. But the wife has a brother with whom she keeps playing around. Hard to say whether in jest or incest. And the secretary is—what? Teasing our hero? Playing dumb? Actually dumb? Wife and brother-in-law come to work for our hero—or to haunt him. They seem to consort and conspire even with the secretary. Or he may just be having delusions. Even his children by his former marriage taunt and defy him; or is he imagining it? He is losing his eyesight even though his ophthalmologist can find nothing wrong with his eyes. Of course, the doctor, too, behaves in a faintly ominous way. At a final tea party, the man demands that his eyes be bandaged; even his hearing seems to be fading in and out. Or there may be a whispered cabal against him. He is symbolically castrated with a Ping-Pong ball and falls into catatonia.

But all this by strange little stages. At one point, in mid-office, during work, out of a clear and seemingly unambiguous sky, the hero proposes to his secretary, "Come on, then, tackle me!" What is this—a sportive sexual advance? Or just an exhibition of male strength and superiority? Or does he intend to tackle her right back and crush her, secret sadist that he may be? Or is he just plain bonkers? The two young sons (circa eleven) converse: "Children seem to mean a great deal to their parents, I've noticed. (*Pause*) I've often wondered what 'a great deal' means.—*I've* often wondered what 'mean' means." Even Henry James wouldn't have made his most ghostridden children discourse like C. K. Ogden and I. A. Richards. But this is theater of the absurd. Fine, but in Beckett and Ionesco I can tell what is being absurdified. Here, are these children older and deeper than their parents? Or are they merely imitating their parents? Or are they imitating Pinter?

In *The Basement,* a young man and his girl move in on the fellow's former roommate. The visitors take over his bed and copulate before him. Soon the men are rivals for the girl, or perhaps woo each other through the girl. She switches over to the host, then pits the two viciously against each other. Finally, the story begins anew with roles reversed: the former host, with the girl, arrives in the same apartment—in which the other chap is now the put-upon host. In this one, Pinter rather tips his hand: the play telescopes itself, and through the wrong end of the telescope: we not only see what is coming, we are also made aware of how small it is.

James Hammerstein has directed adequately, and the canny Ed Wittstein has designed sets that can perform anything: turn themselves inside out, take off this way or that, be two different things at one time; whatever a TV camera can do, they can do better. Hitherto Wittstein's performing sets had been in the service of producers' economy; now they have ascended into the higher realm of author's metaphysics.

The acting in *The Tea Party* is not up to that brooding yet split-second finesse that Pinter requires. Only Valerie French is, besides being ineffably alluring, always able to suggest emotional chain reactions that may blow up a world; and John Tillinger has an idiotic affability so unilaterally disarming that his smile must be a secret weapon. In *The Basement,* alas, all three performances are base.

Baudelaire saw man traversing a forest of symbols, but that is much more manageable than a jungle of ambiguities at the center of which lurks a dreadful nothing. Everything is made to seem both harmlessly banal and fearfully menacing—in fact, Pinter is writing fearjerkers. We may say of him what the bidet manufacturer, blowing up at his wife's sinister praises of her, says of his secretary: "She's not so bloody marvelous. She's all right. But she is not so bloody marvelous."

"OUR PRESENT business is general woe"—thus Albany sums up the Lincoln Center production of *King Lear*. It is unwise for a company that has been having trouble with plays of average difficulty to undertake what is probably the most profound and arduous play ever written. A large and respectable body of critical opinion holds *Lear* to be unproduceable, and if the current mounting achieves anything, it is to corroborate that opinion.

But *Lear*, I persist in believing, can be done; even in this lamentable version there is some good. Ming Cho Lee's sets—though they are heavily influenced, like almost everything else here, by the Peter Brook-Paul Scofield production—nevertheless have great dignity and sweep. The three semidiaphanous gray panels, pockmarked walls with the wattles showing through like the skeleton of a decomposing cadaver, ascend obsessively out of sight. The suggestions of pillars and ceilings that are variously added to the raked, jutting trapezoid of the main stage thrust out at us like a jeering gray tongue, are austere almost to the point of blightedness. When lightning tears across this décor during the heath scene, the entire set becomes a ghostly colossus come to haunt that exiguous puppet, man.

John Morris' music is mostly an electronic hum, sometimes rising to a martial flourish, but generally remaining a discomfiting, almost subliminal rasp, as of distant, indifferent gods filing their finger nails. It is properly chilling, except when it tries to double as thunder and becomes an antiphonal gong prissily punctuating Lear's outcries. But, then, the storm scene is a well-nigh insoluble problem.

There is one good performance: Philip Bosco's Kent. I wish the vocalism did not come so close to being a Gielgud impersonation, but as eclectic sounds go, that is a good one. Mr. Bosco has clear, crisp speech, a presence that cleaves its surroundings like an ice breaker in polar waters, and whether he is showing tender concern for his liege or gruffly challenging scoundrels, the manly ripeness that, according to the play, is all. (But if that famous line wasn't actually cut, it certainly was thrown away.) Tom Sawyer's Oswald was not uninteresting with his petty official's snottiness, and John Devlin would make a lithe, supple-voiced Cornwall if he could forget for a moment that he is supposed to be a villain and allow his actions rather than his attitudes to speak for him.

Beyond these, disaster. Except for a handsome head, Lee J. Cobb has nothing of Lear about him. Like Scofield, he chooses to underplay the part, but whereas Scofield had a characterization (however much I disagreed with it), Cobb has, or conveys, none. His Lear is one long, weary shuffle. From the start, he seems tired, defeated, unregal—not even a foolish autocrat, only a slow, rusty steam engine rolling over the most magnificent part in our poetic theater and painstakingly flattening it out.

Cobb is given to slouching, standing pigeon-toed, and making commonplace gestures (except for one memorable trademark of Willy Loman: a prankish *shtetl* elder tossing two bent fingers over his right shoulder and about to launch into a dance—fine in *Salesman,* out of place in *Lear*), and he shows no real energy anywhere. Even when he fulminates, he does so in a synthetic, earthbound way, never quite shaking off a basic lethargy. His line readings are arbitrary, prosaic, with a laggardly pacing exacerbated by a prodigality of pauses popping up all over, as if he were reading from very fine print in growing darkness. Moreover, he forces his voice into a double-bass register, where it often becomes an amorphous rumble; at other times, as if to escape from this manhandling, his voice flings itself into a giddy falsetto, inappropriately equipped with a Jewish singsong. Finally and most gravely, neither the lapse into madness nor the purified emergence from it is given apprehensible contours: Cobb's Lear does not grow in stature, he merely inches into oblivion.

The rest of the cast is bad; not undistinguished, spotty, or weak, but bad. Stephen Elliott's Gloucester is one of the emptiest performances I have ever seen: rote garbling untouched by human mind. Robert Stattel's Edgar is shifty and churlish enough to damn him without Edmund's machinations, and Stacy Keach's bastard is a squeaky, moonfaced yokel. Charles Cioffi's Albany is an ambulatory hoarse whisper, and René Auberjonois' Fool more of a Pantaloon. Patricia Elliott, as Regan, postures like a silent movie star and, though her elocution is good, speaks with gooey affectedness. Barbette Tweed, as Cordelia, is an insipid debutante with quavering voice and listing stance. As Goneril, Marilyn Lightstone is all blatant attitudinizing, and possessed of a face that cannot be countenanced.

Much of the blame must rest with Gerald Freedman's catastrophic staging, which is one part Peter Brook and two parts nothing. Freedman, who is quite good with farce, often makes *Lear* into one. In the heath scene, he will have four actors moping in a straight line across center stage, with absolutely no suggestion of man's smallness in space. He can make the noble Kent behave like a petulant child in the stocks, the blinded Gloucester wriggle about as if he were doing an Irish jig on his back, and Lear, through much of the sublime closing scene, sprawl like a sack of potatoes across Cordelia. Always at a loss with poetry (his *Tempest* in Central Park was a similar fiasco), Freedman actually cuts some of the noblest lines. In a sense rather different from Shakespeare's, he gives us a great stage of fools.

THE ADVANTAGE of *Promises, Promises* over Billy Wilder's film *The Apartment,* on which it is based, is that it cannot be taken seriously. The slimy young man trying to succeed in business, in the greater reality of film, really did pimp for his adulterous superiors, even if he was prostituting only his apartment; and when this hero was proffered as being cute as a button, a blighting moral twilight fell on the whole operation. In the musical, a genre in which there is as much built-in alienation as anywhere from Kabuki to Brecht, moral sleaziness becomes a shoeboxful of shenanigans, tunefully Terpsichorean turpitude raises chuckles rather than hackles, and victims don't get shafted—merely goosed.

The difference is sealed by the casting of the protagonist. Jack Lemmon made C. C. Baxter into a squirt as slippery as a banana peel. As Jerry Orbach plays him in *Promises, Promises,* you feel he is lending his apartment to the executives out of sheer philanthropy and expects it to harbor nothing worse than advanced handholding. Orbach once played a puppeteer in *Carnival,* and long exposure to those jiggling dolls gave him an incurable case of puppetitis. His face has assumed an all-purpose expression of bittersweet astonishment, his head dangles forward, his limbs flail, flutter and shuffle— the whole thing is done with rather lax strings. And it sets the tone for this roundelay for machiavellian marionettes.

What comes out is an amiable show. Neil Simon piles his own, somewhat more palliative gags on top of those of the Wilder-Diamond screenplay, but because the Niagara of wisecracks has to be interrupted for songs and dances, it never becomes so stultifyingly nonstop as in straight Simon farce. This makes the songs welcome, even though Burt Bacharach's score is ground out ad infinitum by a fancy note-grinder—from Bloomingdale's, not from the neighborhood hardware store. The songs provide a sort of tintinnabulous respite from the relentless one-liners, comic turns, and blackout sketches of the book; and when the music's monotony becomes numbing, there again is Neil Simon for comic relief.

Promises moves along briskly under Robert Moore's intelligently casual-seeming direction, Robin Wagner's sets have a workmanlike chastity, and Donald Brooks's costumes are sassy even if not up to his *couture*. Best, perhaps, are the dances of Michael Bennett, worked around the rough edges and into the crevices of the plot with smoothing, filling ingenuity, arising from situations that beg to be choreographed and doing them full comic-poetic justice. The cast functions with flair—although Edward Winter is too wooden a villain to drive even the dumbest broad to suicide, and Jill O'Hara rather brightens that part, anyway, though her usually lovely voice (*Hair, George M!*) here sounded, owing to a condition that I hope is temporary, as if her dentist has forgotten his drill inside her throat.

There is one truly alive musical number, "Where Can You Take a Girl?" for a quartet of randy executives, rattlingly well performed and staged. And there is one thoroughly canny performance by A. Larry Haines as a disheveled doctor whom any girl would like by her bedside as a teddy bear. A show that has Haines delivering lines like "You know, Baxter, for a fink you've got a lot of class" is not all tin. Things being what they are (and don't ask me what!), *Promises, Promises* is the least negligible musical around.

MURRAY SCHISGAL's *Jimmy Shine*, on the other hand, is so puny a play that if it were not extended in all directions by Dustin Hoffman's life-giving performance, it would barely be discernible to the naked eye. Mr. Schisgal, whose fame rests on his ability to infuse bloodless old contrivances with the plasma of pseudomodernism, specializes in the portrayal of lovable failures. We've had the lovable failure as rapist, typist, intellectual, suicide—everything but microwave physicist—and here he is now as a pristine archetype: the lovable failure as universal lovable failure. Of course, the whole thing (apart from not being a play but a series of more or less labored skits) is a huge lie. If Jimmy Shine were so lovable and bright, he could not be such an ecumenical failure at everything from school to girls, from New York to San Francisco, from painting to living. And if he were propelled by such a categorical imperative to fail, he could not reek lovableness out of every pore. But Schisgal knows his audience, which seems easily as useful as knowing how to write a play.

What does it mean that in less than a week we have had three openings in which the hero is (sometimes openly, sometimes in thin disguise) a young Jewish schnook—*Promises, Promises, The Goodby People,* and *Jimmy Shine?* It means that these shows are tailor-made for the typical Broadway audience: Jewish is what they are, young is what they imagine themselves to be, and the lovable schnook is what they can feel luxuriously superior to. Producers know this unholy audience hunger, and cater to it with a zeal verging on scrupulousness. Now, there is nothing wrong with plays tailor-made to fit an audience if you think of plays as three-piece, or three-act, suits; I like to think of them as art.

Of course, it is not so simple as that. There are the organizations (charitable or uncharitable) that offer theater parties, and the mighty handful of booking agents who lead their equine customers to the same muddy waters. But, finally, it is the customer who could refuse to drink, or, rather, refuse to gaze at his face patronizingly reflected by a stagnant pool.

But to get back to *Jimmy Shine.* In the supporting cast, Rose Gregorio, Eli Mintz, and especially Cleavon Little stand out under the sight-gag-filled direction of Donald Driver (with an assist from Harold Stone). As Jimmy, Hoffman elaborates the film role that made him famous, Benjamin in *The Graduate,* and he is a thoroughly charming actor with sufficient off-beat idiosyncrasies to make him a spiny delight. He has his own truth, but the role is merely a Jewish fantasy figure: the successful failure, the yearned-for antiself of all dissatisfied successes, a figure to cosset as well as patronize. Out of such contradictory but not irreconcilable impulses, one creates a languorous, lukewarm footbath for the soul.

SPEAKING OF LUKEWARM, there is the hit of last year's London season, and thus the almost axiomatic hit of this year's New York one, *Hadrian VII* by Peter Luke. Luke has taken Frederick Rolfe's imaginary autobiography and stressed its wish-fulfillment aspect even more by sandwiching it in between a prologue and epilogue showing the starving "Baron Corvo" as an odd, slightly uncouth, but brilliant little man—a sort of misfit of genius or a greater Jimmy

Shine. The far-flung and abstruse range of Rolfe's mind, the tortuously eccentric but captivating style of his writing have been simplified and toned down. Whereas the novel is worldly, complex and learned, the play is neat and homespun. In both, an obscure Englishman who flunked out of the priesthood has miraculously become pope and shocks the College of Cardinals by his humane reforms, until, having finally won them over, he is gunned down by a fanatical enemy. But, for example, in the novel a cardinal who asks what is to become of the reformed priesthood if the faithful do not provide free-will offerings, is told by Hadrian, "Then starve and go to Heaven, as Ruskin says." The play omits the dependent clause, and the line gets a big laugh. In other words, an erudite reference to the grave Ruskin is turned into a bluff, papal wisecrack. This is the leveling process that informs the adaptation.

The supporting cast, like the staging and set design, are undistinguished—though Christopher Hewett, as the Prepositor-General of the Jesuits, carries on as if wearing a soutane made one automatically guest of honor at a drag party. But the play's cynosure is the gushed-about performance of Alec McCowen in the title part, which had disappointed me in London, but there I sat in the front row, an unfair vantage point. From farther back, I was confirmed in my belief that this was not great acting, only craftsmanship of a very high order. I was particularly aware of a vise-like technique visibly cramping the character to be given life, of a finely tooled artistry never allowed to melt into art. The difference, I suppose, is this: a solid, technically accomplished performance is one in which the actor does exactly what you imagine yourself, *mutatis mutandis,* doing with the part; a great performance is one that surprises you with things that would never have occurred to you. McCowen, who was an admirable Fool in Peter Brook's dubious *Lear,* performs Rolfe-Hadrian like clockwork. Art races ahead or lingers; McCowen makes everything tick.

THE MINNESOTA THEATRE COMPANY has brought us Aeschylus' *Oresteia,* renamed *The House of Atreus.* The play seems a questionable choice, but its adaptation is unquestionably a fiasco.

Tyrone Guthrie, who staged this *House* is a clever director, whose work is, with some honorable exceptions, ingenious, hearty, and vulgar. His laudable aim is to make the classics popular, but his dubious method is to lower the works to the most common denominator rather than to raise the audience to the level of art. "English-speaking communities," Sir Tyrone once wrote, "are, like the Romans and unlike the Greeks, fundamentally philistine"; and, like the noblest Roman he is, he proceeded to give us an Aeschylus pitched midway between Seneca and Plautus.

On the noble hand, there is the authenticity: masks, cothurns, men in the women's parts, choric song, etc.; on the philistine hand, there is much farce wantonly introduced, the actors in female roles camping around, and real women popping up in the chorus after all. To make characters like the Nurse and the Delphic priestess into grotesques is bad enough, but when the goddess Athena nancingly falsettos, "Here I see an assembly bizarre, to say the least" or "Hmmm, it's a dilemma," something mighty funny seems to have happened on the way to the Parthenon.

There is, I think, reasonable doubt whether something as static, ritualistic, and—let us drop the *gros mot*—antiquated as Aeschylus' drama can still hold its own on our boards. But it should surely have been done in one of the several good available renderings rather than in this by John Lewin, who is neither a classical scholar nor a poet, but merely, it would appear, Sir Tyrone's lackey. His stabs at grandeur are as awkward as his shots at wit already quoted; thus we get "lying open-mouthed to the icy stars" or "an altar stone swilled with my father's blood."

But the main trouble with Guthrie's production is that it fails even in its attempts at authenticity. The mask and cothurns were used in the Greek theater largely because the enormous distance from spectator to actor would make unaided human features and statures appear indistinct and puny. Similarly, the use of masks with their built-in megaphones, and avoidance of actresses with their voices weaker than men's had to do with increasing the audibility. In the much more intimate confines of a modern theater these effects, aside from seeming alienatingly archaic, emerge out of proportion—yet proportion or measure was the very ideal Greek drama strove to achieve.

When one is in such fundamental disagreement with a production, it would be petty to itemize grievances, though a protest must be lodged against the flat, commonplace quality of many of the voices, and against the catamite-like performances of Cassandra and Electra, both by Robin Gammell. As in his film of *Oedipus Rex*,

Guthrie tried to make *House of Atreus* look even pre-Aeschylean, mythic; alas, it takes a lot more to make this *House* a Homer.

From what I read and hear about Jerzy Grotowski's Polish Laboratory Theater, it is a mixture of epigonous expressionism, displaced Catholicism, some Eastern influences, and a good deal of Artaudian ritual of cruelty. This may or may not work on stage (I have not seen it), but it came an absolute cropper on ninety minutes of Ford Foundation-sponsored prime time, when Public Broadcast Laboratory played host to the Polish Laboratory Theater in a gesture of alembics across the sea.

Televised for us was *Akropolis,* a monumental drama of 1904 by Stanislaw Wyspianski in which Biblical and Homeric tapestries in Krakow Cathedral come to life on the eve of Christ-Apollo's triumphant resurrection. Grotowski has changed this into a black concentration-camp comedy in which Auschwitz inmates enact the story of Jacob and the tale of Troy. Done in Polish, and as an attempt to use the audience and auditorium in a spatially revolutionary way, the event fell conventionally flat on American television.

The telecast began with an off-screen voice trumpeting in heraldic tones the name and date of the program. We then saw Lewis Freedman, a producer of PBL, assuming for this occasion the look and tone of someone whose eyes had just seen the coming of either the Messiah or the invaders from Mars, but was not yet quite sure which. In a constricted, portentous voice he introduced us to Peter Brook, the advanced British director, who was to prepare us for the work of the even more advanced Polish director.

For the next half-hour, Brook, looking like a hieratic Cheshire tabby, proceeded to tell us about a theater that (as he wrote in his book) "responds to a need the churches can no longer fill." Actually, close to half the time was devoted to pregnant pauses while Brook's brain braced itself for the profundities it was about to propound, making these pauses one of the most expensive quarter hours of dead air ever televised. Yet the utterances so elegantly framed by golden silences were, if anything, even more vacuous. Thus Brook told us that Grotowski's greatest contribution was a kind of rhythm that would make our very breath come in a different way—which I took to mean that instead of breathing in iambs we would forthwith breathe in trochees.

We would witness, we were further told, genuine horror, a sort of black mass. This again made me wonder why the mass, black or white, should be put on the stage. Before I could pursue my speculations about equal theatrical opportunities for masses regardless of color, creed, or raison d'être, I was brought short by the tidings that it was not necessary to be moved by this kind of theater, any more than the Negroes in Harlem had to be moved while watching from their windows a murder being committed. While Brook was thus, apparently, integrating the Kitty Genovese case, I was trying to puzzle out what would be left to the New Theater; it had already abrogated rational persuasion, and was now divesting itself of emotional suasion as well. But presently I was informed that to applaud this theater, as was done in Edinburgh, was a cop-out, the craven reduction of vatic reality to mere histrionic entertainment.

This raised even more questions in me, but they were all quashed by the exhortation that one had to watch Grotowski's troupe with an open mind, lest the great new beauty pass one by. Why, I wondered, are we never ordered to keep an open mind when, let's say, *King Lear* is shown us, every bit as difficult and eternally new as *Akropolis* though it be? Doesn't genuine art ravish us whatever position we keep our mind in—provided only we have one—and require no special pleading for that abandonment of critical standards that masquerades as openmindedness?

Brook's mystagogic pronouncements were intercut with scenes from *Akropolis* flashed at us out of left field; they seemed bewildering this way and déjà vu later, when they were repeated verbatim and picturatim. Freedman reappeared to usher in the play with voice and face even more solemn than before, and here for an hour were the denizens of Auschwitz playing the violin while being pushed around in a wheelbarrow, batted back and forth between fellow inmates like human punching bags, miming grotesque copulations in a bathtub, and prancing about in little mincing hops. There was much Polish dialogue, but we got no subtitles, only an occasional snippet of Freedman's awestruck voice explicating that Jacob was now wrestling with the angel or that Helen was being abducted by Paris.

But you could not identify any of them: everyone was in burlap shifts and clodhoppers, women's parts were played mostly by males (the one actress looking just as masculine and homely as the men), and there was not a moving, expressive face in the lot of them.

Well, not quite. Grotowski plays to audiences of about fifty, broken up into clusters of two or three, around whom the actors circulate, perorate, gesticulate, and all but wrap themselves. For this London filming, a charmingly youthful audience was assembled, and doubtless indoctrinated with the sanctity of this ritual Brook calls "Holy Theater." A lovely, touching sight they were, all those mod kids reverently frozen in their Cecil Gee or Tuffin & Foale finery. Hopping around them in Polish were Grotowski's scarecrows, reducing both the concentration-camp nightmare and the theatrical experience to a Keystone Komedy with a dash of bitters. And on the small home screen this emerged as the reduction of a reduction.

One approves in theory PBL's decision to import Grotowski in effigy after the State Department foolishly reneged on promised entrance visas for the troupe. But suppose that suddenly, for political reasons, an embargo were placed on Russian caviar. Would it help to have a jar of it displayed on television for ninety minutes—even in full color? At that, this might be better than an hour of hermetic Polish cavortings prefaced by half an hour of hermeneutic English gibberish.

THERE IS A WORLD of difference between novelty and newness, a new look and a new substance. The musical *Celebration*, with book and words by Tom Jones and music by Harvey Schmidt, has a sleek up-to-dateness about it but no innovation, to which it desperately pretends. Schmidt and Jones, two Texans whose initial New York gusher, *The Fantasticks*, proved a veritable Old Faithful, specialize in a kind of artful simplicity, a bluff Texas folksiness with just enough of a show-biz veneer to create a seeming new-found land on the musical map: Tin Panhandle Alley.

Newness, genuine newness, is a state of mind, not a new suit with a different cut to it. You cannot, on the one hand, write *110 in the Shade* and *I Do! I Do!*, their almost archetypal commercialism bedizened with such tricky novelties as hiding the orchestra behind the backdrop or reducing the cast to two; and, on the other, try to bring the theater—the musical-comedy theater, at that!—back to ritual. Yet that's what Schmidt and Jones imagine they have done with *Celebration*. It is extremely doubtful whether ritualizing is what our theater needs, but in any case *Celebration* is to ritual as a Wassermann test is to Aztec human sacrifice.

Not that it doesn't try. The set is a proto-Shakespearean stage surrounded by a dark, shaggy, patchwork cyclorama looking like a giant crow's plumage turned outside-in. In the prologue, the twelve

Revelers, who will later assume a variety of ancillary roles, appear in Pogoish prehistoric garb on top of latter-day Panty Hose and Capezios. Then the combination Harlequin, *gracioso*, *raisonneur* and M.C. steps forward—for some reason he is called Potemkin, perhaps because to Schmidt & Jones, Eisenstein is still the *dernier cri*—and sings the title song, which draws a parallel between a prehistoric New Year's Eve celebration and a modern one (after all, as the lyric says, "We're like those ancient people in a way . . . If you'll just assist us with your imagination,/ We'll make this place a celebration"), but there's something bankrupt about a celebration that has to borrow a cup of imagination from its clientele.

We get Ed Wittstein's cunningly devised masks, totems, props, and bits of scenery affixed to long staffs carried on like the standards of Roman legions but with cutouts and paste-ups instead of SPQR on top; we get a truly barbaric torch flaming downstage and a jagged, antediluvian sun in the sky; but what do we get by way of ritual? A schmaltzy fairy tale about a brave little orphan fighting for his orphanage and for a sweet young girl who, in order to rise as a star, is willing to fall as an angel (or so she thinks, but Schmidt and Jones and we know better). Fighting whom? A vulgar, jaded, mean old zillionaire called Mr. Rich. Ah, but innovative invention is at work even here: his full name is Edgar Allan Rich, which students of American literature and show-biz Southern will recognize as a po' pun. Assisted by Potemkin, later betrayed by him, then again magically saved by this mercurial fellow, Orphan wins Angel (so named because she was to have enacted a fallen angel at Rich's New Year's entertainment—but, of course, it's more symbol-minded than that!) away from ruthless, randy Rich. How? With nothing more than his lovable pubescence and the help of God.

For Jones, in both book and lyrics, has a remarkably flatfooted imagination—if I may be permitted to make two not very distant extremes meet in metaphor. Just think what Giraudoux or Anouilh could have done with this contest of youth and eld; with an innocent young girl who wants to be rich, famous, and fallen; with the elaborate stratagems to bring back a senescent nabob's virility. Jones comes up with nothing better than Orphan singing "Hey, Mr. Somebody in the Sky,/ Would you guide me to/ What you can do/ For this orphan in the storm"; Angel singing and talking about what she wants to achieve "before these golden days,/ These Lolita days are through" by means of exercises for her breasts: "They're still a bit small by *Playboy* standards, but they're on their way." Rich com-

plains, "I haven't had an erection in twenty-five years," and sings
about his lost youth, "Where did it pass? [Chorus echoes: "Arse,
arse, arse!"] All those days of tender/ Splendor in the grass?/ Those
endless one-night stands,/ Those ever-ready glands?" (The show is
full of those tedious clean dirty jokes.) And what is Potemkin's
remedy? He has Orphan and Angel sing a love song and embrace
in front of Rich. A kindergarten aphrodisiac!

Mr. Schmidt's music finds keeping up with the Jones lyrics quite
easy. There is almost no melodic line whatever; it all sounds like
a figured bass waiting for a musical idea, and instead getting orchestrations. The invisible nine-piece brass band tinkles, jangles, bangs,
boings and glockenspiels for all it is worth, while the singers go
through their unending *recitativo*—not quite *secco;* let's say demi-
secco.

But I'll tell you where the innovation does come in: in the shape
of God. Never have I been exposed to a more God-ridden musical:
in lyrics, repartee, stage business, plot development—everywhere
there's God. Not, of course, without some confusion: in one song,
Darwin, along with Marx and Freud (rhymes with "void," but then,
most of Jones's rhymes are veud), is accused of killing God. In
another, called "Fifty Million Years Ago," the whole theory of evo-
lution is submitted as proof of the divine spark in man. Now, the
resurrection of God on the stage of the Ambassador would indeed
be quite a ritual, but, coming from Schmidt & Jones, God is no
more convincing than any other innovation.

If these gentlemen wanted to write a truly modern fairy-tale or
ritual musical, how about one where Little Orphan Jackie rejects the
dashing English leading man for hoary Mr. Aristotle Socrates Rich,
and the whole thing ends, not, as here, with a prayer, but with a
great pagan ritual celebrating Mammon? On Broadway, *that* would
be avant-garde.

SPRING, 1969

RIOT
by Julie A. Portman

BIG TIME BUCK WHITE
by Joseph Dolan Tuotti

CITIES IN BEZIQUE
by Adrienne Kennedy

MORNING
by Israel Horovitz
NOON
by Terrence McNally
NIGHT
by Leonard Melfi

CEREMONIES IN DARK OLD MEN
by Lonne Elder III

ADAPTATION
by Elaine May
NEXT
by Terrence McNally

A PRODUCTION OF HAMLET
by William Shakespeare
produced by the APA-Phoenix Repertory Company

Quoat-Quoat
by Jacques Audiberti

Hamlet
by William Shakespeare
with Nicol Williamson, directed by Tony Richardson

In the Bar of a Tokyo Hotel
by Tennessee Williams

The theater in our time has been such a parade of trivia and ephemera that it has considerably shortened the critical life span. One after another, Mary McCarthy, Eric Bentley, Susan Sontag, Robert Brustein, Richard Gilman (I am naming the more interesting figures, without endorsing them equally) either gave up completely on drama criticism or drastically limited their activity in the field. Specific reasons for these total or partial withdrawals are various, but behind all of them may be found disenchantment with our New York (or American, or world) theater, and a sense that covering it regularly is not an occupation worthy of a serious critic—in fact, the more seriously he takes *the* theater, the less worthy of taking up his time.

I have often wondered whether I should apologize—to my readers, to Thespis or to myself—for obdurately persevering, year after year. Besides covering the local theater for *The Hudson Review,* I have done so, at one time or another, for *Theatre Arts, Commonweal,* educational television and now for *New York* magazine. The chief argument against this kind of endurance is that one eventually finds oneself reviewing the same play over and over again. There are some honorable exceptions, needless to say, but basically it is the same Hydra-headed monster that keeps rearing further brainless heads, regardless of how many of them adverse criticism, public displeasure, and time itself have amputated. Again and again the same play with footling variations: with music or without, with literary pretensions or without, with or without a homosexual angle, lurching into sensationalism or sliding into sentimentality. Favorite types have been the Jewish family comedy, the generation gap comedy, the pseudo-absurdist farce (genuine absurdism is comparatively rare), the Negro problem play (serious or satirical) and, of course, the marital, pre-marital and extramarital sex caper. What all these genres usually have in common is cynical or simple-minded, audience-pleasing or self-indulgent manipulation of reality. As a result, critics find themselves running out of epithets, images, and epigrams with which to express their unchanging fundamental revulsion. And they quit.

Why, then, do I persist? Is my stock of synonymous pejoratives, derogatory tropes, antipathetic aphorisms inexhaustible? Is this, in other words, the triumph of rhetoric over good sense? Or is it force of habit, stubbornness, masochism? Or is there simply nothing else I can do? The real reasons, I think, are unflagging (and perhaps unholy) curiosity combined with an unquenchable hope, and an enjoyment of arts and crafts other than those of the dramatist. The curiosity centers on just how the theater will appropriate, digest, and, in most cases, vulgarize current issues and ideologies. The hope, obviously, attaches to the rare good play that finally does show up, no matter how bad things are. By other arts and crafts, I mean, of course, everything from direction and acting to lighting and design. And I also mean the occasional ability of the commercial playwright to construct something less than art but pleasing in its skillful workmanship.

But there is also something else. My position is, I suspect, comparable to that of the writer in a totalitarian state who prefers life under an almost unbearable system to emigration to a liberal but foreign land. He clings, first, to his roots, and, secondly, to his language. For better or worse, I feel at home in the theater—and where else would I go? Only film and literature are, among the arts, in better shape than theater, and I write film and literary criticism for other publications. But theater is my first love, and to it I must always return. As for going into other aspects of the theater, yes, I do a little teaching and lecturing now and then, but drama criticism is my language, and I cannot settle down where that language is not spoken. To be sure, there is a difference: the, let us say, Russian writer is, however stuntedly, engaging in a dialogue; whereas the noncommercial critic is cut off by a thick wall from the predominantly commercial theater. Yet there is a hope in this very fact that is the Russian writer's undoing: even the walls have ears.

One of the newer phenomena in New York theater is Negro militancy, and the two most militant Negro plays of the season thus far are both by whites; you are free to draw your own conclusions.

Riot, an improvisation conceived by Julie A. Portman, was highly successful in a Boston church basement but much less so in a New York
one. It is a piece of central staging that switches back and forth
between a panel discussion on racial violence and the enactment of
ghetto conditions, rioting, counterattack by the National Guard, and
finally chaos. The debate is among a white Jewish liberal, a white
Buckleyite conservative, a Negro moderate, and a Black Panther.
They are all perfect clichés. As for the choreographed interludes,
which range from extracting live but doped rats from trash cans to
troops sticking bayonets almost into the customers' faces and, in the
end, a blackout punctured by strobe lights and hideous siren wails—
this has been called "gut theater," and if one could stay at home and
send only one's guts to the show, they might indeed respond to it.

The problem with agit-prop theater, quite aside from the fact that
it has nothing to do with art, is that it can be used only as an incen-
tive (to incense), but not as a preventive. You can leave a theater
stirred up to strike, loot, burn or start a revolution; but how can you
be aroused to passivity: conciliatoriness, moderation, tolerance, or
what have you? There is no inflaming into coolness. As for horrible
warnings, there is no evidence that anything you can fling before
today's audiences (hardened by movies and TV, where the horrors of
war and violence have become the daily pap) has much of an effect,
short of drawing their blood with those bayonets. But even Kenneth
Tynan has not yet advocated that. One of the doped rats, by the way,
recovered sufficiently to wander off into the vicinity of my legs, but
the only lesson I derived from this was to avoid further plays about
race riots in church basements.

A POTENTIALLY more effective piece of political theater is *Big
Time Buck White*. A Negro organization with many white members,
the Beautiful Alleluiah Days, or B.A.D. for short, is about to hold a
meeting. The leader is one Jive, a shrewd operator, and the guiding
spirit is an agitator named Big Time Buck White (a typical sample
of the verbal wit) whose coiffure seems to have been designed by
Buckminster Fuller out of clock springs. B.A.D. is funded by Whitey's
government and foundations, with their customary suicidal wisdom.
The theater audience, which includes several plants, represents the
black and white members and supporters of B.A.D. The first part of
the play has four of the group's officers trying to enlist one another's
help to supplant Jive. As they jockey for power, they insult or threaten

one another, the audience, Negroes and whites in a spate of racial jokes of all colors: black, white and off.

Finally, Jive enters and puts them all in their places. Then Big Time stalks in and proceeds to answer questions from the audience. Some of these come from actor-plants, others are real. If they are easy or stupid questions, Big Time deals with them with quiet smugness. If they are difficult, the rest of the cast irrupts with jibes and jeers, getting him off the hook. The underlying message is clear enough: "We'll snuff out your souls like white birthday candles." The play was conceived in Watts, where apparently there are several writers' workshops, some acting as lightning rods, some as tinder for racial revolt. The most interesting thing about the play is that it was written by a white, Joseph Dolan Tuotti, which makes *Big Time Buck White* a play either of self-hate or of self-protection for the come-the-revolution days. The white liberals and black liberators in the audience perform an unholy ritual. They laugh explosively at every shallow joke ("We'll put you on the white list"; "He owns a white dog"; "Rubber Band [a particularly unbalanced type] is going to be our next pope"; "If thirty million Negroes . . ." "Thirty million? Shit, I know a million myself!" etc.); they jump literally out of their seats, if not their skins; at every bit of inane braggadocio they applaud and cheer convulsively. Yes, the audience is integrated all right, but for what? For a political black mass, and from mass to massacre the distance seems appallingly short. Let us have thoughtful plays on the subject, even satirical ones, but none of this facile fanaticism.

A GENTLER type of Negro protest play, I gather, was *God Is a (You Know What)*, which, however, I was unable to catch. But I did see *Cities in Bezique,* by Adrienne Kennedy, at the Public Theatre. This is the opposite sort of thing: the Negro masochist play. Mrs. Kennedy's earlier work, *Funnyhouse of a Negro,* was also a psychodrama in which a Negro girl is haunted by ghosts like Patrice Lumumba and realities like her boyfriend and family whirling around before her real or mind's eyes. In the first play of the new double bill, *The Owl Answers,* a light-skinned Negro girl (Mrs. Kennedy is half-white) daydreams on the New York subway when Shakespeare, Chaucer, William the Conqueror and Anne Boleyn burst in on her. They have been her tutelary deities, but now proceed to judge her. The scene shifts almost simultaneously to St. Paul's in London, where the girl's white father is being buried; and to the Tower, where the four aforementioned worthies are detaining the girl; and also to the South, where she was born from her black mother's affair with the richest white man in town, only to be palmed off on the black minister to whom her mother is married. Interwoven with these imaginary scenes is the real situation: the girl has picked up a young Negro on the subway, taken him home to her Harlem hotel room, but becomes hysterical when he tries to have sex with her and throws him out. Above the revolving stage on which all this swirls about hovers a papier-mâché dove backed up by a corpulent Negro clad in white feathers—presumably two-thirds of the Trinity (which is you know what). They flap their wings and arms from time to time, and the man makes pregnant but inscrutable pronouncements.

To complicate matters further, figures peel off their outer layers and become other figures; thus Anne Boleyn strips off her Boleyn gear, leaves it standing on stage, and becomes the girl's mother. The sarcophagus is removed from around the dead father and he becomes the living white father; he strips off a mask and becomes the putative black father. The heroine herself is identified as "She who is Clara Passmore who is the Virgin Mary who is the Bastard who is the Owl," and the other characters have similarly multiple identities one inside the other, like those Russian peasant dolls that keep yielding further, smaller dolls, down to a tiny, doll-shaped sliver. The language is all desperate pseudopoetry, and the tone is harrowing, harried self-accusation and an occasional striking back. Rather than move linearly, the play tries to spiral inward, but actually just revolves in place, or in no place. The language is pretentious and obscure, the metaphors either banal or impenetrable. And the second play of the bill, *A Beast's Story*, is even more arbitrarily arcane. The painful thing about this is that it seems to justify its utter lack of drama by calling itself poetry, and tries to prop up its poetastery with theater devices for buttresses. And those flying buttresses out of Mrs. Kennedy's centrifuge can really knock you unconscious. It is a depressing thing when poetry and drama are played off against each other to the detriment of both by people capable of neither.

The most satisfactory play on the Negro question was Israel Horovitz's *Morning*, the opening one-acter of the triple bill by three authors, *Morning, Noon* and *Night*, Circle in the Square's first venture onto Broadway. (*Noon*, by Terrence McNally, is dazzling but sticky and oppressive; and *Night*, by Leonard Melfi, is opaque and inscrutable, and mostly good for sleeping.)

In *Morning*, a Negro family wakes up one day turned white by a miracle of God. A white bigot with a gun is seeking Junior, the family's teenage son, for allegedly deflowering his daughter. The white man ends up painted black and becoming the victim of the new whites. The idea is simple and symmetrical, and though one condones its premise—*plus ça change* . . . —it is hardly news. But Horovitz has style. For one thing, he uses obscenity in a creative way, turning it into incantation, into an obsessive, funny, nightmarish obbligato. For another, his wit can brush you lightly even as it cuts deep. Someone says in passing, "for although black, God is a light sleeper . . ." In the most off-handed way a huge assertion is introduced; the wildness is heightened by the notion of God anthropomorphically in Morpheus' arms; and final absurdity is achieved by the seemingly meaningful collocation of "black" and "light," which traps us into a non sequitur. Ultimately this suggests that the whole black and white dichotomy may be likewise nonsensical. A playwright who can cram so much so comfortably into so little is to be watched with attention and delight.

What also makes *Morning* (originally called *Chiaroscuro*) remarkable is what it does with language. The white Negroes begin by sounding like minstrel-show characters but end speaking in toney Park Avenue accents. At first they use obscenities as casually as conjunctions; by and by, their language is purified and elevated. But, ironically, as their speech becomes more refined, their behavior becomes more outrageous—more outrageously white—and the comic disparity of form and content in human beings constitutes the play's strongest comment. It was extremely well acted by three of its five actors: Sorrel Booke, Jane Marla Robbins, and Robert Klein. In the other two plays on the bill, which need not occupy us here, these three fine actors also did well against crippling odds.

NATURALISM IS A TOUGH old bird: no sooner had it died out of Ireland in the twenties than it was reborn in America in the thirties. The fifties saw it rise from its ashes in England; in the sixties, still mottled with cinders, it begins to unfurl its wings in the Negro theater. From Synge and O'Casey to O'Neill and Odets; from Osborne and Wesker to Lonne Elder III there is a line to be traced, and Elder's *Ceremonies in Dark Old Men* at the Negro Ensemble Company is a hearty reminder that a play can have solid contemporary significance, dramatic as well as social, without obligatory obeisances to the avant-garde. Chronicling the disintegration of a Harlem family after the death of the materfamilias, it manages to be honest, amusing, angry and sad; if it scales no artistic heights, neither does it sink below a respectably craftsmanlike level. Only when this absorbing comedy-drama reaches for tragedy does it lose its footing. But we can say that on new ground the phoenix of naturalism has been reborn. It is a phoenix too infrequent.

In a sinewy, no-nonsense way, *Ceremonies* presents the untenableness of any type of ghetto existence. Without preaching militancy or resignation—or anything else—it holds up typical lives for our fellow feeling, self-recognition, and truer understanding. It is directed in an admirably workmanlike way by Edmund Cambridge, and has three faultless performances by Douglas Turner Ward, William Jay, David Downing. Mr. Elder has a remarkably sure way of weaving together grave and frivolous strands, and his ability is confirmed by the fact that, though his concern is with a minority, his voice is for all men. When the protagonist, an aging widower, refuses to believe that a scheming girl may not really love him, he exclaims defiantly: "When I love 'em, they stay loved." To which his son replies, "Nobody's got that much love, man!" and the theater is forthwith neither black nor white, but drenched with the hard, untinted light of truth.

What makes *Ceremonies in Dark Old Men* even more fascinating is the audience. While the whites are enjoying it for the sound play it is, the Negroes are, for deeper reasons, ecstatic. At last they recognize their own hopes and frustrations, their own problems and strategies implanted on the stage; the jokes have a familiar seasoning, the tears a known taste. Watching an audience draw from the theater something that sustains and humanizes it is a joy to behold for anyone—for anyone, that is, who has been less and less able to see the temple for the moneylenders.

AN EQUALLY, though differently, happy occasion is the double bill at the Greenwich Mews, *Adaptation* and *Next,* a sassy but over-extended skit by Elaine May followed by a remarkable play of Terrence McNally's, both aptly staged by Miss May. *Adaptation* derives its title from what appears to be a TV participation game in which the contestant enacts his life, but soon proves to be a garishly typical American life trying to make like a laugh-riddled TV game. Under the cheerily blighting eye of a Games Master, the Contestant moves from square to square, accumulating or losing putative points. The secret, we are slyly told at the outset, is that the security square, which he must find, could be any one he chooses to consider so—a handsome conceit, which Miss May, unfortunately, fails to follow through on.

She does, however, put the amiable square of a Contestant through a concatenation of prototypical outrages from birth to death (from a premature coronary—from overwork and overworry—for which the technical term in America is "natural causes"). The trouble here is that a cabaret sketch does not take kindly to being stretched into a one-act play, and that these mundane disasters have already been explored a little too sedulously by, among others, Miss May and her former partner, Mr. Nichols. Moreover, these problems are beginning to have a fifties look about them, whereas we have progressed, as Robert Graves foresaw, "to yet more boastful visions of despair." Gabriel Dell plays the Contestant with such Candide-like charm that the lack of technique or development in his performance is barely perceptible, and his supporting cast is quite adequate.

Next, however, is a small but invaluable treasure-trove. A fat, messy-lived, middle-aged assistant cinema manager is being given a grueling physical and psychic induction test by a fat, robot-like female sergeant. The army has clearly fallen on lean times, but this particular fat morsel fights with comic desperation to stay out. It is hard to say which are funnier: the questions, with their dehumanized yet scarcely exaggerated absurdity; or the answers, with their mixture of anarchic innocence and ironic grotesquerie. Starting out realistically, the play climbs by slow but sure steps into a surreal realm in which the uproarious and the horrible blend into a huge belly laugh that is also a heartache. The playwright accomplishes the almost impossible feat of making every line tearingly funny, yet at the same time relevant to both character and deeper significance. Uncannily, jokes top jokes, gushing forth so fast that you almost don't dare laugh lest you miss something funnier still. But simultaneously a life is unfolded before us, riotously and pathetically real, and downright sinisterly close to our own.

If the play—with the possible exception of the ending, which, though justified and effective, is perhaps a bit too rushed—works as well as it does, the achievement is in no small measure James Coco's. Mr. Coco, who was immensely funny earlier this season in another McNally play, *Witness*, here creates a tragicomic characterization that is both meaningfully large and lovingly minute. At no point does the actor allow us to feel only amused or, later, only chilled; there is always a portion of pity in our laughter, and of admiration in our queasiness. The performance, in its complexity, is Kafkaesque. Only one other actor in America could have played this part, Zero Mostel, and Coco has the advantage of greater self-discipline. *Next* is the funniest—and pointedly funniest—play I have seen in some time, and if McNally can keep piling comic play on play as he here manages to pile comic line on line, he may yet graduate to Parnassus.

The APA's latest offense is rank; it smells to heaven. It is *A Production of Hamlet* [*sic*] by William Shakespeare, based partly on the corrupt First Quarto of 1603, and partly, I would guess, on the First Folio of a play by Tom Stoppard, entitled "Hamlet, Ophelia, Claudius, Gertrude, Polonius, Rosencrantz and Guildenstern and the APA Are Dead." We begin with the rest of the cast lying dead onstage as Horatio delivers their epitaph; gradually, the corpses rise and proceed to enact a series of *tableaux mourants*. The text is vile, the cutting is vicious, and the staging, acting and elocution could not be disimproved on. This is not even a production, merely a traduction of *Hamlet*. Ellis Rabb, the artistic director of the APA, both directed and stars in it, and I can merely echo Hamlet's prophetic soul: "Let the doors be shut upon him, that he may play the fool no where but in's own house."

Take a typical example of Rabb's drawn-and-quartoed staging, the encounter with the Ghost. The Ghost looks like a creature begotten by the Maharishi Mahesh Yogi on a Tibetan mountain goat: it comes in crawling on its belly surrounded by dry ice, then rises and lunges into caprine capers. Its shredded shroud billows about it like a homemade tickertape reception. Its voice comes out of the p.a. system; so far, so good—or, rather, so far Gielgud, in his production. But Rabb provides an echo chamber and multiple tapes, so that the Ghost can chant trios with himself and sound like Peter, Paul and Mary. When Barry Bostwick, playing the Ghost with characteristic APA diction, pronounces "Adieu!" as "Hat-choo!" it sounds like a hay-fever epidemic among loudspeakers. Hamlet exclaims, "Rest, rest, perturbèd spirit," and promptly lies down to take a nap himself, with the Ghost briefly mounting him. No mere Oedipal Hamlet this, but one suffering from passive necrophilia—something undreamt of even in the First Quarto's philosophy.

Rabb's delivery of his lines cleaves the general ear with horrid speech. He carefully accentuates the least important word in any phrase, puts in pauses where none is conceivable, and races over the most poetic passages as if they were difficult tongue twisters he had triumphantly conquered. He tends to slink about with a glazed expression, as if he were doing Lady Macbeth in her sleepwalking scene. He may, actually, be suffering from sleeping sickness, for he frequently stretches out on the floor, or on the two benches that serve as the production's entire furnishings, in recumbent postures that would look good only in a sarong. His eyebrows continually attempt to out-ogive a Gothic arch, and he is enormously fond of suddenly dropping to his knees, which should soon, like the time, be out of joint. Watching Rabb's Hamlet places one at the midpoint between uncontrollable laughter and intense nausea, which cancel out into stunned silence.

The rest of the cast is no better. Richard Woods's Polonius and Richard Easton's Claudius are a pair of mobled queens; Michael Durrell's Laertes looks common and is well-nigh unintelligible. As Horatio, Donald Moffat has at least the honesty of *looking* senile, so that we are prepared for the torpor of his speaking. Amy Levitt's Ophelia, truly "of all ladies the most . . . wretched" seems to be afflicted equally in lymph, thyroids and adenoids. Her diction is lamentable ("horrors" becomes "Horace"), her accent plebeian, her appearance such that it is surprising to hear her directed to a nunnery rather than to Slenderella. Betty Miller's Gertrude is barely noticeable in the early scenes, which makes me doubt her ability to do much with the later, bigger ones—but by the midway intermission I realized that this heavy-handed revel was more honored in the breach than the observance, and decided that by leaving I myself might my quietus make.

James Tilton's black drapes, ascending and receding to seeming infinity, are effective as well as economical, and, combining with his beams of light descending from vertiginous heights, give the stage a nicely Gordon Craigish look. But against such austere and awesome backgrounds, the APA actors look even punier, perhaps in emulation of Craig's supermarionettes. The costumes, by Nancy Potts, are a disaster: either Carnaby-Street goods, or plain street clothes over which are draped travesties of academic gowns. The latter are made either of moth-eaten banquette covers from Tad's Steak Houses, or from the latest flower-pattern Martex towels (highly absorbent). Truly, these were the trappings and the suits of woe. Conrad Susa provided some routine alarums and excursions along with some more alarming excursions into electronics. All in all, it would be hard to imagine more matter with less art.

It is well known that every comedian's secret ambition is to play Hamlet. I therefore ardently hope that Ellis Rabb's *Production* will not be seen by people like Woody Allen, Jackie Gleason, Milton Berle or Carol Channing—it might provide them with the final, catastrophic encouragement. The people—the *only* people—who should see it are the foundation executives and private citizens who have showered money on the APA, when they could, more profitably, ha' fatted all the region kites, or endowed a cat hospital. To think that the powers at Lincoln Center once invited Ellis Rabb to take over their repertory company! It is a thought more chilling than anything seen on the Lyceum stage, and most of that is sub-zero.

What is behind this is obvious enough. Rabb and his troupe are trying to make their *Hamlet* as daringly different as possible. What they don't realize is that their most orthodox attempts to hold, as 't were, the mirror up to past *Hamlet*s would result in a difference quite sufficiently glaring.

IT HAS BEEN a week in which the New York theater has done nothing—nothing in the literal, not the usual figurative sense. For drama, one had to go to the Met, where productions of *Wozzeck* and *Peter Grimes* proved not only good musical theater but fine straight theater as well. So I will write at some length about Le Tréteau de Paris, a visiting French company (every year a different group is sent over under this aegis), even though by the time these lines appear the program will consist of two wretched little plays by Arrabal and not of the far more interesting opening bill, *Quoat-Quoat* by Jacques Audiberti.

Quoat-Quoat is the work of a poet whose torrential verbiage mounted the stage without paying much attention to the requirements of the theater. Audiberti's plays, except for a descent into boulevard comedy like *L'Effet Glapion,* are weird mixtures of symbolism and surrealism, absurdism and vaudeville turns. What distinguishes Audiberti from the absurdists proper is his immensely greater concern, indeed preoccupation, with language. At its worst, this degenerates into logorrhea; at its best, it produces brilliant sallies of wit or lyricism; in between, it secretes inkily opaque whimsies that are nevertheless fascinating.

In *Quoat-Quoat,* a young man of the past century sets out on a sea journey to Mexico on a secret mission, which results in his being condemned to death by the quirky, sinisterly quizzical Captain, to whose daughter he betrayed his secrets. After much odd behavior from these and other queer personages, it emerges that, unbeknown to himself, the young man is not a secret agent after all, and doesn't have to die. It also turns out that the Captain is no ordinary captain but God, who, when the young man insists on being shot anyway, gets disgusted with his boat, his passengers, human suffering, and the endless repetition of it all. By means of a magic fragment from the sacred stone of the now departed Mexican god Quoat-Quoat, our Captain blows everything to bits.

In this sort of abridgment the play makes more sense than in its actual gyrations, permutations and self-contradictions, which bedevil us with continual veering from sense into nonsense, from poetry into prolixity. But Audiberti has a superabundance of what our American theater so sorely lacks and foolishly rejects: language. His words sparkle, incandesce, shoot up in flames; in a twinkling, they have changed from St. Elmo's fire into a conflagration, from a glowworm into a fire-breathing dragon. Take a couple of random examples, rather on the simple side for Audiberti. The Captain tells the young man, "*Avant de vous plaindre de l'injustice, attendez qu'elle vous aie distingué.*" ("Before complaining of injustice, wait for it to have singled you out" or "honored you.") Now, the idea of misfortune as a badge of honor could not be expressed more concisely and evocatively than by the verb *distinguer,* which implies both selection and distinction. But *distinguer* also means "to take notice of," and forthwith the young man is punningly reduced to a nonentity: someone so puny that misfortune might not even be able to spot him.

Or consider, simpler yet, the young man's passionate, anguished outcry to the captain's daughter: "You are pink as a crocodile!" A crocodile is anything but pink, yet the very coloristic absurdity, the metaphorical color-blindness, admirably conveys the young man's frenzy. To call a girl pink is to praise her, flatter her: for our mere flesh-coloredness to be elevated to the hues of the rose is a compliment. But this compliment is here revoked as quickly as it is issued, countermanded so vehemently that it is sent hurtling into preposterousness. In fact the very pinkness, the color itself, is incriminated, unmasked as it were, by being identified with something hideous, false and carnivorous.

The staging by Georges Vitaly in Jacques Marillier's elegantly unfussy set and costumes was persuasive, and there were tidy performances by everyone, with special accolades due Jacques Dumesnil as the Captain and Jean-Pierre Leroux as the quixotic youth. M. Leroux, from the profile, bears quite a resemblance to Jean-Louis Barrault, and his stage personality and acting technique are no less reminiscent of that great actor in his youth, which was his best period.

Actually, language is not completely missing from the contemporary American theater. Tennessee Williams, in his privileged moments, could manage it superlatively. In Albee's best plays, *The Zoo Story* and *Who's Afraid of Virginia Woolf?*, there are some formidable flights of word power; the fact that they are often at the service of bitchiness does not diminish their lacerating splendor. Jack Richardson, in *Gallows Humor,* did estimable things with language; Sam Shepard, John Guare, Israel Horovitz, Terrence McNally and a few others are not exactly strangers to it, either.

Nevertheless, language—or rather the lack of it—has tended to be the undoing of the American drama. A playwright like Clifford Odets, who was at least aware of the problem, could not cope with it, except in dialect, which, for all its sure-fire short-range effects, is ultimately a decomposing agent. His attempts at fine writing always turned into verbal pratfalls; much the same tumbles have overtaken Arthur Miller. Others, like Lillian Hellman, were at least clever enough not to try for anything special in that direction, in which their talents manifestly did not lie. Some of our woollier avant-garde playwrights use language oafishly even in its lowest registers, resembling in this no one so much as their opposite numbers, the commercial Broadway scribblers they like to anathematize. Even our greatest dramatist had to struggle titanically for control over anything but the plainest words. It is not until his very last plays, and even then intermittently, that Eugene O'Neill was able to command a more elevated, more poetic style.

This is the era of the withdrawal of the word from the theater. The word has been superseded by everything from grunts to mere stage directions, or stage indirections and pandemonium. Yet the living word is more alive and more durable than a barrelful of so-called Living Theatres.

THE PORTRAYALS of Hamlet through the ages constitute a psychiatric nosography. There have been Oedipal Hamlets, homosexual Hamlets, transvestite Hamlets (played by actresses), Hamlets suffering from aboulia, dementia praecox, and diverse other ills the mind is heir to. But it remained for Nicol Williamson's Hamlet to suffer from an acute sinus condition. Williamson has a tendency to sound like an electric guitar twanged away at, with fearful symmetry, high-low, high-low, high-low. It is a maniacal singsong, so stringently nasal that the lips seem to part only for visual effect.

Add to this the accent. It has been called Midlands, North Country and Cockney with a loose overlay of culture. Only Henry Higgins could correctly place it South of the Beatles or North of the Stones and identify the veneer as grammar- or council-school. But even Colonel Pickering could tell that it isn't Hamlet. I am not against modernizations, and am all for trying to find a contemporary equivalent for the Sweet Prince; but surely Jimmy Porter or Bill Maitland or some other Osbornian professional griper is no conscionable correspondence for the exacting idealist turned cosmic malcontent.

Then there is the appearance. The equine head with the mad Viking locks jiggling behind the nape and neck; the unweeded, piratical beard and brushwood mustache; the obstreperously lower-class features; the gangling, skulking body; the legs, not exactly spindly, but with more than a hint of octopus about them—all this is unsettling and finally disruptive. It is not tradition that I cling to, nor am I indulging my snobbery: in real life, a prince can look and behave very unlike a prince. But as our innovators are first to point out, a play is not real life but an artifact that creates its own universe and laws, and though these can be bent to accommodate certain idiosyncrasies, scant good can come of breaking them.

Which is not to say that the dogged Williamson doesn't have some very effective moments. The entire business with the Players, the Play Scene itself, the scenes with Rosencrantz and Guildenstern work very handily, with the real sparks flying when Hamlet rubs R. and G., those two dry sticks, together. Even in some of his weakest moments, as in the Closet Scene or in the soliloquies, Williamson will erupt from among some shabbily or indifferently read lines with one or two that possess marvelous shrewdness, animal vitality or insidiously ironic scorn. And there are times when the tenor of querulous fault-finding does rise to metaphysical exasperation, and the play becomes—not quite poetry, but a superb prose translation. Not for long, however. The good prose soon collapses into aborted poetry.

What about Tony Richardson's staging (if Richardson's it be, for rumor has it that with Williamson for a star, you don't need a director)? A few things work: best of all, the Play Scene (particularly the truly clever dumb show done as a cheerfully Anglicized *commedia dell' arte*); almost as good are the scenes leading up to and away from this. In other words, the production has a substantial middle and extremely rickety extremities; for rising action, it substitutes bulging action. The crowd scenes, with the noted exception, are dully staged, partly perhaps because the production was arena-style in London, and insufficient time was allowed for tucking it behind a proscenium. The courtiers are few in number and pallid of aspect; they mostly hold poses, rather like a frieze in very low relief.

Even bravura scenes get badly mangled. The killing of Polonius falls flatter than the old man's corpse, which never gets dragged around by Hamlet. The near-demise of Claudius at his prayers lacks all suspense and punch. The Hamlet-Ophelia scenes substitute sexual horseplay for authentic feeling. And the final holocaust is perfunctory, with the King standing about like a fatted calf, just waiting to be slaughtered, and no one in the entire court thinking of coming to his defense. When there is directorial invention, it is likely to be of the foolish kind, as when Hamlet's letter is delivered by the sailors way-laying Horatio, one of them jumping him and sticking a dagger at his throat, while the other tauntingly holds up the missive before him —sheer nonsense. Worst of all is the Ghost, who does not even seem to be the ghost of Hamlet's father, but that of Ellis Rabb. He is her-alded and accompanied by electronics that sound like Kennedy Airport at peak-traffic time, and remains invisible somewhere way above our heads, presumably in a Boeing 707. His (Williamson's) voice is heard on a multiple-echoed, fadeout-ridden sound track left over from some C-grade horror movie.

The supporting performances are mostly quite insupportable. Francesca Annis is lovely and charming as the sane Ophelia, but un-moving as the mad one. Patrick Wymark's Claudius is a bloated gnome who keeps chopping up, indeed garbling, his lines; Mark Dignam's competently old-hat Polonius would be equally at home in any *Hamlet* from Betterton's to Irving's; Constance Cummings' Gertrude is both wooden and inconspicuous—a bashful marionette; Gordon Jackson's Horatio might as well be his Scottish simpleton schoolmaster in *The Prime of Miss Jean Brodie;* Michael Pennington's Laertes is a brash mod lout; and Peter Gale's Osric a faggot's night-mare. Roger Livesey is a delightful actor who tragically lost his voice; to cast him here (First Player, Gravedigger) is less to help than to pillory him. Jocelyn Herbert's set is pedestrian and unadapt-able; her costumes plagiarize the dawn: the whole cast seems to go about in russet mantles clad. But it's good night, sweet prince, all the same.

•   •   •

For some time now, any number of epigones have been turning out better imitation Tennessee Williams plays than Williams himself has written lately. As a result, Williams was forced to abandon self-imitation for self-parody and produce several rather unsuccessful Williams pastiches. But *In the Bar of a Tokyo Hotel* does not even qualify as poor parody: it makes *The Seven Descents of Myrtle* look, by comparison, like a triumphal ascent of Parnassus. It is a play by a man at the end of, not his talent (that was long ago), but his tether —a man around whom the last props of the dramatic edifice have crumbled and who, in an impotent frenzy, stamps his feet on the few remaining bricks. That someone who was a major American and world dramatist should come to this is a tragedy almost unparalleled in the annals of literature, never mind drama; it would have been a fit subject for a play by the former Tennessee Williams.

In a sense, to be sure, Williams has always been a confessional playwright—and even a confessional being, going from psychoanalysis to Catholicism. But the trouble with his quasi-confessional plays is that they are not honest confessions. In them, Williams appears either as a middle-aged hysterical woman (archetype: Blanche DuBois), or as a sensitive, oversensitive young man, a little too good (*Orpheus Descending*) or too wicked (Sebastian in *Suddenly Last Summer*) for his milieu. These are the two sides of the same trick coin (it always comes up tails): on the one hand, the fear of aging and death and the insatiable hunger for sex as both specific and panacea; on the other, the artist's victimization by society or his own overexacting vision. While Williams was in command of his art, these disguises and fragmentation hardly mattered. Now, in this play, he comes closer to fusing the two falsely complete personas into his one genuinely incomplete one; but, alas, he still lacks the guts to do it, and besides it is too late.

In the Bar of a Tokyo Hotel has aging, man-hungry Miriam trying to seduce the Japanese barman while, unseen by us, her celebrated painter-husband, Mark, wrestles in his room: naked but for a spray gun, he is trying to evolve a new abstract style on canvases spread on the floor. Miriam, amid reminiscences, philosophizings and boasts ("To absorb Kyoto would not take me long. I am a woman of great vitality . . . I can absorb a pagoda in five minutes"), tempts the engaged and faithful barman with four hundred of a currency named— especially for Williams, it would seem—yen. She wants to hold his private parts, which has become one of her favorite activities; she recalls a young man she met at a Long Island party, "and I manipulated his genitals all night long . . . mmmm, yeees!" "Reverence is sinking," she tells us; "I leave it in the hands of a reverend."

These existential and essential gropings are interrupted by her paint-besmirched husband's stumbling into the bar. He is suffering from some unnamed mental and physical breakdown, keeps falling down, and has to have his drinks poured into him like a baby its milk. "I didn't know it till now!" he raves; "The possibilities of color and light discovered all at once can make a man fall over in the street." (To say nothing of the number of times they can make him fall over on the stage.) There are virulent recriminations between husband and wife—she wants him to fly back to the States for treatment while she rattles through Japan for a treat—and as he collapses, she goes off on an assignation, or looking for one.

Here, again, all the old Williams paraphernalia is hauled out. Thus recollections of how Miriam first seduced Mark come straight from Maggie the Cat's hot tin roof, and Mark's outcry, "When I heard you clipping flowers outside my studio, I sometimes wished that what you were clipping were . . ." conjures up the castration motif from *Sweet Bird of Youth*. (By the way, unfinished sentences such as the above are the stock-in-trade of this play; there are scores of them lying around supposedly pregnant and tremulous with the burden of the unsaid. Actually, a platitude with its tail chopped off is nothing more than a bleeding platitude.)

In the second act, Mark's art dealer, Leonard, arrives from the States at Miriam's summoning. Besides being oily and faggy (he obviously deals mostly in oils and fags), he has no character and adds no dimension to the play, but chiefly mouths commonplaces: "A painter with Mark's talent is a restless creature that lives in his own private jungle. . . ." Mark staggers down again, this time with his face mottled with bloodied bits of toilet tissue he has applied to his shaving cuts, and we get three-way recriminations and philosophizings. Williams now indulges in constructions like "Nobody ever gave me a magnum, or a quart, or a baby's bottle of confidence" or "I know [death] will have to remove, wrench, tear the bracelets off my arm," which may be described as piling anthills upon molehills. Finally, just before I did, Mark expires, and Miriam, realizing that she and Mark were one and the same person, instead of feeling liberated, moans out Williams' most autobiographical line: "I have no plans. I have nowhere to go."

Two other dismal devices need recording. One is the arbitrary irruption of cheesy fag-barroom jokes like " 'Never worry, never fear!

Someday you'll meet a rich old queer.' A recent addition to the Mother Goose book." The other is splintered dialogue that proceeds thus: "Something has . . ." "What, Mark?" "Affected my . . ." "Affected your . . . ?" "Vision . . ." This could perhaps be called hemistichomythia. As for the acting, with the exception of Jon Lee's pleasantly straightforward barman, it is every bit as awful as the play deserves. Particularly intolerable are Anne Meacham's distastefully uninflected, foghorn monotone (people have flunked out of drama school, in other days, for better performances than this), and Lester Rawlins' gallery owner, spineless down to his very delivery. Herbert Machiz has directed as is his wont: mostly downstage-center and belting it out at the audience. It's the worst scandal to hit Tennessee since the Monkey Trial.

Summer, 1969

Che!
by Lennox Raphael

No Place to Be Somebody
by Charles Gordone

Promenade
by Maria Irene Fornés

Oh! Calcutta!
by Kenneth Tynan and Jacques Levy

Three Sisters
by Anton Chekhov
produced by the American Shakespeare Festival
Stratford, Conn.

Black Electra
based on Sophocles' Electra
produced by the New York Shakespeare
Festival's Mobile Theatre

Twelfth Night
by William Shakespeare
produced by the New York Shakespeare Festival

Chushingura
produced by the Grand Kabuki Theater of Japan

A Patriot for Me
by John Osborne

THE THEATER seems to have become self-conscious about its laggardliness. It has rightly been accused of trailing behind the other arts; and though, frankly, being behind music and the fine arts may be one of the few points in its favor, catching up with the movies would be all to the good, if only the theater could do it spontaneously, easefully, without that self-awareness that always characterizes writers to whom innovation is more important than writing. And if it only knew which way is forward.

Nowadays, forward tends to mean diving headlong (I use the metaphor advisedly) into sex, nudity and aberration. The pinnacle of this so far (and at this writing I haven't yet seen *Oh! Calcutta!*, which may delve deeper, or, at any rate, lower than anything hitherto) was an ephemeral little item called *Che!* (Where, one wonders, would the avant-garde be without the exclamation mark?) Written by a twenty-nine-year-old West Indian, Lennox Raphael, but one who has lived in New York many years—or, in any case, long enough to learn the uses of publicity—it was preceded by a feelthy-whisper campaign heralding the performance of real live sexual intercourse right before the audience's eyes. Moreover, *Che!* was being done at the Free Store Theatre on the Bowery, a place that looks *louche* enough to suggest one of those dives in pre-Castro Havana where, indeed, not plays but players were mounted.

Whoever had heard about the promised goings-on, and could afford the tickets that came up to $10, crowded into the previews. The drama critic of *Time* was there with Alan Brien, the former London drama critic turned columnist, and both reported rather despondently that the proclaimed intercourse did not come off. To be sure, the management had announced that coitus would occur only when the actors felt like it—presumably so as to preclude prosecution under the Fair Trade Act. From other preview-goers I gleaned the same doleful refrain: "No penetration!" Came the opening night, and so scarce were tickets that, even as a critic, I was given only one seat, despite the danger of autoeroticism to which this was exposing me. There were bleachers rising on three sides of the acting area, and in the middle of the front row of the center section sat, once again, the *Time* critic. Not far from him was Irene Papas, the actress, flanked by two very young hippies, one of whom she kept clutching as things got steamier.

The theater was swarming with men wielding still or film cameras, most of them from news media that were clearly not going to use this material except perhaps for office orgies. A man from Channel 5 later boasted that they had even got the striped cat that crossed the stage during the copulation scene.

After the bleachers were full to bursting, the sporting event commenced. It was performed without intermission or intromission of which only the former was regrettable, as it prevented a hasty departure. *Che!* has four characters: El Presidente (ostensibly LBJ), who is nude except for a belt and an Uncle Sam hat; Che Guevara, who is dressed in something halfway between fatigues and hippie gear, which he removes when a climax is in the offing, though for mere rising action he just takes out his penis; a Nun, who sometimes wears only a coif and sometimes only panties, and, briefly, neither; and an androgynous creature, Mr. Mayfang, who apparently represents the C.I.A., and is enacted by a girl in a sort of silver-shimmering space suit with transparent plastic cups over her breasts. In the center of the acting area stood a studio bed, a few other props were scattered about (such as an urn for simulated defecation), and in one corner stood a cage in which sat a man in a gorilla suit who occasionally strummed a guitar.

Che! consists of the characters' spouting two kinds of dialogue at one another. Either pseudoprofound, e.g., "Put your pain in mine.—I adore conscience!" or "My identity will resort to violence"; or sexual and pseudowitty, e.g., "I am up to my arse in lovers," or "I am the Bride of Christ.—The chosen clit?" or "You taste like colored rain.— I used to taste like tequila.—The vintage has gone sour." (The last during oral intercourse.) Mostly there are gleeful word games: "After a while even the sun goes down"; or "You deserve the best.—His deservation is a ten-minute head." One gathered that the author is illiterate from this "deservation," from "Pulling rank will impotentize your perfection," from "Responsibilization is futile" and, in a general way, from the entire play. For the recordization, I'd like to quote a few more samples of Raphael's wit: "I came like hurricane and rain.— It is your Latin background." "Nobody sleeps with an ape for kicks.— I'd sleep with a rhino for a fuck." And here is some of Raphael's imagification: "His tongue is a laser" or "Passion is cunning and blue."

The action consists of an endless series of simulated copulations and minor perversions in performance groups of one to four, from autofellatio to the Nun being mounted by the gorilla (well, let's be generous; this might be a major perversion), from the men alternatingly performing fellatio on each other to continual grabbing of penises which, however, invariably fail to rise to the occasion. During the supposed *real* sex scene, the gorilla plucked his guitar with simian soulfulness, the lights turned discreetly purple, and Che and the Nun went at it hammer and tongues. But for all their dedication to Thalia (or, in case of malfunction, is it Melpomene?), and for all the aphrodisiac dialogue abetting them ("That's better than my Jesus Christ!" the Nun exclaims), and for all the cameramen's frantic leaping about the bleachers in pursuit of better angles (giving one intimations of a stampede by a herd of rutting chamois), the performers failed: the Nun remained, like the script, impenetrable, Che's organ proving, like the author's pen, a flaccid tool. The play ends with El Presidente shooting Che in a fit of sexual jealousy. The critic of *The Village Voice* devoted several pages to the play, which he found a serious drama about the sexualization of politics. The police, on the other hand, found it "public lewdness, consentual sodomy, and dissemination of indecent materials to minors." The show was closed after some three performances (no doubt to the grief of the *Time* critic who was so determined to get his kicks even by double proxy that he sent his girl friday to a press conference at which the penetration was to be conclusively consummated—but, once again, wasn't); the actors and staff were arraigned, and the case comes up in Criminal Court shortly.

If I go into all this in such detail, it is to show you what a ludicrous pass we have come to. Needless to say, theater of this type elicits condign criticism: most of the remarks I heard or read were lamentations on the ugliness of all four visible performers (the man in the gorilla suit may have been as beautiful as the Apollo Belvedere, but never disrobed), or accusations of "fag" and "dyke" hurled at Che and the Nun for never actually making it. It would all be funny if it weren't so sad; or sad, if it weren't so funny; or both sad and funny if it were not so imbecile. After the police closing, one more private performance was given for a group of assorted notables to solicit signatures on a petition in behalf of the play; very few, I gather, were obtained. But *Che!* has made theatrical history, and those involved with it will be able to make political if not theatrical capital out of it once the legal skirmish is over.

No Place to Be Somebody is a play that would pass more or less unnoticed were it written by a white dramatist. It is written, however, by a black playwright, Charles Gordone, and being hailed as something just short of a revelation. Most extravagant in his praise was Walter Kerr, who compared this first play not to the younger or lesser Albee, but to "the already ripe and roaring Albee of *Who's Afraid of Virginia Woolf?*" Well, roaring, to be sure. If I were Albee, I'd sue.

Gordone's play centers on Johnny Williams, who has made it out of Harlem to Greenwich Village, where he owns a bar, has a black and a white hooker working for him, and sleeps with the latter. He is awaiting the release from jail of Sweets Crane, crook and father figure, with whom he wants to make the big time. But Sweets comes out a dying and reformed man, who only picks pockets for sport and returns the spoils. Johnny is so furious he almost kills him. But in the meantime Johnny has become the lover of Mary Lou Bolton, a white college girl and political activist, daughter of a crooked judge who helped the Mafia. The Mafia is crowding Johnny, who decides to take them on. His white whore, in jealous despair, commits suicide. With Mary Lou's help, and despite her subsequent betrayal, Johnny almost makes it, but ends up, after numerous melodramatic twists, killed by his friend Gabe Gabriel, a young Negro actor-playwright. Gabe executes Johnny at the behest of Machine Dog, a black militant who, though he exists only in Johnny's mind, manages to be an extremely obstreperous symbol. Of course, the whole play may exist only in Gabe's mind, for he introduces every act with a monologue from which, alas, I could not deduce whether what followed was an act of invention or reminiscence.

There are various subplots: the efforts of Gabe, almost white though he is, to land a black part on Broadway; Shanty Mulligan's, (the white dope-addict bartender's) yearning to be a drummer and a Negro, and his eventual discarding of both the dream of blackness and his devoted black girl friend, Cora. There is the story of Cora, who ends up marrying a rich Negro and setting out to educate herself. There is also Melvin, the short-order cook who would be a ballet dancer, but is so shocked by the immorality of white society as to relapse definitely into cookery. There is the white whore who loves Johnny and dies for him, and the black whore who vainly yearns for him and kicks him in the crotch. And there is the ending, where Gabe does a transvestite act in widow's weeds that also manage to shroud the meaning of the symbolism.

Gordone has written a typical protest play, but he has chopped it up into short scenes to give it a novel-like quality, and he has added the monologues, the transvestite bit and the imaginary militant to raise the play out of naturalism. The attempts at heightening miscarry, and even the realistic foundation is shaky. I sympathize with Gordone's bitterness and understand his pent-up rage; it is his dramaturgy that I have little use for. He has tried to cram at least three plays into one; his characters, especially the white ones, tend to be schemata if not automata; his dialogue, though sometimes juicy, often deteriorates downward into banality or upward into grandiloquence. It is all rather like *The Time of Your Life*, with the rosy spectacles traded in for shades. As for Ted Cornell's direction, it is mostly a new kind of weightlifting, using decibels for dumbbells, and getting all the characters to beat their fists on whatever piece of furniture is nearest, as if they were *all* frustrated drummers.

The acting is wild and wildly uneven. Ronnie Thompson as Shanty and Laurie Crews as Mary Lou are hopeless; Paul Benjamin as Machine Dog rants on incomprehensibly; Ron O'Neal is unpleasantly narcissistic as Gabe, but Nathan George would be fine as Johnny if he could control his diction. Marge Eliot is a warmly convincing Cora, and Henry Baker a resonant image of injured dignity as Melvin. The others are passable or by-passable. But there is nothing in this play to make a big fuss about; if you want a true work of the imagination, read Walter Kerr's review.

Obviously, one cannot write a play as if no play had been written before. But one cannot even write a nonsense play as if none existed already. The three archetypal, seminal nonsense plays are Jarry's *King Ubu* (1896), Apollinaire's *The Teats of Tiresias* (1917) and Ionesco's *The Bald Soprano* (1948). From them, directly or indirectly, derive all our cubist, surrealist, dadaist, absurdist and whatthehellisthisist plays; most of them, alas, no mere derivatives but duplications, dilutions, defilements. For it is a mistaken notion that in the realm of nonsense (and I use the term in its widest application—one that includes a good deal of sense under the heading "nonsense") there is no danger of being an epigone, of bluntingly repeating past perception.

To be sure, it is easy to assume that in the domain of the illogical, the fantastic, the subconscious and oneiric, variety is inexhaustible, and that every new and slightly different juxtaposition of unrelated elements constitutes a new departure. On the contrary, I would say that nonsense is most repetition-prone: "My left shoe is an armadillo" and "A sacristan is a flying hexagon" strike me as much more nearly analogous statements than, let us say, "I want you" and "I need you." True differentiation—and, therefore, originality—exists only in the region of the rational, or that part of the nonrational that is susceptible to rational interpretation. It is in our consciousness that we are individuals; our subconscious is substantially unindividuated. That is why psychoanalysis is possible, and why so much of modern art is not. A Cage, a Rauschenberg, a Merce Cunningham (to pull three names out of the hat; it could as easily have been Warhol, Oldenburg and LaMonte Young) are not artists, just walking redundancies.

The avant-garde musical *Promenade* is a piece of attenuated camp that Clive Barnes has declared "a great show" and "a joy from start to finish." Maria Irene Fornés, the author, is a primitive. Now, you can have primitives in painting, but not in writing. For representational painting has a created world preceding and underlying it, so that the naïve artist (who is frequently a child, a crone or an illiterate) reproduces what he sees, and his very simplifications and distortions become his originality. But writing, imaginative writing, cannot merely trace the outlines of the objective world; it is creation *ex nihilo*. "His universe is his play," says Apollinaire of the dramatist, "inside which he is God the Creator." This requires an intensity of mind acquired, generally speaking, through culture and training, not available to the primitive.

In the preface to a couple of her other plays, Miss Fornés writes: "A true work of art is a magic thing. To comprehend magic we must be in a state of innocence, of credulity. . . . If art is to inspire us, we must not be too eager to understand." This could just as easily be a plea for spiritualism and the occult sciences; it is, in fact, the language of the quack. *Promenade* is an amphigory in which two prisoners escape from an imbecile jailer who pursues them; they arrive at a party of the rich where everyone is bored, jaded, promiscuous and vapid; with the help of a maid, they abscond with assorted valuables. In a park, they meet a quasi-demented old woman searching for her long-lost babies about whom she remembers nothing. All the characters somehow end up at the feebleminded but despotic mayor's party, where they must perform for their supper, indeed for their very freedom. The escapees end up in jail again; the mother pronounces them her children and inquires whether they have found evil yet. When they tell her they haven't, she abandons them with a song from which I quote because it is typical of both the lyrics and the dialogue of the show:

"There are many poor people in the world./ Whether you like it or not./ There are many poor people in the world./ But I'm not one of them./ I'm not one of them./ Someone's been stealing my apples./ But I'm not one of them./ I'm not one of them./ . . . People believe everything they hear/ Not what they see. Not what they see./ People believe everything they hear./ But me, I see everything." None of it approaches the wit and imagination of the three nonsense plays I cited earlier. Instead, it sounds like bad Gertrude Stein, and even good Stein is fairly hopeless.

Except for Al Carmines' music, which is a meretricious pastiche of everything from Puccini to Hanns Eisler, from the repertoire of ships' orchestras of the thirties to the scores of today's swinging Italian movies, the production is pitifully good. I say "pitifully" because it makes one bemoan the waste of talent. Though there are some quite incompetent performers (Madeline Kahn, Glenn Kezer, Pierre Epstein, Edmund Gaynes, Art Ostrin), there are others who are marvelous—especially Ty McConnell, Gilbert Price, Margot Albert, Alice Playten, Florence Tarlow and George S. Irving. They sing, act and cavort with prodigious bravura under Lawrence Kornfeld's infectiously impudent direction. Splendid too is the orchestra, lustily led by Susan Romann in the excellent Eddie Sauter orchestrations that often succeed in making Carmines sound like music. Jules Fisher's lighting is, as ever, brilliant painting and sketching with light and shadow; Rouben Ter-Arutunian has designed highly original and decorative scenery, and Willa Kim's costumes are at least intermittently charming. All this is in a brand-new showcase, as handsome as it is comfortable, named, after the show, the Promenade Theatre. It is a good thing that "promenade" is a sufficiently unspecific, noncommittal word to allow us to enjoy this theater in the future without being haunted by memories of Miss Fornés' unmemorable concoction.

OH! CALCUTTA! is a meager little show that should nonetheless be seen by anyone concerned with where the theater is going, might be going, should not be going. It is an "entertainment with music" and without clothes, "devised" by Kenneth Tynan and "conceived and directed" by Jacques Levy. If we take "devised" as a synonym for "begotten," we know forthwith who was the father and who the mother. As a glint in Father Tynan's eye, the show may have seemed bright enough; but, as so often happens, it was spoiled rotten by both parents, and particularly Mother Levy. And not only by them, who authored some of the skits, but also by the nine co-procreators, whose names, however, are not attached to particular sketches. In view of the overall quality of the progeny, almost all feebleminded, some stillborn, the reluctance to claim paternity is understandable enough. Especially as there are some pretty potent names involved.

Among the stillborn sketches, let me count "Suite for Five Letters," a concert reading from aberrant agony columns that ends with mass masturbation; "Four in Hand," which is all mass masturbation plus projections of the accompanying fantasy-less fantasies; "Jack and Jill," in which the sex play of two children of bygone days results in the death or catatonia of the little girl—one cannot tell, or care, which; "Who: Whom," wherein sadism is shown to thrive as happily under a democracy as under a tyranny (did anyone doubt it?); and "Will Answer All Sincere Replies," the adventures of two oafish wife-swapping couples, surpassed in oafishness only by their author. That leaves four skits with a smattering of commendability: "Dick and Jane," in which a man's fantasy life races hopelessly ahead of his girl friend's physical complaisance; "Delicious Indignities," in which a Victorian maiden's virtue is shown to survive all genuine assaults, but not a failed attempt that looks incriminating; "Was It Good for You Too?," about a Masters-Johnson type of sex study, which could have been very funny if (as I suspect) Levy had not camped it up; and "Rock Garden," wherein a young and an old hillbilly exchange confidences too racy for the elder.

There remains a montage of projections of erotic paintings by one Clovis Trouille, who I sincerely hope is a hoax—for if he exists, he will have to be uninvented. This is accompanied, like the dance numbers I am coming to, by music from The Open Window, a rock trio that includes Peter Schickele, who might never have happened if Bach, besides his P's and Q's, had also watched his D's. The music is sometimes moody and abrasive, but as often shapeless and inappropriate. The naked dance numbers include two comic group shuffles and scuffles (one punctuated with mildly amusing throwaway lines), one wistful group interweaving and twining, and one languorous *pas de deux*. They were choreographed by Margo Sappington, and are more decorous than libidinous—except for the *pas de deux*, which looked less like an orgy whose participants had accidentally swallowed saltpeter and more like *Nacktballet* (as I understand it was practiced by Mary Wigman and her disciples). This number was sexy, and at times enthralling. Alas, the accompanying rock ballad was bumptious and distracting, and almost vitiated the sensuality of the dance executed beautifully by Miss Sappington, passably by her partner, George Welbes.

On the technical side, beyond the poor direction of Jacques Levy (not even in flowers, only perhaps in butter, is there such difference between fresh and unfresh as in cleverness), there were the shrewd yet simple sets of James Tilton; the costumes of Fred Voelpel that made even second-rate nudity seem preferable; the nicely various lighting of David Segal, and all kinds of audio-visual effects, clever but mostly obtrusive. The performers are severely burdened: naked, you have to be beautiful as well as talented. Thus Miss Sappington has a lovely figure but sappy face, Raina Barrett a most suasive head but much less eloquent body, Mark Dempsey superb looks but no acting ability, and so on. The new breed of gymnothespians may require not only special training but also special breeding.

What does *Oh! Calcutta!* teach? As theater, that nudity alone is meaningless, a piece of information as otiose as they come. As sexual stimulation, that the shock value wears off in the time it takes to slip out of a bikini; that group nakedness is considerably less arousing than the nudity of one desirable person; and that the law still stands there, like an invisible traffic cop, forcing anything like genuine carnal contact into a detour around the erogenous zones. Thus the pornographic possibilities of legitimate theater are still extremely circumscribed, except in comic, and therefore unarousing, contexts. But the possibilities of naked dance and ballet strike me as esthetically and erotically powerful, and as yet barely adumbrated.

The one thing that did worry me about *Oh! Calcutta!* was the name of Samuel Beckett among the "contributors." Whichever "contribution" may have been his, it is sad to think of the master of the almost bare stage doing so little with the fully bared body.

KNOWING FULL well what the American Shakespeare Festival does with—or, rather, *to*—Shakespeare, I was nevertheless curious to find out how it deals with a great modern playwright, and journeyed there to see Chekhov's *The Three Sisters*. I doubt that I have ever seen a major production, however bad, in which something, however small, could not be praised. This version of *The Three Sisters* is unredeemed across the board. Another first for Stratford, Connecticut.

Let me qualify that. Initially, it looks as if Marian Seldes' Olga and Len Cariou's Andrey might work handily; but Cariou soon settles into dusty sameness, and Miss Seldes gives less and less, until one assumes she is saving up for a grand finale—which, unfortunately, never comes. William Ritman's sets start out acceptably, go into a speedy decline, and end disastrously. The fourth-act set— the Prozorovs' garden, part of a terrace, woods and a far-off river— becomes an almost empty parking lot, with a backdrop seemingly made of enormous building blocks: perhaps the Pyramids when they were new.

Chekhov's plays, more than those of any dramatist, aspire to and achieve the condition of music. Instead of into acts, they might as well be divided into movements. Perhaps that is why there are always four: the perfect sonata form. But it is a threefold music. There is the music of speech: people going into their unsolicited, slightly off-key arias that never quite connect with anybody else's because they are merely the comic-pathetic monologues with which the speaker tries to assuage his sense of futility. Secondly, there is the music of silence, precise as the shape of space between people and objects in a great painting; the silences that are filled with loneliness and frustration must acquire their proper rhythm and duration— silences that can be solos, duets, and even chorales. Lastly, and hardest to convey, there is the music of time. There are visible watches and clocks in *The Three Sisters,* but it is that invisible and inaudible Time that haunts, envelops and carries off these characters that must somehow be made present—an ominous, indifferent metronome.

Of all this, Michael Kahn, the director, has caught little or nothing. Let it be said for him that at least, unlike Lee Strasberg in his production, he does not bring carnival mummers on stage. But the viscous boredom he conjures up and thinks to relieve by infantile tantrums (five characters are accorded one major tizzy each), almost makes one wish for a dancing bear or two. The staging, instead of being orchestrated, seems crudely joisted. Even Chekhov's stage directions are often ignored. Irina's second-act curtain line, "Moscow, Moscow, Moscow," is marked in the text (I am tempted to write "score"): "with intense yearning." Maria Tucci delivers it rather like Napoleon urging on his troops. When Vershinin and Masha are supposed to make coded love by humming at each other—perhaps even arranging a tryst—Kahn has them camping up an aria from *Eugene Onegin.*

I never even got the feeling that these three sisters were part of the same family. Marian Seldes' Olga is a gaunt, ascetic prioress, muzzling her every emotion; Kate Reid's Masha, looking like Winston Churchill *en travesti* and barking out most of her lines ("You can look angry . . . but not sad," Chekhov instructed his wife, who created the role; yet he never commanded her to bite off people's heads); Maria Tucci's Irina, a gushy debutante who ends up comatose and looks like a chubby Eugene the Jeep—what have these three to do with one another?

Brian Bedford, an able actor, is allowed to play Tusenbach as if he were a Noël Coward character. Instead of an awkward, impassioned dreamer, we get a sophisticated farceur; his "Let's go away together and work!" to Solyony sounds like "How about another snifter, old chap?" The shoulder-length hair, moreover, possibly appropriate for his Hamlet, makes Bedford an uncountenanceable Tusenbach. As Chebutykin, Morris Carnovsky (an actor whose reputation strikes me as one of the American theater's profounder mysteries) makes the opposite mistake. He plays the lightweight parasite and quack as a tragic Shylock figure, and his speech patterns are never far removed from Yiddish.

Charles Cioffi's Solyony, instead of blending the sinister with the absurd, oozes fatuity and ludicrousness; Mary Doyle's Anfisa and James Greene's Ferapont emerge much too young and unmoving; Michael McGuire's Vershinin is a center-stage elocutionist. Roberta Maxwell's Natasha is both of Cinderella's wicked sisters rolled into one for the sake of economy; Joseph Maher turns the topheavy Kulygin into a skittering dayfly—even the sure-fire bit with the false beard falls flat, though this is partly the fault of the make-up; and Michael Parish, as Fedotik, manages to mangle his equally sure-fire fire-speech in act three. What may be even more amazing is that the usually dependable Conrad Susa has composed a few bars of connecting music that has absolutely nothing to do with the mood and locale of the play.

They say that Stanislavsky, in the original production, wanted Tusenbach's body carried across the stage. In Michael Kahn's mounting, the stage is littered with Chekhov's scattered bones.

I THINK IT is no longer possible to put on a truly successful production of Greek tragedy—certainly not with American actors. Euripides can still provide a *succès d'estime;* Sophocles can perhaps be done as a concert reading; Aeschylus is a lost cause. However, the

New York Shakespeare Festival's Mobile Theatre production announced as Black *Electra* sounded promising. I imagined it to be a reworking of Sophocles, transposing the play into an African setting and getting the full significance out of its tribal and ritual character. In the interest of vitality and imagination, I was prepared to sacrifice purist values—these being forfeit anyway, since the translation used was H.D.F. Kitto's.

The program ominously read "Sophocles' *Electra*." Still, the beginning was auspicious enough. A chorus of extremely handsome, lithe, well-costumed Negro girls, their faces dramatically streaked with white paint, accompanied by the restrainedly barbaric rhythms of John Morris' protomusic, went into Louis Johnson's ethnically suggestive choreographed movements on Ming Cho Lee's pedestrian but inoffensive set, no doubt limited by the requirements of a Mobile Theatre. Theoni V. Aldredge's russet or terracotta costumes and coifs struck me as an evocative blending of Minoan, Mycenean and West African styles, and there was something distinctly Afro-Hellenic about the dancing. But, alas, the moment Mel Winkler, as Paedagogus, started to admonish Orestes, whose helmet derived all too clearly from Greek vase painting, my hopes were dashed. I don't know what Mr. Winkler is like in other parts, here he was absolutely dreadful. He was not old, he had no inkling of how to speak verse (how many American actors, black or white, have?), he obviously did not look Greek, and words like "Argos," "Lycean" and "Pelops" sat about as comfortably on his lips as a man who discovers he is using the women's toilet.

Worst of all was the speech pattern, which sounded like the Mobile, Alabama, Theatre. Even the best American speech lacks the pronounced melody of British English, which approximates ancient Greek, at least as we vocalize it. American speech is flat, and the Southern accent that adheres to much of Negro speech is even substandard American, and, whether we like it or not, suggests nothing more than Athens, Georgia. Winkler was not alone in this. Thurman Scott, as Orestes, spoke of sharing Electra's "sorra." Clee Burtonya, as Aegisthus, uttered the mysterious line, "May no nimences attend my words." After some speculation about what "nimences" were, I guessed them to be Nemesis.

There was one impressive performance, Olivia Cole's Electra. Miss Cole is a stately, sinewy young woman, with features of a heroic mold, a piercing gaze, superbly elongated hands, and commanding diction—she studied at London's R.A.D.A. She had the energy and passion of Electra, and it is not her fault that she was, or seemed, taller than anyone else, man or woman. She does not yet have the range, the sheer variety needed to sustain such a part, her eyeballs roll overmuch, and her walk tends to be a lollop. But she is, like a Damascene blade, finely tempered and honed. Even so, I had difficulty believing that she was Electra, daughter of Agamemnon, princess of Mycenae.

None of the other performances works, though a special word of censure must go to the lovely and supple Josephine Premice, who has done fetching things as a dancer and singer, and has been delightful in musical comedy. Her reading of Clytemnestra, however, was a campy imitation of Tallulah Bankhead's Cleopatra, and, even without a Nile at her disposal, she managed to sink. The voice and mannerisms were very much those of a female impersonator, and several of her lines got wholly uncalled-for laughs.

Some of the blame for this, of course, devolves on the director. Gerald Freedman, confronted with the demands of tragedy and poetry, once again demonstrates his impotence. Thus he has the appalling idea of letting Clytemnestra have a protracted and raucous fit of laughter at the news of Orestes' death. Or he will let the off-stage Clytemnestra, in the process of being slaughtered, protest feebly, as if the visitors were muddying her carpets. When Orestes and Pylades reappear after the murder, they are covered with gore; the queen's corpse, however, is immaculate, as if just taken out of the cellophane wrapper, the arms and ankles tidily crossed. When Electra is supposed to clutch the tutor's hands in gratitude, the fellow stolidly hangs on to his staff and can spare only one hand, though Electra keeps apostrophizing his "hands, those faithful hands." Pylades, though he has no words to speak, smirks most of the time, so that he is allowed to become an actor who—never mind *speak*— cannot even *look* tragedy.

John Morris' suggestions of music are judicious and effective, but often manage to drown out the words. To think that the vast Greek amphitheaters, without electronics, were far better acoustically than this tiny Mobile Theatre with its modern sound equipment—which, by the way, seemed to be hissing the show much of the time.

As Dürrenmatt said on another occasion, this was not so much a production of a tragedy as a tragedy of a production.

I used to think of Joseph Papp as a director who cannot direct. But with sufficient time and unlimited opportunity one can learn almost anything up to a point. And indeed, the first half of the

New York Shakespeare Festival's *Twelfth Night* is, on its own terms,
quite well directed. A person leaving at intermission (as many do)
might rightly think that Papp is now a director who can direct. What
he cannot do is think.

For Papp conceives of *Twelfth Night* as outrageous farce, full
of sound and flurry, signifying nothing. Even a cursory glance at
contemporary criticism of the play could clue Papp in. Take a random sampling. Robert Graves: "an acknowledgment of defeat"; Wilson Knight: "a melodic pathos"; Middleton Murry: "a silvery under-
tone of sadness"; W. H. Auden: "Shakespeare . . . in no mood for
comedy"; John Wain: "a sharp nipping air blowing from the tragedies"; Clifford Leech: "disturbing reverberations"; C. L. Barber: "a
dark outline"; Quiller-Couch: "the play, for all its gaiety, is agonizing. . . ." But no need to go to the critics; a play that begins
with the *last* of the twelve nights of Christmas revels in its title,
and that ends with Feste abandoned by all, singing alone on the
stage about the rain that raineth every day, is not likely to be all
milk and honey. Papp ignores such hints; his production emphasizes
the subtitle, *What You Will,* with an arbitrariness that Will would
never have willed; and as for Feste's closing song, it is done to a
slaphappy rock rhythm with all the players coming back on, cavorting, curtsying and kissing away.

There is an older school of thought—say, from Hazlitt to Cham-
bers—that regards the play as a supremely sunny comedy. Even then,
however, high comedy is not campy or knockabout farce, delighting
in such hoary gags as one character pulling out chairs from under
another. And beyond this absurd director's choice, Papp does not
ratiocinate. What is the period of this production? Turn-of-the-century, Papp tells us, but I cannot for the life of me tell which century is turning. A jester makes little sense in the costume of a Left
Bank artist of the *belle époque,* and even less so when flanked by
a sailor out of *Billy Budd* and an admiral out of Gilbert and Sullivan. The music is equally schizoid: vaguely Elizabethan roundelays
and Second Empire operetta, a fiddler-ridden thirties hoedown next
to the latest rock with onstage electric guitar. The locale is no less
perplexing. In Sir Toby's and Andrew's carousing scene, we are in
a thriving harbor town: the nocturnal chitchat is basted with flatu-
lent foghorns and whimsical ship's bells; but nothing of this later, and
the characters, for all their occasional naval uniforms, exhale none
of that salty breath they are presumed to be inhaling. Though the
set is a delightful tangle of latticed arches, we can never tell whether

we are at Orsino's or Olivia's. And the tiresomely repetitious games of hide-and-seek the characters keep playing further befuddle the issue.

The characterizations are not only wrong but also self-contradictory. Robert Ronan gives us his usual "I Was a Teenage Pederast" routine, which ill accords with any meaningful conception of Malvolio; but when, at the curtain call, Papp brings him on towering at the very pinnacle of the set, an ominous Puritan repeating his threat of revenge, the gesture is such a turnabout as to be a slap in its own face. The lovely and haughty Olivia is played by the adipose Sasha von Scherler (in her farthingales she looks like something begotten by a centaur on a horsehair sofa), all croonings and swoonings, campy tones and postures befitting the Brighton and Blackpool music halls. As she falls more in love with Cesario-Viola, instead of becoming more involved she becomes more attitudinizing and fluttery. As Orsino, Ralph Waite is the villainous saloon-keeper of second-rate Westerns (perhaps bucking for the roles relinquished by Steve Cochran), and his way with a line of verse is that of an exterminator with a cockroach. His falling in love with Viola is no different from his languishing for Olivia, but if the point is to convey a hopeless philanderer, this is not transmitted either.

Barbara Barrie's Viola is a parody of Katherine Hepburn at Bryn Mawr; unlike most Violas, Miss Barrie makes us believe only in her *boy*hood; her womanhood remains under wraps. She is misdirected into low-comedy routines, such as pulling one foot up flush with the opposite knee, and doubling up with mock laughter. As for her sumptuous verse—the willow-cabin and patience-on-a-monument speeches—M. Jourdain could not have made it prosier. As Belch and Aguecheek, Stephen Elliott and Tom Aldredge have some funny moments, which, however, should take out accident insurance against all the others that collapse like tons of bricks around them. Jennifer Darling's Maria is *de trop* in several directions; Charles Durning is an amusing and accomplished Feste; if you like your will-o'-the-wisps walrus-like, the pointed becoming embonpointed. The rest are rank amateurs.

Theoni V. Aldredge's costumes dazzle with their charm, Martin Aronstein's lighting scintillates, Douglas W. Schmidt's scenery is resplendent (two violet-upholstered chairs of the same wood as the set and same color as Olivia's dress are a typical delight), and even Galt MacDermott's music has an intermittent, incongruous sparkle.

Only man is vile. I doubt that Joseph Papp, as director, will learn any better; but perhaps, as producer, he might stop rehiring himself.

SUPPOSE THAT you had no use for cricket but were, by some mischance, obliged to write a cricket column. You could do one of two things. You could read up on the game in Neville Cardus, Edmund Blunden and the rest of the chaps, then go to the match with some loquacious connoisseur, and keeping your indifference well tucked in, assume the robes of the adept and spout, at second hand, hypocritical paeans. Or you could face up to your boredom and distaste, and to the opprobrium reserved for the unconverted outsider by refined initiates, and vent your honest displeasure. Now if the thing you are attacking happens, instead, to be Kabuki, the traditional popular theater of Japan, you may also be accused of parochialism and racism. But here goes: Kabuki bores me stiff. As stiff as the movements of a Kabuki actor.

Let me start by quoting from a review of a film by Satyajit Ray I wrote some years back: "To a large extent, Oriental philosophy is to blame. Where nirvana is the condition to aspire to, where quietism, denial of the self, submergence of the individual in eternity are the order of the day, the day becomes unimportant—to say nothing of the hour or the minute. But to the enlightened Westerner it is the moment that is of supreme importance; the problem, as Pater clearly saw, is 'how shall we pass most swiftly from point to point, and be present always at the focus where the greatest number of vital forces unite in their present energy?' Having scuttled eschatology and risen above resurrection, most Westerners have traded in a fictitious marriage to eternity for a passionate embrace of the moment, fleeting but real."

The New York opening of the current visit of The Grand Kabuki began about 7:30 and ended around 11 P.M. Unlike Kabuki-goers in Japan, we did not spend the entire day and night to see the whole of *Chushingura;* but also unlike in Japan, we did not have waiters circulating among us with food, nor did we bring our own box dinners. I felt immersed in an unhappy mixture of stasis and hunger, and although Faubion Bowers' running translation and commentary over the transistor radio was a help, the temptation grew to transfer the transistor from the ear to the mouth and nibble on it.

It is not that nothing happens in Kabuki; a great deal does, but it is all stylized down to a vast expanse of immobility fitfully fretted by an outburst of eyebrow-raising; and even the most towering rages are reduced by protocol to maniacal minuets. Whereas Western stylization tends to make things bigger and busier than they are—the enormous tirades of classical drama, the bedroom chases of French farce, the mincing of a Restoration-comedy fop—Kabuki slows down, fixates, makes microscopic, and takes the sting out by schematizing. In this respect, it closely resembles the two-dimensional, perspective-less planes of Japanese graphic art. Everything is given almost equal value and emphasis, whether it is the reading of a letter or an inno-cent man condemned to committing harakiri. Kabuki, to my taste, comes off best in the Japanese woodcuts depicting it, where the vivid hues of fabrics and elaborate patterns of stylized movement create an ornate, swirling magnificence of color and form—which, moreover, does not demand several hours for its viewing.

I doubt that The Grand Kabuki brought along all of its scenery from Japan; certainly there was no revolving stage at the City Cen-ter, and even the improvised *hanamichi* (the ramp along which entrances and exits are made) has been shortened to half the audi-torium's length. But the costumes are the same, and even they appear frail, stiff, overextended, and seem to drape the stage rather than the actors.

And what am I to do with the various Kabuki conventions? That the good man's face should be painted chalk white makes him, to me, more repulsive than the villain, whose face is allowed at least some patches of its natural coloring. That the women's parts are played by men, because the women or boys who acted them prior to 1653 gave rise to hetero- or homosexual lewdness, strikes me as a small advantage; that the art of *onnagata* (female impersonators) may be consummate and their lives blameless, does not compensate me for the lack of the clumsier, less distilled femininity of a mere authentic woman. Or take the *kurogo* (hooded stagehand) who squats behind a sitting actor, just so as to be able to carry away the stool when the actor gets up, and replace it when he sits down again. Stylization is all very well, but if one of its typical aims be-comes to spare us the sight of such a piece of vulgar reality as a chair, I'd rather have the chair. Nor do I find solace in the language, which, at least as translated by Mr. Bowers, adds up to things like "Wafting through the peonies comes the music of the lion"—not to mention inadvertent puns like a man dying of harakiri being told of his "mortification." And that all this is accompanied by plinking samisens and plonking woodblocks goes a long way toward not making it music to my ears.

There remains the traditional authenticity and the great antiquity of Kabuki. Personally, I would rather see Shakespeare's Cleopatra, to cite an analogue, played by an actress, even if the part was originally done by a boy. So much for the authenticity. As for the antiquity, the first crude version of Kabuki dates from 1603. In England, a year earlier, I could already have seen *Hamlet*. Still, you can go for the exotic curiosity value. Only be sure you have three and a half hours' worth of curiosity in you.

JOHN OSBORNE's *A Patriot for Me* is about as unnecessary a play as I have ever seen. If you want to find out about the curious story of Colonel Alfred Redl, the chief of Austrian Imperial counterespionage whose homosexual activities led to his being blackmailed by the Russians into doing some under-the-counterespionage for them, and to his suicide when this was discovered, you can read *The Panther's Feast* by Robert Asprey and find out much more that way. If you want an imaginative re-creation of the splendor and misery of life in the Imperial Austrian army, a novella like Schnitzler's *Lieutenant Gustl* will prove incomparably more revealing. If you want to learn about homosexuals, there are by now hundreds of works of fiction, drama and even poetry that will afford you keener insights. And if you just want to see a decent play, you certainly won't find it among Osborne's later works.

Altogether, Osborne is a perfect example of a playwright who voices the mood of a particular moment in history: *Look Back in Anger* was, to a degree, the expression of English working-class anger against the upper classes, which at last could be reviled with impunity. But it was even more the venting of a self-destructive rage such as overtakes a country that sees itself fallen from political eminence to feeding on memories. And to men too young to have lived them, such memories become a source of especial irritation. Osborne had not so much written a play as tapped a vein.

But there was something that he genuinely possessed: a gift for raillery, invective, lacerating tirades whose victims could be anyone or anything, and whose power, though rhetorical rather than dramatic, could nevertheless buffet the stage. When the time of heroes and statesmen is passed comes the time of the jeerer; Osborne became the beloved Thersites of the British theater. As the climate changed, he did his best to change with the times, and became more and more successful, wealthy, upper class and conservative. But his one true note—his fulminations—no longer fitted the new perspective.

England, its upper crust somewhat reshuffled, was becoming a homogeneous place again, and with Osborne safely ensconced in his room at the top, nothing remained for him to do except inveigh against the middle class (*Inadmissible Evidence*) or the lower class (*The Hotel in Amsterdam*).

In the latter play and in *Time Present*, Osborne goes to absurd lengths to find something to assail, even as his development into a reactionary proceeds apace: in *A Bond Honoured* even God comes off scot-free. In *A Patriot for Me*, the only thing Redl, on the verge of suicide, can harangue against is—the Spaniards! His psychologically and dramatically unwarranted attack on them is surely the most gratuitous farewell speech ever written. In future Osborne plays the characters may be reduced to denouncing cigarettes or the London telephone directory; the objects of invective have become so remote or stale that a late Osborne play is just a bunch of sour gripes.

A Patriot for Me seems to deal with ambition and self-indulgence fighting it out against the background of a similarly schizoid but also narrow-minded and corrupt society. It is some kind of dance on top of the volcano, some sort of *Walpurgisnacht* hurtling into *Götterdämmerung*, in which social orders, races, sexes, even fellow homosexuals oppose, torment and persecute one another—but of all these things Osborne tells you no more than a high-school sex orientation lecture tells about human relations. We do, however, learn in one scene that the homosexual Siczynski read foreign newspapers, and, in another scene, that the homosexual Redl did likewise. The conclusion imposes itself: the cause of homosexuality is reading foreign newspapers.

What Osborne cannot do is write about tenderness and love, hetero- or homosexual. Consider Redl's outcry to his former mistress who has just married the youth he adored: "You'll never know that body like I know it. The lines beneath his eyes. Do you know how many there are, do you know one has less than the other? . . . And the hairs in his nostrils, which has the most, what color they are in what light? The mole on where?" Let us pass over the anacoluthon and the four other grammatical errors in this brief passage; what is so awful is the concept of tenderness as counting nasal hairs. So those monocles worn by Austrian officers were actually microscopes?

Feeble vignettes succeed one another: *A Patriot for Me* is as superficial a passing parade as *Luther*, without even an Albert Finney to hold things together. The wit is pathetic ("You were born with a silver saber up your whatnot") and only the pathos is good for a laugh ("It's the time of night when people die. People give up"). Loosely and flaccidly, the play follows a fascinating career, and ends with a bang from a Browning and a whimper from Osborne. The production is no better or worse than the play, but two performances (and nothing else) are outstanding: Dennis King's charmingly decadent Baron von Epp, and Ed Zimmerman's suavely sinister Judge Advocate Kunz.

You might expect a play whose high point is a drag ball to be a bore; what you would not expect is that even the drag ball is a drag.

WINTER, 1969-1970

PEER GYNT
by Henrik Ibsen
produced by the New York Shakespeare Festival

PRIVATE LIVES
by Noël Coward

LAST OF THE RED HOT LOVERS
by Neil Simon

THE LAST SWEET DAYS OF ISAAC
book and lyrics by Gretchen Cryer
music by Nancy Ford

HARVEY
by Mary Chase

SHOW ME WHERE THE GOOD TIMES ARE
book by Lee Thuna
music by Kenneth Jacobson
lyrics by Rhoda Roberts

THE PRODUCTION of *Peer Gynt* by the New York Shakespeare Festival in Central Park last summer put in question the viability of the entire American theater as it now stands. It was a dismal, a shameful fiasco, but the elements that went into making it extend into the farthest reaches of our theater and culture.

Where in America today could *Peer Gynt* be properly performed? In my time, there have been two mountings of the play in New York: one in 1949, an ANTA production with John Garfield as Peer; one in 1960, at the Phoenix, with Fritz Weaver. Both were artistic and audience failures—the one illustrative of Broadway's insufficiency, the other of off-Broadway's—and Robert Brustein's mournful remarks on the latter production (*Seasons of Discontent*, pp. 218–221) are painfully appropriate to the recent Central Park shambles. There is even a historical link: the Phoenix production was directed by Stuart Vaughan; Vaughan was a foundation-supported director who staged some of the first Shakespearean offerings in the Park; later, his disciple and ex-wife, Gladys Vaughan, became Joseph Papp's chief director at the new Delacorte Theatre, and it is from her that the current artistic director, Gerald Freedman, who staged this production, took over. The Vaughans, Stuart and Gladys, have mercifully faded from sight; Freedman, less happily, is in full swing.

Could *Peer* be done on Broadway these days? Out of the question. Broadway does not present classics unless, as very rarely happens, some tremendous box-office "name" takes it into his spacious head to do a Lear or Hamlet or whatnot; or unless some successful London production is transferred to Broadway for a limited engagement, and usually with even more limited success. (The most recent such disaster was Nicol Williamson's *Hamlet*, directed by Tony Richardson.) An archetypal Broadway producer, Arthur Cantor, once declared publicly what a sorry state of affairs it would be if several Broadway theaters were playing Lope de Vega. The real meanings of his remark were a) Who needs the classics, anyhow? and b) Aren't you impressed that I know all about Lope?

Off-Broadway has proved itself equally uninteresting in reviving the classics; in many cases this is justified by lack of financial and histrionic resources. Though it can do such campy things as an updated musical version of Aristophanes' *Peace*, a straightforward production of that play would be beyond its means. Last season, for example, I attended a staging of *The Dance of Death* at the Roundabout Theatre. This much-lauded playhouse in the Chelsea district had received praise for its recent productions of *King Lear* and *Candida*, and its current Strindberg venture was enthusiastically reviewed by, among others, Howard Thompson of the *Times*, who compared it to Laurence Olivier's production at England's National Theatre. This Chelsea *Dance of Death* proved a sickening travesty, and I felt mortified for having dragged to it a distinguished visiting Yugoslav drama critic. And what are the difficulties of that play compared to those of *Peer Gynt?*

The Lincoln Center Repertory Company has often toyed with the idea of staging *Peer*. In the company's very first year under Blau and Irving, the former spoke of his desire to do it; more recently, *Peer* would appear as one of several plays under consideration for the following year. Next year inevitably came around; *Peer Gynt,* equally unfailingly, did not. This is less than surprising when you consider that under the sole guidance of Jules Irving we get either plays in which some transient star expressed interest (*Cyrano,* because Richard Basehart wanted to do it, though by opening time he was so scared that he lost his voice and Robert Symonds had to play the part—execrably, in a wretched production; *Lear,* because Lee J. Cobb wanted to do it and, worse luck, actually went through with it—under Gerald Freedman's direction: one part watered-down Peter Brook, two parts nothing); or plays which, for one reason or another, are considered foolproof. Such, last season, were a previously unproduced play by the commercial playwright William Gibson, and Molière's *Miser* in a production replete with crowd-pleasing horseplay. *Peer Gynt* could not make it in either category.

Having written the introduction to a new translation of *Peer Gynt* (by Jurgensen and Schenkkan; Crofts Classics, 1966), I have no wish to reanalyze the play here. But any production, and any critique of that production, must start with a brief interpretation of the work. For example, Kenneth Tynan sees the play as "a study of the fallacy that is inherent in total dedication to self-fulfilment." Robert Brustein sees Peer's life as "a tragedy of waste," a gifted man having chosen "to be neither a great saint nor a great sinner, only an opportunistic mediocrity." Frank Wedekind perceived the play as "the fate of a man who, by becoming intellectually hypertrophied, runs morally to seed." I myself would stress the unfortunate upbringing of Peer, which undercuts his physical courage with moral cowardice. Yet the play regards that cravenness with ambivalence. Because of it, Peer walks out on Solveig, unable to confess his affair with the Greenclad; but, then, it is this cowardice that makes him boggle at undergoing the irrevocable eye operation of the trolls, or at revealing his identity to the Lean One and getting carted off to hell. And it is this pusillanimity that saves Peer in the end—if indeed he is saved—for he summons up his courage to face Solveig not for the sake of salvation through her love, but for a list of major grieveances that would help him elude the Buttonmoulder's ladle. Thus Peer seems to stumble across his redemption.

Though the various interpretations I have quoted strike me as, in the main, correct, an irony must also be noted. Moritz Prozor, Ibsen's French translator, was right in saying (as quoted by Rolf Fjelde), "To be oneself is not to be Peer Gynt or another; it is to be a man, to kill in oneself what Peer vaingloriously calls the Gyntian self, in order to bring to life the human self." But the play also intends to show that man learns almost nothing from experience, that it is luck and, finally, the self-sacrifice of some ideal creature like Solveig that saves him—if he is to be saved at all. Peer's opposite, the unnamed peasant boy who mutilates himself to stay out of the war and cultivate his garden, is probably the better man; but his life is atypical and he is rejected by society. Peer, on the other hand, is in most ways archetypal: almost all other characters reflect his egoism, hypocrisy, and greed.

What sort of a guiding idea of the play did Gerald Freedman, the director of *Gynt* and artistic director of the now year-round New York Shakespeare Festival *cum* Public Theatre, evolve and proceed upon? His program note demonstrated not only poverty of style but also paucity of ideas. In fact, what ideas the note did contain were lifted from Rolf Fjelde's introduction to his translation (Signet Classics, 1964), and then watered down, truncated or misunderstood. When Freedman writes, "Ibsen encompassed all the devices of the romantic theatre and used them to service what is essentially a non-romantic play," he is paraphrasing Fjelde's more succinct reference to "this antiromantic work that employs the full resources of the romantic theatre." When Freedman, with clumsy ambiguity, writes that "Peer's life suggests that one creates one's own world, not Fate," he is merely vulgarizing Fjelde's "Ibsen suggests that . . . the world we never made is, often to a surprising extent, the outgrowth of our own human powers or a denial thereof . . ." Freedman speaks of self-discovery coming "when one breaks out of this cyclical pattern of ego and truly relates to another"; Fjelde proposes two possible solutions: "One . . . would be to break the cycle of repetitions," he begins, and these are the words Freedman latches on to. But Fjelde develops even his first alternative into a broader, more philosophical conception; Freedman settles for simple psychologizing couched in psychiatric jargon: "relate" without the reflexive pronoun. Although Fjelde is quite a reliable guide, undigested regurgitation of a single critic, without anything of one's own added, is hardly a solid starting point. And, typically, Freedman nowhere acknowledges his debt to Fjelde.

Now for the casting. For the role of Solveig, Freedman had what he thought was the brilliant idea of getting Judy Collins, the folk singer. "She truly comes with innocence," Freedman was quoted in the *Times*, "with wonder still about the whole art and idea of acting." Having heard one of her records and seen her picture on the album cover, he felt he had found the true Solveig, "So at one with herself when she sings . . . a flower child and an earth mother." And he asked the casting people for *a* Judy Collins. Unfortunately, they got him *the* Judy Collins. He gave her the part without having her read for it! And so we had a woman of thirty, who looked it, playing the teen-aged Solveig not with the wonder *of* acting, but with wonder *about* acting. Virtually every line of Solveig's was read the way a frightened bride in a big church pronounces her "I do!"—all one hears is the silence stretching itself a little. Miss Collins is a large woman (or appears large on stage), who, from the front, does look like a handsome senior flower child, going on earth mother. But let her turn her profile and she becomes mother earth: lumpish, common clay. Her movements lack poetry, and she has no pantomime. Most shockingly, she could not even sing the songs Freedman and his composer, John Morris, had written into the play for her. Her voice is small, uninflected, and ventures out of her throat with the tentativeness of a novice tightrope-walker who finds the safety net is missing. This is the irony of a top popular concert and recording star who—without fancy enough electronics or a small enough high-school auditorium—cannot put a song across.

Solveig was, of course, deliberately not fleshed out by Ibsen. That is sound strategy: the ideal girl-wife-mother figure best achieves symbolic stature in complete diaphaneity, which every man can fill with the image of his yearning, and every woman with her image of herself. What Peer recalls of Solveig throughout his wanderings is the vision of a girl, eyes downcast, clinging to her mother's gown, and carrying her hymnal wrapped in her kerchief: the shy, neat, pious, dutiful, modest maiden. He was once the silver-hasped book in her hands, Peer tells the madman Hussein. To be enfolded in such devout, pure love is the secret dream of the restless, acquisitive, lecherous adventurer. And this image of selfless dedication was simply not forthcoming from Judy Collins.

The part of Aase was assigned to Estelle Parsons, best known for her portrayal of the stupid, hysterical sister-in-law in *Bonnie and*

Clyde. Moon-faced, corpulent, with a flat voice that turns rancid around the edges, Miss Parsons is best at comedy, but like so many comics, ill-advisedly sees herself as a serious dramatic actress. She has nothing of the "small, delicate" Aase, one moment a severely puritanical parent, the next a doting glosser-over of her son's faults, ready to defend him, wrong though he be, against men and trolls. Aase's moral ambivalence and Jon Gynt's overindulgence and recklessness bred and coddled the inconsistency that grew up to be Peer Gynt. But Estelle Parsons never captured the span between force and fraility in Aase, the divergence of her extremes; instead, she wrapped the character in a muffler of cozy dullness from one end to the other. Her death—a scene of unequaled pathos—was about as moving as that of a mosquito slapped to oblivion on one's forearm. But she illustrated the limitations of a typical American actor: not only is he not given a chance to train and develop in a generous variety of parts, he is in fact encouraged to wallow in the ditch of his specialty, which, narrow though it be, has always room enough for some great classic role to be dragged down into it.

No better—perhaps worse—was Olympia Dukakis, who played Ingrid, the Greenclad, and Anitra, the three representative "other women" in Peer's life. It is probably from the 1962 Old Vic production of *Peer Gynt* (whose cast list is reprinted with the Michael Meyer translation used in the Park) that Freedman got the idea for his tripling; but in that production the actress was Adrienne Corri, an attractive and versatile performer. Miss Dukakis is unsuited for these parts by virtue of age and crudity; even if she was merely implementing Freedman's absurd notion to coarsen and burlesque all three roles, the personal vulgarity she brought to the process of perverting the text compounded the offense. James Cahill's Troll King was plain oafish, and John Heffernan's Buttonmoulder as flavorous as boiled water. In several lesser parts, Michael Baseleon and Robert Stattel ranged from the inconsequential to the ungainly.

This brings us to Stacy Keach in the title part. Peer is a curious combination. He is a poet and a dreamer—in part Ibsen himself—but also a self-seeking opportunist; he is boldly and indefatigably enterprising, but also generally misguided and ultimately cowardly. "It is the expression of fantasy," Raymond Williams has written, "which he understands as the expression of self," and he will fulfill himself "not by fighting but by dodging." This requires an actor who can oscillate between contradictory impulses and sometimes interweave them into bizarre spider webs. Keach worked hard on Gynt, and had some good moments, but he did not encompass the part. As the young Peer, he lacked the headlong lyricism; as the old Peer, he could not make the tragicomic struggle with the Buttonmoulder and the falling into Solveig's lap achieve the proper bittersweet tang, the wry pathos. But he remained an actor throughout—not, like most of the others, a buffoon, and the fact that he often could not be heard was presumably the fault of the inadequate sound system.

Freedman cut the play mercilessly and illogically. The way to do *Peer Gynt*, especially in the Park, is, I would think, to leave it more or less uncut with a long intermission for a picnic or frankfurter-stand dinner. But if cutting there must be, you cannot, for example, omit the unnamed boy who chops off his finger in III, i; then bring in his funeral in V, iii, but chopped down to about one finger's worth: a few closing lines of the Pastor's eulogy. Even Benedetto Croce, who did not like the play, considered that eulogy "admirable." Freedman not only jettisoned a character meant to counterbalance Peer, he introduced a meaningless fragment of a scene. The actors were deployed all over Ming Cho Lee's unit set, which looked like a psychotic Bridge on the River Kwai, spiraling upward and ending in a jungle lookout platform. The cast was equipped with coats and umbrellas, and it looked as if any moment they would go darting up and down this structure in a musical number entitled "Dancing in the Rain."

Or take the madhouse scene, IV, xiii. Freedman staged it, in amateurish imitation of Brook's *Marat/Sade*, as a noisy, swirling tempest in a teapot, but without the least meaning. It was not made clear that the asylum director has reversed the order of things, imprisoning the guards and freeing the madmen. Huhu and the Fellah were cut out completely, and the bit with Hussein (a difficult topical reference that should be explained in the program note) was obscured by being taken out of context and by the general hubbub surrounding it. The significance of this climactic scene was totally lost: that only in the madhouse can Peer become the Emperor of Self. He has just sent one madman into the jungle and two others into suicide; to be Emperor of Self means, as Robert Brustein has said, "madness . . . the triumph of the ego over external reality." It also means the destruction of others, as Peer's life, in this scene even more clearly than elsewhere, demonstrates. The mania of selfhood ends in frenzy, and Professor Begriffenfeldt can well pronounce the prostrate Emperor of Self to be *beside* himself. All this is lost on Freedman, and thus lost to the audience. But not only was the cutting of scenes deleterious, so too was the cutting of connecting matter between them. Thus the logical stages by which Peer becomes a Prophet ended up, as it were, on the cutting-room floor; gone too was the meeting between Begriffenfeldt and Peer at the Sphinx, which explains Peer's coming to the Cairo asylum. Likewise lost was the important censure of Peer by the Broken Straws for his negative—i.e., undone— deeds; this states Peer's guilt most clearly: it lies largely in sins of omission. So too does Freedman's.

But Freedman's sins of commission were just as vast. The first of these was actually a sin of both omission and commisson. It was the lyrics Freedman wrote to the four longish songs Solveig was made to sing. Ibsen wrote only two very simple and extremely short songs for her, and they were set by Edvard Grieg as part of his score for the play. John Morris' score for the Park production is not bad at all, but it is not Grieg; when a score is as immortal as the play it was written for, it deserves to be revived along with the play. The music for the new lyrics is not bad either—certainly not by prevailing Broadway musical standards. But the lyrics are trash, e.g.: "The endless joy of love,/ It makes the mountains ring with laughter/ And makes the moment that comes after . . ." I couldn't get down on paper what the endless joy of love makes the moment that comes after; but I do not doubt that it was something equally platitudinous. Next, Solveig sings: "To wander over a field of longing/ And gather blossoms of belonging . . ." Blossoms, except in archaic usage, are to be found on fruit trees, not in fields, but alliteration is clearly more important than accuracy. "A field of longing" would surely not yield blossoms, or even flowers, of any kind, being a field of unfulfillment; as for "blossoms of belonging," it is an image that belongs in the herbal of a Victorian spinster. And because of these Freedman songs a good scene or two of Ibsen had to be cut!

With the very opening scene, the duologue between Peer and Aase, Freedman probed the depths of dullness. The director is mortally afraid of words; however dramatic, poetic, psychologically searching, intellectually stimulating they may be, words are his dreaded enemy, and he either chops them out of the play or tries to upstage them with any kind of business he can dream up. But from this first scene of the first act not much can be chopped and no gimmicks come ready to hand—you cannot, for example, bring the reindeer buck onstage, or have Aase do the tarantella while Peer tells her of his exploits. Moreover, Ming Cho Lee's set was not only aesthetically deficient, functionally it was also extraordinarily unversatile. It

did not adapt itself to being other things—an interior, a desert, the
sea, a madhouse, a ship or whatnot—and failed even to evoke what it
was most supposed to be: a mountainside. That is what it was meant
to be in this scene, a hillside with leafy trees near Aase's farm. We
were to see a cascading creek and an old millhouse. Above all, we
were to feel the summer heat. But all we got was a set of chopsticks
afflicted with rickets and winding up into nowhere.

The costumes, too, were a problem. Theoni V. Aldredge is a
good costumer but not, I think, a brilliant one. Given the fact that
Estelle Parsons is too young and buxom for Aase, and that her make-
up didn't age her either; given the further fact that she was petulant
rather than exasperated and exasperating, it was the "little old lady"
aspect of Aase that needed emphasizing; instead, Mrs. Aldredge gave
her the look of a strapping, almost coquettishly dressed, by no means
ineligible country wench. As for Peer (with his wig or hairdo, whichever it was, Keach looked rather like an overstuffed Prince Valiant),
he was dressed rather too shabbily and fairly un-Norwegianly—where,
for instance, were the puttees? After all, his mother was quite decently
gotten up, and she does dote on him. True, his breeches should be
torn and he should look dirty, but there should still be the mark of
former quality about his appearance, all the more so since Keach
found it hard to convey the charm and appeal of the youthful Peer.

What with these visual handicaps, Freedman might have been expected to come up at least with some interesting blocking, and with
tempos that build to an emotional climax. There is poetry and character revelation aplenty in this scene; it needs only a good directorial eye and ear to endow it with life. But no such luck. Then with
the Ingrid scene (II, i), we landed in real trouble. Freedman chose
to direct this as farce; as Ibsen wrote it, it is barely even comedy. It
is one of those scenes in which spouses (or, in this case, an abductor
and his willing victim) torment each other—scenes at which Scan-
dinavians from Strindberg to Ingmar Bergman have excelled. It
establishes, on the one hand, Peer's irresponsible, unstable personality
—having just deflowered Ingrid, he already longs for Solveig. It also
shows, on the other hand, his romantic unwillingness to settle for a
perfectly good, middle-class existence—he insists on the ideal, Solveig
(whom he will later likewise manage to lose). Freedman, however,
had a loutish, boorish Peer running from a heavy, gross, fortyish
Ingrid, the two of them carrying on like Punch and Judy. Yet according to Walter Kerr, who was full of praise for this production, Freedman "had the wit to play Peer's first really treacherous act, his

seduction of the about-to-be-married Ingrid, as comedy. Because the act is treacherous, it immediately becomes black comedy, the groan at dawn after quite a bad night that is funny because it is so awful and so commonplace." One must admire Kerr's economy: with one fatuous piece of cleverness he can reveal his misapprehension of both *Peer Gynt* and black comedy.

It was with II, iv that Freedman really perked up: bring on the trolls, or dancing girls (or, as he could do here, both) and he is in heaven. But the overrich costumes killed the meaning. Against the set that continued in its paltriness, there appeared, popping out of the Troll King's long train, a procession of monsters. They derived from Bosch, Dali, Tchelitchew: there were creatures with one huge revolving eye, or with a long crimson tongue that ended in claws and served as a leg, or weirdly compounded Siamese troll-twins. As the Greenclad, Olympia Dukakis was made to look even more unprepossessing by the three artificial breasts bursting out of her bodice. And all this in various shades of bilious, poisonous green. Spectacular, yes, but topheavy. Certainly the trolls are eerie and the scene is meant to be fantastic, but it must not overshadow with baroque lavishness everything else yet to come. And the trolls, or at least the Troll Princess, must be alluring as well as garish.

But Freedman does not require a whole scene to wreak havoc; he can do appalling things with single details. Thus after Peer's waltzing off with the three cowherd girls, there is a scene (II, iv) in which our hero finds himself surrounded by glittering, snowy summits; the sight makes him wild and distraught—*yr og forvillet*. Freedman (perhaps misled by Michael Meyer's translation, "dazed and bleary") had him come on all postcoitally tuckered-out from his Lucky Peer act; there were no mountains around, and the soliloquy was cut. We were left with a crass sexual innuendo, which got a cheap laugh from the audience. Again, in III, i, Peer is chopping away at a powerful fir with twisting branches. It can't be all that hard to create such a tree on the stage; Freedman, in any case, preferred the easier and "funnier" business of having Peer hack away at a three-foot log, lopped clean of bark and branches, which he was apparently trying to convert into kindling. The battle with the huge fir fits in with his soliloquy about the marvelous mountain hut he is building; it has no application, except perhaps comic incongruity, to the belaboring of a small piece of horizontal timber. On opening night, this silly bit of business did not even get a meretricious laugh.

One more example: when in IV, vi Peer beckons Anitra to approach, so he can measure her braincase (*hjernekiste*), what did Freedman have Keach do? He had him grab her behind! Big laugh from the audience. The scene is meant to be comic, but under Freedman's aegis brain-humor is reduced to bottom-farce.

Sometimes it was total visual misrepresentation that made mincemeat of a scene. The Boyg is supposed to be an audible but invisible something against which Peer, lashing out in the dark with a branch, comes up short. He seems to collide with an unseen but ubiquitous living wall, whose voice gives him the fatal advice to "go around." This is to become his life-style and undoing. Freedman, however, had some departing trolls from the previous scene fasten one end of a string of colored streamers to the ground, the other to Peer's inert form, so that Peer became, as it were, the hub of a varicolored wheel. When he came to, he tried unsuccessfully to free himself from the streamers. Quite aside from the fact that ribbons cannot be made to say things that an invisible barrier can, the malign "Go around!" that leads to Peer's circumambulation of his true objective, Solveig, did not even make geometrical sense coming from these twirling bands of color.

Most injurious of all, probably, was the outrage perpetrated on IV, i. The Englishman, Frenchman, German and Swede whom Peer is entertaining with dinner were transmuted into an admiral, general, industrialist and diplomat. This is not a serious offense, though Ibsen's satire on the four nationalities is still applicable and a pity to lose. But the scene itself was transferred from a palm grove on the coast of Morocco to a burlesque ship at sea: literally a round washtub with Peer at its improbable tiller. As he related his life story since Act III (important for our understanding of his character), the tub kept bobbing up and down on imaginary waves, and he kept jerking away at the tiller. Meanwhile the four others, reduced to burlesque comics, shot one another with water pistols, and one repeatedly bopped another's head with a slapstick. As a result, we did not really hear Peer's story, but we soon saw the four knocking him out, transporting him to a disk with a mast and a coffer full of gold on it. This was attached to the tub and was meant to represent a dinghy; but why Peer would keep his fortune on a dinghy trailing after his yacht, God and Freedman only know. Stripped of his very clothes, Peer was set adrift on the dinghy, and forced to row ashore by means of his knuckles, rather as impoverished *cul-de-jattes* manipulate their four-wheeled pedestals. Not only was this scene unspeakably vulgar, preposterous and confusing, it also clashed disturbingly with the shipboard scene (V, i), which Freedman, conversely and perversely, staged so that it seemed to take place on dry land.

For sheer burlesque horror I commend to you also the Anitra scenes (IV, vi–viii). These were compressed into a single scene, and as Anitra, Miss Dukakis—middle-aged, obese, and ridiculously gotten up—did a takeoff on a belly dance while the dancing girls disported themselves like chorines in a strip joint and the audience bellowed with laughter. In almost no time at all, Anitra had plucked Peer clean, and he was again abandoned in his undergarments. Totally lost was the complex significance of this episode: first, the absurd quest of an aging man for his lost youth in the love of a young girl; secondly, his inability to inculcate a soul into woman, average woman, who sees man only as something to fleece; lastly, the foolishness of a man who purports to vaticinate and philosophize instead of living. Anitra's dance and treachery are not wholly unlike Salome's; far from being an excuse for campy vaudeville, the scene is a prime example of what Thomas Mann meant when he spoke of Ibsen's *"Poetisierung des Intellekts,"* the ability to render concepts in images.

Again, the shipboard and shipwreck scenes (V, i & ii) were so cut that their entire significance was lost. The flightiness, phony generosity, and cowardice of Peer were excised; the Strange Passenger changed from a herald of death, a *memento mori*, into a meaningless figure; and the Cook, whom Peer causes to drown, was cut altogether. But, you may be sure, we were given a highly picturesque shipwreck: dancers running around under a large billowing blue sheet on top of which Peer and the Stranger seemed to be adrift. Lost was all the bitterness and misanthropy of this scene, which Ibsen is not afraid to vent on his hypothetical alter ego, Peer. There may have been some truth in Max Beerbohm's remark that Ibsen "was an ardent and tender lover of ideas, but mankind he simply could not abide. Indeed, I fancy he cared less for ideas as ideas than as a scourge for his fellow-creatures."

The philosopher Ludwig Wittgenstein admirably identified Ibsen's tone as "the tone of a man possessed by the truth." It is this tone that Freedman managed to sabotage and finally destroy. But there is one further problem, one that makes a truly fine *Peer Gynt* in English as good as impossible: the unavailability of a worthy translation. Take such a simple line as Peer's comment on the dancing Anitra: *"Ei! Hun er sannelig lekker, den taske,"* which means, literally, "My, she is truly dainty [or "savory," a tasty morsel], the pouch [i.e., wench, as in the English "baggage"]." Meyer's drearily prosaic translation renders this as "Mm. She's a nice piece of delicatessen, that girl." Rolf Fjelde has "Ah, she's a tasty dish, the minx!" If anything, this "minx" is worse, though it must be said in Fjelde's defense that he tries to reproduce or suggest Ibsen's rhymes, which the other translators generally ignore. Norman Ginsbury offers, "She's a tasty piece of flesh, the hussy." Jurgensen and Schenkkan come up with "Yes, she's delicious enough, the hussy!" None of these versions quite works, even for so undemanding a line. The most recent translation, Peter Watt's for Penguin Books, comes closest: "Ah, but she's really delicious, the baggage!" Yet it too sounds unhappily literary.

Here now are the closing verses of the Parson's eulogy from V, iii as rendered by the same translators.

MEYER:
The metal of which God made him rang most true
Until the end. His life was as a lute
Whose strings are muted. Peace to thee, silent warrior,
Who strove and fell in thy small humble war.
It is not for us to search the heart and veins.
That is no task for dust, but for its Maker
But freely I hope and firmly I believe
This man is not a cripple in the eyes of God.

FJELDE:
His inborn note was steadfast as a star.
His life was music, like a muted bell.
So peace be with you, silent warrior,
Who fought the peasant's little fight, and fell.
It's not our place to sift the heart and soul—
That's not for dust, but for the judge of all—
Still I believe—and here it must be said:
This man stands now no cripple to his God!

GINSBURY:
The substance of the inner man rang true.
His life was music played on muted strings.
So, rest in peace, you silent warrior,
Who fought the peasants' little fight and fell.
We will not search into his heart and veins;
That is no task for us but for his God.
But freely, and in all sincerity,
I hope that, as he takes his place before
His God, this man no longer is a cripple.

J. & S.:
His native metal, to the end, rang true.
His life was like a song on muted strings.

> And therefore,—peace be with you, quiet fighter,
> Who fought the farmer's little war, and fell!
> It's not for us to scrutinize the heart;
> That's not a task for dust, but for its Maker;—
> Yet I stand here and firmly voice my hope:
> Before his God, this man is not a cripple.

WATTS: The metal he was forged from, there rang true.
> His life was one long tune on muted strings . . .
> So—peace be with you, silent warrior
> who fought a peasant's little war—and fell.
> We shall not probe his heart—his inmost thoughts;
> that is no task for us, but for his Maker.
> But confidently I proclaim this hope:
> he stands, uncrippled now, before his God.

What are the salient features of these translations? Meyer's is loose, uneuphonious, unrhythmical; Fjelde's wanders off (there is no Keatsian "steadfast star" in Ibsen, no "muted bell") and the versification is on the singsong side; Ginsbury's is perfect doggerel, the last three lines unutterably flat—not to mention that nine lines are required for the original eight; Jurgensen and Schenkkan's tends to gloss over, make bland, oversimplify. Watts comes off best, but I do not think that his "one long tune" quite conveys the quality of perseverance to the end, and I rather miss the reference to mortal dust. The last line, however, works very handsomely.

Still, what *Peer Gynt* desperately needs is an Auden or a Richard Wilbur to translate it, and someone other than Papp and Freedman to produce and direct it. I was tempted to write about *Peer* as Shaw did to Ellen Terry: "*It will be done*, if I have to play it myself." But there is better news: Ingmar Bergman, who staged the play in Malmö in 1957 (with Max von Sydow, Ingrid Thulin, Naima Wifstrand, Gunnel Lindblom—brilliantly, by all accounts), has announced that he is making a film of it, in English no less. I could not ask for more. (P.S. 1975: Bergman told me that the project has fallen through. When I expressed regret at the loss of what might have been a definitive version, he pooh-poohed this by saying, rather impatiently, that a definitive version would have to be a stage, not a film version. Potential adapters of all kinds, please note!)

LOOKING BACK at his 1930 play, *Private Lives*, many years later, Noël Coward wrote, rather self-depreciatingly: "It was described in the papers variously, as being 'tenuous,' 'thin,' 'brittle,' 'gossamer,' 'iridescent,' and 'delightfully daring.' All of which connoted, to the public mind, 'cocktails,' 'evening dress,' 'repartee' and irreverent allusions to copulation, thereby causing a gratifying number of respectable people to queue up at the box office. There is actually more to the play than this, but on the whole not very much." I hope that this comment was prompted by British modesty rather than parental blindness, for *Private Lives* is as wickedly winsome four decades later as it was when, a newborn babe in its cradle, it strangled the twin serpents of didacticism and social reform—the two trends that ruled the Anglo-Irish theater (there was no English theater) of its day. With *Private Lives,* Coward proved that if one was enough of an artist, one could be frothy and droll and still say something about one's age that was unassumingly true and ruefully lovely. *Private Lives* is the modest but legitimate heir of *The Way of the World* and *The Importance of Being Earnest.*

I need hardly tell anyone what happens in *Private Lives,* but I would like to say what I think it is about. It is, first, about the impossibility of loving. Ever since Byron damned women for his not being able to live with them or without them—and since, earlier yet, Casanova wrote a twelve volume memoir proving that one could not, for very long, stay either passionately in love or dispassionately out of it—it has dawned on us that the price of romantic fidelity is mediocrity; and the price of romantic infidelity, melancholy. *Private Lives* offers one tentative solution: to keep falling in and out of love with the same partner, thus combining the pleasures of faithfulness and promiscuity. The play is really, as the title of another Coward work has it, a design for living.

But it is also a play about a cultural stance, a fashion in feeling. *Private Lives* epitomizes an era when sentiment, like the female bosom, had to be constricted to the point of concealment. Thus, for example, the great love scene in Act I is played against the grain. Rather than talk about their feelings for each other, Elyot and Amanda play an elaborate question-and-answer game about his trip around the world. The brightness and sophistication of their duologue masks the renewed longing beneath—"Small talk," as the heroine of Coward's *Shadow Play* observes, "with quite different thoughts going on behind it." In the current revival, Brian Bedford tries to convey this touching duplicity; Tammy Grimes doesn't even seem to be aware of it.

But there is something else about *Private Lives:* it reflects the world as the insouciant, frivolous upper classes between the wars wanted it to be. A stylish, snobbish repartee-ridden world in which the few were made for play and the many to be played with. When Amanda wonders whose illuminated yacht is bejeweling the Riviera night, Elyot answers: "The Duke of Westminster's, I expect. It always is." Something in such a line goes beyond mere flippancy or autobiography (Coward's friendship with the Duke); it suggests a world in which a few cosmopolitanly ubiquitous figures could be depended on to brighten the corner where one was.

The current production is adequately directed by Stephen Porter as far as stage movement and business are concerned, but the performances, except for Suzanne Grossmann's highly effective Sibyl—bright surface, brittle pleasantness, irritating sweetness—are inadequate. David Glover's Victor is a mere boob. Brian Bedford's Elyot is not dapper, sexy, upper class, or just plain prepossessing enough; there is little of that exquisite, weary finesse the part cries out for. But the disaster of the evening is the Amanda of Tammy Grimes: this always mannered actress has turned into the paragon of a butch, gay-bar diseuse, all growls, lisps, shlurps and honkings; all strutting, sashaying, swishing and posturing; and nothing whatever that is ladylike or feminine. Not very comely or alluring to begin with, she emerges as an absolute freak for the delectation of flagrant male homosexuals who want women to be as outlandish, outrageous and monstrous as possible. And the frenzy with which the screaming queens, as well as less frenetic inverts, salute this wretched performance is as sorry an exhibition as you can see in any grind-house.

ACCORDING TO a famous schoolboy boner, Shakespeare wrote tragedies, comedies and errors. Neil Simon has yet to write a tragedy, but his comedies and errors are legion. Actually, the man can write funny lines as well as any jokebook, and he can arrange them into the semblance of a plot, which a jokebook can't. But his people, though superficially recognizable, are errors—in observation, psychology, or judgment; the ring of truth is regularly sacrificed for the ring of laughter. Some years ago, Last of the Red Hot Lovers would have been correctly called a farce; now it is billed as a "New Comedy." The New Comedy, we gather, rose with Menander and declined with Neil Simon. This is a play in which it is all for laughs, and the world well lost sight of, but as a middle-aged, married and faithful nonentity looking for one sweet bout with adultery before age and irrevocable fidelity engulf him, James Coco, though physically unsuited to the part, gives another of his magisterial performances. I think that Coco is as good a comic actor as our stage possesses. Not only are his timing, inflections, gestures, facial play and body movements under perfect comic control, he can also make every effect a little bigger, more grotesque than strictly necessary, without, however, going beyond that credibility and dignity whose abandonment reduces comedy to buffoonery.

IF I OVERESTIMATE *The Last Sweet Days of Isaac*, please forgive me. We live in an age of minimal art, where a line is no longer the shortest distance between two points but the shortest way to fame, fortune and enshrinement at the Metropolitan Museum. *Isaac* opened just after *Unfair to Goliath*, an Israeli revue that made me laugh one and a half times, and before *Joy*, an overextended night-club act posturing as theater. There are two amusing performers in *Goliath*, Jim Brochu and Hugh Alexander; the scenery and lighting of C. Murawski is a model of inventiveness on a shoestring; and Menachem Zur's music-making was at least as effervescent as it was eclectic. In *Joy*, Oscar Brown, Jr., demonstrates a winning way with his own lively songs, and Jean Pace an even more winning way or two. A character called Sivuca, described by the program as an "Albino Brazilian" and "hip Buddha," but looking really like a Burl Ives full of *brasilidade* and (coffee) beans, is most astonishing of all. He cavorts about playing several instruments, and vastly augments their range with his own growls and screeches, coming across as a Moogified Yma Sumac. But unless you are a rabid aficionado of minimal theater, you will find this little more than an intermezzo's worth.

When, thereupon, you turn to *The Last Sweet Days of Isaac*, you feel triply relieved: you are in the hands of theater professionals—young ones, to be sure, not yet certain of what vessel will hold their bubbling invention best; you are confronted with something which, both by its imagination and its workmanship, endeavors to continue and expand the theater—musical theater, if you like; and you witness partial failures that stem from daring leaps, not from pusillanimous settling for old hats and small beer.

The construction of *Isaac* is fascinating, tantalizing, and not quite satisfactory. It splits into two one-acters trying hard to relate themselves to each other, sending out greedy feelers but finally failing to merge. Yet this is also the theme of each playlet in itself, and thus becomes an emblematic breakdown. In the first play, Isaac, a crazy, coruscating, marvelous mess of a thirty-two-year-old young-old man, is caught in a stuck elevator with Ingrid, an innocent whom one husband and one lover have made even more innocent. Isaac, who seethes with the gentlest of existential angers—a rage for living and a lust for reality, but a rage that could hardly stir a leaf on a sapling— almost convinces Ingrid to have an instant affair with him in that moment between, say, the 22nd and 23rd floors that he aggrandizes into suspension between life and death.

Isaac, you see, wants to live intensely and recordedly—he is loaded down with cameras, tape recorders, musical instruments; he would not so much burn his taper at both its ends as tape his burning from birth to death, the latter of which, he feels, is imminent. But he is also bright enough to know that when you've got it taped, as well as filmed and canned, life ceases to be life; and his musing about a future society of performers and spectators, nothing but performers and spectators, are funny, frightening, and already very nearly true. All this is interspersed with songs performed by Isaac, Ingrid, and a group that hovers over the stage and is aptly called the Zeitgeist (which can be defined as what ambushes you on the way from Engelbert Humperdinck to the Steppenwolf). A song during which Ingrid, converted to the Walter Pater philosophy of life, exults, "Love, You Came to Me," while Isaac tries unsuccessfully to undress her (in this age of specialization, who is polymath enough to know how to dismantle a Courrèges belt?), is as charming, ridiculous and heartbreaking as anything today's stage can offer.

The second play has Isaac at nineteen in a prison cell next to that of Alice, an activist who seems to get herself busted for the sheer sake of making contact with another being—even if it is only a cop with "meaty" hands. Isaac, again obsessed with media and their rape of our lives, is now the complaisant victim of television. He protests on TV, is arrested on TV, sits in a cell without even a cot, only a TV set that somehow emits as well as receives (Sartre's hell in *No Exit* was a picnic to this!), knows his mother merely via TV, just as he does Alice in her adjoining teeveed cell. He also watches his own death on TV, and is furious only because his name is constantly mispronounced. The details and implications of this Kafkaesque and neo-Einsteinian hallucination defy both my space allotment and my comprehension, which, with Isaac-like smugness, I shall blame on the play. In this one, Nancy Ford's music, so gorgeously superior in the first to the rock-of-the-mill stuff, begins to sound humdrum, but still with a pleasant hum and drum in the ear.

Austin Pendleton's Isaac, displaying the most fertile stammer since Demosthenes', is an owlishly belligerent, sweetly unreasonable, mental-tic-ridden young man, actually a teddy bear weaned on Martin Buber and Marshall McLuhan. His performance would be perfect if it were not a trifle cluttered. But Fredericka Weber, as Ingrid-Alice, is perfection, and when she suddenly picks up a horn to blow her own accompaniment, she rises to whatever comes beyond perfection. I beg you not to believe me but to find out for yourselves.

The true heroine of the evening, however, is Gretchen Cryer, who wrote the book and lyrics. She is gifted with a mind that exudes cunning prosody through every pore, shuttles wittily between insight and second sight, and, when finally hoist with its own petard, goes up in a catherine wheel of utter, inordinate lyricism. I have undoubtedly overpraised *Isaac;* but this, in its funny way, is just what it deserves.

THE RASH OF revivals this season has become a veritable impetigo, if not erysipelas. The latest carbuncle is *Harvey,* an unassuming little comedy that occasionally tickles you, but more often makes you feel itchy. The revivals are meant, of course, as a desperate remedy for Broadway's inability or unwillingness to undertake something better, and therefore, presumably, riskier. So the cure for stagnancy is to be soft-core revivals: what could be safer than to appeal to the sentimental nostalgia of the middle-aged middle-class middle-brow? To take him back to the mediocrities of his younger days, to which he loves to slink back like a criminal to the scene of his prime. The revivals represent the unholy matrimony of box-office greed and audience mushiness, and if this remedy continues to be applied, Broadway has the choice of dying of the disease or the medication.

Harvey, Mary Chase's comedy that won the 1945 Pulitzer Prize over Tennessee Williams' *The Glass Menagerie,* is named after a giant rabbit who at first is visible and intelligible only to Elwood P. Dowd, the lovable drunken loafer whom his sister, Veta Louise Simmons, ashamed of him, would confine to an institution. But eventually, sister, chief psychiatrist and the rest become cognizant of the existence of this 6′2½″ white rabbit endowed with prophetic powers. And the bibulous bonhomie of Elwood, who gives out calling cards to everyone he meets, with invitations to join Harvey and him at one of his many beloved bars, wins out over the loveless world of assorted curmudgeons who do not believe in the rabbit and his stewed friend. In this, unlike in the original Broadway production, we do not get a final glimpse of the creature, but doors open and close manipulated by his invisible paw.

The play presents two problems. The more obvious one is that whereas art does not age, artifice does. Even in Denver, the locale of Mrs. Chase's somnolent whimsy, time does not stand entirely still, and we wonder whether today, even in a genteel comedy, Veta Louise can misidentify an overzealous mental hospital orderly thus: "He was a white slaver. I know he was. He had one of those white suits. That's how they advertise." Of the psychiatric staff, she complains: "They kept asking me a lot of dirty questions about sex urges and stuff like that." Is that still funny? Was it ever? In any case, the never-never land of the play's "real world," in which "Nuts!" is the strongest expletive, has become as unreal to us as Elwood's fantasy world, robbing *Harvey* of its minimal conflict.

But the deeper problem is a moral one, if we may look this fantasy squarely in its pink eyes. Are we to accept without demur the superiority of the shiftless and useless Dowd, his love for people scarcely more than a need for fellow boozers and card partners? Is this mindless, companionable crapulence truly as lovable as the play would have us believe? Frank Fay, as I recall, at least gave the character some tartness; as James Stewart plays him, he is a case of tenderly arrested development in limb, speech and mind. "I wrestled with reality for forty years, doctor," he says, "and I'm happy to state I won out over it." If the hard-won victory over reality is achieved in the name of a potted leporine liaison, the unreality may be inferior to reality.

The part of Veta Louise in the current Phoenix revival is played by, as it now seems obligatory to advertise her, "Miss Helen Hayes." That is not a categorical imperative, but a tribute to one of the *grandes dames* of our theater, who here essays what may be her first unsympathetic—or at least less than predominantly sympathetic—role. With knowing technique and adorable fussiness galore, she succeeds in depriving the protagonist of his antagonist, and converting Veta Louise, whom you should love to hate, into someone you hate to love. In the supporting cast, rather too anodynely directed by Stephen Porter, only Marian Hailey and Henderson Forsythe convince me, and I award one ear of the rabbit to each.

•   •   •

SHOW ME WHERE THE GOOD TIMES ARE is a typical American musical of our day. It is presented at a new theater of which it is impossible to say whether it is on or off Broadway; it is based on a successful work in another medium (in this case, Molière's *The Imaginary Invalid*); and it is no good. A typical current musical, to reiterate, is not much different on or off Broadway, is based on something else, and is bad. This particular one is very bad. Imagine a Princeton Triangle Club show (before this year, when girls were admitted; in *Show Me* there are no noticeable girls, only travesties of women and a few girlish men), which gives you one triangle. Now take another triangle, an inverted one, and place it over your first. You get a Star—correction—*Thtar* of David. And that's what *Show Me* is: a faggoty, Jewish, collegiate musical.

Seventeenth-century Paris has become the Lower East Side in 1913, Argan has become Aaron, Béline has become Bella, Angélique has become Annette, and the story has become nonsense. What was an attack on the charlatanism of the medical profession, and, through it, on hypocrisy and gullibility in general, is now a simplistic plot to which has been added a subplot, the love affair of Gloria, Aaron's sister (based partly on the maid, Toinette, and ever so slightly on the *raisonneur*, Béralde, who however, is missing from the musical, reason having scant place in it). Gloria carries on with Kolinsky, a Jewish Art Theatre actor-manager, who is played, for no intrinsic reason, as a raving queen. Though doctors, real and unreal, still appear in *Show Me*, nothing much is said about them, and the voraciously pill-taking Aaron, if he belongs anywhere, fits into a post-Smith Brothers era, well after Carter's Little Liver Pills became as obsolete as time capsules.

But this is what most Broadway and many off-Broadway musicals still strive for: instead of acceptance of the new ideological and musical landscape in which we live, we are given show-biz songs and plot formulas with beards longer than the aforementioned Brothers'. One of the more unsavory of these formulas is that of gearing a show at as many major minority groups as you can corral. Nine years ago, when *Purlie Victorious* appeared as a play, I wrote: "The one show that could run forever on Broadway would be a big, vulgar musical about Jewish Negroes." There have been frequent attempts at combining these elements; fortunately, one or the other is always missing. In *Show Me*, we have a *small*, vulgar musical (strike one) about Jews but no Negroes (strike two), and though there are compensatory homosexuals, these are faintly disguised, which today is not enough for a selling point (strike three).

Needless to say, there is nothing wrong with a show involving any of the above features or groups if this stems from an intrinsic necessity. But if it is merely slapped on, adventitiously and meretriciously, there goes your show! Sheer shameless audience appeal may still work in the movies, which are relatively inexpensive, but in the costly theater, I fervently believe, people want something more substantial for their money. Cowardice and bets as hedged as a formal garden will no longer pay off. Such cowardice makes musicals out of successful novels, films, plays and gave us, in rapid succession, *Gantry* (*Elmer Gantry*), *Georgy* (*Georgy Girl*), and this. Or it may not be cravenness, just lack of imagination—the inability to think up a story. But why should people who lack courage and originality in one major area presume that they will have it in others?

The best musicals on and off Broadway are those rare birds based only on themselves. Thus, for all their obvious deficiencies, *Hair* and *1776*, and thus, despite some harmless shortcomings, *Salvation* and the pick of the litter, *The Last Sweet Days of Isaac*. The one exception is the charming *Your Own Thing*, which is based on *Twelfth Night*, but the adaptation is very free, and the unisex theme happens to be more apposite today than ever before. But in all these shows, except in *1776*, something else, supremely important, is at work: musical contemporaneity.

Let me make it clear: I am no rock enthusiast—if anything, the opposite. But the sound of our musicals must change. Even if this sound is not so glaringly derivative as in *Show Me Where the Good Times Are* (at which the only fun is to be had by playing a game of "Show me where the good tunes come from"), it is nowadays almost always antiquated. Certainly there are some sentimentalists—the middle-aged nostalgia-mongers and the homosexual camp-cravers—who are a hard-core market for this soft-core drivel. But not enough of one; the new must prevail. Yet must the new be rock?

Not necessarily. Just as we are now in a period of avid, though hitherto not generally successful, experimentation in "serious" music, there could and should be something comparable in musical comedy. The latter desperately needs its Webern, Boulez, Henze; or, more moderately, its Françaix, Carter (not of the Liver Pills) and Britten. Especially, perhaps, a Britten. Someone who can combine the old with the new, who becomes ever more daring as he goes along, who has a fine sense of how to match English words with music (not nearly so easy as matching Italian, French, or even German ones). We need someone who has a musical education as well as facility, and is willing to work unwhorishly in a popular idiom. And who will resolutely not musicalize *John and Mary, The Love Machine* or *Forty Carats*. If there must be adaptations, let them be of something more challenging—say, *Samson Agonistes, The Cabinet of Dr. Caligari,* or *Soul on Ice.*

SPRING, 1970

INDIANS
by Arthur Kopit

THE FRONT PAGE
by Ben Hecht and Charles MacArthur

THREE MEN ON A HORSE
by John Cecil Holm and George Abbott

THE TIME OF YOUR LIFE
by William Saroyan

OUR TOWN
by Thornton Wilder

BORSTAL BOY
by Brendan Behan

THE EFFECT OF GAMMA RAYS
ON MAN-IN-THE-MOON MARIGOLDS
by Paul Zindel

THE ME NOBODY KNOWS
by Will Holt and Gary William Friedman

CHILD'S PLAY
by Robert Marasco

WHAT THE BUTLER SAW
by Joe Orton

COLETTE
by Elinor Jones
music by Harvey Schmidt
lyrics by Tom Jones

IN TRYING to see the New York theater of this season in perspective, we come all too quickly to the vanishing point. True, even halfway serious observers have been complaining about the death of Broadway, the Broadwayization of off-Broadway, and the unconscionable frivolity of off-off-Broadway for some years now. But the first half of the 1969–70 season truly represents some kind of record in triviality, worthlessness, and sheer paucity of shows. The number of Broadway openings so far this season is far below that of previous half-seasons—so much so, in fact, that even the staid *New York Times* saw fit to run a symposium on whether Broadway is dying. The situation is getting harder and harder to dismiss with the usual crying wolf, for even in the fable the wolf finally does turn up; nor is there consolation, necessarily, in the saw about the "fabulous invalid," for even fabulous invalids eventually die.

Interesting but scarcely successful was Arthur Kopit's *Indians.* First produced in London, then in Washington, D.C., and finally on Broadway, the work underwent continual changes, apparently for the worse. This is a play about Buffalo Bill, friend of the Indians and their betrayer, who hobnobbed with many a chief but also exterminated the buffalo herds off which the Indian lived; who put on Wild West shows that enabled him, and the rest of America, to purge their bad consciences by sentimentalizing the redskin. The play alternates between scenes at the rodeo and scenes in which a Presidential Commission, under the guise of hearing grievances, further insults and cheats the red men. Interspersed, too, are outrageous episodes involving comic-strip characters like the Ol' Time President, Wild Bill Hickcock, Annie Oakley, Jesse James, and the Grand Duke Alexis of Russia on a buffalo-*cum*-Indian-shooting expedition. This material tries to be absurdist but generally manages to be only sophomoric.

For this is the problem with Arthur Kopit: a bright, amusing, talented young man seemingly frozen forever at the clever Harvard sophomore level at which he produced *Oh Dad, Poor Dad.* It is only partly Kopit's fault. The American theater is so hungry for new playwrights—or, if you prefer, for success stories—that it will extol and exalt an impressionable young man so quickly and absolutely that he has to be an extraordinarily strong character not to become an *enfant terrible,* a famulus of fame, a playboy of the Western Coast, or some other form of arrested development. *Indians* contains a good, dramatizable concept: our duality toward, and double-dealing with, the Indians—ruthlessness for their living selves, infantile mooning over the idea of them. And the same, of course, applies to our dealing with the Negroes and with Vietnam, though the parallels are less glaring than some slapdash liberals have hastily assumed and praised this play for.

But, alas, Kopit is not very good at bringing his concept to genuine theatrical life. For one thing, he keeps the characters he likes—Buffalo Bill, Sitting Bull, Chief Joseph, etc.—not wholly sympathetic but at least more or less realistic; whereas the ones he dislikes or wants to have fun with become garish caricatures. For another, he and his clever director, Gene Frankel, have gone all out for fancy theatrical effects—abetted by the set design of Oliver Smith (a circus arena that can transform itself in a trice into a number of other things); the lighting of Thomas Skelton (which includes cunning strobe lights during scene changes, so that one image does not exactly flow but teasingly jerks itself into the next one by tiny, jagged reshufflings between flashes of light); the outlandish and exaggerated electronic music of Richard Peaslee (who has never equaled his contribution to *Marat/Sade*); the impressive but too serious choreography of Julie Arenal (including a terrifying Indian dance of self-immolation); and elaborate sound effects that include Buffalo Bill's subconscious addressing him stereophonically. It is all a visual and aural feast—I haven't enumerated the half of it—with the mind, regrettably, cast in the role of Lazarus.

THE MOST SIGNIFICANT feature of the season, as I have already mentioned, is its desperate reaching for revivals. The first of these, a carry-over from last season, was *The Front Page,* which began as a semistar-studded revival at a small New Jersey playhouse, was beefed up and transferred to Broadway, where it proceeded to pros-

per despite its general sleaziness and mainly undistinguished staging and acting. This 1928 play by Hecht and MacArthur is full of
the least attractive ideas of its time: American chauvinism, contempt
for culture, condescension to the intellect, sentimental affection for
crooks in and out of government. And, vilest of all, the notion that
newspapermen are the toughest, shrewdest, meanest and ultimately
cleverest guys in the world. The hell of it is that these smartalecky
or simply asinine attitudes are still cozily alive among the public,
which lapped up this brash, tawdry and essentially unfunny farce.

YET THERE IS at least a low-level knowhow with which *The Front
Page* is put together, a reasonable manipulative proficiency. What
can be said for a revival of *Three Men on a Horse,* a play that must
have drawn precious few laughs from intelligent customers even in
1935, when this John Cecil Holm-George Abbott farce first became
a hit? Abbott, at eighty-two, was again directing, only this time in
slow motion; Sam Levene was repeating his original role of Patsy,
a performance he has since made famous in every play he has been
in; all ages were upped considerably—the young lead, Erwin, was
played by Jack Gilford as a spry fifty, while his ornery, tightfisted
boss was played by Paul Ford as a last-ditch stand in the war
against senility, with flubbed lines dropping all over like falling hair
or teeth. It was, in short, less a revival than an embalming; an evening not of dramatics but of geriatrics. But this mirthless shuffling
about so delighted our senile or prematurely senescent drama reviewers—and especially that most senior of juniors, Richard Watts, Jr.—
as to garner a set of excellent notices and achieve an estimable run.
Yet the play is pitiful in its want of wit, and merely confirms the
unhappy suspicion that, however bad most present theater may be,
that of the good old days must have been even worse. Only then
it did not have to compete with television and a vastly improved
cinema.

REVIVALS KEPT coming at us. Over at Lincoln Center, where an
all-American season is in progress, they began with Saroyan's *The
Time of Your Life,* the hit of 1940. This is a curious play, dripping
with sentimentality on the surface, and full of bitterness underneath.
But it is a comic, absurd, lovable bitterness—with only one character
among the many truly evil, and he dispatched in the most jovially
improbable way at the end—a bitterness which, when it is not an

outright joke, merely serves to remind us how beautiful life is never-theless. I am not suggesting that this is an impossible stance; yet there is something uncomfortable about looking at life as at a pitiful nag, Rosinante, and forcing Quixote-colored spectacles over one's knacker's eyes. In fact, it is hard to say what is real here, the senti-mentality or the disenchantment: whether the play is a cynic's men-dacious daydream, or a sloppy sentimentalist's determination to over-look repeated kicks in the groin. Either way, it is an uneasy, double vision, and neither its mooning nor its moaning rings true.

This dramatic oxymoron was performed by a spotty cast under the less than idiomatic direction of John Hirsch, the Hungarian-born Canadian director. But Douglas W. Schmidt's saloon setting was in-toxicatingly atmospheric, down to its last lovably untidy, rickety detail, and only the marble game seemed less versatile than the au-thor specifies. Characteristically, a lot of patronizing references to Wesley, the Negro piano player, were cravenly omitted, because though one wanted nostalgic period-authenticity, one did not wish to run afoul of anyone. Granted the casting was unfortunate, espe-cially on the distaff side—the beefily unpathetic Kitty of Susan Tyrell, the blandly trivial Mary L. of Priscilla Pointer, the freshman-debat-ing-society Elsie of Laura Esterman—the tinseled look and tinny sound were nonetheless the play's own, and demonstrated how the jewels of American playwriting are designed for instant tarnish.

It is high time that someone publish a judicious reevaluation of the drama of the thirties, or for that matter of the entire literature of that period. In the theater, at any rate, nothing of indisputable merit will emerge. The attitudinizing melodramas of Sherwood and Kings-ley will fare as poorly as the folkloristic revels and urban pastorals of Marc Connelly and Clifford Odets, or the vastly overrated farces of Kaufman and his various collaborators. Nor is there much po-tential for survival in the touching efforts at sophistication of S. N. Behrman, the historical pastiches of Maxwell Anderson, or the coy psychologizings of Philip Barry. The earnest strivings of Sidney Howard will prove as artless as the artsiness of Saroyan, or as the thirties' works of the man who was to emerge as America's one great dramatist with his earlier and, particularly, his later works—Eugene O'Neill. The thirties could be excised from the history of American drama—assuming that it has a history—and no one, except the over-praised authors, would be the worse for it.

•   •   •

STILL ANOTHER revival, also originating in the suburbs, Long Island this time, was another semistellar production of Thornton Wilder's perennial favorite, *Our Town*. Now, it is a well-known fact that perennial favorites take a terrible beating, but it is a moot point whether they get it undeservedly, or are in fact asking for it. If you write a play that is just perfect for high-school dramatic clubs, chances are that it will be performed to death, both quantitatively and qualitatively, by high-school dramatic clubs. But further chances are that if it appeals quite so much to the little darlings and their teachers, there must be something infantile about it in the first place, and so there is about *Our Town*. It is another thirties' product (1938) and may be viewed as a conservative answer to the general leftism of the contemporary theater. The play is, as Wilder said in his introduction, "an attempt to find a value above all price for the smallest events in our daily life." It is precisely of such inflation that sentimentalism is made, and when one of the dead people in the play's last act opines, "My, wasn't life awful and wonderful," we get the philosophy and malady of both *Our Town* and *The Time of Your Life* in a nutshell. In *Our Town*, where the dead can hardly wait to forget all about it, life is wonderful but awful; in *The Time of Your Life* it is, despite all the social ills and private meanness and suffering, somehow as marvelous as the people in it, awful but wonderful.

There is, perhaps, nothing inherently wrong with this view, whichever end is up, as long as you do not use it as a formula for oversimplification and falsification, or just simple fudging. "Oh, earth, you're too wonderful for anybody to realize you," Wilder's freshly deceased Emily apostrophizes. Next, she asks the Stage Manager through her tears: "Do any human beings ever realize life while they live it?—every, every minute?" To which the Stage Manager, who is more than a Greek chorus, and rather like God or Thornton Wilder, responds, "No. [Pause] The saints and poets, maybe—they do some." Well, then why this apotheosis of Grover's Corners, N. H., circa 1900, if people there do not fully realize life? Why not focus on Paris or Rome or Florence, where the incidence of poets, and probably even saints, is greater? And how can the "value above all price for the smallest events" be found in a context of simpering or platitudinizing nonentities who clearly do not realize—in either sense—the worth of living?

And while *Our Town* sloshes about in warm-hearted muddle-headedness, *The Time of Your Life* (notice, by the way, that conspiratorial *Our* and folksy *Your* in the titles) gives us a whore, Kitty, the perfect embodiment of the play's absurd tergiversations. "She is a small powerful girl, with that kind of delicate and rugged beauty which no circumstance of evil or ugly reality can destroy." There follows something about her having that immortal element "which is in the seed of good and common people," as if the yoking of "good" and "common" were the most natural thing in the world. "There is an angry purity, and a fierce pride, in her." Joe, the central character of the play, who is more than a Greek chorus and rather like God or William Saroyan, "recognizes her as a great person immediately." So above the whore with the heart of gold, an old lie we have learned to digest, we now get the whore who is immediately recognizable as a great person, a new and uncooked lie that sticks in the most undiscriminating craw.

But the play is full of such lies. There is the Arab, who fulminates against the stench of the world, but finds ready consolation in the stars and his harmonica. There is Elsie, the nurse who sees nothing but death at its meanest and doesn't believe in love, but who runs off hand in hand with Dudley to find happiness in a cheap hotel. There is Kit Carson, who is obviously a liar and a phony, but who performs the one truly heroic deed of the play—shooting the villainous cop, Blick—and gets away scot-free. There is Nick, the tough bartender, who weeps at "None but the Lonely Heart"; and there is the lovable cop, Krupp, who thinks that "in this wonderful world . . . we're crazy. . . . We're no good any more." And after listing a string of horrors, our cop cops out—concedes that his wife is wonderful, his boys "the swellest," and asks that his foregoing outburst be forgotten. And so it goes, seesawing schematically, the whole thing glibly summed up by Joe: "Everything's right. Right and wrong."

This, of course, is too easy. Yet the general public, the You whose life and We whose town it is, are not even likely to remember this facile ambivalence. They are more likely to be left holding on to an exchange about a plucky little newsboy who dreams of being in show-biz and heartrendingly renders "When Irish Eyes Are Smiling," Greek though he be. Comments Nick: "Joe, people are so wonderful. Look at that kid." Joe answers, "Of course they're wonderful. Every one of them is wonderful." Except that they are also crazy, nuts, dissatisfied, lousy, no good, wanting to make some kind of killing—all terms applied to them by the decent Officer Krupp. It all resolves itself into the gratuitous, meaningless schematism of "My, isn't life awful and wonderful" and all that jazz.

As for the production of *Our Town*, it was passable, except for the hysterical Emily of Elisabeth Hartman, and the occasional anachronistic lapse in Donald Driver's direction. Some of the parents were, like the cast of *Three Men on a Horse*, a bit overripe for their parts but clearly such sentimental revivals appeal to old-timers, so any little cheating that will endear things to them is par for the course. Henry Fonda's Stage Manager was as comfortable as an old felt slipper, except in the area of the New England accent, where it pinched a little.

Why all these revivals, more of which are scheduled, and a couple of others of which I am coming to anon? They represent the hideous marriage of sentimentality and greed. When there is little new stuff that seems suitable for Broadway and the affluent, middle-of-everything audience that alone can foot its bills and stomach its fare, revivals are in. The delicate average stomachs may indeed be upset by the new, though it has never been proved that they could not be slowly accustomed to it; they are presumed to enjoy ruminating on their youth, and in the theater this is the drama of the thirties and late twenties. So if you join the sentimentality of these prosperous middle-everythings to the cupidity of the Box Office, to the unlimited greed of the producers and investors (many of whom partake also of the aforementioned sentimentality), you get the unholy matrimony I have in mind—a calculating marriage of convenience that is also incestuous, sterile and stultifying.

THE ONE TIME I met Brendan Behan, a bunch of us were sitting in the Algonquin lobby, fairly late, when somebody—his waiter, or keeper—came up and asked whether we would kindly keep Mr. Behan company while he ate his dinner. Apparently this helped him eat, just as his witty and variously informed conversation helped us down our nightcaps. He twitted us all with that bellicose charm of his, and I still cherish the oxymoron "Balkan Metternich" that he coined for me.

It was therefore sad, beautiful, and a little frightening to see Niall Toibin revealed on the Lyceum stage, and—excellent actor that he is, and friend of Behan that he was—not just re-create the man, but simply be Brendan Behan. Perhaps death did not, after all, have a sting-aling-aling (to recall the end of *The Hostage*), at least not when his adversary was a man of Brendan's mettle. Death was defeated; for here was not only Behan, with that lopsided, diffident self-assurance of his, cheerily twinkling and tweaking away at us; here, too, was a new play of his—or something very near to it— dazzling and warming us out of his grave.

Frank McMahon has adapted *Borstal Boy*, Behan's memoirs of how, as a sixteen-year-old would-be I.R.A. bomber, he is apprehended in Liverpool, brutalized in an English prison, and finally sent to the Borstal (house of correction) for three years—years that proved as much education as punishment. The resulting stage work is certainly episodic and sprawling, and finicky purists may quite rightly point out its weaknesses as drama; but as a sheer theatrical event bursting with humanity, slyness, fury and good humor, who will find me its equal these days? The first act, mostly in prison, could be harrowing—indeed, parts of it are—but even here you are slowly but surely overpowered by an inner merriment that the play implants in you and intermittently releases in sweet but wondering laughter. How can delight survive among all this nastiness and violence? But it does—for this was always Behan's special talent: to be like one of those crazy spring days on which everything from hailstones to rainbows come lurching at you out of the sky.

McMahon has hit upon the simple, happy devices of having the grown Behan act as sidelines chorus to his immature self's predicaments, and the young Brendan is played, with scarcely less expertise than Mr. Toibin's, by Frank Grimes, a youthful actor of the most forthright, uncloying charm and an unswerving but easygoing conviction. The conversations, or near-conversations, that these two privileged beings have with each other across time and space are instinct with ripeness; they embody before our eyes and ears an image of what it is to come to terms with life, while also making it come to terms with you. And what gives this interrupted but never squelched dialogue something to feed on is, of course, the swirling action that Walton Prison provides.

The second act, at Bay Borstal, is much funnier and easier to take. Yet it, too, has its dark sides and tragic vision, not wholly abandoned for the sake of some of the most exquisite hijinks I have seen on any stage. For that is what makes *Borstal Boy*: Behan's compassion, intelligence and sense of humor are all equally there, whether the matter at hand is grave, agonizing, or ludicrous. What this means in effect is that he pays close attention to people and what they say, do and have done to them, and that he always has a comment on everything, an Irishman's inalienable right to the last word. Except that the word is not insistent; rather, it is like light through Venetian blinds, streaky and unobtrusive, but quite enough to tell you whether it is night or day. And with a zebra'd charm to boot.

It would be ungrateful to carp at the few weak links in the large Anglo-American-Hibernian cast that produces such lovely ensemble acting under Tomás Mac Anna's direction that you begin to think that national and ideological gulfs must surely become bridgeable one day. I particularly liked Bruce Heighley and Michael Cahill, but there are any number of splendidly colorful others against Mr. Mac Anna's austerely simple, minimal but evocative scenery. That this production was the hit of the Abbey Theatre in Dublin I mention with hesitancy, for if you let this suggest to you parochial interest that does not export well, you would be dead wrong. *Borstal Boy* is theater down to those melancholy but infinitely nourishing songs Mr. Toibin sings from time to time—just as Brendan did—and with the same tuneless quality as somebody whistling in the dark. It does not often happen—in the theater or in life—that a whistle can conquer the darkness and transport us to a place where, ultimately, mellowness is all.

What was particularly significant about this dramatic event, however, was that despite its genuine artistic value and condign success abroad, its apt and absorbing blend of the humorous and serious, its historic and contemporary meaningfulness (the I.R.A. as our own militant radicals, black and white), the generally enthusiastic reviews and numerous awards, and a reasonable amount of advertising, it could not survive. It should be fairly obvious, then, that a play cannot succeed on Broadway unless it meets one of these four conditions: 1) it has major stars in it; 2) it has some kind of sensational aspect; 3) it brazenly caters to the values, religion (Jewish), or nostalgia of the theater-going majority; 4) it is a belly-laugh a minute. Since *Borstal Boy* was only a good play in a good production, it failed.

STILL, THEATER keeps popping up, modestly and almost inconspicuously, and encouraging us—perhaps foolishly—to hope. There is the case of Paul Zindel's *The Effect of Gamma Rays on Man-in-the-Moon Marigolds,* a rather tricky title that sounds dragged in by its stamens, but actually makes sense. *Marigolds* concerns an embittered, slatternly divorcée and widow, Beatrice, and her two disturbed daughters. Ruth is sexy, aggressive, dumbish, and has been institutionalized once; Tillie is introverted, homely, shy and brilliant, especially in science. Beatrice, an emotional cripple at war with the world, bullies her daughters, inveighs against fate, and delights in making telephone callers the butts of her irony or fulminations. In the course of the play, Ruth, betrayed by her mother, is once again reduced to a gibbering idiot; Tillie, similarly betrayed, finds strength in scholastic achievement and may work out her salvation. Beatrice schemes to convert the pigsty they live in into a tea shop, knows she is fooling herself, and despairs. That is the simple framework.

The story is not very original, nor is it worked out all that carefully. Though we see a crone whom Beatrice has taken on as a boarder for fifty dollars a week, and Ruth may make a pittance as part-time secretary at school, it is not clear how the family can survive, even shabbily. Nor is it clear how old these teenagers are, and their being played by mature actresses makes for slight confusion. The characters do not belong in quite the same play: Beatrice and Ruth are out of realistic comedy-drama; Tillie is out of some poetic play like *The Glass Menagerie;* a fellow schoolgirl is out of farce. There is a certain unsureness about how much to tell of a character's past: there is a little too much psychological justification of Beatrice's bitchiness to make us take it for granted and attend to other matters, but not enough to make us fully sympathize with what she has become.

But when all this is subtracted, there still remains a very engaging though small play. Its first strength lies in the sympathy and humor with which Paul Zindel views all his characters, even the nonspeaking, doddering crone who is kept on honeyed water, but whose heart belongs to beer. He has sensibly grasped the lesson of *Long Day's Journey into Night:* to show a family destroying one another unwillingly and even apologetically, but with impotent relentlessness. Some of the hostilities, though filigree, are genuinely frightening, particularly the frustrated Beatrice's begrudging of Tillie's modest successes and gratifications. There is a curious, shimmering quality to these characters as they are spun around so fast that you can hardly tell whether what you are seeing now is their bright or dark, tormented or tormenting side.

There are other virtues: an unassuming, leisurely sense of humor, and a pathos under strict surveillance lest it jerk obscuring tears. The symbol of the marigolds works very handsomely indeed—a trifle too neatly, perhaps. There is a nice sense of the stage image, as when Beatrice, close to the breaking point, is fanatically sorting out and folding napkins; or when a flashlight, on a stormy night with the electricity dead, takes over the stage and becomes importunate in its prying. There is an equally knowing orchestration of voices and sounds. Best of all, there is the ability to make the barest utterance grow into the stature of poetry, as when, at the end, Beatrice looks up from her napkins to say point-blank, "Tillie, I hate the world. I hate the world." And her daughter, sitting in the same world yet seeing it through a rose-colored microscope, exclaims, "Atom. *Atom.* What a beautiful word!"

Sada Thompson does ample justice to both the ugliness and the remnants of humanity in Beatrice's character, and manages the comic undertones as securely as the overtones of metaphysical horror. As Tillie, Pamela Payton-Wright knows how to stop an almost too lovable character from spilling over into soupiness, and is utterly persuasive. Judith Lowry is fine as the pitiful but grotesque crone; only Amy Levitt strikes me as less than an actress, despite having all the shrill and grubby requisites for Ruth. Under Melvin Bernhardt's capable direction, *Marigolds* may be no more than a dram of drama, but a dram of the true elixir.

A MUCH BETTER and fresher musical than most Broadway ones is to be found off-Broadway: *The Me Nobody Knows,* adapted from a book by the same title, a collection of poems and prose compositions by schoolchildren between the ages of seven and seventeen in ghetto districts. A part of this material was arranged into a loose concatenation of songs and brief monologues or dialogues and interspersed with cheekily down-to-earth dances by Patricia Birch, dances that are extensions of street games. Will Holt fiddled a little with some of the texts to convert them into lyrics, and Gary William Friedman wrote a score for them that is so good you hardly notice that it is rock. Robert H. Livingston's staging is sensibly plain, and the rest is up to a dozen youngsters, eight of them Negro or Puerto Rican, almost all of them talented, and some six or seven of them first-rate professionals.

I could write paragraphs about what young Melanie Henderson can do with a single, precociously illusionless yet equanimous expression; what eleven-year-old Irene Cara can do with a sassy bit of grown womanhood hard-bought on the installment plan; what José Fernandez can do with the eloquence of inarticulateness; what Douglas Grant, who must be ten or eleven, can do in sheer all-around professionalism without a hint of puerility or preciosity. But I want to express my chief gratitude to Northern Calloway, for portraying a Negro youth with that ironic flexibility and mercurial resilience that I have never seen so well translated into song and dance and just plain bearing. And to pretty, blond Beverly Ann Bremers, for her vocal mastery—from comically fluttering falsettos to low, soul-shaking fortissimos that are yet full of subtle musicianliness and give you warm chills, if there is such a thing. (There is now.) And please do not, because of her unassumingness, overlook Laura Michaels, a performer with a quiet but all-pervasive fervor, an authority that stems from selfless dedication—even to making someone else look good.

The mood shuttles between drama and comedy, but, in a sense, is always simultaneously drama and comedy, for though these kids surmount most of the horrors they face, which is joyous, the mere fact that they should have to tangle with them is unutterably sad. *The Me Nobody Knows* gets it all across with the directness, illiterate poetry, touching unadornment, flashes of extraordinary originality, spontaneity even in banality, which make the writings of children, like the drawings of cavemen, what the sight of the dawn is to eyes accustomed to sleep till noon.

SOMEWHAT OLDER, and considerably worse, children are to be found in Robert Marasco's *Child's Play*, probably the only 1970 dramatic offering to emerge as a hit on Broadway. This is a rather pretentious affair about good and evil epitomized by two teachers in a Catholic boys' school, a good and an evil that mutually destroy each other, much as in *Billy Budd*, only here the good at first appears to be the bad, and vice versa. This conflict is supposed to have a fell effect on the pupils, who perform horrors of sadistic and masochistic mutilation upon one another or themselves. There is much kitchen-sink metaphysicizing à la Graham or Julien Green(e) among the various priestly or lay members of the faculty, which includes a young, innocent gym teacher and a bibulously cynical young priest (tidily played by Ken Howard and David Rounds, respectively). There are overtones also of Henry James and Joseph Conrad; Marasco, who himself taught at such a school, seems to be digesting two years' worth of the curriculum in this, his first play. It comes out, as I remarked elsewhere, as Claudel rewritten by Chayefsky.

Child's Play is full of glaring improbabilities that cannot be explained away with recourse to slogans like "symbolism" or "heightened realism." One simply does not accept a psychopathic teacher's defying detection for thirty years, or another's fundamental goodness remaining unsuspected for decades. Even Tertullian's faith would be taxed by a school teeming with perverted teenaged martyrs, their autos-da-fé unleashed by a mere dimly sensed presence of cosmic injustice embodied in the rival teachers. And why should the mysterious carnage have waited so long to burst forth, and why must it reach the proportions it does before it is comprehended and combatted? But at least Marasco's dialogue is generally literate, captures the flavor of a seedily waspish faculty room, and tends to avoid the obvious. There may be real talent here if it ever gets beyond this first stage of overstylized autobiography into the free field of untrammeled creation.

What is truly notable about the production is the performance of Fritz Weaver as the maligned martinet, the basically pathetic classics teacher. It starts on a high level of crotchetiness verging on hysteria, then, in defiance of probability, keeps building on it, though just sustaining it would be a remarkable enough accomplishment. The voice is a tormented trumpeting, almost providing the words with a musical score, and the movements seem to be carved out of a large block of pain. There is an awesome deliberateness about it all, bordering on overelaboration, but there is something wonderful about acting that goes beyond truth into a sheer display of mastery over a medium, like the *entrechat dix* Nijinsky would put in where ordinary dancers did a mere *six*. By contrast, Pat Hingle's assured but routinely realistic performance as the popular, easy-going, seemingly good teacher is just mellowed Method acting, fluent and unmemorable. Moreover, Hingle has given this same bumptious performance so many times by now that one feels one is watching not Hingle but some comic doing an impersonation of him. Jo Mielziner's set has the right combination of massiveness, mysteriousness, and motheatenness, but Joseph Hardy's staging is calculatedly greedy for stunning effects.

JOSEPH HARDY has also directed the last play of the late Joe Orton, *What the Butler Saw*, and put the finishing—and, alas, diminishing—touches on the unfinished second act. Orton was a very promising playwright developing by imaginative leaps and bounds, whose domain was the confluence of satire, absurdism and camp. His manner was part homosexual protest, part magnificently morbid imagination, part cynical laughter, and there was marked improvement from play to play until a homosexual roommate's bludgeon descended before the thirty-four-year-old playwright could complete his third full-length work. Nevertheless, *What the Butler Saw,* at least in its first half, could be great, grating fun—showing a society with every one of its moral values stood on its head, and people hanging upside down, like sloths or bats, to make it all seem right side up. Unlike most absurdists, Orton never lets us forget that the face in the fun-house mirror is our own. But as Hardy has cast and staged it, the play does not work. The actors either do not look their parts, or do not sound them (genteel British), or cannot act—most notably in the case of Lucian Scott, an old acting teacher of his, whom Hardy has cast in a key role, and who cannot even remember his lines, much less deliver them properly. Furthermore, Hardy does not maintain a fast enough tempo, and worse yet, does not have his actors behave as if they meant what they are doing. Now, the cardinal rule of farce is that the actors must not think of themselves as inhabiting some world of brittle make-believe, but must play the screamingly funny, outrageous, preposterous situations in dead earnest. Failing that, one invites bloodless pastiche, which is just what Hardy, who is rapidly becoming our town's most overrated director, ended up with.

I WONDER WHAT Mme. Colette, fair playwright and first-rate drama critic that she was, would have thought of *Colette,* a biographical entertainment Elinor Jones has fashioned from her works. Well, not from her works—Mrs. Jones has clearly not read the fifteen large volumes of the *Oeuvres complètes*—but from such bits of them as Robert Phelps chose to translate for his one-volume selection, *Earthly Paradise.* A nice anthology, that, but not intended to be put on stage —least of all by this adapter.

Théophile Gautier defined himself as a man for whom the physical world exists; Colette was a writer for whom *only* the physical world existed. She was a genius of the second-rate, which is much better than being a second-rate genius, and is not meant as a slight on the physical world. But the novelist-essayist's exclusive preoccupation with people and animals as sensuous and sensual creatures, with sometimes a glowing landscape around them, does not account for other aspects of existence that cannot be ignored with posthumous impunity. Still, within her sensory bailiwick, this *poète dionysien de la sensation,* as René Lalou dubbed her, was matchless and, to me, vastly preferable to second-rate geniuses like St.-John Perse.

But to take a great albeit somewhat limited writer and translate her into a "character," an "original," an eccentrically theatrical "personality," is an odiously commercial, sacrilegious undertaking. Mrs. Jones, like the inept show-biz gate-crasher she is, has picked up her opera glasses by the wrong end and given us a diminutive, cute, trivial Colette, of an artistic stature midway between Fanny Hurst's and Sophie Tucker's. Joining in this family enterprise, Mrs. Jones's husband, Tom, has written some of his usual saccharine lyrics, for which his partner, Harvey Schmidt, has provided supererogatory tunes. He has also devised a piano accompaniment for the action that is genuinely nauseating: a few precious melodies maniacally reiterated, basting the stage dialogue or monologue with dripping "lyricism"—a case of an incontinent piano ceaselessly tinkling all over the stage.

This is not to say that a good, all-encompassing selection from Colette's works read by one brilliant actress could not afford us a lovely evening in the theater. But these sophomoric attempts at dramatization, using such strictly-from-hunger stratagems as the interview by onstage reporters, repeated memory-flashbacks to Colette's beloved mother pottering with her potted plants, and one sample melodramatic skit in which Colette the music-hall actress camps around, are paltry devices for cashing in on surfaces at the expense of the human and artistic core. Not only does Colette not emerge as a genuine artist; she does not even become a true human being. When you add to (or subtract from) this the performance by Zoë Caldwell, the outrage is compounded. Miss Caldwell is an actress of glibly spectacular competence, who once, working at the Tyrone Guthrie Theatre, exhibited something more than that. In New York, she merely exhibits herself, whether in *The Prime of Miss Jean Brodie* or the crime against Mme. Colette, a performance that is all shoddy histrionic trickery.

Listen to her as the adolescent Colette asking her mother, Sido, permission to touch a butterfly "Only just light-ly." That breathless pause between "light" and "ly"—held for enough of a silent beat to explode on your inner ear—is hamminess itself. Listen to her saying, "I did have the habit, and still have, of maaaaaarveling..." with enough a's in "marveling" for three bowls of alphabet soup. Or catch her switching on her poetic-nostalgia voice in "Always, always my thoughts take me back to Sido," like a double bass vibrating away close to bursting. And when she intones the *arietta*, "Mother, I luuuuvvv him!," that melismatic monosyllable is clearly aimed at echoing down the corridors of time. On top of which, Miss Caldwell is fat and unattractive in every part of the face, body and limbs, though I must admit that I have not examined her teeth. When she climactically bares her sprawlingly uberous left breast, the sight is almost enough to drive the heterosexual third of the audience screaming into the camp of the majority. Colette had sex appeal; Miss Caldwell has sex repeal.

The rest of the cast, except for Keene Curtis, ranges from worst to bottomless, with Mildred Dunnock, as Sido, contributing that selfsame droning performance of hers which by now should bore even her to tears. Gerald Freedman's staging staggers between frenzy and catalepsy, the scenery is scurvy, but a black-and-white cat in the second act (ignore the reddish one in the first) shows real wit and acting talent.

Summer, 1970

Rabelais
by Jean-Louis Barrault

Boesman and Lena
by Athol Fugard

Awake and Sing!
by Clifford Odets

Amphitryon
by Peter Hacks

Endgame
by Samuel Beckett

Terminal
by Susan Yankowitz

The Devil's Disciple
by George Bernard Shaw
produced by the American Shakespeare Festival

The Wars of the Roses
based on Shakespeare's Henry VI, 1, 2, 3 and
*   Richard III*
produced by the New York Shakespeare Festival

Golden Bat
by the Tokyo Kid Brothers

Coco
book and lyrics by Alan Jay Lerner
music by André Previn

In a letter to Antoine Hullot, François Rabelais refers to the good Lord "who never created Lent, but did create salads" and other goodies. Going God one better, Jean-Louis Barrault has created a "theatrical game" that is both meager Lenten fare and a gaudy fruit salad, and named it *Rabelais,* after the genius whose treasury he plundered for the show and whom he chooses to call the first hippie. If anyone was a hippie in those late medieval days, it was the *vagantes,* the wandering scholars; Rabelais was more like a combination Dickens and James Joyce, and like them, totally unsuited to the stage.

There are four salient virtues in Rabelais' writing: the visual exaggeration, the ironic gigantism too huge and multifarious for anything but the mind's eye; the parade of esoteric learning, the prodigality of information and documentation to lend dignity to some jest or whimsy; the daring with which Christian dogma and practice are challenged; and the language in which all this is couched—torrential and frolicsome, awash with cunning archaisms and neologisms. The stage can neither contain such visual abundance, nor convey such verbal tumult. Barrault has simplified, modernized, sifted and, above all, chopped away at *Gargantua* and its sequels; dressed up the remnants in elaborate costumes but no scenery; and, with the addition of rock music and snatches of simple dance movement, turned it all into an undernourished extravaganza, a thoroughly unspectacular spectacle that looks like a cross between Grotowski and the Latin Quarter. Even the glimpses of nudity have a tarnished, touristy, Bal Tabarin quality about them.

But it could all be forgiven if *Rabelais* served some purpose—whether as a useful compromise between new and old forms of stagecraft, or simply as a verbally and visually stimulating theatrical event. Instead, we get the aging Barrault's lame gesture in the direction of youth, and the venerable actor-director's prancing and cavorting in these short-winded revels is almost as melancholy a caper as the Dance of Death.

•   •   •

AN OFF-BROADWAY production of value and distinction is *Boesman and Lena,* the final section of a trilogy about South Africa's outcasts and losers, by Athol Fugard, a white South African playwright. *Blood Knot* dealt with the blacks, *Hello and Goodbye* with the whites, and this play, by far the best of the three, with the in-betweens, the coloreds. These products of Dutch fornications with native women are now equally excluded from fellowship with the whites and the blacks. Boesman and Lena are a middle-aged "colored" couple of itinerant scroungers, living off the prawns they hunt on the mudflats of a number of rivers whose beds form the boundaries of their world. A few measly towns in which they trade with the whites before whom they cringe are the circuit around which these paltry existences keep shuffling. Their abode is a shack they continually set up and disassemble and carry about on their backs; even a snail is not obliged constantly to dismantle and re-erect its domicile—which, besides, is much better constructed.

The only solace for these wretches is quarreling with each other; more precisely, a fight between the stolidly taciturn Boesman's fists and Lena's garrulous tongue. The pair are too old and tired for love, and love, even if it could survive this round of humiliations, deprivations and, worst of all, repetitions that is their life, could not afford them the desperately needed outlet for their great bottled-up rage. What Fugard has accomplished—and it is no mean trick—is to have made an event out of the eventlessness of these lives by means of Lena's attempted rebellion when Boesman brutalizes a wretched old Kaffir who has come to their campfire to die. For in this old man who stumbles upon them in the night, with whom language barriers make communication impossible (though Lena, touchingly, gets him to repeat her name), Lena has found someone even more miserable than herself. When, deprived as she is of faith and hope, Boesman would deny her her last chance at charity, she erupts.

In this eruption, as well as in the more subduedly aching scenes surrounding it, the play gives us a glimpse of hell on earth in the most nearly objective terms in which such harrowing injustice can be evoked. Fugard manages, furthermore, the difficult feat of finding a language for Lena that is neither flatly naturalistic nor unduly and unconvincingly poeticized; that there are a few lapses is not surprising —what is surprising is that they are so few. The play is really Lena's monologue and monody that astoundingly eschews monotony. For this we must thank also Ruby Dee's extraordinary performance, sounding depths one would not have suspected within this actress's reach, and maintaining an exemplary humanity in abjection, an undercurrent of melody in the shrill stream of complaint. There is even an ounce of hopefulness in the play: the cloddish Boesman, from whom she finally cannot detach herself, may—just barely may—realize something of Lena's worth, her dignity, her rights. John Berry has directed the play with straightforwardness and eloquence, and Boesman was well played by James Earl Jones, and is probably even better played now by Zakes Mokae, his genuinely South African replacement.

Now, by way of further demonstration of what is wrong with the theater of the thirties, we get *Awake and Sing!* It is a bad play, badly produced, but I would suggest that anyone who has any delusions about thirties' playwriting see it and weep. The trouble with these plays is that though they were written out of laudable discontent with the insufficiencies of our society, they were works of people who could not write. Drama looked like a fine crusading weapon to the thirties playwrights, and though they were on the side of the angels, they were unfortunately not on the side of art.

The plot of *Awake and Sing!* is a commonplace, each character a cliché, and the mind behind the play an all too ordinary one. But this would not matter so much if the language were that peculiar blend of realism and poetry, of common speech and those barely perceptible shifts that make the quotidian extraordinary. Study a play like Hebbel's *Mary Magdalene* or Hauptmann's *Rosa Bernd;* look at the speeches in which Master Anton talks about "shaving away the whole guy" or Rosa about being too alone on this earth, and notice how out of common speech poetry is being made. But when Odets' Ralphie keeps repeating things like "We don't want life printed on dollar bills" and "Gimme the earth in two hands," this *is* the way such people of the time talked, and it does not transcend the commonplace. Odets' needle points to the true, unpoetic north, alas; not to the magnetic north of poetry. When he did try to write "poetic," however, as he attempted to do more and more in his later plays, the dialogue merely became punctuated with verbal pratfalls.

Equally disastrous, I think, is the naïveté of Odets and his fellows. He—they—really believed that the solution was to "get enough teams together" in the warehouse and, pronto, instead of being printed on dollar bills, life would be hand-illuminated on vellum. But it is *Awake and Sing!* that gets revived, not *The Wild Duck, To Damascus* or *Leonce and Lena.* The production is condign punishment for the play. In a generally undistinguished cast, stolidly directed by Arthur A. Seidelman, I must point to two particularly insensitive performances, those of Phoebe Dorin and especially Salem Ludwig, who with fanatical consistency can reduce every part he touches to exactly the same shade of gray.

I wish I could say better things about *Amphitryon* by Peter Hacks, which the experimental branch of Lincoln Center is currently sprouting at the Forum Theatre. For this is an urbane, eminently civilized play, literate to a fault—or several faults—but with absolutely nothing new to accomplish. In a prefatory note, the German playwright acknowledges his debt to four other *Amphitryons*, those of Plautus, Dryden, Molière and Kleist, and proposes, somewhat immodestly, to offer this version as combining the prime virtues of the others. And so it does—I will even give him another set of virtues, which he prudently omits to mention, those of Giraudoux's *Amphitryon 38*, which his play resembles even more parlously. But that's just it: Hacks's Model No. 39 reads and plays exactly like a highly civilized tour of the monuments of refined Western comedy; yet what the theater needs is explorers, not tourists.

Even so, a visit to the Forum will reward you with certain minor forensic delights. You will hear the merits of husbands' either remaining lovers or transforming themselves into gods—for the sake of satisfying their wives' emotional and sexual needs—defended in courtly disputation and with elegant language. Ralph Manheim's translation is, barring minor mishaps, smooth enough, and there are two fetching performances, by Philip Bosco as a most chivalrous amorist of a Jupiter and Harold Gould as a philosophical slave adept in all the slavish uses of philosophy. Unfortunately the others are much less good, with Priscilla Pointer's Alcmene the Platonic idea of a high-school soubrette, James Patterson's Amphitryon sounding like a buzz saw trying to speak, and James Ray's Mercury mistaking a god for a fairy. Robert Symonds' direction is at least uncluttered, but the décor and scenery have, like the play itself, aspirations to which no amount of sidling up can ascend. Kleist's version would have been far better; ironically, his *Broken Jug* was scrapped because no character actor could be found for Old Adam. So understaffed, the company is condemned to sacrificing genius for Hacks.

• • •

Alas, it is when our theater promises most that it becomes most disappointing. Joseph Chaikin's Open Theatre is proclaimed the best the American avant-garde has to offer. Well, the best it may be, but it is not very good. Last year, I caught the OT's production of *The Serpent*, Jean-Claude van Itallie's adult-comic-book retelling of Bible stories. The writing was undistinguished, but some of the modern-dance movements and idiosyncratic sounds with which the company brought to life these biblical vignettes were ingenious and impressive —though for an evening of full-bodied theater it seemed a bit lean, too much bone and sinew and not enough meat. Now I have caught the OT's *Endgame* and *Terminal*, and both strike me as subserpentine stuff.

Endgame is one of Beckett's most effective pieces, but it is almost always ruined in its productions (I have now seen four) by attempts to undercut its very raison d'être, for which it was produced in the first place. The play concerns the end of the world, both as something to come and as something always already present; to be effective, it must show the recognizable tatters of *our* world flapping about in epic emptiness, and the overwhelming nausea of living, crisscrossed only by dazzling flashes of gallows humor. The play is a desert of brilliantly dramatized boredom and despair, and the first thing the director must do is leave it substantially as it is. Instead, Roberta Sklar has chosen to put in all kinds of comic business—for example, a Clov who keeps making funny little piping sounds and who indulges in old routines like folding a sheet with fanatical methodicalness only to let it drop on the floor. Such devices detract from the grand design of the play, from the heroic starkness that is its noblest feature. The acting, too, is poor; under better direction, Peter Mahoney might be a good Clov, but Joseph Chaikin, as an actor, left me cold even in the old Living Theatre days; now his Hamm is an insufferable roundelay of vocal and facial cuteness and affectations, utterly devoid of either sad or funny dignity. As for the two parents in their dustbins, their performances are so amateurish that it would have been best for the lids to remain permanently sealed.

Of course, Beckett is a master of words, and words are what the OT's performances are least able to cope with. The words in *Terminal*, by Susan Yankowitz, are hollowly portentous when not downright banal, and they are mouthed by the cast with either the overconfidence of street-corner orators or the hesitancy of someone breaking in new dentures. Otherwise, this sequence of more or less grisly revue sketches about dying in America is performed by what amounts to a moderately skillful group of modern dancers and pantomimists, who would not, however, give Martha Graham and Marcel Marceau even a sprint for their money. The images of death are either too known or too far-fetched—Jessica Mitford's book *The American Way of Death* is more devastating by far. But this is what happens when a work does not have a supreme creator behind it and is merely improvised by a group, with assists from hither and yon.

Just as the set of *Endgame* does not convey *our* world as falling apart, the performers in *Terminal* do not sufficiently suggest *our* dying. If they do not actually look like grotesques, their accouterments are outlandish, and they carry on in ways that produce distancing rather than involvement. When there are words by Bertolt Brecht to contemplate, distancing may be fine; here an increased dose of recognizable humanity would be a great boon.

In answer to an inquiry by the *Strand Magazine*, Bernard Shaw wrote: "The most effective situations on the modern stage occur in my own play, *The Devil's Disciple*," but, great drama critic that he was, Shaw was nevertheless unreliable on two dramatists, Shakespeare and Shaw, the second of whom he kept placing above the first. Yet he was quite right in calling *The Devil's Disciple* a melodrama; only he might have gone even farther and counted it, as does Robert Brustein, among his "shameless potboilers." Still, Shaw's successor as the *Saturday Review*'s drama critic, Max Beerbohm, was also right in declaring that Shaw "has done a romantic melodrama better than it is done by gentlemen with romantic hearts and melodramatic heads . . ."

At the American Shakespeare Festival in Stratford, Connecticut, *The Devil's Disciple* is unfortunately done by people with no discernible heads or hearts of any kind, and emerges neither romantic nor melodramatic. By which I mean that the production stubbornly refuses to elicit either heartthrobs or thrills, and settles for the slacker's notion that a "classic" can take care of itself without any directorial assistance—which is about as safe as going to Ireland without a raincoat. Cyril Ritchard's direction is lackadaisical to the point of slothfulness, the only exertion having gone into staging the tea-drinking scene as if it were the tea party in *Alice in Wonderland*. For the rest the play seems to have been shaken off the page onto the stage: let the chips fall where they may, and the devil, or his disciple, take the hindmost. William Ritman, an able designer of contemporary sets, has created less Colonial atmosphere than you can find in a Second Avenue antiques shop, and Jane Greenwood's costumes, like General Burgoyne's soldiery, could barely pass muster. Conrad Susa's score of nostalgic clarion calls is charming but all too brief.

Lee Richardson gave a sound, straightforward performance as Pastor Anderson, resisting, like a true man of the cloth, the temptation to overplay. David Selby was pleasant and manly as Dick Dudgeon, though a little more variety and polish would not have been amiss. And John Tillinger was a most savory rogue of a Sergeant. But Margaret Hamilton played Mrs. Dudgeon in what I can describe only as a low dudgeon, James Cromwell as Christy was a king-size Mortimer Snerd, Joseph Maher a very minor Major Swindon, and Mary Wright's Essie contained enough whining, sniveling and bawling to furbish an entire Dickensian orphanage. As for Cyril Ritchard's General Burgoyne, he was (when he chanced to remember his lines) too lightweight for the part: not a gentleman soldier with a ready, cynical wit but a Jeevesian butler in the wrong uniform. Ever since John Gielgud elevated him from the chorus line to play Scandal in *Love for Love,* Ritchard has remained fixated at that stage, and has played everything from the Emperor Romulus to Captain Hook as scandalously as possible.

Jill Clayburgh, the Judith, had to be replaced by her understudy, Maureen Anderman. We have all heard the story where the understudy goes on and becomes a star overnight. This is not Miss Anderman's case. She mouthed, mugged, strained and hammered away at her part, birthing every line with almost as much pain as it was for us to bear. But at least even G.B.S. would have had to recognize that at Stratford, Connecticut, Shaw and Shakespeare are reduced to the same level.

I am not against Shakespeare in the Park, which is now doing *The Wars of the Roses:* the three parts of *Henry VI* compressed into two, and *Richard III.* It is, after all, free, and as the crookbacked king reminds me, there are some who would give their kingdom for a gift horse. I even tried not to look in the mouth of this unhappy nag, but as it kept neighing, I could not but note its almost total toothlessness.

The *Henry VI* trilogy is apprentice work, but Messrs. Barnes and Kerr notwithstanding, modern scholarship recognizes all of it as the young Shakespeare's, and so it may be worth an occasional whirl. And how giddily it swirls about, all thud and blunder, war and intrigue, heroism and treachery, with foully severed heads dropping on the stage like chestnuts in autumn! While the houses of York and Lancaster, France and England, peasant and noble, ambitious upstart and scheming Machiavel have at one another, there is little time for true drama and poetry to get their licks in. But Shakespeare being who he was, or was to become, rays of wit, pathos, humanity and even some lyricism do enter through the chinks of the busily clashing armor.

Now, if you are going to mount these plays—as Peter Hall and his Royal Shakespeareans so brilliantly did some half-dozen years ago—it behooves you, at the very least, to be able to do battle scenes expertly. It helps, further, if you have an overarching vision, which in the case of Hall and his company was the sinister bestiality of war and absolutist politics. To this end, battles were made not only huge and murderous, but also sneaky, dishonest, thoroughly contemptible, with much ingenuity devoted to the devising of bloodcurdlingly villainous maneuvers both in single combat and group mayhem. And of course it helps even more to have directors and actors who can raise Shakespeare's juvenilia to full-grown terror. None of these requirements, sad to say, is met by the New York Shakespeare Festival.

The swordplay is staged in sluggish slow motion; warfare, with deadly, predictable repetitiveness. Armies either burst through the upstage-center gate of Ming Cho Lee's uninspired permanent set (so permanent that it seems to have served for at least twenty other Park productions), or else they come creeping up the steps surrounding the platform stage. They are scraggly and few, in rubber armor, and they would not chase a lone Central Park mugger off his prey. As for the duels, while the fell antagonists reposition themselves after a blow, you can study the handy genealogical table supplied in the program and figure out the exact degree of kinship between chopper and chopped in time to see the next blow fall.

But the noncombatant passages are staged no better by Stuart Vaughan. Take the famous scene where Henry VI watches a son discover that he has just killed his father in these civil broils, while a little way off a father realizes that he has slain his son. It is a rather awkward, schematic triptych, but it works when sufficiently stylized—as corresponding couples in poignantly painterly poses deliver their antiphonal laments musically rather than dramatically, with the sorrowing King hovering above and behind. Vaughan cramps the internecine pairs into small facing areas enclosed by pillars, so you can barely see the speakers, keeps their delivery doggedly realistic, and when a father finds it hard to lift his son's body, allows the corpse to trudge alongside helpfully. Throughout, the King squats inelegantly downstage center, has to crane his neck backward alternately to the left and right, and is forced to speak away from the audience.

Or take the scene on the eve of the battle of Bosworth Field, when Richard is haunted by the ghosts of his victims. There are numerous ways of making this baleful and harrowing. Vaughan merely throws in a bit of dry ice and has the dead parade down the tiny space that separates Richmond's tent from Richard's (absurd enough in itself) as if it were the boardwalk at Atlantic City, and they the contestants for the title of Miss Revenant. Or what of the time when a messenger (Young Talbot) managed to remain blocked from my view during his entire presence on stage; or when Margaret is actually allowed to do a cancan over the fallen Gloucester? I haven't the space for anything like a full catalogue, but I must point out that Vaughan has cribbed enough master strokes from Olivier's film version of *Richard III* to make me regret that apparently he did not see the Stratford *Wars of the Roses* as well; at least we might have had a richer conspectus of other directors' inventions.

As for the acting, mostly amateurish, it does occasionally scale the heights of mediocrity. The competent but routine Richard III of Donald Madden actually manages to tower over the rest of the cast, although Robert Gerringer, Tom Sawyer, David Snell and, before she turns Margaret into a minstrel-show act, Barbara Caruso have some good moments. In most cases, however, one does not even get to the acting, past the speech, of a commonness, prosaicness and fuzziness that would be inconceivable in a provincial British repertory. At least Theoni V. Aldredge's costumes rise nicely above an undoubtedly impecunious exchequer, though I did rather miss the exploitation of the possibilities of Richard's coat of arms, the black boar. It may have been omitted to deprive the reviewers of an easy pun.

There are two scenes in which a character stands or sits on a molehill that remains invisible to the audience. Alas, it is the emblem of a production that cannot even make a molehill out of a mountain. Yes, Shakespeare in the Park must be preserved, but not like a stillbirth in formaldehyde. Yes, it must be saved, which includes saving it from itself and from ignorant reviewers who would kill it with kindness.

IT WAS IN Belgrade, Yugoslavia, on the eve of World War II. The Comédie Française had come to Belgrade, but on this evening they were not performing a play in a theater; they were reciting French poems in a concert hall. French actors recite poetry beautifully—as most European actors can and most American actors cannot because they are not trained for it—and in that packed hall many of us Serbs of all ages were reaffirming our cultural bonds with France. Quite a few of us were high-school students, to whom French literature, poetry and drama were as familiar and important as our own. It is a marvelous experience, which regrettably is not available to American youth: familiarity with and love of another language, another culture, through which one feels the brother of people beyond one's boundaries, a citizen of the world.

The last poem of the evening was a simple *chanson* by Paul Fort, who had been crowned *prince des poètes* by his colleagues on the eve of another world war. This prose poem is called, like Schnitzler's *Reigen* in its French translation, *La Ronde,* for which there is no good English word. It means a round or round dance (like the Serbian *kolo*) in which all participants form a circle and hold hands; it is also a round or roundelay in music, a short song in canon; and a roundelay in poetry, a little poem with a regularly recurring refrain. It runs:

> *Si toutes les filles du monde voulaient s' donner la main, tout autour de la mer elles pourraient faire une ronde.*
> *Si tous les gars du monde voulaient bien êtr' marins, ils f'raient avec leurs barques un joli pont sur l'onde.*
> *Alors on pourrait faire une ronde autour du monde, si tous les gens du monde voulaient s' donner la main.*

Or in English (which loses all the terminal and leonine rhymes): "If all the girls in the world were to take one another by the hand, all around the sea they could make a round./ If all the guys in the world were to become sailors, they'd make with their boats a pretty bridge across the waves./ Then one could make a round around the whole world, if all the people in the world were to take one another by the hand."

The applause was beyond compare. It was the cannonade that meant to keep the Nazis away from our respective borders; it was the cheer of a small nation to its big sister nation by whose side, if necessary, it would fight for survival; most of all, it was hearts overflowing with love of life and hatred of war and death erupting in an orgasm of hope and good will. The reciter—who, I like to think but cannot swear to it, was Pierre Dux, the superb actor who plays the chief of police in Z—had to repeat the poem. Once again the applause exploded and would not stop, it seemed, until the walls of the building collapsed, until all walls, barriers and boundaries came down, and all men and women were one under the one sky. The French actors stood up and cheered back at the audience; everybody laughed and wept both at once; it was a great and simple moment, and it was theater. Theater not in the sense of make-believe and escapism, but of an art so immediate and universal that, if only there were a way of perpetuating and expanding it, there would be peace and love forever, and all life would be a stage bestridden by kindly giants.

The other night I saw *Golden Bat*, a curious, amateurish little "rock celebration" devised by the Tokyo Kid Brothers, a young Japanese avant-garde group, many of them college dropouts. As art, it was minimal indeed, though some of these twenty-plus-year-olds were not unprepossessing or without theatrical promise. Still, what came across in English was paltry stuff, and there was reason to believe that the Japanese was not much better. But as the youthful performers themselves reminded us, their parents were the ones who were killing, or killed by, some of us in the audience only a quarter-century ago. And suddenly, in the very last number, where the kids, their arms linked, sat on the floor in two concentric circles and began to writhe, to raise and lower their arms, and it was all like a flower opening and closing in extreme close-up as in a Walt Disney True Life Adventure, something took me back to Belgrade and to that French actor speaking of all the people in the world taking one another by the hand.

These kids under Yutaka Higashi were really taking the actors of the Comédie Française by the hand, across real oceans and oceans of time. A bridge was formed by one theater reaching out to another theater, as by those boats in Paul Fort's poem, a pontoon bridge across which we could all learn to walk into one another's arms.

De Gaulle is gone, les Halles have vanished, the old novel, which was good enough for Proust and Gide and Malraux, is no more (superseded by the unreadable *nouveau roman*), but Danielle Darrieux is still Danielle Darrieux, and she is right here at the Mark Hellinger Theatre, doing *Coco*. If this summer you cannot afford a trip to Paris, or what is left of it, you might treat yourself to the imperishable essence of the city come to meet you, as miraculously and gratifyingly as if that mountain had come to Mohammed.

I was still attending the gymnasium (as the Central European

high school is called) when a very young Danielle Darrieux was already becoming the sweetest and sexiest—what an unusual combination—*vedette* of the French cinema. I remember weeping for her in
Abus de Confiance, lusting for her in something that was called, I
believe, *Club de Femmes,* in which I seem to recall her bare shoulders
and back in a "daring" shower scene, and singing along with her (and
the charming Albert Préjean) the title song of *Un mauvais Garçon,*
and especially that demented ditty, "*J' ne donnerais pas ma place
pour un boulet d' canon*"—I wouldn't swap my place for a cannonball
—whose meaning still eludes me, though I can sing the opening bars
with brio. I still see clearly the high, almost austere forehead across
which perfectly arched eyebrows spread their curvilinear grace; the
eyes, an enormous clarity, with upper lids that seemed practically
ogival; the long, fine nose with its round fleshy tip, like a slightly
bottom-heavy exclamation point; the sedately sensual mouth with its
aspiring flared upper lip that seemed to reprise the eyes. The oval of
the chin was invaded by a soupçon of foxy pointedness, and around
all this quivered an ebullient mass of chestnut curls, a miniature
ocean just large enough for a lover's kisses to sail on for a lifetime.

When I saw Mlle. Darrieux step out on the stage the other evening, my first fears were immediately allayed. Other women grow
older; she only grows womanlier. Not that she is old, in any case, but
she has reached that age where an American actress would be obliged
to fight back, to stiffen and claw for the reassurance of applause loud
enough to be blinding. Mlle. Darrieux is not only effortlessly ageless
in herself, she gives us all back our youth. But then I became anxious
again. She was having trouble with her English. It is a very pretty
French English that has crossed the Channel several times and picked
up some British flavoring; it is delicious on the tongue but a trifle
hard on the ear. Aware of the handicap she was laboring under, the
actress labored a little too hard, flinging her body and semaphoring
with her arms more than the stage traffic required. Perhaps there was
also the sense that the part was not really right for her: at least as
Alan Jay Lerner evokes her, Coco Chanel is rather masculine and
formidable, whereas Mlle. Darrieux was always the most feminine of
actresses.

Here, again, my fears proved unwarranted. I should have known
that a trifle like the English language could not prove a barrier to
Mlle. Darrieux for very long. She did not exactly hurdle it—she
walked around it with a smile, soared over it with a song. Some lines
continued to be lost, some merely bounced a trifle oddly and you had

to station your ears in somewhat out-of-the-way positions to catch them. In the end, what was sacrificed in epigrammatic sting was made up for in flavor, charm and sweetness. This was not quite what the part called for, but Mlle. Darrieux's wholesomeness is greater than the sum of all the parts in *Coço*.

And how well she moves; with what winsome musicianliness she sings; and when she has a few words of French to utter, even if it is only Parisian street names she enumerates in a song, it is as if the theater filled up with that quintessence, or fifth essence, better known as Chanel No. 5. Observe her as she becomes a child again in a scene in which the image of her father makes grand promises to her: with one facial expression and a single gesture she has built a time machine that takes her and all of us back into childhood. And in the song in which she voices her disappointment at the broken promises—even when, later on, crumpled on a couch, she reprises a mere snatch of it —something much deeper than anything in *Coco* comes across the footlights, something the equivalent of Baudelaire's great verse *"Que c'est un dur métier que d'être belle femme"*—what a hard job it is to be a beautiful woman! But look closely, later, at the end of her exultant dance number "Ohrbach's, Bloomingdale's, Best and Saks," where she sprouts a series of half crapulous *moues,* half beatific smirks. It is the triumph of being a woman reasserting itself: Hepburn played it indomitable; Danielle Darrieux plays it adorable.

I must desist. As the admirable Colette wrote in 1934 in a play review of which I change only one word, *work* into *performance,* "One simply cannot gather into a concise summary a performance that scatters like an untied bouquet, that expands like a chattering wave." I can tell you easily enough about everything else in *Coco:* the crafty Lerner lyrics and occasionally telling lines, Beaton's shrewd scenery, Chanel's gowns (the originals, not those Beaton embroidered around them), the nonchalantly sketched-in choreography of Michael Bennett, the witty insolence of Charlene Ryan's danced provocations, George Rose's performance so ripe and mellow that you eat it up on the spot—good things that have become even better since opening night. I can as readily tell you about the unchanged mediocrity of the rest of the show, the weakness of the Previn score and of two or three key performances. But about Danielle Darrieux I have told you —I can tell you—nothing. You must see for yourself.

Autumn, 1970

Othello
   by William Shakespeare
   produced by the American Shakespeare Festival,
      Stratford, Conn.

Bob and Ray: The Two and Only
   by Bob Elliot and Ray Goulding

The Happiness Cage
   by Dennis J. Reardon

Alice in Wonderland
   by Lewis Carroll
   produced by the Manhattan Project

Trelawny of the "Wells"
   by Arthur Wing Pinero

Charles Dickens
   by Emlyn Williams

Sunday Dinner
   by Joyce Carol Oates

Two by Two
   book by Peter Stone
   music by Richard Rodgers
   lyrics by Martin Charnin

The Good Woman of Setzuan
by Bertolt Brecht
*produced by the Repertory Theater of Lincoln
Center*

It is too bad that the American Shakespeare Festival in Connecticut doesn't produce wine instead of plays. The much-lauded *Othello*, extolled in particular by Walter Kerr, which the ASF brought from Stratford to New York, could then claim that it does not travel well. But unlike, for example, an Orvieto, a potable *Othello* should prove portable as well. What is decanted at the ANTA Theater is pure vinegar, and the sort of thing that gives festivals, Shakespeare, indeed theater itself, a suicidally sour taste.

One would like to sympathize with this production. It takes none of the stupid spatial and temporal liberties with the text that the old ASF efforts used to revel in: Venice and Cyprus have not been turned into San Francisco and Alcatraz, the time has not been moved forward to the Italo-Ethiopian war. Nor does the production take the new Jan Kott-Peter Brook type of liberties, whereby the entire action is situated in a pretzel factory or atop a condemned launching pad. But, alas, a straight production nowadays requires more inventiveness than a gimmicky one, and invention (never mind imagination) is as scarce in this *Othello* as gondolas are in Hoboken.

Michael Kahn, who directed, is not only artistic director of the ASF but also head of the Interpretation Department of the Drama Division at Juilliard. I am not sure about what gets interpreted there —dreams, tea leaves, or signs in the sky—but I'm fairly certain that it cannot be plays and the characters in them. Anyone who can have Desdemona prepare for bed, and Emilia brush her hair, not at a mirrored dresser in the bedroom but on a bare bench in the middle of a vast, empty stage; who turns the killing of the heroine from the tragically resigned death of a loving victim into a brutal, ugly, undignified scuffle; who can have a wounded man sit around as if he were playing with his pocket watch rather than trying to staunch the blood pouring from his side; who can make another wounded man, slashed in the leg, walk away with a little support from others; who has the noble Cassio stab both Montano and Roderigo in the back; who can completely ignore the martial background and war-like atmosphere of the play; who gives us a mounting so short on extras, settings and clothes (virtually no costume changes for the principals) as to make the whole thing look like bourgeois melo-drama rather than heroic tragedy; who once actually permits Desde-mona to skip off the stage in little hops; and who, above all, allows *these* performances from both leading and supporting players—would make a splendid head of a Department of Misinterpretation, a per-fect Lord of Misrule.

Moses Gunn's Othello is passing strange and wondrous pitiful. This actor, who has moved me in such plays as *In White America* and *Song of the Lusitanian Bogey*, here gives a performance (with the director's connivance, if not his active instigation) that from a white actor would be considered a flagrant racist outrage. Gunn's Othello never walks when he can skulk, shuffle, lope, or titubate; his basic stance befits not a Venetian commander but a karate instruc-tor; his madly quavering voice sounds like a theremin solo played during an earthquake, and most of the time he seems to be vocal-izing not from a script but from a score. He uses his hands and arms more than a deaf-mute, but in gestures that look like a cross between some ancient Japanese dance and a windmill sculptured by Tinguely. At times he seems unable to decide whether to stick an arm inside or outside the other one's sleeve, and on one occasion he makes his gesticulating upstage arm cross over his downstage one, like a pianist performing a piece with complicated fingering. That many of his line readings, often punctuated by inapposite laughter, make little sense, seems, in context, almost a minor transgression.

No better is the Desdemona of Roberta Maxwell, an actress I admired in *Whistle in the Dark*. She starts out as a kittenish Juliet, turns into a shrewish Kate (with overtones of Women's Lib, as in "O, these men, these men!" screamed out supine with frenzied rage), and gets killed in a grisly bout of catch-as-catch-can. She sounds now like a querulous hoyden, now like a boy soprano whose voice is breaking, and always more like a senator's charwoman than his daughter. Her stature and countenance are unsuited to tragedy, and the fact that she is so much shorter than Othello combines with her tomboyishness into making her appear to be his adopted child.

Lee Richardson's Iago is competent, even impressive, in a sturdy, soldierly way—but is it Iago? I am not so much concerned with the actor's finding motivation for what may be, after all, motiveless malignity; but I am unstirred by an Iago who seems so extroverted,

bluff, uncerebral, and who makes the greatest and blackest of villains merely gray. Yet it is an intelligent and robust performance,
and leaves me wondering what Richardson might do with the Moor.
Peter Thompson's Cassio is handsome, straightforward, and not ill-
spoken, yet rather on the colorless side even for this part; of John
Tillinger's Roderigo I felt that his interest in Desdemona was just
a cover for his true craving to be mounted by Othello. Karl Eigsti's
scenery could have benefited from Brechtian placards explaining
whether we were in a Venetian palazzo, a Cypriot garden, or a
parking lot, to all of which it bore a remote resemblance.

It is related in Madrid that the postman once duly delivered
a letter marked "Calle Viejo Idiota" to its addressee living on the
Calle Echegaray, named after the Nobel Prize-winning Spanish playwright and dullard. Mail addressed to an actor c/o "Crashing Bore
Theater" should just as surely reach him at the American Shakespeare Festival.

THE THINGS a drama critic is supposed to review these days! If
there is no theater for a while, I would be content to attend things
like the Bartók Memorial Concert at Carnegie Hall, which was ex-
citing and required no review from me. Neither, though for different reasons, would I have expected to review two Boston disk
jockeys who worked themselves up to a fifteen-minute spot on radio
in which a fictitious interviewer grapples with fictitious interview-
ees. But there are all those empty Broadway playhouses, and nature,
as we know, abhors a vacuum—so in rush two near-vacuums to fill
it, and we get *Bob and Ray: The Two and Only* on Broadway.

Bob Elliott and Ray Goulding were probably fine for the days
when all of you people out there in Radioland yearned for something
to break the monotony of the standard DJ fare. Even television, however, proved too visual and demanding a medium for the pair to
succeed on, except with their cute commercials as the voices of,
say, the Piel Brothers or Skippy peanut butter. But the stage,
the big legitimate stage, where things have to be roughly life-size,
longer than fifteen minutes, eye- as well as ear-catching, and somehow justify the expenditure of time and money—what can it do with
this monochord scraped by two bows? Bob and Ray are radio, which
makes them ancient; they are the forties and early fifties, which
makes them antediluvian; and they are, by current standards of
even minimal intelligence, unfunny, which makes them obsolete.

Before something can become worthy of laughter it has to be, in some way, true. The paradoxes of Oscar Wilde may seem to be mere bits of contrariness (as they did to Robert Benchley, who wrote an uncomprehending and fatuous takeoff on them), but they are actually the far side of truth arrived at by circumnavigation. They are the remoter, less perspicuous truths—minority truths, perhaps—but as real as the other side of the moon. Nichols and May were funny; but that perhaps was satire, a league Bob and Ray do not aspire to. *Beyond the Fringe* was funny, even when it was only mildly satirical—a ribbing, say, of inept Shakespearean productions, and of the Bard himself when he nods a little. This was funny because it was essentially true: it was the Old Vic somewhat exaggerated, or Stratford, Connecticut and Central Park slightly underdone. Or take Flanders and Swann: there was truth in them thar hats, however outrageously bloated, teased, or kneaded. A Flanders-Swann warthog, for instance, is a human being, warts and hoggishness and all.

But these Bob-and-Ray airwave personas are either no longer true or never were, and, in any case, do not get beyond the puddle of pre-FM radio: its street-corner interviews and intramural chitchat. The current show at the Golden Theater is all about radio, too, except when it is about radio disguised as television (a sheep in goat's clothing). When the Two and Only finally do an encore about a waiter and a customer not on a radio program but in a restaurant, it is as if a door swung open on a whole new world; unfortunately, the skit is even less funny and more primitive than the rest. And equally untrue.

For example, there is a skit about a talk-show regular who cannot remember the punch lines of his stories, or else the story that goes with his punch line, and so cannot get any tale finished or started. Does this ever happen? The trouble with the professional talk-show windbags is that you cannot shut them up: they ooze anecdotes and are so punch-line-happy that nothing except a mallet or station break full of commercials can knock them to a halt. In another skit, the founder of the society of Slow Talkers of America puts the interviewer to sleep with the dullness of his discourse riddled with gaping pauses. In truth, it is the slow thinkers of America that we are prey to, whose speech, however, is very fast, very hot air: a veritable simoom in the midst of which any pause would prove a blessed oasis.

Again, we are treated to an interviewer who for the sake of a little sidewalk human interest—talking to a dim cranberry packager —neglects the street-corner drama (violence, police cars, fire engines) that goes careering by. The cranberry man is an imbecile who has never heard of cranberry sauce or juice, and it is significant that Never-Never-Land imbecility rather than earthly folly and stupidity is Bob and Ray's territory. If the skit had any relevance, the interviewer would be chasing after every possible vileness and violence, and the cranberry man would have figured out ways of manufacturing and wholesaling juice and sauce made of pure artificial flavoring. Or take the skit where a surprise long-distance call from a radio program brings the disappointed recipient only chatter and no money. Surely the joke and tragedy of such programs is the absurd amount of inappropriate goods and cash lavished on people who don't need it, while human deprivation rages all around.

There is, ultimately, something even worse about this show than its mirthlessness and banality. I mean its troglodytic benightedness, its refusal to see or say anything of the world outside the studio, of the ills which, if we cannot combat them with anything else, we might at least prick with our ridicule. It is not only a stupid show but also a cowardly one, and its appeal is to brainless nostalgia and ostrichlike escapism. Joseph Hardy is credited with the staging, which consists of gimmicks like a stage piled high with campy bric-a-brac suited less to Bob and Ray than to the Collier brothers, and to have all this motley junk (mostly old radios) remain there absolutely untouched, throughout the show. To me, this suggested that if the bric-a-brac isn't part of the show, Bob and Ray must be part of the bric-a-brac. But what unites these performers and their audience may indeed be a Collier brotherhood of the mind. The Two and Only are not even radio any more, merely static.

One can tell at whatever the aural equivalent of a glance is that Dennis J. Reardon has talent. The young playwright's *The Happiness Cage* begins with an authentic, instantaneous sense of drama, character and language, which is sustained without lapses almost to the very end of the play, a play stuffed with plot, people and palaver, with abundant opportunities for fumbles, slacknesses, dead spots. But with the adroitness and aplomb of a veteran practitioner, Mr. Reardon attacks his material without shirking or trickery, and without any modish shenanigans. The greatest tribute I can pay him is to declare that he makes all those procedures, time-honored to the point of being time-worn, look young, compelling, and very comforting to anyone who inevitably has worried about the future of the theater.

There are certain plays—even very good ones, though, I dare say, not the greatest—to which even partial telling of the plot is a disservice. I shall, therefore, say merely that *The Happiness Cage* concerns an experiment to control our brainwaves electrically, and induce schematic, prefabricated happiness in human beings whose natural right it is to be individualized, anfractuous and, when appropriate, unhappy. Obviously, the army is very interested in the application of this leveling of the mental landscape to efficient soldiering, and the experiments are conducted under the auspices of a general in a veterans' hospital by a zealous neurosurgeon, Dr. Freytag. Opposing this cerebral regimentation is a lowly ex-GI, Reese, in the hospital with a broken arm. An intellectual without a family, slightly paranoid, usually less than effectual in times of crisis, Reese is intelligent and courageous in his stand against mechanized and electrified philanthropy. He is an entirely believable contemporary hero, whose heroism is thrust upon him rather like a strait jacket.

The play ends badly, in both senses: badly for humanity, and less than well for the playwright. From the start, Reardon has rigged the general into a somewhat too easy, conventional military villain; I am sure they come like that in life, but for the purposes of art even generals need a little more transmuting. (In all fairness to the author, there is a potential for complexity in the part, and someone like George C. Scott would have found it; unfortunately, Paul Sparer is not only a supremely obvious actor, he also lacks all grace, even the satanic kind this role cries out for.) Toward the end of the play, my credulity gets truly overtaxed (but, again in fairness to Reardon, things do work at least on a solidly melodramatic level, which, in a lesser play, might just be enough). And the final minutes are an anticlimax—a deliberate and cruel one, to be sure, but for my taste lacking the forcefulness available to a truly inspired anticlimax.

But this is all relatively unimportant compared to the fact that the playwright already has, in this his initial phase, three cardinal virtues in an advanced stage of development. First, he can make even a minor character, however short his onstage span, come to palpitating, insinuating life, not only as a personal truth but also as one that thematically fits into the play as a whole, echoing through and enriching even the scenes in which the character does not appear. Second, the author is fair even to characters he dislikes. Not to the general, perhaps, but God himself would have a hard time with him; certainly to the scientist, who is allowed truthfulness and a conscience in the midst of his fanatically one-sided dedication; and also to such a piece of sinister human wreckage as the weird, cynical hospital orderly. Last, Reardon not only writes totally assured dialogue—succulent, pointed, literate without being literary, and finding the rock-bottom poetry even in inarticulateness—he can also, best of all, make a philosophical debate catch fire onstage, as in the shattering dialectical showdown between Dr. Freytag and Reese. Playwriting that can do this has everything and will travel.

The production is the best Joseph Papp's Public Theatre has given us since its inception with the original, non-O'Horganized *Hair*. Tom Aldredge, whom I have never enjoyed as an actor, proves himself a more than competent director, and both the looks and sounds of this fairly elaborate staging (with the possible exception of the handling of the walk-ons) are tidy and purposive. Moreover, Aldredge does justice to yet another sovereign asset of the play, its ability to modulate back and forth between drama and comedy with verbal and psychological musicianliness.

Lewis J. Stadlen, as Reese, still has a lingering trace of his brilliant Groucho Marx impersonation (in *Minnie's Boys*) about him; but he is a winning and cogent performer who, even if he overdoes something easy, comes through admirably with something difficult. As the guiltridden hillbilly, Miles, Ronny Cox is very nearly perfect. He does, in times of stress, slip out of his accent; otherwise, this is acting of uncanny sensitivity and precision, of dynamic shading, and still instinct with rough-hewn humanity. As Freytag, Henderson Forsythe provides his usual oblique, slippery, cunningly throwaway delivery with nicely spaced chinks to reveal the churning abyss below; here, buttressed with an uncustomary dose of despairing tenacity, the performance is unusually appealing. There are also immaculate supporting performances from Bette Henritze and Charles Durning, whose work tends to be a workout for the edges of my teeth, but who here contribute exactly the nightmare or somnambulistic qualities required.

On top of all this, Reardon is on to an important topic, and one that, as we gather from the experiments of Dr. Delgado at Yale, is rather closer to reality than to Mary Shelley.

Alice in Wonderland, performed by something that aptly calls itself The Manhattan Project, is a bomb. André Gregory has worked for two years with this handsomely subsidized ex-N.Y.U. group. The two Lewis Carroll books, timeless as they are, have been made ostensibly timely here by making sct, costumes and performers as rickety, grubby, mush-mouthed as possible—and by making the sounds and movements garbled, begrimed, gloatingly mean-spirited enough to give them Contemporary Relevance. It is simply kindergarten Grotowski, a sort of stunted Polish joke. The only interesting performance was that of the director, André Gregory, who sat down front in a mod workingman's cap, acted out the whole event with his facial contortions, and kept peeking back at the audience to see if they were getting the full benefit of them.

Whenever one of the six threadbare histrions had to speak lines—as opposed to making assorted noises—the evening grew rife with inarticulateness. Gregory strikes me as one of the most modishly eclectic directors going: rather like Peter Brook, but without Brook's lightfingeredness, he has filched from all possible sources—Brecht, Kott, Grotowski, the Becks, Chaikin—and turned *Alice* into a cross between a playpen and a pigpen.

Externally, there is an interesting visual concept here and there, as in the group grope that represents Alice's descent down the rabbit hole, or in the manner in which four bowed backs form a mushroom for the caterpillar to sit on, the twisted arm of one of the bowed fellows becoming the caterpillar's hookah. Internally, however, the show revels in turning Carroll's world into a psychopathic or social morass—not in the subtle way of Empsonian analysis but as instant muckraking, not so much for the sake of the raking as out of love for the muck. Gregory's *Alice in Wonderland* is a shallow cataloguing of human meanness and sickness seen through a jaundiced eye, whereas Carroll's was a child's-eye view of the human condition, nastiness *and* decency included.

TRELAWNEY OF THE "WELLS" is a well carpentered play by a second-rate mind, and Pinero's insistence that the 1860's be evoked with all their ludicrous fashions in clothing and furniture does not lessen the double nostalgia, about the past and about the good old theater, which permeates the play. The subject, in fact, is the gypsy life of the stage versus the solid respectability of Cavendish Square, and I need hardly tell you which one wins out. I can ascribe it only to disingenuousness on Shaw's part that he praised *Trelawny* in his review of its 1898 première: the sort of accolade one gives to a lesser but highly popular competitor to prove what a good sport one is. Yet Shaw objected to Dion Boucicault's conventional way of turning Sir William Gower into a stage stereotype of the old man (which, in the current revival, George Bartenieff does with a vengeance), and remarked that "It is no more like a real old man than a worn-out billiard table is like a meadow." I am afraid that Pinero's view of life resembles reality about as much as a brand new billiard table does a meadow; and to give the play an amateurish, un-British (in all but Theoni V. Aldredge's costumes), imprecise and unevocative production makes it all rather like a billiard table with the felt ripped off.

AN ITEM FROM England called *Not Now, Darling* is too demeaning even to discuss; about its unappetizing star all I can say is that if this is Norman Wisdom, I'll take Saxon folly. About another British import, Emlyn Williams' encore as Charles Dickens, with some of his selections by now twice-told tales and some new—what can I say? I have, in recent years, had two evenings with Dickens and two with Mark Twain, and one each with Oscar Wilde, Dylan Thomas, Bernard Shaw and John Aubrey. I welcome encountering these literary worthies, but I cannot affirm that I did not enjoy reading their works as much as, or more than, having their effigies half reading, half acting them out at me. And in snippets. Still, for people who cannot or will not read, and who enjoy Williams' snappy way with a snippet (quite generous snippets, too), *Charles Dickens* may be as pleasant a way of not reading a book, and of not going to the theater, as anyone could ask for.

I HAVE BEEN an early fancier of Joyce Carol Oates's fiction, which struck me as that always admirable thing: writing possessed of feminine sensitivity that in no way harps on such sensitivity but simply and hardheadedly puts it to work. And surrounds it with other good, solid virtues, neither feminine nor unfeminine, such as looking at the world steadily and long, and blinking only when absolutely necessary.

Still, I am not yet certain whether Miss Oates's novels and stories, for all her sizable talent, will reach the heights of a Flannery O'Connor, or come to a halt somewhere in the hilly and daley terrain I triangulate with the names of Katherine Anne Porter, Eudora Welty and Jessamyn West. So it is with mixed pleasure and apprehension that I watch Miss Oates wildly sowing her gifts in all directions: essays, reviews, poetry, plays, film criticism, and probably a few other genres that slipped by me on the pages of every known and several unknown magazines. It is not so much the variousness as the sheer bulk of these outpourings that worries me: I respect a polymath but not a polygrapher. And I wonder whether this material, as uneven as a fever chart in quality, is the product of a steamily teaming brain, or of a bureau full of assorted literary productions that has dogged Miss Oates since college and has finally been unleashed on the world.

Sunday Dinner, Miss Oates's second produced play, but the first I could catch up with, is a one-hour one-acter presented by the enterprising American Place Theater. It is an attempt at an absurdist play, without, I am afraid, the grim lucidity that lurks at the core of good theater of the absurd. We know well enough what Beckett is telling us with that grinning despair that stroboscopically illuminates his most lunar landscapes; and, except in their dizziest moments, Ionesco and Genet shed their masks like Salome her veils in a dazzling dance for which we have a shrewd idea whose head will be forfeit. The creepy Midwestern family that returns from a visit to Mother's grave and settles down to the usual gripes, bickerings and pontifications to be consumed with the Sunday dinner, is a bunch of tolerable Oatesian grotesques, with one foot in Babbittry, the other in Grant-Woodsy gothic. But when a possibly blind census taker, who is possibly not a census taker and possibly the long-absconded Father, arrives, joins in the dinner, asks bizarre questions and obtains even queerer answers—not to mention confessions of sins as inscrutably symbolic as they are extravagantly purple, and the whole thing erupts into violence when an idiot son who will not accept the stranger's message of universal guilt scoops out the old man's seeing or unseeing eyes, which roll (unseen, thank goodness!) on the floor, and when this young idiot then assumes the role of the now departed blind man only to be bitterly disappointed at his first crime's not having changed his countenance—I tell you, I don't know what I'm telling you, or what I have been told.

Miss Oates provides some funny and well-written lines, but they prove merely that she knows about words, not necessarily about theater. And there is a cast of ordinarily able actors who, with the exception of Brooks Morton, seem to know *how* it is done even if they don't know *what* it is they are doing. The scenery and lighting, like the staging, may be right; but the play is an equation with too many x's for me to figure out any of the why's.

•   •   •

LET US CONSIDER the ingredients of *Two by Two* one by one. There is Peter Stone's book, a considerably rewritten and updated version of Clifford Odets' 1954 play, *The Flowering Peach*. That was a respectable but dull opus about Noah, since which time there has been a veritable flood of Noahs, thanks to Britten, Stravinsky and now this jaunty version. Odets' Noah family inhabited a spiritual Bronx, Stone's are denizens of Broadway; the distance is smaller than one might think, but it is still a distance. The main troubles here are all those clean dirty jokes and cautiously blasphemous God gags, which produce few yoks and fewer shocks. The music is by Richard Rodgers, and there are three mouth-watering songs in it—"An Old Man," "I Do Not Know a Day I Did Not Love You," "As Far As I'm Concerned"—and one almost as good, the title song. The rest are fair to piddling, and include the musically senile "You" and the mawkish "Hey, Girlie." Which brings us to Martin Charnin's lyrics, not exactly dazzling in their command of language, but generally spunky and peppy. They do, however, tend to suffer from echolalia, and in "Hey, Girlie" and "The Golden Ram" they lapse into tastelessness.

Joe Layton's staging and rudimentary dance movements for a cast of eight nondancers are adequate but lacking in any sort of distinction, to say nothing of innovation. David Hays's sets are well enough conceived but indifferently realized. They are overshadowed by a backdrop that is a large, square, white cardboard tray with upturned edges, on which one usually gets French fries but in this case gets projections by Cris Alexander. These chiefly illustrate the words of God, who speaks in pictograms; at other times, they simply supplement the scenery. To achieve this, slides of practically all great Western art, and not a little Eastern, are dizzyingly flashed at us; if they went by a bit more slowly, they would be a splendid refresher course in art history, but would also dwarf the show into all but invisibility. The costumes are as witless as only Fred Voelpel can make them, and look mostly like crazy quilts that have been raped and slashed to ribbons by a crazy-quilt fiend. The excellent Eddie Sauter's orchestrations are not his best, but still good; John Gleason has done better lighting, but at least cannot be blamed for that pop-art or hard-edge rainbow, the last and least pleasing of the projections. This semirecumbent mixture, however, gets a leavening from the mostly delightful performances. Danny Kaye just about redeems himself for his appalling rendition of the Ragpicker in the movie *Madwoman of Chaillot*. Here he is essentially restrained, even dignified, flavorous and funny enough when called for, but above all quietly likable. And that is a very nice thing to have in the middle of a brassy musical. As for his three sons, Harry Goz cuts a merry, fat figure as Shem, the first postdiluvian capitalist; Michael Karm is rather too oafish a loafer as Ham; but Walter Willison is in gladdeningly fine voice, figure and dramatic fettle as the rebellious idealist, Japheth.

As Mrs. Noah—a far cry from the shrew of the Wakefield mystery cycle, this lovable Jewish mama!—Joan Copeland is the mellowest of matriarchs, though somewhat harsh in her singing; Marilyn Cooper is a sweetly squeaky termagant of a Mrs. Shem; but Madeline Kahn, who has at least two forty-inch busts, is an outrageously vulgar caricature of a Mrs. Ham. The Rachel of Tricia O'Neil, however, is the most huggable, crunchable, bitable apple of a girl to drop on Broadway in many a fall: her singing voice as sturdy as her athletic body, her features so well limned that just gazing at them seems a shamefully inadequate tribute, her movements instinct with the grace of those various wild animals whose presences are merely mimed by the cast. Add it all up, and *Two by Two* is not half bad —only two fifths.

A VERY DIFFERENT god, or gods, must tangle with mortals in Bertolt Brecht's *The Good Woman of Setzuan*, a play with songs about an imaginary Setzuan—Chinese, European, universal—to which come three gods looking for one good human being, necessary for the continuation of the world. These are no mighty Old-Testament thunderers, but pitiful, ineffectual gods, foolish and buffeted about by uncaring human beings. And the good person they find is no worthy patriarch but a lowly prostitute, Shen Teh, who alone provides them with lodging for the night. She is rewarded with enough money to buy a small tobacco shop, but being a decent businesswoman proves very hard, what with hordes of spongers, greedy landladies, overcharging workmen and sundry other social evils to which a body can oppose only a frail buckler of goodness. So Shen Teh invents, and disguises herself as, a ruthless male cousin, Shui Ta, who can squeeze some good out of the worst oppressors and parasites—at the very least a good riddance.

The gods make impossible demands on a human being, asking for goodness that is socially impracticable and self-destructive. The laws of economic necessity make equally impossible demands, forcing a person to suppress his inclination toward good and become the hated exploiter of his fellow men. There is no way out: faced with the problem, the gods withdraw in comic apotheosis to their cloudy kingdom, all the while dribbling pious, melioristic platitudes. In a world full of works purporting to offer solutions to insoluble problems, we must venerate a play that simply stops in front of great, crushing irreconcilables; but a play that confronted with this bitterness does not lose either its sense of humor or its sense of poetry —such a play deserves more than veneration: unstinting love. Unfortunately, it gets much less than this from the Lincoln Center Repertory Company.

To be sure, Shen Teh-Shui Ta is performed by an able actress, Colleen Dewhurst. But she is, alas, a large, somewhat ungainly woman, rather short on charm, who looks, if anything, more appealing as the tough male cousin. Since goodness, apparently, involves a good deal of smiling, Miss Dewhurst gives us a lot of her smile, even though it has an unhappy way of corrugating her overabundant face. Moreover, when she forces her voice down into a mannish register, her elocution suffers and she frequently becomes inaudible. For all that, she is a true professional, with vitality and skill, and towers over the rest of the cast, not only literally. Yang Sun, an unemployed aviator loved by Shen Teh and merely exploiting her, is played by David Birney. Bullied by Shui Ta, this loafer likewise develops an altered ego, that of a slavedriver, and echoes the heroine's simultaneous twofoldness with his own evolved otherness. Birney is a gifted young actor, but is not yet able to muster the variety and pliability the part requires. In smaller roles, Elizabeth Wilson and Sydney Walker perform creditably.

But the rest! There are even performances like those of Ray Fry, Maury Cooper, Eda R. Merin, Michael Levin, Elizabeth Huddle, Frances Foster, Herbert Foster, Joseph Mascolo, Priscilla Pointer, and a few others, which, for merely observing them, made me feel less like a spectator than a guilty accomplice. Even Philip Bosco, an actor of proven ability, seems to have ceased to grow in this ambience, and is content to repeat his whinily Gielgudian mannerisms.

Ralph Manheim's translation is only mediocre, but then Brecht is just about any translator's undoing. Manheim is especially insecure with slang, and often unduly coarse; thus *die Hand am Busen* is not "my hand on her tits." John Lewin translates the lyrics tolerably, though Herbert Pilhofer's music, fascinating in the background, becomes overbearing and unbearable as a setting of the songs. It is regrettable that Paul Dessau's tunes for the original German production were not retained, regardless of the added hardship on the translator. Robert Symonds' staging is at best routine; John Gleason's lighting works better here; and Carrie Fishbein Robbins' costumes are amusing in their discreet patchiness. Douglas W. Schmidt's set is as ingenious as it is atmospheric. Do see *The Good Woman of Setzuan:* the play's virtues can absorb the deficiencies of any production, and you may find this the rare kind of dramatic event that prevents the gods from destroying the theater altogether.

Winter, 1970-1971

COMPANY
book by George Furth
music and lyrics by Stephen Sondheim

SLEUTH
by Anthony Shaffer

HOME
by David Storey

LES BLANCS
by Lorraine Hansberry
completed by Robert Nemiroff and
Charlotte Zaltzberg

ORLANDO FURIOSO
by Ariosto
adapted by Eduardo Sanguineti
produced by the Teatro Libero of Rome

ODODO
book by Joseph A. Walker
music by Dorothy A. Dinroe

THE GINGERBREAD LADY
by Neil Simon

ONE NIGHT STANDS OF A NOISY PASSENGER
by Shelley Winters

THE PLAYBOY OF THE WESTERN WORLD
by John Millington Synge

A DOLL'S HOUSE
by Henrik Ibsen

NO, NO, NANETTE
book by Otto Harbach, revised by Burt Shevelove
music by Vincent Youmans
lyrics by Irving Caesar and Otto Harbach

HEDDA GABLER
by Henrik Ibsen

THE POSITION of the drama critic becomes queerer and queerer by the moment. There is precious little of any importance opening in our theaters month after month, yet one believes in the theater, clings to it, hopes for it, feels that there is something worthy buried there—and wants to believe that it is buried alive. At some point it will try to break out of its coffin, and one wishes to be there to help it come back among the living. But in the meantime one feels like a second-class citizen, envying one's colleagues in the other arts. In the fine arts and music, after all, there is always the good old stuff showing up, and in film and the dance something new is actually happening. (I do review films for *The New Leader*, so I get some relief there.) But the New York theater has virtually no past on display, its present is exiguous, and living on the future makes for a very frugal diet indeed.

To be sure, some New York drama critics and reviewers have an easier time of it. Thus, Stanley Kauffmann and Elizabeth Hardwick write about the theater only when something in it moves them to write; otherwise, they concentrate on film or literature. Among those who pronounce regularly on theater, there are two dispositions that make life easier: one is to belong happily to the rear guard and exult in the commercial claptrap Broadway spews up; the other is to enlist in the avant-garde and discover a new wonder off- or off-off-Broadway every week. There are even some reviewers who manage to straddle both these manias, and others who can drum up a "serious concern," such as the Future of the Musical, and fill their columns with worrying about it. But if you are merely interested in good theater of any kind, if you will oppose the excesses and absurdities of both commercialism and avant-gardism in the name of certain standards of excellence, you find yourself not only disconcerted and depressed by most of what you see, but also cut off from practically all your colleagues, who, knowingly or not, adhere to some version of the aforementioned party lines.

The most pseudo-encouraging event in the late spring of 1969 was the applauded arrival of *Company*, a musical with music and lyrics by Stephen Sondheim and a book by George Furth, based on some short plays of his that were apparently recast to the specifications of Sondheim and Harold Prince, the producer-director. *Company* tells the story—in what was generally considered highly innovative dramatic and musical terms—of marital and nonmarital relations (pre-, extra- and, as it were, contramarital) in Manhattan, more specifically on the chic Upper East Side. The protagonist, Robert, is a desirable bachelor in his mid-thirties, very much badgered and lured into marriage, but put off by the grim connubial relations of five pairs of friends, and by the ease with which he acquires girls, thanks to his attractiveness, charm, sophistication, elegant apartment and other virtues with which the authors and director deck out their imaginary alter ego.

The importance of the show—an alleged new lease on life for the musical—lies in its supposedly novel musical style, and in the fact that its cast of fourteen sings, dances and acts in a series of connected skits, the usual story line being dispensed with much as the customary singing and dancing chorus. Unfortunately, the five couples are all types with archetypal flaws: alcohol, trying to swing on pot, getting divorced only to stay together as lovers, ending a long affair with getting married only to have the bride skip out on the way to church, etc. etc. All these failings are schematic plot devices, and develop neither characters nor situations. There are some bright lines in the book, but they are bright rather than perceptive, clever rather than illuminating, extremely parochial (East Sixties, show business, middle-aged and middle-class, but ever so with-it) and, finally, too few and far between.

As a lyricist, Sondheim is always thoroughly accomplished and sophisticated, here no less than before, and the antiphonal effect with which the book interrupts the lyrics, or vice versa, creating a sort of fugue, is often stimulating. For a *lyricist,* Sondheim knows a good deal about music; I remember, for example, how amazed I was to hear Alan Jay Lerner say a few years ago that he had never heard any Orff. But for a supposedly daring and innovative *composer,* Sondheim may not know enough; I was equally amazed to hear him say once that he did not know the marvelous operas of Janáček. Still, that may not be important; what does matter is that he has here tried to incorporate some of the newer sounds—rock, bossa nova, etc.—into the Broadway idiom, but has done so in such gingerly, timorous fashion as to make it sound rather like a spinster saying "Damn!" and feeling very brave about it. The score of *Company* is the musical wedding of Stan Kenton to Herb Alpert, with a bit of Beatlified Bernstein, in the guise of best friend, lurking in the foreground, and like the other *ménages à trois* in the show, it does not work. Sondheim seems happiest writing a typical show tune like "Side by Side by Side," or a patter song like "Getting Married Today," to which he adds a little dissonance or antimelodiousness. Otherwise, the toe-wetting forays into the sea of modernity merely produce some peculiar tonal intervals to make things harder for the performers.

It is nice to have a musical in which a small cast does its own singing, dancing, and even acting. Or it would be nice if all were up to snuff. Some are, and I found Barbara Barrie, Susan Browning, Elaine Stritch, perhaps Donna McKechnie, and especially Beth Howland admirable. Indeed, among the women, only Pamela Myers is offensive and well on the way to becoming a two-cent Barbra Streisand, which to be sure is only a penny less than the original is worth. The men tend to merge into a single blur of undistinguished competence, with the exception of Dean Jones as the protagonist, who manages the unlikely achievement of further draining a vacuum. Yet for the conjoint efficiency of this unequal cast, credit must go to Harold Prince's staging, and even more to the choreography of Michael Bennett. Mr. Bennett has the gift of making old things look new, simple things look prodigiously difficult, and dance look like inspired sculpture in motion rather than, as usual nowadays, junk sculpture in disintegration.

Yet the most innovative aspect of the show is Boris Aronson's set, which against a background of acrophiliac skyscrapers presents their stylized guts in the shape of gleaming platforms among sleek girders, along which small sections of the floor ascend and descend —a veritable forest of skeletal elevators. With people posted on various levels of this larger-than-playroom-size erector set, or traveling up and down while delivering their songs and cute sayings (*bonbon mots?*), the effect is stylish and fascinating, and does convey a sense of some sort of newness in the theater. It is heartening to see such an old-timer as Aronson, whose décor was always substantial but also ponderous and old-fashioned, daring to undertake so graceful and radical a departure, and fully succeeding.

The main weakness of *Company* is its protagonist, who is mostly a passive bystander, sometimes less than innocent and always less than interesting. It is of as little concern to us whether he becomes sold on marriage or lingers on in bachelorhood as it is whether the brawling, bitchy, arch or inept couples that surround him stay together, separate or vanish into the not so much thinner air. In the last analysis, real innovation takes risks; Sondheim, Prince & *Company* are much too prudent to take them.

To the question just what does the expression "too clever by half" mean, Anthony Shaffer's *Sleuth* will serve as answer. Not only is its almost every line, including many of the interlinear pauses, pure cleverness, but the play is also so constructed that you cannot explain its weaknesses without giving away the plot, which in the case of a thriller constitutes breach of minimal critical etiquette. Let me say only that though the mystery play always stretches a point or two, this one stretches them into lines. There is one character in it who is not only beyond belief, but also well beyond willing suspension of disbelief, and the number of plot reversals would make a shuttle pale with envy—but that, I guess, is how such yarns are spun.

The problem with this superficially most enjoyable play is that a world in which nothing is what it seems is almost as predictable, exasperating and depressing as a world in which everything is exactly what it appears to be—and considerably farther-fetched. But *Sleuth* has one great virtue, just about sufficient to compensate for its vice, and oddly indebted to, made possible by, that vice. Because the plot and at least half the characters are frankly preposterous, Shaffer is free to indulge his practically outrageous verbal facility to its witty, irreverent, rococo extreme. His style is sheer chinoiserie, piling lacquered screens of paradox upon pagodas of hyperbole—

sometimes a trifle schematically, but with unquenchable verve, bravado, and iconoclastic bravura. To sophisticatedly caddish laughter like this you could find the equal only in vintage Noël Coward. From *Sleuth*, the playwright's person emerges as that of a hypercivilized, ultra-urbane bounder, a rather attractive combination in a theater populated almost exclusively by well-meaning bores.

The production could not be better, although Carl Toms' good set seemed to fit a little more snugly into London's St. Martin's Theatre than into our Music Box. But Anthony Quayle's and Keith Baxter's unabashedly, gloriously theatrical performances are here intact, as is Clifford Williams' meticulously timed and spaced direction. I do wish the author had not turned serious, well-nigh metaphysical, in the end; otherwise, *Sleuth*, a play about games-playing, is plotted by a master games-player to whom we must doff everything from our cricket caps to our hunting hats.

Home, another English import, is perhaps equally clever in a precisely antipodal way. David Storey writes about people who are as painfully ordinary as Shaffer's are painfully extraordinary. It is no mean feat to construct a drama out of indirections, involuntary insinuations, utterances stillborn as platitudes or aborted into silences. Like Bond, Jellicoe, Livings and a number of younger English playwrights—largely, I suppose, in reaction against the British Empire style—Storey writes a gray, chilly, discomfitingly damp prose, occasionally clearing into wistful little patches of sunny amiability, the exact linguistic equivalent of English weather. The atmosphere is one of postwar English equity's cheerless triumph over pomp and circumstance, as a classy society gallantly sinks into raucous classlessness. In *Home*, five variously affected victims of train sickness in a society in transition, and amid values in transit to oblivion, discover madness as the only outlet for uprooted mediocrity.

There is something extremely exquisite about the diverse ways in which these people juggle their despair; whether it is colored balls of delusion, knives of nastiness, or just common garden chairs balanced in one hand, whatever sails, hurtles, or hesitates in this air (and these airs) is the identical desperation. There is humor here as well as touching awkwardness; there are the fuzzy edges of quotidian trivia in gruesomely sharp focus as well as discreetly uninsistent, self-effacing bits of symbolism. The only trouble—and it is serious—is that the material is basically undramatic, and cannot sustain more than a one-act play without becoming diffuse or dissolving into banality. Still, the music of the play's silences and near-silences is superbly orchestrated and performed. Lindsay Anderson directs, or conducts, with the most tactful musicianliness, making full use of the two incomparable first violins of John Gielgud and Ralph Richardson, the two crafty second fiddles of Mona Washbourne and Dandy Nichols, and the nice, dopey cello of Graham Weston. This string quintet is all marvelous tone clusters, cagey silences, shrewd rubatos, and shimmering polytonality. *Home* does not really work as a play, but as a concert it is close to sublime.

THE LATE LORRAINE HANSBERRY had three salient features: she was black, she wrote one successful Broadway soap opera, and she died young. All three of these facts have their very real pathos, but they do not add up to significant dramatic talent. And when Robert Nemiroff and Charlotte Zaltzberg, with unmistakable hackery, try to make a play out of something that, despite numerous rewritings, the author could neither carry off nor even finish, the result is unmitigated disaster. *Les Blancs* (the very French title in what is clearly a British African colony testifies to the utter confusion) is not only the worst new play on Broadway, of an amateurishness and crudity unrelieved by its sophomoric stabs at wit. It is also, more detestably, a play finished—or finished off—by white liberals that does its utmost to justify the slaughter of whites by blacks, and fails both as a cautionary tale and as a piece of expiation. It is a malodorous, unenlightening mess.

ORLANDO FURIOSO will have left New York when you read this, but the battle it stirred up still rages. *Orlando* was housed in a bubble-shaped structure erected in Bryant Park, which gave you the feeling of being inside a Zeppelin cross-bred with its own hangar. The show is a reduction of Ariosto's immense epic to puppet theater; but the puppets are blown up to human size, and on close investigation prove to be human beings; and the theater has been blown up to a three-or-more-ring circus. Whether one liked this depends on whether one considers a puppet's becoming an actor, and a theater's becoming a circus, an enlargement or a diminution. My own belief is that size without soul is the essence of vulgarity, and that the inflation and hubbub of this *Orlando* are closer to

Macy's Thanksgiving parade with its overblown balloons and jabbering children than to poetry and theater.

Ariosto was a great poet; the youthful Sir Walter Scott wrote an essay setting him above Homer. Of his sixteenth-century epic, C. S. Lewis justly noted, "It is 'God's plenty': you can no more exhaust it than you can exhaust nature itself." Not only is the work endowed with sweeping fantasy and fine irony, there is also in its descriptions of love, fighting, wonders of chivalry and magic, and just nature itself, a marvelously sensuous realism. Coleridge wrote of it: "We seem not to be reading of things, but to be in the very midst of them." But this adaptation of the poem by Eduardo Sanguineti, and staging of it by Luca Ronconi for Rome's Teatro Libero, departs fundamentally and demeaningly from the spirit of the original. It is a banalization that may well be performed by Sicilian puppets or carnival mountebanks in an Italian town square; it does not then purport to rejuvenate the serious theater, or invite critical assessment. In the present context and with the arrogations made in its behalf, I resent this vulgarization just as I would turning Shakespeare into a circus attraction in order to "revivify the theater."

But there is worse. In a letter to Boccaccio, Petrarch gave his fellow artist good advice about poets, like bees, "not storing up the flowers, but turning them into honey, thus making one thing of many various ones, but different and better." The Teatro Libero's *Orlando* does the exact opposite: it takes one good thing, chops it up and strews it across any number of simultaneously used acting areas. These are so many wooden crates that, like building blocks, can be reassembled in ever new combinations, or even raced along by people pushing from inside or around them while others, mounted on tin horses atop them, represent knights errant, Saracens, Charlemagne's paladins, and actors making fools of themselves. There are two proscenium-like stages at opposite ends of the bubble where different cantos of the poem are churning, while three or four other crate-created acting areas, stationary or charging at you, may carry the burden of a few more cantos and subplots hither and yon among the audience. For the audience stands or mills around, or enters actor-filled chicken coops representing a labyrinth, or, most often, hurriedly escapes from knights on crate-pedestaled steeds charging them at the speed of amusement-park bumper cars, and rather more ferally. The result, to return to Petrarch's precept, may be different, but it is distinctly worse.

It is all very well to be, as Coleridge said, not "reading of things, but . . . in the very midst of them." For a book exists more in permanence than in space and time, and we can slow down, re-read, pause and think in the *seeming* midst of things. In this theater, in the *actual* midst, we can do nothing but run or be run over. We cannot follow the plot or prosody—even if we know the story and the language—because it moves too fast and is scattered all over. We cannot get good work from the actors, performing stentorianly to attract our attention, or mechanically because they know that in other areas more crowd-pleasing episodes are in progress, or gingerly because a little more zeal will tumble them off their platforms. Even so, the nurse who is always on duty is no idle spectator.

But to what end all these hippogriffs clumsily flapping Erector-Set wings over our heads, these marine bears splitting in two as if Museum of Natural History mammoth skeleton replicas were coming apart, these warrior virgins banging away wooden swords to the sound of splintering *ottava rima,* all these maidens and audience in distress? Ariosto, part yearningly, part ironically, celebrated the *"gran bontà de' cavalieri antiqui";* but no goodness of ancient knights, only great gullibility of modern audiences, is at stake here. As John Lahr, that particularly rabid beater of wooden drums for the avant-garde, wrote in his *Village Voice* column, this *Orlando* allows us "to see . . . primal theatrical energy," to be "staring performing energy in the eye." And he upbraids our culture "which likes to keep things 'normal' . . . and puts its 'psychotics' out of sight." "Emotion," laments Lahr, "is kept at a safe distance."

Hogwash. Art is never raw energy to be stared in the eye (a single eye, it seems, like the raging Cyclops'), but is the molding, shaping, channeling and controlling of energy. "Primal theatrical energy" is in the mind of a Shakespeare, Chekhov or Beckett, and no one can stare it in the eye or beat it out with wooden swords against tin horses. And if this kind of audience participation exercises the legs, it unhappily bypasses the brain. As for our society, I don't see it keeping many things normal these days, or emotion at a distance. And where would Lahr have us put our psychotics? Into the drama reviewer's seat, no doubt.

IN THE DECEMBER 10 *Village Voice,* John Lahr attempts to answer some of my charges against *Orlando Furioso* and, implicitly (I refer to the answers, not to the charges), against John Lahr. About the quality of the counterarguments you will have to make up your own minds—but do not miss the quasi-equation of what a unique genius like Shakespeare does with his source material, which he recasts entirely, and what a bunch of spoofers from the Teatro Libero do to Ariosto, which, you have Lahr's word for it, consists of changing the third person singular to the first, and indirect discourse into direct. There is a vast difference, clear to most people, between a great man's using the work of lesser men, and lesser men's tinkering with that of a great one.

But one aspect of Lahr particularly disturbs me. In his peroration against me, in the very climactic last paragraph, he accuses me of "inferring" something, though what he means is that I *implied* it. The first sentence of Lahr's new book, *Up Against the Fourth Wall*, begins: "The body, so long the brunt of the Church's bad joke . . ." The word, of course, is butt, not brunt. And so it goes with Lahr, from first sentence to last paragraph. Now, I can see that judiciousness, learning, maturity, taste, style, etc., might be considered luxuries in a critic in this youth- and pop-oriented age, but I would have thought that such a basic tool as the English language might still be held indispensable.

ODODO, which the Negro Ensemble Company is currently performing, is a scandal. It has a shapeless, poorly written book by Joseph A. Walker, and derivative, pedestrian music by Dorothy A. Dinroe. It is a black supremacist, racist show in which blacks claim to be sole possessors of a valuable commodity called "soul," against which white art and science and culture are as nothing. The cast informs us, after reviling Abraham Lincoln, that they propose to wipe their arses with the Constitution, and that there will be "No more pigs, niggers, or rhetoric,/ Only black men standing tall." If there is anything wrong with blacks, it is because "The honky has taught us a whole lot of bad habits." History is blithely rewritten: "Your Mayflower is a fraud: black prisoners of war watched it anchor." Finally we are told in tuneful numbers, "Who cares about America?/ . . . No glory in their rhythmless hearts./ Who cares about zombies, dead before you die?/ Suffer your death without consolation!"

This random sampling (there is much more where it came from) raises several ponderable points. First, "pigs" and "niggers" may cease to be, but rhetoric clearly will not vanish as long as Joseph A. Walker and his likes are around to supply it. Secondly, what is this "soul" the blacks have a monopoly on? I am reminded of the man who was selling a fabulous plot of land, which turned out to be only a yard square; when questioned about these measly dimensions, he pointed skyward and said, "But look how high it is!" Thirdly, if the whites have taught blacks "a whole lot of bad habits" (which, on the evidence of this show, must include poor use of language), how can superior beings have been so susceptible to contamination by inferiors? And how can we be sure that a musical like *Ododo* is not yet another bad white habit dyed black? Fourthly, what is this about "rhythmless hearts"? Can you always tell a white heart by its marvelous lack of rhythm?

But the scandal is not in that *Ododo* (the Yoruba word for truth) gets written and performed. Oppressed minorities have the right to hate back, and one can write shows just as well—and just as ill—out of hate as out of love. I would, however, point out a bit of unconscious symbolism the N.E.C. might consider. After the liminal pronouncement of the show, "Africa was the cradle of creation," the composer strikes some rather soulful chords on—a piano. Now, the piano is a white creation—at least until the N.E.C. gets around to rewriting the history of music, too—and it is a very interesting, I am inclined to say relevant, instrument. It makes music by using black and white keys equally and harmoniously.

To get to the scandal, however. It is that long list of donors to whom the N.E.C. devotes a special folder inside the program. They are twice referred to as "doners." This may be either subliteracy or humor, making a portmanteau word out of "donors" and "boners." For it is rather a scandalous joke that such a high proportion of the names listed should be those of white individuals and corporations, who have hit upon the felicitous solution of allaying their guilt feelings by subsidizing murderous antiwhite propaganda. True, if you liquidate the person who feels them, you do away with the feelings, too. Still, I have my doubts about endowing a show that advocates militant "marching among the cockroaches" (i.e., whites), whether because one is so stupid as to think one can buy oneself off with a subsidy, or because one is so suicidal as to be willing to suffer one's "death without consolation"—indeed, invite it.

I wonder how many in the audience notice the confused thinking in *Ododo?* In one relatively friendly remark, we hear: "If you

won't be what you claim to be,/ Then we will see that you won't
be *at all!*" Hypocrisy apparently is the unpardonable sin. But is
Ododo what it claims to be? If it is, why should the whites tolerate it? If it isn't, it stands condemned by its own mouth, and why
should blacks accept it? If anyone who cannot quite live up to what
he claims to be must die, none shall 'scape whipping to death. Let
me put it another way. Dick Gregory once explained the Negro
demands with a parable: if a man takes a size 8½ shoe, and for
years you force him to wear an 8, as soon as he gets the power,
he will insist on a 9. That always struck me as faulty thinking:
wear shoes that are too big for you and you fall on your face—or,
worse, shuffle along. Why not 8½ for *all* who need it?

WHEN WILL playwrights learn that it takes more than a string of
funny lines to make a comedy? Actually, Neil Simon's *The Gingerbread Lady* purports to be more than a comedy, and the lines, for
the most part, are less than funny. Less than funny for several reasons. 1) They traipse over the same old terrain, from sex-starvation
to unquenched-thirst jokes, from kinky-sex to show-biz in-jokes, from
Mafia to Polish jokes. (There are no elephant jokes.) You may not
have heard precisely these jokes before, but your surprise is no
greater than at hearing the triumphal march from *Aida* played on
water glasses. 2) There are too many of them. Hardly ever is anyone,
regardless of age, background, or calling, allowed to speak in anything but funny lines. Whether he is touched, anguished, or crushed,
it is all converted into jokes. They end by tripping one another up,
and a joke slipping painfully on the peel of the previous joke is no
laughing matter. 3) The jokes do not, except superficially, rise out of
character or an individual way of looking at the world. Thus, homosexual to nymphomaniac: "I know you, Evy. I wouldn't leave you
alone with the Pope during Holy Week." Nymphomaniac to homosexual: "We could live together in Canada. They don't do sex in
Canada." The butts of the jokes vary, but the diction, sensibility
and underlying mentality remain entirely interchangeable.

Jokes are not really funny in a vacuum; or at most are funny only
one at a time. Is there a greater bore at gatherings than the man who
incessantly tells jokes, even funny ones? Jokes must grow out of some
meaningful human soil, must tell us something also about the teller,
about a society, about life itself. They need the resistance of a hard
surface off which to bounce: bits of dialogue, realities, that are not

funny. And if the play is to have any value, they must aim at something more ambitious than a mere detonation in the auditorium—something, perhaps, resembling the truth. They *do* do sex in Canada; it is only in a Neil Simon play that, salacious allusions notwithstanding, they don't.

In any case, *The Gingerbread Lady* pretends to be more than a farce. It is about a once-popular pop singing star, now a man-hungry alcoholic, divorced and abandoned by the world, whom a coalition of two friends (an unemployed homosexual actor and a fading narcissistic beauty, herself ditched by her husband) and a fanatically dedicated teenage daughter may eventually save from drink. Or may not. The plot outline is: on the wagon (after a stay in a sanatorium), off the wagon (when everyone, in perfect synchronization, loses a job, a lover, or a husband), on the wagon (when filial love flowers with tropical lushness). In *The Country Girl,* it was a wife and a director; here it is a daughter and an actor who do the rescuing. But in that unremarkable Odets play certain relationships at least underwent significant changes; here, the progress of Evy Meara is just up and down that wagon while she and her trio of helpers exchange gags and occasional outbursts. Matters are not helped by Maureen Stapleton's neither looking, nor moving, nor sounding like a famous pop singer of only a few years ago. The actress delivers her lines with impeccable timing and emphasis, but she sorely lacks any sort of grace, charm, poise or sexiness that would suggest either music or glamour in her past.

But of course it is Neil Simon who has failed to provide the character with dimensions, let alone stature. Whether this particular person is saved or goes under interests us only insofar as she is sufficiently particularized and developed for us, as it were, to sink along with Evy; or conversely to the extent that her predicament is seen in the context of show business, society, or some other larger force that brings the individual to her knees. There may be extrinsic reasons for Simon's reticence: he may want us to view Evy as modeled on one or another famous show-business figure, and fear that if the analogy comes too close, it will prove libelous; if too remote from the known facts, devoid of piquancy. His recourse is to lapse into vagueness and gags. When Evy's daughter becomes foul-mouthed and cites her mother's example in her defense, Mother replies: "I talk this way. It's a speech impediment." No matter what his subject, Neil Simon talks in gags. It's not so much a speech as a thought impediment.

As the unsuccessful homosexual actor, Michael Lombard gives a warm and accurate performance, exemplarily avoiding both the maudlin and the obviously campy. The best work, though, comes from Betsy von Furstenberg as the declining beauty who puts her faith in cosmetics until, faced with the loss of her husband, she is persuaded to make up her mind to be herself instead of making up her face to be another. In this implausible role, which would have self-worship and altruism as miscible as gin and vermouth, Miss von Furstenberg hits on the admirable solution of encasing her character in glass: her brittle gaze, tinkling voice, and general air of translucency and frangibility provide a crystalline envelope for a very ordinary little life within, a life the actress presents absolutely straightforwardly inside its glass case. And that voice of hers: a glockenspiel made funky by a head cold!

Finally, even if the play were better than it is, would not the subject matter still seem both exhausted and puny? Even if we were made to care about the possible downfall of this sodden chanteuse, would we care very much?

Whistle-stop drama: *One Night Stands of a Noisy Passenger*, three loosely connected one-acters by Shelley Winters. Miss Winters' heart is in the right place: I have often heard her excoriate the commercialism of our theater, censure that I heartily applaud. But faced with the choice, Miss Winters, I dare say, could not tell a work of art from a turquoise-browed motmot. Such, at any rate, is the evidence of her three ostentatiously and embarrassingly autobiographical playlets in which she modestly equates her fly-by-night fornications with the Three Ages of Woman (green, ripe, gamy), with three stages in the history of this country and the world, and most improbably, with art.

The first of these encounters takes place on a snowy St. Valentine's Day night in 1940 in an Eighth Avenue basement room. A young girl who is an unquestioning Communist but a questionable virgin loses her putative maidenhead on the soiled sheets of an up-and-coming actor. The second play takes place in 1953 in Paris (in April, of course, which is all it ever is there); the girl is now a woman and a fairly successful actress who gets involved with a prominent movie director about to face HUAC. He will give her a screen test if she will act as some sort of cover for him, and the point, as far as I could unscramble it, is the loss of political innocence or idealism. The third episode takes place in Hollywood (now, of course, which is all it ever is there); the somewhat overripe actress has gone on a binge upon winning an Oscar. She ends up in the pad of a hippie head who plies her with sex, acid and coke, tries to make her get him into big-time movies and, when rebuffed, harshly berates her. These are all manifestly *pièces à clef*, but though a blind Hottentot could identify the heroine, only those plugged into the grapevine could identify the men as the celebrities they presumably are. Nobody could identify them as human beings.

Miss Winters is capable of turning out an occasional funny line, as when the hippie offers the wary actress a morning-after cigarette and assures her: "It's a straight one: no fantasy, just cancer." But even plays that ran for only one performance usually had a few funny lines in them. What is distinctly wrong here—besides all those other unfunny lines—is the earnest, loquacious pointlessness of it all, coupled with colossal self-importance. To whom, except to the author, could these narcissistic navel-gazings be of interest? Stendhal's definition of the novel was a mirror on the roadway; Miss Winters' notion of drama seems to be a paillette in the umbilicus—or still farther down. These plays are so boring that they make not only theater-going, but also, much more perniciously, sex itself look like a waste of time. The acting is undistinguished in the first play (which does, however, afford you a rare chance to see Sally Kirkland clothed, or nearly), wretched in the second, and rather good in the third, with both Diane Ladd and Robert DeNiro giving stylish performances. Patricia Carmichael's staging shows a mote of invention in the first play, but proves to be a one-mote affair. The whole thing exudes a certain fetid, intramural smugness, as of an Actors Studio exercise, which is really what it is. To Browning's famous question, "Ah, did you once see Shelley plain?" I can reply, "Thrice. And plain is an, ah, understatement."

I HAVE ALWAYS loved the man John Millington Synge; I wish I could do as much for the playwright. It is impossible not to be stirred by that nobly handsome face, by the shyly quiet yet bold personality, by the perceptively progressive views on art, by the unstinting dedication in the face of a long foreseen tragically premature death. But, for me, the promise of Synge, great and real as it was, lies "with O'Leary in the grave." When Synge, not yet thirty-eight, died in 1909 of Hodgkins' disease, the finest Irish dramatic talent was extinguished unfulfilled. His four comedies of Hibernian peasant life are apt and wry, rambunctious but aware of a dark underside; they are also, however, slight, and like other plays about peasant life, perishable goods. This leaves the two tragedies, *Riders to the Sea* and *Deirdre of the Sorrows*. Pronounced "one of the finest, if not the finest, of all modern short plays" by Una Ellis-Fermor, *Riders*, with its numerous uniform deaths packed as tight as sardines in their tin coffins, fatally skirts travesty. But in *Deidre*, unfortunately left unfinished, Synge may indeed have come, as Allardyce Nicoll suggested, "close to the genius of Shakespeare."

Probably the most rounded of Synge's plays, though, is *The Playboy of the Western World*, which is remarkably Chekhovian in spirit, but not, alas, in language. Language, admirably, was Synge's great love and concern (next to, of course, the people who spoke it), and it became both his glory and his ultimate downfall. That he could control it sovereignly is most perspicuous in some of his lyrics—one of which, "A Question," remains for me Synge's true masterpiece. But in the plays, though he shrewdly picked prose as the vehicle for modern dramatic poetry (thereby proving pawkier than any number of poetic playwrights from Yeats to Eliot), Synge chose a syntax and rhythm derived from the peasant speech of the western Irish counties. Now, the trouble with this lingo—and to what extent Synge did or did not transform it need not detain us here—is its lulling incantatory quaintness which, for all its charm, is ultimately stultifying. It is the sort of lilt that, *mutatis mutandis*, puts us to sleep in certain compositions of Tchaikovsky's; it is the same kind of one-note bizarreness that makes the otherwise brilliant paintings of Soulages finally boring. Yeats cites with apparent satisfaction a sentence where someone is "the like of the little children do be listening to the stories of an old woman, and do be dreaming after in the dark night it's in grand houses of gold they are, with speckled horses to ride, and do be waking again in a short while and they destroyed with the cold, and the thatch dripping, maybe, and the starved ass braying in the yard." Even in a dream, I wouldn't want to ride a speckled horse through a house of gold: it's apt to slip and leave droppings.

Ken Tynan wrote about *Playboy*: "I concede its soft lyricism; but where is its hard meaning? Synge is often praised for his mastery of cadence, and for the splendor of his dying falls. Dying they may well be, but they take an unconscionable time doing it. Synge seldom lets a simple, declarative sentence alone. To its tail there must be pinned some such trailing tin can of verbiage as—to improvise an example—'the way you'd be roaring and moiling in the lug of a Kilkenny ditch, and she with a shift on her would destroy a man entirely, I'm thinking, and him staring till the eyes would be lepping surely from the holes in his head.' Nor can I bring myself to devote my full attention to a play in which all the characters are numskulls—and quaint, pastoral numskulls at that." Yet when this is said, it must be added that there is in *Playboy* much of the "mischievous wisdom" that, according to Yeats, characterized Synge, this "audacious joyous ironical man."

And what of the production the Lincoln Center Repertory Company has mounted at the Vivian Beaumont? Rule number one: if you cannot reproduce the speech melodies of the western counties, forget about doing Synge; the cast sounds not so much like County Mayo as like a cross section of the patients at the Mayo Clinic. From Boston- to Brooklyn-, from stage- to non-Irish, everything bubbles in this cacophonous pot; if you think a Babel of tongues is a bad thing, just try this Beaumont of brogues. Then there is the direction by John Hirsch, even more lacking in rhythm than the speech. Cinematically speaking, it is all slow motion, when not downright freeze shots. And it deprives the play of its three main ingredients: violence, sexuality, humor. Hirsch, who staged the same company's *The Time of Your Life*, another barroom play, has once again reduced a pub overflowing with raucous lusts to a pleasantly edulcorated Hirschy bar. What emerges is less *Playboy* than *Ryan's Daughter*.

The performances are mostly disappointing. Stephen Elliott, to my taste a basically cheap actor, nevertheless does the best job as Old Mahon: funny and pathetic and crazy—just right. But David Birney, perhaps from struggling with the brogue, is often incomprehensible, and though he acts cogently, he is much too handsome and virile for Christy, whose pipsqueakery is one of the main points of the play. There is a desiccated, sexless Widow Quin from Frances Sternhagen, and a strangely muffled Michael James from Sydney Walker. Martha Henry, whom I have intensely admired in Shakespearean roles at Stratford, Ontario, misses both the humor and the pathos of Pegeen Mike. In the trio of love-smitten colleens, Susan Sharkey is delightful, Elizabeth Huddle oafish beyond the call of duty, and Tandy Cronin devoid of the least spark of talent. Worst of all is that archetypal non-actor, Ray Fry, whose repeated presence in important parts would alone disqualify this company from being taken seriously.

•   •   •

IT WAS THE young Hugo von Hofmannsthal who put his perceptive finger on the sort of lives Ibsen's characters lead. He described
them as living "in unbearable, painful, depressing little yellowish-
gray relationships," and that eminently applies to the marriage of
Torvald and Nora Helmer in *A Doll's House*. For eight years, and
during the breeding and rearing of three children, Torvald has
treated Nora as a charming little plaything whose delight must be
to delight him. And Nora has risen, or descended, to his expectations
and convinced herself that this way lies not madness but happiness.
For Torvald, the marriage has a pleasing, yellow candlelight glow,
and even Nora manages to overlook the spreading gray beneath. But
we are allowed to see the full dirty yellowish gray, a dismal color
we sometimes find on book bindings the sun has bleached and that
almost deters us from reading what is in those books.

A Doll's House chronicles the end of a dehumanizing game. It
is too bad that Christopher Hampton perpetuates the mistranslation
of the title, which Rolf Fjelde was, I believe, the first to translate
correctly as *A Doll House*. For this intransigently probing yet always
imaginative and poetic play is not concerned with a house in which
a doll is living, but with the reduction of life to that particular toy
that is a miniature house in which tiny human effigies are manipulated by children—a doll house. It is in terms of this image (which
John Bury's setting regrettably fails to evoke) that the play acquires
its pathos and its poetry. The Torvald who plays with his doll-wife,
doll-children, and doll-friends is not a man but a superannuated baby,
a seemingly innocent creature living a shriveling lie. But in an even
deeper sense, Torvald is himself a doll, manipulated by misguided
and antiquated mores into exercising a paternalism that he is not
thoughtful or humane enough to question. He may not dance the
tarantella like Nora, but he too dances according to a doll-like,
mincing choreography that custom and society have foisted on him.

That a play Ibsen wrote close to a century ago should strike us
as so fresh and vital today, so ineffably more contemporary than
what most of our dramatists and avant-gardists peddle as the *dernier
cri*, is much more remarkable than that, say, Euripides or Shakespeare should affect us in that way. For it is easy for us to see the
truth of our remote and illustrious forebears, tastily preserved in the
aspic of history. Our fathers, however, we tend to rebel against—
almost have to rebel against if we are to move forward. Yet there
is simply no getting ahead of Father Ibsen, who as another great
poet, Rilke, put it, "measured the scarcely measurable."

It redounds to Ibsen's lasting glory that he was able to compress Nora's awakening—about Torvald, the world and, most of all, herself—into barely more than twenty-four hours. It is made as believable as dramatic foreshortening can make a cataclysmic psychological change, but the burden on the actress and the director is also great. In the current revival, Claire Bloom is an extremely fetching, diaphanous yet real Nora. She uses a minimum of vocal and behavioral props, but manages not only to age but also to come of age in a matter of minutes before our eyes. It may be that Miss Bloom and her able director, Patrick Garland, have overstressed Nora's fluttery childlikeness in the beginning, or that, at any rate, they have not quite conveyed her potential for growth. But what is truly admirable in the final phase is that a good deal of the innocence, vulnerability and grace of Nora is preserved even in the hour of hard lucidity, of maturely sober resolve. What Miss Bloom gives us is a firmness that is still a little tentative, a determination that is more hopeful than fully formed. It makes the concluding scene profoundly and believably moving.

Although Garland has directed most of the play sensitively to overtones, and nimbly avoids heavy emphases, he fails with Donald Madden's Torvald—as, I suspect, any other director would, too. Madden is an honorably but thoroughly second-rate actor; he is never absolutely wrong, but his effects come hard to him, he never disappears into his role or vice versa, and he cannot, in an unsympathetic role, still somehow make us like him. In this case, it would be nice if, besides exulting with Miss Bloom's limpid, flexible Nora, we could also feel compassion for this lumpishly well-meaning mediocrity of a Torvald. Instead of being overwhelmingly ordinary, Madden looks and acts somewhat creepy, at times even Dracula-ish, and when he approaches his wife with an "Exceptionally lovely, isn't she?" we tremble in anticipation of the imminent puncturing of a fragile neck by a pair of intimated fangs. This Torvald's behavior goes from faintly sinister to downright malefic in his final outbursts, which makes the ending a too facilely happy one. There is an interesting Kristine from Patricia Elliott, but the Krogstad and Dr. Rank are barely acceptable. That master craftsman, John Bury, has come up with his least suggestive set and lighting; Christopher Hampton's English version, though it has brio and sinew, is sometimes too English ("My opinions . . . are quite different to yours") and sometimes not English enough ("It's time for you and I to have a talk"; "that must mean that I am as well petty"). But what Ibsen and Miss

Bloom achieve here, in lovely concert, must be heard and seen and cherished.

RELEVANCE, IN MY critical vocabulary, is a moderately unappetizing term. It is not dirty to the point of giving off mephitic effluvia, but it does suggest an orchestration of five-o'clock shadow, black-bordered fingernails and begrimed shirt cuffs to match. Yet when I see something like *No, No, Nanette,* I feel like reaching for the nearest plywood gun and rushing to the first street corner to enlist in the guerrilla theater. For though it seems smug and fatuous to make a fetish of mere relevance, reveling in this kind of mindless, soulless and gutless irrelevance is even more offensive. And when I consider the sociopolitical implications of an audience of palsied graybeards; paunchy businessmen; overdressed, made-up and made-over women; Byzantinely decked-out queens and caterwauling catamites; retarded drama reviewers; and the passel of plain good folk with whom there is nothing wrong that a little extra brain and taste could not cure—when I consider these hungry legions devouring *No, No, Nanette* as though it were a combination of Mom's apple pie, free soda pop, and manna from heaven, the spectacle takes on a ghastly sort of relevance.

For it is these tacky (not even elegant!) faggots who hoot with coloratura jubilance each time Ruby Keeler appears on stage looking flustered by receiving the Catholic Mother of the Year award; these solid, nay, ossified citizens who burble with infant delight as Patsy Kelly sputteringly waddles on; these truss-trundlers beating their palms like cymbals whenever they recognize in the orchestra pit the stirrings of a moldering melody being prodded back into life—they are the ones who help the Vietnam spectacular become an unlimited engagement, contribute through apathy to the permanent S.R.O. of our slums and ghettos, applaud an incompetent leading man like Nixon into the limelight (and would clap as loudly for his understudy, a gnu). They would happily carpet the theater with wall-to-wall revivals of ancient idiocies, would forget Song My for a Youmans song, and render unto Irving Caesar that which is God's.

Then, of course, come the Beautiful People who think this atavism clever, lovely, and (having bought their indulgences from Walter Kerr) innocent. After all, aren't these twenties clothes as new as today, these wilted stars as with-it as tonight's *Late Late Show,* these jokes (compared to which a doornail is bursting with life) absitively posolutely reeking with the prestige conferred on those who recognize yesterday's inanities? Behold Ruby Keeler, who cannot and never could act, and whose concern over this is her one unvarying expression, who looks every one of her sixty-odd years, but who defies the passage of time, old age, our very mortality, by dancing on! How well? As Dr. Johnson put it, Ruby dancing is like a dog walking on his hind legs. It is not done well; but you are surprised to find it done at all. In supporting parts, Helen Gallagher and Bobby Van are at least slickly professional; but the juvenile, Roger Rathburn, is wood trying to pass for Styrofoam; and the ingénue, Susan Watson, is only halfway acceptable (the upper half). The chief comic, Jack Gilford, could make a laughing hyena weep, and Patsy Kelly, the lead comedienne, is a duffel bag full of devaluated jests. The chorus girls, hand-picked by Busby Berkeley, are a tribute to his apparently failing eyesight; the chorus boys divide evenly into the wooden progeny Weber has begotten on Heilbronner for display behind plate glass, and elderly Corybants who have donated their manhood to Cybele.

Busby Berkeley is credited with supervising the production, but seems to have de-Camped, leaving the choreography to Donald Saddler, and the revision of the book and its staging to Burt Shevelove. The dances look authentic, and Gallagher and Van give them a sheen, but the book was beyond salvaging even by the savvy of Mr. Shevelove. Let there be light entertainment by all means, but let it have at least remote bearing on the world we live or once lived in. The Bible publisher who keeps three girls in as many cities and never sleeps with them, the bright young lady who wants a fling before marriage consisting of a trip to Atlantic City with a bunch of camp-fire girls and Fire Island boys, the model modern marriage that threatens to break up over a slight misunderstanding—is this a valid travesty of people who lived A.D. 1925? Or even 1925 B.C.? A farce by Feydeau, an Offenbach operetta, an Aristophanic spoof have some bearing on humanity, but *this?*

Even the tunes by Vincent Youmans are, for the most part, musically thin, and the lyrics by Irving Caesar and Otto Harbach have, to quote a line from the show, "Ooh-ooh! A soft center!" The celebrated "Tea for Two" could have been written by a computer with a sweet tooth (Brendan Gill, in *The New Yorker*, has undertaken a splendid textual anlaysis of it), and only "Too Many Rings Around Rosie" can afford to show itself denuded of mothballs. Apropos balls, there is a mildly amusing number with girls precariously treading beach balls; otherwise, the enterprise is sorrily ball-less.

The period sets and costumes by Raoul Pène du Bois are convincing enough, and convinced me that the period was one of the low points in the history of aesthetics. Yet there remain all those people who rejoice in the fact that the production is not camped up. *No, No, Nanette* is to camp what the *objet trouvé* was to Dada: a perfect ready-made. You cannot gild a lily that is pure ormolu. Any way you twist it, *Nanette* is a no-no. And with the mint sunk into producing and promoting this abortion, three young playwrights could have enjoyed useful showcases. The waste! The shame!

HEDDA GABLER is one of Ibsen's more difficult masterpieces to come to grips with: if you have a strong, dominant Hedda, as you almost must have, it is hard to keep the other characters from turning into negligible motes jiggling in her beams of cold light. If you try to curb your Hedda and keep her fairly ordinary (which, in a sense, she also is), you may lose not only the pathos of the situation but even its credibility. And what makes the part of the heroine so taxing for an actress is that she has to be at once a rather empty, unsatisfied woman who feels she is not getting her due from life, and also something much bigger, more terrifying and pitiful: destructive and self-destructive on the grand scale, with an inner turbulence that can tear the roof off other people's houses as well as her own. So Hedda is both endemic and demonic, and the play easily becomes too mundane or too far-fetched.

As most responsible criticism now recognizes, *Hedda Gabler* is much less a play about a bizarre psychopath than one about an environment so stifled by its own closeness that its chief outlet is a petty power struggle: by what means and to what extent can I control the lives of others, or acquire a dominant position in my dreary little ambience? Some, like Aunt Julia and Thea Elvsted, try to achieve this through good deeds—though these, upon inspection, are less unselfish than self-serving. Others, like George Tesman, try to scale, through academic preferment or the elegance of their home and wife, the eminence their feeble talents cannot achieve. An Ejlert Lövborg, for all his visionary ideas, is an existential weakling, whose prophetic book is an attempt to use the future as a stick with which to get revenge on the present. And Hedda pours her vast frustration, her festering ambition, into a vessel named Lövborg, hoping to fuel him into a servo-mechanism for her indirect triumph or, failing that, his spectacular death.

Claire Bloom is a charming actress, but there is something girlish, almost filigree about the emotions she can convey; it is all there, but made out of exquisite Steuben glass rather than out of flesh and desperation. There is, after all, another side of Hedda which Ibsen did not fail to stress, as when he urged the director of the Christiania Theater to cast a Miss Bruun as Hedda at the world première, because she could "express the demonic aspect of the character," rather than a Mrs. Heiberg who, for all her "natural talent" could not. Miss Bloom, alas, is a Heibergian Hedda, who reduces the character —very accurately, very proportionately—to doll-house dimensions. Donald Madden, as Lövborg, looks wonderfully Scandinavian, even Strindbergian, but lacks the poetry and appeal that could make this brilliant but unstable person endearing and therefore moving. The supporting cast is consistently one-dimensional, and, in the case of Tesman, even that single dimension heads the wrong way. Roy Shuman makes this merely plodding character into a dodderer and ditherer, twice his age and half his wit.

Christopher Hampton's translation would be fine, except for the unfortunate change of a key image. Judge Brack now wants to be the only bull in the arena instead of the only cock of the walk, and though a tauromachian trope sounds more prestigious than a barnyard one, it misses the point. The rooster treads hens and survives; the bull puts on a show and is killed. John Bury's set is at best rudimentary, but his costumes for the women are tasteful. Patrick Garland has directed poorly: instead of rising to a series of climaxes, the play drags along anemically and ends not with the general upheaval Ibsen specifically asks for, but with a jaded listlessness that all but engulfs its true meaning.

SPRING, 1971

A MIDSUMMER NIGHT'S DREAM
  by William Shakespeare
  produced by the Royal Shakespeare Company

ABÉLARD & HÉLÖISE
  by Ronald Millar

ALL OVER
  by Edward Albee

FOLLIES
  book by James Goldman
  music and lyrics by Stephen Sondheim

HOW THE OTHER HALF LOVES
  by Alan Ayckbourn

L'AMANTE ANGLAISE
  by Marguerite Duras

METAMORPHOSES
  by Ovid
  adapted by Arnold Weinstein
  produced by Paul Sills's Story Theatre

LONG DAY'S JOURNEY INTO NIGHT
  by Eugene O'Neill

AND WHOSE LITTLE BOY ARE YOU?
  by Rod Parker

SCRATCH
  by Archibald MacLeish

ANTIGONE
  by Sophocles
  produced by the Repertory Theater of Lincoln Center

GODSPELL
  book by John Michael Tebelak
  music and lyrics by Stephen Schwartz

DO MASTERPIECES need to be reinterpreted for every revival? Are there, perhaps, no more masterpieces left at all—as Artaud proclaimed and some eminent critics and men of the theater were only too eager to corroborate lately? What is needed, according to Robert Brustein, the most intelligent and temperate of the antimasterpiecers, is "willing[ness] to approach classical works with complete freedom, even if this means adapting them into a modern idiom." * Oddly enough, Brustein seems to see no significant difference between directorial reinterpretations—as when, say, *King Lear* is so edited, staged, and acted as to make it resemble a work by Beckett (Peter Brook's production); and authorial versions, as when Dryden or Giraudoux writes a wholly new *Antony and Cleopatra* or *Electra*.

In his new-found role as producer and director, Brustein seems to contradict, or at least relax, his former critical standards. Thus, to bolster his argument in favor of irreverence to masterpieces, he is perfectly willing to adduce numerous examples for which he himself has no use: why, for instance, bother to mention such experiments as Dryden's with *Troilus and Cressida*, which, as Brustein states, was "a hash" of the original? And I cannot fathom what the

* "No More Masterpieces," in Robert Brustein, *The Third Theatre*, Knopf, 1969.

difference is between the Stratford, Connecticut, *Much Ado,* set "in Spanish Texas around the time of the Alamo" and reprehended by Brustein; and Lowell's version of *Prometheus Bound,* as staged by Jonathan Miller, with the Greek setting or Caucasian crags abandoned for "a vague seventeenth-century background—probably Spain during the Inquisition" and defended by Brustein—indeed produced by him for the Yale Repertory Company.

The objection to leaving masterpieces more or less as they are is that they were produced by "companies . . . more often dedicated to perpetuating the past than illuminating it, and, as a result, ended up looking more like museums than living organisms." Brustein is writing here about the Old Vic and Comédie Française, and though his intent is to decry old-fashioned productions of classics, the subject of the sentence is "companies"; in truth, it is they who end up looking like museums (and presumably blameworthy), not the practice of letting a masterpiece remain itself. This, of course, raises the question of what is wrong with a museum as long as it preserves and displays its treasures accessibly and tastefully? Do we have to repaint a Cézanne or rebake a Minoan terra-cotta to bring it up to date?

The main issue, however, is precisely how to maintain the quality of a living organism in a play. The failure to do this in so-called conventional productions does not stem from setting and staging the play logically and consistently, from not manhandling the author's text and intentions (to the extent that they are knowable), and from not being palpably and provocatively different from every other mounting of the play that ever was. The failure—and it is common enough—lies in offering a routine, bloodless production along well-trodden lines, in which the play's sights and sounds and ideas are not experienced afresh. Certainly a good production is one that suggests that we are enjoying the play with new eyes, new ears, new minds; but this does not mean that it should be revamped beyond recognition, beyond respecting at least the basic intentions and givens contained in it. To be sure, it is much easier to dazzle by doing things differently with a vengeance—say, converting outdoors into indoors, Venice into Vienna, women into men, romance into satire, etc.—but true artistry is to make things both the same *and* different.

Take, for example, *A Midsummer Night's Dream,* these comments being a preamble to a discussion of its new production by Peter Brook for the Royal Shakespeare Company, now imported by David Merrick. *Dream* can be laid in Athens, in Shakespeare's England or in an imaginary world of the poetic fancy. Or any two of these, or all three places may be combined, and suggestions of time present can of course be legitimately introduced. All of these valid options allow for an individual vision on the part of the director and designer, yet would not clash with what is in the text or with the best tradition of *Dream* productions. Within this set of plausibilities one can work wonders of resourcefulness and empathetic sensitivity.

Indeed, Peter Brook has not taken significant liberties with the time of the play. Although Puck looks like a character from the commedia dell'arte, and the lovers wear mod tie-dyed togs, the period of the production is pleasantly indeterminate. But something jars even here: the costumes (by Sally Jacobs, who also designed the scenery) tend to have an inexpensive, humdrum look about them: not quite Grotowskian poverty, but a kind of flimsy, school-production economy. Where the licence—or licentiousness—comes in is with the locale, the spatial concept of the production, which is topsy-turvy, cute and perverse without shame or surcease. To revert to Brustein: " 'No more masterpieces' means treating the theatre as informally as a circus tent, a music hall, a prize ring—a place in which the spectator participates rather than worships, and offers the stage something more than the condescension of applause."

I find that remark genuinely puzzling. Why is applause a form of condescension? It is a convention as good as any other—say, shaking hands or tipping one's hat—and has a perfectly acceptable symbolic value. It is, moreover, boisterous and informal in character. Furthermore, at the circus and the music hall, two of Brustein's suggested locations, applause is very much the order of the day. At prize fights it is not, but I doubt whether Brustein would be happy if one of his stage productions were constantly interrupted with shouts of "Sock him!" or "Kill him!" and the various jeers and howls the punched flesh is heir to. And what about audience participation? In none of the mediums Brustein describes does the spectator participate in any tangible way; indeed, Brustein has treated with just contempt most audience-participation theater. Clearly what is meant is some sort of emotional involvement, and this is available from any good play in a decent production, however unexperimental it may be. The key word in Brustein's statement, I dare say, is "worships": he is rightly incensed by the sheeplike audiences that flock to the various temples of culture, absorb their monthly quota of self-improvement (or self-promotion), dutifully clap their hands where they are supposed to, and remain basically uninvolved throughout.

But the trouble with a theater that wants to jolt the masses out of their torpor is that it tends to see the problem in simple black-and-white terms. Over here the snobbish, bourgeois audience in their black-and-white evening regalia, pompously or jadedly applauding their fiftieth *Romeo and Juliet* in which an effete Romeo and an elocutionary Juliet vow their love under and on the identical balcony with the selfsame pear-shaped B.B.C. diction all over again. But over there the *Romeo and Juliet* that takes place in the bohemian section of some modern city, with a drug-pusher Romeo wooing the daughter of the illegal liquor-traffic king, the words emerging tough and nervous from the top and bottom of a fire escape, and the audience all involved young people in unregimented clothing and at the edges of their seats with excitement. Not so. One can get radical productions that are absolutely awful, whereas an essentially traditional mounting may be brilliant, its conventionally attired audience genuinely aroused. Innovation can take place subtly, in details, in peripheral matters, slight shifts of emphasis or interesting new technical devices, or a lovely new musical score. Such innovation is less spectacular and more difficult to achieve, yet it will make the tenth go at a great play perfectly rewarding for an intelligent audience. How often, after all, do most of us get to see even so popular a classic as *A Midsummer Night's Dream?* Surely not more often than we hear in concert a major piece of music, yet we do not expect that to be rewritten. What I am saying is that we must not allow our justified indignation with boring productions or complacent spectators goad us into senseless retaliatory measures that cannot reclaim a blasé or boorish audience, but may obscure and destroy the meaning and beauty of a play.

Oddly enough, Brook's *Dream* has strong suggestions of the circus and music hall, and even some of the physical violence of the prize fight. The stage is a dazzling white box set with two swinging doors in the back wall, narrow black ladders bisecting the side walls (these ladders can be pushed aside and thus make a passage), and where the side walls come closest to the proscenium, a further pair of ladders and poles. A narrow gallery runs around the top edges of the set. There the actors not in a given scene tend to congregate and watch their colleagues act; from there too they create such special effects as lowering huge wire coils suspended from fishing rods to become the trees of the enchanted forest. Also up there are a brace of musicians who produce mostly percussive or electronic obstreperousness; onstage, there is a chap who follows the actors around playing a flamenco guitar; the fairies will perform a raga while slowly rising and descending on swings—at other times, they may launch into a rock concert.

The air above the stage is troubled. Titania, on her bed made of one enormous scarlet feather, is sometimes afloat in it; Oberon and Puck swing through it on trapezes or ropes, sometimes passing a whirling disk to each other from wand to wand, a disk that represents the flower with the magic juice; Hermia is hoisted up into it by ropes and pulleys (all visible to the audience) when Lysander suspends her from a crossbar; the fairies, as noted, go up and down in it, making music. But the aerial traffic is not only in bodies: there are silver and blue tinfoil planes shot through this space by the actors on the catwalk; when Titania's body is being belabored by the donkey-fied Bottom, and a p.a. system blares out a deliberately scratchy rendition of Mendelssohn's Wedding March, all kinds of streamers and paper plates are hurled at the stage, a litter that Puck is seen sweeping up with a rake as the curtain descends.

Let us dwell for a moment on Titania and Bottom. The ass's head here consists of a pair of hound's or faun's ears, a bulbous Mickey Mouse nose, and heavy wooden clogs suggestive of hooves. A fairy then sticks an arm ending in a fist through Bottom's thighs, so that he seems to have a huge erect phallus topped with a monstrous glans; thus accoutered (the arm waves up and down), he falls on Titania. Now this is clearly, like much else in the production, influenced by Jan Kott, whose essay on *Dream* makes it out to be Shakespeare's most bestially erotic play. According to Kott, Shakespeare picked the donkey because it "was credited with the strongest sexual potency and among all quadrupeds was supposed to have the longest and hardest phallus." Kott then goes on to visualize Titania as one of those very fair, flat-chested, tall Scandinavian girls he used to see in the Latin Quarter "clinging tightly to Negroes with faces grey or so black that they were almost undistinguishable [sic] from the night." The "grey" was thrown in, I suppose, because it is the color of asses; otherwise, the statement makes perfect sense as the utterance of a sniggering puritanical clod. Titania, according to Kott, then rapes the ass Bottom, "the lover she wanted and dreamed of" without daring to admit it; their lovemaking is meant "to rouse rapture and disgust, terror and abhorrence." We can now add to the other characteristics of Kott his proneness to absurd sexual fantasies. How does our critic gloss Oberon's line about the next thing Titania will see: "She shall pursue it with the soul of love"? "As a punishment Titania will sleep with a beast." I would not have thought that "the soul of love" was instant intercourse; even less plausible is it to assume that Oberon expressly destines Titania for the largest-membered beast there is in the Renaissance bestiaries, since his list of possibilities includes the monkey, the lynx, and the cat, with which she could scarcely have had sex at all. The encounter with the ass-headed Bottom—and surely Shakespeare was largely motivated by the pun arse (ass), bottom—was pure accident. Moreover, as the scene is written, there is not the slightest need to suppose that the transmogrified tinker and the Fairy Queen ever consummated their love.

And now here is Peter Brook, in an interview, discussing "the most extraordinary demonic notion of having the Queen fornicate with a physically repellent object—the Ass. And why does Oberon do it? Not out of sadism, anger or revenge—but out of genuine love. It is as though in a modern sense a husband secured the largest truck driver for his wife to sleep with to smash her illusions about sex and to alleviate the difficulties in their marriage." Well, that's a mighty queer concept of genuine love and the ways to alleviate marital difficulties—to say nothing of it as an interpretation of the play. Oberon, I repeat, does not know what chance will turn up before the waking Queen, and it would be a sorry truck driver indeed whose organ would be the size of a cat's. And of course what one may do under the spell of the magic juice has nothing to do with one's secret yearnings, which is made explicit when Titania, disenthralled of the drug, looks at the sleeping Bottom and says, "O, how mine eyes do loathe his visage now." No comment on the phallus, which only the fevered Freudianizing of Kott and Brook dragged in in the first place.

But that other Pole, Jerzy Grotowski, is equally and no less dismally relevant to this production. The glaringly white set, which gives one a bad case of snow blindness, is the kind of environment Grotowski dreams up for his productions. It also reminds one of Peter Brook's remark in his book, *The Empty Space:* "A true image of necessary theatre-going . . . is a psychodrama session in an asylum." And so an asylum ward becomes the sole setting for all of A *Midsummer Night's Dream* (why not? it worked for *Marat/Sade,* didn't it?), an asylum that is also a circus, and a nice place for an orgy: the floor is conveniently strewn with cushions. From Grotowski, too, Brook may have derived the idea of doubling his actors. Theseus becomes Oberon; Hippolyta, Titania; Philostrate, Puck; Aegeus, Quince. The first three doublings can be defended as stressing the parallel between the fairy and human worlds. But is this underscoring desirable? Surely the play wants to point to certain differences as well as similarities; to make the aerial and Athenian rulers identical obscures the interplay of likeness and unlikeness, and reduces much of the playing to mere tours de force. There is no reason whatever, though, for Aegeus' becoming Quince, especially since the actor in question is questionable enough even in a single part.

This brings us to the performers. The Athenian lovers are all remarkably unprepossessing. Lysander, like Aegeus, is portrayed as a lisping fag; Demetrius looks like a faintly brutish mod cab driver. Hermia is a mousy nonentity; Helena a gawky, plain, desperately sex-starved tomboy. Like most of the other actors, they speak with commonplace accents, often with poor diction, and their lovemaking is of the crudest sort: wrestling bouts, pratfalls, leaps on top of one another, strangleholds, even an occasional travesty of a *Pietà*. Often the actors cannot be heard at all. Words are blithely mispronounced: Theseus, rather unbiblically, gives us an eye for an aye; Helena pronounces erring as airing—which admittedly is as arrant as it is errant. Titania's attendant fairies include one lumpish fattie, Theseus-Oberon is pallid and unregal, Titania vaguely dumpy. Puck is a chunky fellow who comes on rather tougher and more domineering than usual, but who swings well from ropes, walks nimbly on stilts, and juggles passably: when the spinning plate drops on occasion, it is impossible to tell if this is an accident or a deliberate comic effect. The artisans, on the other hand, are made much less undignified than usual, but whether in order not to offend a working-class audience or to help contribute to the general upending of the play is open to question.

By confining the entire action to a white box, by making various characters interchangeable, by using drab actors and flat speech, etc., Brook systematically depoeticizes the play. Much acclaim has been given his avoidance of cardboard forests, fake moonlight, winged fairies, and so forth—as if we could now finally see what the play is all about and hear the words properly against an uncluttered background. But this is sheer nonsense: an imaginative set designer, a stylish costumer, a good lighting man can create images that are suggestive rather than factitious, not ineptly naturalistic but stylized and bewitching. And only in a suitable setting can Shakespeare's lines exude their full meaning and poetry. A bare stage might just do it, too, but a *mise en scène* that contradicts the words or overillustrates them—as when Hermia is called a puppet while being hoisted aloft by a bar on which Lysander suspended her—draws attention to the director's cleverness or capriciousness, to a superimposed absurdism or demented literalness, but not to what Shakespeare wrote. Alas, a Brook for a Shakespeare is not a fair exchange.

So the comedy is reduced to farce in the first half of the play—but farce with nasty overtones. In the second half, the comedy is turned into something rather somber and depressing, again only to demonstrate that the author is putty in the director's hands and that the director really knows what a modern audience needs. So the mechanicals' play becomes less ludicrous, almost pathetic; the comments on it by the wedding couples are made to come out sour, even mean, instead of merely ironically bantering; the final arrival of Oberon, Titania, and their train is imbued with a kind of melancholy, and accompanied by the ominous soughing of the wind: it is as if the fairies were abandoning the mortals forever to their mortality. So Brook turns this airy pageant (with some serious overtones, to be sure) into a dark comedy, which it was never meant to be. Even the songs, which might be presumed to defy Brook with their lyricism, are brutalized by Richard Peaslee's musical settings: drum beats, weird echo-chamber effects, rattles and crashes, rock, unmelodiousness.

The enchantment stamped out, the performances divested of magic, love turned into lust, the *Dream* changed into nightmare—what remains when everything is overthrown, dismantled, shattered? There remains the supreme magician, Peter Brook, who fancies himself the Prospero of the occasion but is really its Sycorax. And what exactly is Brook's fascination with the male arse all about? In *Marat/Sade* he gave us Marat's bare behind; here it is Snug who is twice stripped to tiniest briefs made from a Union Jack. Why does Helena duck when her suitors are about to kiss her each from his side, with the result that they end up bussing each other? Why does the waking, bewitched Demetrius reach passionately for Puck's genitals—especially since none of the mortals except Bottom is at any other time able to see the fairies? Why do the fairies wave about colored plastic tubes of a vaguely phallic sort? But never mind the epicene aspects of this production, which may, after all, be quite harmless. It is the eclecticism, the contrariness, the helter-skelter of it that makes it self-defeating. Peter Brook once surprised a young film maker by telling him that he should shoot his film both in black-and-white and in color and then intercut the two. Why? Because it would create an interesting effect. A mania for injudicious experimentation is what characterizes the director's work in the theater too. In the case of a minor play like *Marat/Sade* or *Titus Adronicus* this can work well enough; with *King Lear* and even *A Midsummer Night's Dream* it undercuts and diminishes the playwright's achievement.

But, say the champions of reckless innovations, this brings new audiences into the theater. What kind of audience, however, would come just to see Brook's cleverness? And how could they see the forest for the coiled-wire trees? And would this lead them to the appreciation of respectable theater (by which I do not mean long-faced and anemic), or would they remain fixated at this anal level? These are questions that cannot easily be answered; still less can they be easily dismissed. I believe that a passable revival such as the current one of *A Doll's House,* ably and conservatively staged by Patrick Garland serves the theater better than all these Brookish fireworks. (The attendants at the Theseus-Hippolyta nuptials actually bring in tapers surrounded by Christmas sparklers.) It may be that there won't be large theater audiences without this kind of bait; and it may be that the days of the theater as a popular art are numbered, or even over. Would that be so bad? If the theater became an élite art, like architecture or contemporary poetry or classical music, giving it few company but fit, I for one would not grieve. Render unto television, popular movies, rock concerts what is theirs and *who* is theirs, and let the rest of us get down to the serious business—or art—of theater.

RONALD MILLAR has adapted three C. P. Snow novels for the stage. One such adaptation may be considered a mere lapse; two constitute a relapse; three, total collapse. With *Abélard & Héloïse* he continues his career as purveyor of middlebrow ponderousness to semicultivated audiences. The play is billed as "inspired by" Helen Waddell's novel, *Peter Abélard,* though "inspired" is hardly a word I would use in this context. All I remember of that dryish book by a fine scholar and translator but unwieldly novelist is the character of Gilles de Vannes, modeled on Miss Waddell's beloved teacher, George Saintsbury; significantly Gilles is the only character in the play who has any life. Abélard and Héloïse have fired the imaginations of such diverse writers as Alexander Pope and George Moore, and there are respectable but uninspired plays on the subject by Roger Vailland and James Forsyth. To these, Millar's work can be appended as the last and least.

For Millar does not convey anything to us: neither life in the Middle Ages, nor the conflict of God and Eros during the heyday of the Church; neither Abélard the great dialectician and teacher, nor

Abélard the masterly poet. But perhaps one could by-pass all these in favor of the tragic love story (and castration is arguably more tragic than death), if only one had the language, the poetry, the fervor. But if you write lines like "Of course I don't want to be a stupid, sublimating little monk," or "Héloïse has no more vocation than the Pope's cat," or grandest of all, "How absurd that we should come to this: two lovers in fancy dress wondering what we should say to each other," you are not fit to write a play about these lovers—at best, perhaps, about the Windsors or the Onassises.

What is left? A nude scene carefully staged and lighted so that the concept of nudity should be more in evidence than any actual flesh, a minuscule homosexual subplot that comes to nothing, a jaunty Irish nun who speaks medieval French with a brogue and vocabulary straight out of O'Casey, some transcripts from the letters of Abélard and Héloïse (letters which, even assuming that they are authentic, are less than dramatic), and a few fancy stage effects, such as a swaying chorus of nuns and monks in the background sibilantly murmuring some key word like "Huzzzzband!" Robin Phillips' staging is pedestrian when it is not pretentious; Keith Michell is a poised but rather unimpassioned Abélard; Diana Rigg, the Héloïse, is built, alas, like a brick basilica with inadequate flying buttresses, and suggests neither intense womanliness nor outstanding intellect. But the dialogue is no help to them; only Ronald Radd has flavor as Gilles, and Jacqueline Brookes some depth as the Abbess of Argenteuil (pronounced argent-toy by everyone). Daphne Dare's costumes look believable, but Christopher Morley's sets seem rather too tidily symmetrical and sanitized. *Qui pereunt in se, vivunt per scripta poetae*, wrote Abélard in a poem for his son: those who die in their persons live in the poet's writing; those who are castrated by their wife's uncle are gelded again by the playwright's pen.

Edward Albee's *All Over* is about the dying of some unnamed and unclassified great man behind a screen in his living room, while in front of the screen his wife, mistress, son, daughter, lawyer, doctor and nurse talk, wrangle, and have an occasional tantrum. The play is so eventless, pointless, and, above all, lifeless that it could actually have been improved by being turned around on its axis. Then, at least, we could have witnessed some hemorrhages, bladder discharges, oscultations, injections, perhaps a death rattle—none of them my idea of drama, but all positively enlivening compared to what we do get.

The anonymous characters this side of the screen, i.e., the supposedly living, have, with the possible exception of the mistress, no more personality than they have names. The wife is a typical cold, upper-class powerhouse, the daughter is a standard hysterical bitch, the son an emotional castrato, the lawyer-friend a thudding nonentity. The mistress has a bit of theatrical spunk and memories of a love affair at sixteen with a boy of fifteen to lend her some lurid color. The doctor is eighty-six and still practicing, which is *his* one point of interest; the nurse was once the mistress of some famous (and yet more anonymous) suicide, which is *hers*. The mother is steadily beastly to her children, and fitfully to the doctor and nurse; the daughter is raucously and clumsily nasty to everyone, the mistress is superior and ironic all around, the lawyer equivocates or acts the straight man, the son is silent and pitiful except in his more eloquent moments, when he waxes monosyllabic. He does, however, have one tear-choked outburst in which he is allowed to itemize passionately the contents of his father's bathroom, which moved me only a little less than the mistress's musings about her boy-lover's penis and how they used to make love "whenever, wherever." The doctor and nurse don't get a chance to be nasty to anyone, which in an Albee character virtually insures invisibility. After two acts or several eons, the doctor announces that it is "all over," and the curtain falls on the play and whatever might still remain of Albee's once deserved reputation.

The play, I repeat, is about nothing. There is no plot, no problem, no conflict, no character. The dramatis personae are a set of attitudes, and their talk is made up mostly of digressions: about parents and grandparents, gardens and travels, dreams and childhood recollections. And when one of these humanoid nebulae launches on yet another irrelevant reminiscence of an even hazier ancestor, it is like watching a gas being superseded by a vacuum. That leaves language. But language (as opposed to snide or lacerating repartee) is what Albee has always been deficient in—and I don't mean anything as simple as incorrect usage, though there is that too, as when "verbal" is used in the sense of "oral." I mean that this language huffs and puffs and bloats itself up to be poetic, doubles up and contorts itself out of any resemblance to human syntax in order to be distinctive, and sounds in one character's mouth almost exactly as in another's. And unless the actors speak in constricted or staggering rhythms out of sheer awe, I must assume that the play is written in free verse, a free verse that should be locked up immediately.

Take these three typical consecutive lines: "He said he thought not." (Poetic for "He said he did not think so.") "Drone, drone!" "It is the ritual that gives me the sense." There are poetic inversions like "Little girl I was when he came to me," profundities like "The silences and the goings-on came later; the tightness was still engaged," wit like "Death! Death! Death! Death! . . . Well, it gets us where we live, doesn't it? or "Death is such an old disease!" (though perhaps this should be classified under profundity rather than wit), and sheer well-turned phrases like "This is what I have come to love you so little for: that you love yourself so little," verbal play as dead as the play itself. When the Mistress happily recalls her affair with the fifteen-year-old boy we learn that their "sex was . . . strong, practiced and assisting," which is psychologically improbable and linguistically gray. She goes on about "a penis I could not dismiss from my mind when I was not with him," which merits a little scrutinizing. That it is more homosexual than heterosexual is unimportant. What is interesting is that it is intended as the most passionately erotic, loving, positive moment in the play, and yet isn't in the least loving or even erotic. It represents, in fact, a bankruptcy of language as well as of feeling. What sort of love is this, and what sort of emotion recollected in tranquillity, that latches on to mere genitalia and disregards all other features of the beloved? What would it say for any of us if all we remembered of an absent lover were a penis or a vagina? And if the best verbiage we could find to express that third-rate longing were as clinically detached as this.

Having in his last few plays thoroughly de-dramatized life, Albee now succeeds in taking the dramatic sting out of death. If *All Over* is anything, it is an argument for euthanasia: had the unseen hero been put to sleep before the writing of the play, the audience would not have been put to sleep—or to the torture—for two hours.

Jessica Tandy gives a bravura performance as the wife, all the more so since it must be done with delivery rather than dialogue. Colleen Dewhurst, as the mistress, is almost as good, though I find her speech unattractive (e.g., "naw" for "no"). Madeleine Sherwood is a curious choice for the daughter, looking somewhat older than her mother, and speaks her lines unvarnished, which here spells disaster. John Gielgud, who has directed the whole thing as if *he* were the great man dying behind the screen, has nevertheless given her a repertoire of squatting or recumbent positions, as though she were practicing for the *Kama Sutra* before the arrival of her partner. James Ray plays the son with a cumbersomeness that must, at least in part, be a vengeance on the role, and George Voskovec, who has long been the gray declivity ("eminence" hardly applies to him) of the American theater, contributes his familiar shade of deadly gray. Betty Field recites Albee's "poetry" as if it were "Thanatopsis" (which perhaps it is), and Neil Fitzgerald, as the old doctor, could have made Lionel Barrymore seem a juvenile. Rouben Ter-Arutunian's set is the essence of anonymity, and being considerably smaller than the stage, appears to be merely camping out on it.

THE ONLY original musical of any consequence—though questionable merit—in a field of nostalgia-laden revivals and pseudorevivals (shows imitating the lunacies of past shows) is *Follies,* which after a shaky start has picked up enough second wind, through publicity and gushy word of mouth, as well as enthusiastic magazine reviews, to make it handsomely in the nostalgia sweepstakes. The show has a cardboard embryo of a book by James Goldman about a Flo Ziegfeld-like figure who throws a quasi-posthumous party in his already half-torn-down theater for all his pre-World War II stars and showgirls. The plot gradually focuses on two formerly friendly showgirls and their fellow-student boyfriends, who once formed a triangle within a square. At this strange reunion, their not very successful marriages are by way of getting cross-entangled and realigned. Yet except for some shadow-boxing, nothing happens. But even as the quartet act out their present troubles, four other performers representing their youthful selves reenact scenes from their past. Similarly, ghosts of former showgirls and entire ghostly follies acts intertwine with scenes from the party, at which the aging performers go through their old numbers, or act out bits of imaginary, stylized autobiography. The stage is aswirl and awash with past and present, real people, former selves, named or just anonymous ghosts of bygone showgirls, singers, dancers, with pasty make-up and in black-and-white ghostly costumes, holding odd, showgirl attitudes in the background or even foreground, crisscrossing with real people, providing mirror images to dances by the living oldsters, sometimes even seeming to communicate across the decades or deaths that separate them from one another. It sounds interesting and confusing, and it is both, though mostly the latter.

There is a great deal of cleverness in Michael Bennett's choreography and in the staging he and Harold Prince jointly devised. Florence Klotz's costumes hover with shrewd campiness between lavish splendor and outrageous pastiche, while Boris Aronson's scenery is awesome in its towering, massive, yet kaleidoscopically shifting structures. Stephen Sondheim's lyrics are often pertinent and always polished; when they are soggy, we may assume that this is their parodic intent. Sondheim's music is mostly over-cerebral spoofs of the popular composers of the period, never happily outright parody, always cluttered up with an overlay of fussiness. Near the end, when all four principals are allowed to enact a production number, a mini-Follies of their own, through which they comment on their real or imaginary lives, *Follies* does come to brief though belated life. But this happens at the end of a very long, intermissionless evening, and the fun is quickly dampened by an ending in which both couples emerge from this *Walpurgisnacht* improbably chastened, mature and together.

The concocters of *Follies* and the champions of the show vie with one another in denying its basis in camp and nostalgia. Instead, we are told about Proustian overtones, the New Plotless Musical, time as the sole subject matter, the Past as a metaphor for . . . I forget what, a Fellini phantasmagoria translated to the musical stage, and more such pioneering palaver. The truth, as I see it, is that some eight hundred thousand dollars were spent on visual opulence, the digging up of old favorites of stage, screen and television, and a large cast of oldsters and youngsters whooping it up with agility or endearing arthritis all over an immense stage. The music and lyrics tend, however remotely and distortingly, to sound like the good (i.e., bad) old stuff; and to see venerable crones capering about and hear them belting out numbers announcing that they have survived everything from Franz Lehár to J. Edgar Hoover, is agelessness equally irresistible to aging burghers and to pederasts clinging desperately to their youth. So despite some up-to-date inventiveness, *Follies* reeks with nostalgia, and the epochal innovations claimed for it ring in my ears like the sound of protesting too much.

One thing, however, is unqualifiedly in the show's favor: the lean, tough, earthy, elegant resiliency and loveliness of Alexis Smith. Handsome but cold and unspectacular in her now almost forgotten movie career, Miss Smith, at forty-nine, reappears as a singing and dancing stage actress of great charm and finesse, and as a woman of paradoxically mature as well as girlish beauty. There is something of a miracle in this, but you cannot be nostalgic about miracles: nostalgia feeds on repetition; miracles are unique.

*   *   *

THE BASIC CONCEIT IN *How the Other Half Loves*, an otherwise ordinary farce, is to make the same set serve as the house of two quite different couples. Distantly related by ties of business, acquaintanceship and adultery, they inhabit the same stage space alternately or even simultaneously, but the Fosters do not see the Phillipses and the Phillipses don't see the Fosters—that is, when they are not visiting each other. There is also a third couple, the pathetic Detweilers, used and abused by both the others. These wretches are even seen at dinner parties at both the Fosters and the Phillipses on consecutive evenings, but seated at the same dinner table that stands for two different places on two different nights. This clearly makes the British author, Alan Ayckbourn, the conqueror of space/time, the Einstein of farce. If marital capers pay off handsomely at the box office, how much more Emolument is there in marital capers squared, for which his formula is $E = mc^2$.

The play works also on a simpler mathematical basis, giving you the bargain feeling of watching two sleazy farces for the price of one. Even so, I would think television is cheaper. Here, though, you get Phil Silvers in the flesh, if you want him; and then there is Sandy Dennis. Miss Dennis' main expression is the smile of a calf's head in a butcher's window, but this sometimes yields to a cold fury that could not so much chew up the scenery as gnaw the padding off a cell. The actress seems to suffer from an advanced case of galloping infantilism, and she reads her lines as if from a cuneiform inscription antedating the invention of punctuation. The voice is always precariously balanced between hysterical sobs and maniacal laughter, and Pauline Kael has aptly observed that Miss Dennis has "made an acting style out of postnasal drip." But if an actress who points her finger more rudely than Uncle Sam and who can ham up a scene with her bare toes is your cuspidor of tea, by all means go. The supporting cast works valiantly, and Gene Saks has staged it all in proper farcical earnest.

I HOPE SOME readers remember my review of the Tréteau de Paris on its visit last year, in which I extolled Madeleine Renaud for her performance in *Happy Days*. This year, Mme. Renaud is back, but by the time you read this, her show will have proceeded beyond New York. It is, to be sure, nothing like Beckett this time; only Marguerite Duras' *L'Amante anglaise*, seen here in English as *A Place Without Doors* earlier this season. Mlle. Duras' play is just as pseudophilosophic, parapoetic, militantly antitheatrical and dizzyingly vacuous in French as it was in English. It concerns a real-life murder case that was solved but never explained, and Mlle. Duras has been so haunted by the character of the simple-minded but complex-psyched provincial murderess that she has rewritten her story at least three times in various modes. But for all her worrying of the subject, she sheds no light on it, only enough verbal ash to have buried Pompeii without the help of Vesuvius.

The two men in the play, Claude Dauphin and Michel Lonsdale, fine actors both, do well by their thankless roles. But Madeleine Renaud takes the somewhat better part of the woman (Mlle. Duras cares much more for women than for men) and makes it into a creation all her own, so beautiful, touching, and human that you feel, as it were, that a reading from the telephone book is turning into *Hamlet*. The part calls only for sitting in a chair and answering the insistent questions of an investigator with archly portentous verbiage or desperate, emaciated clevernesses. Mme. Renaud's face, hands and voice, three marvelous instruments, proceed to play an extraordinary trio. You can literally see a phrase begun on one of them be picked up by another and provided with an obbligato by the third. Now one, now another carries the theme; now all three blend in a crashing chord or a sustained, heart-dissolving cantilena. Feelings suddenly ravage the face, but ravage it quietly, undemonstratively; the voice taunts and tickles with ancient peasant cunning; the forearms rear up with remembered pleasures, or the hands burrow into each other in search of eroded certitudes. Tremors from the eyelids are laid to rest in the fingertips; an ache of the voice reverberates in the gaze; an absurd little hope swells up the words, the arms, the mouth that hungers for smiles. It is an imperiling performance, for it makes almost every other acting this season look like a half-hearted charade. But to see it is to regain faith in the indestructibility of the theater.

PAUL SILLS's Story Theatre enterprise has gone from fabulous to mythic in its new venture, Ovid's *Metamorphoses*, and the result is less metamorphosis than transmogrification. Fairy tales and animal fables lend themselves merrily to story-theatricalization, a mixture of narration and acting out, of pantomine and song. The world of the child and the childlike folk mind can well be recaptured by such innocent and mock-innocent playacting. But myths as reinterpreted by that most elegant and sensual Roman poet, Publius Ovidius Naso, are something both too subtle and too mature for this bouncy and bumptious technique to cope with.

First of all, Ovid's poems were adapted into English by Arnold Weinstein, the most anachronistic Roman of them all. Though some of his versions are not without a verbal facility of their own, a coyly smirking contemporaneity often asserts itself—even more so in the trendy lyrics Weinstein interpolated into the proceedings, looking down his nose or Naso. These songs are insufferably cute and perfectly attuned to what Sills & Co. do to Ovid's spirit. They turn something that the history of art and literature has made wonderfully cosmopolitan and universal into something parochial, Broadway-and-Bronx-oriented (if that is redundant, I can at least plead that redundancy was one of Ovid's foibles too). Now, transposition is fine as long as it is not a lessening. Thus when Paul Sand, looking like a Grand Concourse street urchin, transforms himself into a poor mutt out of a Grimm tale, the comedian's dishevelment nicely bridges the dislocation, and the tale is properly still wagging the dog. But when this same, very likable but nebbishy comedian pretends to be that supremely ambitious youth, Phaëthon, the tragic ride in the chariot of the Sun-God is reduced from overweening to underweening. Similarly, when Pygmalion, the archetypal artist yearning to reconcile the fleshly, mortal beauty of life with the ideal and imperishable beauty of art, becomes Avery Schreiber, the epitome of the Jewish cab driver, trying to lay a Galatea never closer to ideal art than a *Playboy* centerfold, I feel that euhemerism is carried to ridiculous extremes. It may be my limitation, but I cannot conceive of Yiddish hexameters.

But even if you cannot tell an Ovid from an ovine, *Metamorphoses* lacks variety: rape upon rape, transformation upon transformation, is not sufficiently diverse stuff for dramatic life; moreover, despite overlapping, this company is not so multifariously talented and winning as the *Story Theatre* ensemble. Valerie Harper and Paula Kelly have a few very good moments, some of the others have one or two good ones, but Regina Baff and Penny White are eyesores: there is a world of difference between being funny and merely ludicrous. H. H. Poindexter's lighting and a few of Sills's staging ideas again work quite handsomely—notably a silhouetted frieze of anthropomorphic constellations in the night sky—but it isn't enough. A colleague of Ovid's, Horace, prided himself, in his most famous verse, on having erected a monument more lasting than brass. These *Metamorphoses,* alas, are more brassy than lasting.

·　·　·

I WILL NOT DO Eugene O'Neill's masterpiece *Long Day's Journey Into Night* the insult of trying to analyze it in a short space. The greatness of this long play—which cogently makes its very length work for it, suggesting how long a thing a day is in the lives of people who keep reliving it without surcease—is such that it precludes instant exegesis. The playwright's family, here called the Tyrones, are simply shown in their loving, hating and suffering interaction, spread out across an interminable summer's day and night. Into this space is crammed the miserliness and real-estate hunger of James Tyrone, an actor who could have been great but chose to be successful and rich; the emotional starvation and dope addiction of the good Catholic mother, Mary Tyrone, a sculptor in monumental self-delusion; the despair of an elder son, Jamie, who takes to drink, whores and outbursts of violence; and the anxiety of a younger son, Edmund, who carries in him the germs of consumption, the seeds of genius, and the curse of loving his three tormented and tormenting kinfolk. The implications of the August day in a ramshackle beach house are enormous: they spell out a set of interlocking dooms—personal, familial and social. O'Neill has orchestrated them sovereignly around a simple leitmotiv: the harsh truth hurled into a dear detested one's face and the immediate agonized apology that follows. Twenty-three times, if my count is correct, someone hurts someone else with a no longer containable truth, and as many times he or she is reduced to self-lacerating pleadings to be pardoned. In this binary rhythm of injury and forgiveness, like systole and diastole, the great heart of the play beats on toward irremediable exhaustion.

Arvin Brown has staged this revival conscientiously but unoverwhelmingly, in a set that, partly because of inadequate space, does not work. Stacy Keach gives us a Jamie who gets progressively better, and James Naughton is a perfectly likable Edmund, but disastrously unable to suggest the great dramatic genius lurking within. Geraldine Fitzgerald is, despite trouble with her lines, superb as the mother, investing the part not only with the necessary pathos, but also with an unexpected humor that enriches it and the play immeasurably. All would still be salvageable but for Robert Ryan's amateurish Tyrone, vocally, gesturally, emotionally impoverished as only a second-rate movie star can be. Ryan is a cavern at the core into which this worthy undertaking collapses. Come back, Frederic March!

• • •

A PERFECTLY GHASTLY PLAY, *And Whose Little Boy Are You?*, opened and, by the time you read this, should not only have closed but also been blotted out of human memory. The work of one Rod Parker, it concerned the return of a Vietnam veteran to his common-law wife to find her pregnant. By whom? *By God,* by God! Her good Catholic priest believes this, her good Jewish landlord believes this, her mother believes this *ex officio.* Soon the soldier's congressman father, and plenipotentiaries of the Catholic, Protestant and Jewish faiths join the near-believers, willing to exploit the potential Second Coming for their respective benefits. Of course, it turns out in the end that the girl, lonely and high at a party, was jumped by a George Something, who impregnated her.

Now, this play, apart from being rotten in every way, is also preposterous. I can perhaps believe that the extremely unappetizing Helen Kurowski, played by a condignly unprepossessing actress, could be the second Chosen of the Lord. After all, when told that in one day the embryo has grown two months' worth, the soldier wonders whether God is Japanese; if he can be Japanese, he can surely also be blind. But what I absolutely *cannot* believe is that by being administered a quickie by a George Something (even if it were Plimpton) at the one and only party she attended, a girl becomes pregnant. Biologically, of course, this is possible, but it is also highly improbable. What makes it more improbable still is that any number of questionable plays, movies, novels have hinged on this since the first hack put quill to papyrus. The hinge has grown too rusty for use.

In the theater, when skillfully manipulated, we believe the impossible; what we can almost never believe is the improbable. Thus, when Rod Parker, in his autobiographical sketch, claims to be descended from thirty-five Swedish kings, two emperors and Henrik Ibsen, I can believe both the kings and the emperors, but not Ibsen. Maybe David Belasco. Enough about Parker, but the question of the improbable and the impossible in the theater is worth considering. You have heard about Brecht's V-effect; now hear about the Preposterousness factor, or the P-factor, as I shall call it. The P-factor is that preposterous something which, much more than impossibility, makes a play unbelievable.

Let me illustrate. In a show like *Follies* there is much that is impossible—for example, the basic premise of a party given in a half-torn-down theater. Can you imagine ancient Follies girls, whose caducity must be propped up by a silver-topped cane in front and a uniformed chauffeur in back, tripping among the rubble? Can you see waiters with trays picking their way among rampant girders and sliding bricks? And can you trust the followers of Thespis, scarcely less devoted to Bacchus, not to fall off some rampless platform right into the arms of Thanatos? Such a party is quite impossible, but thanks to the staging and set design, not noticeably preposterous. Where the P-factor comes in is in the plot. We are asked to believe that two unhappily married couples, who in this *Walpurgisnacht* reach the breaking point, can also find in that same improbable night a *Karfreitagszauber*, enabling them to walk out, if not wiser and better people, at least with their marriages miraculously salvaged. The P-factor registers like crazy on your built-in Steiger counter (I have named the instrument after a distinguished actor who has given us quite a few improbable performances).

The P-factor, alas, works retroactively: it can enshroud all that went before in a miasma of poisonous preposterousness. That is how the ending of *Follies* functions. But the more usual depredations of the P-factor come at the beginning and can be in the production as easily as in the play. In the mounting of Wedekind's *Spring's Awakening*, staged as his final requirement for an MFA degree from Columbia, the extremely promising young director Robert Mandel was obliged (I presume) to cast as Wendla another MFA candidate who shall be nameless. Now Wendla is a girl of fifteen, a kind of irresistible, naïve, but already quite womanly, impetuous but deeply sensitive, turn-of-the-century Juliet, who dies tragically of a surreptitious abortion into which an oppressive society forces her. But the actress playing this delightful girl was so profoundly charmless and graceless that I had to leave after the first act, lest my furiously signaling Steiger counter have me rooting for her earliest possible quietus, by abortion or anything else, and the whole production fall victim to the P-factor.

To be sure, a truly apt playwright can abort the P-factor before it can take over. Thus in *The Philanthropist*, Christopher Hampton posits a society of terrorists whose aim is to rid the world of its twenty-five most highly regarded writers, as purveyors of that "deceitful idealism" that is at the root of all our troubles. The society is a means of suggesting the absurdity of the world, and also of revealing the odiousness of a character in the play, the novelist Braham Head. Now, in themselves, F.A.T.A.L. (Fellowship of Allied Terrorists Against Literature), and in the letter they send to twenty-five writers announcing their aims as well as the imminent demise of the recipient, are highly improbable. But Hampton puts them to good use. When

Braham reads about the sudden deaths of several colleagues and finds that he himself has not received the fatal missive, what is his reaction? He is furious at the moronic list of victims F.A.T.A.L. has compiled, and insulted at his not getting the letter. *This* we believe, and the P-factor has been squelched.

OUR NOSES CANNOT be rubbed often enough in certain commonplaces. One of them runs: we see things as we want them to be, not as they are. This demon takes much resisting. Only last week Archibald MacLeish yielded to the demon's whispering "Playwright!" in his ear by giving us a play called *Scratch*, that had to be scratched after four performances. It was based on Stephen Vincent Benét's story "The Devil and Daniel Webster," and might have been more aptly entitled "The Devil and Archibald MacLeish."

MacLeish is a worthy minor poet, nothing to be ashamed of. But even in poetry he has delusions of majorness. Thus Edmund Wilson's "The Omelet of A. MacLeish" was more than a parody of that pretentious poem "The Hamlet of A. MacLeish"; it was a dexterous nosography of the tics and poses that made up MacLeish's majoritis. Particularly telling was the line "The celluloid tower with bold intonations defended," which neatly anticipated what was wrong with MacLeish's Pulitzer-Prize-and-Tony-Award-winning play, *J.B.*: an attempt to retell the story of Job in contemporary terms—to scrutinize God and the devil, good and evil, in an updated metaphysic. Yet for all its artful intonations, the play contained little art and less wisdom; its tower not even of ivory, merely of celluloid. But it established MacLeish as (to use a phrase from John Donne's Second Prebend Sermon) "the little great philosopher": a man who seems to tell us great things, because we desperately want to see greatness, and find his pious posturings encompassable by our little minds. *J.B.* was a peanut that thought itself a zeppelin.

In *Scratch*, MacLeish takes another protoliterary source, Benét rather than the Bible, as the basis for his contemporary parable meant to comment on our present political and social chaos, and the result is an olio of Webster, Benét and MacLeish, where it is hard to know which is which, and even harder to care. Again Wilson's parody has proved prophetic. Wilson's MacLeish speaks: "And at last I drew close to a land dark with fortifications:/ Men shrieking outlandish reproaches till all my blood tingled:/ It was ragged and harsh there: they hated: heart horribly quaked in me:/ Then I thought 'I have staved off the pricking of many a sting./ These perchance I may placate too': I put in at that place:/ I met them with scorn and good-natured agreement mingled . . ." And so in *Scratch* MacLeish is trying to pronounce on our catastrophic war and civil dissension via Webster and the impending Civil War in a tone of mingled scorn and good-natured mollification—without clear thinking about the mess we have made into our bed.

Benét's story was simply a good yarn in the tradition of many folk tales (e.g., the one Ramuz turned into a text for Stravinsky's *L'Histoire du soldat*), in which some clever fellow outwits the Evil One—or, in the Rabelaisian formula quoted in *Scratch,* speaks the truth and shames the devil. But the trouble is that Benét's jolly tall tale does not lend itself to a moral interpretation, unless it be the amoral one that Yankee ingenuity, rather than strict truth, overmasters even the powers of hell: sophistic dialectics triumphant in a Satanic dialogue. And not only dialectics: the triumph of oratory—a dangerous, because top-heavy, thing to put on the stage. MacLeish thinks nothing of Benét's purpose; his devil, Mr. Scratch, sneers: "Nothing, in heaven or on earth or elsewhere, is more intelligent than a Bostonian." No, his intent is to give us a Webster so hellbent on becoming President (which presupposes maintenance of the Union, i.e., Law and Order) that he disregards the need to free the slaves. When Jabez Stone, having made a bargain with the devil, is about to forfeit his soul, Webster sees both himself and America on trial (for he convinces the devil to have the case tried), and in using his rhetoric to save Stone, he finds also for—or so MacLeish thinks—the incriminated but lovable United States of today.

But the thinking is deeply confused. Even the peg on which it is hung is poor. Jabez Stone is a nonentity, and there is no sufficient moral ground on which to save his soul. Worse than that, there is no good way of connecting this errant individual with America today: if both have sinned through greed, have sold their souls for seven years of prosperity, Jabez nonetheless is one and homogeneous, whereas America is the heterogeneous many, guilty in different ways and degrees. Neither is Webster America, since the disregard of minority rights for the supposed greater good of the country (actually the power élite) is only one of our problems. A greater one is the sheer lack of intellect in our leadership, and Webster—Benét's, MacLeish's or Webster's—was anything but stupid. In his poem, "Hypocrite Auteur," MacLeish rightly warns: "A world ends when its metaphor has died." Onstage, too, a play ends when its metaphor proves stillborn.

Not only is the whole thing dull, wordy, hollowly grandiloquent, but also the defense of Jabez is a piece of overextended, banal rhetoric that boils down to not consigning a country or an individual, however culpable, to hopeless damnation. The Hamlet of W. Shakespeare said it much more modestly, succinctly and sensibly: "Use every man after his desert, and who shall 'scape whipping?" The major failure of the play is its exiguity of thought and action, but there is also another important lapse: except as bit players, there are no women in it. And it is hard, indeed impossible, to create a representative microcosm without women.

Sophocles' *Antigone* seems to be most relevant to our time. It dramatizes the conflict between the individual and the state, and what, in the here and now, could be more pertinent? But the pertinency is not nearly so total as it appears. Antigone's rebelliousness stems neither from sociopolitical causes nor from a justifiable or unjustifiable assertion of individuality. Rather, it comes from a piety, sisterly as well as religious, but mostly religious, which opposes itself to Creon's autocratic pursuit of political expediency. We are not even remotely in the realm of the rebellious young, but in the midst of a clash between *pietas* and *auctoritas* that could not be further removed from current thinking and struggling.

That is not to say that the play has nothing to teach us, but that the current of its lessons must be run through a converter before it can be plugged into our consciousness. Thus today we cannot readily embrace Antigone's position, because divine right has become all but meaningless to us (God was on our side in World War II, but has not been heard from in connection with the Vietnam war); nor, obviously, can we fully grasp Creon's position, for political despotism, though very much with us, is no longer in the hands of a single autocrat but in those of an ill-defined, polypoid organism, of which it is hard to say how many are its tentacles, and whether it has even one head.

But there is a motif in *Antigone* that can still be telling. It is courage, determination, and above all dignity in its confrontation with rashness, unimaginativeness and obstinacy; in this sense, neither Antigone nor Creon is readily identifiable with the factions that are warring at present. In fact, the danger today is not so much a single Creon as Creons on both—or all—sides: creeping Creonism. But to convey such an abstract—yet real—danger, *Antigone* should be kept on the loftiest, most universal level: epic rather than insinuating,

Homeric rather than conversational. (It may be useful to remember that Diogenes Laertius called Sophocles "the Homer of tragedians.") From this standpoint, it was already a major mistake for the Repertory Theater of Lincoln Center to choose the Fitts-Fitzgerald translation, which is subject to fits of violent modernization. Thus amid some quite decent language, we are suddenly jolted with Creon's outcry to his son, "By God, he wants to analyze me now." Let us not confuse the Age of Oedipus with that of the Oedipus complex.

John Hirsch's direction, which I believe errs on every possible count, manages even to ignore the very text. Repeatedly, the chorus is referred to as a goodly number of old men. Yet what we see onstage is three men and three women: two of them middle-aged, four young. The stage movement can never decide whether it wants to be naturalistic or ritualistic, and there is no consistency whatever in acting techniques or manners of speech. Some actors are Shakespearean, some Stanislavskian, some high-school valedictorian. As the male chorus leader, Charles Cioffi tries to be realistic, yet a line like "But see, Ismene comes" cannot be delivered realistically. Pauline Flanagan, however, as the female chorus leader (Fem Lib having liberated even the Greek chorus), speaks as if every syllable had to be a pear shaped out of Parian marble, e.g., "beyond" pronounced beeOHnd; a performance that invites not so much criticism as strangulation. But no one else—thanks to lack of training, direction or, in several cases, talent—comes off unscathed. By striking a happy middle between extremes, John Harkins, as the messenger, fares best; could we accept a naturalistic Haimon, David Birney, too, would pass muster.

Nothing, however, makes sense here. Not Douglas W. Schmidt's handsome set, with a giant frieze of semiruinous figures: why should an architrave be dragging its feet on the ground? And why should the Palace at Thebes be in ruins? Not Jane Greenwood's costumes, partly out of Buck Rogers; and not Lukas Foss's music, which sounds like the death rattle of a Moog Synthesizer.

But if the week fails Hellenically, it succeeds Hebraically. *Godspell*, a rock musical based on The Gospel According to Saint Matthew, is a frisky, exhilarating little show, full of ozone and lightheadedness. The opening sequence, in which the young cast chants the words of sages old and new, from Socrates to Buckminster Fuller, is absolutely awful. The last part, with the obligatory crucifixion scene, is, though understated, beyond the reach of the medium, and thus awkward and anticlimactic. But in between, and there is a great deal of in between, things are as frolicsome as kittens, and more fun than a barrel of well-schooled monkeys. *Godspell* is part clown show, part minstrel show, part vaudeville, part *Hair*, and it works on all those levels and several more of its own.

John Michael Tebelak has conceived and directed a crackling musical funhouse, in which the Biblical parables leap to childlike, distorted, rough-and-tumble life—but life such as you haven't found it in Scripture since you first read The Song of Songs for its sexy passages. Not that *Godspell* is sexy; it is just lovably playful, turning everything into very dedicated, funny but serious games, as only highly inventive, innocently impudent children can conceive and play them. Stephen Schwartz has supplied lyrics nicely balanced between godliness and sassiness, and tunes that head for your ear with the ineluctable assurance of an earwig. Well, I can't vouch for earwigs, but I can for Schwartz' melodies. Susan Tsu's costumes and Lowell B. Achziger's lighting are eye-tickling, and the young performers blend with the show into a sweet, long cry of joy.

SUMMER, 1971

THE TRIAL OF THE CATONSVILLE NINE
by Father Daniel Berrigan with Saul Levitt

THE PHILANTHROPIST
by Christopher Hampton

THE HOMECOMING
by Harold Pinter

THE BASIC TRAINING OF PAVLO HUMMEL
by David Rabe

CYMBELINE
by William Shakespeare
produced by the New York Shakespeare Festival

As I LOOK AROUND the theater at present, the best thing on the boards is barely a play at all. It is *The Trial of the Catonsville Nine,* Father Daniel Berrigan's own condensation, with some help from Saul Levitt, of the trial record of the famous draft-file-burning case in which he, his brother Philip, and five other men and two women were convicted. The defendants in the Catonsville, Maryland, case did not in the least deny that they poured homemade napalm over a goodly number of draft files at the local draft board and set them on fire; they merely contended that it was better to burn paper than people, and that this gesture, besides being a kind of symbol speaking all civilized languages, actually made it harder to draft a fair number of young men. The judge, himself a Catholic (both Berrigans are Jesuit priests; the other defendants, Catholic laymen), wept when he had to condemn these men and women to rather stiff jail sentences. But it was the law, and it was not up to him or anyone else to disregard the law. Yet that was precisely what the Catonsville martyrs were after: to demonstrate the inhumanity of the Law, even if it meant losing years of their lives to accomplish it.

I have not followed the case closely, and cannot say how much rearranging the play required. A few explanatory speeches have been added, and of course very much had to be omitted; there are also changes of chronological order. But facts have not been altered or testimony rewritten, and the main point emerges gradually with increasingly powerful clarity: the actions of these nine people are based on a reasoning and language totally different from the reasoning and language of the Law (the capital letter seems painfully necessary). The prosecutor and judge might as well be talking Chinese to the defendants; and they, in turn, volapük at the Law. With the help of the defense counsel's questioning, the nine recount their past lives: how from artists, nurses, students, or missionary priests and nuns who gave up their orders when the Church interfered with their charitable work in Africa or Guatemala, they became slowly, almost reluctantly, but inevitably freedom fighters. How our support of inequity abroad alerted and sensitized them to injustices at home, until they could no longer endure in silence foreign and domestic malpractices whose crowning embodiment was Vietnam.

Over and over the judge keeps repeating that the government of Guatemala or Whathaveyou is not on trial here, that the defendants' parents' experiences in Nazi Germany are not relevant here, that the Church's restrictions on the Maryknoll order's reform work is not being tried here. Over and over the judge, more exasperated than hostile, wearily claims irrelevance and implores the defendants to get closer to the actual case, from which they seem to be straying many miles and years afield. But the defendants and their attorney keep affirming that the poverty and exploitation seen in remote places abroad, and in cities and hamlets at home, *are* relevant; that the deaths in Latin America and Africa and Asia, and their repercussions in human hearts, are relevant; that the meditations of priests and laymen about their priesthood and religion are relevant; that burning souls are as relevant as hands that burn documents. And later, when the jury is out, and the nine gather around the judge to try to reach him in basic human terms, they come very close to success, but finally founder on the Law: inflexible, immutable, inaccessible to mere common sense, humanity and horror of useless bloodshed. After all, couldn't every other infringer of the Law then argue that his conscience gave him the right, etc. etc.?

The play is staged by Gordon Davidson in a church, and there is something particularly poignant about a pulpit becoming the judge's chair, a pew turning into the jury bench. We are reminded that official religion (in this case Catholicism, but it could be any other) is on the side of the Law against its own saints (for that is what these nine are), as it always was. And Davidson has found a technique that lets testimonies blend aurally into one another even as the physical presence of one defendant on the witness stand is suddenly, in mid-sentence, superseded by another's: the same effect is achieved by a lateral wipe in the movies. This rapidity and fluidity suggests the length and endlessness of the trial, as well as the seamless oneness of the eternal agon between the Soul of Man and the Law, that necessary robot policeman or Frankenstein monster man had to invent. Like any weapon or monster more powerful than its inventor, it may end up by destroying him.

This forthright, moving piece of documentary theater has vast implications and sets up tremendous reverberations. Not only do we see that sainthood represents common sense far more truly than does the Law; not only do we see the failure of democracy in action, for these inspired men and women try every way of reaching the elected lawmakers of this land and fail, just as they fail in getting the silent majority on their side. The play takes us further: to a clear view of the preposterousness of the *condition humaine;* these nine people acted out of brotherhood with all men, and it is their brothers who imprison them and decimate their days of freedom. These nine speak out against the injustice of an unnecessary war, and only achieve the further injustice wreaked on them. These nine were particularly moved by the state of black men, and a black attorney represents the State against them. These nine achieved the wedding of compassion with passion, only to elicit the divorce of legal reason from human common sense. And we, all of us who allowed them to be arrested without coming to the defense of their courage and goodness, are powerless, pusillanimous and guilty.

This is a terrible awareness, but the play makes us aware of something even more terrible: that we are not, and probably never will be, citizens of one land. Not only cannot the people's will end this war—

it is not even enough people's will to end it. From what the nine tell us, we sense how little serious opposition to the war and other forms of injustice there is around. And we feel vividly that we are the victims of dual citizenship. Each one of us is living not only among his friends or friendly enemies with whom, despite disagreements that may not be all that friendly, he can still comfortably share the same world, breathe the same air. One is also, alas, a citizen of a realm of fools—or a ship of fools, heading for shipwreck—peopled by those with whom one has nothing in common, and of whom, with the best of intentions, one cannot say *humani nihil a me alienum puto*. *The Trial of the Catonsville Nine* happens to be well directed and well enough acted, but this is of no greater importance than whether it is, strictly speaking, a play or not. It is a shattering experience emotionally and intellectually: it glues itself to your brain and forces you to think about it. I doubt whether art—pure, certified art—can do any more or better.

THE MOST INTERESTING by far of the current "real" plays—those, at least, that are not revivals—is Christopher Hampton's *The Philanthropist*. Unfortunately, I don't know the twenty-four-year-old English author's two previous plays, which sound, at the most modest estimate, interesting; the present play is lively, likable, intelligent and provocative, even if not devoid of flaws. It reveals a mind coming to grips with genuine problems, a mind at work even in the midst of small talk, and no matter if it is to some extent a collective mind, the mouthpiece of a culture: Oxford's, literary London's, England's. There is personal invention here, and a true concern for assessing the relation of the life of the mind to life in general, a subject seemingly beyond the capabilities of any American dramatist of comparable age.

The title is the key to the intention: the play is a pendant, a counterpart to Molière's *The Misanthrope*. Hampton's hero is Philip, a philologist-don at an unnamed English university in the near future. Philip knows himself to be boring by the simple fact that he bores himself; he remedies this as best he can by being inordinately nice and complaisant to everyone around him. He speaks, sees and hears no evil, likes everyone, and is in all ways the opposite of Alceste. Whereas Alceste tells a bad poet just what he thinks of his work, Philip is able to make himself like a bad play a student reads to him. Whereas Alceste resists the overtures of Célimène's friend Arsinoé, Philip, out of sheer desire not to offend, yields to Celia's fellow student Araminta. Whereas Alceste wants to shun society, and so loses his beloved Célimène, Philip is desperately gregarious, and so—here comes the switch—likewise loses his betrothed Celia: he invites over an impudent novelist who proves to be the straw that breaks the engagement's back.

The point here is that excessive affection for humanity and utter contempt for it come finally to the same thing: you cannot live for people any more than you can live against them. But beyond that, the play questions the very possibility of human goodness. Through a number of narrated events outside the immediate purview of the stage action, we are given a picture of a world gone mad, in which every kind of assassination, political and even literary, flourishes; in which students become disgusted with what learning reveals to them and set fire to their apartments; and Philip, the good man himself, spectacularly lets down a beggar who has become dependent on him. Within the stage action proper, violence and absurdity likewise prevail. A student shoots himself bizarrely, and no one pays much attention to it. People drop into bed with perfect strangers for no particular reason, and leave each other next morning perfect enemies. Worst of all, people, for one reason or another, dislike themselves. They may be as unself-confident as Philip, who says, "I am a man with no convictions—at least, I think I am." They may, like Celia, get engaged to a safe, staid fellow out of mistrust of their emotions. Or like Donald, Philip's fellow don, they may observe that there are two kinds of people, "those who live by what they know to be a lie, and those who live by what they believe falsely to be the truth"—after which Donald cheerlessly numbers himself among the former.

It would be a world of total despair if its absurdity did not make it funny. The swinish novelist Braham Head is "one of those writers who has been forced to leave the left wing for tax reasons"; Philip the philologist specializes in silly anagrams with the rapid improvisation of which he entertains his friends; masturbation can be justified as "the thinking man's television"; seemingly fake guns go off and seemingly real ones do not. Those anagrams, it appears, are significant: everything can easily rearrange itself into something else, even its opposite: "I think there's nothing cruder than an excess of subtlety," the odious novelist remarks, and, indeed, *les extrêmes se touchent*. If Alceste made an enemy out of Oronte by faulting his sonnet, Philip angers a young playwright no less by awkwardly liking his play. If Alceste's jealousy annoys Célimène, Philip's lack of jealousy annoys Celia just as much. The man who is too soft on mankind produces no better effect on it than he who is too hard on it; in the end, "philanthropist" is just an anagram of "misanthrope," a reshuffling of ingredients that produces a different concept but the identical unhappy results.

The verbal anagram with which the play ends is Philip's discovery that "imagine the theater as real" is an anagram for "I hate thee, sterile anagram," which suggests that Hampton considers the theater a game of anagrams with reality, but a game that is ultimately sterile. Yet life itself is anagrammatic, too. The play (or life) ends with a visual anagram: a seeming toy gun, in the first scene, kills someone with no particular reason to die; the real-looking pistol in the last scene, with which we expect Philip to kill himself (he has lost three girls, including his fiancée, all in one day, and has been unwittingly betrayed by his best friend) proves to be a mere cigarette lighter. He has just announced that he is about to do something terrible, so we expect suicide. Instead, he lights a cigarette. But, anagram of anagrams, even cigarettes spell suicide, albeit in a roundabout, slower way.

Do not assume, however, that Hampton has only cleverness going for him—though he can cleverly sustain a funny idea for several lines of good repartee, witticisms topping one another, which is the sine qua non of the true comic dramatist. He can also write a good serious scene, such as the final parting between Celia and Philip, or, in another key, the painfully constrained colloquy between Philip and Donald in the closing scene. Neither love nor friendship works for Philip and his nonlovers and nonfriends, and these scenes, though still subtly comedic, are fraught with a grave pathos. In the end, Philip emerges, very much like Alceste, a comic figure with tragic overtones. Or to put it more precisely, though the fanatic of scornful truth and the fanatic of good will and accommodation may be comic figures, the fact that their consistency damns them in the eyes of an inconsistent world is a kind of tragedy. Molière's play is an analysis of the nature and failure of honesty; Hampton's very nearly is an analysis of the nature and failure of goodness.

I say "very nearly" because, for all its aptness, the play is not quite so strong as it might be: the violent, absurdist world outside is not completely successfully integrated with the absurd little vehemences of Philip's seemingly somnolent world; Philip himself, though a good man, is probably too weak and ineffectual to embody a fully valid critique of goodness. Alec McCowen plays him with a barrage of brilliant little comic inventions: overachieving gestures, pauses panting for pregnancy, artful vocal diminuendos, looks that could melt a pound of butter on the spot. But these clevernesses are finally self-defeating: they invest individual moments with indisputable bravura, but they detract from easeful flow in the characterization, from attention to the core of personality. Jane Asher is quietly affecting as Celia, suggesting both the cynical coolness that might make a dazzling girl latch on to a stodgy do-gooder, and the very genuine melancholy that briefly pervades even such a clever young butterfly upon realizing that the comfortable old toadstool is no flower for her to suck. Penelope Wilton, who re-created the jolly nymphomaniacal Araminta here (like McCowen and Miss Asher, she had been in the London production), was unfortunately soon sent packing by a foolishly xenophobic Equity ruling. What a bouncy lump of overripe femininity was thus lost! As Donald, Ed Zimmerman, one of the more interesting young American actors, caught the essence of a decently self-doubting academic (as opposed to Philip's more crippling form of the malady) very deftly. Only Victor Spinetti, as Braham, was too obviously crass, and in a small part Paul Corum was quite deplorable. The sad thing is that despite laudatory notices, the play is doing poorly, and may well have vanished by the time these further praises reach print.

T<small>HE</small> R<small>OYAL</small> S<small>HAKESPEARE</small> C<small>OMPANY'S</small> original production of Harold Pinter's *The Homecoming*, transferred here in 1967, was so brilliant that I could fathom the fair reception the play managed to finagle: the current revival is deplorably staged, miserably designed, and shakily acted. Even so, it elicited from the first and second strings of the *Times* a rapturous double stop that gave me quite a start.

The least of *The Homecoming*'s troubles is that it does not make sense. This only stirs the interpreters, professional and amateur, to greater heights of interpretative madness. Ambiguity and implication are, of course, valid and potent artistic devices, but if the whole scenario, on almost all levels, has to be supplied by the critic or spectator, who then is the playwright? Pinter's play, like all his others, depends on tricks of diametrical reversal, going from one extreme to the other and saying vague, hostile nothings that can be made menacing, portentous or deep.

The basic flaw of *The Homecoming* is that it is totally formulaic and predictable: every character, sooner or later, becomes the opposite of himself. Max bullies his sons most of the time, even beats the strongest of them into submission; sure enough, he ends up crawling to them. Lenny is a slimy, totally nonintellectual pimp most of the time; suddenly he challenges his brother Teddy, the philosophy professor, to a fancy dialectical duel, full of recondite concepts and terminology. Equally uncharacteristically—and predictably—Teddy claims to be out of his element and clams up; inconceivable, if you have ever known a professor of philosophy. Teddy seems to be concerned about his wife, Ruth; when she suddenly decides to become both the family whore and a public prostitute, and abandon her small children, he goes back to America perfectly unruffled. Ruth herself at first seems vulnerable and withdrawn, and doesn't want to get involved with her husband's family; moreover, she is tired on arrival at the paternal home. Next thing, however, she is going out on a walk; a little later, she is seducing Lenny; the following day she is a hard and calculating slut. Joey the boxer seems to be the toughest son of the three, so naturally he has to be the one who cowers under his old father's stick, and who in two full hours cannot go "the whole hog" with Ruth. Sam is a consistent nonentity while standing up, but when in the end he keels over, there are as many signs pointing to a faint as to death. And even the dead revolve—not in their graves, but in the evaluation of the living: Jessie and Mac shuttle between decency and vileness.

These instant contradictions extend to the whole play. Peter Hall proudly declared, "Any proposition we draw from one side of the play we can contradict or modify by a proposition from some other side." Now, people are often inconsistent, but they are not schematically self-contradictory. Nor are they, and this is the second big flaw here, all profoundly repulsive or utter nullities. But those are the only kinds of characters you tend to find peopling (or, rather, insecting) a Pinter play. Pitiful worms or poisonous adders: nobody you can care about in the least; not even when, as invariably happens, the worms lengthen into adders, and the adders shrivel into worms.

This leaves the language. But there hardly is any in Pinter: only commonplaces, repetitions, insults, non sequiturs and pauses. This too is a language, I grant you, but is it a language for human beings? Take Ruth's speech: "I was born quite near here. (*Pause*) Then . . . six years ago, I went to America. (*Pause*) It's all rock. And sand, it stretches . . . so far . . . everywhere you look. And there's lots of insects there. (*Pause*) And there's lots of insects there. (*Silence. She is still*)" The words clearly mean very little; but the pauses, ah, those famous Pinter pauses! How minimal can minimal art get? That is where you, dear spectator, fill in the play. And if others can have *their* interpretations, you won't be caught with your mystagogic pants down either, by gum. During the original run of *The Homecoming*, the *Times* letter columns were brimful of rival exegeses, each more fanciful than the last; now John Lahr has edited *A Casebook on Harold Pinter's The Homecoming*, in which a number of contributors, known and unknown, compete at inventing thoroughly contradictory and illusory explications. As for all those gratuitous pauses, if they serve any purpose, it is to stretch Pinter's meager, stunted inventions into full-length plays.

The current production is directed by Jerry Adler as one part carbon copy of Peter Hall's, one part old gags, and two parts deadly stasis. Dahl Delu's set is shabby without any power of suggestion, and no one is credited with the costumes, which indeed are to no one's credit. In the cast, Norman Barrs and Danny Sewell at least know what they are doing; Eric Berry's Max is all meaningless bluster, and Lawrence Keith's Teddy is oily, boring, and un-British. Conversely, Tony Tanner's Lenny is standard English music-hall slickness. Janice Rule, beautiful as ever (too much so for this part), plays Ruth as a cross between *Strange Interlude* and *Sweet Bird of Youth*, and quite misses the Pinterian pointlessness.

Most noteworthy is the play's intense though latent homosexuality. Once again the motif of the same woman (and what a beastly woman!) shared by two or more men somehow involved with one another—in rivalry, kinship or love-hate—appears; just as it did in *The Servant*, *Accident* and *The Basement*, among others. And as so often is the case with homosexual sensibility, the action oscillates between affectlessness and sadomasochism. Instead of a casebook on *The Homecoming*, I'd like a case history on its author.

THE PUBLIC THEATER gives us *The Basic Training of Pavlo Hummel*, a not unrewarding play by David Rabe. It concerns a confused young man who briefly comes to tragicomic life in the Vietnam war, then goes down in it to absurd and anonymous death. Rabe knows the war, having been through it; and knows, what is more, how to write. His able play nevertheless suffers from splits down the middle in two directions. Horizontally, it tries to be as much about the war and the sad and comic grossness of army life as about the peculiarities and tergiversations of a funny little man trying to find himself. It even wants, I think, to relate the home front (or lack of one) to the battlefront. In these dualities and overextensions it often manages to stretch beyond the breaking point. Vertically, though it is in perfect control when dealing with its subject as a piece of artfully heightened realism, it is also drawn into modishly antirealistic devices over which it exercises insufficient control, and which have a way of becoming top-heavy and crumbling.

Nevertheless, to my mind this is much the best play about the war so far, leaving the *Viet Rocks*, *Summertrees*, *Pinkvilles*, and the rest several lengths (or shortnesses of wit) behind. Rabe impressively avoids easy pathos by making the protagonist anything but prepossessing, and by making the bad guys—smarmy officers, Napoleonic noncoms, and brawling GI's—as human as villains can be, and often are. The play's horror tends to be comic, as is a nightmare that is so outrageous as to be almost amusing, except that it devastates all the same. What is frightening here is the semblance of logic, of benevolence even, about the inhumanity; the cheerfulness, or at least casualness, with which the worst befalls and befouls us. The dialogue has an assurance that gives it historic authority; it is also marshaled in a way that endows it with artistic dignity.

But there remain the problems of the above-mentioned rifts, as well as the difficulty of making a drama about armies, wars, and senseless death differ from other such plays, however superior to them it may be. *Pavlo Hummel* is, nevertheless, greatly helped by exemplary direction and performing. Jeff Bleckner has staged it with a quiet inventiveness and purposefulness that would do credit to a much more experienced and acclaimed director, and the cast performs as a flawless ensemble that does the Public Theater—and the theater in general—proud. I single out only as *primi inter pares* William Atherton as a perfectly befuddled Pavlo, sympathetic squarely in spite of himself, and Lee Wallace, as a legless, one-armed cripple, whose sneering, sardonic despair is one of the most moving creations in a small part I have ever seen.

Cymbeline, unsatisfactory as it is, is still a considerable enough play to make the foolish liberties taken with it hurt both it and us. There is an instructive insight into how the play was staged to be gleaned from a profile on Joseph Papp in the August 15 *New York Times Magazine*. According to this eyewitness account, A. J. Antoon, the director, comes into Papp's office to inquire how much he can "screw around with" the play. Papp instructs him to "start out by trusting Shakespeare." Later he may find out "what bends," and can, if he gets very sure of himself, "really break it up." Then Papp proceeds to explain the character of Imogen to Antoon, and what must not be cut from her speeches: "She says, 'O brave Sir, I would they were in Afric both together, Myself by with a needle, that I might prick The goer-back.' And here she says, 'Thou shouldst have made him as little as a crow.' This is the way she sees her lover, this is a woman's idea of loving, of pricking him with a needle, of making him small enough to eat up."

Well, the needle passage refers to a sword fight the oafish Cloten has picked with Imogen's gallant husband, Posthumus. Imogen is saying that she would like to be in a desert spot with the combatants and have a needle with which to prod whichever abstained from fighting (as her husband did, out of kindness) back into the duel, which of course would then lead to Cloten's undoing. And the crow passage is from Imogen's questioning of the faithful Pisanio about what Posthumus' sailing into exile was like. She gently chides Pisanio for not having watched the departing ship long enough, even to the time when her husband's figure was no bigger than a crow—"or less, ere [he] left To after-eye him." None of this has anything to do with a woman's idea of loving being to prick her man with a needle, or making him as small as a crow so she can eat him. It is Papp who should eat crow for this kind of explication. And with the blind leading the halt, you can imagine what we got.

The play is a fairy tale subsuming mythic elements. It thus needs to be played with the innocent gravity with which a fairy tale is told and believed by its teller and hearers. There may indeed be humor in it, but this must not outweigh the element of wonder; and though everything may have a happy end, the dangers, heroism and endurance by which that end is gained must not seem a mere self-indulgent charade. There is, for instance, a good deal of bird imagery in *Cymbeline,* but from this to turning the British army into a flock of oversized birds, the Roman forces into a pack of large animal masks, and the battles into a traffic jam in a Carnival procession, is to have no concept of the play beyond bending it into misshapenness when not breaking it into smithereens. Galt MacDermot's setting of the songs was lamentable, the design chaotic, and the acting ludicrous. To Afric with the whole thing and a needle to each and all.

Autumn, 1971

Where Has Tommy Flowers Gone?
by Terrence McNally

Jesus Christ Superstar
music and lyrics by Tim Rice
and Andrew Lloyd Webber

The Incomparable Max
by Jerome Lawrence and Robert E. Lee

To Live Another Summer, To Pass Another
Winter
by Hayim Hefer, Dov Seltzer and Jonaton Karmon

The off-Broadway season opened with Terrence McNally's *Where Has Tommy Flowers Gone?* From the author of *Next* and several other not uninteresting one-acters, this came as a distinct disappointment. But there lies part of the problem: *Tommy* is a full-length play, and most of today's playwrights can write only, in however many acts, one-acters. The explanation, though I and many others have nibbled away at it, remains to be more comprehensively stated. McNally's play is dragged out beyond any shape or structuring: it concerns a kind of hippie living on charming conmanship, petty thievery and air. He is given endless monologues and comic solo turns, and is intermittently joined by his English sheepdog, Arnold; by his current girl, Nedda Lemmon, whom he met as a fellow shoplifter at Bloomingdale's; and by an old-time bit player whom he adopted off the sidewalk. But we mostly see Tommy's momentary encounters with shadowy passers-by from whom he tries to get money; watch him doing an impersonation of Marilyn Monroe in heaven, or going into recollections of his family, with his various kinfolk in Florida seen and heard on three screens showing simultaneously the identical footage. Why so much of those fugitive strangers, why the irrelevant and campy impersonations, why three screens when one would do as well, and none at all better yet?

There is a desperation about this kind of playwriting: garrulity posturing as content, gimmickry pretending to be form, bizarreness mistaking itself (or hoping to be mistaken by others) for an original voice. Actually, Tommy is a type, a mode, a subculture, far more than he is an individual. But there is also another difficulty: Tommy is presented as a heterosexual in one principal and several peripheral involvements; yet neither as McNally wrote him, nor as Robert Drivas acts him, does our hero suggest a heterosexual. Not only does he go in for female impersonation (aside from Marilyn Monroe, he'll give you Pat Nixon's meeting with a dying Puerto Rican girl, and for shoplifting purposes he dons his ever-handy disguise as a nun), he also relishes every kind of campy list-making. Surely we must recognize by now a new version of the Homeric catalogue: the homoerotic catalogue. This consists of enumerating pell-mell old movies, movie actors, names from yellowing gossip columns, song titles, show titles, cartoon characters, antiquated locutions, and other verbal paraphernalia from the magpie's nest of the campy memory. Such one-upmanship through *faisandé* data is the special pride of a certain type of homosexual, and is quite rare among heterosexuals. Moreover, there is a kind of brittleness, affectlessness, cuteness about Tommy (both written and acted) that does not ring true in a heterosexual context, and his involvement with Nedda is evoked only in the most surface-skimming terms.

Jacques Levy's staging is gimmicky without being really clever, and the set and costume design are undistinguished, but the supporting roles are well enough played by man, woman and dog alike. I particularly cherished the bouncy freshness a newcomer named Barbara Worthington brought to a number of girls who flit through Tommy's life. One would be strongly tempted to urge Mr. McNally to write the kind of play he really has a feeling for, and do it forthrightly; but when one remembers *And Things That Go Bump in the*

Night, which seemed to fill this bill, one is stopped shudderingly short.

Meanwhile, the Broadway musical scene also swung into action with the arrival of *Jesus Christ Superstar.* This is the highly touted "rock opera" by two young Englishmen, which as a record sold two-and-a-half million copies; in a concert version toured America with loud and lucrative success; and had an advance sale of over a million dollars at the box office. (It may be interesting to note that, in the words of its shrewd producer, the recording of Tim Rice and Andrew Lloyd Webber's "rock opera" sank in London "like a stone." No one can be a rock prophet of the Lord with honor in his own country.) The show has no book, and merely relates the last seven days of Christ in today's lingo set to occasional rhymes and to trendy occasional music. The latter is medium-hard rock with overtones of an older Broadway idiom, as well as of medium-serious composers: in the orchestral finale, for instance, I kept hearing Massenet. But there are no tunes that impress forcefully, except perhaps for Herod's Charleston, about which more anon. A notch or two below the music are Rice's lyrics, for example, making Christ sing, "It was nice,/ But now it's gone," or "Then I was inspired,/ Now I'm sad and tired," or "My time is almost through,/ Little left to do/ After all I've tried for three years—/ Seems like thirty!" And this about Mary Magdalene, a reformed Supergroupie with whom our Superstar lives in carnal knowledge: "Who are you to criticize her?/ Who are you to despise her?" She, in turn, intones: "Don't you think it's rather funny/ I should be in this position?/ . . . Yet if he said he loved me,/ I'd be lost and frightened:/ I couldn't cope." And Caiaphas concedes: "One thing I'll say for him:/ Jesus is cool."

But it is not so much the blaring obviousness of the music or the mangy doggerel of the lyrics that is to blame; rather, it is the general crassness and opportunism of the conception. At a time when religion of a dubious sort is staging a comeback among Jesus freaks, what could be a better investment than a show that features a rock-singing, long-haired and barefoot enemy of the Establishment—for that is virtually all this Christ is—who loves his girl manfully and handles his mike like a pro? And how those Jewish priests and Roman governors, to say nothing of the spear-carrying pigs, hate his guts! But he just keeps crooning and shrieking his guts out, and is finally crucified in style on an inverted golden triangle, while above him, in a large, winged contraption housing four seminude angels (the metamorphosed Judas and three black cuties, clearly the Celestial Supremes), chant his praises and the chorus bops out its hosannas as "Sanna ho! Sanna hey!" It is not sacrilegious, merely meretricious and silly.

The most spectacular aspect of the show is the staging by Tom O'Horgan, who clearly imposed his conception on the set and costume designers, as well as devising the rudimentary choreography. O'Horgan thinks big, which wouldn't be bad; but he thinks big without actually thinking. Take the opening stage image. Three huge, Art Nouveau, backward-slanting panels form a sort of curtain; together, they look like one side of a towering *fin-de-siècle* pyramid with its tip lopped off. Suddenly we notice four scantily clad bodies wriggling across the high top edge of the panels, and painfully making their wormlike way down as the three panels slowly sink back toward a horizontal position. They never quite make it, forming instead a sharply raked floor, over whose far horizon more and more bikinied bodies emerge to dance some kind of prehistoric tribal dance (shades of *Lenny,* also directed by O'Horgan). This is admittedly clever, but is it in any way germane? You might say it represents pagan revelry before the coming of Christ. (Even then, what's all this crawling down from snub-nosed pyramids?) But not so—for next, a large silver chalice rises out of the floor and from it emerges a smaller silver chalice that turns around and turns out to be Jesus Christ in a high-collared cape, made, it seems, out of numerous thin silver ropes. Now the ensemble is suddenly clothed, but proceeds to indulge in the same gyrations as in the previous pagan ritual. If the point is that Christianity is merely paganism made superficially respectable, the point, besides being very doubtful, is not made sufficiently clear. It is all merely a grandiose O'Horganian visual non sequitur.

And there is an unbroken chain of these. Bits of scenery, whole sets, actors are continually rising or descending through the air; large objects of peculiar shapes are carried on, sometimes with people stepping out of them. A huge portrait of Caesar unfurls upward like an accordion, until the image has six foreheads and as many pairs of eyes, for no reason whatever. Herod comes out of a mighty carapace whose insides may be a weird maw or the cross section of a uterus. Pilate is suddenly provided with an enormous pewter elephant's trunk, but inverted so that the thicker end faces the audience; from it hangs a big pewter tongue. The object requires a couple of men to carry it on. Occasionally cloths or gauzes billow forth from nowhere to cover a person or the entire scene. For the Gethsemane song, a plastic box the size of an upright piano comes down from the flies and hangs above Christ's head; at the end of the number, it is slowly hoisted away. It glitters like a fancily wrapped candy box sent to Gargantua on his birthday, but what it means is anybody's guess. Many objects look like bones or genitalia, others like gold or silver lollipops of giant size and embossed with faces (mostly sylized suns and moons); a pair of silver dentures the size of cocktail tables is carried on in a procession and used more or less as cymbals. On and on come the monstrosities, inspired by Beardsley, Félicien Rops, abstract expressionism, pop art, with an occasional touch of Odilon Redon or Gustav Klimt. And there are gaudy projections on the backdrop as well as strange cutouts in it, and always moving platforms. But all it proves is O'Horgan's megalomania, which is hardly news.

Since all the singing is through microphones whose wires are disguised as shaggy ropes, there is no judging the voices. There is no acting to speak of, though Ben Vereen's Judas wiggles well on the floor in remorse, and Jeff Fenholt is a good enough pop Jesus, with a voice that can slither and quaver up and down the octaves. Yvonne Elliman has a certain visual and vocal innocence as Mary Magdalene, and Barry Dennen exudes a convincingly cold worldliness as Pilate. King Herod (Paul Ainsley) has the best number: emerging from a portable sea monster, he is a bloated outlandish ogre in drag, with Carmen Miranda headgear and huge cerulean wedgies the shape and size of a couple of Roman triremes. He sashays and cavorts in a malicious Charleston, with which he taunts the bound Christ; capering along with him are two tiny priests in effeminate, diaphanous gowns, and they are vocally joined by the entire chorus. Here, for once, the doggerel bites as well as it barks, the music wallows in lilting derivativeness, and that huge, fat, mincing figure, supported by two cavorting little book ends, all combine to make some genuinely obscene merriment. But they cannot redeem an evening of bloated, eye-and-ear-boggling mindlessness and tawdriness.

BY SOME STRANGE mathematics peculiar to the theater, two half-playwrights do not add up to a whole one. Now, a man who can write plays only in collaboration is a half-playwright, whether his name is Hart or Hecht, Kaufman or Caillavet, Connelly or Crouse, Berney or

Richardson, Lawrence or Lee. If you put two of these together on a project, what comes out may be a play of sorts—sometimes even, God save the mark, a hit—but never a playwright. Labiche, you may say, but Labiche, such as he was, could often go it alone. Beaumont and Fletcher, I suppose, were as near as two halves ever came to making a whole dramatist, but have you read any really good Beaumont and Fletcher since you left college, or even before? Of course, there have been some pretty good plays written in collaboration— *Eastward Ho!* or *The Changeling,* for example—but Jonson and Chapman and Marston were all individual dramatists first and collaborators only afterward. Beware, however, of your full-time collaborator, who flocks together with another bird of his feather and kidney; at best, this hybrid can produce a gag-filled farce—a work of art, never.

There is something unnatural about two men, neither of whom can write a play, assuming that together they can. They can whip up a commodity, a *You Can't Take It With You,* for instance; but can you image a *Misanthrope* by Molière and MacArthur, a *Spring's Awakening* by Wedekind and Ryskind? The authors of the present play, *The Incomparable Max,* are Jerome Lawrence and the Robert E. Lee whom he had been waiting for to write fourteen plays or musical books with, as the program tells us. Their biggest hit was *Inherit the Wind;* their second-biggest, *Auntie Mame;* their third-biggest, *Mame.* You will note that the first was the retelling of the notorious Monkey Trial, as dramatic a case as ever hit that secondary form of theater known as the courtroom, and with such great actor-directors improvising for you that all you need is scribes to take it down. *Auntie Mame,* for what it was worth, was the adaptation of a campy best-seller into a campy boulevard farce; and *Mame* was a musical adaptation of that adaptation. But what of the rest of the Lawrence and Lee roster? Most noteworthy are the book for *Look, Ma, I'm Dancing,* containing some limp ballet-world injokes, and *The Night Thoreau Spent in Jail,* which turns Thoreau into a yippie *avant la lettre,* and had 132 productions all over the country because New York didn't want it. Just previously, there was a ghastly musical adaptation of *The Madwoman of Chaillot* and an item about Evita Peron with some orchidaceous title that I have happily managed to forget.

But to get down to *The Incomparable Max,* and very far down it is, too. The authors refer to it as a play about Max Beerbohm, and someone—a single someone—could perhaps write a charming play about that dandy, wit, essayist, esthete, critic, caricaturist, *flâneur* upon whom, according to Oscar Wilde, the gods bestowed the gift of eternal old age. Indeed, Max lived to be eighty-four, and was a sprightly, crabbedly amusing old man from the age of twenty-four on, when he brought out, with precocious senescence, a slender volume entitled *The Collected Works of Max Beerbohm*. Sixty glorious years of being satirical, critical, imperturbably snobbish and offhandedly puncturing—in short, full of elderly virtues—is a life that might provide a neo-Shavian playwright with something to play with. But Lawrence and Lee have done nothing of the sort; they have merely taken two of Beerbohm's essay-stories about two curious characters and turned them into a couple of stage acts, eking them out with a little anecdotal material about Beerbohm and some gags of their own about America, computers and critics.

Now these stories make delicious leather-armchair reading, and blend exquisitely with a book-lined library setting; on the stage, they are as out of place as Coleridge's *Table Talk* would be. On top of this, to take two quite unrelated stories of totally clashing moods, in which Max appears only as an interlocutor, and to force these into some kind of supposed whole, presupposes not only half-playwrights but half-baked ones as well. Gerald Freedman—a farce-director if ever there was one—was a second strike against the enterprise; the third was the casting. Clive Revill is grand in vulgar parts; in *Irma la Douce* or as Fagin in *Oliver!* he was splendidly coarse. But refinement is not his trough of tea, and here he was clearly Max's greengrocer rather than Max himself. Even his looks were wrong, to say nothing of those vestigial down-under tones originating at the root of a nose looking rather like the map of New Zealand.

David Mitchell's set and Martin Aronstein's lighting were fine; but, oh, that supporting cast. Michael Egan was an acceptable Rothenstein, and with better material Fionnuala Flanagan, I know, could do a great deal more. Most of the others, regrettably, fitted their assignments as to the manure born. Four performances by two actors, doubling, and doubling me up, were particularly painful. Richard Kiley will do for straight parts or musical tear-jerkers, but he is an actor sadly dependent on surface effects and devoid of the least magnetism; here, especially when playing an oddball, he made me cringe even more for him than for myself. Worse yet, however, was Martyn Green, who could actually ruin the one part no actor has ever managed to louse up, that of the Devil. Green's Horned One is actually a cow, so boring that if the play has any kind of run (which I doubt), he may end up converting more hell-bound souls than Billy Graham.

An unnatural thing, I repeat, is a composite playwright, rather like a centaur: a bit of a human head, to be sure, but ever so much more horse's arse.

THOSE ILL-STARRED Arabs have goofed again! What a machiavellian masterstroke it was to concoct a pseudo-Israeli musical out of the most revoltingly unmusical clichés, occasionally leavened with Levantine modalities, and lyrics that are so gruesomely simplistic as to give goose pimples even to Mother Goose—plus, by way of a non-book, a slapped-together bunch of Jewish jokes culled from the sere leaves of an ancient Anti-Semite's Manual. To this were added rudimentary scenery and costumes ranging from drab to dismal. A singing and dancing chorus of unblemished amateurishness was then assembled, and phonetically coached in Hebrew and dancing—all but one blonde *première danseuse*, that is, whose professionalism put the rest to even greater shame. Three men and two women—presumably the only prisoners of war the Arabs ever took—were then hypnotized into believing themselves to be performers rather than army cooks, mailroom clerks and ambulance drivers, and brainwashed into doing the aforementioned drivel.

This mess was ascribed to some fictitious Israelis with ingenious and only slightly improbable names like Hayim Hefer, Dov Seltzer and Jonaton Karmon (this last being a phonetic near-palindrome for "no mark, not a notch"), and packed off to the U.S.A., so as to make, by way of retaliation, all shipments of arms, money and even sympathy to Israel cease forever. But the best-laid plans of Mahdis and Yemen can misfire. The Arabs did not reckon with the taste- and gutlessness of our reviewers or the Hadassaishness of Broadway audiences. This inflammatory garbage, called *To Live Another Summer, To Pass Another Winter*—there was even a sickening pop song about the massacre of the Six Million, rendered by a mugging grimace-monger—managed to be greeted with such hasidic huzzaing as to prove, ultimately, worth its weight in bonds.

Winter, 1971-1972

The Black Terror
  by Richard Wesley

The Sty of the Blind Pig
  by Phillip Hayes Dean

El Hajj Malik
  by N. R. Davidson, Jr.

The Two Gentlemen of Verona
  by William Shakespeare
  produced by the New York Shakespeare Festival

Murderous Angels
  by Conor Cruise O'Brien

The Ride Across Lake Constance
  by Peter Handke

There's One in Every Marriage
  by Georges Feydeau
  *adapted by Suzanne Grossmann and
    Paxton Whitehead*

Vivat! Vivat Regina!
  by Robert Bolt

GREASE
book, music and lyrics by Jim Jacobs
and Warren Casey

SHADOW OF A GUNMAN
by Sean O'Casey

TWELFTH NIGHT
by William Shakespeare
produced by the Repertory Theater of Lincoln Center

THE DUPLEX
by Ed Bullins

O FF-BROADWAY is currently offering a whole spectrum of black theater. To start at the bottom and work our way up, there is *The Black Terror* by Richard Wesley, with which the Public Theater is undercutting its splendid record of two David Rabe plays showing alongside and above this fiasco. The remarkable thing about *The Black Terror* is that, whereas productions at the Papp emporium are always at least professional, this offering, with the exception of Marjorie Kellogg's apt stage design, is totally and depressingly amateurish. The play is a boringly predictable, dry-as-dust in spite of its blood-and-thunder rhetoric, political tract, concerning itself with whether a heavily armed black militant movement should go all out for immediate and complete war on the White Establishment, or continue with guerrilla tactics, sniping down whites whenever and wherever it is convenient.

Aside from the fact that he seems to have no writing ability whatsoever, Mr. Wesley has one other great shortcoming: he has either studied the archetypal play of this sort, Camus' *Les Justes*, too closely, and tried too hard to be different, or he hasn't studied it at all. Either way, he has made his black terrorists too different from the Russians of 1903, whom Camus so conscientiously scrutinized in his play and still failed to make dramatically viable. But what Camus realized is that for a play about assassination and terror to have any human dimensions, the audience had to respect the terrorists: "The greatest homage that we can render [the men of 1903] is to say that we could not, in 1947, put to them a single question that they hadn't already put to themselves and to which, in their lives or by their deaths, they haven't in part given an answer." The characters in Wesley's play never concern themselves with the basic question: their right to kill. The chief conflict is between Keusi, an ex-Vietnam sharpshooter, who believes in selective and judicious sniping, and the whole rest of the cell, who are, to a varying degree, for an all-out uprising. Previously, Keusi has killed a bestial, fascist police commissioner (cleverly called Commissioner Savage) with a bow and arrow and with the greatest of ease—the black-militant version of Steigian dreams of glory! Keusi, who has performed this feat in Savage's back garden and got away scot free, boggles merely when his next victim is to be a respectable black leader who believes in cooperation with the whites and has even denounced a few black terrorists. Keusi is not for blacks' killing one another. The others are; even his girl M'Bahlia, perhaps the most dedicated terrorist of them all.

Even Camus, as I said, failed; maybe because the conflict in a terrorist cell is inevitably overburdened with questions of strategy, schematic party-line rhetoric, fulminations of formless rage, and systematic repression of the full scale of human thought and emotion. But Wesley's language is particularly dreary—almost exclusively made up of stuff like "Kill the oppressor beast!" "Now this lapdog seeks our death!" "The faggot lackey must die." "A pig is a pig is a pig!" and so on, down to the ritual repetition of certain cozy obscenities. For poetry, Wesley gives us "Oh, they were beautiful, man—I mean, Ramon with his face blown off . . ." and for wit or insight (I am not sure which): "I am a black terrorist; sex isn't a thing with me any more." "Yeah, baby, but we all have to do some sacrifices sometimes." This may be the true talk of the black terrorist cells, but it is not the stuff drama is made of.

Some of the language is further debased by the appallingly sloppy diction of the entire cast. Susan Batson, for example, says "your cowardness" and "sit idelly by" (which may be illiteracy as much as bad elocution) and something about a "useless female raising sibyllines" which may be "siblings" or "zibellines" for all I can tell. Paul Benjamin, an actor who suffers from what I would call absolute histrionic illiteracy, compounds his ineptitude with a "hum?" that he gratuitously appends to every third phrase. Don Blakely shouts an entire scene at the top of his voice (even though he is bleeding from wounds) in the muddiest of elocutions, Kirk Young has almost no variety in his delivery, and an actor who calls himself Kain mumbles away into his own navel. Kain, by the way, seems to imitate Marlon Brando at his worst, and Blakely and Batson have actually been members of the Actors Studio; how sad if potentially bright young Negro actors were to be saddled—as these are—with the tiresome ballast of outworn Method mannerisms!

If the actors, except for Earl Sydnor, are dreadful, much of the blame must go to Nathan George's inept direction. But why shouldn't the rave reviews George got for his mediocre performance in that less than mediocre play, *No Place to Be Somebody,* have gone to his head? Just as the rave reviews for this boring and maniacal play from Barnes and a number of other white reviewers practicing the art of bending over blackward are bound to go to Richard Wesley's head. It is typical of the dishonesty of this playwriting that even at the end of the piece, when large-scale street-fighting breaks out, none of the "good," i.e. militant, blacks in the play is allowed to die, a fate reserved for the whites and Uncle Toms exclusively. And yet some of my perceptive colleagues have praised this play for its impartiality! They seem to be no brighter than the character in *The Black Terror* who shouts enthusiastically in bad English and worse logic: "For every one of us who falls there will be ten oppressors!" Actually, the syntax is so faulty that the meaning is the opposite of what the playwright intended. And this, alas, may be exactly what would happen: for every dead black terrorist, ten living white oppressors.

The Negro Ensemble Company's *The Sty of the Blind Pig* is a more serious attempt at playwriting, but the author, Phillip Hayes Dean, errs in two serious ways. For two long acts he gives us atmosphere and background, and then frantically piles all the revelations and activity into the short third act, making part of his play tedious and part of it ludicrous. Also, he tries to wed naturalism to symbolism, and the result is obviously not a happy marriage but unholy acrimony. Clarice Taylor and Moses Gunn perform capably, though not without a certain monotony; Frances Foster overacts, and Adolph Caesar is unskillful and obvious. But Shauneille Perry continues to prove herself a most sensible and proficient director.

• • •

EL HAJJ MALIK, given by the Afro-American Studio, is an adaptation of Malcolm X's speeches and autobiography into something that is a cross between Brecht and the Oberammergau Passion Play, an oratorio without singing and a living newspaper. There are passages in doggerel verse, some music and dancing, much rhythmic marching and chanting, and an aura of ritual. The play is ascribed to one N. R. Davidson, Jr., about whom we are told nothing, and who may be a nonpen name for what may have originated in group improvisation, like some productions of Joan Littlewood. But just as Littlewood could work wonders, so clearly can Ernie McClintock, the Studio's director, and his lively assistants and actors. As art, the play is midway between a folk ballad and a political poster (leaving the biggest questions unanswered), but it is so brilliantly directed and lovingly performed that even the dull passages, of which there are a few, go by bearably, and the rest rousingly. Here the black theater is alert to the fact that audience identification with characters onstage, its mainstay hitherto, is not enough. Something bigger, deeper, truer is what drama calls for, and though *El Hajj Malik* doesn't quite get there, it's on the way.

WHAT A LONG way we have come—backward! From the nineteenth century on, great progress was made in ridding Shakespearean productions of the accretions, subtractions and alterations that had been calamitously visited on the plays ever since the Restoration. Scholar-critics and actor-managers earned lasting glory by clearing the originals from the happy endings, musical-comedy interludes, farcical subplots, spectacular tableaus and other extravagances and banalities that defaced the master's works the way billboards, motels and curio shops mar our noblest landscapes. Names like that of Nahum Tate became synonymous with theatrical ignominy: emblematic of fashion-mongering or audience-courting hacks who would slap a happy ending on *King Lear* as quickly as wanton boys dismember a fly.

But does humanity ever take a step forward without two steps back? Soon the "advanced" critics and directors were vying to produce the most ingenious reinterpretations of the Bard—to squeeze further meaning, newer relevance, more unheard-of implications from the plays. Some of this, of course, is legitimate: a masterpiece is a masterpiece because it is both eternal and mutable—can, without changing its fundamental meaning, yield overtones that are variously suggestive to each successive age. But for chronic innovators this isn't enough. Soon after the merriment over those misbegotten Nahum Tates of yesteryear died down, directors were once again competing at reinterpreting, adapting, rewriting Shakespeare in the best tradition of little men living off improving their betters. Even as our history out-Herods Herod, so does our theater out-Nahum Nahum Tate.

What was needed was the conjunction of two truly deplorable sensibilities: that of a benighted, untalented Polish pseudocritic—a man who could not read Shakespeare in English—Jan Kott; and that of a director whose adroit vulgarities were surpassed only by his megalomaniacal brazennesses, who was instantly influenceable by any theatrical mind, good or bad, that he could crib from and exaggerate—Meyerhold, Brecht, Artaud, Grotowski were all grist for his fast-grinding mill—Peter Brook. Brook read Kott's semiliterate lucubrations, *Shakespeare Our Contemporary*, and promptly started giving us distortions of Shakespeare that, though more skillful than those of the old-time hacks, were in no significant way different from them. The basic purpose, once again, was to provide a pleasurable shudder of novelty and to exalt the cleverness of the adapter-director at the expense of the underlying masterwork; all this to the parasitical cheers of shallow reviewers and un- or misinformed audiences. A prime example of Brook's unscrupulous malpractices is his current film version of *King Lear,* compared to which *The Two Gentlemen of Verona,* as adapted by John Guare and Mel Shapiro, who also directed it, is harmless fluff indeed.

The musical, with a score of Galt MacDermot, despite additional songs and scenery, some refurbishing of the original choreography, and two cast changes, is still essentially what was seen in the New York Shakespeare Festival's production last summer in Central Park. Consequently, my original strictures still hold. Because *Two Gentlemen* is one of Shakespeare's earliest and least plays, the sophomoric tampering with the text is less noxious than when a better play is taken for a ride. The extensive cutting and rewriting here have to do with turning the two loving couples into Puerto Ricans and blacks respectively, the setting into a mixture of today's New York and Never-Neverland, and the "message" (originally a flimsy but not wholly uninteresting examination of the jarring interaction of passion and friendship) into the shoddiest and shabbiest of homilies: Love, love, love—everybody love everybody! The score, though abundant, is undistinguished and mostly unmelodious; the lyrics, by Guare, contain sporadic clevernesses and much immature self-indulgence; the staging goes from resourceful to merely cluttered. The final effect is of an above-average varsity show, rather lavishly gotten up for a college production.

The cast, however, is enthusiastic to the point of irrepressibleness, and the firm pivot and pinnacle of the production is Raul Julia's Proteus. Julia deliciously exudes a blend of bonhomie and bumblingness that overcompensates for the latter by bumbling ahead and over everything with a sturdy confidence in its ability to outbumble everyone in a world full of imperfect bumblers. It is as if very fast things were filmed in slow motion: the resultant speed is roughly normal, but the shape of the movements and the sound of the words (enhanced by a spicily incongruous Spanish accent) are just a trifle off—distorted, travestied, cartoonish; Mr. Julia's Proteus is a lovable, flummoxing lummox. As Valentine, Clifton Davis is manly and forthright but unexciting; the Silvia of Jonelle Allen, though vocally somewhat clouded, radiates life-force as she prowls and pounces with the best of pumas. Diana Davila, alas, plays Julia as a terminal case of Parkinson's disease: the movements and utterances a perpetual tremor verging on paroxysm, the mind seemingly collapsing, the entire performance one giant, doddering simper. Miss Davila is perhaps the most mannered actress on the New York stage, and her manners are very bad.

Alix Elias' Lucetta is apparently inhibited by this Julia, whose breaking chirrups are what Miss Elias herself does, but does better. Conversely, the funny Frank O'Brien now outrageously overdoes Thurio, while Norman Matlock's Duke remains muffled and amateurish. John Bottoms is a fair Launce, José Perez a nice Speed, but Phineas, who portrays the dog Crab, is a mutt of sheer shaggy and contrary genius.

DOCUMENTARY DRAMA is an attempt to present historic events on the stage as factually as possible. The movement started in Germany, and three of its important specimens—Hochhuth's *The Deputy*, Weiss's *The Investigation*, and Kipphardt's *In the Matter of J. Robert Oppenheimer*—have been seen in New York. There have been also domestic examples—*Inquest* and, more notably, *The Trial of the Catonsville Nine*—and we are about to see yet another German effort, Enzensberger's *The Interrogation of Havana*. The form approximates the movies' *cinéma vérité* (or reconstructed *cinéma vérité*, as in *Battle of Algiers*), and differs from the older form of the historical play, like *The Royal Hunt of the Sun* or *A Man for All Seasons*, where historical material is used loosely, subordinated to poetic invention or dramatic intention.

The current entry into this field is *Murderous Angels*, by the Irish diplomat, historian and man of letters, Conor Cruise O'Brien. It concerns the bloody events in the Congo after its becoming independent from Belgium (June 30, 1960), leading up to the violent deaths of Patrice Lumumba and Dag Hammarskjöld in 1961. The argument is that Prime Minister Lumumba, seeking to rid the Congo of all foreign encroachment and financial exploitation, asked for Russian help and so fell afoul of U.S. and U.N. interests. U.N. Secretary-General Hammarskjöld, acting in what he believed to be the interests of the U.N., world peace and humanity (which would have been gravely endangered had the Congo triggered an all-out East-West conflict), allowed Lumumba to fall into the hands of his assassins. Later, Dag himself died in a mysterious Congolese plane crash, which O'Brien sees as a deliberate expiatory sacrifice.

The three main problems facing the documentary play are that the events to be depicted may not lend themselves to stage presentation, that there may not be enough documentary evidence, or that there may be too much—too voluminous and contradictory to boil down to suitable length. To cope with this, one may pick an incident of a relatively localized sort—at the risk, however, of losing scope and ecumenical significance. Or one may choose something that unfurled in a court or similar place of investigation, thus giving the action both unity of place and the traditional excitement of courtroom drama. Or one may invent fairly freely, and stick in relevant facts where they seem appropriate. In any case, there will be much compression of happenings, conflation of characters, and rearrangement of time sequence, raising doubt about how "documentary" the work really is.

O'Brien's ambitious and well-intentioned play falls into just about every pit lying in wait for documentary drama. These events in the Congo seem remote to most of us and, having taken place in the darkness of the heart of Africa, remain shrouded both by lack of information and deliberate obfuscation. But the concomitant world crisis obliges O'Brien to jump around various parts of Africa, Europe and New York, and so diffuse his impact. The actual circumstances of the deaths of both his heroes were hidden from view, forcing him, in his eagerness to remain historically accurate, to jettison both *scènes-à-faire*. Similarly, there were no physical confrontations between his two heroes, and O'Brien scrupulously avoids inventing any.

Nevertheless, he does invent some happenings and characters—notably a white secretary-mistress for Lumumba, and a black male assistant-lover for Hammarskjöld—and here his imagination proves to be that of an intelligent amateur, not of a dramatist.

The big problem, though, is that *Murderous Angels* does not, despite conveying certain terrible events, manage to be about much of anything. O'Brien seems to know Dürrenmatt's dictum that in our world "Creon's secretaries liquidate the Antigone affair. The state has lost its embodiment . . . and is representable only by statistics." So Lumumba and Hammarskjöld are almost less visible here than the various political and economic string-pullers and their puppets, and this makes for comedy rather than drama. Thus the minor characters do become figures of absurdist comedy, while the principals remain almost Schillerianly noble. The result is hodgepodge.

The basic point seems to be that the cold, cerebral humanitarianism of a Scandinavian saint and the hot-blooded, impractical heroism of an African liberator are both equally, ineluctably destructive—of each other and of themselves. This, though old hat, might be interesting if there were real interaction between the two murderous angels; without such interplay, there is no play. In short, this is a problem play with a rather hoary problem and almost no play. Moreover, the published text has undergone drastic changes and cuts at the hand of either the author or his director, Gordon Davidson. Though in this case shortening may well seem amelioration, the loss of a few ironic complexities makes the play even thinner. Davidson, in fact, seems to have reduced it all to an irreconcilable clash of whiteness and blackness—not, I think, the author's point at all. Most damagingly, Lumumba's black antagonists were heavily cut, the sinister Munongo eliminated altogether. If this was done to placate local black extremists, no use: the theater was picketed.

This may have been the reason for a mediocre performance from the excellent Lou Gossett as Lumumba; from Jean-Pierre Aumont I did not expect—or receive—much more than a slick, aging matinée-idol presence, with a thick, barely scrutable, accent. Accents and nationalities were particularly badly managed, and in a generally uninspired cast, which sank to the ludicrous depths of a Barbara Colby, Joseph Moscolo and John Baragrey, only two Richards, Easton and Venture, held their own nicely.

WHEN IS A PLAY not a play but a fraud? When, in fact, is any so-called work of art not a work of art but a piece of trickery, a hoax, a nonsensical game, a fraud? This question comes up—is the only one that comes up—in connection with the Lincoln Center Repertory Company's production at the Forum Theater of Peter Handke's *The Ride Across Lake Constance,* which begins, continues and ends as utter self-indulgent nonsense. The author is a twenty-nine-year-old Austrian writer who made a name for himself in 1966 by attacking a group of established German writers at one of their big gatherings when he was only twenty-four and still passed for an *enfant terrible.* That same year Handke's "play," *Publikumsbeschimpfung* was published. Michael Roloff, Handke's translator, calls this *Offending the Audience,* but *Beschimpfung* is really a much stronger word in German: abusing, reviling, insulting the audience would be nearer the mark.

Handke is a writer of some small talent, as at least one of his novels, *The Goalie's Anxiety at the Penalty Kick* attests. But his plays, with the possible exception of *Kaspar,* are all audience-insults of one kind or another, hailed and adulated by the very people who are being abused by them. But this has become the very condition, the very model of modern "art." We live in an age where an insolent, incompetent dauber like Barnett Newman gets museum retrospectives, has highfalutin books written about him and passes for a major painter. A fey farceur and effete solipsist like John Cage, playing campy games with silences, is proclaimed a serious composer, lectures at universities, has books of musical theory published, and becomes a major influence on modern music. A vulgar little window decorator like Andy Warhol, without a single idea or vision in his head, plays perverse little jokes that are first proclaimed paintings and later taken seriously as films.

I could go on citing abuses upon abuses—such as Claes Oldenburg's having a hole dug in Central Park with an invited audience watching, all with the blessing of Mr. Heckscher, the Parks Commissioner, and to the oohings and ahings of his staff of radical-chic cognoscenti—but this is not the question. The question is how does this sort of thing come about? What or who has created the cultural climate in which the "experts" and, following them, the public, no longer know a work of art from a hole in the ground? Let me say that I am against neither the innovative nor the difficult in the arts. In my doctoral dissertation, for example, I tried painstakingly to elucidate some of the most radical and arcane prose poems of Rimbaud and Mallarmé, and my enjoyment of truly innovative theatrical works like Jarry's *Ubu Roi* or Apollinaire's *Les Mamelles de Tirésias* is sweet and unalloyed.

But the trouble began with the Surrealists. The "surreal" fantasies of a Lautréamont, for example, had real human value, being the only form in which the libido—wearing the mask of dreams and visions—dared appear in the light of that still-puritanical day. But the puritans were finally, if not defeated, at least held at bay, and by the time the official Surrealists under André Breton took over, the only thing that still needed disguising was lack of talent. Not that there wasn't some real talent among the Surrealists—Paul Eluard's, for example—but by and large what the movement codified and promulgated under the guise of art was dreams, free association, automatic writing, the parlor game of *cadavre exquis* elevated to the status of art. Everybody was not taken in; a fine novelist and critic like Jean Prévost warned, almost half a century ago, against literature that was "printed matter founded on other printed matter" and added: "The literary work has value only by virtue of the human substance it contains. As for the modes of expression, they vary according to the circumstances. A literary technique never has any value by and of itself . . . no form of style is essential."

But there may still have been a slight justification for Surrealism as a demolisher of the few remaining literary taboos. Theodor W. Adorno, a modish German critic whom I do not much admire, may be right when he describes Surrealism as a movement "where art batters down art." In any case, good or bad, useful or useless, Surrealism did its job and there is nothing—repeat nothing—that epigones like Handke can add to it. Once the novelty of the non sequitur has worn off, once the thrill of nonsense images—in this case, for example, a group of people chanting out, in barbershop harmony, "Oh, let the drawer be stuck!" over and over again—has worn thin (if nothingness can be said to wear thin), there is no point in the enterprise. Surrealism has smashed the last remaining window panes; what's the point of throwing stones at empty frames?

The point is the pretentiousness and pusillanimity of contemporary criticism which sanctions such claptrap. Read, for example, Clive Barnes's review of *The Ride* in the *Times* of January 14. He goes to great lengths to say that he did not understand a word of the play from the very beginning but hastens to add that he was "oddly, compulsively interested." And he concludes, "Yet the inconsequentiality had a certain weight of consequentiality about it. It could be a fraud . . . but I suspect that Mr. Handke is too clever a writer, and too ingenious a man, to have perpetrated a fraud." In other words, if the Emperor rides through town naked, all he has to do is advertise that his nakedness was designed by Pierre Cardin or Bill Blass, and all is forgiven. "A hole dug by Oldenburg is not just a hole," say his exegetes. I agree: it is also a major, swinish imposture.

THERE'S ONE IN EVERY MARRIAGE, which comes to us from Canada, is farce as it wants to, dreams to, demands to be written. It is an Englishing of *Le Dindon* by Georges Feydeau, whom Eric Bentley called "possibly the greatest writer of farce of any country at any time." The plot of this, as of most, Feydeau plays is adultery: alleged, feigned, imaginary or remembered adultery—always past, future or potential, and always averted in the nick of time. Feydeau can make out of the contemplation and plotting of adultery the most elaborately architectonic structures, with schemes and counterschemes stacked up on top of one another as in a prodigious card castle, until one bottom card is pulled out by coincidence, dramaturgy or Fate, and the whole thing comes cascading down into respectable everyday solidity.

But until this collapse into conventionality, what intrigues, cross purposes, misunderstandings and mismatings! What all-but-real human grotesques; what penetrating, barely oversimplified *aperçus;* what terrible comic truths! The basic subject is the intoxicating delusion of deviltry, the grand fantasies of philandering, the Casanova and Messalina complexes with which a good little bourgeois society tries to leaven the dough of fidelity. And neatly arranged around this central theme are innumerable human foibles affectionately but unblinkingly lampooned. The structure of it is as intricate, multifarious and precise as the Taj Mahal.

In this Stratford National Theater of Canada production, the play is fetchingly adapted by Suzanne Grossmann and Paxton Whitehead, joyously staged by Jean Gascon, and designed with witty *outrecuidance* by Alan Barlow. Not all the performances are up to the commandingly saw-toothed vocalizing of Roberta Maxwell, the Olympianly blustering doltishness of Tony van Bridge, or the oozingly relaxed slatternliness of Patricia Gage; but Richard Curnock and Peter Donat have some magisterial moments in two of the key roles, and several other performers are not to be sneezed at either. Indeed, it is only Jack Creeley's unconvincing show of virility, and the dullness of Tudi Wiggins and Joseph Maher that cast passing shadows on the proceedings. Otherwise, it is all a lambently innocent orgy of laughter, beautifully lighted by Gil Wechsler and illuminated by the finest French *esprit*. Only one other Frenchman, an exact contemporary of Feydeau's, could have made it funnier: Georges Courteline. But then it would have been comedy, not farce.

ROBERT BOLT IS an eminently reasonable man: a former schoolmaster, he remains a literary pedagogue, in the best sense of the word. The introduction to his new play *Vivat! Vivat Regina!* is a humane, sensible, downright moving essay about theater, history, art and life today, and how all these matters interrelate. I wish this admirable introduction were widely read. I even wish it could be performed in preference to the play that anticlimactically follows it.

Bolt has had one deserved success in the theater with *A Man for All Seasons*, whose circumspect protagonist, Sir Thomas More, was, to some extent in reality and to a greater one in Bolt's play, a schoolmasterly hero: a champion of realistic prudence rather than headlong heroism, a just and reasonable man whose one mistake was to believe in the power of a rational law to keep irrational monarchs in check. This protagonist was your very best kind of Oxbridge don, and around him the stage became an embattled senior common room, rather as in a C. P. Snow novel, only better. It was history writ small, but in a fine, cursive hand, neat and purposive.

With *Vivat! Vivat Regina!*, however, Bolt is in trouble. He has two decentralizing heroines here, Mary Stuart and Elizabeth I, who, moreover, never meet; and almost three decades in the histories of two countries to cover. Being an honest teacher, he wishes to tell the truth, at least insofar as it can be reconciled with the invention and pruning required by the play form. He does not want to cheat like Schiller, who manhandles history for the sake of drama, highly moral drama at that; nor does he want to compete with Schiller's majestic *Mary Stuart,* and so must go out of his way to emphasize what Schiller didn't, and vice versa. This is the death blow to Bolt's dramaturgy: not only does his play lose itself in pageantlike scope and the Keystone Kops tempo with which it gallops through time and space, it also denies itself such great and natural climaxes as Mary's tragic end, which is reduced to two gestures, one epigram and one apothegm. Drama in farce-time, history as speeded-up cinematography.

The writing, despite its somewhat bastardized diction, is respectable enough, though lacking in any special distinction. There are no long speeches and most of the dialogue is stichomythic, crisp and sometimes witty; but just as the play lacks focus, the words lack poetic power. Besides providing a painless history lesson on a propaedeutic level, the play serves mostly to convince people of average, humdrum lives that the great and mighty pay dearly for their greatness and might. This being a lesson that the public is only too predisposed to embrace (the mediocre having all along found it a soothing poultice for their mediocrity), the play's didactic value seems to me no greater than its poetic.

The New York production is serviceable on the whole, faithfully mirroring the work's exemplary mediocrity. For some reason it follows the earlier Chichester version of Bolt's text, rather than the revised London one, but my only major discomfort came from the accents. The opening scene, in France, is played in bad, musical-comedy Gallic singsong, which even makes some of Claire Bloom's lines incomprehensible. And why Mary cannot lose her French accent after years in Scotland is quite beyond me. In the Scottish scenes, garish pseudo-Lallans croakings cling like burrs to the actors' speech. The worst offender is Alexander Scourby, whose John Knox is straight from the Bronx Highlands.

But Peter Dews's direction moves swiftly and lucidly, though without compelling imagination, and Eileen Atkins' Elizabeth is wonderfully tart, pawky, consistent underneath her neurotic variousness; I just wish she did not make the learned, polyglot queen sound a trifle plebeian. Miss Bloom is as keen, capricious, exalted and sensual as required, and it is probably the play's fault if she does not add up to a fully touchable, tastable, smellable Mary. Douglas Rain's Cecil is fine until he becomes repetitious, Lee Richardson's Bothwell is amusing as well as formidable, and Peter Coffield invests the sketchily written Darnley with dignified pathos. The others were mostly adequate, except for Scourby's jocular Knox and Robert Elston's utterly inept Leicester. Is it merely from doing Van Heusen commercials that Elston has become an overstarched shirt with nothing in it? Carl Toms's sets are functional but pedestrian, his costumes a good deal better. But both as spectacle and as writing, how very much finer was Schiller's *Mary Stuart* at Lincoln Center earlier this season, to which Bolt's play might have served as prologue.

GREASE is an *objet trouvé*, just like a toilet bowl displayed at a Dadaist art show. Yes, it is funny, this musical about the carryings-on at a typical high school in 1959, when rock-'n'-roll was in its infancy, having leapt, more or less ready-made, from the pelvis of Elvis Presley. Most creatures, including even the human, are adorable in their infancy, but rock-'n'-roll was a little beast that looked merely ludicrous. It had a duck's tail on its nape, a head and torso that kept up a perpendicular wobble like a worrybird's, pipestem legs that shook from a chronic birth trauma, and it made absolutely hideous noises both with its mouth and with its instruments. Rather like the amphisbaena, its behind was indistinguishable from its head, which may have been just another, less developed butt.

What *Grease* is good at is mimicry. Either by faithful reproduction or by the slightest of exaggerations, the show manages to be a compendium of the wails, wiggles and witlessness of the fatuous fifties. And the curious thing is that all fatuity—when, as it were, put behind glass—is funny. All, that is, except the current model. Funny as some of the things onstage were, I was almost more amused by the garish hair, horrendous gladrags and outlandish pseudo (or genuine) transvestism that constituted the façades and charades of the first-night audience. How many of them, I wonder, saw themselves faithfully reproduced on a stage a dozen or so years hence, and eliciting everything from tintinnabulant titters to booming belly laughs in an audience bedizened in future fatuity?

But I suppose they would not mind being tomorrow's laughing-stocks any more than today's *succès de scandale*, as long as they can be the centers of ill-gotten attention. Anyway, at the appropriately named Eden Theater, across the gap of scarcely more than a decade, two outrageousnesses were noisily flirting with each other. *Grease* is the *Jesus Christ Superstar* of the post-under-thirties or the *No, No, Nanette* of the presenescent, whichever way you want to look at it. Its book is total nullity, and should, if this were not an act of redundancy, be ignored. But its music and lyrics are often fraught with demented fun, especially in numbers like "It's Raining on Prom Night" and "Beauty School Dropout." Better yet are the hair styles by Jim Sullivan, and the Douglas W. Schmidt and Carrie F. Robbins sets and costumes, whose limitations are surely not their designers', only the budget's.

Although Tom Moore has staged this Warren Casey-Jim Jacobs musical without particular distinction, the choreography by Patricia Birch is the dazzling jewel in the toad's head. Slowly but surely, Miss Birch has evolved from a charming dancer into a vital and inventive choreographer: *You're a Good Man, Charlie Brown, The Me Nobody Knows*, and now *Grease* mark her *gradus ad Parnassum*. If the show is remembered for anything, it will be for her dances and dance movements during the song numbers. In all of these, preposterousness is piled on preposterousness—but always with a fine period sense—until the whole thing resembles a mighty pyramid standing, nay, dancing on its head. Among the performers, Carole Demas, Barry Bostwick, Adrienne Barbeau, Timothy Meyers, Jim Borelli and Alan Paul seemed especially worthy, but the whole event can be enjoyed as a raucous joke that, alas, wears thinner as it chortles along.

THE REASON Sean O'Casey's masterpiece, *The Plough and the Stars,* is never done hereabouts, whereas his first-produced and much less worthy play, *Shadow of a Gunman,* is revived from time to time, is simple and sad: *Plough* requires four sets, *Gunman* only one. And so *Shadow of a Gunman* it is again, now that violence in Ireland is again front-page news, and O'Casey's prophetic relevance can be presumed to excuse a poor production.

After the Abbey had turned down a few of O'Casey's firstling efforts, the playwright was advised by Lady Gregory, "Mr. O'Casey, your gift is characterization." Though this was sound counsel, O'Casey at first heeded it too well. Accordingly, *Gunman* is almost all characterization—or, to be precise, an unending parade of characters popping in to do a comic turn and promptly dropping into oblivion —but no plot, no development, no thrusting into the depths. If the play can be saved, it is only through all-encompassing ensemble acting that holds together these wandering potsherds; and through atmosphere—getting the brogues, the lilt, the language to poeticize and unify this rogue's gallery in play form.

But the language here is even worse than the acting, ranging from pure Americana to concoctions whose origin is more mysterious than Cuchulain's. Some of these performers must have looked up the wrong definition of "brogue," and promptly put their foot in it. Most peculiar was the lingo of Estelle Omens, the kind of Irish seldom heard outside the Warsaw ghetto. In this respect, only Bernard Frawley sounded right as the timid Mr. Gallagher, and coincidentally or not, gave the best performance. Still, Jacqueline Coslow was a likable and, in the main, believable Minnie, and Paddy Croft, while overdoing both her Irish and her histrionics, was quite amusing nevertheless. But, oh, the leads! Leon Russom, playing the poet mistaken for a gunman, did not strike me as mistakable for either a gunman or a poet—or even an actor: dullness never had more fitting monument. John Heffernan, who also co-produced, was merely irritating in the juicy part of the cowardly peddler. Heffernan used to be an interesting actor whose work was marred by mannerism; now fidgets have irreversibly gained the upper hand.

Philip Minor has directed pedestrianly, and there are moments when the footwork gets out of control: Miss Omens, for example, is permitted to do a whole jig where a little standing pat would work wonders. Lloyd Burlingame's set is uninventive, but at least it does not move around for no good reason. Eileen O'Casey, Sean's widow, charitably remarked about the equally messy Actors Studio production of *Gunman* that a good play "can be acted in several different styles." But surely not all at once.

MOSES GUNN, as Orsino, stalks onto the Vivian Beaumont stage and delivers the famous opening line, "If music be the food of love, play on," and *Twelfth Night* is lost. Until then I was rapt in admiration for the set conceived by Ellis Rabb, the director, and Douglas W. Schmidt, the designer. The vast stage is laid bare and curtained and carpeted with the same unending, circular blue—the blue of Romantic yearning, set here in some legendary Persia of the miniatures blown up to human, or slightly superhuman, size. Fat, sassy stars are twinkling in low and heavy clusters; suddenly, from under and behind them, a happy phalanx of merrily outlandish masquers invades the scene. And then Gunn has to open his mouth and spoil everything with his characteristic mixture of croak and quaver, establishing within the scope of a single line four depressing truths.

First, that he mouths words without the slightest apprehension of their meaning; second, that his vocal cords are among the most unstrung on the American stage; third, that the reviewers who have claimed that he is the finest black actor in our theater must be out of their minds; and fourth, that casting a black in a white Shakespearean role is a hopeless proposition. Let the liberals rant to their bleeding hearts' content, a black does not work as Orsino, even if you turn Illyria into some kind of overexposed Persia, with double inconsistency: Persians are not black; still less, like these Iranian Illyrians, are they indiscriminately either black or white. Neither the looks nor the sounds of a black actor fit in with the logic of the plot or the rhythms and tonalities of the language—historical significance, psychological credibility, appropriate speech melody, all is forfeit. Just imagine an all-black play by Jones or Bullins cast half with defiantly white actors!

But all of this is supposing that the black actor is doing a good job. Not so here. Gunn's stare is empty, or his eyeballs roll around wildly; on top of a short, stiff neck, the head is cocked absurdly; the movements lack even a barbaric fascination. Then, with the vowels emerging sticky, quailing and muffled, you begin to wonder whether music is not indeed some kind of food—mush, for example—that Gunn's mouth is full of. And the other blacks in the cast are worse yet. A colleague of mine has already correctly identified Cynthia Belgrave's Maria as pure Butterfly McQueen, a black stereotype well worth avoiding. On top of this, Miss Belgrave is an agonizingly limited and crudely unappealing actress. Much of the time her squawkings remain indecipherable, in which respect she is surpassed only by the black Fabian of Harold Miller, a performance almost totally lacking in intelligibility, never mind grace or minimal polish.

This is not to say that all is well among the white actors. Blythe Danner is a charming Viola: her poetic climaxes are somewhat short-changed, but she has such honesty, verve, innocence and unstinting involvement, such true girlishness submerged in such believable boyishness when she becomes Cesario, that one barely notices the lack of some ultimate lyricism. Martha Henry is a technically strong actress, intelligent and womanly; why, then, is her Olivia an unful-filled performance? She has been given a most unbecoming wig or hairdo, some unfetching costumes, and has been, in part, directed for crass farce. Though she can flit springily on elegant bare feet (as I vividly recall from her Stratford, Ontario, Miranda a decade ago), she alone among the unshod females in the cast must wear clodhop-perish sandals. But all this is only a part of it; something vibrant and captivating curled up inside Miss Henry is never unclenched.

Leonard Frey, even if not quite right for the part or the period, does many droll and winning things as Aguecheek. René Auberjonois' Malvolio lacks the initial weight and gravity to make his subsequent fall appear ludicrous and pathetic enough without having to resort to farcical exaggeration. Still, there is technical glitter here, and as much as can be done without truly feeling the part. But in the crucial role of Feste, George Pentecost exudes a gray superficiality, a snide unloveliness that is neither humane, nor witty, nor genuinely cerebral; even though it is proficiently enough tossed off, this clowning neither touches nor delights us. Pentecost's singing, incidentally, seems better than his acting.

Nothing good, however, can be said for Sydney Walker's dismally routine Sir Toby, or for Stephen McHattie's clod of a Sebastian—how could he ever be mistaken for his flavorous and frolicsome sister? The others manage to make their small parts look even smaller. And why should Curio, patently a man, be played by a woman?

Rabb's direction is helter-skelter. To make the long entrances and exits on the large open stage faster, the actors leave and enter in whipped-up canters or gallops; they then arrive in an Illyria before the invention of the chair (such is Rabb's empty-stage concept) where no one properly sits, although some perch occasionally on a semicircular ramp. This doesn't bother Rabb, who, as I recall from his largely recumbent performance as Hamlet, likes nothing better than the floor; accordingly, everybody sooner or later flops down or sprawls out, as if Illyria were hit by an epidemic of sleeping sickness. There are other oddities: the idea of putting Malvolio into a bird cage is not even for the birds, since the cage keeps malfunctioning. Cathy MacDonald's music starts pleasantly but quickly descends into the lower reaches of show-biz; Ann Roth's costumes are hit-or-miss affairs. Only Schmidt's scenery and John Gleason's lighting remain steadily bright.

ED BULLINS' *The Duplex* was brought by the playwright and his chosen director, Gilbert Moses, to Jules Irving for his Forum Theater; shortly before the play was to open, and without having seen a run-through, Bullins sent out a blast to the *Times* about how his serious play was being changed into a coon show—that the production turned a *Lower Depths* into a *Pal Joey*. Other Bullins broadsides were dispatched in various directions, and thunderbolts were hurled at all but Gilbert Moses, who, after all, is black. Yet if debasement there was, surely it would have had to be his doing.

Bullins could have stopped the show from opening, but that clearly was not his intention. Rather, he wanted to have it both ways: be the scourge of white Establishment theater verbally, while cashing in on it financially and in prestige. As of this writing, he has refused to see the production despite warm invitations; he continues to have his hate and eat it too. All these maneuvers would be less deplorable if there were anything seriously wrong with Moses' direction, or anything seriously right about the play itself.

The Duplex is part of a cycle of twenty plays. I can only hope that future installments, or such past ones as I have missed, achieve more. For this is mere commercial theater, rather slow and faltering in the first two acts, quite slick in the second two, and brought to a sudden end without much of a resolution. It is, to be sure, *black* commercial theater, which in these confused times easily passes for art in both black and white circles. To me, it looks like second-rate William Inge, with the significant difference that Inge would not have required two acts for the kind of exposition that two scenes could have taken care of.

The play concerns two roommates in the sublet half of a Southern California duplex during the early sixties. Marco is good-looking, frivolous and cynical; Steve is sensitive, studious, literary and of course modeled on the author. Marco and his friends mostly drink, play cards and wench; Steve has a serious, troubled love affair with Velma, his middle-aged landlady, an unhappy wife whose shiftless husband, O.D., keeps beating her up, taking away her money, occasionally raping her, and living with a younger woman. There are various friends, neighbors and more or less footloose females who weave in and out, and the second-movement curtain (Bullins calls his acts "movements") comes down on three couples copulating in unison. There is a wearisome elderly couple from next door who keep butting in for purposes of ponderous comedy, and provide unrelieved stretches of comedy relief. Things get pretty hairy between Steve and O.D., whom Velma, in the last analysis, can't stop loving; all of a sudden, the play is over as unexpectedly and brusquely as it rattled along interminably until then.

There is nothing embarrassingly bad or unendurable about the play—with the possible exception of some of the old woman's maunderings; but neither its insight nor its language, neither its dramaturgy nor its perspective, is in any sustained way compelling. Its laughter is routine, and its poignancies, with one or two exceptions, are perfunctory. Yet there is a smooth functionalism about its better parts that is certainly less amateurish than what we have to sit through in a play like *Night Watch*. The chief virtue of Bullins' work is that black audiences can doubtless identify themselves with it wholeheartedly—as the black part of the opening-night audience noisily did—but here hides a danger. Recognition of yourself up there on the boards is not the end-all of art, at best the beginning. It is understandably satisfying for the audience of an emergent theater to see itself raised to the heights of the stage, with the social and cultural importance this implies. But for the work to become art, it must take the audience beyond mere self-recognition, identification with mirror images. It must do, say, envision things that in some profound sense have never been done, said, envisioned before, and this *The Duplex,* in terms other than its negritude, fails to do. It is all basic minimums. If drama-turgy were cobblery, you might say that *The Duplex* does not rise above the sole—though it does undeniably have plenty of sole.

Gilbert Moses has staged the play with prestidigitation only occa-sionally smacking of glibness. The four song numbers that some re-viewers took to be his interpolations are of course Bullins' own; they do not contribute anything much, especially as the lyrics tend to get slurred. Moses makes one serious error, though: he does not respect the "roomness" of the separate rooms suggested by the set; instead, people see, talk and even walk through walls, which is disturbing in an essentially realistic work. The acting is uneven, throwing together finished performances with what seems to be first stabs or final fiascos. Kert Lundell's set appropriately marries Southern California blatancy to low-budget flimsiness, and features some of the most aggressively phallic flowers that ever bloomed in plastic. It is refresh-ing to see a black play not take white-baiting for its principal theme or tone, but what Bullins has substituted lacks even the impact of some of his earlier agit-prop offerings.

SPRING, 1972

OLD TIMES
by Harold Pinter

THE SCREENS
by Jean Genet

STICKS AND BONES
by David Rabe

FINGERNAILS BLUE AS FLOWERS
by Ronald Ribman

LAKE OF THE WOODS
by Steve Tesich

A FUNNY THING HAPPENED
ON THE WAY TO THE FORUM
book by Burt Shevelove and Larry Gelbart
music and lyrics by Stephen Sondheim

SMALL CRAFT WARNINGS
by Tennessee Williams

SUGAR
book by Peter Stone
music by Jule Styne
lyrics by Bob Merrill

Captain Brassbound's Conversion
by George Bernard Shaw

Lost in the Stars
book by Maxwell Anderson
music by Kurt Weill
lyrics by Maxwell Anderson

The Real Inspector Hound
by Tom Stoppard

The Crucible
by Arthur Miller

Two established contemporary dramatists have recently had their latest works produced here. Typically, Harold Pinter's *Old Times* had the shortest of waits before arriving on Broadway in an important deluxe production; Jean Genet's *The Screens* had to wait a decade before being put on for a few performances by The Chelsea Theater Center of Brooklyn in an inadequate ambience and with a domestic and rather obscure cast. I find both these playwrights overrated, but at least in Genet there lurks a genuine poet, even a dramatic poet, who unfortunately cannot shake off the pederast and criminal he has to carry with him as ballast. In Pinter, I see only a clever ex-actor turned playwright full of surface theatricality underneath which resides a big, bulging zero. But Pinter knows how to make his nothingness look portentous, whereas Genet undercuts his strongest linguistic and visual gifts by yielding ostentatiously to his aberrant impulses.

Old Times is even emptier than the usual Pinter product. There has, in the past, been an aura of glittering sinisterness around his work, which people could equate with some inscrutable anguish or horror festering at the heart of existence—or whatever phrase best dignified the hollowness at the core of Pinter's plays. But here we have Deeley, who says he is a film maker, and his wife Kate, living in an elegantly converted English farmhouse, and both characters

and place are too tidily slicked down to generate unclassifiable anxieties. The pair talk, or rather muse, about Anna, who was Kate's
roommate twenty years ago, then married a rich and eminent Italian,
and is about to return on a first visit. She is seen during this conversation with her back to us, immobile in the upstage shadows. Presently she joins the couple, and the rest of the play is the customary Pinterian battle of wits in which words are devious and indis-
tinctly allusive: precise about odd, irrelevant details, but reticent and
evasive about anything essential. The purpose is to entice the other
person into some sort of damaging self-revelation and manipulate him
or her into moral and physical subservience. For example, if A asks
B about C, "Is he away for long periods?" the answer is, "I think
sometimes. Are you?" By taking "to be away" in a figurative rather
than literal sense, the answerer has presumably made the questioner
feel ridiculed, humiliated, bested. But we may well wonder what sort
of gain this is: is there any real victory here, and at what? A parlor
game, at best.

We care neither about the characters nor about the issues. It appears that there may have been a lesbian relationship between the
two women when they were roommates. There also seems to have
existed a struggle for dominance between them, and perhaps an exchange of identities, which manifested itself in Anna's stealing Kate's
underwear. Deeley and Kate met in a suburban cinema where both of
them were seeing, apparently for the first time, *Odd Man Out,* after
which they struck up a conversation; later it emerges that Kate and
Anna had seen the film together beforehand. It emerges also that
at a party, Deeley once stared up the skirt of a woman wearing his
future wife's underwear—Anna, one presumes. There may, in fact,
have been something between him and Anna, and Kate may have
married him on the rebound, after she was rejected by Anna. And
so on, through a set of imperfectly remembered or wishfully imagined
incidents. What is Anna up to now? Has she come to reclaim Kate?
Or would she rather snatch Deeley from her? Or does she intend
to subjugate both?

But of what consequence are these shadowboxing shadows? Why
should anyone give a tinker's damn about such nebulous figures with
wispy, indefinable, and probably illusory problems? Memory and
oblivion, at any rate, do not work in this way. Typically, someone
will declare, "I was interested once in the arts, but I can't remember which ones they were." This gets a cheap laugh out of an absurdity that has no bearing on human reality. You might say that

Pinter is not trying to write realistic dialogue. Yet even if absurd, or absurdist, the statement must have some human relevance. The joke here is purely verbal, based on the fact that "arts" is a plural noun, requiring that pronominal "they" that, in this context, falls estrangingly, comically on our ears. If the line were deprived of its grammatical idiosyncrasy and ran, "I had an artistic interest once, but I can't remember what it was," most of the humor would be gone, and most of the pseudomeaningfulness as well. Now, when Beckett's Estragon answers Vladimir's question about what to do while they are waiting with, "What about hanging ourselves?" the remark is certainly absurdist, and part of the humor surely lies in the casual formulation of so dread a notion. Yet there is a human truth in this: people have been known to kill themselves out of sheer frustrating ennui. But no one who once dabbled in poetry or was a concert- or museum-goer forgets this—ever. Or consider the moment in *The Importance of Being Earnest*—as antirealist, antinaturalist or absurdist a play as you might ask for—when Algernon tries to see Cecily's diary. "Oh no," she exclaims; "you see, it is simply a very young girl's record of her own thoughts and impressions, and consequently meant for publication. When it appears in volume form I hope you will order a copy." On the face of it, this is simply an absurd, funny paradox. Forthwith, however, three shocking truths emerge: 1) A young girl's private life is really a highly marketable commodity; 2) The modest young lady herself is the first to wish to exploit it; 3) The young man she loves and wishes to marry is to be her first paying customer. Though you may dispute the exact amount of truth in Wilde's cynicism, the proposition holds at least as a queasy human possibility; Pinter's joke is just a quibble on words.

Worse than that, *Old Times* suffers from what I can only call spiritual shallowness. It is of the greatest possible unimportance with whom one of these figurines spouting dim witticisms or pregnant silences (false pregnancies, as I once called them) has slept, is sleeping or will sleep. In a good bedroom farce, the problem becomes one of stratagems and timing, of dramaturgy becoming geometry, of plotting becoming the cogs of a complicated, fascinating clockwork. In a decent comedy, we get involved with the people and so care about how they bed down. But here it is merely a question of ascendancies among puppets; we might as soon care about which horse on a merry-go-round will come to a halt ahead of another. When, in the second act, the scene shifts to the bedroom of the cottage, Deeley explains the furnishings to Anna: "The good thing about these beds is that they are susceptible to any amount of permutation . . . It's the casters that make all this possible." What is the point or joke? That by means of harmless-sounding badinage Deeley is trying to generate an atmosphere of seductive sexual innuendo—*ménage à trois,* perversion, orgies. Any hack farce writer can do as much.

But what about the language? Pinterites will ask. Well, what about it? Like Albee, Pinter is linguistically *nouveau riche.* Anna uses the word "lest" and Deeley is startled: "The word 'lest.' I haven't heard it in a long time." Later, there is a similar reaction: "Gaze?" "The word 'gaze.' You don't hear it very often." Accordingly, we get a certain overwriting whose verbosity is supposed to impress the audience as much as the dramatis personae; it may take any form from euphuism to bureaucratic jargon. While Kate is taking a bath, Deeley expatiates to Anna: "She gives herself a very good scrub, but can she, with the same efficiency, give herself a good rub? . . . I have not found this to be the case . . ." The purpose, again, is to create an aura of enticing sexuality for three (i.e., Which one of us gets to dry that lovely body we both desire? Couldn't we perhaps do it together?), but the mock-serious grandiloquence about trivia is again only a verbal trick, not worthy of being—as, alas, it is—one of the comic mainstays of Pinter's oeuvre.

There is also something rather pitiful about a sixty-minute play like *Old Times* being stretched by means of those Pinter pauses to a little over seventy; then, furbished with a twenty-minute inter-mission, being peddled as a full-length two-act play. It is interesting to note, by the way, how our full-length dramas have shrunk from the five acts of the Renaissance to the four of the romantics and earlier realists, then to the three acts of most twentieth-century theater un-til, most recently, the two-acter became prevalent. But at least *Waiting for Godot* is an honest two-act play, not, like *Old Times,* a one-acter with delusions of grandeur and genuine *longueurs.* There comes a point when the paying customer can feel swindled, and a nonpay-ing critic no less so; this is the sort of play one used to feel entitled to getting two or three of per evening. It is as if Pinter had come to a party dressed in nothing but a pair of shorts, which, quite aside from the quality of the shorts, is not really sufficient attire.

But the playwright is lucky in his associates. Peter Hall knows how to stage these plays so that they assume a semblance of mean-ing. He gets from the actors all kinds of rubatos, crescendos, dimin-uendos, overtones and soft-pedalings; he works out effects of move-ment in space worthy of a kinetic sculptor, of light and shadow to do an old Dutch master proud. John Bury executes the lighting plot as if it were a grand conspiracy (which it is), and designs his dependably brilliant sets—in this case, sparse modern furniture arranged somewhat bizarrely, proportioned a little discordantly, and surrounded with rather more space than customary. The colors, too, are a mite too coolly understated; the floor is raked; the walls given exaggerated foreshortening, so that our eye is fed more perspective than is its regular diet; one corner of the acting surface protrudes disquietingly from behind the curtain. The total effect is a refined malaise, as in those puzzle drawings where we are told that something is wrong, but are hard put to track it down. This is the exact visual equivalent of Pinter's dramaturgy, and is managed rather better by the designer than by the author. The acting is not the very best British acting, but a more than acceptable second best: Robert Shaw seems a bit unduly mechanistic at times, Mary Ure uses her voice a bit too much like a Yo-Yo, and Rosemary Harris turns Anna into someone a trifle more smug than mysterious.

"Listen, what silence!" we are told at the very beginning of the play, and I suppose the strongest pleas on behalf of Pinter are based on his supposedly innovative use of silence. Very well, I grant Pinter the title of Grand Pauseur, but actually Jean-Jacques Bernard started a school of playwriting known as *l'école du silence* in the early twenties, in which the characters revealed themselves more through their silences than through their words. But these were, so to speak, communicative silences, and a character like the eponymous Martine (1922) bared her soul by means of what she did not say. Pinter's silences are as stingy as his words: both withhold rather than impart things. But this lack of generosity is indispensable to Pinter, precisely because he has nothing to say. In any case, the value of silence is greater to poetry than to drama because it can be put to more spectacular use within or against a metrical structure than in the looser aggregate of prose, where it stands in less clear contrast to its surroundings. Poetry, moreover, is sound appropriately framed by silence, but theater is also action and interplay not necessarily suited to such framing and apt to get lost in lacunae. With his mania for silences, Pinter is to drama what John Cage is to music and Ad Reinhardt to painting. It might be called a case of premature silence. All true art finally abuts on the ineffable, where there is nothing left but stillness, meditation and awe; but putting the silence before the words (or tones, or colors and shapes) is no better than putting the cart before the horse.

.　.　.

QUITE THE OPPOSITE problems confront us with Genet's *The Screens*. Here was a work which, with one intermission, lasted about five hours, and the first trouble was that, so far from getting too little, we were getting too much. There are seventeen scenes in the play, which Genet wanted performed outdoors on four levels, the highest of them representing eternity and the afterlife. The plot ostensibly concerns Algeria and its fight for independence; the real theme, however, is yet another exaltation of evil, a celebration of the elegance of vice. "It's not the meek shall inherit the earth," we learn, "but the abject and the vile." Accordingly, the hero is Saïd, a poor thief, who can obtain in marriage only Leïla, the ugliest girl of all. Their relationship is sheer sadomasochist love-hate, and Saïd, in the war, turns traitor so as to experience abjection beyond that of prison, which even Leïla, turned thief to share his fate, could attain to. Executed by his own people, Saïd is an outcast of sorts even in the realm of the dead; Leïla, though no longer alive, never even makes it to the other world. Saïd's mother, a garbage-collector who hates and is hated by people, becomes a heroine by mistake; Warda, a whore and a bawd, complains: "At the butcher's and the grocer's women say hello to me. I am less and less a somebody."

If the trouble with Pinter is that underneath his portentous pose we sense utter emptiness, the trouble with Genet is that though he says a mouthful, often with great poetic gusto (albeit with prolixity and repetitiousness), it happens to be something that most of us cannot accept. As much as any playwright, Genet represents for me the problem of how to come to terms with a work whose content—yes, content in the outmoded, discredited sense of something that might just refuse to become blithely identical with form—I can neither accept nor even feel much sympathy for. Interestingly enough, Genet himself makes fun in *The Screens* of another playwright who presents a similar difficulty, when he has one of the *colons* describe the ideal slave state with "thousands of Moslem boys reciting Claudel in the original." Claudel, too, could rise to great heights of poetic drama, although I (like Genet, obviously) find his message of Catholic asceticism based on self-denial repellent. But is the paean to self-sacrifice perhaps a fraction more endurable than the extolling of evil and rhapsodizing about dirt? Claudel's figures are mostly self-destructive, whereas Genet's upside-down utopia is a threat to everything I stand for.

In some ways, Genet rather resembles Oscar Wilde—is, in fact, a Wilde whose paradoxes dare speak their name. It would probably be

quite fruitful (no pun intended) to make a study of the relationship of the paradox to homosexual drama (Cocteau, Stein, Joe Orton come immediately to mind): a distinct relation seems to exist
between sexual inversion and the inversion of values as embodied in
the paradox. "At bottom, all ways are alike," says Saïd, and at bottom this may be true, but not necessarily elsewhere. *The Screens* is
called, in French, *Les Paravents*, and I sat there wondering whether
Les Par-derrières would not have been a more fitting title. Otherwise, however, the play is often extremely witty, its language almost
always charged with poetry. There are frequent irrelevancies and
dawdlings, but our flagging interest is always revived and never allowed to conk out during this endless, sticky, mazy, maddening marathon of a play. Sometimes it is the satirizing of the *colons,* sometimes the vertiginous involutions of intimate relationships; at other
times, it is the lowlife comedy of whores and thieves, or the serenely
cynical vision of the dead that delights us. I suspect that the pederastic view of the French army could have been good for a few raucous laughs too, had John Granger, who played the Lieutenant, been
better. What really captures the imagination is the flaring up of verbal and visual images, of scenic devices like that of natives hastily
painting conflagrations on screens while down front the European
landowner prattles and postures on and on. Genet gives us pure and
ardent sarcasm, fury blown as deftly and exquisitely as Venetian glass.

Minos Volanakis is credited with the translation, and it is hard to
believe that a Greek who has been working in England could come
up with such racily idiomatic American talk, but however this came
about, it was splendid. Volanakis' staging was equally good, allowing for the limitations of the small, shabby box that is the theater on
the fourth floor of the Brooklyn Academy of Music, and of a pick-up
cast that was considerably less than stellar. But among these forty-
three or forty-four actors (counts differ) playing as many as five or
six different parts, the level of performing managed to be surprisingly
far from contemptible. There were weak performances, to be sure,
notably that of Robert Jackson, who made Saïd into a hysterical eccentric: a fidgety eel who did not change in the course of the action
except to become shriller and more hysterical. Several performances
were stereotypes, especially Despo's Kadidja, but at least one had real
stature: Julie Bovasso's Mother. It is regrettable that Miss Bovasso
wastes much of her time and energy on writing godforsaken plays,
when she can give such stylish, slightly mannered but shrewdly insinuating performances as this. The effective costumes of Willa Kim

and the unassumingly inventive stage design of Robert Mitchell aided the general effort handsomely; The Chelsea Theater Center of Brooklyn is becoming more and more professional in the finest sense.

THE TWO OTHER recent theatrical events of distinction and good augury also took place off-Broadway. Both were second plays confirming the gifts of their young authors. At the Public Theater, Joseph Papp, while still showing *The Basic Training of Pavlo Hummel*, mounted another play by David Rabe, *Sticks and Bones*. This, though written before the very fine *Pavlo*, was revised subsequently, so that it is both an earlier and a later play. While in *Pavlo* Rabe considered the effect of the Vietnam war on its participants, in *Sticks and Bones* he examines the disasters of the home front. A Vietnam veteran, David, comes back blind to his silent-American family—parents and a brother—who manages to be far blinder than he. Their names derive from television: Ozzie, Harriet and younger brother Rick; it is Rabe's double nelson on America. The protagonist tries to convey to his kin the horrors of war, but Ozzie is lost in bittersweet dreams of what he might have become, and bitter anxieties about the frustrated life he leads. Harriet is merely plying her family with her cookery, her beloved Father Donald (the family confessor), and friendly, homespun platitudes. As for Rick, he is a domesticated dropout, dispensing robotlike pieties to his parents, gulping down their food, and for the rest concentrating on his guitar and the seduction of not-too-nice girls. At first, the family cannot accept David's blindness; later, they cannot tolerate what he keeps seeing with his mind's eye. Neither by persuasive eloquence nor by shock tactics can he penetrate their carapace of obtuseness; when they summon the smarmily unorthodox Father Donald to cure him, David finally sets on him with his blind man's cane. In the end, the family prevails with a stratagem that may push black comedy a little too far: they provide David with a razor and basin and make him slit one of his wrists. While he bleeds to death, they settle down to their chattily pointless daily existence.

The play functions on three levels. There is a kind of heightened realism much striven for by Arthur Miller, but more successfully managed by Rabe. Here, for example, belong Ozzie's reminiscences about the great runner he once was (with a double entendre no doubt implied), and his repeated references to Hank, a friend we never see, whose archetypal American values and success drive Ozzie to admiration, envy and despair. Here, too, belong the outbursts of vindictiveness and castration that flash forth from beneath Harriet's placid kitchen-and-church surface. The next level is that of adroit black comedy (except for that final scene), and includes Rick's larger-than-life stupidity, Father Donald's supposedly enlightened obscurantism, and any number of ferociously funny scenes and speeches. Lastly, there is a level intended to be pure poetry for David's scenes of painful self-searching and despair at his family; here the writing fails to rise to its intentions: "And then I knew that I was not awake but asleep, and in my sleep there was nothing and nothing"; or "The seasons will amaze . . . Texas is enormous; Ohio is sometimes green." Most disturbingly, the transitions between any two of these three modes are at times precipitous and jarring. And Rabe is youthfully prodigal of good ideas insufficiently worked out: he brings the Vietnamese girl David left behind onstage as a ghostly image that follows David around fitfully; except at the very end, the figure does not yield anywhere near its dramatic potential.

But the people live and the dialogue works because Rabe is aware of all the tics, absurdities and sadnesses that go into the making of his characters: he does not limit himself to the most obvious imbecilities or nastinesses to be punctured one after the other. Even pigheadedness is allowed to have its pathos. The recital of the horrors of war does not quite come off, though there is a powerful scene in which David projects what he sees as a film of the ravages of war, but the family and we perceive as blank frames coming from the projector, except for here and there a greenish spot. Throughout, the atmosphere of specious solicitude covering up genuine self-absorption is expertly caught. But the real strength of the play lies in its ability to satirize fiercely without losing a residue of sympathy and even compassion—except, perhaps, for the priest, of whom Harriet says, "I called Father Donald seven times and he never answered. He's beginning to act like Jesus Christ: you call him and you never hear from him!" Rabe attacks with wit, passion, fury turning into despair, but not with hate and still less with modish self-righteousness.

The production is up to the play except for David Selby's somewhat monotonous David, with an unpleasing whine in his voice. Tom Aldredge overdoes Ozzie, but has the right basic quality; Elizabeth Wilson's Harriet and Cliff de Young's Rick are perfect; the others are more than adequate to lesser roles. Santo Loquasto's set manages to be simple and yet not tasteful, which is absolutely right here, and

Jeff Bleckner has directed a trifle too frenziedly but with great clarity and authority.

THE AMERICAN PLACE THEATER inaugurates its new home—an improvement over St. Clement's, but somewhat disappointing for a playhouse devised by a real theatrical designer, Kert Lundell—with a double bill, a case of very mixed doubles. Ronald Ribman's *Fingernails Blue As Flowers* is a by now conventional exercise in bargain-basement absurdism, ponderously directed by Martin Fried and ruinously enacted by Albert Paulsen, who turns a blustering U.S. tycoon of the Edward Arnold-Eugene Pallette variety into a skimpy South American clown with language difficulties. The supporting cast boasts a child actress whose untalentedness and repulsiveness set a new low even for that queasy profession. But things look up enormously with the second, much longer, play, *Lake of the Woods* by Steve Tesich.

Whereas Ribman's play is diluted, denatured Ionesco, Tesich's 125-minute opus is a lesson from Beckett, well learned. *Lake* concerns a typical megalopolitan advertising man whose vacation and automobile bring him to a touted scenic resort, Lake of the Woods. His retinue consists of a faded, put-upon wife, a catatonic daughter and a sassy houseboy. There are no woods and there is no lake; all that is left is a sign reading "Lake of the Woods," an outdoor grill and a sandy wasteland. A discarded handbill announces that a rock festival is about to take place here, and at one point a scraggly straggler of a rock musician does wander onstage only to pass out promptly. A faintly comic, faintly ominous old forest ranger appears and disappears periodically. For the most part, Winnebago, the hero, argues with his houseboy, who also disappears from time to time, leaving Winnie to argue with himself. Winnie's wife, Juanita, comes and goes disconsolately between the dried-up lake and the dried-up daughter in the trailer. Eventually, some offstage rock musicians dismantle the trailer and strip Winnie of everything, but a night of self-communion has regenerated him. He turns the shield reading "Lake of the Woods" into a stretcher on which he and Juanita carry their daughter, with the grumbling houseboy loaded down with camping equipment, their last possessions, bringing up the rear. Winnie is leading them to whatever green wilderness may still be left. The houseboy gripes, Juanita is weary and worried, the daughter is lost to the world, but Winnie is indomitably hopeful: after a night of sarcasm, rant, distraught questioning, righteous indignation, soul-searching and running around in circles he has fought his way into a new-found sanguineness.

The point of the play is simple and unremarkable—except perhaps in its unexpected plea for a hope born of despair, when most of contemporary theater prefers fashionable despondency. What is outstanding is the dialogue, which manages to go from outrageous farce to gravity and even sadness—though still laced with spurts of absurdist humor—to end on a note of striving onward. The positive note may not be entirely earned by the foregoing demonstration, but is at least in the tradition of this Midsummer-Night's-Dream kind of play, where a night spent in a haunted and haunting place turns you into someone happier and better. Tesich skillfully manages the transitions between moods and their partial interpenetration, so that the almost ghostly forest ranger and quite trivial rock musician manage to inhabit the same theatrical world without splitting it in two.

The comic dialogue ripples along: "There was supposed to be a lake here." "There probably was; the hole is still here." "It's not a hole, but it's not a garden of Eden either." "What is it then?" "Something in between." "Something in between is always a hole." And the comic monologues are no less fluent, as when Winnie, in the middle of this sandy waste, feels an ant crawl up him: "An ant! Other people run into deer and elk and black and brown bears. I run into an ant. It's probably the same one that has been following me since Kansas. I wonder," he adds with reference to other previous encounters, "where his friend the fly and mosquito are?" Tesich can toss off a well-turned phrase, as when he describes tourists confronting the fauna: "They surround the poor beast and shoot it full of film"; and he can be just as effective with a simple non sequitur: "But as my poor father said just before he died, 'So what?'" Yet what I like most about *Lake of the Woods* is that it makes Winnie's improbable conversion almost believable; that it finds a way of making idealism more attractive than cynicism by keeping it unsentimental; and that in Winnebago it gives us a character of stature whom we can remember with affection.

Frederick Rolf has staged the play competently against Kert Lundell's rather too literal scenery. The acting is very creditable, with Armand Assanto doing a particularly fine job as the houseboy, an emblematically confused youth of our times wavering between crassness and decency, between dropping out and pitching in. And Hal Holbrook, an actor whom I previously found mediocre, seizes the long and taxing role of Winnie and makes him funny, moving and real in a performance as intense and many-sided as I have seen in a long, long time. *Lake of the Woods* is even more original than Tesich's trenchant previous play, *The Carpenters,* done last season by APT. If Tesich and Rabe continue to develop as they promise to, America will soon have two genuine new playwrights, and *two* swallows just might make a summer.

BEFORE GOING ON about the revival of *A Funny Thing Happened on the Way to the Forum,* let me say that it is still, or again, the most pleasing show on Broadway. In his second-most-famous book, *Roman Laughter,* Erich Segal refers to *Forum* as "an unabashed *contaminatio* of the *Pseudolus, Casina,* and *Mostellaria";* actually, at least three other Plautine comedies and possibly some of Terence's seem to have influenced the plot and infected the spirit of the show. And if there is any stricture to be made about it, it is precisely that it is somewhat abashed: Burt Shevelove and Larry Gelbart, the co-authors, are apparently, slightly afraid of their own formidable cleverness, and are fastidious purists to boot. They are particularly hard on what they consider anachronistic, and have accordingly eliminated some very funny lines from successive versions of the show. In the current one, I particularly missed the awestruck question about a multiple conqueror of Northern Greece, "He raped Thrace *thrice?*" And to a man with a wine cask, "Was one a good year?"

If you have been wondering about the *contaminatio* in Prof. Segal's statement, it seems a spoiling, or simply a mixing of several extant plays into a new one of your own. This Messrs. Shevelove and Gelbart have done with wit, aplomb and a sophisticated vulgarity that is indeed unabashed, imperious and triumphant. It is the vulgarity of highly civilized people who can use it as a spice or leavening, and not as a lumpy, indigestible dough. The book of *Forum* continues to be lavish with laughter that is as honorable as it is merry, and with situations that emit a radiance even in between the actual laughs. Stephen Sondheim's score remains his best because it is his least pretentious; he has even improved it by adding two jolly new songs and subtracting one infelicitious old one. The fact that one of his good melodies stems from a Brahms trio is quite appropriate to the general atmosphere of *contaminatio.* And Sondheim's lyrics are the best anyone writes these days, full of the verbal play that Plautus so zestfully reveled in. The new sets and costumes are lackluster, even seedy, however, below Tony Walton's for the original production.

Said production had for its center Zero Mostel—an extraordinary center that at times became coextensive with the circumference. Had not Plautus himself, after all, written his *Mostellaria* with this unique superclown proleptically in mind? But Plautus never wrote a *Silversaria,* and Phil Silvers as the wily slave who spins the plot is quite a comedown. Whereas Mostel is burlesque plus poetry, Silvers is merely burlesque. Nor does he convey the lecherous side of the character: when he stares at the luscious, semi-nude body of one of Lycus's courtesans, he is not mentally undressing her, only metamorphosing her into one on Hugh Hefner's calendars. His singing voice crumbles in the ears like shredded wheat between the fingers. Even his lines lose their impact: I can still hear Mostel fawning: "You, Lycus, are a gentleman and a procurer," or exclaiming about a fellow slave's impending demise: "A pyre? A fire pyre?" Yet I could barely hear those lines when Silvers was actually delivering them. And I am sorry to say that George Abbott's original staging, especially in the chase scene, seemed to me more resourceful, or at least better implemented, than Shevelove's is now.

Still, the principals are on the whole very good. I particularly relished Carl Balantine's urbanely rascally pimp, and Larry Blyden's prissily befuddled when not priggishly cocksure chief slave, funnier than Jack Gilford's in the original version. Among the courtesans, Lauren Lucas and Charlene Ryan are outstanding, though Ralph Beaumont's choreography is an even paler version of Jack Cole's pale original. Three people from the initial production I miss enormously: the pellucid, deliquescent Philia of Preshy Marker, now replaced by Pamela Hall, who looks like Ruth Gordon in drag; the powerful and powerfully amusing Domina of Ruth Kobart, now shrunken in every way to the skimpier compass of Lizabeth Pritchett; and that sexiest of all Broadway dancing girls, Lucienne Bridou—whatever became of her? But it would be poor form to miss even this poorer man's *Forum.*

WHAT CAN I SAY about Tennessee Williams' *Small Craft Warnings* that I have not already said about his three last plays? It is the work of a man out of touch with the changing world, yet unable or unwilling to write honestly out of the depths of his true, immutable self. The result is feeble self-parody, dilution of his former glories.

The nine nonentities drifting in and out of this broken-down bar in Southern California are not new, fully realized creatures but ghosts of Williams characters past; they monologize drearily about their clichéd pasts and presents, and if they engage in conversation at all, it is only the bandying of depleted words, not a dynamically structured progression of relationships and ideas. It is clearly the play of a man who has lost all sense of give and take with life, except for dimly recording the mumblings in barrooms from Tokyo to New Orleans. Pitiful decals are rubbed, row upon row, on a smudged, rickety background.

The only forthright thing about *Small Craft Warnings* is its title: it warns the theatergoer about the small craft that is left to the play's author. I suppose it is useless to urge Williams to take the homosexual relationship here between a fading, rich dilettante and an idealistically searching young drifter, and turn it into an entire play, the one play Williams might still endow with originality and significance. But let me at least urge those near to and concerned for him to guard Williams against himself, and save his fine and important plays from burial under these incontinent droppings. His future is at stake.

SUGAR is the best nonmusical musical I have ever seen. Consider it straight comedy—fast, funny, unassuming—with incidental or accidental music, and all is well. You do not get the bonus of really good songs, but you do get the most diverting, stylishly mounted, smoothly acted, brilliantly staged and endearingly danced comedy in many a season. And a comedy with dancing—surely this is a bonus, after all.

Let me get the unpleasant verities off my chest first. Bob Merrill has never been my favorite lyricist (or composer): anyone who could write "Doggie in the Window" deserves to be swept into a large tin pan and dumped in the nearest alley. Still, his lyrics for *Sugar* are his best so far, and actually have their moments. What grounds them finally is not so much lack of cleverness (though there is that, too) as a certain goody-goodiness that is the bane of lyric writing. Yip Harburg to the contrary, song lyrics are not poetry; in fact, I doubt if true poetry has ever been written for a composer, even of operas, to set. Probably the finest such texts are Hofmannsthal's librettos for Strauss's operas, and even they are either prose or well below what Hofmannsthal wrote as straight lyric poetry. W. H. Auden has written some appealing lyrics for *The Rake's Progress,* but compared to his nonlibrettistic poetry, they are mere wisps. When music has true poetry underlying it, you may be sure the poem was written first, with no aspiration to appear at the Met, Carnegie Hall, or on Broadway. Only when it is under no obligation to another art can poetry be itself.

So if show lyrics are at best occasional verse and at worst doggerel, they can best elude the long shadow of Hallmark cards by being saucy, naughty and irreverent. This is why your Cole Porters and Larry Harts stand up so much better than your Hammersteins and Merrills. By act two, Merrill's wits are truly flagging; happily, Jule Styne's tunes now awaken to at least an imitation of life. Styne has written some juicy songs, but you won't find them in *Sugar.* Yet there are, in this second act, some passable ones, like the affectionate parody of a Coward song—or of a Sandy Wilson parody of a Coward song—called "Beautiful Through and Through," followed by a jolly combination of the offbeat and beaten-to-death "What Do You Give to a Man Who's Had Everything?" Pastiche though it was, I also liked "When You Meet a Man in Chicago"; but in between there was a horrible number, worthy of Joe Darion and Mitch Leigh, called "It's Always Love," for which I would urge the authors to substitute something else at a not-too-late later date.

The book is based on the Billy Wilder-I. A. L. Diamond movie, *Some Like It Hot,* which I disliked at any temperature. Peter Stone's adaptation of it seems to me both funnier and in better taste than the original, from which some dialogue, including the legendary last line, remains. Though all the film's comedy situations are there, no comic turn has been left un-Stoned; for every one of the film's strangulated chuckles, the show gives you a resoundingly unstoppered laugh. But this is also in large measure the achievement of Gower Champion, whose direction is one of the few consummate pieces of musical staging I have witnessed. Champion is the master of at least three highly useful skills. First, the integration of dances into the show's overall movement. Although for some time now song numbers have flowed imperceptibly in and out of the plot, choreography still tends to look arbitrary and adventitious. Champion has done more than anyone to break down the barrier between the prose of mere blocking and the poetry of dance—think of those waiters in *Hello, Dolly!* Here the connections between machine-gun salvos and tap-dancing, between oldsters being wheeled about in armchairs on casters and a veritable Dodgem ballet are jubilantly exploited.

Champion is also expert at using large groups of dancers as one flesh-and-muscle kinetic sculpture, a pullulating, polypoid mechanism shaping and reshaping itself before your eyes but remaining fixed around one pulsating center. Lastly, he is perhaps the most creative user of props for dance numbers—in this instance everything from instrument cases to wicker chairs, newspapers to car horns, spotlights to Pullman berths and their curtains. In some ways he may remind you of Busby Berkeley, but if so, he is that very much superior thing, a Berkeley with brains and taste. And he must be the first choreographer to have put even a corpse to productive work—as a stagehand. Hail, Champion!

Scarcely less satisfying are the costumes of Alvin Colt, the lighting of Martin Aronstein and especially the sets of Robin Wagner. Here is scenery that is modest, limberly mobile, witty and graceful, and whose color sense is as daringly simple yet challenging as was the Creator's when he designed the first rainbow. And the performers in *Sugar* are good and attractive down to the last chorus girl and boy. Tony Roberts and Robert Morse are versatile and winning as the two jazz musicians dragging themselves away from pursuing gangsters, and they take to their confining and precarious drag with resigned gallantry, like a fish to a water closet. Roberts sometimes reminds me a little uncomfortably of Walter Matthau; Morse I don't know how to begin to praise adequately: what do you give to a man who's had, and still has, everything? The two are charmingly matched by Cyril Ritchard, who made me feel that Ivor Novello was alive and well and more winsome than ever, and by Elaine Joyce, as the eponymous Sugar. She may also have talent, but is so utterly lovely that neither she nor I required it. With all this going for a musical, does it need songs?

NOT EVEN MAX BEERBOHM, Shaw's able successor as the *Saturday Review*'s drama critic, whose respect for his predecessor was sincere and enlightened, could find anything to like in *Captain Brassbound's Conversion*, either at its première in 1900, or at its 1906 revival. The play has an amusing female central character, Lady Cicely, surrounded by men who are indeed peripheral and half-realized; it also changes locales and tonalities so readily as to remain jerky and unsatisfying. Lady Cicely represents the formidable aristocratic Englishwoman at her most graciously, awesomely incontrovertible; the part, then, requires an actress whose heartiness is both playful and regal, supremely poised yet able to infiltrate anyone's skin, whatever its color or toughness. This dominant mother figure has figured out every masculine foible; her remarks always hit the male on the head. Ingrid Bergman is a charming and elegant actress, but her artifices have not become second, let alone first, nature; she is commanding, but not with that witty, crystalline English power one associates with such great British ladies as Mary Wortley Montagu. Miss Bergman is as Swedish as crayfish with aquavit, and the evening's best laugh for me came from someone's addressing her with "It is easy to see you are not Scots, milady." The production around the star is almost totally overcast or undercast, depending on whether you are speaking meteorologically or histrionically.

ALL IS LOST in the revival of *Lost in the Stars* except Kurt Weill's music, and even this takes a considerable beating. Two songs have been excised, and one put into the wrong mouth in the wrong act. Weill's orchestrations for Broadway (unlike his European ones) always sounded a little tinny to my ears; in the current revival, they sound even tinnier and the tempos seem eccentric. Moreover, Karen Gustafson was having a hard time keeping singers and orchestra together. And what singing! The Reverend Stephen Kumalo is a part calling for an acting singer rather than a singing actor, and certainly not a nonsinging actor. Brock Peters acts the part convincingly, but his singing voice is gritty, blaring, unmusical; in a sweet song like "Thousands of Miles," it sounds as if it had dragged itself barefoot over just that distance. The chorus had some ragged moments; in an important dramatic number like "Fear," its enunciation was so muffled that the only fear it left us with was that of the unknown. Gilbert Price sang the lovely "Stay Well" well enough, but dramatically and psychologically it belongs to Irina in the second act. Margaret Cowie would have sung it beautifully, as she did the no less ravishing "Trouble Man," with exquisite musicianliness and flawless diction.

But Weill's music can take more killing than ever Rasputin did, as the fact that it could survive Maxwell Anderson's book and lyrics proves. Alan Paton's novel about the miseries of apartheid, on which the show is based, is moving despite its mediocrity; Anderson reduced it to so much synthetic *veldtschmerz*. Yet the last scene remains affecting, thanks in no small measure to the performances of Brock Peters and Jack Gwillim. Gene Frankel's direction is uninventive and clumsy, including the worst staged murder I have ever seen; Oliver

Smith's set—a bagel in cross section—is unevocative and ugly; Paul Sullivan's lighting is garish, and Louis Johnson's choreography a bad joke. That Clive Barnes could extol these dances shows him at the top of his dance, as well as dramatic, form.

Tom Stoppard's new double bill consists of *After Magritte,* a curio of a curtain raiser, bumptious, roundabout and endearingly outrageous by turns. Its somewhat sophomoric glee is not without some genuine glitter. The longer play, *The Real Inspector Hound,* is a thoroughly ingratiating spoof on the "levels of reality" and "truth or illusion?" themes, with which *Rosencrantz & Guildenstern Are Dead* dealt rather too self-consciously and pretentiously. Part satire, part persiflage, the construction here has the jewel-like precision of a maniacal timepiece that tells you exactly how out of joint the time is. Nothing makes sense, yet all is perfectly believable—as logical as a nightmare to the dreamer caught up in it. A murder mystery is enacted before two commenting and bickering critics who get sucked into the play; while mystery melodramas are deliciously parodied, critics are devastatingly lampooned. But it is in the interweaving of the two levels that the fun becomes truly dizzying and insidious; clichés are hilariously smashed to smithereens, and these piled up again into towers of seductively treacherous artifice.

The Real Inspector Hound is today's best game for adults. It is funny and civilized, involving despite its detachment, and, by God, there even lurks an indefinable but necessary extra dimension in it, like that bit of truffle at the heart of a goose-liver pâté. It is all enticingly acted by expert tricksters, my favorite being David Rounds. Joseph Hardy's staging is a bit lumbering, even campy, but William Ritman's décor is canny, and nothing can deflect the mischief from its course.

I have always considered *The Crucible* Arthur Miller's best play, even when the partly true (and so partly false) analogy between Salem witch hunts and McCarthy Communist hunts made it hard to hear the play amid the shouting. Two decades later, when we can savor the artistic merit first, and the still not invalid social relevance second, the work emerges flawed but forceful, anachronistic and somewhat repetitious but essentially well constructed; it makes shrewd use of an absorbing and appalling chapter of our history that never ceases to be maniacally rewritten, and it holds the stage with tooth and nail, as good plays must.

Miller faced the difficulty of having to convey simultaneously the tragedy of an individual and that of a whole society, and of having to keep the relationship between the two in constant focus. Sensibly, he picked for his protagonist a man who has sinned in his own eyes, and allows a minor, expiated transgression to make him vulnerable in a major, social context, in which he is innocent; it is thus the individual's decency and conscientiousness that make him the victim of hypocritical mass-righteousness. John Proctor, the former adulterer but never diabolist, is both an Aristotelian hero complete with *hamartia,* and a Freudian hero made incomplete by a nagging sense of guilt. He is so human and interesting that we feel cheated when other characters come, as they must, to the fore, and deprive us of closer companionship with Proctor. Unlike, say, *Death of a Salesman, The Crucible* leaves us hungry for more, and if that is a failing, it is surely the nicest there is.

But, as usual with Miller, only more patently, the play also contains a totally unendearing flaw: linguistic insufficiency. Next to a tone-deaf musician, a word-deaf playwright is the saddest thing I know. Not that Miller completely lacks language—that would have killed his Muse in the cradle. But he loses control over it as soon as it steps outside the quotidian and ordinary. Here, to bridge the gap between 1692 and 1953, he concocted a pidgin-Colonial to make your eardrums buckle. Bits of actual or simulated Colonial verbiage and syntax pop up in an otherwise modern diction like horses yoked to an automobile. Historical drama must either find a language that transcends time, or translate into a flexible up-to-date idiom; a full antiquarianism is incomprehensible, a partial one indigestible. When, at the climax, Proctor's morally impeccable wife speaks her husband's clipped eulogy, "He have his goodness now," that *have* makes a dent in the play's very compassion.

The Vivian Beaumont production is unusually good. True, Robert Phalen still haunts rather than acts, and Pauline Flanagan and Ben Hammer are stodgy; as Mary Warren, a key role, Nora Heflin acts intensely but without a period sense, turning a Salem courtroom into a discothèque; and Jerome Dempsey is too soft as Reverend Parris. But Robert Foxworth is a splendid Proctor, down to that peasant heaviness that beautifully offsets the man's ultimate intelligence, courage and humanity. He is finely matched by Martha Henry's Elizabeth Proctor—a shade stronger on the reticence than on the emotion underneath it, yet deeply compelling; and by Pamela Payton-Wright, who can make Abigail horrible without forfeiting her pathos. Miss Payton-Wright is rapidly becoming one of our most valuable all-around actresses.

There is sterling work also from Philip Bosco, Stephen Elliott, Aline MacMahon, Sydney Walker and Wendell Phillips, among others, and for such rare ensemble acting on the Beaumont stage as well as for his simple and uncluttered direction, John Berry is to be thanked. Jo Mielziner's sets contribute little, and his lighting at the end fails to evoke the inexorable approach of a terrible dawn; Carrie F. Robbins' costumes are self-effacing and correct.

SUMMER AND AUTUMN, 1972

DONT PLAY US CHEAP
  words and music by Melvin Van Peebles

THE HUNTER
  by Murray Mednick

THE BEGGAR'S OPERA
  by John Gay
  produced by the Chelsea Theater Center
    of Brooklyn

JULIUS CAESAR
  by William Shakespeare
  produced by the American Shakespeare Festival,
    Stratford, Conn.

MAN OF LA MANCHA
  book by Dale Wasserman
  music by Mitch Leigh
  lyrics by Joe Darion

MASS
  music by Leonard Bernstein
  lyrics by Leonard Bernstein and Steven Schwartz

JOAN
  words and music by Al Carmines

H<small>AMLET</small>
by William Shakespeare
produced by the New York Shakespeare Festival

P<small>RESENT</small> T<small>ENSE</small>
by Frank D. Gilroy

M<small>UCH</small> A<small>DO</small> A<small>BOUT</small> N<small>OTHING</small>
by William Shakespeare
produced by the New York Shakespeare Festival

J<small>ACQUES</small> B<small>REL</small> I<small>S</small> A<small>LIVE AND</small> W<small>ELL</small>
<small>AND</small> L<small>IVING IN</small> P<small>ARIS</small>
songs by Jacques Brel
adapted by Eric Blau and Mort Shuman

O<small>H</small> C<small>OWARD</small>!
words by Noël Coward
adapted by Roderick Cook

T<small>HE</small> C<small>ITY</small> C<small>ENTER</small> A<small>CTING</small> C<small>OMPANY</small>

T<small>HERE ARE STILL</small> many places where the black man's lot is hard, unjust and unenviable. In the New York theater, however, it is not hard and unenviable, merely unjust. There Melvin Van Peebles, a black man of virtually no talent whatever (unless self-promotion be counted as one), manages to have two musicals of zero value running concurrently on Broadway. I wrote briefly and dismissingly about *Aint Supposed to Die a Natural Death:* a bunch of untuneful, gratingly monotonous and generally hate-riddled Van Peebles songs, fairly cleverly illustrated with stage movements devised by Gilbert Moses, pasted together and, without anything resembling a book, served up as a musical. When the Tony awards came along, this bookless, graceless musical was nominated in every conceivable category, including one inconceivable one: Best Musical Comedy Book. Clearly, if it hadn't been a little black book, it wouldn't have had a Chinaman's chance. Interestingly, *Aint* didn't win a single, measly Tony.

What is the basis for Van Peebles' reputation? Three movies, all of them critical and two audience flops, and *Aint*, which has been kept huffing and puffing to papered houses by puffery such as having black celebrities like Shirley Chisholm take over a part for an evening, by white foundation monies being poured into it, and by uncritical raves from awed white uncritics. So now we get a new Van Peebles musical, *Dont Play Us Cheap*. This does not resemble *Aint* in any way, except that, from *aint* to *dont*, it continues Van Peebles' war on that white chauvinist status symbol, the apostrophe. Otherwise, the new show differs in that it has a book, and that, abandoning the previous message of hatred for whitey, it proposes to celebrate the joy of being black. These apparently laudable undertakings prove, in the event, even less appealing than their opposites.

Dont Play Us Cheap starts out with a rat and a cockroach crawling through a hole in the wall beside a huge, i.e. man-sized door, and with the rat intoning a general lament about his and the roach's life, which turns into a comic—but still totally unmelodious—song duet. So far, so passable; we assume that we are heading for an animal fable with music, a genre that would be relatively new on Broadway, and might yield some whimsical, hortatory fun. But presently the two pests complain about their own worst plague: the Devil's imps assuming the shapes of rats and roaches to wreak havoc on human beings, for which innocent, real rats and roaches are persecuted. Forthwith, Aesop is forgotten, and we get a tenuous story about two minor devil's advocates who change from rat and roach into men to break up more efficiently a happy Saturday-night party in Harlem. One of them is won over by love to remain human and humane; the other, unreconstructed, changes back into a roach and is swatted to death. The Devil is assumed to be so powerless as to have to turn his envoys into tiny creatures to enable them to infiltrate human residences; he cannot make them pass through locked doors. This feeble device provides a cute opening number and a convenient though unconvincing conclusion.

The plot is so trivial and banal as actually to benefit from a thumbnail précis: the young girl whose aunt gives the party falls in love with the better little devil and he with her; he stops being a metaphysical saboteur and she finally prefers him to the scion of a rich, upwardly mobile, Uncle-Tomish family, who become the laughingstocks of the party. Mostly stock, to be exact, for there is very little laughing in

Van Peebles' book. When the more diabolic imp shows up to un-straighten out the first one, he, too, very nearly falls—for the wise and lovable aunt; but he remains unconverted and pays for it. The party itself is an excuse for bringing on an assortment of black stereotypes and having them crudely manipulated by obvious song cues into even more obvious songs—this time more of the gospel variety, as opposed to the jazzier nonscore for *Aint*. The music ranges from the platitudi-nous to the mercilessly teased-out and unmusical; Harold Wheeler's able orchestrations try valiantly to make silky purrs out of rasps more suited to a sow's ear.

But the greater disaster is the words, both book and lyrics. They turn the principal characters into nonentities, while leaving the lesser ones insulting clichés. I shudder to think what would have been said of a white author, had he portrayed blacks like this. The writing ranges from a devil's saying, "When I give her what she really wants, all hell will break loose," to the aunt's remarking about her modest social status, "It may not look like much to you, but you just don't know how far back I had to start"; in other words, from the indubit-able bottom to dubious heights. There is an abundance of apothegms like "If you aint [*sic*, no doubt] got rip-off in your heart, the Devil cant [ditto] rip you off." The singing is exuberant but untidy, the acting for the most part amateurish. Many sung words are indeciph-erable; there are even performers, like Robert Dunn, whose very spoken words remain impenetrable. Joe Keyes, Jr., is so wooden in the male lead that he must have confused a devil with a cigar-store Indian. Even the experienced Avon Long, as his diabolic cohort, is at best a deviled ham. Only Esther Rolle and Rhetta Hughes, as aunt and neice, perform with style. And Van Peebles the director makes still less of what little Van Peebles the playwright provides.

Black theater, like any other, must be allowed and helped to grow. But it is not the tired formulas and tin ear of Melvin Van Peebles that will bear fruit. The current show merely shows that if there is anything drearier than Van Peebles' hate, it is Van Peebles' love.

IN *The Hunter*, by Murray Mednick, two young men in battered Civil War uniforms recline on cots in an abandoned cemetery with one blank tombstone in it; there is also one stunted tree. It is night. They talk in contemporary jargon of the grayest, least imaginative sort; Lee is mooning about a lost girl, Harry tries to fend off the tirades so he can sleep. A hunter appears with a bagged hawk. He claims to be lost, but is in no hurry to ask directions, and keeps the youths covered with his shotgun—first casually, then with menacing deliberateness. He spouts away about hunting or rattles off lengthy accounts of Civil War battles. The men try to appease him with anec- dotes from their love lives, then switch to military drill in which he joins. They jump him, take his gun and nail him to the tree. He howls but doesn't bleed.

In act two, Marianne, a cowgirl, appears; she shoots a watermelon in two, recounts a dream about two World War I soldiers horribly dead and loses her pistol to Lee. While Lee covers the jealous shot- gun-pointing Harry with it, he also leads Marianne into the bushes, where they copulate noisily. The crucified Hunter has vicarious orgasms listening to them, while the frustrated Harry relieves tensions by symbolically raping the watermelon with his fist. In act three, the slain Hunter stinks and requires burial. Marianne refuses sex with Harry and urges Lee to kill him. From their cots, the men keep each other covered and exchange insults as Marianne leaves. One of them finally kicks the corpse off the main stage. They are about to shoot each other when Marianne reappears as a World War I nurse, and a slide projection strews the stage with countless crosses.

The meaning is simple to the point of banality. Men, though friends, are potential rivals—not having versus having sparks the con- flict; women, seeming balms, are actually bones of contention. The world is a large, thinly veiled graveyard in which past and future fighting intermingle; memories of former wars, uneasily swept under the rug, only help stir up future ones—until the earth becomes one vast, unmistakable necropolis. The hunt—murder of animals described in glowing terms by both the Hunter and Marianne—is the bellicose peacetime link between wars. There is no progress: the men are both Civil War deserters and modern hippies in army surplus uniforms; the girl is the Old West, World War I France (Marianne) and Europe, and a swinging chick of today. Military drill—playing at sol- diers—is the way the real warfare begins.

What does Mednick do with this skeleton, which is no better or worse than any other lying around a would-be playwright's closet? For obviously it is the fleshing out that matters. He gives us four pup- pets that do not come to any sort of life, real or surreal; dialogue of staggering flatness and triviality; situations that do not arouse our interest; and resolutions, if that is what they are, that hold no sur- prise. In fact, listening to Mednick's flavorless verbiage is tantamount to counting sheep. Like his Hunter, the author howls, but does not bleed: there is no real blood in the play. Instead, Mednick throws in mystifying devices; call them symbolic, surreal, absurdist or just poetic—by any name, they smell as sour. A typical example: the blank tombstone onstage left in act one appears onstage right in act two, turned around and reading "I Keep Thinking It Is Thursday." In act three, it is blank again and back where it started from. So are we. The play gets nowhere, even though it leaves no headstone unturned.

This sorry farce is worth noting because Mighty Joe Papp not only produced it, but also prefaced it with a fighting manifesto to the critics, in which he declares that the "new" playwright, like Mednick, "expresses the unspeakable." Actually, I think, he does better than that: he does not merely express it, he *is* it. Then, on NBC, Betty Rollin pronounces the play "brilliant," but provides no explanation. In the *Times,* Barnes announces that though he will "probably never know what the play was about," he "enjoyed it a great deal more than innumerable plays" he understood and damned. In *Women's Wear Daily,* Martin Gottfried describes the story as "irrational," but finds that the "events flow . . . logically." A scene where talk is "either a complete irrelevance or an unsuccessful effort" at meaning, Gottfried cannot complain about because it "works very well." For Jack Kroll's encomium, see a future *Newsweek.*

Is it asking too much of our reviewers that they understand something before they leap to extol it? What would these critics say in praise of a play in Arabic? Most of them, probably, nothing, because there is no prestige in hailing Arabic. But there is every sort of glory in jumping on the avant-garde bandwagon: you are ahead of your times, you are a swinger rather than an old fogy, you damn well won't be another Eduard Hanslick who damned Richard Wagner because he didn't understand him. But suppose Mednick is no Wagner? I know two other plays of his, and find them equally execrable. And suppose our critics are not even as good as Hanslick, who wrote perceptively about Brahms?

Well, if you admit you don't understand something but are still for it, you can at least be praised for your open mind. Some minds, however, are so open as to be positively wall-less; only wind blows about in them. And in any case, ladies and gentlemen, you don't get off that cheaply. If you don't understand, abstain from evaluating. If you think something is nonsense, denounce it. You may in due time be proved wrong. But that is the risk of a profession that could at least be dignified, if only its practitioners were not hellbent on playing it safe.

The Beggar's Opera (1728) was our first musical comedy and has arguably not been surpassed in the following 244 years. John Gay's satire is exemplary: light enough to have us gulping it down and barbed enough to have us gasping as it sticks, not in our craws but in our consciences. For it is a brilliantly intransigent kind of satire that provides alternatives for behavior that turn out equally unethical. The *dramatis personae* are so mired in evil that dwells both around and inside them that they cannot escape corruption. And since most of them profess to be doing right, they add to their several vices the ecumenic magma of hypocrisy.

The dashing Captain Macheath is a highwayman, and a gallant undoer of women eventually done in by them. This Byronic hero *avant la lettre* has secretly married Polly Peachum, and made Lucy Lockit, upon promise of marriage, publicly pregnant. Whichever of them he does right by, the other will be wronged. As it happens, he has no intention of doing right by either, only by his own insatiable appetite for women. In one of his most famous songs, he declares: "How happy could I be with either,/ Were t'other dear Charmer away!" That sounds like opportunistic insouciance but is in fact worse: a lie. For whenever Macheath is close to one woman only, he soon runs off to the brothels for a little group sex. Polly, the nicest person in the play, is loyal to Macheath, but at the expense of disobeying parental commands. Yes, but her father, Peachum, is a shopkeeper whose real trade is receiving stolen goods from a stable of thieves and, whenever one of them loses his touch, turning him in for profit. His wife is no better, and not even legally his wife, so their instructions to Polly to turn in her husband for the reward and inheritance were best left unheeded. True, but even the good Polly would rather see her dear Captain hanged than unfaithful.

Lucy is crasser about it; she offers Macheath Hobson's choice: herself as wife or the noose. She too plots against her father, Mr. Lockit, the Newgate jailer; also, she tries to poison her rival, Polly. To make herself an honest wife, Lucy will gladly become a murderess. As for Lockit, he has made a thriving business of being a turnkey, entering into lucrative collusion with his chief informer, Peachum, and charging unhappy prisoners large sums for such amenities as lighter chains and less chafing manacles. Love, marriage and bringing criminals to justice are thus seen as essentially selfish acts, quite possibly worse than their guilty opposites. Greed and self-advancement are the only motives; the choice is merely between double- and triple-dealing. If Jenny Diver, Macheath's favorite whore, turns the Captain in, she is aiding the law only for gain and to avenge her ego; as for the law, it is as nefarious as any outlaw and far more hypocritical.

The Beggar's Opera is something much more remarkable than a satire on Walpole and the social conditions of the time: a sharp critique of the middle and upper classes. Macheath and his gang of robbers are *lumpen*-aristocrats living as fecklessly as the real nobility; and the Peachums and Lockits embody all the socially virtuous vices and morally vicious virtues of the mercantile middle class. So besides writing the first musical, Gay wrote perhaps the first Marxist play—no wonder Brecht and Weill picked it as the basis for their equally dazzling and not so very different *Three-Penny Opera;* except that in Gay the proletariat fares no better than its betters. For his work, like all great satires, laughs (or weeps) not at prevailing conditions, but at the *conditio sine qua non*—the human condition itself.

As a sample of Gay's method and subtlety, consider this couplet from one of his verse epistles. Londoners are trooping to the country in springtime: "Then Chelsea's meads o'erhear perfidious vows,/ And the prest grass defrauds the grazing cows." As in the musical comedy (which is also a good spoof of grandiloquent *opera seria*), the irony here cuts two ways: the townfolk are not ennobled by the country, and lie to their heart's content; and by lying on it, deprive the cows of their proper fodder and so wreak ecological damage. The spectacular achievement of *The Beggar's Opera* is that, like this couplet, it confronts the bitterest truths about life with graceful polish. It delights the foolish with its bubbling farce while offering the connoisseur the dark splendor of its insights and the high sheen of its stylistic refinements.

But for the production to do justice to the work, it must be respectable and polished. The bourgeois elements must be prim and proper, even as the proto-aristocrats must be refined and graceful. The values that are turned upside down must always be present in their righteous or romantic hues; it is only from behind those sensible or exalted façades that the ignominy must quietly radiate. That is why surface proprieties and elegancies—of speech, attire and comportment—must be adhered to; in the simplest terms, the play is about the indecencies of decorum. Hence Rabelaisian and Bruegelesque excesses are anathema here. Unfortunately, Gene Lesser, who directed this Chelsea Theater of Brooklyn production now transferred to Manhattan, has ignored the eminently applicable Miesian dictum "less is more"; his more proves painfully Lesser. He makes the bourgeois drip malice and ugliness, the aristocrats wear their appetites on their sleeves—if not stamped on their foreheads. The whole cast tumbles and wallows, blusters and grovels incessantly; the voices (especially when they unsuccessfully imitate British speech) have no gentility; the set and costumes, though very cleverly executed, are near-shambles and tatters. If Lesser could not learn from William Empson's penetrating (though stylistically nearly impenetrable) essay on the work, he could at least have heeded Eric Bentley's plain speech: "The lightness of John Gay's manner is in direct, not inverse, ratio to his seriousness as a satirist."

Lesser gives us a foul slattern of a Mrs. Peachum; a ponderously obvious Peachum (played with oily self-indulgence by Gordon Connell); a Macheath who, though he can act and sing, lacks the ultimate finesse and command; a Lucy awash in repulsiveness; and a Polly and Lockit who are at best ciphers. Still, Timothy Jerome's Captain is personable, Jill Eikenberry's Trull is desirable, and Tanny McDonald has a strong moment as Jenny, even if it derives too noticeably from Peter Brook's movie version of the play. The small McAlpin stage is woefully insufficient for this sweeping spectacle, and Ryan Edwards' scoring of the ballads for three players is a bit rudimentary. All the same, to Empson's conclusion, "It is a fine thing that the play is still popular, however stupidly it is enjoyed," I add that seeing this masterwork on our stage, however shorn and trammeled, is yet a modest gain.

What is done at the American Shakespeare Festival in the name of Shakespeare should be stopped in the name of common decency. Right now at Stratford, Connecticut, the season has begun with *Julius Caesar*. Since it is not the best Shakespeare, I assumed that it was less susceptible of desecration. I was proved quite wrong. The moment the lights went up on Robin Wagner's respectable but unthrilling set, and two cut-rate histrions in nightshirts and flat New York accents purported to be Roman tribunes in togas, I had that familiar sinking feeling variously diagnosed as *eructatio Stratfordensis* or the dry heaves. Soon there was a whole clothesline's worth of nightshirts, and also soldiers equipped with helmets like medieval cuspidors, ensigns left over from *Jesus Christ Superstar* and armor that made them look like Michelin trademarks. There were also commoners wearing weird buff cloth helmets, tight buff overalls, and, since they usually came climbing up out of a hole in the floor, looking like a cross between Martians and moles.

Presently there appeared a small man with a face, voice and demeanor lacking anything resembling strength or nobility, but who did strut a little more than the others and wore his nightshirt as if it were something special—say, a veterinarian's apron or a Klansman's sheet. My date thought it was Bobby Morse about to go into a *Sugar*-y dance, but it turned out to be Bernard Kates playing Caesar. Some crazy East Village hippie shook his fright-hair (one hardly dares hope it was a wig) and shrieked something about "Beware the dykes of St. Mark's!" He was a most supererogatory soothsayer in a production in which everything augured ill. I noticed a gawky fellow (with good legs, however) who turned out to be Mark Antony, which was bad enough, and also Paul Hecht, which was worse, because I had previously always liked Paul Hecht. But this Antony was unmagnetic, lacked heroic or aristocratic stature, spoke with an acceptable accent but with a voice devoid of poetry, passion or mere excitement, and later delivered a funeral oration for Caesar in the tone in which a pious Jew might address himself to the Wailing Wall.

I became aware also of a Dracula-like creature—tall, gaunt, stooped—who, frustrated by the script in his ambition to suck the exposed necks, contented himself with swallowing the beginnings and ends of his lines. He did, however, deliver all those Shakespearean middles with a middling British accent, somewhat clouded by the fact that it imitated the mannerisms of several well-known English actors. This turned out to be Cassius, as portrayed by Josef Sommer. Gradually and dimly, one also noticed another Thespian, who did everything very conscientiously and correctly but, alas, so boringly that one yearned for him to commit one really interesting error. This was James Ray doing Brutus, that noblest Roman of them all, as if he were the most average Poughkeepsian of all.

Soon there were also women to be seen, especially one who preened and postured hideously. This was Sharon Laughlin as Portia, who may have sounded so mushy because in preparation for her demise by swallowing burning coals she kept a glowing ember or two secreted under her tongue. Diction, as always here, was generally poor, and when one of these rusty Rosciuses blared out, "I am the son of Marcus Cato, ho!" my date incredulously inquired: "The son of marzipan potato?" But I must say that the battle scenes limped the diction a close second, being as muscle-bound as the latter was throat-bound.

WHEN *Man of La Mancha* reopened at the Vivian Beaumont the other night, it garnered, along with a standing ovation and a garland of sundry critical praise, the epithet "unpretentious" from Betty Rollin, the NBC drama expert. To me, that is a climactic achievement. When a thousand-page classic whose complexity is such that its meaning is still argued over some four centuries later is whittled down to a two-hour musical comedy that carries its simpleminded message stamped all over it; when a mass-pleasing piece of commodity theater usurps the prestige of Cervantes and one of the greatest and most ambiguous figures in all art (literary, pictorial, musical), Don Quixote, to produce a string of single entendres—well, *unpretentious* is the last modifier that comes to my or any mind.

The history of the show is itself, to borrow a term from Cervantes, a *novela ejemplar* of human folly. After doing nicely in the tryouts at the Goodspeed Opera House, the show opened in New York in November 1965 to dubious preview audience response and hardly any advance sale. It was a likely prospect for an early closing, and Walter Kerr, in the *Tribune*, gave it a barely lukewarm review (though, God knows, Kerr loves big Broadway musicals). But the *Times* had, among its various gray eminences, a veritable gray declivity of a drama critic, Howard Taubman, whose time on the job was almost up, but who rallied his flagging forces for a Parthian hyperbole: *Man of La Mancha* was at least the equal of Cervantes. As the *Times*' former music critic, Taubman should have known twice better.

Now, the *Times* cannot always turn a mediocrity into the global hit *La Mancha* became. But when you get a classic that everyone has heard of and almost everyone feels guilty about not having read; when this is reduced to a small, simple package that any child— especially any child—can cope with; when there is crass music and dancing too; when, in short, you can indulge your untutored palate and pass for a refined gourmet, then it's lapping-up time at the old corral. If *Hamlet*, a much shorter and less honored-in-the-breach classic, were similarly musicalized and supplied with a happy "inspirational" ending, blessed with raves from the *Times* and a raving "unpretentious" from television, all would go equally well. Grab people both by their pretentiousness (Cervantes! Shakespeare!) and their appetite for brashness (Zap! Zowie!), add a few eminently brushable-away tears, and you're in.

My notice in *The Hudson Review* back in 1966 began: "In *Man of La Mancha*, Dale Wasserman has framed a comic-strip retelling of *Don Quixote* with an imaginary incident from the life of its author: to stop rough fellow prisoners of the Inquisition from burning the manuscript of his masterpiece, Cervantes gets them to act out the highlights of the novel. This enables Wasserman to be simplistic about life in the main story, and pietistic about art in the frame. Mitch Leigh's music is consummately unmusical, its gray monotone squeezed out like dirty water from a kitchen mop. To this, Joe Darion has provided sickeningly sanctimonious lyrics, e.g.: 'And yet how lovely life would seem/If every man could weave a dream/To keep him from despair . . .' (You said it, Darion; back to the loom!) or 'To dream the impossible dream,/to fight the unbeatable foe,/ . . . To right the unrightable wrong,/To reach the unreachable star,' etc. etc. As Pablo Neruda wrote in a poem, *'mi corazón fué interminable'*—there is no end to the melting heart of *Man of La Mancha:* it sweats, oozes, dribbles or gushes out of every pore of this spongy mass. In his dances, Jack Cole tries to right the unrightable balance by introducing bits of nastiness, say a sadomasochistic gang rape, which only proves distasteful in a different way."

But then, as now in this more or less original-cast revival, I did and do praise some production values. Albert Marre is one of our cleverest, earthiest directors, and it is too bad that Broadway has not used him more consistently where earthy shrewdness is required; they have often put him to other tasks with less happy results than in this gorgeously and appropriately gimmicky staging. Howard Bay's scenery works sweepingly with its bluffly bold strokes, and only the windmill episode falls as flat as the Don in that misadventure. The cast remains able, and I was delighted that Edmond Varrato had to pinch-hit for Irving Jacobson as Sancho: Varrato's looks and manner may not reach La Mancha, but at least they go farther than the last stop on the Lexington Avenue IRT. Richard Kiley is absolutely right as the Don, having a gently ceremonious grandness and a wilted but willing youthfulness that are sweet without being sticky. Joan Diener as Aldonza-Dulcinea remains a problem. She has the vocal requisites, but even they emerge with a certain heaving and forcing that slightly curdles the sound. Histrionically she mugs, pushes, moans and labors so achingly that one feels each nascent line to be begging for a Caesarean section. Not only does she make a monosyllable into a monologue, she hits every terminal consonant so hard that it booms and reverberates like J. Arthur Rank's gong. Diction has become addiction. But looking like a tarnished Raquel Welch, she is physically right for the part.

Cervantes ends with a piously dying hero who recants his noble folly, while even his few loved ones preserve their relish for food, drink and good cheer at the prospect of a tidy inheritance. There is no redeemed Dulcinea at his bedside (as she is in the show), ready to carry on with his faith and ideals; no large chorus blaring out a soppy and saccharine message. But there is no better formula for mass success than a really impossible dream ground to pleasingly palpable, easily digestible pulp.

If you had six colored chalks, a piece of pavement, and no knowledge of perspective, would you undertake to paint the Isenheim Altar? No. If you were suffering from frostbite, had several dead keys on your piano, and could not read music, would you perform the *Appassionata* in Carnegie Hall? No. If you were Leonard Bernstein, would you compose a *Mass* that is not only a setting of the Roman Catholic Mass but also "a theater piece for singers, players and dancers"? Certainly. And the result is on display at the Metropolitan Opera House. This theater-mass would not bring anyone a step closer to religious sentiment, but it could easily drive people out of the theater in droves.

Mass has a kind of plot. A sacerdotal figure, the Celebrant, tries to celebrate the Mass among worshipers seated in bleacher-like pews upstage; mysteriously garbed dancing figures center stage; and, down front, a bunch of oddly assorted hippies, flower children, activists and Damon Runyon characters. A group of kids periodically bounces and tumbles on and off the stage; they are dressed as acolytes and behave like baboons. The Celebrant, himself a guitar-strumming hippie turned hierophant, is continually interrupted by various individuals or groups doing their specialty acts, by the two onstage pop groups or strolling musicians, or by invisible, recorded choirs blaring away stereophonically from the far corners of the auditorium. Or he may interrupt himself to go into one of his solo turns. It all has to do with people losing their faith, or having the wrong kind, or not knowing where to look for it.

Finally the Celebrant stumbles up a mighty set of stairs leading nowhere, but providing him with his private Calvary. Beset by doubt

and despair, he smashes various sacred vessels and then discovers—
I swear it on the Bible—that the Communion wine is more brown than
red, and that glass shines brighter when it is broken. The entire cast,
from the rosiest choir boy to the blackest Harlem swinger, is understandably awed into silence by this miracle; the Celebrant tears off
his robes and departs, perhaps into death. But the leading boy soprano
discovers his cast-off guitar strap, and carries on for—presumably
becomes—the Celebrant. The old Celebrant, or his spirit, returns, and
as all members of the cast join in a love-in (consisting of almost as
much hugging and kissing as went on among Bernstein, the cast, and
the co-creators down to the lighting designer during curtain calls),
the new and old Celebrants exchange meaningful glances from opposite sides of the stage, which may or may not be Life and Death.

Musically, *Mass* ranges from the nethermost regions of Orff to
typical show tunes, several of them self-plagiarisms from *Candide*
and *West Side Story*. Some of this music, with better and more secular lyrics, might work handily in a musical comedy; some of it is
merely derivative and attitudinizing drivel. The trouble is not so much
that it is eclectic or disparate as that it is banal, inappropriate and
rather vulgar. And that it is set to ideas by Bernstein and lyrics by
Bernstein and Stephen Schwartz that are simplistic, pretentious, pedestrian and not a little distasteful. Quite aside from their obviousness ("I believe in one God,/ But then I believe in three;/ I'll believe
in twenty Gods/ If they'll believe in me!"), they have that awful
smell of the rhyming dictionary about them, as when we get short,
consecutive lines ending in *season, reason, treason,* or are treated to
couplets like "When my spirit falters/ On decaying altars" and "So
earnest, so solemn,/ As stiff as a column."

Mass works in layers. On top are those choric worshipers going an
occasional bit of pantomine straight out of *Carmina Burana* or *Catulli
Carmina*. Below them are those quasireligiously bedizened dancers,
doing one of Alvin Ailey's quasiballetic choreographies. Below them
are the other dancers and singers, performing some of Ailey's more
hectic, show-bizzy numbers. And way down front are the solo turns,
out of the night club and cabaret worlds. This makes for a discordant
cake whose layers are chocolate, rhubarb, molasses and ham: indigestible. The individual performers give their all, the orchestra or
orchestras cannot be faulted, and there is usually something going on
in at least two or three places. But the whole thing is no religious
music-drama based on the litany, merely an inadvertent Broadway
musicalization of the Tower of Babel episode from the Bible. The

overriding sense conveyed is that of self-indulgence: this work, clearly a refugee from show business, has, like immigrants from certain countries, dropped several syllables from its name and doubled its final consonant: the way, for example, Kastenbaum becomes Kass, Masturbation becomes *Mass.*

There is a curious and I think significant parallel between *Mass* and the Reverend Al Carmines' current self-serving, amateurish, melodically derivative and barren, pseudo-religious but genuinely polymorphous-perverse musicalization of the Maid of Orléans story, *Joan.* Both the Kennedy-Center-to-Lincoln-Center and the Judson-Church-to-Circle-in-the-Square shows—high and low camp—insist on God's simplicity.

Carmines' Virgin Mary—a sashaying, miniskirted, bleached-blond countersoprano (or whatever you'd call a voice that shatters glass and drives dogs mad)—protests demurely that she is all simplicity, "And God is even simpler than I." Bernstein's Celebrant advocates "sing[ing] God a simple song . . . for God is the simplest thought of all." (I *think* that word was "thought"; it may have been "sod" or "sot," but I'm pretty sure it was "thought.") Strange what laboriously stylish extravaganzas, what elaborately twisted shows better suited to gay bars, it takes to proclaim the simplicity of God.

Though Gerald Freedman, who staged the Central Park *Hamlet,* may be the director with the greatest number of Shakespearean scalps hanging from his belt, he did not quite perform his customary murder here. I assume that *Hamlet* frightened him more than, say, *The Tempest,* which he reduced to a grinning cadaver by tickling it to death; but less than *King Lear,* from which he backed away in panic, letting it die of neglect. Here Freedman gave the play free rein, did not dare greatly cut it, and luckily lacked the courage to goose it more than intermittently. But, true vaudevillian that he is, he had to turn comic passages into farce, and throw in burlesque or bizarreness where none was required. What finally characterized this production was an essential lack of dignity.

We were treated to a Claudius boozily titubating down a set of stairs while humming to himself, letting out a goodly belch, and literally pushing his knees to make them bend in prayer. His arms would thrash about like a windmill or paw like a scrabbling rabbit, and whenever other people talked too long, he would start a smooching session with his Queen. Gertrude not only joined heartily in the billing and cooing, but also produced some giddy debutante giggles all by herself. Osric was portrayed as a swish bullfighter, Laertes as a quavering popinjay. Hamlet was made to scribble on the floor with his bodkin, assault the King's chair in proxy regicide, double over as if to vomit while listening to the Ghost, and act grossly demented not only during his "mad" scenes. Thus, for example, after his encounter with the Ghost, the awe-struck "O, wonderful!" was directed into a sardonic vocal caper, as of a student activist just informed he was given an F in deportment.

Nevertheless, the scenes with the players, Rosencrantz and Guildenstern, Ophelia, Polonius and the swordplay were acceptably staged; others, like Ophelia's funeral, the gravedigger interlude, the closet scene (though I would have preferred an invisible Ghost here) and some of the chases on the battlements were done at least inoffensively. The Hamlet-Ophelia scenes, despite a welcome ungimmickiness, did not convey a Prince who cared much about the girl.

Yet the main trouble was the absence of an overarching conception. The director must have some governing idea of what the play is about. He may, for instance, decide with the late D. G. James that *Hamlet* "is a tragedy . . . of defeated thought. Hamlet does not know; and he knows of no way of knowing." The Prince then becomes, in Jules Laforgue's penetrating phrase, *"trop nombreux pour dire oui ou non."* Conversely, the director may feel, with Boris Pasternak, that *"Hamlet* is not a drama of a weak character but . . . of duty and self-denial . . . of high vocation, of a call to heroic action in fulfillment of its hero's predestined task." Or the director may opt for any interpretation between these extremes. What he may not do with impunity is to sit back like a dull and muddy-mettled rascal and, unpregnant of his cause, say nothing.

The acting is uneven, often downright odd. Barnard Hughes' Polonius is the most solid performance of all: fusty without fustian, purblind but not dull-witted, pompous but with humanizing glimpses of his own pomposity. Scarcely behind is Kitty Winn's Ophelia. Miss Winn could easily settle for her winning self and fall into an Ophelia who is endearing and pathetic. Instead, she works hard and well at making her more of everything: more childishly trusting; more earnestly, tearingly baffled; and, finally, more lewdly, hideously mad. The result is not just an Ophelia that jerks a genteel tear, but a lost soul that rips up our guts and throat. Splendid—if only Miss Winn's elocution did not get a bit too frayed as her mind becomes unhinged. James J. Sloyan is a persuasive Rosencrantz; George Taylor a good Ghost and a poor Player King.

But what are we to make of Laertes as a prissy simperer, a gum-drop-voiced syllable-sucker, a yokel whose chief expression is pop-eyed hebetude? We are to conclude that Sam Waterston is one of the worst actors on our would-be classical stage and had better stick to playing present-day mooncalves, his specialty. And what of Michael Goodwin's flyweight Fortinbras, who could at best fight the lower-case poles with which the scene designer has tic-tac-toed the stage? (The more this set circles around on a dual turntable, the more it is the same old Ming Cho Lee.) James Earl Jones, a first-rate actor in parts for which he is suited, is an ill-starred Shakespearean King: his built-in-echo-chamber voice roller-coasts aimlessly up and down the octaves; his body is dragged about like a large side of beef by a butcher embarrassed to have strayed onto a stage; his bulging eyes roll around his head in search of that third ball that would make it a game of billiards. Colleen Dewhurst, as Gertrude, acts kittenish or clomps about like a hoplite, and forces her voice down into a whispering baritone.

Stacy Keach is a manly, flexible and sprightly Hamlet, but one who can neither look princely nor sound poetic. His diction is precise, but he splinters long, flowing lines of verse into coagulating tone clusters or elides pauses where they are desperately needed; "a beast, no more" becomes "a beast no more." He moves with vigor, but without finesse, and as the play progresses, he runs out of energy and invention. Repeatedly he will stress the wrong word: "These but the trappings and the suits of *woe*"; "King, father, royal Dane. O, answer *me!*"; "that the Everlasting had not fixed/ *His* canon 'gainst self-slaughter" etc. He plays a decent, confused fellow in need of some psychotherapy; not Hamlet.

FRANK D. GILROY, as he emerges ever so discreetly from his plays (and also movies) is a thoroughly nice man and, perhaps for that very reason, not quite a good enough playwright. This is not meant condescendingly: the world may need truly nice people more than master playwrights. But like it or not, niceness gets into the major dramatist's way. Do you think that Ibsen was a nice man? Or Strindberg? Or Pirandello? Or O'Neill? Or Brecht? Chekhov, who was an exception to many things, most likely *was* nice, and in his best moments Gilroy is Chekhovian. But even if niceness is not always a dramaturgic handicap, lack of niceness is not the only prerequisite.

Present Tense, Gilroy's current bill of four one-acters, strikes me as an almost complete, although completely likable, failure. This does, I'm afraid, hinge largely on Gilroy's niceness. Yet before we get to the present tense, it behooves us to recapitulate the past. Gilroy began with some highly successful television playwriting, and also achieved recognition as a screenwriter. But his true love was the theater, and who but a very nice man would so devotedly embrace a losing cause when he is perfectly capable of making out with a winning one? His first produced play was *Who'll Save the Plowboy?*, and it remains his best. In fact, this simplest and bitterest work of Gilroy's was modestly but unquestionably art. Is it that Gilroy had to pay too high a price for his artistry? The play was done off-Broadway (Broadway having yet again refused something that would have suited and ennobled it), but had only a *succès d'estime* and a skimpy run.

What made *Plowboy* so fine was its spareness. It dealt with a number of interlocking problems adding up to a vision of life as a series of compromises that leave everyone ultimately unfulfilled. And it dealt with its unhappy compromisers sympathetically but unsparingly, painfully but leanly. I think there were more devastating monosyllables in that play than in any other within recent memory. But it was the strategic marshaling of those literal or figurative monosyllables that made the play art. When a frustrated, exasperated housewife said, "Death or a new stove. I'll settle for either one," we more than understood, we experienced her.

Why was Gilroy's greatest hit, *The Subject Was Roses*, so disappointing to me? Because it was, alas, a soap opera. It was a "Short Day's Journey into Night," with a once loving Irish-American family wrangling toward bigger and better outbursts, clashing its way to the son's leaving home. But O'Neill's family chronicle ends with a seemingly beatific vision that is pure tragedy; Gilroy's concludes with some familiar nagging, behind which we are to surmise reconciliation and hope. Of course, in plays, as in life, things may end happily. But in realistic drama happiness has to be made credible; in *Roses*, it depended on a sudden and ephemeral paternal embrace, insufficiently motivated and unable to carry its load of hope—it was unearned. Yet I doubt if a man as nice as Gilroy would simply sell out to Broadway; I think he genuinely yielded to his better instincts and worse sense of truth.

About Gilroy's next, the less said the better. *That Summer—That Fall* was a retelling of the Phaedra-Hippolytus story in terms of simple Italian-Americans, and one of the things you cannot do to great works of art (which can take almost every other kind of beating) is to simplify them. Euripides and Racine have a complexity that fights its way through to simplicity; the other direction on this one-way street leads merely to a crash. Next came *The Only Game in Town,* about two small-time Las Vegas losers: a chorine who is a loser in love, and a honky-tonk pianist who is a loser in everything. Through love and a few other miracles, they make it to the happily-ever-after. It was a pleasantly trivial boulevard confection, about which I wrote in *Commonweal:* "The program describes Gilroy as 'a product of television's Golden Age,' and, like Hesiod, television is entitled to its nostalgic myths, though why this age of iron pyrites should spill over into the theater is not quite clear—unless it be that the stage is more hospitable than TV to moderate sexual boldness." I do wish TV would outgrow its escapist puritanism, so that *The Only Game in Town* and *Present Tense* could go where they belong. Instead, they clutter up a theater that in its time of ordeal needs stronger, truer fare.

Present Tense, besides being gimmicky, is suffocated by niceness. In the first play, an errant husband is driven to ever more ludicrous stratagems of despair by his wife's saintly complaisance; in the second, foolish but lovable pride drives a man out of a perfectly good, normally dishonest job; in the third (and best), the generous permissiveness of a lover allows his partner in adultery the luxury of a phone call that heralds the end of the affair; in the last, the frantic efforts of a husband to delay and cushion some tragic news for his wife make the situation worse—not for her perhaps, but certainly for us who have guessed it all long ago. Despite good acting, the work doesn't belong in a theater struggling for its life, which won't be saved by amiably pseudo-serious trifles.

Gilroy describes in a book the one brief meeting we had. It was pleasant but slightly strained, because I had liked *Plowboy* so much, and we were both a bit uneasy about what *Roses,* opening the following week, would bring. He concludes his short account: "I have this thing about writers and critics. Like baseball players and umpires— I feel they should not socialize." Gilroy may be right in this fastidious, scrupulous sentiment; yet even as I like his plays less and less, I would like to know this nice man more.

· · ·

Too bad that A. J. Antoon, the gifted young director, should have taken the title of *Much Ado About Nothing* literally. For if the play were indeed about nothing, his staging of it for the New York Shakespeare Festival would be quite agreeable. But behind the irony of its title, the play *is* about something: illusion and reality; deception, self-deception and unmasking; the superficiality and mercenariness of a society where semblances could lead to tragedy and only the unlikeliest accidents enable order to reassert itself. I would call it Shakespeare's most Pirandellian play, were it not *lèse-majesté* to liken the greater to the lesser. In Central Park, it comes out not Pirandello but Pinero.

What we see, Shakespeare tells us, is no more real than the hearsay fabricated to delude us. The truth is what we know in our hearts, except that in this Messina the heart is seldom heard, drowned out as it is by everything from the voice of pride and self-interest to mere fusillades of charmingly obfuscatory wit. As Francis Fergusson observed, "The comic vision of *Much Ado* will only appear . . . slowly, and as we learn to trust the fact that it is really there." The trouble with most productions of *Much Ado* is that they do not trust the play. They refuse to set it in Renaissance Europe, where it clearly belongs; or in the present, to which it could be tactfully adapted; and insist on thinking up unlikely times and places to smuggle it into—none more improbable than its current dislocation to our own Southwest, somewhere between the Spanish-American and First World Wars. From the opening moments when the set, a gallimaufry of travestied old posters, is invaded by a Sousa-esquely costumed military band and a plague of scurrying Keystone Kops, to be followed by a "reporter" (for messenger) using old-fashioned flares to photograph the ladies awaiting the return of the Rough Riders, we know that meanings will be ridden over roughshod.

For this *Much Ado* is transposed into an indolent Never-Never-Land where intrigue has no teeth at all, and the elegant wordmongering and lowborn word-mangling proceed as if people had never been invented. The characters, at best, rise from Mack Sennett to Joaquin Miller, and seem uneasy receptacles for Shakespeare's words—assuming these can be heard at all, which is hard over the almost ceaseless interference of Henry "Bootsie" Normand's brass band. Oh, it all looks gladsome enough, what with Ming Cho Lee's uncharacteristically sensuous set (derived perhaps from Douglas W. Schmidt's décor for *Grease*), Theoni V. Aldredge's sparkling yet unexaggerated costumes, the amusing albeit meddlesome score of Peter Link and Scott Joplin, the conscientious lighting of Martin Aronstein, and the serviceable dances of Donald Saddler. Antoon himself has come up with some endearing ideas, such as having Benedick row in in a canoe wafted by the turntable and then imperfectly hiding behind his craft to eavesdrop.

But the direction is not always felicitous even on its own terms. Thus it is out of character for the cool Beatrice to climb eagerly on a chair for a better view of the returning Benedick and army; it is all wrong for Dogberry, who takes himself very seriously (therein lies the humor), to dance around waggishly holding up his coattails as he declares himself, without knowing what he says, "a pretty piece of flesh." Don John, when foiled, would not be reduced to weltering on the floor in a travesty of Chaplin's travesty of Hitler; the old musical-comedy trick of doing a wistful number with umbrellas under the rain is a soggy joke to play on the next-to-last scene; and, in the last, bringing in the women ludicrously swathed and riding carousel horses destroys even the dubious solemnity the moment demands; and the scene in which Beatrice eavesdrops should not be staged less resourcefully than the one in which Benedick is gulled, and so both fall flat.

There are graver problems in the sheer casting. Sam Waterston is good enough for the foppish and fatuous aspects of Benedick (but must there be so many?) until, supposed to grow earnest and manly, he can barely muster up a difference. Kathleen Widdoes, the Beatrice, is always so smugly delighted with whatever she is doing that she has a way of preempting the whole joy of the thing, leaving little or nothing for the beholder. Her Kewpie-doll face oozes a self-satisfaction that seems to have provoked someone into knocking it flat and slightly askew, which has a certain piquancy; but all of those eyebrow wigglings and *oeillades* and adorably pigeon-toed stances finally achieve a mighty *Verfremdungseffekt,* while her line readings remain superficial.

April Shawhan can be very funny as a saucy soubrette, but as the sweet, chaste, maligned Hero, she is about as uneponymous and grotesque as they come. Worse is Glenn Walken's Claudio, conceived along the lines of Andy Hardy Goes to Messina. As Margaret, Jeanne Hepple confuses witty banter with tormented tootlings and grimaces worthy of Belloc's Maria. Bette Henritze's Ursula is drab except when she is scary, and Will Mackenzie's Verges is rather difficult to notice. There is worse. Mark Hammer's Leonato is a performance clotted with gluey amateurishness; Frederick Coffin's Borachio achieves the rare stunt of being both crass and effete; and Tom McDermott's Friar

Francis is a crapulous Irish jig instructor. Somewhat better are Marshall Efron's Balthasar, a cute joke gone slightly off-color, and Barnard Hughes's passable Dogberry.

That leaves a nice, warm, not overdone Antonio from Lou Gilbert; a dignified, well-balanced Don Pedro from Douglass Watson; and a Don John from Jerry Mayer who, directed more appositely, might have clicked. Is Messina in a mess!

Jacques Brel Is Alive and Well and Living in Paris is a potpourri of Brel songs which, after a long off-Broadway and touring career, has set up shop on Broadway. Brel may indeed be all of those things, but I would vastly prefer him to be Brecht and alive or Weill and living. For his tunes achingly lack melody and inventiveness, and try to make up for it with brazen iteration of phrases and monomaniacal propulsion, as if dynamics were all and the power drill as musical an instrument as any. And his lyrics, at least in this Eric Blau-Mort Shuman adaptation, emerge as pretentious platitudes ("The old, old silver clock/ That's hanging on the wall,/ That waits fo us all"); or banalities made "literary" by being interlarded with name-dropping (Sunday at the bullfight: "the day when grocery clerks become García Lorca"); synthetic poeticism (I counted at least three or four instances of "years" rhyming with "tears"); and desperate, portentous attempts at significance (the exclamation "Saigon!" dragged in from left or, Brel being Belgian, Flanders Field).

This leaves the production and the performing. The set, by Les Lawrence, looks like a set of carious mammoth teeth made of cloth rather than enamel, and pretending to be sails on some antique vessel. The central acting area thus becomes the cavity in some monstrous prehistoric bicuspid surrounded by molars billowing in the wind. It is a set that hurts. The staging, by Moni Yakim, consists of making the four singers, singly or jointly, bustle about cutely, grope one another crudely, or assume poses that are picturesque and bathetic. There is a good deal of would-be ingenuity that comes out as self-conscious fussiness. Joe Masiell has a fine voice that has yet to find material worthy of its variety and resonance, and his delivery ought to be stripped of the tricks and fidgets with which the director has bedizened it. George Ball and Henrietta Valor are as competent vocally as they are unwinning visually.

Which brings us to the star, Elly Stone. Genuine chanteuses have, over and above their singing, a special brand of persuasion. Edith

Piaf had an all-embracing humanity, Juliette Gréco a quintessential femininity, Lotte Lenya a shrewd incisiveness, Mabel Mercer a sly sophistication, Greta Keller the ability to convey limitless living. Miss Stone, despite some technique and stage presence, rings false. Her vocal range is limited, her tonal quality a superinsistent tinkle. But the real trouble is that her expressions, gestures and general demeanor do not strike one as truly felt. She turns it all on without losing a basic quality of porcelain-doll-likeness, and her favorite stance—face tilted zenithward, arms coyly half-opened—suggests a less than innocent Danaë inviting Zeus to shower her with aphrodisiac gold coins. But she does have an enthusiastic following, though the clappers seemed mostly claqueurs, and the screamers squealy-mouthed flamingos.

OH COWARD! may be a small diamond, but it is a very nearly flawless one. Like Noël Coward himself, from whose works it is culled, it is all wit, polish, taste and style, and it will no more do to accuse this many-faceted scintillation of being superficial than to reproach a diamond for being all surface. The show, however, is more than brilliant, cutting and, like certain other gems, blessed with sentimental value; it is also profoundly melodious, which even the Kohinoor cannot claim to be.

I have always considered Coward's tunes second only to Weill's, and his lyrics as good as any written in English. But I think I know why his songs have not surpassed those of Kern, Berlin and the rest in popularity: the flavor of many of the lyrics is British, and the melodies are not always easy to hum. Coward is extremely fond of chromaticism, and even trained performers have been known to cut themselves on his sharps or fall flat on his flats. Carrying the tune of your typical hit song is like promenading a package down Fifth Avenue compared to negotiating the modulations of, say, "Zigeuner," "Half-Caste Woman" or "Play, Orchestra, Play," which is more like broken-field running. But how dazzling the result!

There is something else, too, about Coward's work that is not everybody's dish of tea: camp. Now, camp, despite Susan Sontag's obfuscations on the subject, is basically the homosexual sensibility translated into a performing art (or nonperforming art, or general behavior). But we must distinguish between high camp and low camp. André Gide is supposed to have said, *"Je suis pédéraste, pas tapète,"* and just as there is a vast gulf between the pederast and the faggot, so there is between the plays of Oscar Wilde and those, say, of certain off-off-Broadway playwrights. (A good example of low camp would be *Lady Audley's Secret,* a musical that just breezed in and out of town, and about which only the performing of Lu Ann Post deserves honorable mention.) *Oh Coward!* is very high camp indeed, which, practically speaking, means subversive or even anarchic views given the most genteel and soigné expression: impeccably housebroken outrageousness, fastidiously elegant bitchiness, the most *outré* sentiments kept in tight control by a jaded omniscience. It may not be art, but like blindfolded tightrope-walking, it has a blasé bravura all its own.

Roderick Cook has devised and directed this show, which admirably avoids the pitfalls into which similar tributes have tended to hurtle. It is not excessively reverential, and flaunts the fact that Coward thinks of himself principally as an entertainer. It is not pedantic, and handles its material rather cavalierly—abridging, conflating, defying chronology—but the liberties are taken with the letter, never with the spirit of Coward. It effects a neat compromise between familiar and esoteric Cowardiana, and though I could cavil with some of the omissions and inclusions, what two-hour selection from so nearly inexhaustible a hoard would not arch somebody's eyebrow? Above all, *Oh Coward!* is unassuming—from its scenery to its two-piano-plus-percussion arrangements, from its costumes to its staging.

Just as Coward is Coward's best interpreter, so Roderick Cook is the best performer of the revue he has devised. He handles the laconic gestures, minimal facial play, ironically understated verbalizings and vocalizings with that weary poise and attenuated aplomb that are the Coward hallmarks; lacking only are the tremulous falsetto and slightly overglossy good looks of the Master in his heyday. But the variety of accents, the expression midway between sneering and somnolence, and the voice wearing white kid gloves are all meticulously there. What is particularly pleasing about Mr. Cook is that he can take a song like "Marvelous Party," of which Bea Lillie seemed to have uncontested ownership, and by doing it differently but equally well make it his own.

Barbara Cason is almost as good. But she is the only non-Britisher in this trio of performers and, as the only female, has to do both the mature primadonna and the bewitching ingénue numbers. Though she is fine in the former, even if vocally a bit tentative at times, she is less suited to the latter both in age and looks. Yet she compensates for this with a lightness of touch and a nicely subdued impishness.

Jamie Ross, who completes the cast, has a certain Scottish asperity about him, and lacks some of the litheness, both somatic and vocal, that we associate with Coward. But he has stage presence and acting ability, and his baritone has a rich texture; it is just too bad that he is made to take that superb ballad "You Were There" at a stickily slow tempo.

Oh Coward! is not only a potpourri of songs but also a cento of some of Sir Noël's musicless words, and these too are sly, pungent and wisely chosen. It is a show that, while it delights you, leaves you, like Chinese cooking, hungry for more, exhibiting ceremonial tact even in this. And there are so many resplendent Coward items left to do that I hope that this show will not die, only turn eventually into its own sequel.

REPERTORY THEATER being what the New York stage needs most of all, with the possible exception of directors, nothing would seem more welcome than the City Center Acting Company, with six plays in repertory. The group is last year's graduating class from the Julliard School, who have decided to stay together as a group under John Houseman's artistic directorship and perform, under City Center auspices, at the Good Shepherd-Faith Church. After seeing three of their productions, I submit this half-time report.

It seems to me that the group is to be commended for both its intentions and effort. It should be patronized as much as possible just so that people can get an idea of what a joy repertory can be for both performer and spectator. And several of the plays are so well chosen that they make good watching in almost any production. But— and it's a huge but—the level of work here is far from the consistently professional, and one's attitude toward the City Center Acting Company will vary according to one's tolerance for well-meaning, hard-working amateurs spiced here and there with a touch of genuine professionalism.

The opening bill was a cut and slightly recast version—to fit the somewhat small complement of performers—of Sheridan's *The School for Scandal*. This is the kind of play that requires the highest command of stylization and polish, the very thing it is least likely to get from a young, fairly inexperienced American company. Nevertheless, thanks nine parts to Sheridan and one part to enthusiasm, the evening is pleasant enough. The night I attended, Dakin Matthews had to go on suddenly for an ailing colleague in the taxing role of Sir Peter Teazle, and filled the aggregation with apprehenion and apologies. They were wrong: not only did he manage to get through the part without any real hitch, he also gave a nicely tempered, modulated, warm performance in a part that lends itself to easy exaggeration, and proved the linchpin of the enterprise. The other piece of solid work came from Jared Sakren as Moses. Pattie LuPone had much of the verve and sassiness required for Lady Teazle, but a certain lack of charm and a faintly lupine visage militate against Miss LuPone. Mary Lou Rosato, although very un-British and rather quirky, was nevertheless an interesting Lady Sneerwell. But the other major performances went from bad to ludicrous, and there was a curious notion rampant that effete mincing equals English sophistication. Gerald Freedman's direction was less gimmicky than usual, though he could seldom resist underlining the obvious. Douglas W. Schmidt's simple yet suggestive décor testified to the designer's ability, and there was sparklingly appropriate music by Robert Waldman.

The NEXT BILL was *U. S. A.*, Paul Shyre's adaptation of the John Dos Passos novel, a dramatic reading that calls itself a "revue," presumably because it has a piano player, which is fine—it is certainly not him that we should shoot. I consider these reading adaptations of novels and autobiographies—a genre to whose proliferation Mr. Shyre has contributed more than anyone—lazy people's theater and a rather sorry affair. It is a way for the adapter to become a playwright without writing a play, for the audience to see part of a novel without having to read the book, and for a stage to show a modest amount of activity without offering living theater. In the end, you get neither the novel nor a play, and the undertaking falls between the two or more stools on which the performers perch most of the time.

U. S. A. was mainly dreary, given the genre and the graceless reading of the central role by Norman Snow, who confirmed his crude work in *The School for Scandal*. Nevertheless, he was surpassed in ineptitude by Benjamin Hendrickson and Gerald Shaw, while James Moody was merely dull. Mary Joan Negro and Mary Lou Rosato had some good moments, but Leah Chandler is not even just another pretty face, only the same pretty face we have seen freezing the action in many an amateur production. One of the company's performers, Anne McNaughton, directed pedestrianly.

NEXT, WE GOT Brendan Behan's *The Hostage*, which Gene Lesser sensibly, though not always cleverly, updated, and then directed with more brio than finesse. Behan's play is a ramshackle affair, but it oozes drunken, disrespectful fun, and has a tonic effect on an audience. A church, alas, is hardly the right setting for a play that takes place in a brothel, even if both institutions trade in illusions, and Lesser's idea of having an angelic, or at any rate stereophonic, choir accompany the onstage voices from the loft behind the audience makes for undue grandness. The cast struggles valiantly with the Irish and English accents, and here again Dakin Matthews is a marvelously complex, fallible and humane Pat, as Irish as begorrah. David Ogden Stiers, as Monsewer, would be an amusing man indeed if only someone could put a stop to his pulling all the stops and losing the comic pinprick in a haystack of mannerisms. As Teresa, Miss Negro is immensely moving in the first act, but does not rise to the climax of the finale, and Jared Sakren is again competent in a small part. Others fare less well, notably Sam Tsoutsouvas, a flamboyant but hollow actor; James Moody and Benjamin Hendrickson, who succeed in turning campy homosexuals into bores; and Kevin Kline, whose I.R.A. officer gives one-dimensionality a worse name. Worst of all is Cynthia Herman, whose Miss Gilchrist can hardly even be understood. The staging of the last scene is particularly murky, but the general effect is still more enjoyable than not.

The City Center Acting Company is off full steam on the right track; like our railroads, it needs saving.

WINTER, 1972-1973

THE CREATION OF THE WORLD
AND OTHER BUSINESS
by Arthur Miller

ENEMIES
by Maxim Gorky
produced by the Repertory Theater of Lincoln Center

HAPPY DAYS, KRAPP'S LAST TAPE,
ACT WITHOUT WORDS #1 *and* NOT I
by Samuel Beckett

THE MOSCOW CIRCUS

THE GREAT GOD BROWN
by Eugene O'Neill

DON JUAN
by Molière
produced by the APA-Phoenix Repertory Company

THE SUNSHINE BOYS
by Neil Simon

THE PLOUGH AND THE STARS
by Sean O'Casey
produced by the Repertory Theater of Lincoln Center

DON JUAN IN HELL
by George Bernard Shaw

MEDEA
by Euripides
produced by the Circle in the Square Theatre

FREEMAN
by Phillip Hayes Dean

ENDGAME
by Samuel Beckett
produced by the Manhattan Project

EL GRANDE DE COCA-COLA
by Ron House and Diz White

A LITTLE NIGHT MUSIC
book by Hugh Wheeler
music and lyrics by Stephen Sondheim

THE MERCHANT OF VENICE
by William Shakespeare
produced by the Repertory Theater of Lincoln Center

SEESAW
book by Michael Bennett
music by Cy Coleman
lyrics by Dorothy Fields

EMPEROR HENRY IV
by Luigi Pirandello
with Rex Harrison, directed by Clifford Williams

THE ORPHAN
by David Rabe

THAT CHAMPIONSHIP SEASON
by Jason Miller

IT IS NOT surprising that, having been praised to the skies for
even his recent sorry work, Arthur Miller should assault the heavens
with his new play, *The Creation of the World and Other Business*.
It is, frankly, rather foolhardy of someone who has no English style
to tread in the footsteps of the King James Bible and Milton; and it
is downright reckless of someone with very little sense of humor to
try to squeeze jokes out of material that Mark Twain, Bernard Shaw,
Anatole France, Erich Kästner and who knows how many other able
humorists have bled dry of every laugh it contained. Yet on the
Ossa of stylelessness and the Pelion of humorlessness Miller must
pile the Everest of pointlessness.

For in this retelling of Genesis, the playwright cannot even decide
whether Lucifer is the hero and God the villain or vice versa, and
his continual reversals create not complexity but stultifying confusion. And are there still any thrills left in dabbling with the
notions of a pettily despotic God and a libertarian and egalitarian
Lucifer at a time when there are precious few people left who believe in an even remotely anthropomorphic deity and devil, and
those few not likely to be found in a Broadway theater? But even
if an accident brought them there, it would take a miracle to make
them laugh at God's saying about the still innocent Adam and Eve,
"Look at them! They're in the middle of a perfect night and they're
playing handball"; or at the fallen Lucifer lamenting, "For all the
bad I've done, I might as well have stayed in heaven." And this is
still preferable to the vulgarity of God's exclaiming, "He was like a
snake, that son of a bitch, Lucifer. And as for you, schmuck..."
Genesis is reduced to a Jewish joke. And when all else fails, out
comes the trusty anachronism: "ANGEL: But Lord, Notre Dame isn't
for 6,000 years yet. GOD: I know. I'm looking forward."

Miller himself is looking backward, though no farther than *Back
to Methuselah*, or not even quite that far. He sheds not a firefly's
worth of light on the metaphysics of good and evil, and he does not
even write, as he once used to, interesting roles for actors to bite
into. There is not a single part here that would give a bravura actor
a chance to transcend the exiguity of the vehicle, and there are
supporting parts like those of the three archangels who mostly stand
and wait and do not serve at all.

George Grizzard, as Lucifer, comes off best because of that sleek,
languid quality of his that can so quickly flare up into exacerbated
petulance—a quicksilver, ambiguous, ever so faintly and fascinatingly

slimy quality that can make a plodding part become disturbing. Stephen Elliott's God would be better if his omniscience extended to remembering his lines. Bob Dishy amiably turns Adam into a Jules Feiffer-Second City caricature. Zoë Caldwell's Australian Eve does not fit vocally into the Miller milieu, is visually even less dishy than Bob, and allows her speech patterns to become a jag. Barry Primus does his standard tormented bit as Cain, and, unhappily for Mark Lamos, the part of Abel dies of dramatic inanition well ahead of fratricide. Like Miller's language between the Bible and the Bronx, Gerald Freedman's direction shuttles between the reverentially wooden and the resolutely arch. Boris Aronson's scenery, abetted by Tharon Musser's lighting, conjures up an Eden with iridescences worthy of a nickelodeon, though some of the shapes are rather more pleasing. Stanley Silverman's music is a spirited pastiche, but Hal George's costumes have a kind of assertive self-depreciation that merely irritates.

Miller's exercise in manic Manichaeism contains one piece of invention: an archangel named Chemuel, unknown even to Gustav Davidson's exhaustive *Dictionary of Angels,* which does, however, list a Chamuel and Kemuel. Actually, the play most needs a Samhiel, the angel who, according to the cabala, was invoked as a curer of stupidity. Done with *After the Fall* and the fall itself, Mr. Miller may now return to his prelapsarian self.

ON THE MAIN STAGE, the Repertory Theater of Lincoln Center began what was to become Jules Irving's last season with Maxim Gorky's *Enemies,* and the irony of it lies in the fact that Ellis Rabb, the guest director, is one of those mentioned as a possible successor to Irving. *Enemies,* finished in exile on Capri in 1906, is a respectable enough play, though it lacks the haunting, perhaps romantic, intensity of *The Lower Depths.* It seems likely that Gorky followed the advice of Chekhov, who admired the work of his junior but found it "somehow uncontrolled and flamboyant." By the time of *Enemies,* Gorky was certainly unflamboyant, but the control, such as it was, was mostly ideological. Even though the play (at least in its first version, as performed here; later, Gorky rewrote it for the worse) is by no means a piece of agit-prop—the bourgeois are drawn with considerable understanding, indeed some sympathy—there is something programmatic and didactic about it, relegating human values to a secondary position. Human interest is there, I repeat, as well as a good grasp of the spectrum of attitudes that characterized the Russia of the aborted revolution of 1905, but the chief characteristic of *Enemies* is its portentousness, beside which all else unhappily pales.

We are shown a sort of miniature revolution in a provincial textile factory, owned jointly by the weak-kneed liberal Zakhar Bardin, and the tough reactionary Mikhail Skrobotov. When, during an outburst of worker unrest, Skrobotov is shot to death, Bardin tries to placate the workers with various concessions, but a telegram previously dispatched by the dead man brings in the army under the command of the officious and inept Captain Boboyedov of the Gendarmerie, or as the present translators (Kitty Hunter-Blair and Jeremy Brooks) put it, the Security Corps. Leading the investigation, however, is the dead man's brother, the ice-cold Assistant Prosecutor Nikolai Skrobotov. Completing the cast of upper-class characters are Kleopatra, the dead man's wife, now a shrill Fury crying for vengeance, though she used to cheat on her husband profusely; Zakhar's brother, Yakov, an amiable drunkard who has opted out of life; his wife, Tatiana, an actress of some repute, no longer in love with her weak spouse and turned bored dilettante; Paulina, Zakhar's wife, a well-meaning but inflexible woman, decent and unimaginative, to whom Socialists are distant, hardly real bugbears until to her dismay she finds out otherwise; General Pechenegov, Bardin's retired, totally right-wing uncle vacationing at the Bardin estate—a foolish man mostly engaged in domineering his luckless old orderly, Kon; and twenty-year-old Nadya, an orphaned niece whom the Bardins have adopted.

Gorky uses these people admirably to show various degrees on the bourgeois-upper-class scale, from the bullying exploitativeness of Mikhail and the General to the unthinking support given that attitude by Kleopatra and to a lesser extent Paulina; from the lukewarm and ultimately ineffectual liberalism of Zakhar, through what we would now call the radical chic of Yakov and Tatiana, who fence-sittingly flirt with the workers, down to the enthusiastic espousal of the underprivileged by Nadya, whose late mother had herself been impoverished. Among the workers, however, there is nowhere near such variety. There is Levshin, the canny old man who has thought his way through to socialism but cleverly conceals his true feelings; Sintsov, the clerk, a kind of idealized Gorky-figure, who is really a disguised party organizer come to politicize the workers; Pologgy, a miserable, self-righteous little clerk who turns informer; and for the rest, faceless good men who without any false heroics are the noble forerunners of the Revolution and reek with solidarity and the spirit of self-sacrifice.

A play such as this has no heroes in the strict sense. When, in act three, the workers appear before an improvised Army tribunal, their behavior is brave but unspectacular, and Tatiana, the theatrical, ego-centric, but not imperceptive actress, exclaims, "Why do they speak so simply, look at things so simply . . . and suffer? Why? Do they have no passion in them, no heroism?" The play certainly lacks heroes even in the technical sense of the word, and here the observa-tion of Berthold Viertel, the German director-critic, is relevant: "The theme of the Russian theater was not the hypertrophy of individual-ism . . . but life, broad and drastic as it is. Life was the protagonist . . . The issue was the question of the individual's rootedness in everyday reality, in the existence of all. . . . The Russian Christ was the populace. And the suffering of the people begat the drama . . ." All very well, but one can also understand Rilke's demurrer after meeting Gorky on Capri shortly after the latter had completed *Ene-mies*. Much as he was impressed by the Russian, Rilke could not help feeling (as he wrote to Ellen Key) that "the revolutionary is a con-tradiction both of the poet and of the Russian; the one and the other have so many reasons for the inward refusal of revolutions, nothing is more important to them than patience . . ."

True enough, the characters in *Enemies* are not patiently, fully developed; perhaps, in fact, there are too many of them for anyone but a supreme dramatic genius to do justice to all in such short space. But there are further difficulties: for Gorky, the workers have to be absolutely right, the factory owners basically wrong—which means that the more educated, articulate, psychologically complex people have to be essentially villains. Thus Nikolai, the Assistant Prosecutor, is a demon of unfeeling lucidity, just barely tempted from his dogged persecution of the workers by the actress' flesh; the seeming decency of Zakhar has to become tantamount to weakness and opportunistic willingness to make small concessions to forestall greater losses— eagerness to shore up exploitation by means of piddling compromise. Nadya, the young idealist who presumably will become a Socialist, is shown as a zealous innocent, rightly but ineffectually sympathetic to the workers—a character who would become interesting only dur-ing an actual Revolution, when she would probably be caught between two grindstones. Sintsov, the organizer, could have been fascinating, but Gorky lets him get lost in the shuffle.

This leaves us, as the most dramatically viable characters, the couple, Yakov and Tatiana. An ironical wastrel, a boozing, quipping fifth wheel, Yakov betrays the factory owners' stratagems to the workers. He does this partly to ingratiate himself with a new group of people, and partly out of boredom with and spite against the old; but the workers' cause is of little interest to him compared to his mesmerized preoccupation with the crumbling of his marriage. Tatiana is likewise bored with her life—even, it would seem, with the stage—but she may get some pleasure from enacting the cynical teller-off of other people, the morally superior speaker of harsh truths. She is attracted to Sintsov and fairly openly flirts with him, but will not go any farther; she will not even hide evidence that is sure to incriminate him, though she could do this with impunity. Later she toys with the notion of sleeping with Nikolai in exchange for Sintsov's freedom, but this, too, is beyond her: she remains an alert, observant but selfish dilettante. She and Yakov are well matched, in fact, except that she continues to function, however barrenly, while he merely deteriorates.

These two (along, perhaps, with Nadya) are the play's most Chekhovian characters—the most freewheeling and unpredictable, and so the most dramatic. But whereas in Chekhov they would be allowed more limelight—like Masha and Vershinin, or Astrov and Elena—here they remain overshadowed by social events, by the unsuccessful workers' uprising that nevertheless heralds the Revolution. Chekhov, aside from being the greater playwright, was lucky to die before the age of ideology closed in; even Gorky in *The Lower Depths* had partly escaped it; in *Enemies*, despite laudable efforts to the contrary, oversimplification begins to set in. Gorky's characters, moreover, are not so salty, original, pathetically or risibly eccentric as Chekhov's; the General, who may be the oddest, is still only a prankster and martinet; Pologgy, although related to Chekhov's frustrated whiners, is contemptible rather than pitiable.

Finally, Gorky's language and the quality of his invention are less choice than Chekhov's. Still, there are splendid exceptions. Take Yakov's description of what haunts him even in the midst of his drunkenness: "I can see this face, this broad, unwashed face staring at me with enormous eyes which ask . . . 'Well?' Do you understand? Just one word . . . 'Well?'" Or take the observation of Levshin, the old worker sage, "It's the vicious has to be killed. The good ones are no hindrance, they'll die of themselves"—the sort of statement that brilliantly exemplifies what Zakhar fears in the workers when "they look at you with such clear eyes" as if no murder had been committed: "That terrifying simplicity!" Two brief scenes are particularly effective: the one where Tatiana plays with making love to Nikolai to save Sintsov, and Yakov's farewell to his wife, where Tatiana does not grasp that the "anywhere" into which he is going is suicide.

Yet if most of the good bits involve Tatiana, Yakov or both, this is no justification for turning them into the central characters and deflecting the play's socialist realism into bourgeois romanticism. Already the highly successful Royal Shakespeare Company production of the play cheated a little when it added a final offstage pistol shot, providing a neat ending but unduly stressing the importance of Yakov's death. Ellis Rabb's production, however, went immeasurably farther in grotesque wrongheadedness.

Rabb, always more concerned with visual effects than with verbal or psychological accuracy, directed the show so as to put the huge stage of the Vivian Beaumont on pyrotechnical display. In the most intimate scenes, characters were kept at great distances from each other, so that the dialogue crisscrossed the stage in quaint diagonals, as it were. Often several groups of people were relegated to various remote corners of the stage so that dramatic interaction was impossible, and in general much more attention was paid to curious entrances and eccentric exits, to odd collapses onto provocatively positioned pieces of furniture and to picturesque bits of ensemble choreography, than to the meanings of the sundry relationships and of the play itself. Perversely ignored was the helpful hint in the use of the very word "enemies," which Paulina first applies to the opposing lower orders, but which Kleopatra then applies to their own class. While the workers know what they want and stick together, "we," she says, "*we* live like enemies, believing in nothing, bound together by nothing, each for himself."

Instead of concentrating on establishing this distinction, Rabb devised pretty tableaus to make us view the drifting, doomed upper classes with exquisite melancholy. For this purpose he mobilized the Beaumont's revolving stage, so that act two ended not, as in the text, with Levshin's exhortation to a fellow worker to "hurry up and get things straight," but with the turntable revolving from the garden to the interior of the Bardin house, where Mikhail's coffin stood mournfully surrounded by guttering candles. Needless to say, no such coffin figures in Gorky's script. But the worst *contresens* was the second turning of the stage at the end of the third and final act. Here we are supposed to be left with the frightening image of the brave workers having bags put over their heads by the soldiery to cut off their quiet professions of faith (this is actually taken over from Gorky's own 1933 revision of the text, which the English adapters have permissibly added to what is otherwise the superior 1906 version). Nadya cries out at both soldiers and fellow bourgeois, "It's you —you—you're the criminals," and Levshin adds that the killer is he who implants the bitterness. Instead of this, Rabb gave us an offstage shot followed by the turntable's slow revolution (quite the wrong sort, that!) bringing us back into the garden. There we saw, downstage center, Yakov's body elegantly dead on a lounge chair, with a clean handkerchief daintily covering the bullet-shattered head. Not a drop of blood on either the pure white hankie or on Yakov's immaculate white suit; we were to assume that the gallant and decorous suicide had, after shooting himself through the temple, considerately covered up the offending sight. Meanwhile the entire cast—soldiers, workers, bourgeois—slowly filtered into the garden, ending up huddled together in an awe-struck tableau as the lights achingly dimmed.

Now this is vulgar nonsense. The implication is first that this socially useless tippler is Gorky's tragic hero, that his suicide somehow epitomizes the perhaps inevitable but nevertheless profoundly sad passing of an era of gracious living; and second that there was something so exaltedly heroic about this gesture that for its sake the bagging of prisoners had to be dropped so that all characters, regardless of class and persuasion, could be revealed paying silent homage to the departed. Nothing could be farther from the playwright's intentions; nevertheless Clive Barnes of the *Times*, that choragus of the chorus of raving reviewers, was to comment about those plays by Chekhov and Gorky that end with pistol shots—as if *Enemies* were some sort of *Sea Gull* or *Ivanov*.

With the casting, Rabb does no better than with the staging. And what rotten performances on this stage that becomes a veritable battleground for no less than six histrionically hostile armies having it out with one another! The failing forces of Jules Irving's Actor's Workshop are led by Robert Phalen, who reduces a revolutionary worker to a scowling blank, and by Robert Symonds, who turns a well-meaning but weak liberal factory owner into a puling nonentity, featuring that whiny Symonds twang piped in direct from the great tundras around Winnetsk and Grandrapidovsk. The faltering legions of Rabb and the old APA-Phoenix Repertory Company are headed by Sydney Walker, who plays a wily, aged peasant turned hortatory working-class pundit as if he were a Macy's Santa Claus dandling rambunctious children; and George Pentecost, who acts a prissy clerk with his typical fussy externalizations over a central void.

The veterans of Broadway are represented by Barbara Cook, a musical soubrette whose loss of voice is presumed to have increased her straight acting ability, and whose emotional outburst at her husband's murder might just win a prize for Allegiance-to-the-Flag recitation during National Girl Scout Week; and by Stefan Schnabel, who plays a retired martinet of a Russian general as if he were in some farcical Hollywood remake of *The Captain From Köpenick*. The Jewish Art Theater contingent is led by Joseph Wiseman, who plays a bibulous Russian aristocrat exactly as he did Bummidge in *The Last Analysis*, only more Jewish, and who macabrely dances out his drunkenness as a nasally falsettoing, squinty-eyed Specter of the Rose. And Will Lee performs a beleaguered Slavic orderly as a prematurely aged Motel the tailor.

The horrors of Method acting are spearheaded by Christopher Walken, who plays a socialist intellectual by allowing his syllables to dribble down his chin while he lopes and smirks soulfully. The hordes of provincial repertory thespians are present in full panoply, commanded by Josef Sommer, who plays a mean but lecherous district attorney as a cross between an effeminate Count Dracula and some self-pitying Dickensian sniveler. He is matched in effeteness by Tom Lacy's rendering of a Captain of the Security Corps as an overripe version of his Birdboot in *The Real Inspector Hound*.

Partial relief is provided by four performers: Frances Sternhagen, who manages to keep a rich, socially inflexible wife from losing our sympathy; Nancy Marchand, who makes a self-centered butterfly of an actress flirting with revolutionaries also gracious and not devoid of a well-conveyed ultimate awareness; Philip Bosco, who resists making a petty tyrant more obnoxious than necessary (though I wish his voice would not splinter so in the fortissimos); and Susan Sharkey, whose young gentlewoman irresistibly drawn to the people's cause has fine, strong moments, even if the rest of her performance is allowed by the director to lapse into musical-comedy Americana.

Douglas W. Schmidt's scenery was, as always, both appropriate and imaginative; Ann Roth's costumes were pleasing and, for all I know, authentic; and John Gleason contributed consistently evocative lighting. But how can they prevail against Ellis Rabb, who for the sake of a visually gripping ending foists a final tableau on us not only undreamt of by Gorky, but also foolishly contradictory to his very aims. This is a stroke of theater worth twenty strokes of the knout.

·   ·   ·

WHO IS SAMUEL BECKETT? A farcical nihilist, according to Harry Levin; the author of terminal art that is also hilarious, according to George Steiner; the creator, according to Robert Abirached, of a single figure that masticates the same monologue from book to book and exudes without surcease the muttered romance of creature discomfort. Yes, I think, and also Aeschylus in reverse. The Greek tragedian, by inserting a second actor, made drama possible; the Franco-Irish tragicomedian, by returning it to the single speaker, alone or grazed by other alonenesses, made drama impossible again— impossible and still persevering. It is a drama reduced beyond the absurd to the molecular structure of our condition, to atoms of suffering and laughter. Beckettian man is laughing through his cursing and weeping: cursing God, bewailing his birth, laughing at himself.

Yet Beckett is not a minimalist like Gertrude Stein. His human minimums are still full of humanity: they stink of it, choke on it, deprecate it and sometimes even exult in it; but they do not convert it into arch pseudoprofundities, paramathematical formulas, or a game of chicken on the edge of total dehumanization. In Beckett's best plays and novels there is still form enough and a great sufficiency of feeling; only, man is observed from a great, stoical distance, seen in absolute focus but without any ambience. His personal minutiae fill the field of vision: place has ceased to exist and time is reduced to the tick of mortality and the tock of waiting. The only chorus around this lone, pre-Aeschylean protagonist is the voice of mortality speaking in blows to the body and soul, or jeering silences.

In his early monograph on Proust, Beckett wrote of "the wisdom that consists not in the satisfaction but in the ablation of desire," and surely his is an art of ablation, of surgical removal of human faculties and possibilities (thereby emblematizing the work of time), but not always abrogating some blind hope: a hope indistinguishable from obstinacy, an insistence on carrying on even as one is carried off. The hero is "amputated on all sides" but also "erect on [his] trusty stumps." Beckett has made of man's case history a declension and placed man in the last, the ablative case. His life is afflicted, but his ending strongly inflected.

How prophetic, metaphorical and, indeed, Beckettian that the small, experimental Forum Theater in Lincoln Center should have scheduled for what it did not realize would be its swan song a Beckett mini-festival. No one knew that an incompetent board of directors would cause the demise of this precious and necessary theater; yet what more glorious death rattle could there be than

alternating performances of two Beckett gems: *Krapp's Last Tape*
(1958) and *Happy Days* (1961), the latter postfaced by *Act Without Words #1* (1957), the former by a world première, *Not I*.
Truly, this is dying in style—and in good company, too, for Beckett's
great drama itself seems to expire with the dying fall of his new,
very bad, very nonexistent play.

Both evenings were directed satisfactorily by Alan Schneider, and
the performers were the acting couple Hume Cronyn and Jessica
Tandy. The best play of the four surely is *Happy Days*, which becomes brighter and sharper—more touching, hilarious and essential—
with every viewing. Its heroine, Winnie, is, among all Beckett's
dramatic creations, the most winning loser: the most patiently suffering, the most cheerful amid the adversity in which she is literally
buried. Yet in her good-natured adaptability—the sweetness with
which she endures, the absurd gratitude she exudes—lies the horrible
irony of the play, so that we have the potent paradox of a jollity that
breaks our hearts. With her almost completely senile husband barely
within sight and, given his failing senses, only occasionally within
hearing, she is about as isolated, as immobilized, and as stoical as
the Prometheus Bound of Aeschylus. Although no vulture feeds on
her liver, the alarm clock of time—or mortality—harries her with its
strident commands to wake or sleep: to be human, and so to be the
atrophying victim of transience. Lear, off to prison with his beloved daughter, exults, "We two alone will sing like birds i' th' cage";
Winnie actually does sing The Merry Widow Waltz. "What a curse,
mobility!" she will exclaim as she watches her Willie creep back
into his hole; encouragingly, she comments, "I know it is not easy,
dear, crawling backwards, but it is rewarding in the end." This is
the kind of joke at which one does not know whether to laugh or
weep, but in the end one laughs, Just as Winnie and Willie laugh
at the fact that in this sun-lashed desert of theirs an ant still lays
eggs. Asks Winnie: "How can one better magnify the Almighty than
by sniggering at his little jokes, particularly the poorer ones?"

If it is woman's supreme virtue to endure with dignity, to improvise little happiness out of incidentals and leftovers, man, who like
Krapp turns bitter, must seek crepuscular satisfaction in his creative
memory. Memory recorded on tape, for man is an artificer; and
memory relived in the mind, for he is also a cogitator. Of course
Winnie, too, remembers; but to her memory is just a pastime, a
source of a little pride—*amour-propre*. To Krapp, memory is everything, except for the piddling necessities of food and drink, which

one can elevate by desperate stratagems into minor pleasures. But memory is the living past, to be argued with, deplored or endorsed, chewed over and added to, ransacked for whatever might justify the ignominy of having to go on living. Winnie's memory is an album to flip through; Krapp's is Proustian and reconstructs a past whose few choice incidents, culminating in an erotic climax, glow on inextinguishably. Remembering is glory and pain, but not entertainment. He, too, sings—an old hymn that doesn't do much for him now; recalls his authorship, which gained him no money and scant recognition, and is no help either; but the memory of idyllic intercourse in a softly swaying boat, that is the viaticum for the journey through life, and the last viaticum for the journey into death.

Hume Cronyn was a fine Krapp, uncoy and unlovable in his old, corporeal presence, in which he gave out with some of the best stage wheezing I ever heard: a wheeze almost good enough for a death rattle. But on tape the middle-aged Krapp's voice was dripping with bland satisfaction, very much the "stupid bastard," as the old Krapp comments, "I took myself to be." What a magnificent phrase: "the stupid bastard I took myself to be." It is bad enough to *be* a stupid bastard, but proudly to *imagine* oneself being one is doubly stupid. As a result of Cronyn's uningratiating interpretation, the sadness we felt in the midst of this comedy was not for an individual but for old age itself: for transitoriness, mortality, and the Pyrrhic victory that recording a life, on tape or in the memory, represents.

Jessica Tandy was less successful with Winnie. Miss Tandy has a theatrical quality, a larger-than-lifesizeness achieved partly by looking too studiedly lovely for her age (and in this case for her role), partly by having a diction that smacks of the elocution teacher resolutely addressing some particularly backward pupils, and partly by having a certain aristocratic *hauteur* that is really too good, too special for Winnie. Ruth White, who created the part at the New York world première, was better, though she may have gone a little too far in the other direction, giving us a Winnie a shade more doltish and blithering than called for. Perfection for me was achieved by the French Winnie of Madeleine Renaud, one of my greatest theatergoing experiences. Mme. Renaud played her as somewhat lightheaded, frivolous but gallant—in the manner, say, of Yvonne Printemps in something like *Trois Valses*—which made it all the more heartrending to see such a wispy, airy creature the victim of creeping earthboundness. But to our exhilaration, Mme. Renaud seemed to float like a balloon above the string that tied her to mortality.

Beckett's greatness, as has often been noted, lies in his ability to get down to the essentials of unaccommodated man, the bare, forked animal. But as usual, Jan Kott is wrong when he sees *King Lear* as an adumbration of *Endgame;* this is putting a kind of inverse Cartesianism before horse sense. It is the other way around: it is Beckett who approximates *Lear* in that he manages to invest his gallows humor and *reductio ad absurdum* with such a passion and verbal felicity that his sarcastic, fanatically prosaic, quintessential prose becomes a kind of poetry against the grain. When Krapp reflects on his literary achievement, "Seventeen copies sold, of which eleven at trade price to free circulating libraries beyond the seas. Getting known," the sneer is first of all autobiographical. It mocks Beckett's transatlantic success, the academic snob appeal of his work, which ironically led to those twin peaks: inclusion of a wordless scene in *Oh! Calcutta!* and the Nobel Prize for Literature—two accolades Beckett did not so much accept as endure. But there is also something wildly poetic about those absurd figures, 17 and 11, and that marvelously wry, ludicrous conclusion, "getting known."

Beckett's words are mostly plain monosyllables, grayed with age, yet still occasionally kicking up a polysyllable or pun. Worn down with fingering and re-use, these words still achieve ironic stabs, thanks to the art of assemblage into rhythmic sequences, subtle echoes, minute modulations, refrains—and, everywhere, pauses seeping in to reveal the raw material from which this speech was wrested, the menace against which this ablative absolute is erected. In it up to her neck, Winnie can still say: "Yes, those are happy days, when there are sounds. (*Pause*) When I hear sounds. (*Pause*) I used to think... (*pause*)... I say I used to think they were in my head. (*Smile*) But no. (*Smile broader*) No, no. (*Smile off*) [...] I have not lost my reason. (*Pause*) Not yet. (*Pause*) Not all." Even out of context, how sublime the pathos of those last four monosyllables in which a human being bargains with destiny, clings tenaciously to remnants of reality, crumbs of time.

Yet Beckett will go too far—which, in his case, amounts to not going far enough. In *Act Without Words #1* he returns to pantomime, which, for someone who can turn the rags of near-monosyllabic verbiage into a glittering panoply, is a lamentable abdication. In the new play, *Not I*, words are, to be sure, preserved, but everything else is—equally distastrously—jettisoned. The play begins with mutterings in pitch darkness, whereupon the lights go up on a mouth surrounded by blackness: a disembodied female mouth that splashes us with an uninterrupted fifteen-minute stream of words. At some distance from the Mouth stands a tall, faintly lit, shrouded figure, designated as the Auditor "on invisible podium about four feet high," intently listening to the Mouth.

The Mouth pours out in fragments the miserable life story of a woman who was conceived, born and made to live without love and largely without speech. So we get the paradox of a speechless life splattered out in an unquenchable monologue to someone who seems to be the judge of the dead. The Mouth tells of various quasi-incidents in that near-eventless life, sequestered, haunted by a buzzing, prompted to speech only on rare occasions, always in winter. Then the woman would spout forth her story to unheeding strangers, only to crawl back abashed into her hole. There is also something about an April morning with larks in the air, when, her face buried in the grass, words first came to this creature; and something about a trial at which she could not speak up in her own defense; and the time when, at Croker's Acres, she sat staring at her hand and, for once in her life, wept. These and a few other minimal events keep tumbling over one another, submerging and resurfacing, always fragmented and only semicomprehensible, in the Mouth's monologue.

Meanwhile the Auditor remains mute and merely shrugs four times, four decreasing shrugs; the first clear and audible as the arms hit the thighs, the last barely perceptible. These shrugs occur at times when the Mouth becomes flustered in its recitation and stammers the identical sequence of monosyllables: "she— . . what? . . who? . . no . . no! . . she! . . (pause)" after which comes the Auditor's arm movement. The implication is that the Mouth insists on speaking in the third person (not I) about a life that is in truth its—her—own. This *mauvais quart d'heure* (in both senses) ends with the Mouth's jabbering swallowed up by darkness, the speaker never having assumed identification with or responsibility for her life. God (the Auditor?) comes out bad, too; the only time the Mouth laughs is when it mentions God. With characteristic quirkiness, Beckett appends two notes to the typescript of the play. The first is legitimate and describes the Auditor's movements, but the second is a perfect non sequitur and reads *in toto: "Note 2:* 'Any': pronounce 'anny.'" This is not related by asterisk to any (or anny) specific passage of the text, and just hangs there absurdly at the end of the typescript.

Such minimalism is not, I believe, to be countenanced from anyone, not even from Beckett. Up to a point, less may indeed be more; but beyond that point less is nothing. It is all very well for Beckett to return the drama to the Aeschylean essentials, but farther back than Aeschylus no one can go: the terrain there is not merely uncharted, it is no longer terrain. Ionesco may be right in his remark to Claude Bonnefoy, "Beckett's plays seem to be moving toward gimmickry. It's as if now he were making concessions to *his* audience, the audience he formed. . . . He's no longer trying to say what he has to say, but to find gimmicks that will leave the audience gasping. . . . It's a permanent succession of daredevil feats." The only act that can follow painting oneself into a corner is disappearance into the woodwork. Come back, Sam Beckett! It is not easy crawling backward, but it is rewarding in the end.

CONCURRENTLY, A SHOW of a much lesser but still delightful sort is provided by the *Moscow Circus,* which turns clowning and acrobatics into more than spectacle: art. And oh, those great, weightily graceful bears! Apprehensively, I heard they would sing, but there was only one brief solo, no bear-ruined choirs. On bikes, scooters, motorcycles, they are prodigious; so, too, as boxers, jugglers, trapeze artistes. Their movements are primeval and essential; these bears would have Beckett's endorsement.

THE PHOENIX REPERTORY COMPANY is back again, and its first bill, *The Great God Brown,* is a phoenix too frequent. I am tired of reiterating how utterly unworkable the lumbering mammoths of O'Neill's middle period seem to me, although this one is less behemoth than blowfish. O'Neill was staggering through a maze of blind alleys toward his eventual greatness. In *Brown* he was encumbered not only with his insufficiently sublimated neuroses and his inability to digest Sigmund Freud (who keeps coming up in half-chewed lumps), but also with experimentation in expressionism, a chiefly Teutonic style that never became domesticated on these shores. So the play suffers, as it were, from a double German accent, which falls particularly heavily on O'Neill's far from viable English style ("When you have a love to live, it's hard to love livin'" or "Into thine [sic] hands").

The symbolism, expressionism, Freudianism—perhaps even the leaden attempts at prose poetry—might be forgiven, however, if the plot and characters made any kind of sense. They don't. As an *idea,* the notion of the Babbitt-like Brown killing the troubled artist Dion Anthony in order to steal his talent, wife, mistress and identity, may sound fascinatng, but in dramatic terms—at least in O'Neill's—it never conveys a sense of people underneath the symbols, as the characters of Toller, Kaiser and some other better expressionists do. There is not enough plain talk here from which the fancifulness could take off; there are no real people who could make us sympathize with their having to resort to masks. When the face beneath the mask is an automaton's, the only culprit to get unmasked is the playwright.

Harold Prince has staged the play like someone who is either overwhelmed by its magnificence to the point of catatonia, or apprehensive about making his Broadway debut as a director of straight plays—or possibly is quite unsuited to such a task. There is very little movement, and what there is is ritualized, hieratic, pompous; lines are delivered without conviction, and the tempos throughout are unvaried and soporific. Typically, he has the principal sex scene played on a circular banquette, fit only for the mating of croissants. John Glover is too young and lightweight an actor to endow Brown with any notable quality except perhaps pipsqueakery, and John McMartin is so utterly a comedian (and a funny one, too) that he cannot—with all his eyeball-rolling, voice-splintering, slouching around—make Dion into anything but a comic figure. The principal women, Katharine Helmond and Marilyn Sokol, besides being extremely limited and tiresome actresses (the latter a perpetual amateur), are visually unsuited for their parts. In fact, the Phoenx's leadng ladies look rather like a joke on heterosexuality perpetrated by confirmed outsiders.

Boris Aronson's all-purpose set fails all purposes and looks bilious to boot. Carolyn Parker's costumes have the virtue of being unnoticeable, but her masks—grotesque cartoon faces on heavy curved Lucite —belong in a comic strip. Well, at least having to hold up those rebarbative visors exercises the performers' arm muscles.

The Second APA-Phoenix Repertory Company offering, Molière's *Don Juan,* improves on the opening bill. This is a curious play in which the author raises serious questions comically, by maintaining an aura of ambivalence around his hero. His Don Juan is an inhuman humanist, ingratiating atheist, courageous and pusillanimous; a seducer, yes, but one who has made a science and art out of seduction. He defies God as grandly as his servant, Sganarelle, defends religion servilely. Don Juan, then, is an archetypal modern man, flouting tradition and convention wholeheartedly, refusing affection where custom demands it, all passionate effusion where resistance seems insurmountable.

Stephen Porter's translation is smooth enough, at times to the point of archness: "You don't give in to the astounding miracle of the walking-talking statue?" And his staging is swift and unfussy, but questions do arise. Why must the servants be costumed as Bedouins? A misguided tribute to the Moorish conquest of Spain? Why must Doña Elvira be played by an actress too old, sexless and unimpassioned for the part? To arouse facile sympathy for the Don's dumping her? Why must Juan's father deliver his moral tirade in a tiresomely uninflected monotone? To get easy laughs? Or to disguise the actor's inability to deal with the material uncamped-up? Why must both the peasant girls be overage, and one of them obese, unappetizing and untalented enough to turn a satyr into an anchorite? To drive home how unhappy is the professional seducer's lot? And how can Porter ruin the later climax of the statue's walking in by having an earlier scene end with its sauntering off in full view to clear the stage for the next scene? There must be less anticlimactic ways of removing the monument.

Still, the play is as delightful as it is deep, and at least parts of the acting and directing work. Paul Hecht does not convey the Don's sexual irresistibility or the charm that might be a reasonable substitute for it, but he does quite well with the aristocratic haughtiness and better yet with the humorous iconoclasm and wounding banter. John McMartin is a fine Sganarelle, clearly more rag doll than flesh and bone, with more catches in his voice than are in a fraudulent contract, enough shuffles and shiftiness in his footwork for Stepin Fetchit and Charlie Chaplin to claim joint paternity, and eyeballs that seem to revolve sideways, inward and especially heavenward incessantly and sometimes simultaneously. David Dukes, John Glover and James Greene do nicely in smaller parts, and Nancy Potts's costumes hold their own against a low budget. It is unfortunate, though, that enforced parsimony should have done away with scenery. When Juan's feasting is done off a roughhewn table against plain black drapes, it may almost be worth letting the Commander usher one to a place that at least has good fireworks.

NEIL SIMON IS BACK—if he was ever away—with *The Sunshine Boys*, a play of his where gagwriting is ostensibly subordinated to pathos, and underlying the comedy is a supposedly serious theme. Well, after one has been dubbed by Clive Barnes funnier than Bernard Shaw, one has to strive for bigger things—Shakespeare's dark comedies, perhaps. The significant plot concerns a once famous vaudeville team, Lewis and Clark, of whom Clark now vegetates in a ramshackle hotel and still hopes for parts in musicals or TV commercials, while Lewis has stolidly retired to his daughter's New Jersey home. Clark's nephew, Ben, is his uncle's agent, and also lovingly looks after the lovable grump. When CBS plans a spectacular about the history of burlesque, it is mandatory to have Lewis and Clark reunited in their fabled doctor's office skit. The comics have boycotted each other for a dozen years but under Ben's patient ministrations are grudgingly reconciled. Predictably, however, animosity scuttles the comeback, Clark has a heart attack, and all both of them can look forward to is sunset years of bickering in the same old actors' home to which fate, or Mr. Simon, consigns them.

The story is exiguous but presumably will serve as scaffolding for the exploration of such great topics as What Was the Glory of Burlesque?, Where Has That Old-time Humor Gone?, What Is to Become of Beloved Entertainers Grown Aged?, Is Greasepaint Thicker Than Friendship in the Theater? and Can Man Laugh Away His Mortality? There may be one or several worthy plays in this, but none can survive burial alive under 10-Gags-10 per minute—some new, more old, a few funny, many dreadful, but all of them marching, skipping, somersaulting at you without respite. The humor itself is sternly limited in scope: insult jokes, speaker's-stupidity jokes, geriatric sex jokes, and show-biz in-jokes. Although Mr. Barnes has compared this alleged comic masterpiece favorably to Molière and Shaw, one glance at *Don Juan* and the difference slaps you in the eye.

To Simon, the basic unit of playmaking is the joke. Not the word, the idea, the character, or even the situation, but the gag. It kills him if here and there a monosyllable resists funnying up, if now and then someone has to make a move that won't fracture the audience. Note how many lines in *Don Juan* don't try in the least to be funny—which is why those that really are hit us, and why life and thought are allowed elbow room in the play. Can you imagine anything more horrible than an orgasm stretched to two hours? Alan Arkin's direction milks the jokes not only by their udders but even by their tails. Sam Levene's hangdog humor sags too low now, but Jack Albertson does well by Clark, and Lewis J. Stadlen, as Ben, amazed me by conjuring up some humanity out of literally nowhere.

I have always considered *The Plough and the Stars* Sean O'Casey's finest play; the current Lincoln Center Repertory production makes it look like flimsy stuff.

Now, a Polish or French play need not—indeed, *should* not—be done with Polish or French accents, but an Irish play without brogues is worse than a leprechaun without his crock of gold. So the motley cast at the Vivian Beaumont sports brogues, but they seem to come from counties not yet accounted for; when a couple of British soldiers come on with putative cockney accents, the sound is not so much of Bow-bells as of Babels. But the big difficulty with staging *Plough* is that one must suggest the whole violent, heroic, absurd Easter Rising going on offstage, and always show the onstage action impinged on and overshadowed by the gallant madness just beyond. At the Beaumont, instead of the feeling of a terrible beauty being born, the evening must be borne with a terrible sense of duty.

There are serious problems with the play itself. The principal characters are the loving newlyweds Nora and Jack Clitheroe, and the play shows how she tries desperately to keep her husband, an officer in the Irregulars, from participating in the uprising. But patriotism, honor and a wounded buddy call. Jack dies a hero's death, Nora goes mad, and various minor characters live or die, show courage or contemptibleness; life, despite the Dublin Post Office, goes tragicomically on. Unfortunately, Jack and Nora are never sufficiently in focus, never allowed fully to capture our imagination and self-projection, to make these two pillars of the play really hold it up for us. The surrounding buttresses—the droll minor characters—are stunningly there, but they become flying-off buttresses, leaving the Clitheroes shakily behind. The second act in the pub, probably the best-written of the four, has almost nothing of Jack in it, and nothing at all of Nora; this is where the play truly loses them and its chance for homogeneous firmness.

Still, if the staging were more imaginative and the acting better, all might be saved; even this precarious mixture of tragedy and farce, whose secret O'Casey tried so hard and not quite successfully to wrest from Shakespeare, might just work if the performances had greater authenticity and suppleness. But there is Christopher Walken, whose Jack is bereft of every ounce of charm, dash, flexibility and even savor (as for his accent, it is variously American, Scottish and even Yiddish); I do not know how one of the most promising actors in our recent theatrical history could come to so disheartening a pass. Then there is the Nora of Roberta Maxwell, who does not so much speak her lines as resonate them; she seems to have swallowed a tuning fork and every utterance comes out as a *pinnnng*. She rightly tries to play Nora as somewhat hysterical to begin with, to justify her subsequent madness, but, in the process she forfeits all charm and grace and goes from shrewishness directly to dementia without passing Ophelia and collecting our sympathy. Pauline Flanagan plays the fruit peddler Bessie Burgess as if she were Deirdre of the Sorrows crossed with Boadicea, and monotonously even at that. Leo Leyden makes Flynn insufferable rather than a pathetic nuisance, and so on down the line. Kevin Conway, though much too tough a presence for the gangly Covey, is at least straightforward, and that old Gate Theater stalwart, Jack MacGowran, could play Fluther in his Celtic-twilight sleep.

Dan Sullivan's direction is uninspired, especially in the tempos, which tend to be funereal. Perhaps he took O'Casey's dedication of the play "To my mother's gay laugh at the gate of the grave" half seriously; this production would do nicely in the tomb, but never at the Gate. Douglas W. Schmidt's scenery is good, and, so, too, is John Gleason's lighting. But you can't help feeling that romantic Ireland is, with O'Casey, in the grave.

"The best performance of the 1951–52 season was a reading of a single Shavian scene," wrote Eric Bentley about the original production of *Don Juan in Hell*. Even then I was against the excerpting of one act from a four-act play, and even then thought that Agnes Moorhead was too dull and desiccated for Doña Ana, and that Cedrick Hardwicke made the Commander military enough, to be sure, but in a more Blimpish fashion than Shaw had intended. But when Laughton, as the Devil, and Charles Boyer, as the Don, crossed intellectual blades, the old, not so original, not so prophetic utterances nevertheless sparkled with intelligence, wit and dramatic urgency.

Bernard Shaw was arguably one of the least sexual figures among major modern dramatists. Sex was small potatoes to him ultimately, and canniest of Irishmen, he was not going to be the victim of any potato famine. In *You Never Can Tell*, he debunked love; in *Arms and the Man*, heroism; in *Man and Superman* (1903), he set about debunking the greatest hero of romance, Don Juan. Not so much debunking as converting him—to the Shavian doctrines of the Life Force and of the joy and supremacy of cogitation. In short, Shaw turned Juan into a man consumed with intellectual passion, and accepting sex as a necessary adjunct to creative cerebration. This postdeathbed conversion of the Don took root; Henry de Montherlant was to write that Don Juan has, among other things, a need that is "more intellectual than physical," and Max Frisch, in an afterthought to his play *Don Juan or the Love of Mathematics*, observed that were

Juan alive today, he would busy himself with atomic physics. In the very year in which Laughton staged *Don Juan in Hell,* the dream sequence from *Man and Superman,* E. M. Butler, a female Cambridge don, complained in a book that Shaw, "that merciless *raisonneur,* [had] disenchanted and undone the work of Mozart."

Yet even if we consider Shaw's Don Juan Tenorio, alias John Tanner, a disenchanting figure and find the ideas in *Don Juan in Hell* eclectic, eccentric, imperfectly epigrammatic or innovative (and trace them back to Schopenhauer or sideways to Bergson), two superb truths remain. One, that Shaw actually put ideas, ratiocination, intellectual debate, the parturient mind, on our stage; and two, that he succeeded in making it diverting, instructive, dramatic and, yes, even sensual. It will not do to quote, as the *Times* reviewer has done, one or two lines out of context (one of them even spoken by the scene's least intellectual character) as representative of what the thing as a whole, and Shaw's genius itself, could or could not do. And as for Mr. Barnes's carping about Shaw's style, it can hardly be taken seriously from someone who, in that very review, uses the noun "rejoinder" as a verb!

The performances, with one exception, are not up to snuff. Paul Henreid's Commander belongs in a Viennese café, inspecting the passing girls over his *Schlag* and quoting some witticism out of Peter Altenberg. Edward Mulhare plays the devil like a defensive C. of E. parson, uneasily fingering his collar and allowing as how God may not "actually" be dead. Agnes Moorhead, the sole relic from the Laughton production, lacks not only spirited femininity but also the energy to utter more than one word every five seconds. Ricardo Montalbàn, however, is a revelation. This man whom I wrote off as a second-rate star of third-rate movies delivers Juan's speeches with great sonorousness and variety, consummate phrasing and exemplary elocution. True, his accent is thickish (but at least Spanish) and slows him down. But his face is expressive, he moves well, and he creates even in a staged reading a full-bodied characterization. Thanks to Shaw and Montalbàn, this revival may yet prove the worthiest endeavor of the 1972–73 season as well.

MINOS VOLANAKIS SAYS he staged the Circle in the Square's *Medea* because it is the best play about New York he has read. If he means that it is violent and bloody, so is almost any other Greek tragedy; if, as seems likelier, he means that it parallels the women's lib movement, his reading of the play is extremely shallow. At least when he staged Genet's *The Screens* in Brooklyn, he did not treat it as a gay lib tract.

Rather than a women's libber, Euripides' Medea resembles a romantic heroine—the woman scorned, like whom hell has no fury—but even this is only a small part of what is at stake. The play concerns a rational principle (Jason), coolly practical and conforming to social norms but also jejune, bloodless and deficient in humanity, in conflict with an elemental force (Medea), sly but fiercely unwise, comformable only to the primitive energies buffeting the universe. On the lowest level of psychological action, the jilted wife kills the new bride and the children she herself bore the faithless husband. On the higher level of clashing historical opposites, the vigorous barbarian cuts off the reproductive powers of the civilized weakling: without his existing heirs and a new wife to give him others, he can only wither away. On the highest, metaphysical level, the fact that the sun-god's dragon-drawn chariot comes to the child-murderess' rescue suggests a cosmic power holding not with Jason's calculating cautiousness (the exile marrying the local ruler's daughter to give himself and his children status), but with the passionate, primordial Medea, whose demands are incalculable, pristine imperatives.

Volanakis, however, not only misses the point of the play, he also fails to clarify the dramatic development. This hinges on Medea's gradual realization of the all-importance of children: the daughter whom Creon wishes to protect by banishing Medea; the boys whom Jason would take from their mother to establish him as a dynast; the offspring aging Aegeus so yearns to have that he travels to Delphi for counsel; the children whose importance the addled chorus tries vainly to minimize. It is by striking down his sons that, as she slowly grasps, Medea can best destroy the man for whom she vainly sacrificed everything. But in so doing she also kills part of herself.

None of this is conveyed by the current production of this admittedly difficult play, in which the audience is asked to accept Medea's soaringly unnatural act as preferred by nature to Jason's plodding propriety. A further reason for the failure is the director's stylistic floundering. Greek drama can apparently be performed today only at a considerable cost: you either aim for the poetic sublimities and forfeit such elements as a modern audience can identify itself with; or you modernize for contemporary relevance and lose the timeless grandeur. It is not a good bargain either way, but Volanakis' shuttling between the two and adding an element of the absurd is appreciably worse yet. Thus some characters wear masks, some don't; some masks are doffed in the course of the play, some aren't, and still others (the chorus') keep going on and off for no convincing reason. Creon, on exaggeratedly high cothurni, is virtually pushed in and out by two soldiers he uses as a portable conductor's podium, and the effect is grotesque. Medea's children wear Kewpie-doll masks and modern Greek peasant costumes that make them look like those alleged peasant handicrafts sold to tourists on Mykonos, and the effect is comical. Jason's house is now a crater covered with the lid of a marketing basket; when people must emerge, the lid lifts or blows off.

Volanakis embroiders the play with curious conceits, such as the Messenger's almost killing Medea, who then uses his discarded sword to slay her sons with. Worst of these curios is the final apotheosis in which that basket lid becomes the dragon chariot of the sun and half a gilded dummy inside it substitutes for Medea, while the actress' voice comes out of a loudspeaker nowhere near this lay figure. Half a dummy on the halfshell is all that confronts Jason in his final agonizing agon.

The director fails equally as translator. "Hate me, I'm sick of you." "And I'm sick of you"; or "You should have kissed them yesterday when you kicked them out" is rendering Attic Greek with attic English. The choric passages, though better translated and passably directed, suffer from diction that turns question into "queshton" and horrible into "hah-ribble." Which brings me to Irene Papas. After seeing her in a row of plays and movies, I must regretfully conclude that her acting ability is minimal. She does look imperious, though also rather mannish; she can turn on the waterworks at will; and were the play done in demotic Greek, her elocution might be splendid. If you can see Medea in a Vidal Sassoon haircut, Miss Papas may look Medea, but she certainly does not sound it. As T. S. Eliot noted, the part requires "simple force and subtle variation"; although Miss Papas can shout, she seems rather haphazard about when to do it; although her voice can go colorlessly limp (her one form of subtle variation), it does so at equally arbitrary moments. And her English just isn't good enough, unless you are willing to settle for "the boot chair's hand that kills," "drug yourself to the other side," "the basest man on nurth," and so forth. The rest of the cast is American and utterly untrained for such undertakings; Al Freeman, Jr.'s bellowed vocalise is not even intelligible.

Nancy Potts's costumes are hideous when not laughable (Aegeus, wearing a woman's white beach pajamas, removes a leather glove to reveal a blue motoring glove painted on his hand) and made mostly of shoddy, crinkly materials. Only Marc B. Weiss's lighting has imagination, but it lights up things that were better left hidden.

FREEMAN, by Phillip Hayes Dean at the American Place Theater, starts slowly and banally. The squabbles in a precariously middle-class black household in the Michigan boondocks sound either already heard or not worth hearing. There is father Ned, who has toiled out his life at the automotive factory, resigned to his little lot; his wife Teresa, the stock calm, patient, sardonic, dominant black woman who is defeated inside; their son Freeman, who flunks out of school and factory, fails to build his dream house or get elected to the City Council, a talented but downtrodden rebel with too many causes. Freeman's interminably pregnant young wife, Osa Lee, is there to add tragicomic wistfulness. Rex, who when orphaned was raised by Ned and Teresa as a brother to Freeman, is there for schematic contrast: by playing his cards right (as well as a little dirty pool) with the powers that be, he has become a rich, esteemed doctor, an important though not quite upright pillar of the community.

Nothing in the first act really comes off, and very nearly off I went. Although the people are real, they are also obvious; though the dialogue is believable, it is scarcely endurable. But after the intermission, things change radically. One is finally caught up in Freeman's stubborn, amateurish, self-defeating struggle to prevail; one begins to see how those good people around him have, for all their ostensible and even genuine help, failed him almost as surely as the white world that exacts maximal tariff for minimal leeway. This man's failure is more honorable than his quasi-brother's success, and not in any romantic terms, such as those, say, of the movie *Morgan!*, where failure is made fashionable, glamorous, and in truth absurd; but rather in those of *An Enemy of the People*, where the hero is not just a quixotic iconoclast but the man who can save the world if it isn't past saving.

Although the second act works, and holds both your interest and concern, it is still only decent, deserving playwriting. But near the end comes a confrontation between Rex and Freeman, a low-key, kitchen-table wordfight in which the not unlikable and certainly realistic opportunist opposes with quiet reasonableness the defeated, disillusioned but still kicking idealist, the man who is perhaps his own worst enemy and yet radiantly, hopelessly right. This duel between the man who does right in the worst, self-sabotaging way, and his friend, brother and enemy who does wrong in the best and nicest of ways is a perfectly conceived and impeccably executed scene. It is a magisterially sustained collision between people who love and hate and, more than that, grieve for each other. Dean allows both men equal intelligence and eloquence, and lets them say, unturgidly and unerringly, the most concise, pertinent and devastating things with every thrust, parry and counterthrust.

This scene is bewilderingly good. It is way beyond anything Jones-Baraka, Bullins or any other black American—and almost any white American—dramatist today could manage. With uncanny precision and inspiration, the most appropriate and persuasive words fit themselves into the right spaces, as if the muse and the computer worked dazzlingly hand in hand. But no other scene in the play comes near to so leaving your mind and soul breathless, and even the crucial and correct change in the father comes about jerkily and not quite convincingly. Here the author is not helped by the technically inadequate performance of Dotts Johnson, flanked by a much too predictable one from Estelle Evans as Teresa. As Rex, J. A. Preston is embarrassingly limp in his early scenes, but gets better, indeed good, in the end; Marjorie Barnes's Osa Lee is perfectly pitched between wisdom and immaturity. As Freeman, Bill Cobbs grows slowly more interesting and at last overpowering, which is right. Lloyd Richards has directed plausibly in Douglas Higgins' incisive setting.

Every known and some unknown foundations support André Gregory's Manhattan Project, its name as pretentious a put-on as everything else about it. For God knows how much ill-gotten money over a period of years, Gregory has given us thus far his unappetizing *Alice in Wonderland* and now a vomitory *Endgame*. Gregory strikes me as a madman who imagines he is Jerzy Grotowski —as, by the way, does Jerzy Grotowski. For *Endgame*, Gregory has conceived an environment that looks like a chicken coop with a tinfoil floor, and the play becomes a cockfight enacted in the barnyard adjoining a Nestlé's factory. The benighted director who, as befits a Grotowskian, sets himself up as author, completely reorchestrates and misconceives the play. What is meant to be a sardonic, grimly funny vision of ultimate despair now becomes an endless series of nightclub turns, vaudeville routines, dialect jokes, sophomoric running gags, ludicrous sight gags, all grafted onto Beckett's defenseless play like silicone breasts on a grand piano.

Not only do these vulgar, ostentatious, unfunny things have no bearing on *Endgame*, they actually distort the play's meaning. The two last survivors in a dying world are whiling away their desolation with somber, gallows humor—wit and sobriety yielding a combined swan song and hyena laughter. Instead, Gregory gives us two puerile pranksters having a hellishly good time—not the only men on earth but the only idiots who would laugh at each other's jokes. If the foundations have this much money to burn, would it not be more charitable to make a nice bonfire of it for some Lower East Side residents to warm themselves by of a cold winter night?

EL GRANDE DE COCA-COLA or *El Coca-Cola Grande* (as it was called before the attorneys for Coca-Cola, with foolish punctilio, insisted on the title change) is an adorably idiotic show. One laughs at it for no very good reason, as one laughs at the chatter of an adored woman— and just as constantly, just as blissfully. The framework is a floor show in a flea-bitten night club in Trujillo, Honduras, M.C.'d by the impresario Don Pepe Hernandez, and performed with local Coca-Cola backing by Pepe's small but indomitable family impersonating any number of international variety acts. There are essentially two jokes: the show is in Spanish, albeit the most simplistic Spanish interlarded with English words and phrases (except in the French, German and Italian acts, where those languages get their fracturing); and all the acts are inept, fraudulent and in variously outrageous ways a total bust.

Now, why should this be funny? My guess is as bad as yours, but I suppose it has something to do with the shortness, swiftness and demented conviction of the thing; something more with the preposterousness and expertise of the performing; and more yet with catharsis. Thanks to our new, hard-won enlightenment, we can no longer have our fun with most races, creeds and nationalities—either because they have organized against it, or because the thing strikes us as being in bad taste. (Usually the former.) But the Latin Americans—especially when spoofed, as here, by a coolly British group—are still enjoying an open season. There are still enough real-life operettas and melodramas, hilarious or bloody, being enacted south of the border to permit consciences not to quail at such persiflage. And so all our pent-up dialect stories, all our repressed minority baitings, happily disguise themselves as Spanish jokes and come tumbling out here to our delectation and relief.

But it's not all purgation only. Ron House (the one American in a cast of five), who conceived the show together with Diz White, is a hugely funny man. Not only are his vocal and visual Hispanisms histrionic delights, but even his basic expression—a smile that sweatily modulates from unctuous hospitableness to terminal hysteria—is a marathon mirth-begetter. And when he proceeds to do impersonations of Jaime Cagney and such in the original dubbed-in Spanish—well, Don Juan may have gotten the Commander's statue to walk; Don Pepe could get it to roll in the aisles. Of all the White Houses from Washington to San Clemente, this White-House extravaganza is surely the biggest fun house yet.

FORTUNATE ARE THOSE unlucky enough not to have seen Ingmar Bergman's witty and poignant, lyrical and satirical masterwork *Smiles of a Summer Night*. Fortunate, that is, when they see *A Little Night Music*, the operetta Hugh Wheeler and Stephen Sondheim have fashioned from it. The picture has the bittersweet wisdom and elegance of the best of Schnitzler and Girandoux; the musical has a book by Hugh Wheeler.

Wheeler is the archetypal hack: successful mystery writer, author of three Broadway failures, scenarist of one of the most repellent films ever made, *Something for Everyone*, and coscenarist of the wretched *Travels With My Aunt* and the ingeniously directed but indifferently scripted *Cabaret*. Here and there he preserves a sliver of Bergman's dialogue, often rewriting a line for the worse, and for the rest obtruding his own effete drivel. What was dashingly masculine and sinuously feminine Continental humor may now at best pass for wit at the Continental Baths. "Don't squeeze your bosoms against the chair, dear," Bergman's sardonic but profound Mrs. Armfeldt, now turned into a dilapidated Auntie Mame, admonishes her granddaughter; "it will stunt their growth. Then where would you be?" Bosom is, of course, always singular, though the likes of Mr. Wheeler would not know that. But the cheapness of the supposed joke should be apparent to all.

More samples of Wheeler wit. Says Mrs. Armfeldt: "To lose a lover, or even a husband or two, in the course of one's life can be vexing, but to lose one's teeth is a catastrophe." Set this beside Wilde's "To lose one parent, Mr. Worthing, may be regarded as a misfortune; to lose both looks like carelessness," and you have the measure of Wheeler's lack of bite. Or take this bit of obvious, vulgar innuendo from the old lady: "The Baron de Signac, who was, to put it mildly, peculiar . . ." As delivered by Hermione Gingold with a ponderous inflection and broad leer, the line epitomizes the kind of imaginative bankruptcy that is here considered dialogue and, worse yet, wit.

All of Bergman's complex characters are simplified down to monochromes and flattened out into drugstore cutouts. The Count, a Byronic Don Juan, becomes a blustering boob whose stupidity elicits gales of unearned onstage laughter; the Countess, a touching, because wounded, schemer, who sometimes involuntarily reveals the pain beneath her glitter, becomes a typical uneasy, neglected wife; lawyer Egerman, a delightfully sophisticated and ever so slightly fatuous bon vivant, becomes a rather plodding Midwestern would-be philanderer; his exquisite child-wife Anne becomes a somewhat overgrown, vapid drum majorette, and so forth. "Watch him like a hawk," the Count exhorts his wife, and she replies, "Yes, dear. You're a tiger, I'm a hawk—we're our own zoo." Imagine Bergman's Countess spouting such tripe!

Yet all is not lost. If you can forget Bergman, which is hard, and Wheeler, which is impossible, there is still Sondheim. And Sondheim has composed, to his customary polished, easefully and richly rhyming lyrics, some of his best tunes so far. Although their forms are basically simple—waltzes, simulated folk ballads, old-fashioned show tunes—Sondheim has laced their carefree forthrightness with daring little twists in the melodic line: unexpected wry modulations, deliberately wrong notes, a fine gray overcast on the sunniness. Whereas this tended to make some of the music in *Company* and *Follies* ungainly, here it enhances the old, innocent waltz tunes with a jaded, world-weary and then again curiously modern aftertaste, to which Jonathan Tunick's cunning orchestrations add spice.

The first act contains only one weak song, although the invention of a singing chorus that butts in with numbers such as one about a slapdash orgy is out of key and geared to a sensibility very alien to that which informs—or should inform—the basic material. In the second act, Sondheim's musical invention flags both qualitatively and quantitatively, but two numbers are still very fine. The plot may have gotten in the music's way here, even though such sequences as Henrik's attempted suicide and the game of Russian roulette, inspired high comedy in the film, are wantonly and stupidly reduced to near-nothingness.

The director, Harold Prince, is also to blame. In the first act, while not displaying any great resourcefulness, he nevertheless maintains an adequate pace and acceptable stage movements. In the second, things bog down, get cluttered, seem to move in circles and stumble over one another. Boris Aronson's scenery is of little help, finding no valid solution for commingling the outdoors and the indoors, and putting altogether too much faith in rows upon rows of birches painted on sheets of translucent plastic. And another Birch, Patricia, who has done such stunning work elsewhere, has been choreographically hamstrung: the show has no dancing ensemble, and all that the principals apparently could be made to do is some wan, dreamy waltzing around.

But with Florence Klotz's costumes we are once again on safe terrain. There is an opulent but restrained elegance here that is carefully but not excessively calculated; in the clothes, more than anywhere else, the spirit of the original work shines on. The acting? Poor Glynis Johns, a delectable middle-aged tomboy, is disastrously miscast as the embodiment of ripe femininity, and Hermione Gingold continues her career as our leading fag hag, senior division. Victoria Mallory is a witlessly simpering young wife, D. Jamin-Bartlett as Swedish as apple pie, George Lee Andrews a cipher, and Judy Kahan uncomfortable in her role. Len Cariou wears gradually thinner, but Laurence Guittard and Patricia Elliott do much with little.

Both by addition and by subtraction, Wheeler and Prince have turned comic subtlety with serious implications into crude jocularity without reverberations, except for an epicene sensibility that now infiltrates everything. I'd buy the record, though.

Ellis Rabb's production of The Merchant of Venice might be described as rock bottom for the doomed Repertory Theater of Lincoln Center if anything as viscous, pulpy and nerveless deserved the epithet "rock." But bottom it certainly is. Rabb has transposed the action into some present-day but wildly fictitious Venice compounded of L'Avventura, La Dolce Vita and the freak show of Fellini Satyricon. Venetian society now consists of campy homosexuals and idle tourists and one honest, noble Jew, Shylock, a sort of Hamlet or Lear, only more dignified than either, whom the vicious anti-Semitism of the profligate Christians drives to an act of bizarre desperation. He goes about his bloody vengeance in the most restrained, gentlemanly and philosophical fashion, and when he is foiled and ruined bears up with exemplary stoicism. There is also a yacht named the Belmont, on which a swinging jet-setter called Portia gallivants about with Nerissa, a black lady's-companion with one foot in women's lib and the other in the Black Panthers. Here some preposterous wooing game is played by means of three caskets—some new craze, no doubt, to replace computer dating and Russian roulette.

To make a complete travesty of the play, Rabb has ruthlessly cut it, which does not prevent him from adding lines of his own (mostly in German) to suit his absurd purpose. A purpose actually no better than to remake Shakespeare's play in his own anemic and anomic image, which is more scroungy than absurd. And also cowardly, because this nonsensical Shylock was obviously devised to placate various Jewish pressure groups too stupid to see the salutary, therapeutic value of an honest examination of how anti-Semitism works, creating a debased symbiosis in which torturer and victim become indistinguishable.

Rabb must consider it a personal triumph when his mauling of the playwright's intentions succeeds in making a shambles of the play. Thus, for example, Lorenzo, Jessica and Launcelot become part of a neurotic *ménage à trois,* and the great moonlit love scene (V, i), contrary to the manifest meaning of every line, is twisted into a quarrel scene in which Lorenzo and Jessica, when not at each other's throats, literally put each other to sleep. It would be unfair to several other directors to call Ellis Rabb the worst director in America, but he is almost certainly the most perverse.

The motley crew that mills and moseys around the Beaumont stage is certainly one of the aggregates least resembling an acting company I have ever encountered. True, there is Rosemary Harris who, except for being somewhat too old for Portia and putting a lachrymose tremolo into many of her line readings, is an actress with real training and savoir faire; there is Sydney Walker who embodies this incredible Shylock as creditably as possible; and there are, in lesser parts, Philip Bosco and Alan Mandell, performing with urbane professonalism. But for the rest! Josef Sommer does a spidery, blood-curdling, horror-movie Shylock, unfortunately while playing the part of Antonio. As his seemingly unplatonic friend Bassanio, Christopher Walken struts about like a male model showing off the latest Bill Blass collection while mumbling his lines in a barely audible, break-neck monotone, like some lobotomized valedictorian at an idiot school. This is a performance whose evaluation requires not a critic but a neurosurgeon.

There are contributions by Gastone Rossilli, Olivia Cole, Fred Morsell, Robert Symonds and especially Caroline Kava that would not do credit to an Eskimo church pageant, and James Tilton's setting, lighting and projections are shabby-ingenious: though they do make a shoestring look like a full pair of shoe laces, they do not make it Venice, whose colors and moods are not evoked. And Portia's Onassian yacht, "the Belmont," does not look like a yacht at all and remains, sadly, the Beaumont. Ann Roth's costumes fail both as aesthetics and as satire, but Cathy MacDonald has put together a charmingly syncretic score.

THERE IS SOMETHING noble, indeed heroic, about the two character play. It reduces human conflict to the barest, purest essence. In a magnificent passage of *The Notebooks of Malte Laurids Brigge,* Rilke's semi-autobiographical hero blames himself for having written the wrong kind of play: "What an imitator and fool I was to have needed a Third Person in order to tell of the destinies of two people who make it hard for each other. . . . Surely I should have known that this Third Person who weaves through all lives and literatures, this ghost of a Third Person who never existed, has no significance, that he must be denied. He belongs to the pretexts of Nature, who is always at pains to deflect attention from her deepest secrets. He is the screen behind which the drama unfurls. He is the noise at the entrance to the voiceless stillness of a veritable conflict. One would assume that all of them found it too difficult to speak of the Two who concern us; the Third Person, precisely because he is unreal, is the easy part of the task—they could all manage him. Right at the outset of their dramas, one notices the impatience to get to the Third, they can hardly wait for him. . . . And yet there they are living among us, not these Third Persons, but the Two, of whom there would be so unbelievably much to say, of whom nothing has ever been said as yet, even though they suffer and act and do not know how to help each other."

It is greatly to the credit of William Gibson's 1953 play, *Two for the Seesaw,* that it limited itself to a pair of onstage characters: Jerry, a Midwestern lawyer, not quite divorced from his rich wife and not quite over her, trying to find himself and a new life in New York; and Gittel, a thirtyish would-be dancer but acutal seamstress from the Bronx, a vulnerable but resilient, richly feminine but nervously jocular Jewish girl. He is lonely and disgusted with his cushy past set up for him by a wealthy father-in-law; she is surrounded by casual friends and transient lovers and so unsure of herself as to have become a walking handout of warmth and sex. They help each other toward dignified self-awareness through a clumsy-sweet affair. At last he goes back to Nebraska and his wife; she, remaining deeply in love with him, will try not to shortchange herself in future relationships. The sad ending seemed to me unconvincing, and the somewhat smug male superiority, unpleasant; some of this, to be sure, was forced on a newcomer to Broadway by old hands trying to make the play more commercial. Still, it was about the Two, with the Third, the wife, obtruding only via telephone and telegraph, and it did explore fairly singlemindedly the hearty compatibilities and disheartening incompatibilities of two people trying to love each other.

In the current musical adaptation, the title has been shortened to *Seesaw*, but the cast has been extended to include most of New York City in cross section. Once again the rush to bring on the Others has dissipated the impact by diluting the brew. Worse: the additional characters and situations are trivially observed and glibly slapped on. Worse yet: the original dialogue has been about 90 percent rewritten, partly to update it, partly to accommodate the wide-angle perspective, and partly to minimize the poignant probing in favor of harum-scarum humor. The book is credited to Michael Bennett, the director and choreographer, although persistent rumors (insistently denied) have had Neil Simon rewriting it. Since Bennett was brought in to replace Edwin Sherin as director and supersede Grover Dale as choreographer, there must have been some unnamed initial bookwriter as well. And the book remains an untimely hodgepodge; even the serious moments, where it sticks closely to the original, now ring overdramatic and false in this frivolous context. Some of the changes are melancholy comments on our times: a tidy income that in 1953 could be $15,000, had to be upped to $27,000; the affair is now consummated right on the first date. The dollar and sexual restraint have undergone comparable devaluation.

Cy Coleman's score is utilitarian but unoriginal—rather like the book, which now depends on jokes like a Mobile Theater's doing "*Hamlet* in the original Puerto Rican version," or "gay" meaning to the Nebraskan "something like happy?" Still, with one foot in cliché and the other in tunelessness, the music (greatly helped by Larry Fallon's laudably understated orchestrations) is well ahead of Dorothy Fields's lyrics, ranging from banalities lke "I'm not smart enough,/ I'm not fine enough,/ I'm not swell enough/ For him" (note that anachronistic *swell!*) to ear-graters like rhyming *sexual* with *intellectual.*

Bennett's characteristic minimal choreography based on everyday movements slightly heightened or stylized is beginning to yield diminishing returns, though it is still engaging and lively, especially when garnished with useful gadgets like mirrors or balloons. Robin Wagner's décor, depending on Sheppard Kerman's sweeping projections of New York cityscapes, is expansive and exhilarating, and Jules Fisher's lighting is whimsical, even if lacking the master's customary wizardry. Ann Roth's costumes are regrettably humdrum.

Although Gittel does not come so naturally to Michele Lee as it did to Anne Bancroft, Miss Lee sings, moves, acts, speaks and radiates like a true pentathlon champion, deserving fivefold accolades. As Jerry, Ken Howard is that rare thing nowadays, a young leading man who can actually stop a show with a combination of warmth and suavity, quiet charm modulating into dizzying exuberance. And Tommy Tune, as long on talent as on legs, is an exquisitely animated beanpole as well as a gracefully sinuous vine. In a rather barren season, *Seesaw* does have its blessed moments of abundance.

PIRANDELLO's *Henry IV* (retitled here *Emperor Henry IV*) is either the funniest tragedy or the saddest comedy ever written; either way it is a masterpiece, and a peculiarly modern one at that. Dürrenmatt, whose plays are very much in the same spirit, has argued persuasively that the age of tragedy is over, that we live in an era of more or less gruesome farce. The play's protagonist became, for the sake of a masquerade, the eleventh-century German emperor Henry IV; a headlong fall from his horse made him mad, and for twelve years he believed that he was truly that emperor. He recovered his senses, but realized that his beloved had been taken from him by the man who caused his fall and downfall; by now, life had passed him by. He continued to act the emperor's part deliberately, amusing himself by feigning madness. Eight more years later, the lost lady, her lover, and her lovely daughter come to visit him; he parries their every effort to drive him, as it were, sane.

The vision of the woman he loved twenty years ago is reconstituted in the daughter, who is seemingly offered him as a psychiatric dodge. It makes him—what? Sane, because he feels entitled to claim her as restitution for his sufferings? Or insane, because what right has this aging man to snatch at a young girl, indifferent to him and engaged to another? The play's tragically insistent question comes fully alive: what is sanity and what is madness? Can there be an absolute answer to this terrifying question in whose shadow most of recent history has been lived?

The protagonist, about to be foiled again by the same rival, Baron Belcredi, who moves to free the girl from his grasp, goes momentarily mad with rage and kills the baron. Or was it sane to pay Belcredi back for a ruined life? But to avoid trial for murder, our hero must now go on living his mad masquerade forever. Only, now his retainers, who acted out eleventh-century characters and events to humor the madman they served, no longer believe his madness; he can no longer enjoy the role of master illusionist. Henceforth there is to be a monstrous amalgam of madness and sanity: a formal madness beneath which everyone is sane, and knows that the other one knows. Master and servants are trapped in a hideous game in which the former can no longer harbor illusions of superiority, and the latter can't pretend to be helping a poor sick person. "Form," as Walter Starkie noted, has "swallowed Life altogether." The situation is a metaphor for most human lives.

Brilliantly, the play dislocates us: are we in the eleventh or twentieth century? Is the hero perhaps madder when he is sane? Is pretending madness the true dementia? Or are the servants and visitors, who must dress up and play parts, the truly unhinged? Is trying to cure an adjusted maniac the worst insanity? Everything depends on the leading actor: he must carry off mercurial tergiversations and bottomless ambiguity. Of the Henrys I have seen, Herbert Berghof and Sacha Pitoëff were dismal failures; Ian Keith was very fine, and Max von Sydow magnificent. Rex Harrison now is all wrong. Looking and acting like a cross between Paul Scofield's Lear and the Man of La Mancha in the Nicaraguan production, he plays everything on much the same level, except for going very slow at times, and at others speeding up to the point of incomprehensibility. Though he does convey the humorous aspects of the part, the grandeur and the pathos are quite beyond him. Paul Hecht is so much more apt and charming as Belcredi that the play begins to look like the baron's tragedy.

As the fatal Countess Matilda Spina, who is supposed to be "imperious and too beautiful," Eileen Herlie is shrill and painfully homely. And David Hurst plays an Italian alienist like a poor imitation of Sig Rumann in his crazy German psychiatrist bit, which is the way Hurst plays everything. In smaller parts, Stephen D. Newman, Reno Roop, Linda DeCoff and especially George Taylor do nicely. But Abd'el Farrah's sets are dreary, and only four or five of his costumes please. The sometimes able director, Clifford Williams, has directed in a stodgy, mausoleum style.

IN THE AMERICAN theater nothing fails like success. Our recent theatrical history is littered with one- and two-shot men who made it very big with one play or two and then dried up suddenly or watched their inspiration ebb away through numerous failures. One thinks of Edward Albee, Jack Richardson, Arthur Kopit, Jack Gelber, Arnold Weinstein, Kenneth O. Brown, Frank Gilroy, William Hanley, Ronald Ribman, William Snyder, Lewis John Carlino—the list could be extended almost indefinitely. And when you look at them very closely, even our *doyens* fall into that category: despite a few fine patches elsewhere, it is through two plays each that Williams and Miller wield their authority. The problem is that after a success or two our dramatists can no longer write plays; they must write Important Plays. They become awestruck by their genius and are soon struck dumb. The talented David Rabe must not go the same way.

When I read that Rabe's *The Orphan* was an Orestes play set in both past and present and featuring two Clytemnestras, I resolved to expect little, but never, never would I have expected the author of *The Basic Training of Pavlo Hummel* and *Sticks and Bones* to contrive such a strained, pretentious, muddled, clumsy and almost completely flavorless piece of claptrap. The idea, if it can be called one, is that Orestes is reincarnated in Charles Manson; that Agamemnon, Aegisthus, Calchas are the forerunners of the present American Establishment and its materialism, militarism and mumbo jumbo. Clytemnestra is America herself, the traitorous mother who becomes identified with the pregnant Sharon Tate. Rabe was actually seduced by his producer, Joe Papp, into spelling this out in a program note more clotted in its prose than the play itself. The notion is not only an insult to poor Miss Tate, it may even be unfair to Charlie Manson. Aeschylus I won't worry about; to his peripatetic shade, it is merely a stinkweed among the asphodel.

The parallel between the Manson "family" and the House of Atreus is preposterous enough, but Rabe does not even try to work it out properly. In the first act, he tells the myth more or less straight in the standard contemporary mode of demystification, anachronism and gags, with occasional intrusions of the present, mostly in the shape of one of Manson's girls. In the second act, he deals chiefly with Manson-Orestes and the "family," but accords the mythic figures a few brief entrances and a bloody exit. To fret his scraggy texture further, he adds a microphone-carrying Speaker, who incessantly butts in either with smart-alec jibes or with lengthy disquisitions on the current state of science and technology and the latest scientific data on the workings of the human brain and heart. Meant either as Greek chorus or Brechtian alienation, the device creates only an obtrusive vocal palimpsest.

Rabe hits out against both secular and religious authorities; indeed, against God himself in the person of a slippery and unsavory Apollo; but, much as I sympathize with his thesis, it falls between parallels as surely as if they were stools. In the broad or abstract sense, Agamemnon & Co. are such obvious power figures that to spell out elaborately their contemporary relevance is sheer supererogation. When, however, specific analogues and far-fetched correspondences are forced on the Then and Now, the whole thing becomes ludicrously unconvincing. And Rabe cannot come up with a language suitable to both his Atreids and Mansonites; when he sticks to modern idiom, he does well enough, but his attempts at fusion confound him: "Think of yourself as a Vietnamese, Aegisthus; think of yourself as a duck, a squirrel!" Or: "Clytemnestra, you are too rich to have ever been anything but a whore!" Or: "You are incredible—how can I forget that you are absolutely disgustingly unbelievable?" Rabe stoops even to a rather heavy reliance on street-corner obscenities, which he does not even put into the appropriate mouths.

The production itself miscarries. The brilliant Santo Loquasto has come up with a routinely avant-garde set; the dependable Theoni Aldredge, with run-of-the-mill costumes. Jeff Bleckner's staging is busier than an Attic bee and hot in pursuit of *coups de théâtre*, but it all looks premeditated, excogitated, desperate. Even Tharon Musser's lighting is reaching for tenuous effects, and Peter Link's incidental songs bear only coincidental resemblance to music.

One performance stands out gloriously: W. B. Brydon's Agamemnon is worthy of both Aeschylus and the best of modern military monsters—say, Strindberg's Captain Edgar. He is vulgar and shrewd, bloated and earthy, and neatly conveys both the absurdities of strength and the strength of absurdity. His diction is marvelously crisp; his gestures are exemplary in their economy. Mariclare Costello is also impressive as a Manson girl, though she does swallow some of her words, and John Harkins, Carol Williard and Laurie Heineman perform usefully. There is no need whatever for two Clytemnestras—it is a sheer modish theatrical prank, a kind of dramatic featherbedding—and when they are played by Marcia Jean Kurtz and Rae Allen, even one would be rather more than enough. As Orestes, the clever Cliff DeYoung is coasting on previous clevernesses; in the part of the Speaker, where straightforwardness could do wonders, Jeanne Hepple is arch and unpalatably precious. As Calchas, Tom Aldredge confirms that his acting is mostly peculiar looks and untenably oddball phrasings; the Apollo of Richard Lynch is all breathy, wavering voice, meaningless intonations and lack of purposeful energy.

Dear David Rabe, either stick to what you know, or bone up a little more!

IT WAS A GOOD FEELING last spring when the New York Drama Critics' Circle was voting for the best play of the season, to find myself in a quandary: whether to vote for David Rabe's *Sticks and Bones* or Jason Miller's *That Championship Season*. Two good plays do not exactly constitute an embarrassment of riches. But they were both American plays; had both, thanks to Joseph Papp, made it to Broadway; and two good dramas on Broadway in one calendar year was more than we've had in some time. I have already written here about Rabe's play; now for Jason Miller's.

That Championship Season is a necessary play. In a naturalistic way it does more or less the same thing that *Sticks and Bones* does in its absurdist-symbolist fashion: it tells grass-roots America that it stinks. For even in this Vietnam-war-waging, Nixon-favoring, culture-despising year of 1972, when Neil Simon's *The Prisoner of Second Avenue* is the hottest ticket on Broadway, when *The Godfather* is the biggest cinematic money-maker, when Herman Wouk, Taylor Caldwell and Irving Wallace are perching on top of the best-seller list, there remains considerable faith in the solid backbone of America, the good and simple folk back in the small towns, the America that the two Walts, Whitman and Disney, could hear singing, the unspoiled, sweet salt of the earth. And it is these people that Miller reveals to be weak, cowardly, prejudiced, corrupt and sustained, if at all, by self-delusion. What makes the indictment stick is first, that it is made from an evident position of intimate knowledge and understanding of the people portrayed, and second, that the judgment is made regretfully, without rancor, almost with love.

Understanding is clearly necessary for an intelligent verdict. The locale of the play, as we gather from both internal and external evidence, is Scranton, Pennsylvania, where Miller was raised. It is an unprepossessing milieu, this small, cultureless, coal-mining town, and treated without close knowledge (as in Barbara Loden's film *Wanda*), it can strike us as completely dehumanized. But because the author was truly of that world, and now no longer is, he is able to give us both the inside-out and the outside-in view of it, the latter chiefly from the mouth of Tom, whose nomadic life has taken him largely out of the town. But more important even than knowledge is sympathy: a recognition of the humanity of these beings—of that bit of depth even in shallowness, of the stirrings of awareness even in ignorance— which makes the five dramatis personae persons as well as dramatic, worthy of our concern because we cannot quite hide from ourselves that under the superego we are their brothers.

Who are the players in this quintet? There is, first, the old coach, known only as Coach, who twenty years ago guided the other four (along with another boy, Martin) to victory in the Interstate High-School Basketball Championship. The big silver trophy, with all their names engraved on it, stands proudly displayed on a table in the coach's living room, the scene of the action. The coach was sub-sequently retired, and pensioned off for having broken the jaw of a disrespectful student. But he and his boys—always excepting Mar-tin—have annually come together to celebrate a victory that "gave this defeated town something to be proud of," as the coach puts it, a victory on account of which a local cop will still tear up the coach's traffic tickets. The coach became the moral, social and political mentor of his boys for life, and this role is now his only raison d'être. It is his values that have governed their lives in one way or another— and why not, since he has abundantly drilled it into them that life and basketball are essentially identical. When one of the boys, Phil, says, "Politics is not basketball," the coach retorts, "Hell, yes. You get the crowd behind you and you can't lose. Everybody votes for a winner." Again: "Life is a game, and I'm proud to say I played it with the best." And yet again: "You quit on the field, you'll quit in life. It's on the playing fields the wars are won." The pathos of this is that it is, in a sense, true—or at least, widely believed to be so. Be-tween the playing fields of Eton and the basketball court of Scranton there may not be that much difference, and no less a sage than Sir Walter Scott has assured us that "Life is itself but a game of football." But between believing it and living it, there is a world of difference.

The boys are now in their late thirties, and the coach warns them that this is the age of heart disease. (The irony is that they are not so much weak as faint of heart.) He wants them, as he always wanted them, "lean and mean." (Well, they are getting less and less lean, but they are not wanting in meanness.) There is, first, George, the mayor who, with the coach's help won his election by a margin of 32 votes against an old drunk. Now, however, he is up against an appealing, intelligent, honest man: Sharmen, the high-school principal. George is worried, but he covers it up with bravado: Sharmen is a Jew, and a relative of his, as the coach has ferreted out, was a Communist; this and Phil's money should get George reelected.

Phil Romano is the "dumb dago" who inherited his father's strip-mining business and is the town's rich man. Ever since school days, the boys depended on Phil's car to get laid in; now he will provide the required campaign funds. But Phil has lost confidence in George, as has most of the rest of the town, and would gladly support Sharmen, if it were not for the latter's opposition to him as an ecological menace. Then there is James Daley, the junior-high-school principal, who first had to look after his long-dying father, then after his numerous brood, and now even after Tom, his dipsomaniac younger brother, whom he has had to fish out of the alcoholic wards of several cities. James is embittered by having been a constant, dutiful grind, sacrificing himself for others; he hopes for a belated recompense: success in politics. He is George's campaign manager, for which he is to be rewarded with the post of school superintendent. His ultimate ambition is Congress, but like George, he is a loser, identifiable by the sweatiness under his collar.

More obviously a loser is Tom, the drunkard. Yet alcohol has turned him into one of those privileged jesters whom the coxcomb allows to utter sardonic truths intolerable from a sober, responsible person. Tom is a "happy" drinker who finds truth in wine, but he is too weak to be set free by it, except to go off to other cities for his binges. And then James has to bring him back home. Tom uses the truth merely as sarcastic witticisms to be hurled at his fellows, or as innocent-sounding questions that lead them into self-incrimination. But revealing the mud around him does not elevate Tom: a morass can't be used as a springboard; a morass sucks one in. Phil, too, with all his money, is a loser. "I like being rich, okay," he boasts. "I need money. I want two of everything. Cars, boats, women, etc., etc. Around expensive things I get a hard-on, turned on, I want them." But having two of everything is divisive and can be almost as frustrating and depleting as having none. In another sense Phil admits: "I'm so bored half the time, it's killing me." The two things that console him are driving his sports car at suicidal speeds, and girls, mostly very young ones. And something else: "Sit and replay the old games in my head . . . Sometimes I think that's the only thing I can still feel . . . that championship season . . . nothing matched it, nothing."

What Miller does is to let his characters interact and gradually reveal themselves. This is a time-honored basic technique of realistic drama, but Miller handles it with admirable assurance. The two pegs on which he hangs the action are the basketball reunion and the mayoral race, which permits the conversations to oscillate between the blissfully nostalgic retrospect of victory and the somewhat parlous prospect of collaborating on George's reelection. The coach looms as chief strategist in both contests, and the parallel between the game and life is thus forcefully posited. But now details begin to emerge. George is unmasked as an incompetent politically and even humanly: Marion, his wife, has been carrying on with Phil and a good many others in town. It comes out, too, that Phil would rather support the Jew, Sharmen; that James, whom his own young son considers mediocre, would as soon run himself for mayor; that the boys are about to bring in outside experts to run George's campaign and so cut out James; that Tom is not a hopeful but a hopeless alcoholic; that the coach, who claims to have fully recovered from his operation, is actually in precarious health; and that Phil, with all his money, has very little to look forward to.

The game-life parallel begins to fall apart. In the game they were all one harmonious team; now they are squabbling, undermining, insulting, betraying, hitting and even threatening to shoot one another as the evening and the flow of liquor progresses. In this respect, *That Championship Season* is reminiscent of *Who's Afraid of Virginia Woolf?*, where a friendly get-together deteriorates into a drunken orgy of hate and self-hate; but Albee, despite some attempts at making his play transcendent through references to the decline of Western culture, was dealing essentially with private, personal problems. Miller's play, however, takes on a genuinely social character by capturing both the private and the public lives of a town as they intermingle and uneasily fuse. Thus, for example, although Miller ostensibly writes a play about men only, he deftly intimates what the town's women are like. There is George's wife, Marion, with her joyless promiscuity; Phil's Claire, who, in collaboration with her mother, lives the gay life of the rich bitch with continual travel and sex abroad; and James's Helen, who mass-produces babies and sacrifices her talent for painting to her monomaniacal motherhood. Then there was the more sophisticated Miss Morris, the music teacher, with whom the coach had a long-lasting relationship but whom he could not marry because she would not convert to Catholicism and because he had to take care of his old mother. There is even Mary, epileptic and retarded, with whom the boys used to have gang bangs, and who was recently brutally raped. As the feminine side of town comes gradually to life, it too seems to be populated with losers.

Is it, then, a case of the wonderful old basketball days versus the measly, bickering, unfulfilled days of adult life? No; Miller eventually brings life and the game together again in painful harmony. Tom reveals why Martin left town and never came back to these reunions: because the championship was won crookedly. There had been a superb black center on the opposing team, and Martin, on instructions from the coach, broke his ribs ("I told him to get tough under the boards" is how the coach euphemizes it), and this is how the trophy was captured. Now it all fits together: both life and basketball are a fraud, the one merely extending and perpetuating the other. Yet Miller does not allow things to become quite that simplistic, either. He makes the coach himself phrase his philosophy differently at different moments. There is the noble version, when the coach explains why he did not marry: "I never had the time. Teaching the game was not just a profession, it was a vocation. Like a priest. Devoted my life to excellence ... superiority. ... You boys are my real trophies, never forget that, never." Soon after, there comes a more equivocal version, a stoic-masochistic one: "Pain. The price is pain. Endurance. You endure pain to win, a law of life, no other way, none. The pain in my gut. It's been there all my life. It's good to hurt. The mind overcomes pain. You keep your marriage, George. Hold on to it." (It is in such incomplete sentences that much of the play's dialogue unfolds—the syntactic incompleteness becoming the objective correlative of the primitiveness and untidiness of these lives). Finally, we get the third and unvarnished version: "Exploiting a man's weakness is the name of the game. He can't move to the left, you left him to death. Can't stop a hook, you hook away on him. Find his weak spot and go after it. Punish him with it. I drilled that into you a thousand times!" This is the coach's reply to Tom's accusation that they are smearing Sharmen with his long-dead Communist relative; forthwith, we see the application of this sports philosophy to the game of life. It is to be stated even more bluntly by the coach at the very last: "You have to hate to win, it takes hate to win." Dedication, pain, hate; it isn't any one of them but all three together. Two parts bad to one part good—this, alas, is the final truth about the games of basketball and life as they are played in Scranton, Pa., and just possibly elsewhere, too.

Above all, the game theory of life is immature, as the play copiously illustrates. For in stressing the team and the in-group, development is stunted in two directions: toward the single self, leading to self-reliance, self-cultivation, individualism; and toward public-spiritedness, ecumenism, world-citizenship. The coach and at least three of his boys are arrested at the level of parent and child servicing each other's physical and emotional needs—which the sports family, the coach-father and the player-children, reiterates and extends into life. Miller lets us feel the weakness of unhappy families as paralleling the weakness of the in-group's morals and morale in contrast to those of Sharmen. Tom, as we have seen, does not really emancipate himself; only Martin has done so, but we do not know at what price.

This immaturity is neatly epitomized in various small but telling ways. I have mentioned the coach's need to look after his mother as his pretext for not marrying; more revealingly, Phil bursts out at one point: "You know the only woman I ever loved? . . . my mother, fuck the psychiatrists . . . my mother is the only . . . woman I ever knew. The rest are all cunts." (Ellipses the author's. This line, by the way, was loudly applauded by the opening-night audience on Broadway.) These men are inveterate mother's boys. Even more infantile is the unwillingness to accept as true what one doesn't want to believe. When Tom, mocking the coach's semiliterate eulogy of the Greek ideal, observes that the Greeks were homosexual, the coach explodes: "The Greeks homos? Not the Greeks, maybe the Romans but not the Greeks! Don't come around me with that liberal bullshit. I won't listen." "I won't listen" is arguably the motto of the play: the boys will be boys and hear and believe only what they want to hear and believe. George lets himself be convinced that Marion did it with Phil only to raise money for her dear husband; James is convinced that he spilled the beans to George just so that the truth would bring them all together again; Phil is readily persuaded that James would never hurt him intentionally. And the play ends with the coach and his boys pulling together against Sharmen, good government, progress and truth—against anyone who isn't one of them.

Miller is skillful with some important devices. He knows how to make a character or a situation gradually take on a different complexion through a casual remark here, a small revelation there. Thus Marion appears at first as a woman who committed a single indiscretion, but by accretion of information and the change of the coach's way of talking about her, she ends up as a slut. James's dedication to his slowly dying father is spoken of in act one as a great personal sacrifice, such as, the coach declares, not many would have made. In the second act, this sacrifice, which James uses as an excuse for his underachieving, earns only a hollow, rote approbation from George: "We all have great respect for you, James, you sacrificed, well, you know." By the third act, however, when James complains that his father never showed him the slightest respect in return for his sacrifice, the coach lets him have it: "Whine . . . Bitch and whine and blame your life on everybody. You got the eyes of a beggar." Meanwhile we have also heard from Tom that "James never did anything out of . . . love. The word embarrasses him." For James is . . . "just obedient. An obedient man. Press a button . . ." There it is again: obedience, a child's virtue; another great manly sacrifice was, like the coach's devotion to his mother, merely infantile doing what one is told to do.

Feeling is immature in the boys. When George learns of his wife's infidelity, he cries out uncomprehendingly, "Marion. Unfaithful. I'm the mayor, for Chrissakes!" This is pathetic—but for the shallowness, not the depth, of its feeling. What are feelings to George, anyway? When he wants to prove to the others that he has them, he exclaims: "I can understand . . . understand what makes a man take a gun, go up a tower, and start blowing people apart. I know the feeling. All smiles, huh? I have rage in me . . . I hate like everybody, hate . . . things." This is the horrible confirmation of the coach's "it takes hate to win"; yet it is also pathetic. Miller makes genuine pathos out of such inferior feelings, especially of that lame, evasive last word, "things": George does not even have the courage of his hates.

Another device Miller uses unobtrusively but compellingly is the parallel. The key revelation of the breaking of the black center's ribs is prefigured by an incident the coach recalls: "A Communist came through here, 1930 maybe. Bad times. Poverty like a plague. . . . He came to organize. We broke his legs . . . with a two-by-four and sent him packing." So, too, Phil makes a semi-pitying, semi-contemptuous statement about his father, an ignorant immigrant who had only hard work and premature death out of the fortune he amassed—and Phil doesn't realize how this parallels his own boring himself to death with his fast women, fast cars, and the fast demise he is courting.

What emerges is the picture of a society that makes a fetish out of success, but does not know what to do with it or even what it really is. Ultimately it recognizes success only in material terms.

However proudly the coach may talk about the Bach and Shakespeare he heard in his father's house, when he wants to prove the incontestability and value of that championship season he must reach for that prominently displayed trophy and exclaim: "I carved your names in silver, last forever, forever . . ." This echoes his earlier tribute to Teddy Roosevelt: "They carved that man's face in a mountain," which is typical also of the misinformation he frequently spreads. Concrete proof is what is wanted, and Miller deftly brings on a set of concrete, pragmatic evidences of championship with which to cement anew these perennial basketballers' unholy alliance. First is a recording of the last few seconds of a broadcast of that championship game. The coach plays this record that is cracked with age and scratchy from constant replay—but it is evidence, concrete evidence. The boys listen to it raptly, then burst into the school song, and Phil and George even end up crying in each other's arms. Tangible or at least audible success. And sloppy sentimentality, with grass-roots America singing "Another victory for Fillmore"—a school named for a President whose face could at best be carved in a molehill.

After the aural, the ocular evidence. As the coach admonishes them, "No way a man can do it alone. Got to belong to something more than yourself," the boys proceed to arrange themselves around that twenty-year-old, ill-gotten trophy for the annual photograph. Even the unconverted Tom smiles for the coach's camera. Then the boys insist on taking a picture of the coach holding the cup. To make him smile, Tom, recalling the coach's earlier puzzlement at that word, encourages him ironically, "Say cunnilingus," but what dent can Thersites make in Achilles? The lights fade, and only a spotlight is left enshrining the coach. James, the photographer, announces. "I got you, Coach," and the remark is rich in subliminal meanings. The coach responds with the curtain line: "Yeah." The complacency of grass-roots America is engraved on that silver monosyllable.

Did the coach speak true when, early in the play, he declared, "We are the country, boys"? I think the characters are truly representative, created with sympathy, authentic. While Miller reprehends their outlook and behavior, he nevertheless allows them a fleeting self-cognizance, a bit of misdirected decency, some juvenile affection. Even as he makes us aware of their racism, crudeness, jejuneness, he also makes us feel the pity of this entrapment by the pettiness, barrenness and monotony of small-town existence. An author who can be both surgically probing and charitable, both muckraking and forgiving, performs that marriage of incisiveness and generosity from which truths are born. Miller's accuracy as a reporter is mirrored in the persuasive shabbiness of the language. The incomplete sentences, lacunas and aposiopeses, awkward repetitions and omnipresent clichés —all that invincible prosaism that can nevertheless stumble onto some sort of clumsy dignity—these and other traits of speech are instinct with authenticity. Most interesting, perhaps, is Miller's avoidance of that folksy poetry with which writers tend to redeem the speech of plain people. This method is no more wrong than plain folk are incapable of unconscious poetry, yet I admire Miller's refusal to make use of it and still succeeding in making his characters fascinate us. He charges his dialogue with deliberate or inadvertent humor, self-revelation, conscious or unconscious, and the ominous ring of human hollowness. But for all that, he does not encourage glib feelings of superiority in the audience: they recognize too much of themselves in these characters.

To one of them, however, Miller does grant a spurious poetry. Some of the coach's lines have a certain afflatus, a grandiose rhythm, obsessive refrains, and some fairly conventional but charismatic metaphors. This is true especially at the play's end, where the coach is given what amounts to virtually a two-page monologue. But the poetic heightening is undercut by a mixture of nostalgia for a past that was even more reactionary than the present, and a grandiloquence that is more than faintly self-serving. The speech begins with a glowing evocation of the coach's father and the town as it was in his time; it ends with this prognostication about the mayoral race:

> *You won't lose boys—because I won't let you lose. I'll whip your ass to the bone, drive you into the ground. Your soul belongs to God but your ass belongs to me, remember that one, yes sir, we can do it, we are going to win because we can't lose, dare not lose, won't lose, lose is not in our vocabulary! I shaped you, boys, never forget that. I ran you till the blisters busted, ran you right into perfection, bloody socks and all; you couldn't put on your jocks, awkward, all legs, afraid, a mistake a second. I made you winners. I made you winners.*

There is a horrible beauty in that, after all.

But in general, along with the purposive leanness of the dialogue, there is even an almost complete absence of stage directions and instructions about how a line is to be read (e.g. anxiously, softly, etc.). Though there is nothing wrong with such hints to actors, directors and readers, there is also something fine and fastidious

about refraining from them. It allows the director, actor or reader *
to come to his own conclusions and fill in his own details; yet the
movement of a speech is always so clearly plotted that this leeway
will not alter basic meanings or imperil communication.

In Joseph Papp's production, first mounted at the Public Theatre,
then transferred to the Booth on Broadway, the production values
are all of the utmost artistry. A. J. Antoon's staging is as meticulous as
it is resourceful, creating an elaborate choreography of movements
that first delight us by their unexpectedness, then delight us again
by their absolute rightness. A drunk falls down a flight of stairs
almost too spectacularly; an angry man goes out on the porch to
simmer down, and repeatedly sticks his head back in through the
window to hurl further invective at his offender; a bit of violence
erupts so swiftly that it is over before it is really fathomed. All these
events have an uncanny aroma of credibility, of really happening and
happening for the first time. The rhythms of speech are cogently
orchestrated, motion flows freely across the entire stage, and each
entrance and exit has its particular shape and flavor.

The set, by Santo Loquasto, is right to the last detail. The tacky
curtains and doilies, the Persian rugs and flowered wallpaper, the
framed photographs of teams, the Grand Rapids mahogany furniture,
the archetypal dowel post and balusters of the staircase spiraling to
the second floor—all share in a fadedness and mustiness that no
amount of cleaning or polishing could assuage. It is bourgeois respectability going to seed, but gallantly hanging on to every grasp-
able vestige. The very layout of the room, with its unequal spaces
to which further nooks and crannies adhere like pockmarks and warts,
generates an aura of mixed coziness and embarrassment. It all exudes
an uncertain yellowness, which it seems to have absorbed from bygone lives and is now breathing back into the current ones. Ian
Calderon's lighting cannily contributes to this impression.

But the ultimate triumph of *That Championship Season* is in its
performances. The five actors could scarcely be surpassed individually, but are even more astounding together. One might perhaps
object that some look a little younger or older than their prescribed
ages, but this is as nothing to their perfection in every other respect.
As the mayor, Charles Durning gives off exaggerated self-assurance
with every paper-thin smile and briskly tossed-off conviviality. Durning has a jerkiness of speech and angularity of motion that jut out
incriminatingly from under the assumed fluidity. Even crushed with

* *That Championship Season* has been published by Atheneum.

pain or maddened with wrath, he retains that puppetlike pettiness
that makes him in equal measure ludicrous and pitiful. As James, the
junior-high-school principal, Michael McGuire conveys magisterially
an ingrained mediocrity sweatily straining to please. Even his pomposity has a thin, brittle tinkle in it, and his slightly squeaky voice
seems to curl upward as it slowly gathers courage. At bay, he fights
back with the inept but desperately serious anger of an aging tenor
with a second-rate opera company in a grand, dramatic moment. As
Tom, his younger, alcoholic brother—the softly sardonic voice of
defeated reasonableness—Walter McGinn gives a magnificently balanced performance, not allowing the justness of his perceptions to
blind us to his hopeless decay, and infusing his genuine likableness
with a chilling sense of the sodden impotence underneath. His drunkard's titubations are flawless in their underlying somnambulistic
agility, and his cascading down the stairs is splendid and alarming.

Richard A. Dysart's Coach is no less superb. Dysart conveys the
maniacal aspects of the man without losing any of his equally relevant
joviality. Though he can, at times, sound and look like a lesser Old
Testament prophet, at other times, as when he pries esuriently into
the details of Phil's intercourse with Marion, he becomes childlike,
almost Puckish. Dysart wisely eschews the extremes of distastefulness
or cuteness that the part could seduce one into, and makes a marvelously kaleidoscopic jumble out of probity and mean prejudice.
He declines Phil's invitation to watch basketball on color TV: "They
all shoot down at the basket. Not my game," and sees to it that the
line sounds too funny to be moving; then continues with "It's not the
white man's game," in tones of such disarmingly seriocomic distaste
that the underlying nastiness hits us only a second or two later.

But the most dazzling presence onstage—*primus inter pares*—is
Paul Sarvino as Phil. He makes the "dumb dago" shrewd, warm-
hearted, ruthless, amiably oafish and coldly cynical all at once. I
cannot begin to describe how the actor can convey so many conflicting and contradictory characteristics with a single slow expression, one
quick remark, or a solitary dismissing gesture—but he does. He makes
you feel that everything comes from very deep in him, but also that
he is just a huge, overgrown baby whose innermost core is right under
the skin. He is so simple, so obvious, and then suddenly we don't
know where this weeping has come from, or whether that inflection
derives from silliness or great subtlety. And his comic timing is always
exemplary. From all five actors we get ensemble acting of the highest
order, which could hold its own against the finest acting aggregations
of the world.

Jason Miller has written a first-rate commercial theater piece. It is not quite profound or venturesome or novel enough to make it a work of art, but it is the very best example of the sort of play that keeps a commercial theater nourishingly and honorably alive. If it cannot have a long life on Broadway, Broadway itself no longer deserves to live.

ABOUT THE AUTHOR

JOHN SIMON was born in Yugoslavia in 1925, attended schools there, in England and in the United States, and received his B.A., M.A. and Ph.D. in comparative literature from Harvard. Since then he has taught at Harvard, the University of Washington, M.I.T., Bard and the University of Pittsburgh.

Mr. Simon has been the drama critic for a number of magazines and for Public Broadcasting, and currently appears in that role in *The Hudson Review* and *The New Leader*. He has also been a film critic for the latter, as well as for *Esquire*, and at present reviews the medium for *New York*. His book reviews, articles on the cultural scene, and film, drama and art criticism have appeared in a score of magazines, among them *The New York Times Sunday Magazine, Harper's, Horizon, The Reporter, Time, Vogue, Saturday Review* and *The National Review*.

Mr. Simon lives in New York City and is the author of four previous books.